Advancing DEI and Creating Inclusive Environments in the Online Space

Nina M. McCune
Walden University, USA

A volume in the Advances in Educational Technologies and Instructional Design (AETID) Book Series

IGI Global
PUBLISHER of TIMELY KNOWLEDGE

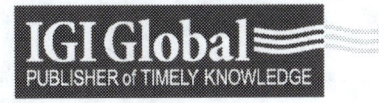

Published in the United States of America by
IGI Global
Information Science Reference (an imprint of IGI Global)
701 E. Chocolate Avenue
Hershey PA, USA 17033
Tel: 717-533-8845
Fax: 717-533-8661
E-mail: cust@igi-global.com
Web site: http://www.igi-global.com

Copyright © 2022 by IGI Global. All rights reserved. No part of this publication may be reproduced, stored or distributed in any form or by any means, electronic or mechanical, including photocopying, without written permission from the publisher. Product or company names used in this set are for identification purposes only. Inclusion of the names of the products or companies does not indicate a claim of ownership by IGI Global of the trademark or registered trademark.

Library of Congress Cataloging-in-Publication Data

Names: McCune, Nina, 1969- editor.
Title: Advancing DEI and creating inclusive environments in the online
   space / Nina McCune, editor.
Other titles: Advancing diversity, equity, and inclusion and creating
   inclusive environments in the online space
Description: Hershey, PA : Information Science Reference, [2022] | Includes
   bibliographical references and index. | Summary: "This book addresses
   topics covering Diversity, Equity, and Inclusion (DEI) ranging from
   creating sites of collaboration and engagement, ensuring and
   pro-actively delivering resources and student support, developing
   hallmarks of inclusivity to support online course design and faculty
   development, and measuring not only the success of these
   transformational initiatives, but measuring inclusion and evaluating
   progress against the institution's mission and values"-- Provided by
   publisher.
Identifiers: LCCN 2022018274 (print) | LCCN 2022018275 (ebook) | ISBN
   9781668451465 (Hardcover) | ISBN 9781668451502 (Paperback) | ISBN
   9781668451472 (eBook)
Subjects: LCSH: Walden University (Minneapolis, Minn.) | For-profit
   universities and colleges--United States. | Distance education--United
   States. | Web-based instruction--United States. | Inclusive
   education--United States. | Minorities in higher education--United
   States.
Classification: LCC LB2328.52.U6 A38 2022 (print) | LCC LB2328.52.U6
   (ebook) | DDC 378.1/758--dc23/eng/20220722
LC record available at https://lccn.loc.gov/2022018274
LC ebook record available at https://lccn.loc.gov/2022018275

This book is published in the IGI Global book series Advances in Educational Technologies and Instructional Design (AETID) (ISSN: 2326-8905; eISSN: 2326-8913)

British Cataloguing in Publication Data
A Cataloguing in Publication record for this book is available from the British Library.

All work contributed to this book is new, previously-unpublished material. The views expressed in this book are those of the authors, but not necessarily of the publisher.

For electronic access to this publication, please contact: eresources@igi-global.com.

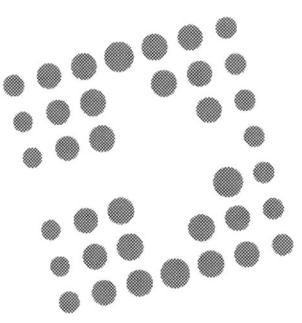

Advances in Educational Technologies and Instructional Design (AETID) Book Series

Lawrence A. Tomei
Robert Morris University, USA

ISSN:2326-8905
EISSN:2326-8913

Mission

Education has undergone, and continues to undergo, immense changes in the way it is enacted and distributed to both child and adult learners. In modern education, the traditional classroom learning experience has evolved to include technological resources and to provide online classroom opportunities to students of all ages regardless of their geographical locations. From distance education, Massive-Open-Online-Courses (MOOCs), and electronic tablets in the classroom, technology is now an integral part of learning and is also affecting the way educators communicate information to students.

The **Advances in Educational Technologies & Instructional Design (AETID) Book Series** explores new research and theories for facilitating learning and improving educational performance utilizing technological processes and resources. The series examines technologies that can be integrated into K-12 classrooms to improve skills and learning abilities in all subjects including STEM education and language learning. Additionally, it studies the emergence of fully online classrooms for young and adult learners alike, and the communication and accountability challenges that can arise. Trending topics that are covered include adaptive learning, game-based learning, virtual school environments, and social media effects. School administrators, educators, academicians, researchers, and students will find this series to be an excellent resource for the effective design and implementation of learning technologies in their classes.

Coverage

- Classroom Response Systems
- Instructional Design
- Web 2.0 and Education
- K-12 Educational Technologies
- Adaptive Learning
- Bring-Your-Own-Device
- Higher Education Technologies
- E-Learning
- Digital Divide in Education
- Hybrid Learning

IGI Global is currently accepting manuscripts for publication within this series. To submit a proposal for a volume in this series, please contact our Acquisition Editors at Acquisitions@igi-global.com or visit: http://www.igi-global.com/publish/.

The Advances in Educational Technologies and Instructional Design (AETID) Book Series (ISSN 2326-8905) is published by IGI Global, 701 E. Chocolate Avenue, Hershey, PA 17033-1240, USA, www.igi-global.com. This series is composed of titles available for purchase individually; each title is edited to be contextually exclusive from any other title within the series. For pricing and ordering information please visit http://www.igi-global.com/book-series/advances-educational-technologies-instructional-design/73678. Postmaster: Send all address changes to above address. Copyright © 2022 IGI Global. All rights, including translation in other languages reserved by the publisher. No part of this series may be reproduced or used in any form or by any means – graphics, electronic, or mechanical, including photocopying, recording, taping, or information and retrieval systems – without written permission from the publisher, except for non commercial, educational use, including classroom teaching purposes. The views expressed in this series are those of the authors, but not necessarily of IGI Global.

Titles in this Series

For a list of additional titles in this series, please visit: www.igi-global.com/book-series

Guide to Integrating Problem-Based Learning Programs in Higher Education Classrooms Design, Implementation, and Evaluation
Pam Epler (Youngstown State University, USA) and Jodee Jacobs (Youngstown State University, USA)
Information Science Reference • © 2022 • 246pp • H/C (ISBN: 9781799881773) • US $205.00

EdTech Economy and the Transformation of Education
Sara Fazzin (Xenophon College London, UK)
Information Science Reference • © 2022 • 294pp • H/C (ISBN: 9781799889045) • US $215.00

Methodologies and Use Cases on Extended Reality for Training and Education
Anacleto Correia (Naval Academy, Portugal) and Vitor Viegas (Naval Academy, Portugal)
Information Science Reference • © 2022 • 300pp • H/C (ISBN: 9781668433980) • US $215.00

English as a Foreign Language in a New-Found Post-Pandemic World
Walaa M. El-Henawy (Port Said University, Egypt) and Maria del Mar Suárez (Universitat de Barcelona, Spain)
Information Science Reference • © 2022 • 335pp • H/C (ISBN: 9781668442050) • US $215.00

Handbook of Research on Learner-Centered Approaches to Teaching in an Age of Transformational Change
Billi L. Bromer (Brenau University, USA) and Caroline M. Crawford (University of Houston-Clear Lake, USA)
Information Science Reference • © 2022 • 385pp • H/C (ISBN: 9781668442401) • US $270.00

Handbook of Research on Teacher and Student Perspectives on the Digital Turn in Education
Sviatlana Karpava (University of Cyprus, Cyprus)
Information Science Reference • © 2022 • 586pp • H/C (ISBN: 9781668444467) • US $270.00

Digital Active Methodologies for Educative Learning Management
Nuno Geada (Public HighSchool of Palmelal, Portugal) and George Leal Jamil (Informações em Rede Consultoria e Treinamento Ltda, Brazil)
Information Science Reference • © 2022 • 313pp • H/C (ISBN: 9781668447062) • US $215.00

Handbook of Research on Teaching in Multicultural and Multilingual Contexts
Erasmos Charamba (University of the Witwatersrand, South Africa)
Information Science Reference • © 2022 • 450pp • H/C (ISBN: 9781668450345) • US $270.00

701 East Chocolate Avenue, Hershey, PA 17033, USA
Tel: 717-533-8845 x100 • Fax: 717-533-8661
E-Mail: cust@igi-global.com • www.igi-global.com

Table of Contents

Foreword xiv

Preface xvi

Acknowledgment xxi

Section 1
Living Theory

Chapter 1
Developing a Learning Model for Caring, Inclusion, and Social Change in an Online Environment ... 1
    William C. Schulz III, Walden University, USA
    Ann M. Morgan, Walden University, USA

Chapter 2
Digital Appreciative Inquiry for Inclusion 24
    Ann M. Morgan, Walden University, USA
    Kathe Pelletier, EDUCAUSE, USA

Chapter 3
Using an Emotional Intelligence Learning System for Person-Centered Curriculum Development
and Teaching 40
    Richard Hammett, Walden University, USA
    Gary R. Low, EI Learning Systems, USA
    William C. Schulz III, Walden University, USA

Section 2
Making Space

Chapter 4
Success and Failures in the Development of an Inclusive Online Learning Environment 63
    Tina Marshall-Bradley, Walden University, USA

Chapter 5
Designing an Inclusive Online Classroom 75
Kristi A. Trapp, Adtalem Global Education, USA
Katherine Strang, Adtalem Global Education, USA
Kathleen Morrison, Adtalem Global Education, USA
Laura Karl, Adtalem Global Education, USA

Section 3
Into Practice

Chapter 6
Advancing Equity, Diversity, and Inclusion Through the Transformation of Nursing Education 94
Todd A. Dickson, Walden University, USA

Chapter 7
Strategies for Doctoral Student Readiness, Student-Centered Support, and Inclusion 110
Laura K. Lynn, Walden University, USA
Melanie Brown, Walden University, USA
Michelle Brown, Walden University, USA
Deborah Inman, Walden University, USA

Chapter 8
The Students We Have: Compassionate Grading in Online Courses 125
D. Gabriela Johnson, Walden University, USA
Sara Makris, Walden University, USA

Chapter 9
The SPII-Hub and Other Initiatives to Advance Online Engagement 138
Rebecca L. Jobe, Walden University, USA
Katherine Strang, Adtalem Global Education, USA

Section 4
Measuring Inclusive Teaching and Learning

Chapter 10
A Framework to Measure Inclusion 153
Rebecca L. Jobe, Walden University, USA
Nina M. McCune, Walden University, USA
Laura K. Lynn, Walden University, USA

Chapter 11
Assessing Institutional Readiness: A Collaboration 166
Kristin Bundesen, Walden University, USA
Christopher Gilmer, West Virginia University Potomac State College, USA
Latara O. Lampkin, Florida State University, USA
Laura K. Lynn, Walden University, USA

Chapter 12
Developing a Rubric for a Person-Centered Approach to Teaching in Inclusive Online Learning
Spaces 186
    William C. Schulz III, Walden University, USA
    Juli K. Konopa, Walden University, USA

Section 5
Systems of Practice

Chapter 13
Framing Higher Education Through the Social Determinants of Health 210
    Aimee Ferraro, Walden University, USA

Chapter 14
Sustainable Strategic Planning for Inclusive Online Teaching and Learning 225
    Sue Subocz, Walden University, USA
    Heidi Chumley, Ross University School of Medicine, Barbados
    Sri Banerjee, Walden University, USA
    Myrna Cano-Wolfbrandt, Arizona State University, USA

Chapter 15
Equity in the Online Space? A Multi-Systems Perspective 248
    Nina M. McCune, Walden University, USA

Section 6
Closing Thoughts

Chapter 16
The Social Determinants of Changemakers: A Commitment to Inclusive Teaching and Learning
and a Positive Social Change Mission 268
    Nina M. McCune, Walden University, USA
    William C. Schulz III, Walden University, USA

Compilation of References 281

About the Contributors 308

Index 315

Detailed Table of Contents

Foreword xiv

Preface xvi

Acknowledgment xxi

Section 1
Living Theory

What kind of theoretical foundation grounds a university's efforts and approaches to create inclusive learning environments?

Chapter 1
Developing a Learning Model for Caring, Inclusion, and Social Change in an Online Environment ... 1
  William C. Schulz III, Walden University, USA
  Ann M. Morgan, Walden University, USA

A clear and explicitly communicated learning model is at the heart of the learning enterprise for a university. In this chapter, the authors present an inclusive teaching and learning model and discuss how its evolution expresses the values and mission of the university and guide it in outlining the behaviors and expectations that the university places on faculty, staff, and learners with respect to supporting inclusive learning relationships, recruiting faculty and staff, professional development, and performance management.

Chapter 2
Digital Appreciative Inquiry for Inclusion 24
  Ann M. Morgan, Walden University, USA
  Kathe Pelletier, EDUCAUSE, USA

Appreciative inquiry is an approach with the power to contribute to inclusion in the workplace. Paired with digital interventions, which share the power to include and the potential to exclude, digital appreciative inquiry offers promising possibilities when used with intention. This chapter presents guidance to help higher education institutions accomplish the goals of inclusion using digital appreciative inquiry, which can lead to greater staff and faculty belonging, trust, engagement, and institutional sustainability.

Chapter 3
Using an Emotional Intelligence Learning System for Person-Centered Curriculum Development and Teaching 40
> *Richard Hammett, Walden University, USA*
> *Gary R. Low, EI Learning Systems, USA*
> *William C. Schulz III, Walden University, USA*

In this chapter, the authors will define and present an emotional intelligence learning system, rooted in research related to transformative emotional intelligence and explore how an online university can leverage this system within an inclusive teaching and learning model to teach emotional intelligence, personal skills, and leadership development. Implications for teaching, course development, and professional development are discussed so that faculty, course developers, administrators, and staff can use the tools to engender flow and positive change within their spheres of influence.

Section 2
Making Space

Inclusive environments in the online space do not happen because they are desired – those environments are intentionally designed. What do some of these designs look like?

Chapter 4
Success and Failures in the Development of an Inclusive Online Learning Environment 63
> *Tina Marshall-Bradley, Walden University, USA*

Developing engaging learning environments for the benefit of all learners is a challenge for online programs. Research has shown that online learning environments are not designed to engage Black, Indigenous, people of color (BIPOC) for value that they bring to academic programs. Walden University and the master's in education (MSED) program have created foundational areas that can be used to create equitable learning environments. Arroyo and Gasman's 2014 model of Historically Black College and Universities' (HBCUs) student support provides a strong plan for institutions to change practices in support of BIPOC and other marginalized communities. Building on the activities of the revised core courses in the MSED program, and using the HBCU-inspired framework and recommendations from external reviewer, a case study is considered. This case study suggests an institution can build an online experience that is inclusive and supports the work of BIPOC and other marginalized communities.

Chapter 5
Designing an Inclusive Online Classroom 75
> *Kristi A. Trapp, Adtalem Global Education, USA*
> *Katherine Strang, Adtalem Global Education, USA*
> *Kathleen Morrison, Adtalem Global Education, USA*
> *Laura Karl, Adtalem Global Education, USA*

In this chapter, the authors share core principles and essential questions for evaluating the inclusivity of the online classroom curriculum and design. The nine core principles are building upon students' individual strengths and assets; exploring, affirming, and embracing diverse voices and students' identities; valuing each student lived experience; empowering positive social change agents; ensuring multiple means of expression; providing meaningful opportunities for feedback for growth; exploring course concepts through the lens of historically marginalized individuals and groups; ensuring designs are not systemically biased; and empowering appropriate responses and feedback to perceived inequities. Theoretical support and curriculum design strategies are provided for each of the principles.

Section 3
Into Practice

Intentional design serves as the blueprint for creating inclusive environments in the online space. In this section, the authors explore how the theory and the conceptualization are put into practice.

Chapter 6
Advancing Equity, Diversity, and Inclusion Through the Transformation of Nursing Education........ 94
    Todd A. Dickson, Walden University, USA

Diversity, equity, and inclusion are intimately connected to social determinants of health (SDOH). SDOH are crucial and can have a substantial impact on disparities in health outcomes. Nurses have a social mandate to address health disparities by recognizing social determinants of health and contributing to the development and implementation of initiatives to eliminate healthcare disparities for individuals, groups, and communities. This chapter defines the principles essential for addressing health equity and highlights the historical importance of nursing efforts in tackling health and healthcare disparities. Next, this chapter talks about the current state of various contextual elements that influence nursing education, with a focus on health equity and issues that will affect nursing education and the nursing workforce in the future.

Chapter 7
Strategies for Doctoral Student Readiness, Student-Centered Support, and Inclusion...................... 110
    Laura K. Lynn, Walden University, USA
    Melanie Brown, Walden University, USA
    Michelle Brown, Walden University, USA
    Deborah Inman, Walden University, USA

Equity in education is instrumental to individual, local, national, and international progress. Walden University exemplifies this through a commitment to support doctoral students with various levels of prior experience. The university scales doctoral resources based on data and communication with stakeholders. Resulting from this effort, Walden has developed centralized academic support services. Students who use these services report better preparation to make progress in their doctoral programs; however, some students have struggled to find and access resources when they need them. In 2019, the concern was addressed through a collaborative planning summit and position paper to create a holistically supportive doctoral journey for all students. The resulting innovative approach is described, highlighting aspects used to foster inclusion through easy access and better preparation for our diverse student body. Recommendations for faculty and administrators looking to enhance their support strategy through increased inclusivity and improved student progress are shared.

Chapter 8
The Students We Have: Compassionate Grading in Online Courses... 125
    D. Gabriela Johnson, Walden University, USA
    Sara Makris, Walden University, USA

Students who choose to enter college in their twenties, thirties, and beyond face the challenges of balancing their academic experiences with busier lives, often with little social capital to guide them through the intricacies of college life. Students may feel overwhelmed, easily discouraged, or overlooked by people within their institution, including their professors. Instructors who, themselves, lack the experience of being first-generation college students may struggle to identify with the behaviors of the students they teach.

They may see their roles as evaluators more than as partners or guides. The practice of compassionate grading and teaching can increase opportunities for trusting relationships to form among instructors and students, and for learning to occur.

Chapter 9
The SPII-Hub and Other Initiatives to Advance Online Engagement 138
    Rebecca L. Jobe, Walden University, USA
    Katherine Strang, Adtalem Global Education, USA

This chapter reviews some of the essential ingredients in creating a post-secondary online learning environment that is diverse, inclusive, and promotes connection and engagement across the program lifecycle. Various initiatives to build student engagement and connection are discussed. The authors also argue that while most of the attention on engagement in the educational setting focuses on student engagement, equal consideration must be given to faculty and staff engagement to create the optimal environment.

Section 4
Measuring Inclusive Teaching and Learning

How can a university measure the efficacy of its diversity, equity, and inclusion initiatives?

Chapter 10
A Framework to Measure Inclusion.. 153
    Rebecca L. Jobe, Walden University, USA
    Nina M. McCune, Walden University, USA
    Laura K. Lynn, Walden University, USA

Inclusive learning environments create a well-rounded education that initiates and amplifies the diverse experiences of all students. In higher education, this requires that all learning spaces, from the point of onboarding and classrooms through social clubs and completion, are designed in ways that promote the active participation of learners, and that students feel a sense of purpose, belonging, and safety to engage fully in the academic process. Institutions working to integrate and assess inclusive teaching and learning need to carefully consider their institutional mission and understand the history and potential challenges of developing systemic, structural inclusion within their organization. Successfully measuring inclusion requires clear operational definitions and comprehensive evaluation that includes both quantitative and qualitative assessment. This chapter reviews the importance of creating an inclusive environment in higher education, the barriers that arise, and the need for reliable and valid means of measuring its effectiveness.

Chapter 11
Assessing Institutional Readiness: A Collaboration 166
    Kristin Bundesen, Walden University, USA
    Christopher Gilmer, West Virginia University Potomac State College, USA
    Latara O. Lampkin, Florida State University, USA
    Laura K. Lynn, Walden University, USA

This chapter examines, introduces, and documents the exploration and initial review of an institutional self-assessment toolkit designed to query and instigate discussion of how institutions perceive equity as they serve "historically-underserved" undergraduate students. A pilot of the toolkit, developed by the

National Institutes for Historically Underserved Students (NIHUS), was evaluated by a working group of the Undergraduate Advisory Council within Walden University. The working group generated feedback to the NIHUS on the toolkit and considered potential wider adoption across undergraduate education within the university. This exploration and collaboration continues.

Chapter 12
Developing a Rubric for a Person-Centered Approach to Teaching in Inclusive Online Learning Spaces 186
    William C. Schulz III, Walden University, USA
    Juli K. Konopa, Walden University, USA

In this chapter, the authors discuss the benefits of developing and deploying a care-oriented, person-centered rubric for supporting effective online learning relationships. The process by which the rubric was developed at the university and a detailed faculty-focused rubric are presented as part of a larger inclusive teaching and learning standards framework, and the implications of utilizing both the rubric and ITL frame for future faculty recruiting, development, and assessment are discussed.

Section 5
Systems of Practice

What systems must be considered to operationalize and institutionalize inclusive practices?

Chapter 13
Framing Higher Education Through the Social Determinants of Health 210
    Aimee Ferraro, Walden University, USA

The mission and organizational structure of a university can employ a variety of frameworks to address diversity, equity, and inclusion. In this chapter, the guiding principles of one online university, and how reframing its approach to higher education through the Social Determinants of Health, allowed the institution to respond to the call for action around educational justice, health equity, and healthier communities. Examples of how to encourage interdisciplinary collaboration and integrate social determinants of health into curricula are provided.

Chapter 14
Sustainable Strategic Planning for Inclusive Online Teaching and Learning...................................... 225
    Sue Subocz, Walden University, USA
    Heidi Chumley, Ross University School of Medicine, Barbados
    Sri Banerjee, Walden University, USA
    Myrna Cano-Wolfbrandt, Arizona State University, USA

It may indeed be time to stop strategic planning, at least as it has most typically been considered and conducted, in favor of approaches that focus on articulating visions for a future built on the individual and collective experiences of learners and future learners of an institution. Instead, it may be time to create operational plans designed to sustain a culture of community commitment and ensure an inclusive teaching and learning environment. Such an inclusive teaching and learning environment is founded on (1) an understanding of learners as whole people with pasts that must be honored throughout the learning process, (2) a set of complex social circumstances that must be considered in the design and delivery of learning experiences, and (3) a future that is unpredictable and ever-changing.

Chapter 15
Equity in the Online Space? A Multi-Systems Perspective 248
   Nina M. McCune, Walden University, USA

As postsecondary institutions develop equity-minded approaches to improve minoritized and marginalized student retention and completion, most literature, case study, and discourse focuses on traditional, on ground, and/or residential schools and courses. More intentional and urgent focus must happen in the online space both in terms of institutional planning, practice, and strategy and in terms of individual/professional development. All individuals navigate systems using sets of ingrained, implicit, or cognitive biases. In postsecondary education, these biases impact student success. For any postsecondary institution with online course or program delivery, individual and organizational development opportunities must target these biases and create space for double-loop learning in order to achieve an equity-minded approach to organizational change.

Section 6
Closing Thoughts

Intentional inclusive environments impact more than the institution and more than the student. Entire communities can experience positive social change.

Chapter 16
The Social Determinants of Changemakers: A Commitment to Inclusive Teaching and Learning and a Positive Social Change Mission 268
   Nina M. McCune, Walden University, USA
   William C. Schulz III, Walden University, USA

The closing chapter of this edited edition puts forward a theory of the social determinants of changemakers – those learners supported by an inclusive educational institution, empowered to create positive social change in the world. Building on previous social change and social determinants scholarship, and through intentional and inclusive institutional organization, planning, and support, this framework is not only possible for postsecondary education institutions to drive positive social change – it is the call to action of our time.

Compilation of References 281

About the Contributors 308

Index 315

Foreword

The COVID-19 pandemic and the social justice issues of the early 2020s forced the trajectory of education to dramatically shift and has required all in higher education to consider different modalities, systems, curriculum, and supports to effectively serve our diverse faculty and students. This critical period highlights that online learning can no longer be relegated as an optional resource, and we, as academic researchers and scholar practitioners, must consider the impact of the online experience for all students. In essence, institutions of higher education have been thrust into a national discourse that not only asks questions about equity but also requires us to act on key inclusive teaching and learning issues that extend beyond brick-and-mortar and into the online space.

As education develops a deeper online focus, recent events have revealed disparities, such as limited student access to computers or internet services, the often-underfunded development and maintenance cost of technical infrastructure for course development and faculty training, the scarcity of inclusive content reflecting and respecting all learners, and the multiple gaps in available resources to effectively train and support faculty and staff. *Advancing DEI and Creating Inclusive Environments in the Online Space* is a pioneer in showcasing how online institutions can create high-quality education programs that work toward achieving equity in higher education. Specifically, it reveals how Walden University is addressing inclusive teaching and learning (ITL) questions and challenges by integrating specific practices in every aspect of online education. The evolution of the university's ITL model and its alignment to the university's strategic plan and organizational structure is paramount in serving as a foundation from which additional initiatives and practices are being built. Initiatives include a thorough evaluation of our curriculum, which has resulted in identifying essential advancements for designing an inclusive curriculum and improving practices for teaching and learning. Additionally, the development of an ITL rubric provides a template to assess how diversity, equity, and inclusion initiatives are being implemented and allow for continuous improvement.

Walden University's ITL model also aligns with a mindset among faculty and staff who value emotional intelligence and empathy within the classroom and in the curriculum it offers. This person-centered learning approach is rooted in the core of Walden University's mission of providing underrepresented groups with access to higher education, developing curriculum that represents a diverse voice, modeling inclusive training for faculty and staff, and delivering personalized feedback. The model also stresses the importance of engagement in the classroom to promote social change, encourage inclusive conversations, and support successful completion of goals. Students, faculty, and staff are also encouraged to share their perspectives as they engage in the classroom, committees, orientations, trainings, and policy-making initiatives to help drive change and improve the learning experience.

Foreword

As more higher education institutions focus on delivering online learning, they must begin with an equity-minded approach that genuinely values access and inclusivity to impact organizational change and student success. If you and/or your organization are seeking strategies to help implement a more inclusive online environment, this book is a must read!

Deepa Shriram
Walden University, USA

Kristy Wake
Walden University, USA

Preface

Online teaching and online learning are not newcomers to postsecondary education. Although an exact start date is fuzzy, the mid-1980s serves as a common point of reference. Perhaps, as some suggest, it was a course at the University of Toronto in 1984 that was the 'first.' Maybe it was 1985 at Nova Southeastern University. More than likely, wherever it started, the course was developed and delivered using the latest Commodore Educator 64 computers with blinking neon-green text against a matte black background. As I write this preface in 2022, almost 40 years have elapsed for online education, and the changes to our networks and user interfaces have advanced tremendously. Yet, practitioners continue to have discussions about best practices that are quite similar, in fact, to the ones I engaged in during my 1995 training on a WebCT platform. The fundamental questions about how to design easily accessible and engaging courses seem to exist as prolonged, unanswerable horizon events, with each new technological innovation causing a reconsideration of previously settled practices.

At the same time, I wonder if we, the postsecondary practitioners, need to shift the investigation from *engaging* practices to *inclusive* practices. Perhaps they are related notions. If we intentionally design online classes to engage students and capture their attention or immerse them in the nuances of our respective disciplines, should we not also design our classrooms to be inclusive spaces, where all learners are not only welcome, recognize their voice and value in the materials, and have every opportunity to succeed? Our discussions about online engagement may have gone in slightly different directions during the past 4 decades to address new technologies or tools, yet we have given attention only haltingly to how we ensure equity outcomes for our diverse student bodies. If we were to say that equity has been addressed since *Brown v. Board of Ed* (1954) or *Swann v. Charlotte-Mecklenburg Board of Ed* (1971) or *Keyes v. School District No. 1* (1973), we would be unable to explain why the United States Government Accountability Office released a report in July of this year finding that schools "remain divided along racial, ethnic, and economic lines throughout the U.S.—even as the K-12 public school student population grows more diverse" (para. 1).

Our world community has been through *a lot* in the past 2 years. There is nary a person over the age of 2 who has not been isolated, distanced, masked, quarantined, soaked in hand sanitizer, perhaps hospitalized, and hopefully vaccinated. We have endured (and still endure) a fast-mutating and highly contagious virus that has forced us to change the way we work, shop, socialize, celebrate, mourn, entertain, exercise, and even learn. The COVID-19 pandemic served as a *backdrop* to increasingly pitched political rhetoric, rearranging what anyone could expect from civil discourse. Embedded within that rhetoric are echoes of a racially segregated American past and present, complete with unfunny rejoinders of blatant White supremacy. We live at a time of great uncertainty, with major dimensions of our shared experiences changing rapidly and unexpectedly.

Preface

This edited collection serves as a starting point for changing discourse about online education. We, as postsecondary practitioners, must begin to consider the implications of all these forces on our profession, our disciplines, our students, and the communities we serve. The chapters in this book are a blueprint for how online educators can change their perspective to create intentionally inclusive spaces for students, colleagues, and even communities. Walden University was founded on the principle of positive social change (Hodgkinson, 1969, p. 2) and to develop scholar practitioners who will advance the betterment of society. This is not a small task – *change* itself is hard, let alone social change. We are resistant to any kind of change, be it prompted by intrinsic desires or extrinsic demands. It is even sometimes hard to *admit* that we must change, insofar as that admission is akin to broadcasting our humiliating defeat or (at least) that something is not working, or not working *well*. We must change our educational systems and practices, however, because we are clearly repeating the same mistakes of the past. If in the year 2022, there are findings of *de facto* or *de jure* segregation in American schools, we must change.

The work and ideas presented here are not leavened by idyllic escapism or by utopian ideations. They are an outcome of fastidious, ruminative work that began with a Diversity and Inclusion working group in 2015 that identified opportunities for the school's diverse community of practitioners and learners to *do* more and *become* a leader for online higher education. Chaired by Dr. Savitri Dixon-Saxon, this group aimed to create a more diverse and inclusive university. They understood that building a diverse and inclusive environment is a challenge for any organization, and recommended the school prioritize diversity and inclusion among all the other competing priorities that are integral to its strategy. They observed that all community members, especially leadership, must *willingly* engage in honest self-analysis of their position relative to those who are marginalized, underrepresented, and discriminated against, as well as one's personal role in the hierarchy of power and privilege. The group further observed that the future of any organization extends far beyond how successful or profitable it is; the future also depends on how the organization does business, who has the opportunity to contribute to the decision-making process, and the likelihood that every person has the opportunity to be developed at the same high standard.

As a leader in distance education, Walden University brings together people from varying backgrounds, cultures, and belief systems. The university encompasses a wide range of work styles, thought processes, and perspectives. By taking advantage of all these dynamics, the working group considered how the institution can maximize creativity and innovation and improve operational effectiveness and efficiency. Administrators as well as faculty and staff members were tasked with developing an educational environment that meets the highly diverse cultural needs of Walden's student body. The educational products included considerations for diversity in curricula; diversity in methods of delivery; diversity of the workforce involved in developing, managing, delivering, and supporting our students; and inclusive systems for engaging all stakeholder groups.

The authors of this book provide an opportunity not only to imagine what change in higher education could look like but also to imagine beyond its pages what change in higher education could do. The authors offer a framework for building inclusive postsecondary learning environments in the online space, which is increasingly important as our delivery of post-pandemic education remains largely online. These chapters are intended to invite professors, course designers, administrators, and academic staff to a conversation about changes we can make immediately for long-term, positive impact. These chapters are intended to guide diversity, equity and inclusion efforts in higher education institutions, the individuals in those institutions, and—through the collective effort of those individuals—inspire sustainable organizational equity outcomes.

In the first section of this book, the authors address the theoretical frameworks that ground approaches to create inclusive learning environments. Will Schulz and Ann Morgan identify the need for a person-centered learning model in Chapter 1, "Developing a Learning Model for Caring, Inclusion, and Social Change in an Online Environment." This learning model comes from the values and mission of the university and drives innovations for inclusion and positive social change. As Ann Morgan continues with Kathe Pelletier in Chapter 2, "Digital Appreciative Inquiry for Inclusion," this kind of learning model thrives through appreciative inquiry, an asset-based approach to organizational understanding that grounds initiatives and innovations in community strengths and opportunities. This empowering model engages members of the university in self-determined change and redesign. Both the learning model and the use of digital appreciative inquiry are complemented by sharpening institutional and individual emotional intelligence, as Richard Hammett, Gary Low, and Will Schulz explain in Chapter 3, "Using an Emotional Intelligence Learning System for Person-Centered Curriculum Development and Teaching."

Once a theoretical framework has been constructed, it is equally important to plan how the theory is enmeshed in the online classroom. Tina Marshall-Bradley shares an experience in the Master of Education program in Chapter 4, "Success and Failures in the Development of an Inclusive Online Learning Environment," and explores how the program can continue to improve practices that support BIPOC and other marginalized communities as a way of impacting positive social change. In Chapter 5, "Designing an Inclusive Online Classroom," curriculum and instructional designers Kristi Trapp, Katherine Strang, Kathleen Morrison, and Laura Karl explore how nine core principles and essential questions have guided the way they design inclusive curricula.

The next section concentrates on what those elaborated practices look like and how practitioners experience inclusive practices in action. Todd Dickson shares how an emphasis on inclusion and on the social determinants of health inform teaching for health equity as well as issues that affect nursing education and the nursing workforce in Chapter 6, "Advancing Equity, Diversity, and Inclusion Through the Transformation of Nursing Education." The material in Chapter 7 argues that instruction alone is not enough in online inclusive environments, and Laura Lynn, Melanie Brown, Michelle Brown, and Deborah Inman discuss how to support doctoral students in "Strategies for Doctoral Student Readiness, Student-Centered Support, and Inclusion." D. Gabriela Johnson and Sara Makris make a compelling argument and identify how care operates in online spaces in Chapter 8, "The Students We Have: Compassionate Grading in Online Courses." Rebecca Jobe and Katherine Strang offer an overview of how online spaces can include student, faculty, and staff in discussions and other forms of engagement to create a community of active learners in Chapter 9, "The SPII-Hub and Other Initiatives to Advance Online Engagement." This section showcases the online classroom, student support services, faculty intentionality, and university-wide platforms for operationalizing inclusive engagement.

But how can institutions measure the efficacy of inclusive initiatives? As postsecondary institutions utilize more and more data to understand their students, the feeling of being included is a difficult measure. Yet, Rebecca Jobe, Laura Lynn, and I offer ways of considering inclusive strategy efficacy in Chapter 10, "A Framework to Measure Inclusion." If an institution is not ready to design its own statistical algorithm, Kristin Bundesen, Christopher Gilmer, Latara Lampkin, and Laura Lynn reflect on a self-assessment tool kit measuring how well an institution serves historically underserved students in Chapter 11, "Assessing Institutional Readiness: A Collaboration." In Chapter 12, "Developing a Rubric for a Person-Centered Approach to Teaching in Inclusive Online Learning Spaces," Will Schulz and Juli Konopa detail how an inclusive rubric reinforces the university's learning model and mission and vision for developing scholar practitioners who will advance the betterment of society.

Preface

To plan a university-wide set of initiatives, however, institutions must engage in systems planning. What kinds of systems must be considered to not only operationalize but also *institutionalize* inclusive practices? The chapters in section five sharply focus on how Walden University has reorganized itself along the social determinants of health to realize healthier communities. Aimee Ferraro explains the origin of the social determinants and why they serve as a logical institutional organization strategy (Chapter 13, "Framing Higher Education Through the Social Determinants of Health"). Sue Subocz, Heidi Chumley, Sri Banerjee, and Myrna Cano-Wolfbrandt in Chapter 14, "Sustainable Strategic Planning for Inclusive Online Teaching and Learning," explore how schools can create operational plans designed to sustain a culture of community commitment and ensure an inclusive teaching and learning environment. I consider how organizations can learn and make change individual by individual and academic unit by academic unit in Chapter 15, "Equity in the Online Space? A Multi-Systems Perspective."

To close out the book, Will Schulz and I propose a social determinants of changemakers in Chapter 16. Walden University's mission is to provide a diverse community of career professionals with the opportunity to transform themselves as scholar-practitioners so that they can effect positive social change. The chapters in this book explain how an online institution produces scholar-practitioners dedicated to positive social change. As Walden produces changemakers, we use the epilogue to investigate what socially determined variables and conditions support their development and success.

Raj Chetty, a professor of economics at Harvard University, works with big data. By using data from the United States Census Bureau and the Internal Revenue Service, Chetty and his team at Opportunity Insights track how the annual income of people born in the late 1970s/early 1980s compares to the income of their parents. With a spreadsheet of more than 70 million rows of anonymized data, this team developed a map (https://www.opportunityatlas.org/) showing economic mobility within all 70,000 census tracts, street by street and neighborhood by neighborhood. These data tell the story of how poverty throttles opportunity for children to earn more than their parents, a theme in any understanding of the American dream.

Chetty was inspired to do this kind of work, in part, because the findings from a large government-run study did not seem to make sense. This was a study that had direct and immediate implications for policy, and the findings would undercut opportunities for impoverished families. The *Moving to Opportunity Experiment* conducted by the U.S. Department of Housing and Urban Development from 1994-1998, was an initiative that impacted 5,000 families, cost $80 billion, and took over 20 years to deliver its findings. The findings suggested there was no impact on adult earnings for the children of families who moved from low-income areas to higher-income areas, and that a neighborhood has little bearing on a person's overall economic achievement (Sanbonmatsu et al., 2011). This finding was curious and contradicted troves of social science research that routinely found that if a child grows up in an environment with excellent schools, nutritious food, and safe built environments, that child would have great economic mobility. Chetty et al. (2016) gained access to the *Moving to Opportunity* datasets and discovered that, in fact, a child moving from a low-income to a higher-income neighborhood had a 31% increase in future annual income, and increased college enrollment rates. The issue was the initial 2011 report was published too quickly, and did not allow enough time to lapse to accurately measure younger children's earnings in adulthood. Chetty et al. made a bold request to investigate the data – something rather uncommon in otherwise definitive studies, especially large-scale studies by the federal government.

Reexamining what has been pronounced as hard-and-fast fact, and reimagining different outcomes are examples of two important ways of creating inclusive change. First, we must be bold and tenacious, to deeply understand how systems interact and play out. Second, we must not only be courageous and dogged to understand why some individuals do not have the same kinds of achievements as others – we must course-correct. In postsecondary education, we have the opportunity to investigate how to build the assets diverse students bring to each classroom, and how to build a community of scholar-practitioners ready to take on any challenge. In this course-correction, we have a framework for inclusive spaces online that can impact equity outcomes positively, and I hope you will be bold and harness the changes recommended herein.

Nina M. McCune
Walden University, USA

REFERENCES

Chetty, R., Hendren, N., & Katz, L. F. (2016). The effects of exposure to better neighborhoods on children: New evidence from the moving to opportunity experiment. *The American Economic Review*, *106*(4), 855–902. doi:10.1257/aer.20150572 PMID:29546974

Hodgkinson, H. L. (1969). Walden U.: A working paper. *University History, 1*. https://scholarworks.waldenu.edu/university_history/1

Sanbonmatsu, L., Ludwig, J., Katz, L. F., Gennetian, L. A., Duncan, G. J., Kessler, R. C., Adam, E., McDade, T. W., & Tessler Lindau, S. (2011, November). *Moving to opportunity for fair housing demonstration program. Final impacts evaluation.* United States Department of Housing and Urban Development, Office of Policy Development and Research. http://www.huduser.org/publications/pdf/MTOFHD_fullreport_v2.pdf

United States Government Accountability Office. (2022, June 16). *K-12 education: Student population has significantly diversified, but many schools remain divided along racial, ethnic, and economic lines* (GAO-22-104737). https://www.gao.gov/products/gao-22-104737

Acknowledgment

There are many to thank for contributing in some way to this book. The authors are incredibly grateful to our editorial team, namely Richard Brunelli, Tanisha Landis, and Paolo Ortega for the impeccable communication, the outstanding feedback, and the unflagging support in reviewing *each* and *every* word in this book.

Given that a picture is worth the proverbial 1,000 words, the authors thank Jose Henriquez for the beautiful illustrations and graphic design work. Thank you Andrew Flatgard and the RAL team for ensuring we complied with proper image use guidelines. Your work helps tell the story of educational justice so much more clearly.

I thank each of the authors for their contributions to this work. Your expertise shines in these chapters. I have learned not only content from you, but have also learned from your professionalism and grace. Most of the authors also served as referees; this book would not be complete without this double task.

This book was written during a time of rapid institutional change, as Walden University became part of the Adtalem Global Education family. During this change, all colleagues were asked to support the transition in various ways, adding tasks to already very demanding schedules. Despite limited bandwidth and time, the reviewers and referees of each chapter contributed to the intellectual strength, quality, coherence, and content of this work. There are few words to express how profoundly grateful the authors are. We recognize the contributions of Judi Blakely, Hillary Blevins, Laura Caramanica, Walter Frazier, Maranda Griffin, Sherry Harrison, Jennifer Kozar, Deb Leggett, Tomekeia Luckett, Jack McDonald, Belinda McFeeters, Jackie Olson, Alina Perez, Angie Prehn, Tika Rai, Fran Reed, Rebecca Stout, Alejandra Stuart, Amy White, Don Yarosz, and Ellen Zamarripa. Additionally, I am thankful to the following for responding to any number of questions to help clarify ideas or to locate resources: Kelley Costner, Pamela Denning, Lyda Downs, Rochelle Gilbert, Michelle Hajder, Jessie Lee, Marilyn Powell, Lana Rocca, Deepa Shriram, and Kristy Wake.

The idea for this book came during an animated, late Friday afternoon meeting. While we were perhaps giddy from anticipating the end of a work week, many in that meeting credited their inspiration to our colleague Karen Milheim, who edited a 2017 IGI collection entitled *Cultivating Diverse Online Classrooms Through Effective Instructional Design*. I appreciate the time you spent with me during the early phase of this book, Karen, and I hope this edited work serves and appropriate postscript to yours. Tom Geckel and Mary Mora, I thank you both for the time and consideration you gave when the book was barely an idea. You guided me in the direction we needed to go, and I appreciate your observations and suggestions.

Acknowledgment

For all those who have contributed already, there are more whose work will begin when the book is published. I thank Eric Brosch, Susan Flower, Ashley Guidone, Katie Heitzig, Janeen Johnally, Pat Kahoe, Bill Taylor, and Meghan Willmore for helping to promote the book. I am sure there will be others on the team who will contribute, and I thank you in advance. Your efforts are meaningful and so appreciated.

Sue Subocz, a co-author in this collection, was instrumental in making sure we had the resources and support necessary to carry out this task. Additionally, her vision for educational justice is not only inspiring – it is an example of how postsecondary institutions can, in fact, make change to become not only accessible, but also equitable. Sue, a *thank you* is inadequate to express my gratitude. Your consummate, unwavering allyship and leadership is what makes a more just future possible.

Section 1
Living Theory

What kind of theoretical foundation grounds a university's efforts and approaches to create inclusive learning environments?

Chapter 1
Developing a Learning Model for Caring, Inclusion, and Social Change in an Online Environment

William C. Schulz III
https://orcid.org/0000-0001-8560-5540
Walden University, USA

Ann M. Morgan
https://orcid.org/0000-0002-7607-2743
Walden University, USA

ABSTRACT

A clear and explicitly communicated learning model is at the heart of the learning enterprise for a university. In this chapter, the authors present an inclusive teaching and learning model and discuss how its evolution expresses the values and mission of the university and guide it in outlining the behaviors and expectations that the university places on faculty, staff, and learners with respect to supporting inclusive learning relationships, recruiting faculty and staff, professional development, and performance management.

INTRODUCTION

A clear and explicitly communicated learning model is at the heart of the learning enterprise for a university. An effective learning model specifies the underlying processes and philosophy that guide a learner to achievement of clearly defined learning outcomes/competencies and provide a framework for identifying productive, inclusive learning relationships between and among learners and faculty members. Likewise, an effective learning model outlines the values, behaviors and expectations that the university

DOI: 10.4018/978-1-6684-5146-5.ch001

places on our faculty, staff, and learners with respect to supporting learning relationships, recruiting faculty and staff, professional development, and performance management.

In this chapter, we will explore how Walden's current model evolved over time, reflecting the shared values and practices of our learning community and how the model was and is both informed by emergent practices as well as research. As such, this chapter is primarily theory and informed-practice oriented, and it provides the general outline from which to better understand the applied elements and examples of Walden's inclusive teaching and learning strategy in action, as discussed in later chapters.

We will discuss the broad framework of the model and explore how this person-centered learning model, already rooted in a community of inquiry and appreciative inquiry development structure, incorporates elements that directly support inclusive teaching and learning perspectives. We also will look at how this system reinforces Walden's scholar-practitioner development approach to our mission, which "provides a diverse community of career professionals with the opportunity to transform themselves as scholar practitioners so that they can effect positive social change" (Walden University, n.d., para. 2).

This emergent learning model both reflects the historical strengths of Walden's approach to online learning, but also outlines a set of practices and organizational commitments that will require further effort on behalf of the university to reach this model's integrative aspirations.

BACKGROUND

Evolution of the Learning Model and Link to Cultural Values and Governance

Walden University's community, culture, and commitments to its students (learners), faculty, and staff, are rooted in clearly stated values that establish what it is, how it engages with stakeholders and each other, and how it implements its current and evolving learning model and inclusive teaching and learning strategy. The university's values drive this learning model, and likewise, this learning model informs the university's values in an iterative and reciprocal way.

Three values—quality, integrity, and student- and learning-centeredness—have traditionally been at the core of the university and are the touchstones for action at all organizational levels. They demand high standards of excellence, uncompromising openness and honesty, and primary attention to the learning progress and outcomes of Walden learners.

When operationalized, these values also define an openness and commitment to learning as an organization and to taking opportunities to clarify those values and grow as an institution. As Walden began an in-depth review of our learning model in 2018—and began to focus more explicitly on issues related to educational justice, inclusion, and equity for our learners and others we serve—it became clear that our emerging learning model would also inform and clarify our values as an institution, which is a process we are undertaking as we write this book.

Having said that, the core values of quality, integrity, and student- and learning-centeredness do, in fact, align with and support the learning model we will be exploring in-depth in the remainder of this chapter. These values and principles give Walden University its unique identity and underpin our mission.

One example of the way Walden puts its values into action is through university-wide initiatives and development designed to meet the needs of learners, faculty, and staff. Since review of the learning model began, values-driven professional development themes have included positive leadership (Cameron, 2008) and wellbeing, with an emphasis on health, purpose, and connection (Ryff & Keyes, 1995;

Seligman, 2018; Cohrs et al., 2013). Training and development opportunities in recent years have been aimed at bringing attention to human potential to bring more balance, empathy, and compassion to the global community and greater appreciation for diversity and inclusion.

Table 1 identifies a few key phrases from Walden's official value statements and commitments and links those commitments to concepts that directly inform our inclusive teaching and learning model.

Table 1. Links between Walden's core values and learning model elements/commitments

Portions of Walden's Value Statements	Primary Learning Model Thread(s)
• All motivated adult learners, especially those who are without opportunity in other venues, should have access to innovative educational services. • Provide options for each student and to meet motivated learners where they are, so that they can best develop. • Are open to diversity and inclusion in all that we do as a university.	Toward Educational Justice—Access & Inclusion • Inclusive • Person-Centered • Appreciative Engagement
• Provide useful, dynamic, responsive programs, services, and resources to support each student. • Be learner-centered, incorporating learners' prior knowledge and allowing them to focus their academic work on their needs and interests. • Provide our learners a respectful, supportive learning environment where mutual inquiry, discovery, and student learning is our top priority. • Find new ways to provide our learners with access to learning solutions that meet their needs. • Inquiry/action model of learning fosters critical thinking and underpins research and discovery for reflective practitioners (bachelor's and master's learners) and scholar-practitioners (doctoral learners).	Support Learners in the Journey • Inclusive • Person-Centered • Experiential • Reflection-in-Action • Mutual Inquiry • Transformational Learning
• Consider education and social change are fundamental to the provision and maintenance of democratic ideals and principles, especially that of the common good. • Learners effect positive social change when they behave as reflective or scholarly practitioners.	Toward Educational Justice & Equity—Outcomes • Reflection-in-Action • Transformational Learning

Looking Forward: The Threads of Walden's Learning Model

Given the foregoing, we now consider the inclusive teaching and learning model and transformational learning framework, which has evolved over time as Walden grew and put its values into action.

The learning model (see Figure 1) is a research-based conceptualization of exemplary educational andragogy that engages the adult learner in developing and building knowledge, skills, and attributes that will continue throughout life and result in development as a reflective scholar-practitioner who affects positive social change.

The model includes five interrelated research and practice-based threads that are woven together to support our learners in achieving transformational learning so that they can affect positive social change. Each research and practice-based thread also drives an element of Walden's implementation of its inclusive teaching and learning strategy.

The model commits Walden to these five core principles:

Figure 1. A Visual Representation of Walden University's Inclusive Teaching and Learning Model 2022
Note. Image credit: Dr. Nina McCune, Walden University

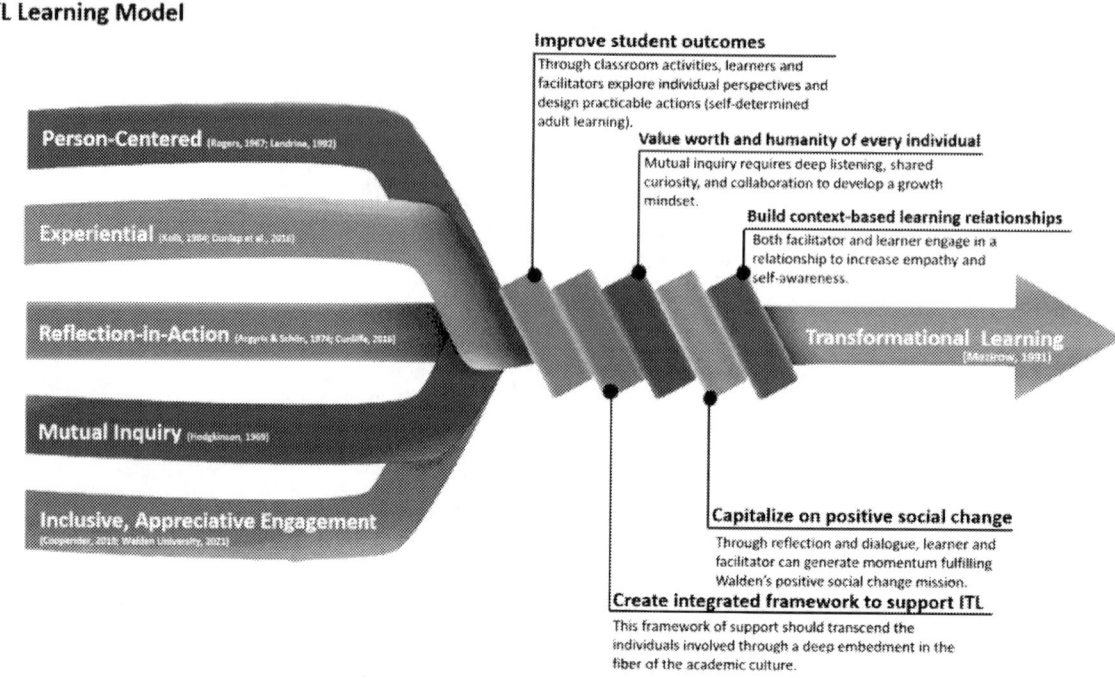

1. That all relationships within the university are **person centered** (Rogers, 1967; Landrine, 1992)—where both learner and facilitator engage in a relationship to increase self-awareness with respect to both the referential self (self at center) and indexical self (self within a social context) perspectives and to support positive regard for others and empathy—with the goal of enhancing mutual learning.
2. That the focus of learning is **rooted in experience and in the integration of knowledge and theory** to create new opportunities for improving our world and affecting positive social change (Kolb, 1984; Dunlap et al., 2016).
3. That we facilitate, through classroom activities, the **exploration of individual perspectives and choices,** and that learners are given the opportunity to reflect on the process of learning itself—that they would become able to **reflect-in-action** as scholar-practitioners (Argyris & Schön, 1974; Cunliffe, 2016).
4. That all learning relationships have **mutual inquiry at their foundation** where mutual curiosity, the ability to listen deeply, and asking questions without judgment are highly valued (Hodgkinson, 1969).
5. That those in learning relationships form an inclusive solidarity, honoring the value that every learner brings for understanding the world better and for **asking positive questions together** where positive affect leads to positive action (Cooperrider & Srivastva, 1987; Morgan, et.al., 2022).

In putting these principles into an integrated, inclusive teaching and learning framework for action, Walden is building on both seminal approaches to andragogy and heutagogy and the most up-to-date research findings available to inform our goal of helping our learners achieve transformational learning (Mezirow, 1991) and become reflective and action-oriented scholar-practitioners who effect positive social change.

Further, this learning model is both informed by, and is part of Walden's formal governance system, and it aligns with regulatory requirements and other university policies and goals to guide the university's improvement practices in andragogy, heutagogy, effective online learning program and course design, and learning technology deployment.

We will now provide a more detailed explanation and research-based grounding of Walden's inclusive teaching and learning model and explore its connections within our mission of serving a diverse community of career professionals so that they can affect positive social change more broadly in the world.

Building a Research-Based Learning Model Rooted in A Mission and Practice

Walden University has been offering educational opportunities for a diverse community of career professionals around the world for more than 50 years and was one of the first doctoral-focused universities to offer such services in a distance-learning and fully online context. Until very recently, Walden concentrated exclusively on the working-adult, a non-traditional-aged learner, and has focused its learning processes and practices to support the adult learner through the application of andragogical principles.

An Andragogical/Heutagogical Context

One of the foundational contexts for Walden's inclusive teaching and learning model is that it is informed by *andragogy*, which is the science and art of adult learning. As initially articulated by Malcom Knowles in the 1980s, andragogical approaches to learning assume that adults (including working professionals) learn differently than children (pedagogy) in at least five important ways:

1. Adults and working professionals generally have a more **mature concept of self** and are more self-motivated and independent in their learning. Adults are more likely to be able to identify most of their learning needs and to benefit from participation in the selection of learning resources and goals.
2. Adults and working professionals have an **increasing level of both professional and life experience** from which to draw upon to make learning analogs and links between practice and theory.
3. Adults and working professionals, based on their increasing maturity and experience, generally have more roles in life, which **increase their readiness and willingness to learn** so that they can be more prepared in those roles.
4. Adults and working professionals tend to be **more problem centered rather than subject centered**. The application of new skills and knowledge for adults must be seen to be relevant immediately in the various roles for which they have responsibility.
5. Adults and working professionals generally **have a stronger internal, intrinsic motivation to learn** and to improve themselves (in addition to learning for problem solving). Adults pursue education rather than having it required of them.

As Fornaciari and Lund Dean (2013) note, "Andragogy principles firmly move power, responsibility, and motivation toward the learner, away from the instructor" (p. 703), and they require that course design, content, and social learning contexts are crafted in such a way as to optimize the learning needs of adults and working professionals.

Traditionally, Walden's learning model has been rooted in principles and practices that straddle traditional *pedagogical approaches* to learning (faculty directed and content centered within a one to many information flow process) and *andragogical practices* for learning (more learner- and problem-analysis centered, with some *many to many* engagements).

As part of Walden's recent revisions and updates to our inclusive teaching and learning model, we are moving much more explicitly to incorporate updated andragogical elements into practice. This includes going even further by incorporating what AlFuqaha (2013) calls Web 2.0 concepts based on heutagogical principles (self-determined and non-linear learning), which leverage mobile platforms with many-to-many and self-determined learning that is rooted in experiential, reflective learning and is also consistent with Kolb's (1984) learning cycle. In Figure 2, AlFuqaha suggests that there is a learning-teaching continuum that moves from Pedagogy to Paragogy.

Figure 2. The Continuum from Pedagogy to Heutagogy and Paragogy
Note. Image based on AlFuqaha, 2013, p. 43, image credit Jose Henriquez, Walden University.

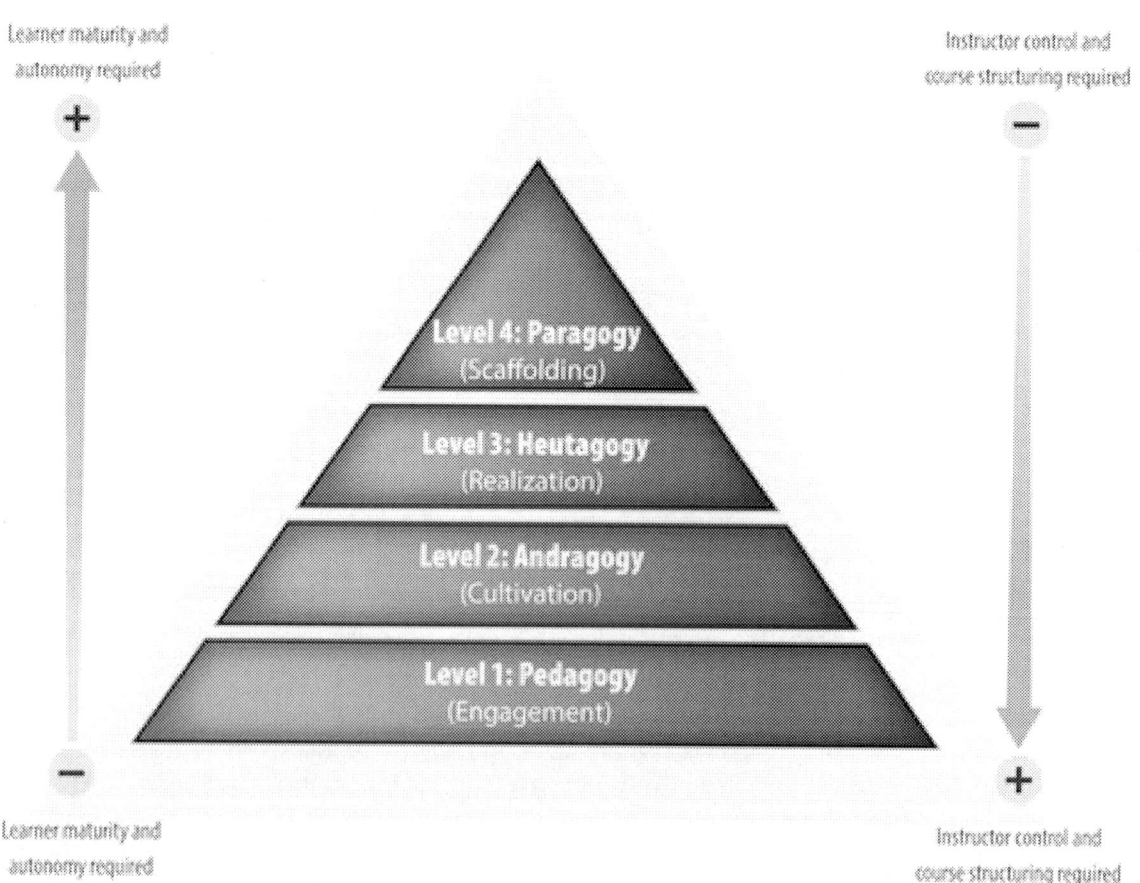

AlFuqaha (2013) describes the heutagogy paradigm shift this way:

The heutagogy (Web 2.0 edutainment) paradigm means 'self-directed or self-determined learning'. It is learner centered too, and involves experiential learning to stimulate meaning, promotes the concept of self-determined holistic learning through critical reflection, and involves encouraging learners to become deeply reflective while developing their abilities.

Experiential learning focuses upon helping learners understand how experiences affect their values, beliefs, goals, habits, conceptual frameworks, and previously held ideals, and to contemplate ways in which the learners might expand their self-efficacy in these areas (2013, p. 42)

However, as Herie (2013, p. 11) notes, there is yet more opportunity to move beyond discrete competency development to more generalized self-learning capability development.

Andragogy, as self-directed learning focused on competency development, is re-conceptualized in heutagogy as self-determined learning focused on developing capabilities. As our rapidly changing occupational terrains continuously advance and expand workforce competency needs, today's workforce requires lifelong learners who are both competent and capable.

No post-secondary program of study can ever really prepare students with all of the knowledge and skills needed (competencies); rather, it is one's capability in determining what knowledge and skills need continuous development, and how to access/master them (capabilities).

Herie argues that learning models and educational services that are rooted in heutagogical principles can help learners better learn to learn and become strong knowledge curators and hyperlearners who develop and continually strengthen their capabilities at effectively accessing and applying knowledge in a nonlinear fashion. This view is compatible with Paul Hanstedt's (2018) call to help create *wicked students* who can address *wicked problems* (Rittel & Webber, 1973). This requires the ability to think beyond the scripted knowledge of a given discipline as well as integrative and reflective learning.

Heutagogical approaches encourage the process of learning over the content (the *how* rather than the *what*) and emphasize networked community learning (many to many) and crowdsource learning. Herie emphasizes that:

Heutagogy's emphasis on developing capabilities in a learner-directed, nonlinear and process-oriented way makes it particularly well suited to today's digital generation, where connectivity, creativity and reflexivity are foundational to global citizenship and collaboration (Herie, 2013, p. 12).

From the brief summary of Walden's inclusive teaching and learning model (see Table 2), one can begin to see how the model builds upon effective andragogical and heutagogical practices. In this model, one of the goals is to support transformational learning, where learners demonstrate capabilities at applying competencies in novel situations and to diverse audiences.

Table 2. Andragogical and Heutagogical Foundations of the Inclusive Teaching & Learning Model

Learning Model Element	Advanced Andragogical Foundation	Heutagogical Practice
Person-Centered	Adults and working professionals generally have a more **mature concept of self** and are more self-motivated and independent in their learning.	Develops capabilities in a learner-directed, nonlinear, and process-oriented way.
Experiential	• Adults and working professionals have an **increasing level of both professional and life experience** from which to draw upon to make learning analogs and links between practice and theory. • Adults and working professionals tend to be **more problem centered rather than subject centered**. The application of new skills and knowledge for adults must be seen to be relevant immediately in the various roles for which they have responsibility.	Involves experiential learning to stimulate meaning, including peer-to-peer learning.
Reflection-in-Action	Promotes the concept of self-determined holistic learning through critical reflection.	Involves encouraging learners to become deeply reflective while developing their abilities.
Mutual Inquiry	Adults and working professionals generally **have a stronger internal, intrinsic motivation to learn** and to improve themselves (in addition to learning for problem solving). Adults pursue education rather than having it required of them.	
Inclusive & Appreciative	Adults and working professionals, based on their increasing maturity and experience, generally have more roles in life. This **increases their readiness and willingness to learn** so that they can be more prepared in those roles.	• Promotes connectivity, creativity, and reflexivity. • Promotes inclusive experiential learning that focuses on helping learners understand how their own experiences, as well as those of others, affect their values, beliefs, goals, habits, conceptual frameworks, and previously held ideals.

Note. This table summarizes how the inclusive teaching and learning model emphasizes both andragogical foundations and heutagogical practices.

A Community of Inquiry and Mutual Inquiry Context

Walden's current learning model and related best practices and quality hallmarks were informed by Karen Swan's 2004 research, *Relationships Between Interactions and Learning in Online Environments*, published by the Sloan Consortium (now called the Online Learning Consortium, or OLC), a consortium committed to quality online education. Swan's analysis focused on how effective learning is influenced, within a community of inquiry context, by three major intersecting interactions, as shown in Figure 3.

This model suggests that effective online learning is dependent on:

1. The need to have an *effective online interface/learning management system* that is intuitive; easy to access and navigate to find important information; easy to read, watch and listen to content; easy to find faculty and peer comments; and easy to find and track both formative and evaluative feedback. The underlying interface can either enhance learning or hinder it if the structure is not optimal.
2. A strong **Cognitive Presence**, where learners can interact with *content that is relevant*, current, and reflective of the state of the art in the discipline or field and where they can engage actively with written and other feedback provided by the faculty in rubrics and other forms

Figure 3. Community of Inquiry Model for Effective Online Learning
Note. This image is adapted from Swan, 2004, p. 1. Image credit Jose Henriquez, Walden University.

RELATIONSHIPS BETWEEN INTERACTIONS AND LEARNING IN ONLINE ENVIRONMENTS

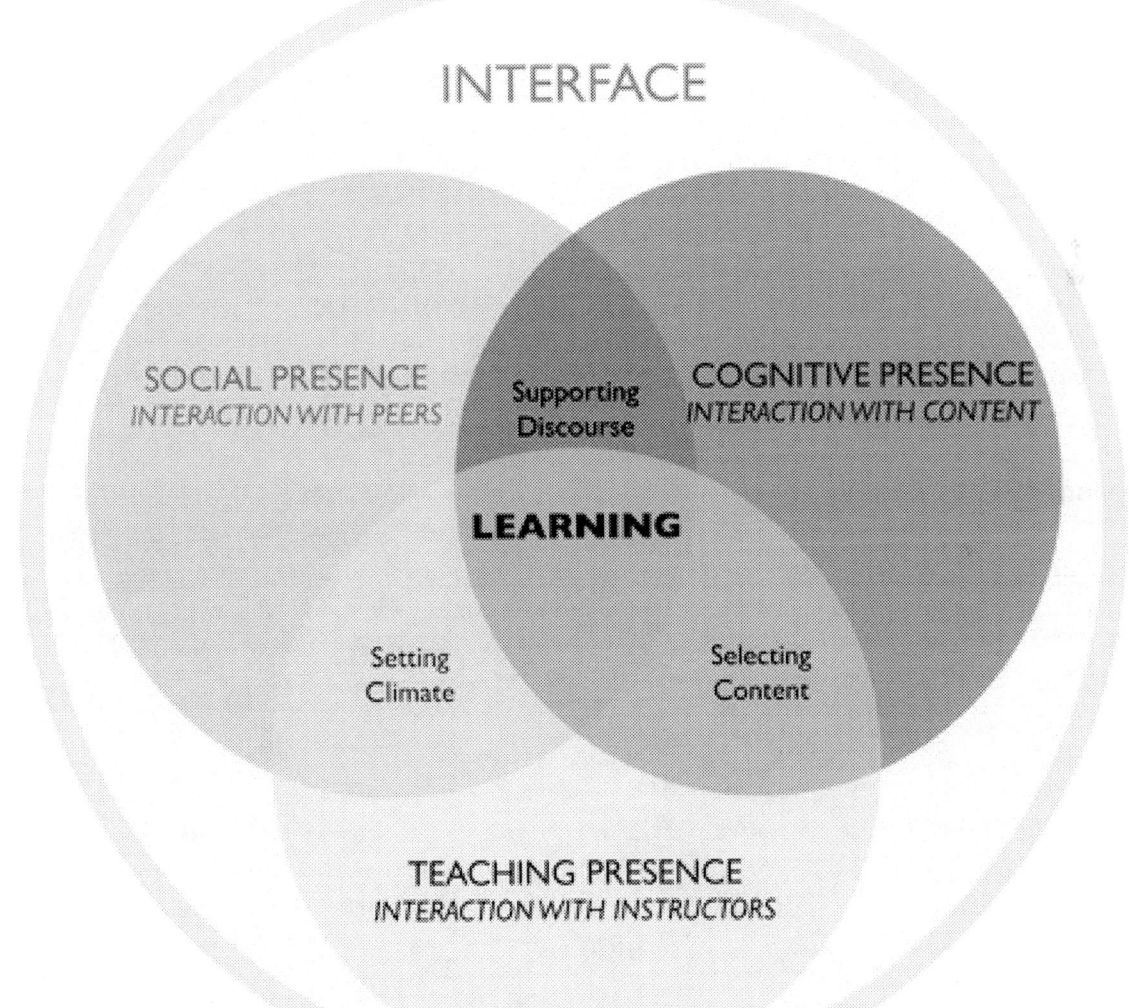

INTERFACE

SOCIAL PRESENCE
INTERACTION WITH PEERS

Supporting Discourse

COGNITIVE PRESENCE
INTERACTION WITH CONTENT

LEARNING

Setting Climate

Selecting Content

TEACHING PRESENCE
INTERACTION WITH INSTRUCTORS

3. A strong ***Teaching/Facilitating Presence***, where learners can interact with faculty on a substantive basis and where faculty can help learners better understand the context and implications of the course content relative to the course and program learning outcomes and professional skill and knowledge development
4. A strong ***Social Presence***, where learners can interact with their peers within a community of practice context and where discussions are more open ended and help learners integrate their practice with newly emerging skills and knowledge

The Swan model is a powerful *transactional* model for effective online learning and has served Walden well over the years. However, given the increasingly diverse nature of Walden's adult/working professional learning community, it was clear that our learning model needed to be more responsive to this diversity and more explicit in addressing how we could improve inclusive teaching and learning across all three primary domains of the community of inquiry framework, but particularly with respect to the social and teaching presence domains.

CONNECTING THE MODEL TO INCLUSIVE TEACHING AND LEARNING ONLINE

The Model Is Inclusive and Person Centered with a Focus on Appreciative Mutual Inquiry

Moving to Support More Substantive Inclusion University-Wide

Research suggests that Walden's diverse learner demographics are an important context from which to assess our teaching and learning practices and learning models. Devlin and Mckay (2018) argue that learners that come from traditionally underserved populations have not only the responsibility for learning the content of their courses of study, but also for bearing the burden of having to learn how to be a university student and to be able to read and understand the cultural capital that underlies university expectations, which are often hidden. They continue:

[This paper] argues that the need to master the student role, to be aware of and be able to respond to and manage tacit expectations and the hidden curriculum, to behave and perform according to unspoken expectations and to have the requisite digital competencies and skills are **key to non-traditional student achievement and success** *(p. 146; bolded text added for emphasis).*

They argue that "students from higher socio-economic strata and traditional backgrounds build familiarity with these tacit assumptions, values and expectations [the cultural capital of the university] over a lifetime," (p. 149) while students with non-traditional backgrounds often struggle to understand what is expected of them (and why), what is assumed about their prior experiences and academic capabilities, and how to navigate the university overall.

In short, many nontraditional learners come to online education and the university assumes that the learners are motivated, know why they are there, what is expected of them, and how to navigate the complex university organization to get answers to questions. The reality, however, is that these nontraditional learners need help in learning to become a university learner (Christie et al., 2008; Collier & Morgan, 2008).

When universities fail to prepare their learners to learn, and to know what is expected of them before they begin their learning journey, then the term *broad access* is a misnomer, as access is not the same as *inclusive*. "The goal of access policies should be successful participation in higher education, as access without a reasonable chance of success is an empty promise" (International Association of Universities, n.d., p. 1).

As such, Walden has pursued a robust inclusive teaching and learning strategy (see Chapter 14, "Sustainable Strategic Planning for Inclusive Online Teaching and Learning") that recognizes that our learners will come to the university with a wide range of experiences and that none of our staff and faculty should make blanket assumptions about their needs. We should strive to provide the opportunity for each individual to flourish in a full, person-centered, and caring learning environment.

This means that we should strive to know each learner as a person (their referential self) and also as a person situated in a larger social and cultural context (their indexical self) as suggested by the work of Hope Landrine (1992) and informed by the broader social determinants of health and learning framework provided by Sanderson (2021). To meet learners where they are and to truly include them, we must seek, as a university, to be culturally sensitive, expansive, and competent.

For example, Landrine (1992) offers a cross-cultural and anthropological analysis, originally meant for clinical psychologists, that is relevant and informative in how faculty (and course-writing teams, in particular) might increase their cultural sensitivity and awareness by recognizing that their learners come to them from a variety of contexts of the self,—ranging from the Western concept of the referential, self-determined self to the indexical self of sociocentric cultures—in which one's understanding of self is deeply embedded within one's familial, community, and national/regional relationships (including learning relationships). Landrine's observations, while aimed at clinical psychologists, resonate well within an educational relationship perspective as well. To know, and support the whole person, we must pay attention to both notions of self that Landrine outlines.

This distinction becomes important because Walden's inclusive teaching and learning strategies and practices are informed by the fundamental goal of ensuring learners know Walden values the inherent worth, humanity, and dignity of *each of them as they engage with our staff and faculty*. Inclusive teaching at Walden is an intentional practice and conscious awareness of the diverse social, cultural, and community identities, knowledge, and lived experiences of all learners.

By sharing knowledge and expertise through mutual inquiry, inclusive learning at Walden empowers and connects each learner with multiple perspectives and ways of thinking about the practices that can benefit a variety of cultures and contexts. In this space, students build upon existing knowledge and advance lifelong skills to create positive social change in local, national, and global communities. Programs and courses are designed to provide the opportunity for each individual to flourish in a person centered and caring learning environment. It is to the person-centered elements of the learning model that we now turn our attention.

A Person-Centered Approach to Teaching and Learning

A fundamental aspect of Walden's inclusive teaching and learning model is that we strive to ensure that all learning relationships within the university are person centered (Rogers, 1967; Landrine, 1992)—where both learner and facilitator engage in a relationship to increase self-awareness (in both the referential-self and indexical-self contexts), positive regard for others, and empathy—and are focused on learning through mutual inquiry.

This person-centered approach applies some of the constructs that Carl Rogers applied within a humanistic approach to psychology and clinical practice, but within a generalized educational and learning-relationship perspective, as suggested by both Rogers (1969) and by Swan et.al. (2020). In applying Rogers's framework to education, he noted in *Freedom to Learn*:

- People [learners] have great **potential for self-awareness, choice, responsibility,** and growth—and have a natural potentiality for learning.
- Self-initiated learning, which involves the whole person of the learner—**feelings as well as intellect**—is the **most lasting and pervasive**.
- The most socially useful learning in the modern world is **the learning of the process of learning**, a continuing openness to experience and **incorporation into oneself of the process of change.**
- Empathetic therapists (**learning facilitators) should help unlock client's** (learners') untapped potential.

You'll note that Rogers's insights closely align with some of the core assumptions and observations related to andragogy and heutagogy, where the learning context should build on strengths and interests, involve the whole person and their thoughts and feelings/emotions (see Chapter 3, "Using an Emotional Intelligence Learning System for Person-Centered Curriculum Development and Teaching"), recognize the need for thoughtful reflection about self and others (Landrine, 1992), and, where learning-to-learn is an important, transformational process (capabilities building, not just competency-development).

Within the Rogerian approach to person-centered learning, the following behaviors must guide both and/or all persons in a learning relationship:

- There must be *congruence* between the learner and facilitator.
  - Presence
  - Realness (authenticity)
  - Genuineness (general courtesy)
- There must be a *level of regard* between the learner and facilitator.
  - Active listening
  - Positive recognition
  - Timeliness in feedback and engagement
  - Contextual and culturally competent feedback
- There must be *empathy in the relationship* between the learner and the facilitator.
  - Reflective callouts
  - Overall caring approach

Rogers argues that through our curriculum and teaching we must reach the whole person and seek to understand and engage with the whole person and their learning context (Rogers, 1969; Landrine, 1992). Hence, this is a person-centered approach, not merely a student-centered approach in which faculty and support staff, working together, help to unlock the client's, or the learner's, untapped potential.

Developing a Learning Model for Caring, Inclusion, and Social Change in an Online Environment

It is everyone's job in the university, through the lenses of this person-centered approach, to provide on-the-spot customization when we can so that learners understand we see them as individuals and that we're working to help them learn best in support of their goals.

For the purposes of this chapter, it is sufficient that these person-centered elements be introduced at this general level. Please review Chapter 12 ("Developing a Rubric for a Person-Centered Approach to Teaching in Inclusive Online Learning Spaces"), in which we explore these relational constructs in more detail and share the outlines of a person-centered rubric to guide development and measurement of these behaviors.

An Appreciative and Mutual Inquiry Context

Of course, the general context in which person-centered learning relationships form is important, and two other of the five threaded elements of Walden's learning model provide some of the institutional expectations that we have in support of building effective person-centered learning relationships—taking an approach to learning that involves both mutual inquiry *and* inclusive, appreciative engagement.

The highly related processes of appreciative engagement (Cooperrider, 2018) and mutual inquiry (Hodgkinson, 1969) set the stage for building person-centered learning relationships, and, interestingly, both center around the process of being curious together and asking and making inquiries into interesting and even beautiful questions (Berger, 2014).

These processes of appreciative engagement (see Chapter 2, "Digital Appreciative Inquiry for Inclusion") and mutual inquiry are at the heart of the learning context and are aimed at transformational learning because, as Cooperrider and Whitney (2005) note, change begins the moment we question, and in doing so together as teacher and learner (and each member of a learning relationship can inhabit both roles!), traditional barriers and power distribution in the relationship begin to change.

Curiosity about others and how we can work together to improve the world is the starting point for an appreciative engagement/mutual inquiry framework. The development and accretion of knowledge is an open, broad activity guided by the need to address complex challenges by learning both within and across discipline and from a diverse range of perspectives. As such, it is important to recognize that the curricula (and the engagement areas within the LMS) makes space and faculty acknowledge, appreciate, and ask for multiple perspectives taken with positive regard and a strengths-based approach. In particular, from an inclusive teaching and learning perspective:

- The curricula make space and faculty members encourage discussion that is culturally expansive
- The curricula and faculty allow for engagement with both the referential and indexical selves of both learners and faculty (Landrine, 1992)
- The curricula and faculty create spaces for sharing and comparing stories
- Faculty honor the disorientation and exploration that leads to transformation
- Faculty and learners ask positive questions together

In Walden's learning model, we have woven elements of an appreciative inquiry framework together with our own historical practice of mutual inquiry. In updating its learning model, Walden has put an emphasis on having its faculty (and staff) behave as positive education leaders whose behaviors are rooted in the appreciative inquiry paradigm. As Johnson (2014, p. 2–4) notes:

As an instructional method, appreciative inquiry has a potential to help bridge the gap between the instructor and student within an online classroom...Appreciative inquiry takes a positive approach to change (Cooperrider, Whitney & Stavros, 2008) and the development of relationships rather than placing an emphasis on employee and organizational deficits...

In appreciative inquiry, as a framework for guiding faculty-learner and peer-to-peer learning relationships, conversations and engagement are based on the "act of appreciation of each [faculty and learner's] values and abilities (*begin with what is good*) and rooted in a process of inquiry that *uses questions as a form of communication*" (Johnson, 2014, p. 4; italics added for emphasis).

Appreciative inquiry also assumes that conversations create meaning, and that the principle of simultaneity relates change to inquiry, whereby questions, as a form of inquiry, set the stage for true change and learning. This simultaneity principle:

acknowledges that when we are genuinely curious, and ask positive and powerful questions, the questions themselves set direction. Good questions point us in the direction of our thinking and action. (Johnson, 2014, p. 8)

In this light, the role of faculty shifts from purveyor of knowledge to expert, curious, positive guides that ask questions within a community of learning and practice and who are focused at every step of an individual's learning journey on ways to support that learner and create a positive emotional state that can sustain the learner's motivation.

As noted earlier, the integration of an appreciative inquiry model into best practices for Walden faculty *is fully aligned with our founding principles*. Harold L. (Bud) Hodgkinson, one of Walden's founding leaders, and principal author of *Walden U: A Paper* (1969) noted:

Basic to the entire program [at Walden] is the concept of inquiry. Inquiry is the bridge between teaching and learning, content, and method. . . Pedagogy [andragogy], therefore, comes to mean the act of mutual inquiry.. . . collaboration, trust, and growth are a part of the educational rhetoric but not a part of the educational scene. . .The rigid line between content and method, teacher and student, ignorance and knowledge, and teaching and research need to be made more interactive and processual (p. 1).

Dr. Hodgkinson's observation that effective mutual inquiry and knowledge creation (and application) requires a process of engagement that is *highly collaborative and fuzzy at the edges*, is an important one, and it is directly consistent with the principles of effective appreciative inquiry processes. For effective and rigorous practitioner-scholarship:

- Is a highly iterative process that requires its practitioners to be able to re-imagine lines of thinking as new insights and facts emerge during learning and research,
- Requires that we make links between seemingly disparate concepts, and,
- Compels us to reconcile differences in assessment and the perceived meaning of other's work.

Effective mutual inquiry *requires mutual curiosity, explorations of thoughts, and the ability to listen carefully and deeply to one another and to avoid a judgmental attitude.* Mutual inquiry requires thoughtful engagement of ideas and a willingness to be *learning-centered*, where both learner and faculty are open to learning, and where both faculty and learner model reflexive and double-loop learning together (Argyris & Schön; Cunliffe, 2016). Faculty must be prepared and willing to ask mutual (and often difficult) questions about ways of thinking—interpreting or understanding events, concepts, and mindsets that differ across various cultural and experiential boundaries (Landrine, 1992)—and they should seek to model and encourage imagination and aspirational thinking for social change.

Likewise, for authentic learning relationships to develop and to increase trust by learners so that they can be more open to transformational learning, faculty must also model and express care and empathy for their learners. They should delight at discovery and the broadening of their learners' and their own thinking and understanding of the world.

To remain competitive and to thrive as a learning institution dedicated to working professionals, especially at the graduate and doctoral level, it is imperative that universities emphasize their focus on some form of appreciative inquiry as a form of mutual inquiry and learning and *recruit and retain faculty that are particularly well suited for a values-based approach to their craft*. For the most part, technical and gatekeeper approaches to the work of faculty must be secondary to strengths-based and servant leadership approaches. In short, hire for attitude, cultural awareness, and reflexive, supportive behaviors, and train for additional skill (where baselines skills are typically the very basic initial screening criteria).

Built on an Experiential Learning Cycle & Constructivist Base

Another of the threads of Walden's inclusive teaching and learning model focuses on is learning that is experiential and constructivist and that again supports transformational learning (Mezirow, 1991). By beginning with the end in mind (to help provide opportunities for practitioner-scholars to apply new insights, skills, and knowledge to addressing social change challenges), the model is built so that there are clear connections between theory and practice, and that the connection starts with an articulated opportunity, need, or problem from the field of practice.

That is, the curricula are structured in such a way that they are opportunity/problem driven. They build on the fact that learners come to learning with a desire to understand the nature of these opportunities and problems more deeply and want to learn how specific knowledge (from the curricula) can help them envision and enact positive change in their life, for their families and communities, or the discipline under study, etc.

The model thus incorporates a variation of Kolb's (1984) learning cycle theory, and does so within a degree level of success context where:

- Learners develop scaffolded competencies that focus on challenges in the field of practice and that are guided by academic knowledge.
- Learners can make informed choices about focus and assessment—driving an emotional connection to the work.
- As appropriate (especially at the doctoral level), learners move toward self-determined learning (heutagogy) and personal choices regarding transformational learning.
- The curricula encourage an interdisciplinary and transdisciplinary discussion and engagement built around some applied knowledge system—such as the Social Determinants of Health (SDOH) framework or the U.N. Sustainable Development Goals—consistent with the mission of the university.

Toward an Integrated, Appreciative, Andragogical-Heutagogical, Recursive Learning Process

If we take the proposition that learning processes are becoming more important in both helping learners master competencies *and* building life-long capabilities, then there is another opportunity to weave these elements into an inclusive teaching and learning model and have it explicitly incorporate such processes.

Dunlap et al. (2016) take this approach in, *Presence+Experience: A Framework for the Purposeful Design of Presence in Online Courses*. The authors integrate Swan's (2004) community of practice approach (which has historically guided Walden's learning model) with Kolb's experiential learning process/cycle model, which they describe as "a more prescriptive model effectively used to structure on-campus and online courses" (Dunlap et al., 2016, p. 145).

The Kolb Experiential Learning Theory (KELT), articulated in *Experiential Learning* (1984), is one of the best-known approaches for addressing how learners develop knowledge and skills through an iterative process (fractal cycle). The process requires individuals to critically reflect on their concrete experiences and current learned knowledge in light of new knowledge and abstract concepts that might help them improve their understanding of a particular problem or gap in understanding and to test their new understanding through the application and exercise of their *new knowledge/skills*. Additionally, individuals are required to iterate again as *theory meets practice* and establishes a new *experience base*.

Kolb's learning theory proposes both the ideas of a *learning process cycle*, and distinct *learning styles*. While there is controversy over the empirical validation of the learning styles elements of KELT (Moores et al., 2004), there remains broad acceptance of the generalized experiential learning cycle process elements of the theory, which continue to offer a strong conceptual basis for understanding experiential learning and for developing even more advanced learning process theories, such as the Co-Constructed Developmental Teaching Theory (CDTT) discussed by Schenk and Cruickshank (2015).

For our purposes, the Dunlap et al. (2016) approach of integrating the Kolb's learning cycle with the community of interest learning model of Swan (2004) seems productive. Figures 4 and 5 illustrate how they have integrated these two learning models, where the central element in gray represents the Kolb learning process and each of the other elements speak presence within the community of inquiry context, which inform how to best set climate, support discourse, and select content within an online course.

Dunlap et al. (2016) suggest the following about their integrated model (*italics our emphasis*):

The P+E framework is particularly helpful for online course designers and educators who are creating courses requiring a high level of interpersonal connection, such as courses in education, counseling, social work, and the like; we believe that the P+E framework may help alleviate educators' concerns about delivering and facilitating the learning of high-touch content online. (p. 151)

These observations support the idea that a *community of inquiry-based experiential learning model* could be a suitable basis from which to move toward a more robust, andragogy-to-heutagogy learning model that builds on the best of all elements of the models (see Figure 6).

This model builds on the general, iterative learning cycle proposed by Kolb (1984) and Schenk and Cruickshank, 2015, and integrates the general andragogical framework of Knowles (1980, items in blue), as well as an inclusive and appreciative inquiry approach, following Johnson (2014). The model reflects:

Developing a Learning Model for Caring, Inclusion, and Social Change in an Online Environment

- the focus on learning processes and the iterative/fractal nature of these cycles of learning and relearning (learning and capability-building at the center),
- a nonlinear approach to teaching and learning that is compatible with emerging knowledge about how neurobiology informs and affects learning (learning at center),
- an andragogical context that incorporates the fundamental experiential and content elements of learning for adult, working professionals (cognitive presence),
- the important elements of recognizing working professional needs to co-create learning outcomes and the learning process with peers and facilitators (social presence, supporting discourse) within a respectful, caring, diverse, and inclusive environment that supports and invites multiple perspectives in terms of both content and outcomes, and
- the important, person-centered dynamic learning relationships and climate that must be built to foster trust and engagement for high-level competency and capability development (teaching presence, setting climate), where learners are free to experiment, disciplined in their self-reflection, and are fully and emotionally connected to the process (see Chapter 3, "Using an Emotional Intelligence Learning System for Person-Centered Curriculum Development and Teaching").

Figure 4. The Presence + Experience (P + E) Framework
Note. Image used with permission. Original image in Dunlap et al., 2016, p. 148.

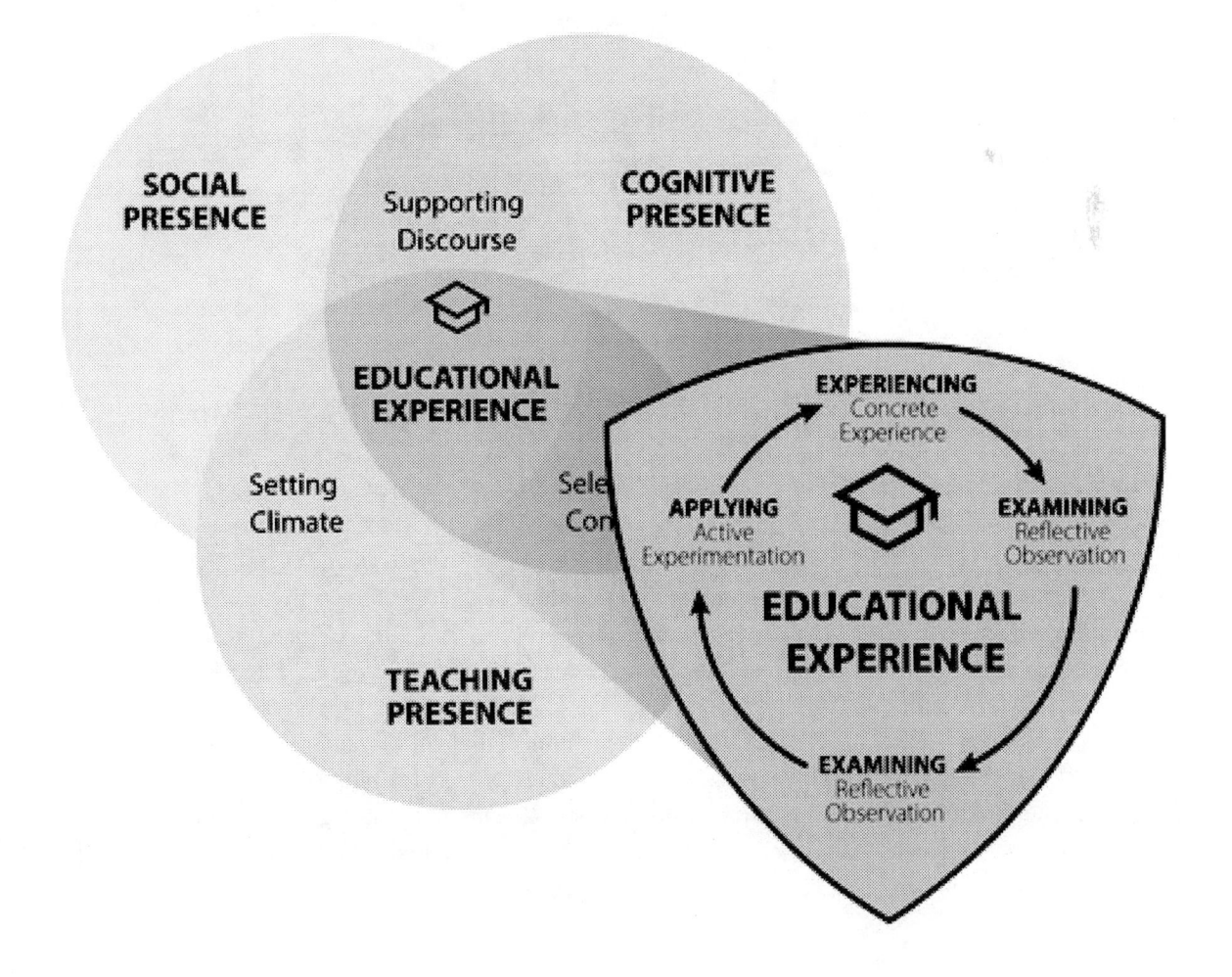

17

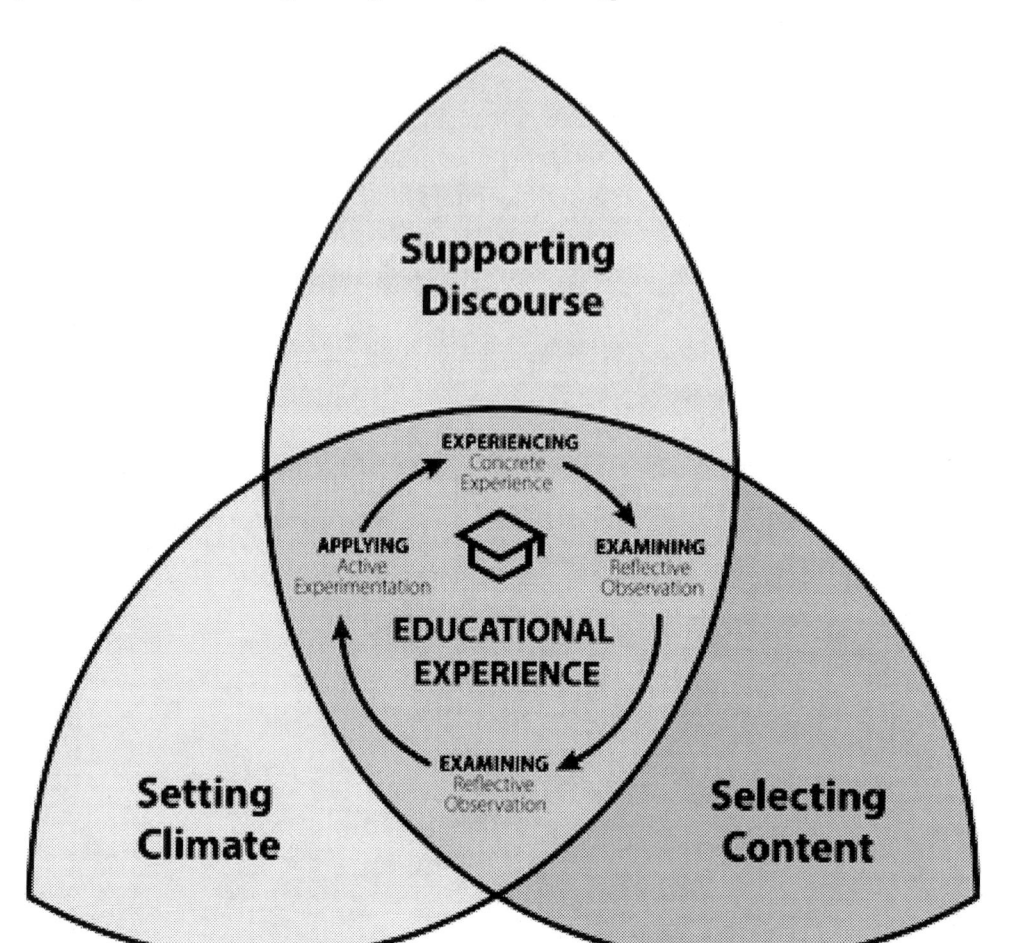

Figure 5. Educational Engagement with Experience is at the heart of the Dunlap et al. (2016) model
Note. Image used with permission. Original image in Dunlap et al., 2016, p. 148.

Toward More Choice-Making, Reflection-in-Action & Transformative Learning

Figure 7 illustrates how the threads of Walden's learning model elements wrap around the iterative, experiential learning cycle and where reflection-in-action helps support transformative learning. In this view, we can see how andragogical principles from Knowles (1980) (outside arrows) align with the Kolb's learning cycle (icons) and where appreciative, mutual inquiry—fueled by positive, interesting, curiosity-based, beautiful questions (asked Socratically or otherwise)—drives capabilities learning.

This is a nonlinear, iterative approach to inclusive teaching and learning that depends on positive engagement by both teachers and learners with respect to the full cycle of feelings rooted in lived experience, meeting reflective observations and thinking/conceptualization, and then experimenting and applying new formulations of knowledge and practice, thereby transforming one's knowledge of self, world, and the possibility for new and transformative action. This integrated model has many implications for inclusive curricula design (see Chapter 5, "Designing an Inclusive Online Classroom"), but the following are worth noting at a general level. The model:

Figure 6. A More Detailed, Integrated Learning Model to Integrate Andragogy with Heutagogy
Note. Image credit: Jose Henriquez, Walden University

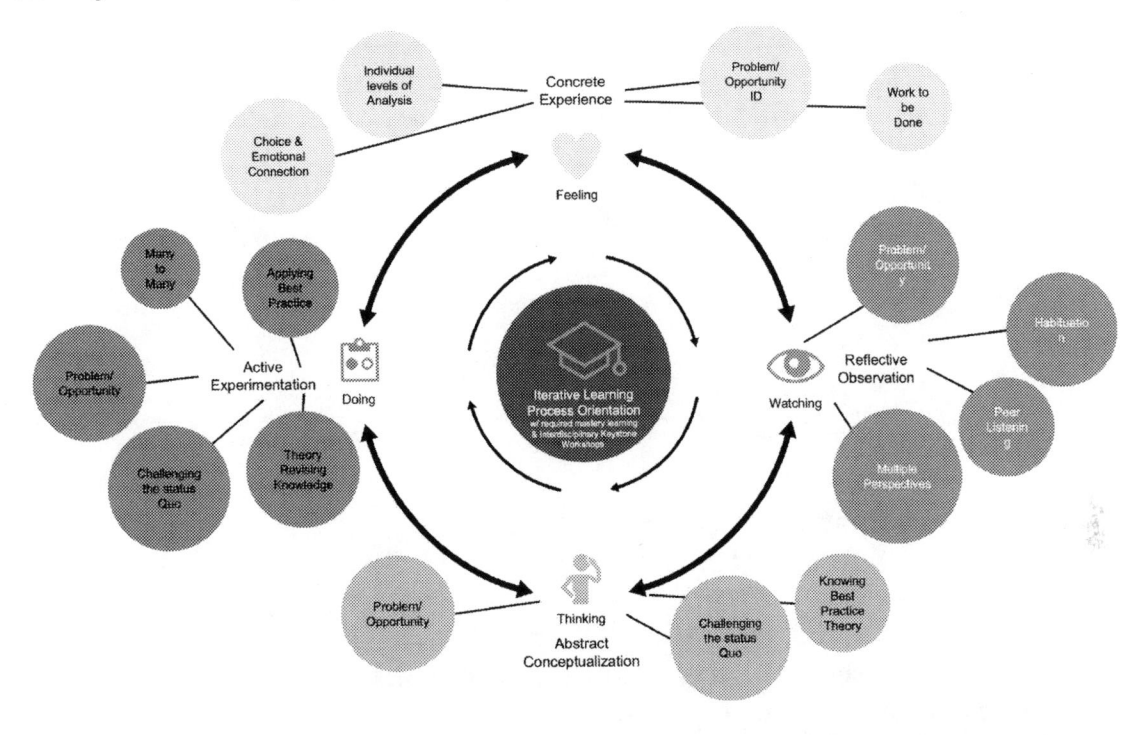

Figure 7. The Learning Engagement Process Within an Integrated KELT-Based Learning Cycle
Note. Image credit: Jose Henriquez, Walden University

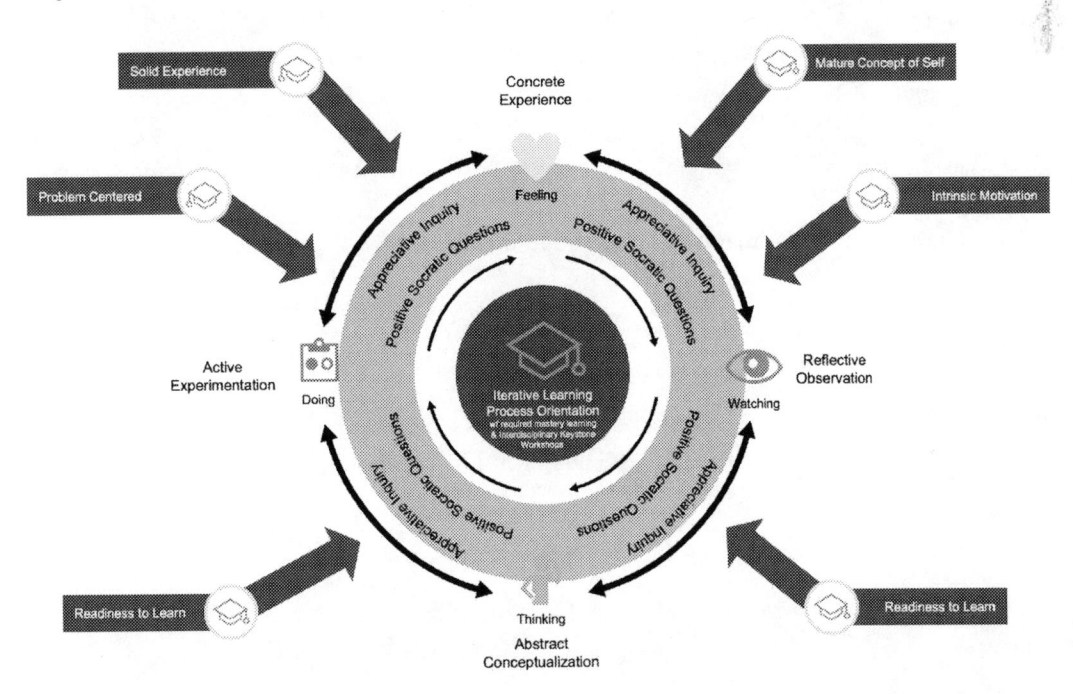

- Provides more opportunities for Choice-Making
    - Emphasizes the integration of learner choice and co-creation of learning pathways within the curricula
    - More choice in identifying and exploring specific opportunities in the field of practice
    - More choice in identifying appropriate learning assessments that meet learning outcomes of course/programs
- Emphasizes Double-Loop Learning or Reflection-in-Action (Schön, 1984; Cunliffe, 2016)
    - Deploy appropriate journaling and other means for building strong self-reflective capabilities in learners
    - Learning to think about and reflect on learning and both the referential self and the indexical self (Landrine, 1992)

CONCLUSION

The Goal is Transformative Learning and Enhancing One's Capability to Engage for Social Change

In this chapter we have explored, in varying degrees of depth, the five central threads of an integrated inclusive teaching and learning model that has been designed to help a large online university implement its inclusive teaching and learning strategies and to help better support students as they seek transformative learning, both in themselves and as agents for positive social change. Figure 1 (at the beginning of this chapter) serves as a visual representation of the general version of the model, and this model appears several times throughout the book.

An important feature of this general model, and of the more integrated and detailed versions of the model also presented in this chapter, is that they are dynamic and iterative because the threads cycle together to weave a self-reinforcing pattern and an inclusive kaleidoscope of potential. Each thread is an important element, but not *the* most important. The model reflects the reality that the whole is much more than the sum of its parts—and that is both the beauty of it conceptually and the challenge of bringing it to life.

It is to that challenge that the many contributors to this book now take us.

REFERENCES

AlFuqaha, I. N. (2013). Pedagogy redefined: Frameworks of learning approaches prevalent in the current digital information age. *Journal of Educational Technology*, 10(1), 36–45. https://eric.ed.gov/?id=EJ1101795

Argyris, C., & Schön, D. (1974). *Theory in practice: Increasing professional effectiveness*. Jossey Bass.

Berger, W. (2014). *A more beautiful question: The power of inquiry to spark breakthrough ideas*. Bloomsbury.

Cameron, K. (2008). *Positive leadership: Strategies for extraordinary performance*. Berrett-Koehler Publishers.

Canning, N. (2010). Playing with heutagogy: Exploring strategies to empower mature learners in higher education. *Journal of Further and Higher Education, 34*(1), 59–71. doi:10.1080/03098770903477102

Christie, H., Tett, L., Cree, V. E., Hounsell, J., & McCune, V. (2008). 'A real rollercoaster of confidence and emotions': Learning to be a university student. *Studies in Higher Education, 33*(5), 567–581. doi:10.1080/03075070802373040

Cohrs, J. C., Christie, D. J., White, M. P., & Das, C. (2013). Contributions of positive psychology to peace: Toward global well-being and resilience. *The American Psychologist, 68*(7), 590–600. doi:10.1037/a0032089 PMID:24128320

Collier, P. J., & Morgan, D. L. (2008). Is that paper due today?: Differences in first-generation and traditional college students' understandings of faculty expectations. *Higher Education, 55*(4), 425–446. doi:10.100710734-007-9065-5

Cooperrider, D. L. (2018). A time for action: Appreciative inquiry, positive peace and the making of a Nobel nomination. *AI Practitioner, 20*(1), 7–18. doi:10.12781/978-1-907549-34-2-2

Cooperrider, D. L., & Srivastva, S. (1987). Appreciative inquiry in organizational life. *Research in Organizational Change and Development, 1*, 129–169.

Cooperrider, D. L., & Whitney, D. (2005). *Appreciative inquiry: A positive revolution in change*. Berrett-Koehler Publishers.

Cooperrider, D. L., Whitney, D. D., & Stavros, J. (2008). *The appreciative inquiry handbook: For leaders of change*. Berrett-Koehler Publishers.

Cunliffe, A. L. (2016). On becoming a critically reflexive practitioner redux: What does it mean to "be" reflexive? *Journal of Management Education, 40*(6), 740–746. doi:10.1177/1052562916668919

Devlin, M., & McKay, J. (2018). Teaching inclusively online in a massified university system. *Widening Participation and Lifelong Learning: the Journal of the Institute for Access Studies and the European Access Network, 20*(1), 146–166. doi:10.5456/WPLL.20.1.146

Dunlap, J. C., Verma, G., & Johnson, H. L. (2016). Presence+Experience: A framework for the purposeful design of presence in online courses. *TechTrends, 60*(2), 145–151. doi:10.100711528-016-0029-4

Fornaciari, C. J., & Lund Dean, K. (2014). The 21st-century syllabus: From pedagogy to andragogy. *Journal of Management Education, 38*(5), 701–723. doi:10.1177/1052562913504763

Hanstedt, P. (2018). *Creating wicked students: Designing courses for a complex world*. Stylus Publishing.

Herie, M. A. (2013). Andragogy 2.0? Teaching and learning in the global classroom: Heutagogy and paragogy. *Global Citizen Digest, 2*(2), 8–14. https://www.centennialcollege.ca/pdf/global_citizen_digest/volume-2-issue-2.pdf

Hodgkinson, H. L. (1969). Walden U.: A working paper. *Soundings: An Interdisciplinary Journal, 52*, 172–185. https://scholarworks.waldenu.edu/cgi/viewcontent.cgi?article=1000&context=university_history

International Association of Universities. (n.d.). *Equitable access, success and quality in higher education: A policy statement by the International Association of Universities.* https://www.iau-aiu.net/IMG/pdf/iau_policy_statement_on_equitable_access_final_version_august_2008_eng_0.pdf

Johnson, B. A. (2014). Transformation of online teaching practices through implementation of appreciative inquiry. *Online Learning, 18*(3).

Knowles, M. S. (1980). *The modern practice of adult education: From pedagogy to andragogy.* Association Press.

Kolb, D. A. (1984). *Experiential learning: Experience as the source of learning and development.* Prentice-Hall.

Landrine, H. (1992). Clinical implications of cultural differences: The referential versus the indexical self. *Clinical Psychology Review, 12*(4), 401–415. doi:10.1016/0272-7358(92)90124-Q

Mezirow, J. (1991). *Transformative dimensions of adult learning.* Jossey-Bass.

Moores, T. T., Change, J. C.-J., & Smith, D. K. (2004). Learning style and performance: A field study of Is students in an analysis and design course. *Journal of Computer Information Systems, 45*(1), 77–85. doi:10.1080/08874417.2004.11645819

Morgan, A. M., Jobe, R. L., Konopa, J. K., & Downs, L. D. (2022). Quality assurance, meet quality appreciation: Using appreciative inquiry to define faculty quality standards. *Higher Learning Research Communications, 12*(1), 98–111. https://scholarworks.waldenu.edu/cgi/viewcontent.cgi?article=1301&context=hlrc

Orem, S. (n.d.). *The five principles of appreciative coaching.* http://www.saraorem.com/5-principles/

Rittel, H. W. J., & Webber, M. M. (1973). Dilemmas in a general theory of planning. *Policy Sciences, 4*(2), 155–169. doi:10.1007/BF01405730

Rogers, C. (1969). Freedom to learn: A view of what education might become. Charles E. Merrill Publishing.

Ryff, C. D., & Keyes, C. L. (1995). The structure of psychological well-being revisited. *Journal of Personality and Social Psychology, 69*(4), 719–727. doi:10.1037/0022-3514.69.4.719 PMID:7473027

Sanderson, C. D., Hollinger-Smith, L. M., & Cox, K. (2021). Developing a social determinants of learning™ framework: A case study. *Nursing Education Perspectives, 42*(4), 205–211. doi:10.1097/01.NEP.0000000000000810 PMID:33935243

Schön, D. A. (1984). *The reflective practitioner: How professionals think in action* (1st ed.). Basic Books.

Seligman, M. (2018). PERMA and the building blocks of well-being. *The Journal of Positive Psychology, 13*(4), 333–335. doi:10.1080/17439760.2018.1437466

Swan, K. (2004). *Relationships between interactions and learning in online environments.* The Sloan Consortium. https://www.immagic.com/eLibrary/ARCHIVES/GENERAL/SLOANCUS/S041202C.pdf

Swan, K., Chen, C.-C. B., & Bockmier-Sommers, D. K. (2020). Relationships between Carl Rogers' person-centered education and the community of inquiry framework: A preliminary exploration. *Online Learning, 24*(3). Advance online publication. doi:10.24059/olj.v24i3.2279

Walden University. (n.d.). *Vision, mission, and goals.* https://catalog.waldenu.edu/content.php?catoid=147&navoid=47257

ADDITIONAL READING

Blaschke, L. M. (2012). Heutagogy and lifelong learning: A review of heutagogical practice and self-determined learning. *The International Review of Research in Open and Distance Learning, 13*(1), 56–71. http://www.irrodl.org/index.php/irrodl/ article/view/1076/2113

Bogler, R., Caspi, A., & Roccas, S. (2013). Transformational and passive leadership: An initial investigation of university instructors as leaders in a virtual learning environment. *Educational Management Administration & Leadership, 41*(3), 372–392. doi:10.1177/1741143212474805

Cavins, B. J. (2006). The relationship between emotional-social intelligence and leadership practices among college student leaders. *Dissertation Abstracts International. A, The Humanities and Social Sciences, 66*(10–A), 3518.

Collier, P., Morgan, D. L., & Fellows, C. (2007, August). *Mentoring as "imported" cultural capital: A program to facilitate first generation students' transition to the university* [Paper presentation]. The American Sociological Association 102nd Annual Meeting, New York, NY, United States.

Delahunty, J. (2018). Connecting to learn, learning to connect: Thinking together in asynchronous forum discussion. *Linguistics and Education, 46*, 12–22. doi:10.1016/j.linged.2018.05.003

DeNoyelles, A., Zydney, J. M., & Chen, B. (2014). Strategies for creating a community of inquiry through online asynchronous discussions. *Journal of Online Learning and Teaching, 10*(1), 153–165.

Pacansky-Brock, M. (2017). *Best practices for teaching with emerging technologies* (2nd ed.). Routledge. doi:10.4324/9781315629292

Schenck, J., & Cruickshank, J. (2015). Evolving Kolb: Experiential education in the age of neuroscience. *Journal of Experiential Education, 38*(1), 73–95. doi:10.1177/1053825914547153

Thomas, L., Herbert, T., & Teras, M. (2014). A sense of belonging to enhance participation, success and retention in online programs. *The International Journal of the First Year in Higher Education, 5*(2), 69–80. doi:10.5204/intjfyhe.v5i2.233

Weimer, M. (2002). *Learner-centered teaching: Five key changes to practice.* Jossey-Bass.

Weimer, M. (2010). *Inspired college teaching: A career-long resource for professional growth.* Jossey-Bass.

Yang, B. (2004). Can adult learning theory provide a foundation for human resource development? *Advances in Developing Human Resources, 6*(2), 129–145. doi:10.1177/1523422304263325

Chapter 2
Digital Appreciative Inquiry for Inclusion

Ann M. Morgan
https://orcid.org/0000-0002-7607-2743
Walden University, USA

Kathe Pelletier
EDUCAUSE, USA

ABSTRACT

Appreciative inquiry is an approach with the power to contribute to inclusion in the workplace. Paired with digital interventions, which share the power to include and the potential to exclude, digital appreciative inquiry offers promising possibilities when used with intention. This chapter presents guidance to help higher education institutions accomplish the goals of inclusion using digital appreciative inquiry, which can lead to greater staff and faculty belonging, trust, engagement, and institutional sustainability.

INTRODUCTION

Organizations, educational institutions, and communities have much to gain from ensuring the inclusion of a diverse set of stakeholders in change management (Dahlvig, 2018), quality management (Morgan et al., 2022), and positive leadership (Dahlvig, 2018). Full inclusion means welcoming in and engaging all types of participants in ways that value their unique styles and approaches (Makoelle, 2014) by removing barriers and providing reinforcement (Vrasmas, 2018). The approach and principles of Appreciative Inquiry (AI) have the power to contribute to these goals of inclusion.

Further, technology offers a digital toolset that enables the inclusion of participants by eliminating the space and place boundaries that exacerbate exclusivity or marginalization of persons or groups (Gale & Mills, 2013). Using digital appreciative inquiry—or AI and technology together—with care and intention can ensure desirable results and a greater sense of inclusion for all those who are invested in the university or organization despite geographical or other boundaries.

This chapter will address the purpose, principles, practices, and possibilities for digital appreciative inquiry, recognizing that both AI and technology have the power to include—and the potential to exclude—if not approached with intention and consideration. Bringing together the principles of AI with the values of inclusion and promising practices for digital facilitation, we will provide guidance that can help organizations accomplish the goals and subsequent outcomes of inclusion in the higher education workplace.

BACKGROUND

Why Inclusion?

Two years into the COVID-19 pandemic, many of us are frayed, stressed out, and isolated—so much so that evidence of stress-induced brain inflammation has been detected even in those who have never had COVID (Brusaferri et al., 2022) and the World Health Organization has reported a 25% increase in anxiety and depression worldwide (World Health Organization, 2022). The murder of George Floyd in 2021 and ongoing racial violence and systemic racism has added to the already weighty collective trauma of Black, Indigenous, Asian, and Latino/Latina people and raised awareness in many of their white counterparts of the longstanding injustices and inequities faced by these groups (Mason, 2021). Individuals with perhaps invisible, increased risk factors for COVID may have needed to remain isolated in their homes when lower-risk individuals started to return to pre-pandemic activities like spending time indoors in restaurants or churches, with dire psychological consequences (Pietrabissa & Simpson, 2020). Legislative rulings in some states prevent open discussion and education about sexual orientation or gender identity, and in other states, record numbers of anti-trans bills were introduced since 2020 (Equality Texas, n.d.).

Stress is high on college campuses, too. Many campuses experienced the sudden shift to *emergency remote teaching*, which required faculty to transition classes historically taught face-to-face, often via lecture, to a virtual setting in a matter of weeks, using tools and design techniques that were unfamiliar and perhaps unwanted (Hodges et al., 2020). Staff may also be feeling the instability and newness of supporting faculty and students through new modalities. Both faculty and staff have been called on to present a sense of calm to students during these turbulent times, and this kind of emotional labor comes with a cost to those maintaining this equanimity while feeling the same stressors themselves (Skallerup Bessette, 2020). Additional uncertainty is felt on campuses where enrollment trends are headed in the wrong direction or when students are facing hunger and housing instability (Khosla, 2020).

Higher education has not been immune to the waves of resignations, retirements, and other departures known as The Great Resignation. Low pay and high stress are the top reasons for student affairs professionals leaving their jobs and, in some cases, the field entirely (Ellis, 2021). Other workers have found the flexibility of hybrid or remote work appealing or are increasingly insistent about work-life balance (Schroeder, 2022). These turnover trends are forcing higher education leaders to reevaluate strategies for employee retention and engagement.

Feeling Included in Higher Education

The state of the world and the shifting higher education landscape present opportunity for growth and positive change. Cultivating a sense of inclusion in the workplace is one lever to help us feel more connected to each other and more fulfilled in our workplaces, supporting workplace retention and success. The benefits of inclusion are significant, both to the individual and to the organization. Pal et al. (2022) found that inclusive practices play a significant role in improved employee well-being and recovery from adverse life events such as those experienced due to the pandemic.

Outside of the context of the pandemic, Brimhall and Mor Barak (2018) noted significant relationships between inclusion and employee innovation and job satisfaction, ultimately improving the quality of care in a diverse human services organization. Similarly, a climate of inclusion has been associated with employee engagement, a critical element of overall workplace well-being (Downey et al., 2015). All of these outcomes of inclusive climate and practices can lead to lower turnover, higher productivity, and the achievement of institutional goals (Rawat, 2020; Dahlvig, 2018; Panicker & Sharma, 2020).

Inclusion is not something that "just happens" in organizations. Developing an inclusive climate requires intentionality, structure, and caring actions. A sense of belonging in the workplace is tied to an individual's sense of identity and identification of themselves in the organization. That connection and organizational identity are built through purposeful and meaningful opportunities for participative decision making (Panicker & Sharma, 2020). Li et al. (2019) investigated antecedents and consequences of an inclusive climate and found value in identity-conscious programming and intentional inclusivity as a predecessor for increasing effectiveness in the organization and producing changes that are proactive rather than reactive.

Involving employees in organizational change is one strategy for contributing to an inclusive climate and for creating positive change. Large-scale change is adopted more readily when more members of the organization are able to contribute and participate (Whitney & Trosten-Bloom, 2010). Additionally, these participatory methods can be empowering and contribute to a sense of belonging and organizational justice (Kostenius & Nystrom, 2020; Panicker & Sharma, 2020).

INCLUSIVE PRINCIPLES

Appreciative Inquiry: A Whole-System Approach to Inclusion

Appreciative Inquiry (AI) is an organizational development and change-making approach that can include the whole system at scale. It is the "cooperative, coevolutionary search for the best in people, their organizations, and the relevant world around them" (Cooperrider & Whitney, 2005, p. 8). AI is a generative approach that intentionally builds on what is working in an organization to create positive change in social systems (Cooperrider et al., 2008). While one of the most important elements of AI is the focus on the positive core, its participatory, strengths-based, generative techniques mean that by its nature, AI is inclusive. The philosophy of AI can be understood through five core principles: constructionist, simultaneity, anticipatory, poetic, and positive.

The key phrase commonly used to describe the *constructionist* principle is *"words create worlds"* (Cooperrider & Whitney, 2005, p. 14). This principle is rooted in social constructionism (Gergen, 2015), which asserts that meaning is created in social structures. Meaning and understanding are found when humans come together in relationships and reflect and communicate. The language, ideas, and behaviors of people comingle to make meaning.

The principle of *simultaneity* further affirms the importance of language and the need for intentionality in inquiry. This principle states that *change or progress begins as soon as a question is conceived.* We are reminded by this principle of the importance of carefully crafting and framing the question in order to set the desired tone (Stratton-Berkessel, 2010; Cooperrider & Whitney, 2005).

Where focus goes, something grows. The *poetic* principle indicates that beliefs of human beings about themselves and the world influence where attention is paid. Conversely, the places where attention is paid influence human beings' beliefs about themselves and the world (Williams et al., 2016). What we choose to study both describes and creates reality. When we focus on individuals, teams, and organizations at their best, we learn valuable insights that can be applied to creating the future.

Positive images and stories inspire positive action and change. Cooperrider describes organizations as having an "automatic tendency to evolve in the direction of positive imagery" (1990, p. 15). With the *anticipatory* principle, people and organizations have to look forward in order to move forward, and AI offers a number of approaches for imagining, brainstorming, and dreaming (Stratton-Berkessel, 2010) that conjure positive images. Human systems grow in the direction of their images of the future.

Positive emotion and/or affect leads to positive action. According to the *positive* principle, organizations perform at their best when the humans in the organizations are at their best. The well-being of individuals and the nourishment of each person contributes to the whole. Cooperrider puts it this way: "While negative affectivity is notably linked to the phenomenon of learned helplessness, positive affect is intimately connected with social helpfulness" (1990, p. 8). Frederickson's broaden-and-build research expands on the notion of helpfulness: positive emotion and finding joy in work can also result in greater inclusivity (Johnson & Frederickson, 2005).

With roots in and alignment to positive psychology (Cooperrider et al., 2018), AI celebrates what is best in people and systems and then uses positive questioning, brainstorming, and imagining to drive transformation or innovation and enhance well-being. AI typically uses a 4-D (Discover, Dream, Design, Destiny) approach (Cooperrider & Whitney, 2005) or a 5-D (Define, Discover, Dream, Design, Destiny/Deliver) approach. Additionally, the SOAR analysis is an approach for continuous improvement leveraging the principles of AI and includes the steps of assessing the strengths, opportunities, aspirations, and results (Stavros & Hinrichs, 2009). Whitney and Trosten-Bloom describe "a menu of approaches" (2010, p. 23) that emphasize on-location facilitation that range from processes that take more than a year, to shorter-term inquiry that might include a smaller team, to a core group in an ongoing innovation team capacity.

Many successful AI interventions have been facilitated in large corporations and have included hundreds of individuals. These large-scale examples of AI, documented in case studies from organizations such as BP, Syntegra Benelux, and Nielsen Media Research, bring participants together in a way that enables them to collectively examine the big picture and create a shared vision and plan while allowing participants the opportunity to contribute fully as individuals and see themselves in the outcome (Cooperrider et al., 2008). This approach ensures that those who are most impacted by the inquiry have a role to play in contributing to the design of a future state (Flavell, 2021).

AI's *whole-system approach* (Whitney & Trosten-Bloom, 2010) honors the voices of each *whole* individual (Rogers, 1979). The whole system accounts for participants in any capacity in the organization: students, faculty, staff, CEOs or presidents, community members, families impacted by the results of an organization, and everyone in between. AI creates space for sharing and honoring individual stories and identities that contribute to a greater understanding of the positive core and story of the whole organization.

The AI approach can clearly lead to an inclusive practice that is designed to build trust and a sense of workplace justice and transparency, create space for the whole person and complexities of identity, and include the entire system (Panicker & Sharma, 2020). Building on what works promotes a culture of inquiry that is anchored in care and compassion (Valli, 2006).

Due to its large-scale nature, AI can introduce us to individuals we might not otherwise have met or interacted with and uncover what might have otherwise not have been known. One AI participant declared, "I have been in this job for four years and I never knew these people existed" (Stone, 2017, p. 37). AI experiences have the potential to reveal the commonalities among departments or participants and reduce the invisible protective boundaries, allowing participants to see themselves as a part of the whole.

Digital Technology: Tools and Techniques for Inclusion

Shutdowns intended to slow the spread of COVID forced remote work and learning and changed the definition of campus and workplace. Despite the abrupt move online, many workers, including faculty, found they enjoyed the flexibility of working from home—or working from anywhere—and that they can do their job as well or better than they did from an office or on campus. Indeed, employers are finding that productivity, innovation, and outcomes have not only remained stable with a remote workforce but in some cases have increased (Sparapani & Ruma, 2022).

During this time, digital tools have allowed us to remain connected. Many colleges and universities that pride themselves on the residential experience are even embracing a hybrid future, not just as an emergency response but as a strategy for sustainability and retention of staff, faculty, and students (Beytekin, 2021). As campuses consider the shifts needed to offer hybrid learning and work on a long-term basis, it will be critical to continue addressing issues of the digital divide. Even after 2 years of learning and teaching during a pandemic, all people do not have access to or experience with certain technology. While digital inclusion efforts are being made, communities, schools, and education systems face complex sociological, ecological, and infrastructure issues.

However connected we may be through virtual means, the social connection may not be a foregone conclusion. For individuals forced into a remote work situation due to a change in policy beyond their control, they might feel the ongoing isolation of the pandemic when the informal watercooler conversations and other in-person interactions are no longer an option. Recent studies indicate, however, the possibility for conscious creation of digital spaces that create a sense of we (Kostenius & Nystrom, 2020) or that hold the space for social and relational interaction.

Additionally of note are studies that indicate the interrelatedness between digital exclusion and sociocultural exclusion. Already marginalized groups are often also facing digital inequalities. Digital inclusion has the propensity to mitigate socially exclusionary factors like age, gender, socioeconomic status, class, and culture (Mascheroni et al., 2022). Further, Mascheroni et al. (2022) recognize "a recursive loop between diverse social and personal inequalities and digital inequalities" (2022, p. 452) calling to the fore the importance of being intentional about full inclusion in digital opportunities.

Digital Appreciative Inquiry for Inclusion

Practicing inclusion—so that all members of your organization feel seen and valued and can contribute to organizational improvement—requires more than just inviting people to the table. AI principles offer cues to create generative, life-giving opportunities while recognizing that individuals will be bringing their whole selves, cultures, abilities, and orientation to the experience.

Digital interventions have their own generative potential. Mascheroni et al. (2022) teach us those digital opportunities need to be plentiful, accessible, and achievable; they also need to be nourishing, strengths based, and empowering. These opportunities can be accomplished through the combination of AI and digital interventions (Tollec, 2021) for *digital appreciative inquiry (DAI)*.

DAI offers flexibility and opportunities for contribution and participation that connect across geography and the complexity of identity to include all members of an organization. Adding a digital aspect to AI practice requires more than just plugging in technology or opening a virtual meeting tool or application; it requires planning for meaningful engagement that equips the people in a system to participate safely and effectively.

The principles of AI have only recently and minimally been investigated for their role in serving organizational diversity, equity, and inclusion goals (Georgakopoulos & Petzold-Bradley, 2021). Likewise, while exploration of how the "digital shift" would impact AI is documented, it is only recently that virtual technology and AI are emerging in research together (Cruz Teller & Sutton, 2021, p. 4).

PROMISING PRACTICES

DAI is potentially best explored for its use in the higher education workplace by examining the ways the AI approach can be brought to life with digital technology informed by inclusive pedagogy (Morina, 2020; Gale & Mills, 2013; Kim et al., 2021). Thoughtful planning of the structure of the agenda and facilitation strategies, as well as consideration of the affordances and limitations of the digital environment, are critical when practicing DAI in order to achieve the experience and outcomes of inclusion. The following practices offer examples and inspiration.

More Is Not Better with Technology

Digital tools can be leveraged to create a collaborative AI experience that intentionally includes both synchronous and asynchronous interactions as well as a potential treasure trove of data from participant contributions to which participants may return after the engagement for collective meaning-making. But while technology offers affordances for inclusion and collaboration for remote participants, decisions about which tools to include should start with setting objectives for the experience instead of just going after the shiny object (Darby & Lang, 2019). Resist the temptation to use all the technologies you have available to you. Instead, find the "right tool for the job" (Darby & Lang, 2019), and "keep it simple and use the basic set of tools" (Boettcher & Conrad, 2016, p. 63). This intentionality in tool selection can also be extended to considerations of access across all participants. The lowest-tech solution is often the most inclusive and least distracting.

In this vein, consider the accessibility of the digital tools used. Digital accessibility training is increasingly being offered as professional development on college campuses, but a gap still exists (Mancilla &

Frey, 2021), so locating accessibility allies and experts and inviting their feedback on your tool selection can help you ensure all can participate fully. Another strategy to promote accessibility and encourage collaboration is to incorporate the principles of universal design for learning that are often applied to course design. Providing alternative means of access where possible is the kind of adjustment that, while making technology accessible for one participant, can also help many others be successful (Tobin & Behling, 2018).

Digital Inclusion at Large and Small Scale

While inclusion is not accomplished merely by inviting a broad group to participate, ensuring you are starting with a diverse and representative stakeholder group is essential. AI is designed to accommodate a large number of participants, so be as inclusive as possible. A representative group or a group of diverse stakeholders (Cooperrider & Whitney, 2005; Gergen & Gergen, 2004) should include all levels of leadership, partnership, and participation. What this looks like will be unique to each organization, but a multicultural, integrated identity approach should be taken. The "right mix of people" will include those who have "the influence and resources to deliver whatever they collaboratively agreed upon" (Whitney & Trosten-Bloom, 2010). Consider a broad stakeholder set that might even be considered tangential to the AI topic but that might benefit from inclusion and ultimately enrich the process, such as family members, community members, or external partners.

Inviting large-scale participation in a DAI experience may seem daunting to manage, but when participants live and work remotely from each other, this kind of intentional inclusion is even more important to embrace. Broad inclusion through DAI can counteract the isolation and loneliness remote staff and faculty increasingly report (Carter et al., 2022) and contribute to the meaningfulness of their work (Cruz Teller & Sutton, 2021).

As social beings, we learn from each other. Interacting with others is vital to building positive emotion and momentum for change. Consider ways to foster robust dialogue and engagement online that we enjoy face-to-face (Darby & Lang, 2019). So, not only should you be thinking about the breadth of participants in DAI, but design for meaningful interactions should also be a consideration.

Creating smaller groups, like using web conference breakout rooms or asynchronous small group activities, is a way to structure DAI to really allow for participant-to-participant interactions. Eyler (2018) encourages placing our social natures front and center: "We can learn things on our own, but we rarely learn them as deeply, because so much of our learning derives from our social nature and visceral need to communicate with each other" (p. 66–67).

When considering the experience of each individual, ensuring that all participants are fully included means facilitators and participants themselves must be skilled, knowledgeable, and aware of the potential for bias in questions, microaggressions, and behaviors in the delivery of questions that alienate or diminish persons or groups in any way (Gale & Mills, 2013).

Digital Storytelling

In most AI approaches, storytelling is used to build trust and an inclusive climate (Langer & Thorup, 2006). Individual stories told and retold and combined and coded and themed lead us to the heart and soul of the organization. This is often done through paired interviews in which participants are encouraged

Digital Appreciative Inquiry for Inclusion

to share back and note the exact words of their partner. Then sharing is done in groups, documented, and made a part of the data collected.

Provide multiple avenues for storytelling, including synchronous and asynchronous, large and small groups, and even potentially some anonymous opportunities. You might leverage tools like a virtual whiteboard, web conferencing breakout rooms, or shared Google documents. Stories might be recorded and shared asynchronously through video blogs or in written blogs that preserve and attend to the expression of individual experiences.

The constructionist principle ensures that voices are honored, and words are regarded as life-giving, "creating the world as we know it" (Whitney and Trosten-Bloom, 2010, p. 53). A rich and diverse stakeholder group is vital, and with it, each member should be regarded as "vibrant and rich sources of resources" (Gale and Mills, 2013, p. 11) bringing value to the co-created result.

Intentional Inquiry

Change or progress begins as soon as a question is conceived. The principle of simultaneity further affirms the importance of language and the need for intentionality in inquiry. We are reminded by this principle of the importance of carefully crafting and framing the question in order to set the desired tone (Stratton-Berkessel, 2010; Cooperrider and Whitney, 2005).

Because the very act of asking questions creates change, facilitators and those in power must recognize—and welcome—questions that have the potential to disrupt the status quo. They must acknowledge and address the places and processes where dominant thinking or ways of knowing might exclude or hinder new meaning that is representative of all (Gale and Mills, 2013). Facilitators can very quickly get a read on questions and language being used in the design of DAI with social media crowdsourcing. Posing a question, for example, to #academicchatter may elicit feedback that points to opportunities for reframing, avoiding bias, and ensuring a positive direction.

Crowdsourcing within the organization through Google Forms or a survey tool may also help with early shaping of the questions and may create interest and momentum around the topic. Recognize that "virtually any pattern of organizational action is open to alteration and reconfiguration" (Cooperrider, 1990, p. 14). Cooperrider suggests that when people and organizations hold the same "conventional" values, expectations, beliefs, processes, and possibilities, they will continue to get the same results.

Involving a more representative group in the planning stages can ensure that equity and inclusion are woven into the questions that guide the DAI experience and not just added reactively. Openness to taking the inquiry in a different direction than originally intended is critical to enable different voices to contribute in a way that recognizes different ways of knowing, being, and doing, and more equitable results are met (Moriña, 2020).

Be an Open Book

Since we create what we study, according to the poetic principle, transparency in the philosophy and agenda of a DAI experience can focus the team to actively engage in the process. Transparency can also serve as a tool for inclusion when expectations for participation are provided up front (Stone, 2017). Establishing expectations for participation requires thoughtful planning and building understanding with participants of the principles, processes, and tools that you will be using in DAI. Gale and Mills (2013) point to the importance of providing stakeholders with a full picture of the planned experience.

In DAI, the process, people, tools, and outcomes are interrelated. While the toolset and approaches are flexible, the ability to adapt comes from awareness of the principles and the intentions behind choices for technology. Many facilitators find value in exposing participants to the principles as a way to bring them along in the process.

Sharing the big picture can be especially important when the DAI activities extend beyond a brief encounter or interaction. Providing an agenda in advance is another example of universal design for learning in action, providing options for diversity in executive functioning styles and preferences (CAST, n.d.). Giving insight into what is planned and why it is planned that way makes space to accommodate flexibility or adjust where needed.

As the facilitator, sharing your authentic or vulnerable self is another way to engender trust and encourage participants to contribute. In a virtual setting, when informal socialization is less likely to happen than when all participants are together in one space, you may need to be more deliberate in making opportunities to expose the human side of yourself, including being willing to expose imperfections (Darby & Lang, 2019). This might involve having photographs of family or pets on camera, including and participating in warm-up activities, and being transparent when technology is not working as expected.

Notice and Embrace the Provocative

AI is known for the way it can unearth provocative propositions and the positive core. Arora (2021) presents AI as an opportunity for moving more deeply into a subject or point of impasse. In DAI, the stories that are told, depicted, or written throughout the process may unearth emotion or tension. Participants may see themselves in the stories of others, or this deep sharing may exacerbate a sense of "otherness" and conflict. AI facilitators and participants are encouraged to *deepen* their listening and their personal exploration and awareness.

Often, when traditionally face-to-face practices transition to a virtual format, synchronous engagement is the default. However, with DAI, embrace the asynchronous opportunities to create space to pause a large group session for personal digital journaling or reflection. This can be another opportunity to leverage tools that allow for anonymous contribution, such as virtual whiteboards. Even though AI is intended to create a safe space for trying out new ideas and reflections, knowing when to provide a more private space can make the experience feel more inviting when topics particularly laden with emotion are being discussed.

For facilitators to adjust when individuals might be retreating or reacting out of discomfort, and to ensure they are framing every facilitation decision with a focus on assets, it is important to follow the cues of digital body language. Digital body language extends beyond just what you might observe in a synchronous video session. It can include other indicators, such as how much time passes between asynchronous responses, word choice or tone, or length of messages (Dhawan, 2021). Noticing digital body language, in addition to more overt feedback, can help a facilitator understand when participants are ready to move on, when there is a need for a break, or when it's time to stop and celebrate learning or light-bulb moments.

Ideally, unearthing the stories of individuals and of the organization also creates a sense of belonging. Bringing together the intersectionality and complexity of each participant or each human in the organization contributes to connection and a sense of care or nurturing of each individual within the system (Li et al., 2019). AI storytelling and sharing of experiences gives way to sharing of values and purpose (Whittaker et al., 2017).

Pay Attention to Diversity

Cultural or racial differences do not disappear with a digital approach. Ignoring diversity may actually work against the goals of inclusion by encouraging power imbalances, which may ultimately prevent participants from having a voice or lead to marginalization (Georgakopoulos & Petzold-Bradley, 2021). DAI facilitators need to be aware of potential power dynamics within the group because of differences in authority, race, gender, or other characteristics.

In accordance with the positive principle, consider the ways in which DAI might "call people in" to positive action through invitation. "Calling in" is a phrase used by Loretta Ross, activist and expert on racial justice and human rights. Ross addressed the behavior of "calling people or organizations out" by "calling in" with radical love. She observed the public (social media) shaming for issues related to racism or sexism in social media, for example, and encouraged a new approach that calls people and organizations into accountability and conversation (Oberst, 2021).

As part of the conditions for a successful event, the facilitator takes a minor role and allows participants to establish relationships, manage processes, and ensure dialog is safe, positive, and affirming (Ludema et al., 2003). Setting expectations at the start of DAI might include participant preparation and bystander training (Haynes-Baratz et al., 2021) that empower reframing negative remarks and reducing microaggressions. Beginning with appreciative interviews and ensuring a narrative-rich environment (Ludema et al., 2003) creates an environment for vulnerability, connectedness, empathy.

In both traditional AI and DAI, the images that inspire action are not meant to be person centered; rather, while they are borne out of the stories of each unique individual, what is produced is "a situational and interactional tapestry…of the whole" (Cooperrider, 1990, p. 14). This understanding provides a way to use DAI approaches that allow participants to decide when, how, and what they contribute to the whole. As a DAI facilitator, you might do any of the following:

- Center the voices of those most impacted by systemic racism or bias (e.g., LGBTQ+individuals or those with disabilities or cognitive differences).
- Draw out and honor each person's lived experience.
- Bring awareness and make adjustments due to the dynamic your own social or racial identity as a facilitator might create.
- Consider preferences in participation. Some individuals may be comfortable engaging on the spot in large groups; others may prefer space and time to reflect.
- Offer opportunities for anonymous participation, especially with sensitive topics.
- Choose a video-optional—or better yet—a "video-invited" approach that communicates the value of using video but gives participants agency as to whether or not they turn on the camera.
- These strategies offer ways that you can maximize inclusive collaboration with DAI to allow participants to live the principles of AI and come together to share and interpret bright spots in their lived experiences and uncover the ways they can design the future state together.

CONCLUSION

Possibilities for Practice

DAI offers an approach to combine the life-affirming practices of appreciation with the potential of digital technology to model inclusive practices that lead to the outcomes and benefits associated with inclusion. The ideation and planning for building more inclusive and equitable opportunities and environments in the higher education workplace requires the voices of those who have not heretofore been included in meaningful ways.

While DAI might have first begun out of necessity and novelty (Tollec, 2021; Cruz Teller & Sutton, 2021), facilitators and organizations are discovering its validity and merit. Campus leaders are still figuring out what inclusion means for them and for their people in the workplace. Hybrid and virtual modalities continue to gain momentum and mature in both the classroom and workplace in higher education. DAI is an approach that can be used to move people and organizations toward belonging, trust, engagement, productivity, and organizational sustainability, but it is incumbent upon facilitators and participants of DAI to mindfully center the principles and practices of inclusion in order to accomplish these goals.

As noted by the poetic principle, as much as DAI principles and practices can enhance inclusivity, organizations that are "committed to an ideology of inclusion, consent, and coevolution" will more likely succeed with it (Cooperrider, 1990, p. 18). An organization that puts the spotlight on inclusivity and takes action to remove barriers or policies that inhibit full inclusion will more likely fulfill its vision for an inclusive organization. Further, an organization that leverages approaches like DAI with the intention to build inclusion will be much more successful in doing so.

In keeping with the flexibility that AI offers, as DAI is practiced more widely, its implementation will continue to take additional forms, both in structure and in the tools that are leveraged for convening and facilitation. Especially as organizations seek transformational goals such as inclusion, it will be important to intentionally evaluate the process, practices, and outcomes of DAI in the context of the individual experience, organizational context, and across the field more widely, so that we can invite ongoing positive change and optimize the power of the combination of appreciative principles, technology, and inclusive practices.

REFERENCES

Arora, U. (2021). Deepen: A new 'd' for a more generative appreciative inquiry. *AI Practitioner*, *23*(2), 73–87. doi:10.12781/978-1-907549-47-2-11

Beytekin, O. F. (2021). Transformation of higher education into new normal. *Higher Education Studies*, *11*(3), 125–133. doi:10.5539/hes.v11n3p125

Boettcher, J. V., & Conrad, R. M. (2016). *The online teaching survival guide: Simple and practical pedagogical tips*. Jossey-Bass.

Brimhall, K. C., & Mor Barak, M. E. (2018). The critical role of workplace inclusion in fostering innovation, job satisfaction, and quality of care in a diverse human service organization. *Human Service Organizations, Management, Leadership & Governance, 42*(5), 474–492. doi:10.1080/23303131.2018.1526151

Brusaferri, L., Alshelh, Z., Martins, D., Kim, M., Weerasekera, A., Housman, H., Morrissey, E. J., Knight, P. C., Castro-Blanco, K. A., Albrecht, D. S., Tseng, C.-E., Zürcher, N. R., Ratai, E.-M., Akeju, O., Makary, M. M., Catana, C., Mercaldo, N. D., Hadjikhani, N., Veronese, M., ... Loggia, M. L. (2022). The pandemic brain: Neuroinflammation in non-infected individuals during the COVID-19 pandemic. *Brain, Behavior, and Immunity, 102*, 89–97. doi:10.1016/j.bbi.2022.02.018 PMID:35181440

Carter, M. A., Hutton, V., Udah, H., & Francis, A. (2022). COVID-19 and the changing higher education landscape: The impact on academics and their well-being. In A. P. Francis & M. A. Carter (Eds.), *Mental Health and Higher Education in Australia*. Springer. doi:10.1007/978-981-16-8040-3_3

CAST. (n.d.). *The UDL guidelines*. UDL. https://udlguidelines.cast.org/

Cooperrider, D. L. (1990). Positive image, positive action: The affirmative basis of organizing. In *Appreciative Management and Leadership*. https://wedgeblade.net/files/archives_assets/20884.pdf

Cooperrider, D. L., McQuaid, M., & Godwin, L. N. (2018). A positive revolution in education: uniting appreciative inquiry with the science of human flourishing to "Power Up Positive Education." *AI Practitioner, 20*(4), 3–19. https://img1.wsimg.com/blobby/go/51efc041-220d-40f6-8781-42c50a059a56/downloads/1d2030t4a_252200.pdf?ver=1599704335266

Cooperrider, D. L., & Whitney, D. K. (2005). *Appreciative inquiry: A positive revolution in change*. Berrett-Koehler.

Cooperrider, D. L., Whitney, D. K., & Stavros, J. M. (2008). *Appreciative inquiry handbook: For leaders of change* (2nd ed.). Crown Custom Publishing.

Cruz Teller, T., & Sutton, S. (2021). Appreciative inquiry and virtual technology: An improbable pair for accelerating the wholeness principle. *AI Practitioner, 23*(4), 4–24. doi:10.12781/978-1-907549-49-6-1

Dahlvig, J. E. (2018). Flourishing for the common good: Positive leadership in Christian higher education during times of change. *Christian Higher Education, 17*(1–2), 97–109. doi:10.1080/15363759.2018.1404819

Darby, F., & Lang, J. M. (2019). *Small teaching online: Applying learning science in online classes*. John Wiley & Sons.

Dhawan, E. (2021). *Digital body language: How to build trust & connection, no matter the distance*. St. Martin's Press.

Downey, S. N., van der Werff, L. K. M., & Plaut, V. C. (2014). The role of diversity practices and inclusion in promoting trust and employee engagement. *Journal of Applied Social Psychology, 45*(1), 35–44. doi:10.1111/jasp.12273

Ellis, L. (2021, August 25). The great disillusionment: College workers are burning out just when they'll be needed most. *The Chronicle of Higher Education*. https://www.chronicle.com/article/the-great-disillusionment

Equality Texas. (n.d.). *Legislative bill tracker*. Retrieved June 7, 2022, from https://www.equalitytexas.org/legislative-bill-tracker/

Eyler, J. R. (2018). *How humans learn: The science and stories behind effective college teaching*. West Virginia University Press.

Flavell, M. (2021). The promise of appreciative inquiry as a tool to developing home–school relationships for secondary Pacific students. *Australian Educational Researcher*. Advance online publication. doi:10.100713384-021-00497-x PMID:34898814

Gale, T., & Mills, C. (2013). Creating spaces in higher education for marginalised Australians: Principles for socially inclusive pedagogies. *Enhancing Learning in the Social Sciences*, *5*(2), 7–19. doi:10.11120/elss.2013.00008

Georgakopoulos, A., & Petzold-Bradley, E. (2021). The craft of mediation: The infusion of multidisciplinary approaches, appreciative inquiry, and cultural diversity. *GPSolo*, *38*(1), 31–35.

Gergen, K. J. (2015). *An invitation to social construction* (3rd ed.). SAGE Publications., doi:10.4135/9781473921276

Gergen, K. J., & Gergen, M. (2004). *Social construction: Entering the dialogue*. Taos Institute Publications.

Haynes-Baratz, M. C., Metinyurt, T., Li, Y. L., Gonzales, J., & Bond, M. A. (2021). Bystander training for faculty: A promising approach to tackling microaggressions in the academy. *New Ideas in Psychology*, *63*, 100882. Advance online publication. doi:10.1016/j.newideapsych.2021.100882

Hodges, C., Moore, S., Lockee, B., Trust, T., & Bond, A. (2020, March 27). The difference between emergency remote teaching and online learning. *EDUCAUSE*. https://er.educause.edu/articles/2020/3/the-difference-between-emergency-remote-teaching-and-online-learning

Johnson, K. J., & Frederickson, B. L. (2005). "We all look the same to me": Positive emotions eliminate the own-race bias in face recognition. *Psychological Science*, *16*(11), 875–881. doi:10.1111/j.1467-9280.2005.01631.x PMID:16262774

Khosla, N., Gamba, R., Taylor, S., Adediji, L., Bovey, J., Engelman, A., Jones-Bey, A., Lan, T. K., Vo, H., Washington, V., & Inch, E. S. (2020). Academic goal-setting among college students experiencing food insecurity, housing instability, and other challenges in a diverse public university. *Journal of Social Distress and the Homeless*, *29*(1), 3–15. doi:10.1080/10530789.2020.1678810

Kim, H. J., Yi, P., & Hong, J. I. (2021). Are schools digitally inclusive for all? Profiles of school digital inclusion using PISA 2018. *Computers & Education*, *170*(104226), 104226. Advance online publication. doi:10.1016/j.compedu.2021.104226

Kostenius, C., & Nyström, L. (2020). "When I feel well all over, I study and learn better" - Experiences of good conditions for health and learning in schools in the Arctic region of Sweden. *International Journal of Circumpolar Health*, *79*(1), 1788339. Advance online publication. doi:10.1080/22423982.2020.1788339 PMID:32663109

Langer, R., & Thorup, S. (2006). Building trust in times of crisis: Storytelling and change communication in an airline company. *Corporate Communications*, *11*(4), 371–390. Advance online publication. doi:10.1108/13563280610713851

Li, Y., Perera, S., Kulik, C. T., & Metz, I. (2019). Inclusion climate: A multilevel investigation of its antecedents and consequences. *Human Resource Management*, *58*(4), 353–369. doi:10.1002/hrm.21956

Ludema, J. D., Whitney, D., Mohr, B. J., & Griffin, T. J. (2003). *The appreciative inquiry summit: A practitioner's guide for leading large-group change*. Berrett-Koehler Publishers.

Makoelle, T. M. (2014). Pedagogy of inclusion: A quest for inclusive teaching and learning. *Mediterranean Journal of Social Sciences*, *5*(20), 1259–1267. doi:10.5901/mjss.2014.v5n20p1259

Mancilla, R., & Frey, B. (2021). *Professional development for digital accessibility: A needs assessment*. Quality Matters. https://www.qualitymatters.org/sites/default/files/research-docs-pdfs/QM-Digital-Accessibility-Professional-Development-WP.pdf

Mascheroni, G., Cino, D., Mikuška, J., & Smahel, D. (2022). Explaining inequalities in vulnerable children's digital skills: The effect of individual and social discrimination. *New Media & Society*, *24*(2), 437–457. doi:10.1177/14614448211063184

Mason, S. (2021). *Shock of a nation: An examination of George Floyd's death as cultural trauma* (Publication No. 28494946) [Master's thesis, University of Colorado–Colorado Springs]. ProQuest Dissertations Publishing.

Morgan, A. M., Jobe, R. L., Konopa, J. K., & Downs, L. D. (2022). Quality assurance, meet quality appreciation: Using appreciative inquiry to define faculty quality standards. *Higher Learning Research Communications*, *12*(1), 98–111. https://scholarworks.waldenu.edu/hlrc/vol12/iss1/5/

Moriña, A. (2020). Approaches to inclusive pedagogy: A systematic literature review. *Pedagogy*, *140*(4), 134–154. doi:10.15823/p.2020.140.8

Oberst, H. (2021, March 24). Loretta Ross calls in the 'calling out culture'. *UWIRE Text*, 1.

Pal, I., Galinsky, E., & Kim, S. (2022). Employee health and well-being after a crisis – Re-imagining the role of workplace inclusion. *Community Work & Family*, *25*(1), 30–62. doi:10.1080/13668803.2021.1987859

Panicker, A., & Sharma, A. (2020). Demonstrating the impact of participative decision making, distributive justice perception and growth opportunities on favorable and unfavorable employee outcomes: Mediating effect of workplace inclusion in Indian HEIs. *International Journal of Business Science and Applied Management*, *15*(1), 30–46. https://www.business-and-management.org/paper.php?id=137

Pietrabissa, G., & Simpson, S. G. (2020). Psychological consequences of social isolation during COVID-19 outbreak. *Frontiers in Psychology, 11*, 2201. Advance online publication. doi:10.3389/fpsyg.2020.02201 PMID:33013572

Rawat, P. S., Lyndon, S., Pradhan, M. R., Jose, J., Kollenchira, M., & Mehta, G. (2020). Employee reactiveness and inclusive leadership: Time to manage emotional diversity. *South Asian Journal of Business Studies, 10*(3), 357–376. doi:10.1108/SAJBS-02-2020-0042

Rogers, C. R. (1979). The foundations of the person-centered approach. *Education, 100*(2), 98–107. http://www.unifiedcommunities.com/ucs/Rogers_Person-Centered-Approach_1979.pdf

Schroeder, R. (2022, January 14). Leadership in the time of the great resignation. *Inside Higher Ed*. https://www.insidehighered.com/digital-learning/blogs/online-trending-now/leadership-time-great-resignation

Skallerup Bessette, L. (2020, March 26). Affective labor: The need for, and cost of, workplace equanimity. *EDUCAUSE Review*. https://er.educause.edu/blogs/2020/3/affective-labor-the-need-for-and-cost-of-workplace-equanimity

Sparapani, J., & Ruma, L. (Eds.). (2022). *Shaping the future of hybrid work*. MIT Technology Review Insights; Dell Technologies. https://wp.technologyreview.com/wp-content/uploads/2022/01/Shaping-the-future-of-hybrid-work.pdf

Stavros, J. M., & Hinrichs, G. (2009). *The thin book of SOAR: Building strengths-based strategy*. Thin Book Publishing.

Stone, M. (2017). Supporting inclusion for all; especially for students vulnerable due to their economic circumstances: Introducing Manuaute o Te Huia. *Kairaranga, 18*(1), 28–39. https://files.eric.ed.gov/fulltext/EJ1240272.pdf

Stratton-Berkessel, R. (2010). *Appreciative inquiry for collaborative solutions: 21 strength-based workshops*. Pfeiffer.

Tobin, T. J., & Behling, K. T. (2018). *Reach everyone, teach everyone: Universal design for learning in higher education*. West Virginia University Press.

Tollec, B. (2021). Digital appreciative inquiry: A whole new relational experience. *AI Practitioner, 23*(4), 18–26. doi:10.12781/978-1-907549-49-6-5

Valli, L., van Zee, E. H., Rennert-Ariev, P., Mikeska, J., Catlett-Muhammad, S., & Roy, P. (2006). Initiating and sustaining a culture of inquiry in a teacher leadership program. *Teacher Education Quarterly, 33*(3), 97–114. https://www.jstor.org/stable/23478896

Vrasmas, E. (2018). For a pedagogy of inclusion: A brief overview of the current research on inclusive education. *Bulletin of the Transylvania University of Brasov, 11*(2), 31–44.

Whitney, D., & Trosten-Bloom, A. (2010). *The power of appreciative inquiry: A practical guide to positive change* (2nd ed.). Berrett-Koehler Publishers.

Whittaker, K. A., Malone, M., Cowley, S., Grigulis, A., Nicholson, C., & Maben, J. (2017). Making a difference for children and families: An appreciative inquiry of health visitor values and why they start and stay in post. *Health & Social Care in the Community*, 25(2), 338–348. doi:10.1111/hsc.12307 PMID:26584790

Williams, P., Kern, M. L., & Waters, L. (2016). Exploring selective exposure and confirmation bias as processes underlying employee work happiness: An intervention study. *Frontiers in Psychology*, 7(878). Advance online publication. doi:10.3389/fpsyg.2016.00878 PMID:27378978

World Health Organization. (2022, March 2). *Covid-19 pandemic triggers 25% increase in prevalence of anxiety and depression worldwide* [Press release]. https://www.who.int/news/item/02-03-2022-covid-19-pandemic-triggers-25-increase-in-prevalence-of-anxiety-and-depression-worldwide

Chapter 3
Using an Emotional Intelligence Learning System for Person-Centered Curriculum Development and Teaching

Richard Hammett
Walden University, USA

Gary R. Low
EI Learning Systems, USA

William C. Schulz III
https://orcid.org/0000-0001-8560-5540
Walden University, USA

ABSTRACT

In this chapter, the authors will define and present an emotional intelligence learning system, rooted in research related to transformative emotional intelligence and explore how an online university can leverage this system within an inclusive teaching and learning model to teach emotional intelligence, personal skills, and leadership development. Implications for teaching, course development, and professional development are discussed so that faculty, course developers, administrators, and staff can use the tools to engender flow and positive change within their spheres of influence.

INTRODUCTION

In this chapter, the authors, Rick Hammett and Gary Low, define and present an emotional intelligence learning system rooted in research related to transformative emotional intelligence (Low & Hammett, 2021). They also explore how an online university can leverage this system within an inclusive teaching and learning model to teach emotional intelligence, personal skills, and leadership development.

DOI: 10.4018/978-1-6684-5146-5.ch003

Positive personal growth and change is a mandate and baseline for all caring educators/learners and is facilitated through solution-focused processes with new learning and constructive thinking supported with transformative emotional intelligence (TEI) skills and competencies. Achieving life and career excellence with growth motivation requires a positive mindset and an environment that provides permission, protection, and potency (personal relevance) for learners.

Developing a healthy, productive, and happy mind for a positive life and career is not a one-and-done process, nor can it be wished into existence. Research and experiential learning support the development and practiced use of EI skills that facilitate wise behaviors to achieve the personal vision and purpose of higher education (Low & Hammett, 2021).

Emotions are natural, but they are not neutral. They drive us toward action. When those feelings are related to the experience of positive growth, excitement creates a flow where teaching and learning happen spontaneously and with little effort (Csikszentmihalyi, 1990). Conversely, when the problematic feelings related to anger, fear, and sadness are experienced, learning becomes difficult, flow is interrupted, and, in their efforts to self-advocate, instructors and learners often resort to coping strategies that can create challenges for themselves and their learning institutions.

In this chapter, we present an emotional intelligence learning system that online faculty, course developers, administrators, and staff can use to engender flow and positive change within their spheres of influence, including the design of online curriculum and the enhancement of person-centered teaching and learning.

BACKGROUND

In Chapter 1 ("Developing a Learning Model for Caring, Inclusion and Social Change in an Online Environment"), the Figure 1 was presented to illustrate how Walden's learning model supports our inclusive teaching and learning (ITL) strategy.

As you review Figure 1, note how four of the five threads are highly process- and relationship-focused, and address the *how* of Walden's learning model. As such, each element is highly dependent on, and assumes, that the human beings at the heart of these relationships have the capabilities to be inclusive, respectful, curious, reflective, and caring of others. But alas, this is likely not the best of assumptions, particularly in an online setting where technology mediates these relationships and many of the engagements occur in asynchronous time and without visual communication queues.

Learning within an online, multi-contextual, inclusive teaching and learning environment places a premium on the need for both learners and faculty to build reflexive, self-awareness skills (such as those discussed in this chapter) that can help them develop and maintain an even larger set of emotional intelligence skills and predispositions.

Learning relationships that tie together to support transformational learning are an important part of Walden's learning model. This model takes an intentional approach to learning in that both facilitator/mentor and learner engage in a relationship to increase inclusion, empathy, and self-awareness. This occurs individually and, as shown in Figure 2, within the larger online community of interest.

The intersection of social and teaching presence infused with both process and content elements sets the learning climate and involves a variety of interpersonal engagements, including one-to-one faculty/student interactions, student-student interactions, and faculty interactions with groups of learners.

Figure 1. How Walden's Learning Model Supports its Inclusive Teaching and Learning Strategy
Note. Image credit: Nina M. McCune, Walden University

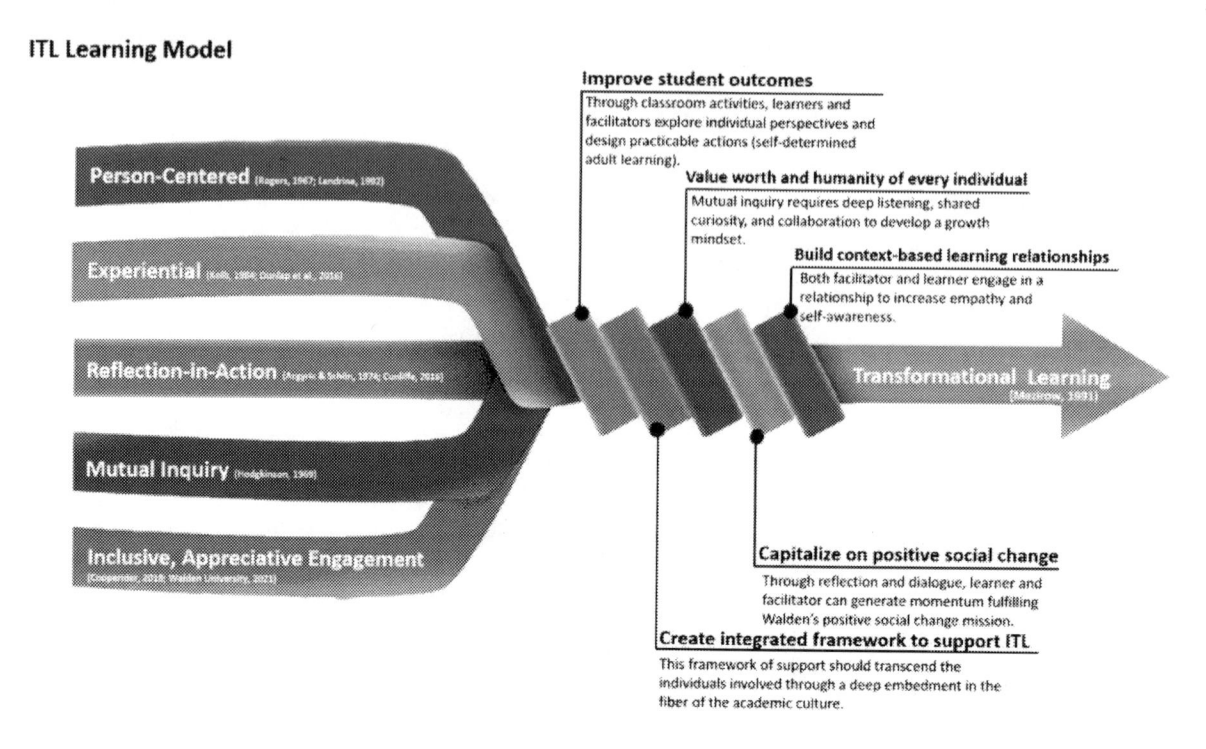

ITL Learning Model

- Person-Centered (Rogers, 1947; Landrine, 1992)
- Experiential (Kolb, 1984; Dunlap et al., 2016)
- Reflection-in-Action (Argyris & Schön, 1974; Cunliffe, 2016)
- Mutual Inquiry (Hodgkinson, 1969)
- Inclusive, Appreciative Engagement (Cooperrider, 2018; Walden University, 2021)

Improve student outcomes
Through classroom activities, learners and facilitators explore individual perspectives and design practicable actions (self-determined adult learning).

Value worth and humanity of every individual
Mutual inquiry requires deep listening, shared curiosity, and collaboration to develop a growth mindset.

Build context-based learning relationships
Both facilitator and learner engage in a relationship to increase empathy and self-awareness.

Transformational Learning (Mezirow, 1991)

Capitalize on positive social change
Through reflection and dialogue, learner and facilitator can generate momentum fulfilling Walden's positive social change mission.

Create integrated framework to support ITL
This framework of support should transcend the individuals involved through a deep embedment in the fiber of the academic culture.

Each of these types of engagements are influenced by specific person-centered characteristics, expectations, and experiences, as well as by broader social determinants of learning elements and cultural contexts (Sanderson, 2021). Within the context of inclusive teaching and learning, it then becomes important to recognize that *every relational interaction* requires an understanding of context and a commitment to care. There can be little authentic inclusion in online environments when people are not sufficiently skilled at knowing their own emotions and being able to understand and connect to the emotions of others. The transformative emotional intelligence framework discussed in the remainder of this chapter is important for developing emotional intelligence to facilitate inclusion in the online classroom.

These relational interactions, which are where moments of truth (see Chapter 12, "Developing a Rubric for a Person-Centered Approach to Teaching in Inclusive Online Learning Spaces") happen in learning, occur in the online world in a variety of asynchronous settings, including emails, in-course announcements, engagements in Discussion forums, ask-the-instructor forums, and in both general feedback areas as well as with assignment-specific proximate feedback. In many online programs there is also a requirement or practice of communicating with learners in real-time, synchronously using video collaboration tools, the telephone, instant messaging, or even face-to-face in some instances.

In *all* instances, however, if one wishes to build and maintain the trust needed to support learning relationships, behaviors by both faculty members and learners must be authentic and rooted in the skills one needs to practice emotional intelligence. It is to those skills, and a transformational emotional intelligence system for online learning, that Hammett and Low now turn.

Figure 2. The Focus of Person-Centered Engagements to Support Learning
Note. Image adapted from Anderson et al. (2001) Community of Inquiry Model. Image credit Jose Henriquez, Walden University.

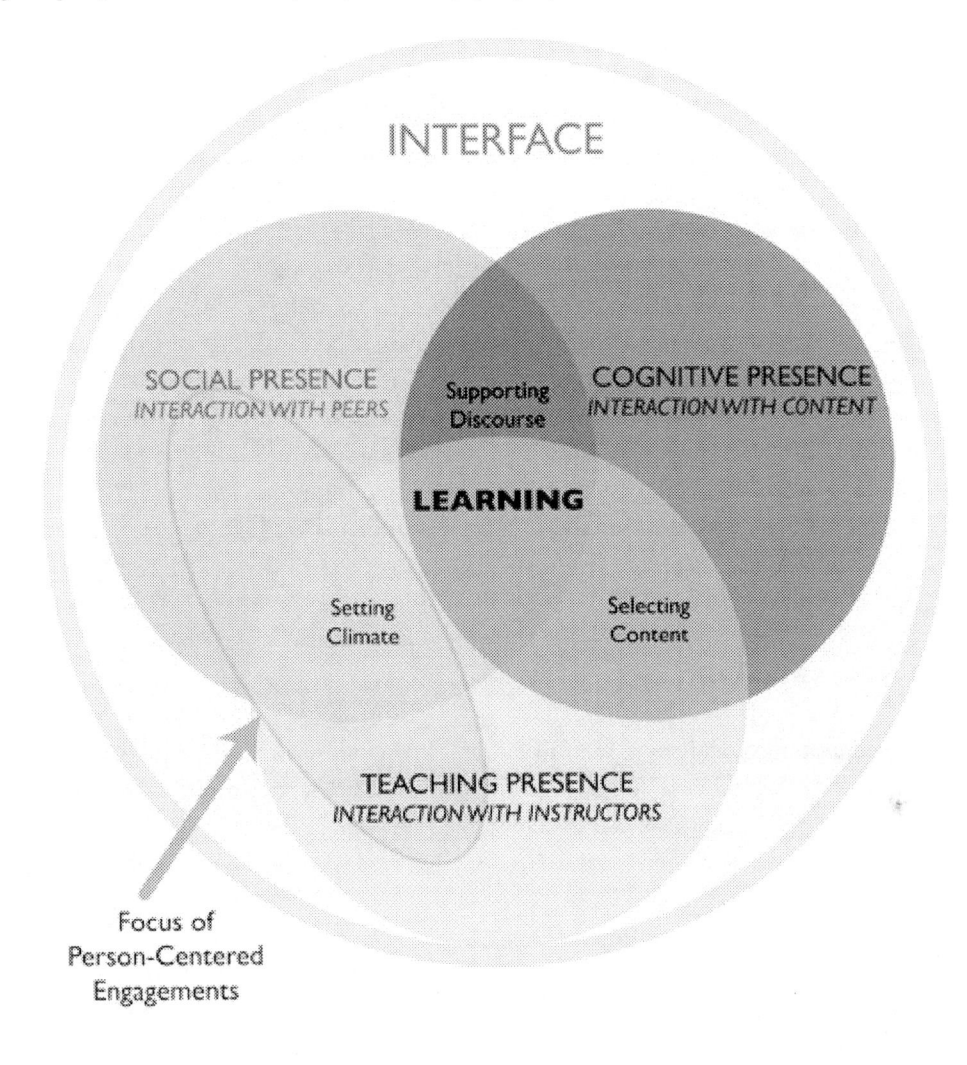

TRANSFORMATIVE EMOTIONAL INTELLIGENCE FOR ITL MODELING[1]

Transformative emotional intelligence (TEI) is a framework for positive growth and change that includes a systematic, five-step emotional intelligence learning and development model called the emotional learning system. While TEI can be explained using Goleman's (1995) seminal, four-pane model of emotional intelligence (EI), we are more closely related to Epstein's (1998) research and resulting two-mind theory of personality and healthy development, his cognitive-experiential self-theory (CEST). Epstein stated something important about emotional intelligence. He said that *the practical application of emotional intelligence leads toward developing smarter emotions*, not just knowledge about the subject of emotional intelligence (Epstein, 2012). The purpose of TEI is to provide a practical way to help people develop their own EI as interpreted by Epstein, so that they can be more self-aware and aware of the emotional states of others, allowing for authentic inclusion and engagement. According to Epstein, constructive thinking is the key to emotional intelligence. Stated another way, people who think constructively are emotionally intelligent and those who don't, aren't (Epstein, 1998).

Our short definition of EI is closely related to Epstein's CEST. Transformative emotional intelligence "is the learned ability to think constructively and act wisely" (Low & Hammett, 2021, p. 38). As first presented by Nelson and Low (2004), "Emotional intelligence behavior involves understanding your immediate experience and learning to think constructively about your behavior choices …" (p. 11).

TEI facilitates the application of the ITL learning model and transformational learning in several ways. First, as will be presented later in this chapter, the main tenets of TEI emphasize the person-centered and relational aspects of learning. Second, TEI's integrated learning model, the emotional learning system (ELS), emphasizes reflection and wise behavior over reactive behavior, which helps to foster trust among online learners and their faculty. Finally, TEI is reflected in thinking constructively about your immediate experience and your behavioral choices in the moment before you act.

Nelson and Low's (2004) longer definition of TEI includes the four domains of (a) self-awareness and appreciation, (b) healthy relationships, (c) being a good team member, and (d) healthily dealing with the demands and pressures of everyday work and life. Transformative emotional intelligence is the confluence of learned skills and abilities that facilitate the four TEI domains. The main tenets of TEI include that it is a positive philosophy that is research-derived, person-centered, skills-based, relationship-focused, facilitates inclusion and positive change, and results in intelligent self-direction (Low & Hammett, 2021).

Origins and Application of TEI

The transformative learning model shared in this chapter began with three research questions posed by two young psychologists, Darwin Nelson and Gary Low, in the mid 1970s (Low & Hammett, 2021). Let's review and reflect on the answers that have emerged through research.

Research Question #1: What Differentiates Healthy, Successful People from Those Not so Healthy and Successful?

The team of Nelson and Low discovered that a major factor was a skills-based approach, specifically personal, emotional, relational, and life (PERL) skills. Fixed factors like traits, types, or temperaments were not so important. These findings guided them in a lifelong mission of learning all they could to create, research, develop, and apply these skills in their life and professional work.

Research Question #2: How Could we Help Others Learn the Key Skills, Strategies, and Behaviors of PERL Skills to Improve their Success, Health, and Well-Being?

From the very beginning, we understood the value and need to engage, motivate, and create passion (interest) for improving our abilities and skills. This personal realization was based in part on our observation that these values were often missing or not evident in courses, programs, and training. We were intrigued and interested in the important works of Carl Rogers (client-centered, fully functioning person), Abraham Maslow (self-actualization), John Gardner (*Excellence,* and *Self Renewal*), and early thought leaders in positive and humanistic psychology, counseling, and human potential and development. From John Gardner's topics on excellence in the 1960s, Research Question #3 emerged.

Research Question #3: Can we be Excellent and Equal, Too?

Influenced by John Gardner's two early books, *Excellence* (1961) and *Self Renewal* (1963), the challenge of becoming and being excellent and equal, too, was a focal point of our education, training, counseling practices, and skills-based learning approach. With research, study, and experience, the action learning construct of personal excellence became an integral element in the personal, emotional, career, and life skills model of a healthy, productive person. *Personal excellence* is the process of developing yourself into the best person you can be. This process integrates an intentional self-renewal and positive change protocol that is self-directed and personally meaningful. Pursuing personal excellence facilitates high levels of achievement, happiness, and physical health.

The three initial guiding research questions provided focused and influencing direction for creating and developing our positive philosophy, theory, and practice that has emerged as TEI. The discovery of positive, enduring qualities, characteristics of personal, career, and life growth and development are now essential elements of our learning model of TEI. Students, friends, and colleagues have extended and added to the substantive research foundation, scholarship, and applications of TEI. For a comprehensive list of more than 125 related publications, we invite you to review Appendix A of *Transformative Emotional Intelligence for a Positive Career and Life* (Low & Hammett, 2021).

Nelson and Low set out in the mid 1970s with their original item pool of more than 1,200 items to help identify the factors and skills involved in success, personal health, and well-being. We were most concerned with constructs that could be learned and practiced (i.e., skills). Our research findings provided a positive direction to guide and develop an emerging and positive philosophy, theory, and practice for healthy being. Central to healthy being is a learning model and related strategies for the continual pursuit of effective behavior supported by PERL skills embedded in four major learning dimensions. These dimensions and related skills are shown in Table 1, along with more information about emotions and emotional intelligence.

Table 1. PERL dimensions and related skills

Dimension (Competency)	Related PERL Skills
Personal	Self Esteem Stress Management Positive Change
Emotional	Comfort Empathy Decision Making
Relationship	Assertion Anger Management Anxiety Management Leadership (Positive Influence)
Life	Drive Strength Time Management Commitment Ethic

Important Influences

As shown in the *Historical Roots, Limbs, and Branches of TEI* (Figure 3), there have been many important contributions from cognitive and related psychologies in the development of our TEI theory and practice. Following along the trunk of our imaginary tree, TEI theory is supported by and supports positive psychology and the continued expansion of our understanding through neuroscience research of how the brain learns best. The three principal areas where TEI has been used are demonstrated in the major limbs of (a) counseling and psychotherapy, (b) training and education, and (c) wellness. Based on the 1,200-plus item pool referred to in the last paragraph, we now emphasize the positive assessment instruments presented in Figure 3 to support the work of good professionals in the six branches of healthy being. Those include (a) relationships ([Relationship Skills Map®] Nelson & Nelson, 1984); (b) personal excellence ([Personal Excellence Map®], Nelson et al., 2007); (c) career and life skills, ([Skills for Career And Life Effectiveness®], Nelson & Low, 2011); (d) emotional skills ([Emotional Skills Assessment Process®], Nelson & Low, 1998); (e) lifestyle skills (Lifestyle Type Indicator®], Nelson & Low, 2014)]; and (f) personal well-being skills ([Well Being Assessment Process®], Nelson, 2012).

Transformative EI is grounded with engaging assessments and person-centered learning frameworks designed to create and enhance self-awareness with positive self-discovery and exploration, and it is guided by an unwavering belief in the capacity of individuals to learn, grow, develop, and strive to achieve personal excellence in their life and career. Positive assessment is a TEI research-derived, self-assessment process to build self-knowledge for intelligent self-direction and positive change. Balancing cognitive development and emotional (experiential) development is essential to achieve career success, personal well-being, and a healthy emotional mind.

Positive assessment is the necessary first step in the learning process but is often missing in education and business organizations. Positive self-assessment provides a method of self-discovery exploration for the individual learner to survey the learning terrain to achieve personal effectiveness. In the tradition of TEI, positive assessment guides meaningful learning and embeds PERL skills, behaviors, and strategies. Specific examples of positive assessment instruments are provided in Figure 3.

Positive assessment and The Emotional Learning System© are designed to explore and identify strengths (first), skill areas to further develop (second), and self-knowledge to understand the impact and influence of personal, emotional, relational, and life skills. This personal learning system provides additional learning and development strategies to understand, develop, apply, and model TEI skills daily. The influence of humanistic psychology has been a foundation in the development of our learning models, positive assessments, and theory of healthy being. These thought leaders ushered in a change in thinking about what it means to be human that deemphasized deficit models in favor of more constructive ones. Their influences informed and shaped our views on healthy, effective, and positive being. Within the humanistic realm, helping practitioners began emphasizing non-deficit models in favor of models that described being healthily human and used these models for helping individuals perfect (here, 'perfect' is a verb, referring to the lifelong process of striving to *perfect* oneself) themselves based on the client's unique life goals and aspirations. Our interpreted goal of humanistic psychology is not so different from the helping goal of professional coaches and caring teachers: to inspire clients/students to maximize their personal and professional potential. As we strive and continue to develop, refine, and integrate a holistic theory of human behavior evolving from research on healthy, productive being, we want to acknowledge the early influences of the theories, thoughts, and works of Carl Rogers, Abraham Maslow, John Gardner, our colleague Darwin Nelson, and others.

Carl Rogers created lifelong interest of a fully functioning person, client-centered learning, acceptance, and positive change. We learned about Rogers and his significant body of classic works and influence from readings, doctoral studies, caring faculty, and from students of Rogers at the University of Wisconsin. Our colleague and co-author on many of our published works and assessment instruments, Darwin Nelson (1942–2017), met Rogers at a national counseling convention in Dallas in 1967 and later visited with him in La Jolla, CA, for insightful discussions about our positive assessment approach for skill development and a person-centered learning framework.

Figure 3. The Historical Roots, Limbs, and Branches of TEI
Note. Image credit: Jose Henriquez, Walden University

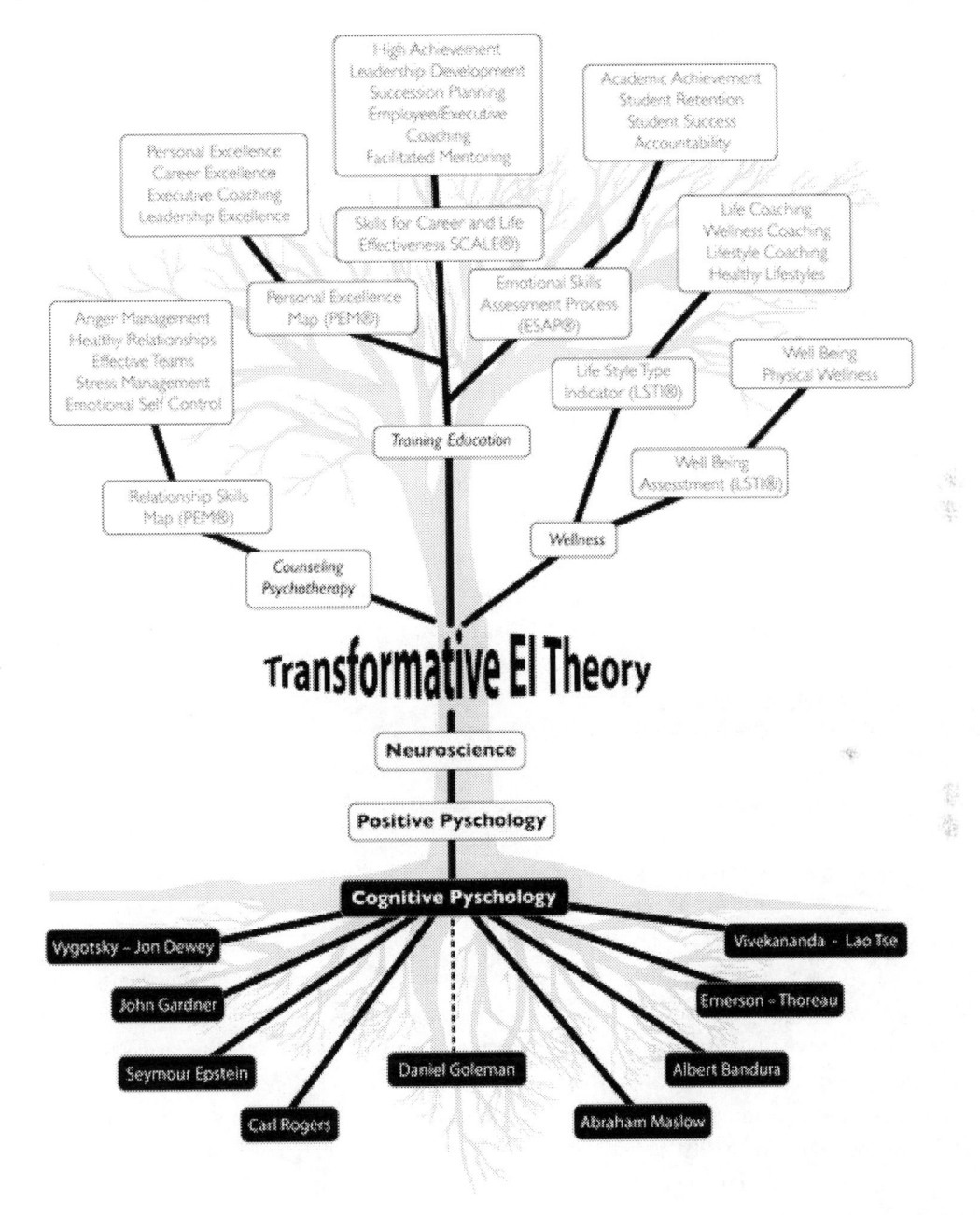

Genuine, authentic relationships are at the center of emotional learning and positive change. Reflective listening and core conditions of inner growth, congruence, empathy, and positive regard are behavioral reflections of personal health and well-being. Like Rogers, we see the conditions of person-centered, relationship-focused learning as key personal and emotional skills that guide wise actions and positive personal change.

Recall Rogers's (1995) curious paradox that, "When I accept myself just as I am, then I change" (p. 17). The quotation reflects an understanding that when he accepted self as decidedly imperfect yet still caring and growth oriented, he created presence. Being more in the present and aware of feelings at any given time guided a purpose of using feelings to connect more meaningfully with self and others. The curious paradox reflects a kind of dynamic self-awareness that is important to learning, teaching, and coaching with emotional intelligence. When you inculcate emotional intelligence in your work, then you work continually with yourself and others to engender the curious paradox on a personal level to pursue goals.

Along with Rogers, Abraham Maslow piqued our interest in healthy, positive human conditions. For Maslow, these included motivation, needs, and the growth of the person. We see value in helping individuals develop to be their best version of self, especially in relationships with others. Striving to grow and develop our abilities to the fullest is important for achieving balance and equilibrium. As shown in Figure 4, each of the key models that have influenced the development of our transformative theory of emotional intelligence can be shown to strive for equilibrium by balancing the cognitive, emotional, and behavioral systems of being human (Hammett, 2013). You may recognize the zeniths of fully being human described by Maslow's self-actualizing (Panel A), Rogers's fully functioning person (Panel B), and Epstein's cognitive-experiential self (Panel C). Congruent with these models, our transformative approach adds three ways of modeling EI through active imagination, self-directed coaching, and guided mentoring (Panel D). Please see Figure 4 for further clarification. As demonstrated in our explanation of using the Emotional Learning System (ELS) that follows in this chapter, we integrate this humanistic framework of healthy being with positive assessment through the ELS to help shape productive teaching, coaching, and learning relationships.

Maslow's hierarchy of needs describes a process of growth and motivation that we view as important for relating the TEI principle of interdependence for developing healthy, productive relationships, key emotional-life skills, and constructive thinking. Our view of the relationship between Maslow's hierarchy and our current views from research-derived, person-centered, relationship-focused, and skills-based models of human behavior and life development are shared in Table 2. Note the PERL skills measured by our positive assessments in the third column.

John Gardner's books (1961, 1963) were carried with us for years. We accepted his challenge to answer his (see Research Question #3, above) and other important questions and, in the process, constructed a healthy model for achieving personal excellence. As a result, our belief today is that there are good ways to approach excellence and equality when we learn to: (a) create personal standards of guiding ethics with intentional, positive, emotional skills to pursue skills-based change; (b) set, establish, and pursue personal goals daily to achieve positive, skills-based change; and (c) develop/use constructive thinking to shape wise behavior with PERL skills for positive personal change. These three research-derived guiding principles that we developed based on Gardner's initial challenge can be useful to inform online education as instructors work with their students to maximize potential. In short, we agree with Gardner that there are multiple ways of measuring people. According to Gardner (1961):

There is a way of measuring excellence that involves comparison between people–some are musical geniuses, and some are not; and there is another that involves comparison between myself at my best and myself at my worst. It is the latter comparison which enables me to assert that I am being true to the best that is in me–or forces me to confess that I am not. (p. 128)

Emotional Intelligence Learning System for Person-Centered Curriculum Development and Teaching

Figure 4. Transformative EI and its Influences
Note. Models that have shaped our TEI approach. Adapted with permission from R. Hammett (2013). Image credit Jose Henriquez, Walden University.

Panel A:
Abraham Maslow's model of personality and growth

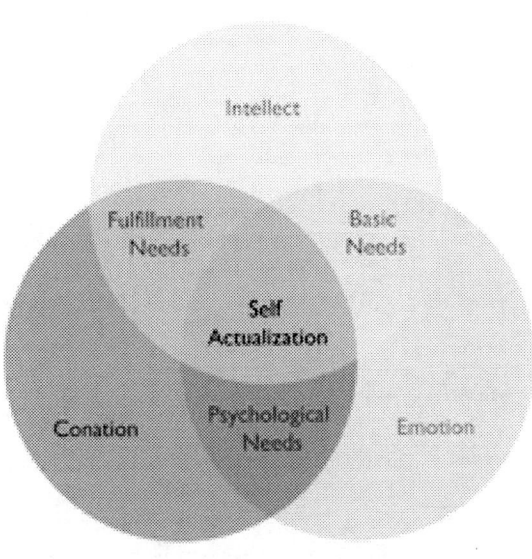

- Intellect
- Fulfillment Needs
- Basic Needs
- Self Actualization
- Conation
- Psychological Needs
- Emotion

Panel B:
Carl Roger's model of personality and growth

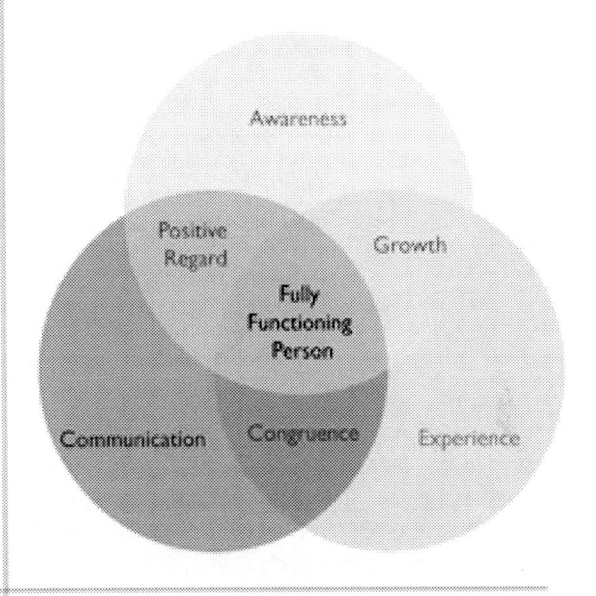

- Awareness
- Positive Regard
- Growth
- Fully Functioning Person
- Communication
- Congruence
- Experience

Panel C:
Seymour Epstein's Cognitive-Experiential Self Theory

- Rational Intelligence
- Wise Actions
- Reframe
- CEST
- Practical Intelligence
- Constructive Thinking
- Experiential Intelligence

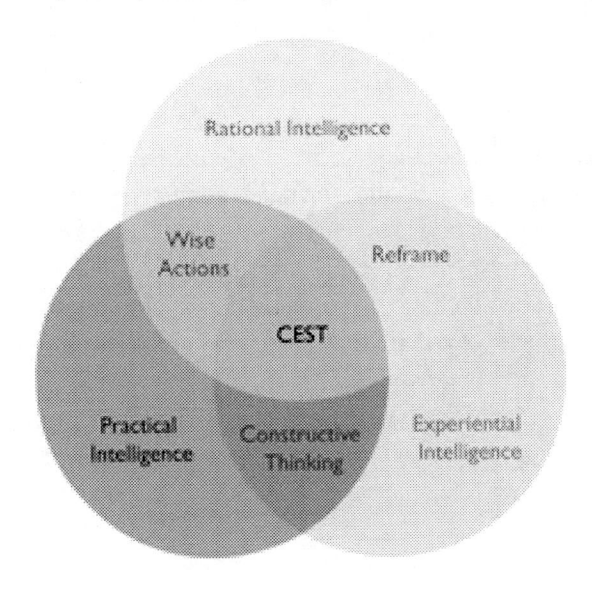

Panel D:
Nelson and Low's skills-based model of emotional intelligence

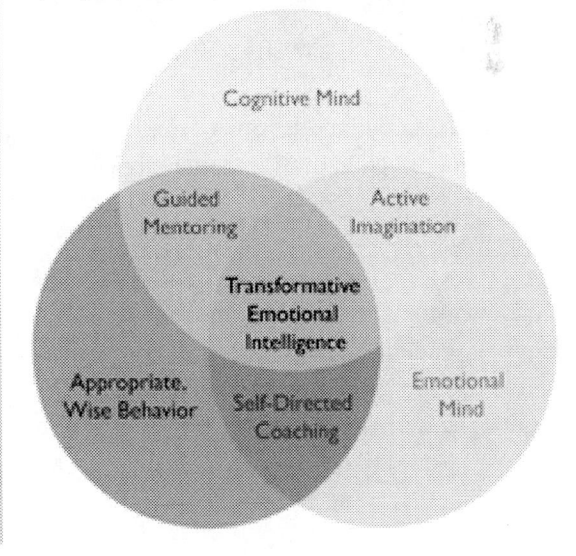

- Cognitive Mind
- Guided Mentoring
- Active Imagination
- Transformative Emotional Intelligence
- Appropriate, Wise Behavior
- Self-Directed Coaching
- Emotional Mind

49

Table 2. Work-life excellence: needs, beliefs, and skills

Need Type	Related Beliefs	PERL Skills
Survival	Obtain pleasure and avoid pain in fulfilling physiological needs essential to life and well-being	Anger Management, Anxiety Management, Stress Management, and Self-Esteem
Safety	To make sense out of your experience and develop consistency and stability in how the world is viewed	Self Esteem, Stress Management, Positive Personal Change, Physical Wellness
Relationship	To seek meaningful connections and emotionally satisfying relationships with others	Assertion, Comfort, Empathy, Leadership, Self-Esteem, and Stress Management
Self-Esteem	To believe that one has value, worth, and dignity; to develop high self-esteem	Self-Esteem
Equilibrium	To seek balance and harmony when we experience distress or perceive deficits	Anger Management, Anxiety Management, Stress Management, and Self-Esteem
Growth	To commit to continuous growth and change as we seek to develop our best self	Self-Esteem, Achievement Drive, Positive Personal Change, Physical Wellness

Note. Maslow's contribution established a frame of reference for thinking about motivation that focuses on the subjective experience of the individual. Our connection, interpreted through related beliefs, emphasizes PERL skills that individuals can use to encounter, satisfy, and, when necessary, revisit needs in pursuit of personal growth.

From our perspective, it is important to include a discussion about our background because those meaningful experiences provided the framework for us to develop our positive assessment instruments and our approach for using them in professional coaching scenarios. With that background, we turn our attention to our emotional learning system, a model that we integrate with positive assessment in our professional teaching, mentoring, and coaching practices.

The Emotional Learning System©

Key to person-centered learning from the perspective of TEI is engagement, and engagement is not formally integrated in most learning models or curricula. Most curricula and course content begin with what we want the students to learn and know rather than what our students want to learn and know. This 19th and 20th century teaching paradigm fails the litmus test of person-centered engagement that we all know is critical to 21st century online learning. The challenge is compounded by complicated online environments and busy instructors who may not have a systematic way to meaningfully engage with their students. The five-step ELS presented in Figure 5 begins with *Step A Self-Assessment: Explore* to encourage discussions about what the student wants to learn and know as the beginning point in courses and lesson plans. We now briefly discuss each of the five steps of the ELS (see Figure 5) for those who would like a concrete ITL implementation model and engagement system they can use daily when interacting with their students.

- **Step A (Self-Assessment: *Explore*)** requires that you develop an intentional self-assessment habit: inquiring, discovering, and questioning. (What thoughts am I having right now? What am I feeling? How do I want to respond best in this situation?) Because self-assessment is the active process of exploring your experience as it occurs, you must pause before you act. Even when strong emotions (e.g., anger, fear, or sadness) dominate your immediate experience, the self-assessment process enables you to pause so that you can follow the path of reflection, not reaction. You will know when you are mastering the ELS Step A when you begin relying on it to get to know and solve problems with your students.

- **Step B (Self-Awareness: *Identify*)** involves the process of identifying your experience as either a thought or a feeling. Accurate self-awareness is the learned ability to correctly identify and label the emotion being experienced. Once the emotion is identified, the constructive thinking process can begin.
- **Step C (Self-Knowledge: *Understand*)** involves insight and an understanding that allows you to make choices about how to behave. Wise actions are the immediate result of conscious reflection and constructive thinking. Occasionally, Step C is a logical and sequential process. At other times, a quick insight pops into your awareness and reveals new, more creative, and better problem-solving options.
- **Step D (Self-Development: *Learn*)** involves learning various ways to improve your behavior. Positive self-development is a learning process in that only seldomly is our behavior correct on the first attempt. Improved behavior requires choosing and engaging in personal behavior that pleases you and increases your self-esteem and your self-appreciation. New and improved behaviors require practice to become intentional habits.
- **Step E (Self-Improvement: *Apply and Model*)** requires that you apply and model emotionally intelligent behavior to achieve personal, career, and academic goals. The ability to apply and model emotionally intelligent behavior is not an *arrival* state. Rather, it is a process of using the preceding four steps to perfect yourself, to achieve your best as a person, and to exercise intelligent self-direction.

It is important to know what you can change and what you cannot. What you can change is to learn and practice new skills in how you think, feel, and behave. Practice is needed, and we do not usually practice emotional skills unless we explore and learn about emotional intelligence. Developing EI skills takes time and practice. Be energized and focused on your journey of your learning adventure and discover the pathways of self-discovery, self-knowledge, self-improvement. Think of yourself as a work in progress. We all are works in progress. We make mistakes. The key is to learn from your experience. One of the skills you will learn is Commitment Ethic (tenacity) as an emotional skill essential for the commitment to learning new skills and behaviors.

The Role of Emotions in Online Teaching and Learning

Emotions are natural and they are experienced by instructors and students alike during their ongoing learning relationships. While they are natural, emotions are not neutral, and understanding them within an online context can be even more challenging. They drive us toward action. When those feelings are related to the experience of positive growth, excitement creates flow where learning happens spontaneously and with little effort (Csikszentmihalyi, 1990). Conversely, when the problematic feelings related to anger, fear, and sadness are experienced, learning becomes difficult, flow is interrupted, and, in their efforts to self-advocate, instructors and learners can resort to coping strategies that create challenges for themselves and their learning institutions. In teaching and learning, flow is the goal!

Figure 5. Five-step Emotional Learning System©
Note. Image credit: Jose Henriquez, Walden University.

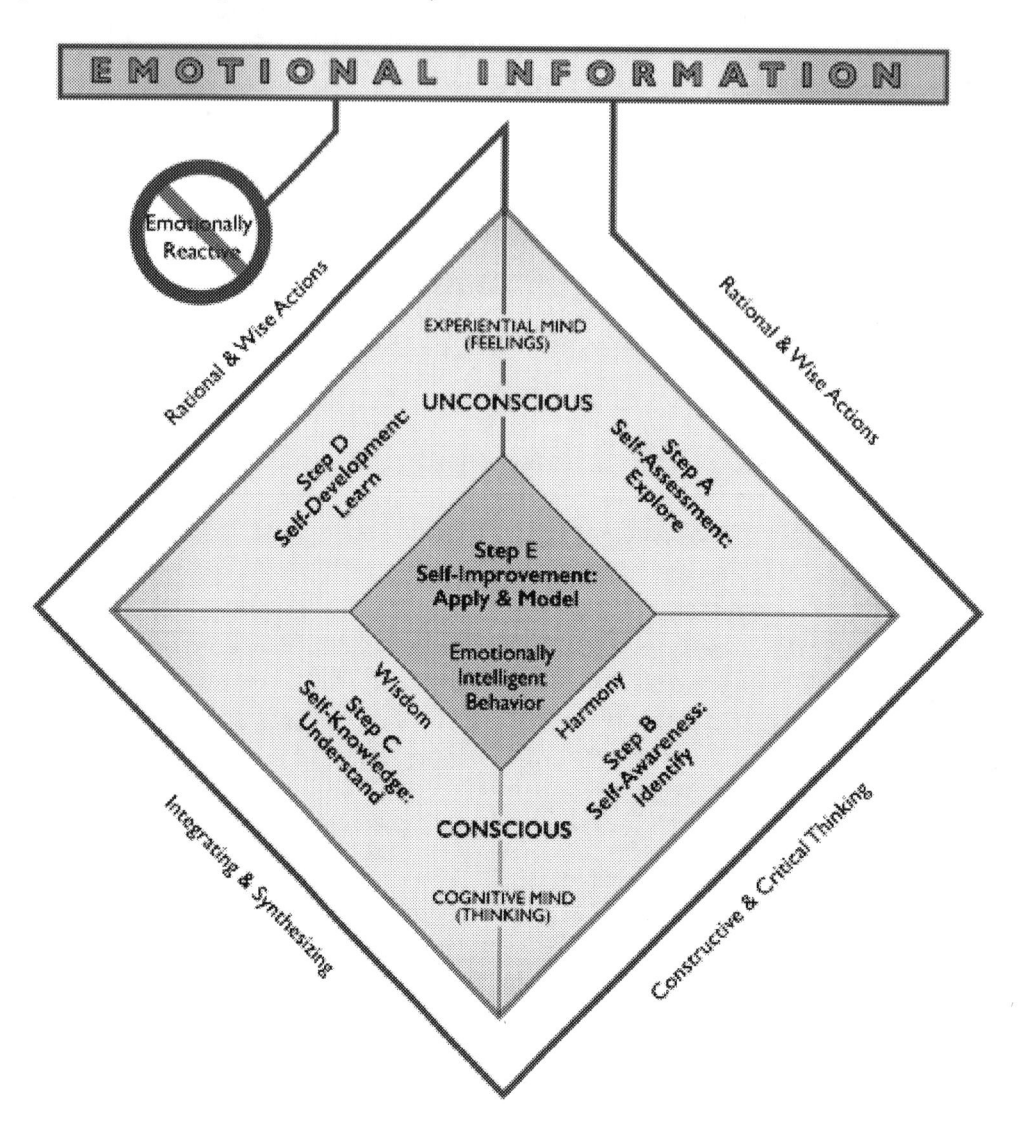

In TEI we focus on the four basic emotions of anger, fear, sadness, and happiness. Our rationale for limiting emotional focus is practical. First, if we focus on are four basic emotions, we increase our ability to correctly identify an emotion when it occurs. This self-awareness is crucial for gaining prominence over our feelings (see Figure 5). Second, the temporal nature of emotions influences the words we use to relate and describe the four basic emotions, but they are not the basic emotions themselves. As reminded by Nelson and Low (2004), anger creates a strong attempt to stop or start an event in the present. But in the past, it can become resentment, and in the future it may be experienced as envy or jealousy. Sadness is a down feeling related to loss. In the past, it may become regret, remorse or guilt; in the future it may manifest as pessimism and hopelessness. Fear is a feeling related to caution and withdraw. Memories of fear in the past can bring fear into the present and, if projected into the future, fear can manifest as worry, stress, or panic.

As you learn to identify and change the thoughts that create basic human emotions, you gain positive and empowering contributions of your emotional system. You are able to learn about basic human emotions of happiness (love, joy), anger, fear, and sadness. You learn that the act of changing your thoughts can calm yourself with a focus on positive skills and positive emotions. When we identify and make these changes, we improve our ability (with skills) to control, manage, and regulate basic, primary emotions. In the following paragraphs, we provide some examples of the basic emotions and their temporal nature.

- **Anger Example** — Anger happens quickly, in the present, and is a strong attempt to change something in the present. Anger is created by destructive thinking and naturally moves us toward aggression. When experiencing anger, it is helpful to practice the skill of anger management by quickly thinking reflectively and constructively. Knowing that our anger is truly *our* anger is a quick step in the right direction. We want to be able to think how we want to respond in ways that are healthy, constructive, and positive. Learning the emotional skills of anger management and constructive thinking are important for creating flow in online environments.
- **Fear Example** — Fear and anxiety happens now, in the present, and fear has a future time element. Always important to know and respect about the emotion of fear is that there is perceived immediate danger. With danger, you need to take action and be safe. However, fear has a future time element. It helps us recognize fear and know that we may need to reflect, plan, and take action to reduce the harmful effects of it. Identify healthy ways to respect fear. Learn more specifics about how to manage fear. We don't want fear to result in us retreating or withdrawing from life. The skill of anxiety management is one key.
- **Sadness Example** — Sadness is a loss of something important. When we experience loss we may feel strong emotions of anger, fear, sadness. Temporary sadness, while truly sad, and its reactive thoughts may take us to more serious and longer impacts depending on what the loss is and how much effect occurs. Knowing sadness is in the present and knowing that sadness has a past time element helps us to reflect, plan, and then act. Being active with specific personal goals help us reduce negative effects of being too sad for too long. Emotional skills enable us to regain balance and equilibrium. We need to stay healthy and engaged with life. Emotional skills are keys to resilience and personal renewal.
- **Happiness Example** — We are happy when we are happy. You are happy when you are happy. A unique aspect of happiness is that happiness resides in each person and may be different from one person to another. In other words, happiness occurs when we create happiness, plan happy things, do happy things. Creating happy thoughts guides us toward the experience of more happiness. When we think about healthy things that make us happy, it is positive. When we feel happy, we are happy and not angry, fearful, or sad. The takeaway is to create happy thoughts, feelings, and behaviors as often as possible. A word of caution: Create boundaries or parameters so that being happy is not harmful to self or others. Learning about positive emotions is an important piece of the happiness puzzle. It is essential to learn as much as you can about health, wellness, and well-being to be healthier and well.

Emotions and how people experience them are the same in both online and face-to-face learning environments. In face-to-face environments, however, synchronous communication and accompanying body language are helpful in mitigating the negative consequences of difficult feelings. In online environments, we must implement strategies to overcome the challenges associated with asynchronous communication. Useful strategies incorporating TEI are offered in the next section.

Applying TEI in Online Environments

One good place to begin applying TEI is to familiarize yourself with the 13 PERL skills that we have found through research to be related to high achievement and satisfaction. As you *explore* the skills, acknowledge those that you already use to make you successful as an online instructor. Next, *identify* one skill that you would like to develop, strengthen, or enhance that, when improved, would help you proactively implement the ITL model (i.e., help make yourself more person-centered, experientially focused, reflective, collaborative, and inclusive through appreciative engagement). Then, take some time to *understand* that skill. Use your active imagination and self-directed coaching and discuss the skill with people who you respect as having high acumen with the skill you chose to improve. Imagine and record on a piece of paper how your teaching or interaction with students would change if you improved that skill. In the next phase, learn the skill. Self-directed coaching and guided mentoring can be excellent ways to practice becoming more skilled. Finally, *apply and model* the skill daily with your students and colleagues to really integrate the five pillars of the ITL model in your daily work. When you feel confident in your use of the identified skill, return to the skill definitions and choose another skill to develop, strengthen, and enhance. We have found that students respond favorably to our attempts to discuss, share, and model PERL skills and they also enjoy discussions about the positive contributions of the emotional mind advocated through TEI. While the 13 PERL skills were presented initially in Table 2, we define and discuss them in more detail in this section. The section ends with a practical example of TEI application in online environments.

- **The Intrapersonal Domain and EI Skills.** Constructive thinking allows you to be imperfect (as all humans are), make mistakes, and remain positive in your evaluation of self. None of us wants to fail or make serious mistakes, and the risk of failure is always a part of high achievement. What we say to ourselves (self-talk), how we explain our behavior, and what we do to improve our behavior all have a significant impact. The first PERL skills we will discuss; Self-Esteem, Stress Management, and Positive Change, are related to the Intrapersonal competency of TEI.
    - *Self-Esteem* is the learned ability to view the self as positive, competent, and successful. Positive self-esteem is the foundation for achievement and a general sense of well-being. It is developed and maintained when one experiences success after effectively dealing with self, others, and the demands of life. Self-esteem serves as a thermostat of how we direct, focus energy, and change.
    - *Positive Stress Management* is the learned ability to choose and exercise healthy self-control in response to stressful events. This skill requires that you regulate the level of emotional intensity and use cognitive coping strategies during difficult and stressful situations. It is an essential emotional skill for health, performance, and satisfaction. How to focus your thinking, feeling, and behavior to develop and improve stress management are discussed in this section.
    - Our published assessment instruments measure a problematic indicator called Change Orientation. *Change Orientation* is the degree to which an individual is or is not satisfied with current behavior and the magnitude of change necessary or desired to develop per-

Emotional Intelligence Learning System for Person-Centered Curriculum Development and Teaching

sonal and professional effectiveness. It includes the degree to which a person is motivated and ready for change. Change orientation must be understood and converted to the *positive change* emotional skill in order to achieve excellence in all areas of life. The change orientation indicator is based on a TEI principle that change can be and, indeed, is positive when it is planned and when people are active participants to help shape change.

- **EI Skills of the Interpersonal Domain**. A major factor in personal satisfaction, academic achievement, and career success is your ability and willingness to establish and maintain healthy interpersonal relationships. Your interactions and associations with others form an important part of the EI curriculum. Friends, peers, teachers, mentors, and professional helpers can have a powerful influence on your academic and career development. The quality of your interpersonal relationships—especially with significant others in the school, career, and life contexts—affects your ability to focus on and complete meaningful academic and career goals.

The ability to act wisely in human relationships is interpersonal competence. Interpersonal competence requires that you apply and model three important emotional intelligence skills. Effective communication (the EI skill of assertion) and emotional self-control (the EI skills of anger and anxiety management), as well as understanding and appreciating the differences in others, are reflections of interpersonal intelligence. These communication and relationship skills allow you to work effectively in groups and teams.

- *Assertive communication* is the learned ability to clearly and honestly communicate your thoughts and feelings to others in a straightforward and direct manner. It is a way of talking to people that lets you express your thoughts and feelings in a way that is not hurtful. Assertive communication allows you to respect your rights and the rights of others and is essential if you are to constructively express and deal with strong emotions like anger, fear, and sadness. Assertive communication is characterized by using *I* language in your communication with others.
- For people who score high on our aggression measures, the skill to develop is anger management. *Anger management* is the learned ability to express anger constructively in relationship to self and others. *Aggression* is the degree to which an individual employs a personal communication style (pattern) that violates, overpowers, dominates, or discredits another person's rights, thoughts, feelings, or behaviors. Aggression is a potential problem area that negatively affects relationships and must be converted to the *anger management* emotional skill. Aggression is characterized by using *You* language in your communication with others.
- For people who score high on our measures of deference, the skill to develop is anxiety management. Anxiety management is the learned ability to manage self-imposed anxiety (fear) and effectively communicate with others. *Deference* is the degree to which an individual employs a communication style (pattern) that is indirect, self-inhibiting, self-denying, and ineffectual for the accurate expression of thoughts, feelings, or behaviors. It involves the fear emotion that must be understood and converted to the anxiety management emotional skill. Changing how you communicate during stressful (anxiety-producing) situations is a major personal change that can bring many emotional benefits.
  - **The Leadership Domain and Related EI Skills.** Effective leadership is people centered, and effective leaders know, understand, and respect the needs, values, and goals of others. A genuine respect for the differences in others and the ability to communicate and accurately understand the differing points of view are the essence of emotionally intelligent leadership.

The ability to quickly establish and comfortably maintain effective interpersonal relationships with a wide range of individuals and groups reflects the social awareness emotional intelligence skill. The ability to accurately understand and accept differing viewpoints requires the skill of empathy. The social awareness and empathy skills are interdependent and necessitate an assertive communication style.

Reasoning and emotions are interactive, and both are essential for effective decision making and person-centered (relational) leadership. Intuitive wisdom, a major contribution of the emotional mind, influences your decision-making ability and provides the energy and stamina that move you toward your goals. Remember that deciding is a process, not an event. When you have a decision that you cannot make, talk it out, get feedback, and pay attention to your emotions and let them help unlock your cognitive thoughts.

One view of decision making is that it should be separated from emotions and be a completely logical and rational process. A similar view perceives good leaders as people with a particular collection of stable traits or personal characteristics. When these views are personalized as negative belief systems, you might hear such statements as, 'I cannot make a decision' or 'I have never been a leader and never will be.' These are isolated views of the cognitive system.

Emotions are the key to creative problem solving. The initiative and goal-directed component of positive influence is also a contribution of the emotional mind. When you apply the positive influence skill, you act more than you react, and you accept responsibility for achieving your academic, career, and life goals.

Meaningful relationships are hard to find if you look for them, and they are sometimes slow to develop if you wait for them to happen. Without healthy and supportive connections with others, our personal resources are often inadequate in times of high stress. Actively seek out relationships with people who are genuinely interested in your success, care what happens to you, and will help you when you honestly need help.

- *Social Awareness* is a by-product of interpersonal awareness and our actual behavior when relating to others. It is the learned ability to affect others positively and develop trust and rapport in relationships. Social awareness is a result of attendant behaviors that are both verbal and nonverbal. Rapport is achieved through good eye contact, a pleasant greeting, and a willingness to self-disclose (say something about yourself to the other person). Active listening is the best way to make a good, comfortable contact with another person—a willingness to attend to what another person is saying (pay attention) and letting that person know that you have heard the message sent. Social awareness enables a person to be confident, spontaneous, and relaxed with others in a variety of situations.
- *Empathy* is the learned ability to accurately understand and constructively respond to the expressed feelings, thoughts, and needs of others. Accurate empathy involves communicating to the sender that he or she has been heard, understood, and accepted as a person. Empathy is the process of letting a person know that you have understood that person's feelings.

When you communicate assertively, your message is clear, honest, and direct. How you speak is important, and your ability to listen and accurately hear what someone else is saying and feeling is essential to establishing and maintaining effective relationships. Comfortable, healthy relationships are created between two people when the talk is straight, the listening is active, and the differences are

Emotional Intelligence Learning System for Person-Centered Curriculum Development and Teaching

recognized and appreciated. When you care about the other person and want to be helpful, accurate empathy is important.

- *Decision Making* is the learned ability to use effective problem-solving and conflict-resolution strategies to resolve issues. It requires using a systematic model to approach the problems that occur daily.

The ability to make quick decisions and demonstrate good judgment has an important emotional component. The experiential mind comes to the support of the cognitive mind when difficult problems require resolutions and important decisions must be made. Much has been said about how emotions interfere with reasoning, and more must be understood about how emotions spark creativity, curiosity, and intuition.

The experiential mind plays an extremely important role in shaping your fundamental values and your characteristic behaviors. Emotions are a source of energy for high performance, motivation, and innovation.

- *Positive Influence* is a behavioral reflection of self-empowerment, interpersonal, and goal achievement skills. It is a set of personal and goal-directed behaviors that create consensus and momentum and gain the active support of others. Positive influence results from a self-directed, internal process that is grounded in positive self-esteem, guided by clear personal values, and observable in proactive, self-confident behaviors. It is a cumulative set of behaviors that are observed by others and evaluated as valuable and meaningful directions to follow.

You are an effective leader when your relationships with others are characterized by honesty, trust, empathy, integrity, dependability, and a respect for diversity. The energy, excitement, and commitment to a purpose necessary to develop these relationships come from the emotional mind. In a sense, positive influence is a learned process that reflects a person's ability to model emotionally intelligent behavior. A person demonstrates harmony (congruence) and wisdom (good judgment) by integrating the experiential and cognitive systems.

- **The Self-Management Domain and Skills**. This domain highlights the skills that are central to the behavior of high achieving, productive instructors and learners who learn to motivate themselves by setting meaningful personal goals, managing their time and resources, completing assignments, and becoming flexible and adaptable in response to unexpected demands and changes. Effective self-management is the key to high levels of academic, life, and career success.

The ensuing discussion's most important message is that accepting responsibility for your own learning and your own success is the first step to improving your achievement. A conscious decision to be the best person that you can be is within the domain of the cognitive mind. The emotional mind provides the energy to achieve your goals and sparks the happiness that results from doing something important to you—and doing it very well.

The drive strength skill incorporates energy from the emotional system and requires that you develop the ability to set clear and meaningful personal goals. The ability to motivate yourself, focus energy, and achieve goals is an initial step toward personal excellence. Commitment ethic is the closure skill that many people fail to develop. The emotional outcome of this skill is experienced internally as pride and observed externally as dependability.

The increasing demands and rapid changes characteristic of an internet-connected world require a level of productivity and personal resilience beyond normal levels. As people respond to the increasing work demands of the 21st century, self-management skills become more essential.

The ability to remain flexible and open to change requires cognitive, emotional, and behavioral skills. The ability to confront problems, go through emotions, and change behavior is extremely important to personal well-being and physical health.

- *Drive Strength* is reflected by goal achievement; it is your learned ability to complete meaningful goals that give you personal satisfaction and positive feelings. Improving your ability to achieve goals involves learning a specific process called action goal setting, which you can apply and practice on a daily basis.
- *Action goal setting* helps a person learn that she can direct and focus energy to accomplish behaviors that are satisfying. This process builds feelings of self-control and reminds you that you can exercise choice in your behaviors. When you want to feel better, happier, or healthier as a person, you must start doing more things that you really like and value. Each meaningful goal that you set and accomplish builds your self-esteem and self-confidence.
- *Commitment Ethic* is an emotional skill reflected by the learned ability to complete tasks, assignments, and responsibilities dependably and successfully. People with a high level of commitment ethic skill are inner-directed, self-motivated, and persistent when completing projects, regardless of the difficulties involved. Commitment ethic is a dedication to task completion that produces excitement and pride, not fatigue and sacrifice.
- *Time Management* is the learned ability to organize tasks into a personally productive time schedule and use time effectively to complete the tasks. Effective time management is the ability to *actively manage* time instead of *responding* to the demands of time.

Positive mental health and productive living require that we actively manage our responsibilities within time restrictions. An important by-product of good time management is a feeling of self-control—we are managing our responsibilities, not being managed by them. In essence, effective time management is self-managed and self-directed behavior that allows us to accomplish daily tasks with less effort and emotional intensity.

In Scenario #1 below, we provide an example of how thoughts and emotions can interrupt flow and cause discord in online learning. In Scenario #2, we demonstrate how constructive thinking, anger control, and assertive communication with empathy facilitates authentic inclusion and flow.

Scenario #1: Instructor-Student Interaction Without TEI
- *Instructor Thinks: 'I've been providing the same feedback to this student for 6 weeks and he keeps making the same errors.'*
- *Instructor Feels: Anger*
- *Instructor's aggressive email response: (Repeats previous feedback) If you do not implement my feedback, you will receive a failing grade in my class.*
- *Student's reaction: Thinks: 'This instructor hates me. I wonder why she has singled me out. She's planning to fail me!'*

Emotional Intelligence Learning System for Person-Centered Curriculum Development and Teaching

- *Student Feels: Anger*

A deferent response could be to quit turning in assignments and withdraw (either officially or unofficially) from the class.

An aggressive response could be an email like the following: 'You keep saying the same thing in your feedback and I keep changing my work and nothing I turn in is good enough for you. Now you are going to fail me and I don't know why you have it in for me! I will talk with my academic advisor about dropping your class immediately.'

Scenario #2: Instructor-Student Interaction With TEI
- *Instructor thinks: 'I've been providing the same feedback to this student for 6 weeks and he keeps making the same errors.'*
- *Instructor feels: Anger*
- *Instructor recognizes the uncomfortable feeling, and recalls reading about TEI. She searches for a constructive way to reflect, thinking, 'Most students give it their best. Perhaps there is something in this student's life that is interfering with his interpretation of my feedback.'*
- *Instructor feels: More positive; more empathy toward the student*

Instructor's empathic email response: I am sensing that you might be having trouble with my feedback and I care about your success in my course. I would like to visit with you to see if I can help you implement my feedback with better fidelity. When will you be available to meet by phone or in Teams?

- *Student thinks: 'I have been having trouble understanding her feedback. This instructor really seems to care about me. I will suggest two or three dates and times to meet in the near future.'*
- *Student Feels: Positive, included, connected*

Student sends a positive email with dates and times to meet with the instructor.

CONCLUSION

Exploring Walden's Inclusive Teaching and Learning Model and Person-Centered Approach Through the Lens of TEI Theory and Practice

The primary focus of this chapter has been to present a transformational emotional intelligence learning system of thinking and practice that can be used as a basis for improving online inclusive teaching and learning. Given the structure and framework of the TEI model that is, in-part, directly built on the work of Carl Rogers and his person-centered approach to learning relationships, it is easy to see how the TEI system resonates with and can amplify the effectiveness of Walden's Inclusive Teaching and Learning Model and can be an important instrument in improving any universities' curricula and approaches to teaching.

The TEI learning and development framework aligns well with Walden University's five dimensions of transformational learning. TEI embraces interdependence as a higher order value for a positive, meaningful, and inclusive approach for meaningful engagement. TEI facilitates the application of the Walden ITL learning model and transformational learning in other ways as well. First, the main tenets of TEI emphasize the person-centered and relational aspects of learning. Second, TEI's integrated learning model, the emotional learning system (ELS), emphasizes reflection and wise behavior over reactive behavior. Finally, TEI is reflected in thinking constructively about your immediate experience and your behavioral choices in the moment before you act.

A fundamental overlap between both the TEI learning system and Walden's learning model is that both focus on transformational learning and take as given that such learning is based on skills development. That is, one can learn specific skills that then lead to more effective emotional outcomes, which then open the door to intentional self-renewal and positive change protocols that are self-directed, and personally meaningful. Pursuing personal excellence facilitates high levels of achievement, happiness, and physical health—all of which are a part of transformational learning overall.

TEI does not use emotional intelligence (EQ) as a guiding model, because that model—like traditional models of cognitive intelligence—can presume that nature dominates nurture. The TEI approach is a transformative, developmental approach in which transformative EI skills anchored in behaviors such as a positive, person-centered, relationships are focused to guide intelligent self-direction and positive change. As such, the TEI learning system is a strong complement as one considers implementing a comprehensive inclusive teaching and learning model such as the one introduced in this volume.

REFERENCES

Csikszentmihalyi, M. (1990). *Flow: The psychology of optimal experience*. Harper and Row.

Epstein, S. (1998). *Constructive thinking: The key to emotional intelligence*. Praeger Publishers.

Epstein, S. (2012). Emotional intelligence from the perspective of cognitive-experiential self-theory. *The International Journal of Transformative Emotional Intelligence, 1*, 108–120. http://eitri.org/2015/11/14/emotional-intelligence-from-the-perspective-of-cognitive-experiential-self-theory/

Gardner, J. (1961). *Excellence: Can we be equal and excellent too?* Harper & Brothers.

Gardner, J. (1963). *Self-renewal: The individual and the innovative society*. W. W. Norton.

Goleman, D. (1995). *Emotional intelligence: Why it can matter more than IQ* (10th Anniversary). Bantom Books.

Low, G. R., & Hammett, R. D. (2021). *Transformative emotional intelligence for a positive career and life*. Emotional Intelligence Learning Systems. https://pubhtml5.com/tene/fdpa

Nelson, D. B., & Low, G. R. (2004). *Emotional intelligence: Achieving academic and career excellence*. Pearson Higher Education.

Nelson, D. B., & Low, G. R. (2011). *The skills for career and life effectiveness assessment*. https://doscale.com/

Nelson, D. B., & Low, G. R. (2014). *Lifestyle type indicator*. https://eilearningsys.com/?page_id=142

Nelson, D. B., Low, G. R., & Hammett, R. D. (2007). *Personal excellence map*. Emotional Intelligence Learning Systems. https://eilearningsys.com/?page_id=218

Nelson, D. B., & Nelson, K. W. (1984). *Relationship skills map: Positive assessment of relationship and intimacy skills*. Emotional Intelligence Learning Systems.

Sanderson, C. D., Hollinger-Smith, L. M., & Cox, K. (2021). Developing a social determinants of learning™ framework: A case study. *Nursing Education Perspectives*, *42*(4), 205–211. doi:10.1097/01.NEP.0000000000000810 PMID:33935243

ADDITIONAL READING

Emotional Intelligence Learning Systems. (n.d.). *Emotional skills assessment process*. http://eilearningsys.com/?page_id=162

Rude, D. A. (2013). Developing emotional intelligence in leaders: A qualitative approach. *The International Journal of Transformative Emotional Intelligence*, *2*, 21–34. http://eilearningsys.com/wp-content/uploads/2015/03/131214-Volume-2-D.Rude_.pdf

ENDNOTE

[1] Portions of this section were previously published by Emotional Intelligence Learning Systems (EILS). The authors of the EILS book and owners of EILS, Inc., are the two of the authors of this chapter, Richard Hammett, and Gary Low.

Section 2
Making Space

Inclusive environments in the online space do not happen because they are desired – those environments are intentionally designed. What do some of these designs look like?

Chapter 4
Success and Failures in the Development of an Inclusive Online Learning Environment

Tina Marshall-Bradley
Walden University, USA

ABSTRACT

Developing engaging learning environments for the benefit of all learners is a challenge for online programs. Research has shown that online learning environments are not designed to engage Black, Indigenous, people of color (BIPOC) for value that they bring to academic programs. Walden University and the master's in education (MSED) program have created foundational areas that can be used to create equitable learning environments. Arroyo and Gasman's 2014 model of Historically Black College and Universities' (HBCUs) student support provides a strong plan for institutions to change practices in support of BIPOC and other marginalized communities. Building on the activities of the revised core courses in the MSED program, and using the HBCU-inspired framework and recommendations from external reviewer, a case study is considered. This case study suggests an institution can build an online experience that is inclusive and supports the work of BIPOC and other marginalized communities.

INTRODUCTION

One of the challenges in online learning environments is developing engaging learning experiences that support inclusivity and promote equity. Black, Indigenous, people of color (BIPOC) face unique challenges in higher education, and institutions must consider the needs of BIPOC student populations to ensure student success (Galán et al., 2021). The questions I center in this chapter is what more can be done in virtual academic programs to honor BIPOC voices and to ensure their success, to make them feel wanted, or to address their professional goals? In current discourse, very little of the literature frames ways to develop inclusive curriculum in the online environment specifically – something I thematize here as well. Yet the literature does address how institutions can bring action to social and educational justice

DOI: 10.4018/978-1-6684-5146-5.ch004

commitments and to equity in teaching and learning. Some professionals have promoted the desire to develop and foster online experiences that challenge and dismantle structural and systemic issues such as racism sexism, religious bias and xenophobia (Evans-Amalu & Claravall, 2021), and these nascent investigations for online teaching and learning continue to evolve.

That is to say, inclusive efforts in virtual environments are yet to be widespread and fully realized. For example, a qualitative study by Salvo et. al. (2019) reported that African American male students identified factors such as lack of interaction with the online instructor and limited feedback as negatively impacting their learning experiences. I have experienced a similar lack of interaction with online instructors - I realized my discussion forum posts did not receive the attention of those from White colleagues. I am not alone in this observation. An analysis of massive online open courses (MOOCs) revealed online instructors are 94% *more likely* to respond to forum posts by White male students than students of color (Baker et al., 2018). For BIPOC students, rather than feeling a sense of excitement and engagement, there is a feeling of dread and disappointment when these kinds of disparities diminish and devalue their contributions. There is a critical need to ensure both BIPOC students *and* faculty feel heard, seen, and valued in the online environment. In a way, I write this chapter to connect the past, present, and future of DEI initiatives at Walden. I know how the experience has been, and I am involved in efforts to improve the learning experience and ensuring all students feel valued and heard. Like all institutions, there is still room for improvement.

It is clear to non-White students when institutional values do not match institutional practices. BIPOC students are accustomed to *code switching* and come to online environments expecting that they will need to adjust their identities, ideas, and whole selves if they are to be successful (Drake & Ogelsby, 2020). They also are accustomed to *not* being engaged beyond what is required in the course, even though factors such as the diversity at the institutional level and a supportive environment beyond the classroom contribute to academic success (Gasman & Arroyo, 2014). Examining inclusivity should extend beyond the boundaries of the individual course or program, and into the systems that support the courses.

In 2016, Walden University initiated a Diversity and Inclusion Working Group that has led to the creation of many foundational tools to promote equity, embrace diversity, and create inclusive experiences. Over the years, these tools have been cascaded throughout parts of the institution, and new innovations have been piloted. For example, there are many features in the master's in education (MSED) program that contribute to a strong foundation for a diverse, equitable, and inclusive environment for emerging teachers to grow and develop. However, tools are *not enough* to realize the institutional goals and visions. There is a need for the *application* and *understanding* of the principles that support DEI environments. Additionally, there is a need to systematically evaluate the extent to which ideas and principles are applied structurally throughout the learning environment (see Chapter 10, "A Framework to Measure Inclusion").

While I am a member of an institution currently working to actualize its DEI goals, I know we have room to improve. This work challenges a deeply entrenched status quo, and requires persistence and unwavering focus. While work has been done on the MSED program, this work will not have the desired effect without dismantling structures that prevent diversity, equity, and inclusion to be fully realized. To realize an inclusive environment, it is critical that all individuals at the institution are offered development opportunities (see Chapter 15, "Equity in the Online Space? A Multi-Systems Perspective") and are held accountable for applying the principles for creating and maintaining inclusive environments. It is also imperative that systems are put in place to monitor the work of individuals and make changes when individuals and programs are not in compliance with the ideas put forward by the institution.

Success and Failures in the Development of an Inclusive Online Learning Environment

BACKGROUND

At the center of the work of any organization are those navigational tools used to define community values, to bond the community to those values, and to frame the work. The navigational tools used at Walden University include its vision, mission, and goals, namely, the commitment to *positive social change*. For Walden, positive social change is defined as "a deliberate process of creating and applying ideas, strategies, and actions to promote the worth, dignity, and development of individuals, communities, organizations, institutions, cultures, and societies. Positive social change results in the improvement of human and social conditions" (Walden University, 2022, para. 4). Positive social change is the cornerstone of the institution and is considered in all its initiatives and programs. In the MSED program, positive social change starts with the mission for the Riley College of Education and Human Services that requires that candidates be able to inspire influence and impact their diverse communities.

In addition to positive social change, institutional values build a framework for community engagement. Walden envisions a "learning community where knowledge is judged worthy to the degree that it can be applied" (Walden University, 2022, para. 1) to address contemporary challenges in society, thus "advancing the greater global good" (Walden University, 2022, para. 1). This vision speaks to the need for programs to create experiences for all members of the community to identify and address issues within society. Supporting the vision of the institution is its mission to provide "a diverse community of career professionals with the opportunity to transform themselves as scholar-practitioners" (Walden University, 2022, para. 2). Included in the goals of the institution are the commitment to "produce graduates who are scholarly, reflective practitioners who are agents of positive social change" (Walden University, 2022, para. 3). The MSED program aligns its work to Walden's mission and vision, as well as the navigational tools of the Riley College of Education and Human Services and the institution.

Positive social change, thus, serves as the framework for DEI initiatives. The framework is built on principles that do not unbuild implicit biases explicitly, or defeat deficit modes of thinking. It is the energy and focus of the community that must do that work, especially in the online setting. Current research using deep neural networks to support BIPOC and other marginalized individuals refers to identifying why these populations do not succeed in online environments (Cheddadi & Bouache, 2021), and institutions would be wise to use the racially disaggregated BIPOC student achievement data to inform DEI efforts. Even as we move forward to use sophisticated technologies to advance DEI issues, there are missed opportunities to embrace information, ideas, and practices that come from marginalized communities who have traditionally and historically *not* achieved success with education systems at the same rate as White counterparts. Until institutions apply evaluative systems that include DEI at the center of the work for *all* members of the community, online environments will continue to miss the mark of promoting positive social change.

OPPORTUNITIES TO GROW

The Student Experience

The MSED program requires candidates to use 11 educator preparation program outcomes in their work actively. Some of the outcomes are based on the knowledge and skills that all educators should have. While there are other specific diversity and dispositional outcomes that are designed to address the affective aspect of the education profession, diversity and dispositional outcomes of the MSED program require candidates to create educational opportunities that are adapted to diverse learners and remove barriers that inhibit learning, and build meaningful relationships to improve student learning through effective planning, communication, use of assessment data, and high-caliber delivery of instruction. This is the opportunity to create positive social change in educational communities. This value informs the development of the MSED program – and in turn, develops opportunities for students to deploy DEI strategies in their development. For example, candidates are required to act in ways that honor multiple perspectives and affirm the dignity and respect of all individuals, internal and external to the learning environment. This includes their work with not only the students that they serve in their classrooms but the families and communities that they serve.

In support of the work that is done in programs regarding positive social change, Walden University's *8 Frameworks for Positive Social Change* (see Figure 1) provide a critical part of the work. In particular, the ideas in the MSED program that are most prominent from this framework are the ideas of systemic thinking, reflection, practice, and collaboration. Examples of systemic thinking in the MSED program include the idea of streams of thought that are used in journal posts in core courses. Examples of reflection include not only class discussions but also reflections on the research that is being done as a part of coursework.

From 2020 through 2022, the MSED program restructured the traditional graduate three (3) credit courses to one (1) credit courses. As a part of the redesign of the program, the core courses were reimagined using features that included traditional graduate study (colleague engagement, scholarly assignments) as well as features that are more closely associated with professional development (i.e., professional learning communities, colleague collaborative projects). In focusing on issues of equity and inclusion, courses were built on universal design of learning (UDL) principles, which have been found to make learning more engaging for BIPOC students (Fuentes et al., 2020).

Synchronous engagements offer students opportunities to experience, in real time, simulations of what they may encounter in the field. Candidates can attend the live sessions and engage with the faculty member and their colleagues, or they can watch a recorded version of a session. For students who are unable to attend live sessions, alternative options are available – expanding the accessibility of instruction. Through the discussion feature, candidates who did not attend the live session can still post their opinions, share their perspective, or ask questions. For group activities, candidates can do the same thing, and they have a dedicated workspace where they can post draft copies of their work, add to existing work, create wikis, post videos, and engage in discussions about the work. This kind of opportunity creatively engages students to experience a variety of scenarios to prepare them for their future work.

A purposeful feature of the MSED program redesign was the blend of graduate study and ideas of professional development learning as promoted in the education field. This line of thinking took into consideration Walden University's commitment to the development of scholar practitioners while also responding to the immediate need for deep and meaningful learning with practical implications. Courses were developed with an eye toward student choice; differentiation regarding content, process, and product as much as possible; and diversity of (and within) the learning resources. Also, callouts to students in the courses aimed to have candidates think about their own practice/teaching environment and its uniqueness as well as how to apply it to what they were working on in the courses.

Figure 1. Walden University's 8 Frameworks for Positive Social Change
Note. Image credit: Jose Henriquez, Walden University.

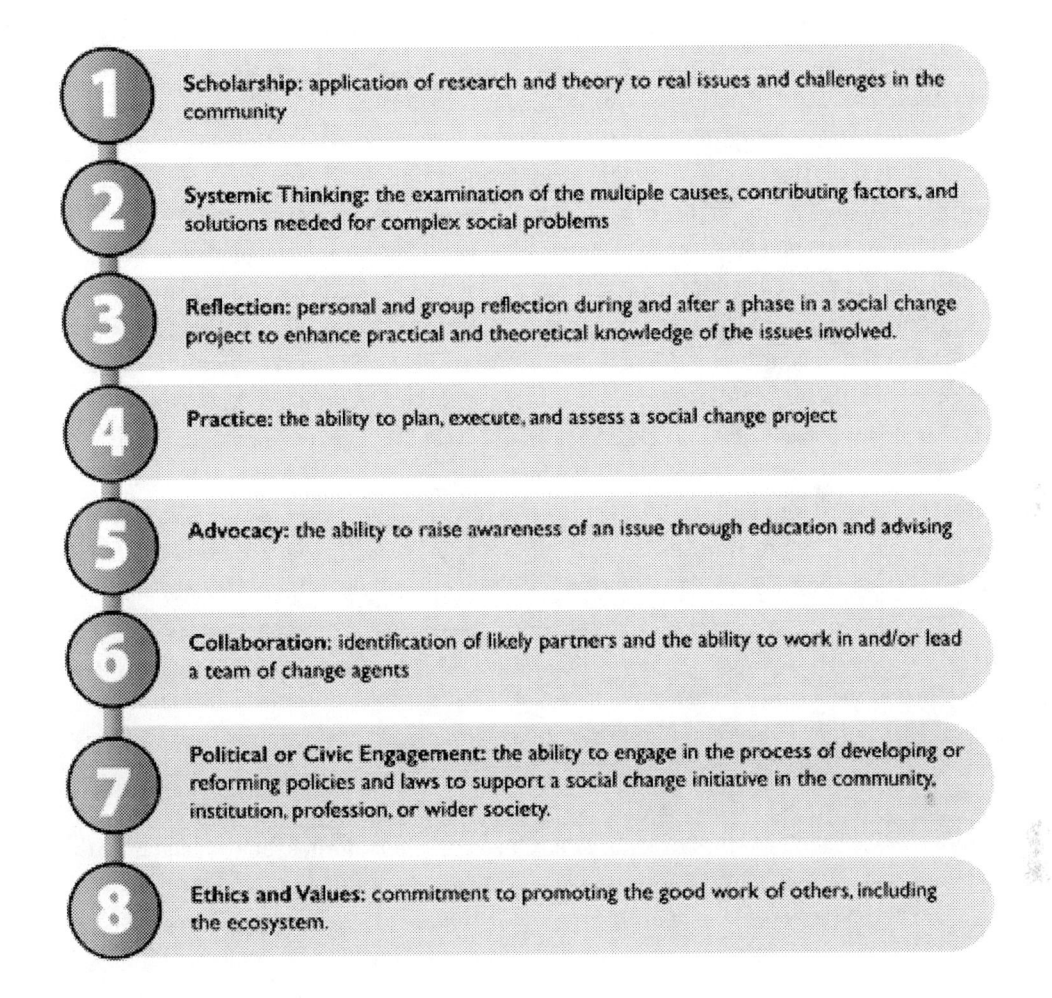

1. **Scholarship:** application of research and theory to real issues and challenges in the community

2. **Systemic Thinking:** the examination of the multiple causes, contributing factors, and solutions needed for complex social problems

3. **Reflection:** personal and group reflection during and after a phase in a social change project to enhance practical and theoretical knowledge of the issues involved.

4. **Practice:** the ability to plan, execute, and assess a social change project

5. **Advocacy:** the ability to raise awareness of an issue through education and advising

6. **Collaboration:** identification of likely partners and the ability to work in and/or lead a team of change agents

7. **Political or Civic Engagement:** the ability to engage in the process of developing or reforming policies and laws to support a social change initiative in the community, institution, profession, or wider society.

8. **Ethics and Values:** commitment to promoting the good work of others, including the ecosystem.

In the first course in the MSED program, *Teacher as Professional* (EDUC 6610), candidates are assigned to groups based on a contemporary topic in education. One of the topics that is on the list to be studied includes diversity, equity, and inclusion in K–12 environments. As evidence of the importance and interest in this topic, every term each section of the course has at least one group of five or six candidates who study this topic. In some terms, some sections of the course have multiple groups studying the topic. One student group discussed the role of technology in the evolution of equity and inclusion. This group wanted to provide reassurance and tools to parents and guardians, insofar as using technology can be intimidating to those who do not interact with it. By developing a website that was easily accessible to those parents and guardians, the student group felt they had succeeded in their goal.

An additional feature of the MSED program is the importance of candidates examining their professional practices through their personal experiences. According to Owen (2015), reflection requires learners to draw on specific backgrounds, beliefs, cultural understandings, philosophy, skills, and knowledge basis. These personal dimensions have a fundamental influence on professional practice as well as on ways of responding to political aspects of their role as educators and mentors (Owen, 2015). For example, an educator's belief about the primary focus within the curriculum and the approach they take to presenting the information or having students engage with the content are clearly connected to the influence of their personal experiences. Although there are specific requirements of the school and school system, there are many ways for classroom teachers to present information from their perspective.

Reflection includes examining personal ideas and biases regarding issues of diversity. The program requires that candidates reflect on past experiences in their personal lives that may have an impact on their professional practices. Some of these experiences include the impact of how individuals were reared, who they traditionally engaged with, enculturation, and just the natural biases that occur in individuals living. The focus of the new core courses is not simply on how educators embrace their teaching practice. There is also a strong emphasis on the idea of reflecting and embracing issues with which there are wide variances in thoughts and beliefs. The nation's current discussion on critical race theory has huge implications for what will be taught and how the content will be delivered. And while school systems and school boards discuss the issue and pass policies, it is ultimately classroom teachers who will make the decision as to what is presented and how the information is presented. An example of a resource that is included in the revised version of the course *Creating Effective Learning Environments* (EDUC 6657) is the inclusion of excerpts from the book *White Fragility: Why It's so Hard for White People to Talk About Racism* by Robin DiAngelo (2018). Candidates post a journal entry in which they consider this passage:

While implicit bias is always at play because all humans have bias, inequity can occur simply through homogeneity; if I am not aware of the barriers you face, then I won't see them, much less be motivated to remove them. Nor will I be motivated to remove the barriers if they provide an advantage to which I feel entitled. (DiAngelo, 2018, p. xii)

Students must wrestle with ideas of diversity, bias, heterogeneity, homogeneity, and how those frames inform how they navigate their daily lives, their internal world, and their interactions with others.

Additionally, MSED program creates resources students could use in their future classes. Scenarios include information based on the content that needs to be addressed. However, underlying features, such as the race and ethnicity of the characters and their situations, are considered. An example of a scenario that was created for the course *Enhancing Learning for Diverse Populations* (EDUC 6650/6616) includes a school-based case that not only presents information regarding the diverse needs of special needs students, but also presents features that cause candidates to think differently about diverse populations and their roles in society. One feature includes making the teacher a person of color and giving her a traditional Nigerian surname. Most of the models of teachers used in courses are White women because they make up 79% of all teachers in the United States (Shaeffer, 2021). The first student in the scenario is an African American boy who is receiving services for gifted and talented (GT) students. The parent who is the primary advocate is his father. This would typically not be the model shown because African American males are underrepresented in GT programs (Vega & Moore III, 2018); the parents who typically are shown as students' advocates are mothers.

All of these approaches to creating a program that embraces student perspectives and lived experiences has, in fact, contributed to positive social change. The work MSED students have achieved has impacted the communities they serve by specifically incorporating DEI strategies. Candidates not only engage their students with the resources and perspectives they have gained in the program, several candidates have designed innovations to support the families and members of the community they serve. Some of the work includes establishing councils consisting of parents for specific projects in their classrooms or schools as well as targeted and specific opportunities for families whose first language is not English to become involved with school environments. For instance, one former student reported that they decided to improve their own Spanish language skills by setting up a special group in Class Dojo for family members of English language learners (ELLs) in her class. Another student sent bulletin board kits home with students whose families earn less than the national median household income, based on qualifications for free and reduced lunch. This allowed those families to participate in school activities without having to adhere to a special schedule of school-related events that often conflicted with part-time job schedules. These are promising examples of the types of social change student candidates can create by innovating and removing barriers all too common in lower socioeconomic communities.

The Faculty Experience

Faculty development and faculty training have been ongoing and purposeful. At Walden University, faculty members are continually trained in processes related to creating an engaging learning environment, promoting the development of technical and specialized skills for disciplines, and advancing positive social change. This training includes the creation of engaging experiences regarding clarification of values and ideas connected to information from the literature. Faculty members are trained to honor the voices of candidates, as they use the activities in the learning environment to craft their own experiences in collaboration with other candidates in the course, colleagues in their work environments, and faculty members. There is still room for improvement, however, and an elaborated discussion of this is included in Chapter 15, "Equity in the Online Space? A Multi-Systems Perspective."

Like other faculty throughout the institution, the faculty in the MSED program consistently participate in training and push the boundaries of extending ideas of diversity and inclusion. Although these activities are commendable, it cannot be lost on student candidates in the program that the ideology of the institution is not always realized, as the population of the student body in the MSED program is overrepresented by African American women, yet the faculty population is underrepresented in terms of BIPOC. This is in a discipline that has historically been the purview of African American women.

Along with faculty members, there are other individuals who are extremely important in the crafting of learning environments. These individuals are learning architects, subject matter experts, and course designers who play critical roles in the identification of the content that goes into courses as well as how that content is presented. Representation of BIPOC in these positions is also critical because of the diverse mindset that they bring to the positions.

Challenges to Overcome

Even with all the exciting features and a solid foundation of providing an inclusive environment, there is more that can be done. Although the new features presented in the MSED coursework show tremendous opportunities, the application of this information is predicated on the faculty members who facilitate the courses, present supplemental information, and guide the work of candidates. Within the MSED program more can be done by the faculty to calibrate feedback that is given to candidates by faculty members. More can be done to provide authentic types of professional development that require faculty members to examine their own biases. These types of professional developments must be more than slide presentations or web resources – they must be truly engaging and create spaces for faculty to reflect and grow.

In an inclusive learning environment, it is critical to develop this kind of underlying trust to ensure all faculty feel included and psychologically safe.

The work of transitioning the MSED into a truly inclusive environment will require program leadership to apply evaluation systems that will transition the program. During a recent review of the MSED program, reviewers commended the program on the longevity of all faculty, even those who were part-time. However, the reviewer noted that the faculty were not diverse, and efforts should be made to provide program candidates with opportunities to engage with diverse faculty. Plans have been discussed to address other areas to improve the MSED program (i.e. upgrade course information and materials). Yet no plan has been developed to address the lack of faculty diversity or the need for all candidates to have access to BIPOC.

Promising Framework of Practice

Although there is an agreed-upon definition of positive social change, the interpretation and application of that interpretation varies widely by individuals and across programs. One of the challenges has been finding a way to clearly articulate the impact that Walden University has had on BIPOC and other marginalized populations. It is difficult to measure quantitative impact, however, alumni relay profound qualitative information. One thing is for certain, and that is to create inclusive learning environments where professionals do their work, they must have programs where DEI is modeled, practiced, and centered. In my experience, and as evidenced in this case study, it is critical that voices of those who are a part of the learning community are *central* to the learning experience and that authentic experiences are embraced.

The MSED program has made strides in addressing issues of inclusivity, diversity, and equity. Still, more work must be done to remove more barriers for more student populations. As discussed in Chapter 5, "Designing an Inclusive Online Classroom," programs like the MSED program can benefit from non-White, non-western values, cultures, and practices as a part of its ecosystem (Ndumu & Walker, 2021). In addition to an Inclusive Teaching and Learning rubric, other frameworks that promote incorporating non-dominant perspectives in courses and programs have existed within Historically Black Colleges and Universities (HBCUs), like that from the Center for Minority-Serving Institutions (CSMI), which includes Hispanic-serving institutions (HSIs), HBCUs, and Tribal Colleges and Universities (TCUs). A pivotal institution-focused, non-Eurocentric, theoretical framework of how HBCUs support students of color finds that BIPOC "students have tremendous power to create transformational movements within institutions…and educational leaders would be wise to recognize and harness their energy" (Arroyo & Gasman, 2014, p. 74). This framework (see Figure 2) can be adopted in any classroom, and suggests that student identity formation and values cultivation are key to BIPOC student success and development within a learning community.

Through the synthesis of information from close to 150 studies, Gasman and Arroyo (2014) identified four characteristics that HBCUs have that support BIPOC. These characteristics are:

1. A supportive environment – This has been defined as providing an environment where students feel a sense of safety and recognition in all aspects of the educational environment (Crooks et al., 2021).
2. Broad, iterative interpretation of student achievement – Along with formal assessments, performance assessments and evaluations are aligned with (1) cultivation of values (Crowley et al., 2021), (b)

Success and Failures in the Development of an Inclusive Online Learning Environment

formation of identity (Johnson et al., 2022), and (c) pedagogy that is culturally relevant (Ragoonaden & Mueller, 2017).
3. A holistic view of success – Even though the institutions and programs have their measures of outcomes, ideas of success can be determined by individuals. While one person's idea of success is career growth, another person's purpose can be social justice and activism.
4. Flexible entry points – This includes considering visibility, accessibility, and affordability of programs (Ndumu & Walker, 2021)

This framework has, in part, informed Walden University's practice of flexible entry points. Entry into the MSED program is accessible to most practicing teachers. Implementing the other characteristics of the framework (a supportive environment; broad, iterative interpretation of student achievement; and a holistic view of success) would move the MSED program closer to its idea of having a positive impact on social change by challenging the current status quo in higher education.

Figure 2. HBCU Framework for Student Support
Note. Image used with permission. Source: Arroyo & Gasman, 2014, p. 65.

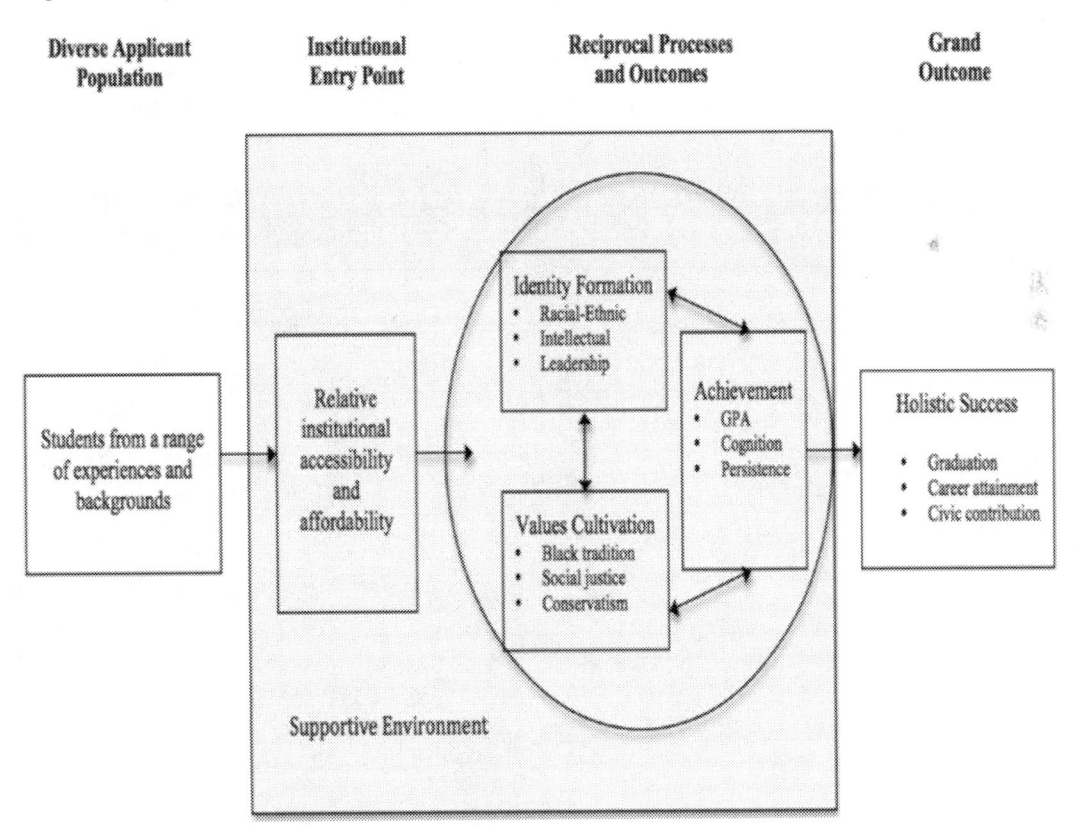

CONCLUSION

Yet, more elements of this framework could be adopted. Along with incorporating this framework, the MSED program could act on the recommendations provided by the external review team in response to its most recent academic performance review, which indicated that candidates should have more opportunities to engage with BIPOC communities. If institutions are to become inclusive environments that embrace, celebrate, and utilize the lived experiences of BIPOC and other marginalized populations, there must be action taken at *every* level to hold the individuals and the institution accountable. Building on the activities of the revised core courses, using the HBCU-inspired framework as well as the recommendations from external review processes, the MSED program can continue to build an online experience that is inclusive and supports the work of BIPOC and other marginalized groups. The success of these initiatives will be an MSED program that is diverse, equitable, and inclusive and that produces "graduates who are scholarly, reflective practitioners who are agents of positive social change" (Walden University, 2022, para. 3).

REFERENCES

Arroyo, A. T., & Gasman, M. (2014). An HBCU-based educational approach for Black college student success: Toward a framework with implications for all institutions. *American Journal of Education*, *121*(1), 57–85. doi:10.1086/678112

Baker, R., Dee, T. S., Evans, B., & John, J. (2018). *Bias in online classes: Evidence from a field experiment* (CEPA Working Paper No. 18–03). Stanford Center for Education and Policy Analysis. https://cepa.stanford.edu/sites/default/files/wp18-03-201803.pdf

Cheddadi, S., & Bouache, M. (2021, August 17–21). *Improving equity and access to higher education using artificial intelligence* [Conference presentation]. 16th International Conference on Computer Science & Education, Lancaster, UK. 10.1109/ICCSE51940.2021.9569548

Crooks, N., Smith, A., & Lofton, S. (2021). Building bridges and capacity for Black, Indigenous, and scholars of color in the era of COVID-19 and Black Lives Matter. *Nursing Outlook*, *69*(5), 892–902. doi:10.1016/j.outlook.2021.03.022 PMID:34092370

Crowley, D. M., Scott, J. T., Long, E. C., Green, L., Giray, C., Gay, B., Israel, A., Storace, R., McCauley, M., & Donovan, M. (2021). Cultivating researcher-policymaker partnerships: A randomized controlled trial of a model for training public psychologists. *The American Psychologist*, *76*(8), 1307–1322. doi:10.1037/amp0000880 PMID:35113595

DiAngelo, R. (2018). *White fragility: Why it's so hard for white people to talk about racism*. Beacon Press.

Drake, R., & Ogelsby, A. (2020). Humanity is not a thing: Disrupting white supremacy in k-12 social emotional learning. *Journal of Critical Thought and Praxis*, *10*(1), 1–22. doi:10.31274/jctp.11549

Evans-Amalu, K., & Claravall, E. B. (2021). Inclusive online teaching and digital learning: Lessons learned in the time of pandemic and beyond. *Journal of Curriculum Studies Research.*, *3*(1), i–iii. doi:10.46303/jcsr.2021.4

Fuentes, M. A., Zelaya, D. G., & Madsen, J. W. (2021). Rethinking the course syllabus: Considerations for promoting equity, diversity, and inclusion. *Teaching of Psychology*, *48*(1), 69–79. doi:10.1177/0098628320959979

Galán, C. A., Tung, I., Call, C., Boness, C. L., Bowdring, M., Mcphee, J., & Savell, S. M. (2021, July 20). *Anti-racist approaches to ensure the retention and success of BIPOC graduate students in psychology* [Conference session]. American Psychological Association Conference. 10.1037/e505642022-001

Johnson, D. J., Chuang, S. S., & Glozman, J. (2022). Identity formation and re-formation: Resistance, growth, and emerging pathways for immigrant youth and their families. In D. J. Johnson, S. S. Chuang, & J. Glozman (Eds.), *Re/formation and identity: The intersectionality of development, culture, and immigration* (pp. 1–15). Springer International Publishing. doi:10.1007/978-3-030-86426-2_1

Ndumu, A., & Walker, S. (2021). Adapting an HBCU-inspired framework for Black student success in U.S. LIS education. *Education for Information*, *37*(9/10), 1–11. doi:10.3233/EFI-211511

Owen, H. (2017). 'The best PLD I've ever had': Reconceptualising professional learning and development. *Professional Development in Education*, *43*(1), 57–71. doi:10.1080/19415257.2015.1085890

Ragoonaden, K., & Mueller, L. (2017). Culturally responsive pedagogy: Indigenizing curriculum. *Canadian Journal of Higher Education*, *47*(2), 22–46. doi:10.47678/cjhe.v47i2.187963

Shaeffer, K. (2021, December 10). *America's public school teachers are far less racially and ethnically diverse than their students*. Pew Research Center. https://www.pewresearch.org/fact-tank/2021/12/10/americas-public-school-teachers-are-far-less-racially-and-ethnically-diverse-than-their-students/

Vega, D., & Moore, J. L. III. (2018). Access to gifted education among African-American and Latino males. *Journal for Multicultural Education*, *12*(3), 237–248. doi:10.1108/JME-01-2017-0006

Walden University. (2022). *Walden university catalog*. https://catalog.waldenu.edu/content.php?catoid=193&navoid=74971

ADDITIONAL READING

Gardner, M. E., Bodiya, E. C., & Subramanian, S. (2021). Remote learning barriers and opportunities for graduate student and postdoctoral learners in career and professional skill development: A case study. *Journal of Microbiology & Biology Education*, *22*(1), ev22i1.2451. Advance online publication. doi:10.1128/jmbe.v22i1.2451 PMID:33953812

Miller, E. C., Reigh, E., Berland, L., & Krajcik, J. (2021). Supporting equity in virtual science instruction through project-based learning: Opportunities and challenges in the era of COVID-19. *Journal of Science Teacher Education*, *32*(6), 642–663. doi:10.1080/1046560X.2021.1873549

Note, N., De Backer, F., & De Donder, L. (2021). A novel viewpoint on andragogy: Enabling moments of community. *Adult Education Quarterly*, *71*(1), 3–19. doi:10.1177/0741713620921361

Reedy, A. K. (2019). Rethinking online learning design to enhance the experiences of indigenous higher education students. *Australasian Journal of Educational Technology, 35*(6), 132–149. doi:10.14742/ajet.5561

Summers, L. L. (2020). The right blend: SEL skills support teacher learning in person and online. *Learning Professional, 41*(4), 32–36. https://bettereducate.com/uploads/file/47595_therightblend-pdf_therightblend.pdf

Walden University. (2017). *Walden 2020: A vision for social change.* https://www.waldenu.edu/-/media/Walden/files/about-walden/walden-university-2017-social-change-report-final-v-2.pdf?la=en

Chapter 5
Designing an Inclusive Online Classroom

Kristi A. Trapp
Adtalem Global Education, USA

Katherine Strang
Adtalem Global Education, USA

Kathleen Morrison
Adtalem Global Education, USA

Laura Karl
Adtalem Global Education, USA

ABSTRACT

In this chapter, the authors share core principles and essential questions for evaluating the inclusivity of the online classroom curriculum and design. The nine core principles are building upon students' individual strengths and assets; exploring, affirming, and embracing diverse voices and students' identities; valuing each student lived experience; empowering positive social change agents; ensuring multiple means of expression; providing meaningful opportunities for feedback for growth; exploring course concepts through the lens of historically marginalized individuals and groups; ensuring designs are not systemically biased; and empowering appropriate responses and feedback to perceived inequities. Theoretical support and curriculum design strategies are provided for each of the principles.

INTRODUCTION

Postsecondary education must do more to dismantle its own inequitable policies and practices, which play a role in perpetuating and exacerbating the injustices in society at large. - Desmond-Hellmann et al., 2021, p. 1

DOI: 10.4018/978-1-6684-5146-5.ch005

Many higher education institutions recognize the need to break down barriers, provide access to education, and help students achieve their personal and professional goals. While online learning can provide access to education for a broad and diverse population, it can also be challenging to create a sense of belonging and foster a truly inclusive learning community (Thomas et al., 2014). Walden University, a fully online institution built on the foundation of positive social change, has a history of addressing issues of diversity and inclusion head on with the belief that "a good education not only focuses on knowledge mastery; it encourages learners to use that knowledge to shape positive change in their workplaces and communities" (Walden University, n.d.). In the spirit of its social change mission, Walden recognizes that as the world changes and unexpected challenges face society, there is an opportunity to reevaluate approaches, consider the diverse needs of students, and engage in dialogue about how to offer a more equitable learning experience for all.

BACKGROUND

To evaluate and continue to improve inclusive curriculum design for the online classroom, Walden University collaborated with O'Donnell Learn, an instructional solutions organization focused on equity and inclusion in learning design, to extensively explore diversity, equity, and inclusion initiatives, documents, white papers, and feedback gathered from Walden faculty and staff. This effort resulted in nine core principles and essential questions for designing an inclusive curriculum, as shown in Table 1.

THE CORE PRINCIPLES

The core principles are used to inform the design of online courses for the purpose of creating an inclusive curriculum and supporting students' sense of belonging. In this chapter, each of the core principles are thoroughly explained and supported by learning theory as well as evidence from research. Additionally, following the discussion of each core principle, specific curriculum design strategies appropriate for all degree levels are shared. These strategies, when used to design new online curricula or to evaluate and revise existing curricula, can help create a learning environment in which students feel welcomed and valued for their unique individual contributions, experiences, perspectives, and identities.

Principle 1: Building Upon Students' Individual Strengths and Assets

Essential Question: How do the course resources, student tasks, activities, and assessments build upon students' individual strengths and assets while also supporting their needs?

Malcolm Knowles, in his seminal work on the theory of andragogy, posits several assumptions about adult learners and why different instructional approaches are necessary when teaching adults as opposed to pedagogical principles for teaching children (Knowles, 1980). Of particular importance is the recognition that adult learners bring a great deal of life experience to their learning. A strengths-based approach recognizes and values the experience, strengths, and assets students bring to their learning rather than focusing on potential deficits. Additionally, extensive research has indicated that adult learners thrive in learning environments that acknowledge and celebrate their lived experiences and that ultimately

Designing an Inclusive Online Classroom

Table 1. Core principles and essential questions

Core Principle	Essential Question
Principle 1: Building upon students' individual strengths and assets	How do the course resources, student tasks, activities, and assessments build upon students' individual strengths and assets while also supporting their needs?
Principle 2: Exploring, affirming, and embracing diverse voices and students' identities	In an attempt to serve all students equitably, how do the curriculum, course resources, student activities, and assessments affirm, celebrate, and validate historically marginalized individuals, groups, and students' diverse, multiple, and intersectional identities by supporting and normalizing these voices throughout the curriculum?
Principle 3: Valuing Each Student's Lived Experience	Do the course resources, student tasks, activities, and assessments create a space where knowledge is developed and co-constructed with students' lived experiences in a way that normalizes the need to share and critique?
Principle 4: Empowering positive social change agents	How do the course's resources, student tasks, activities, and assessments promote, facilitate, and support collaborative alliances, action research, and projects that lead to student agency to effect positive social change?
Principle 5: Ensuring multiple means of expression	Are students offered multiple opportunities to demonstrate knowledge (via assessment strategies) in ways that are best aligned to their own unique abilities and strengths?
Principle 6: Providing meaningful opportunities for feedback for growth	Are assessment and feedback provided in such a way that allows students to self-assess their own strengths, learning gaps, and direction to move forward?
Principle 7: Exploring course concepts through the lens of historically marginalized individuals and groups	How do the course's curriculum and central concepts incorporate historically marginalized individuals and groups?
Principle 8: Ensuring designs are not systemically biased	Is the course free of resources, student tasks, activities, and assessments that may be perceived as oppressive or reinforcing systemic biases and privilege? Is the course free of deficit-oriented, marginalizing, discriminatory, and racist ideologies?
Principle 9: Empowering appropriate responses and feedback to perceived inequities	Does the course have a space that allows students to provide feedback to instructors, and each other, when they feel not represented or valued?

this approach can contribute to a more socially equitable and culturally inclusive learning experience (Gering et al., 2018).

To build on students' strengths and assets, online courses should be designed so that students have opportunities to express their strengths and make choices about activities and assessments that build on such strengths and assets. In addition, learners need resources and opportunities to extend their knowledge, skills, and abilities as they work toward achieving learning outcomes.

Strategies that Support this Principle

- **Ask students to share their strengths, assets, interests, and life experience:** Include surveys, self-assessment activities, or discussions early in the course for students to share their strengths, assets, interests, and life experience, and continue to provide space in the classroom for instructors to interact with students beyond the graded assignments (e.g., Class Café, Ask the Instructor, media elements).
    - Course Cafés, created using the discussion tool, is an open forum for students to introduce themselves, get to know their classmates, and discuss informal topics outside of the formal content of this course. This space can also be used to have students discuss their goals and

share why they are pursuing a degree, what life experiences have motivated them, and what they hope to achieve.
  - Ask the Instructor is a forum to post questions to the instructor about the course—including assignments, due dates, and procedures—so that all class members may benefit from the instructor's response.
- **Ask students to reflect and share their personal thoughts**: Include journals or discussions throughout the course for students to reflect on their career choice.
- **Design discussion topics that draw upon students' personal experiences or interests:** Ask students to connect course topics, concepts, and ideas to their personal experience.
- **Provide resources in multiple formats:** Include learning resources at various levels of depth and complexity and in various formats to support students' individual learning preferences. Use interactive media to introduce topics or complex ideas.
- **Provide multiple assessment format options** that students can choose from for submitting assignments. For example, give students the choice of submitting a video recording, audio recording, or a paper.
- If designing an online course that will be taught by someone else, **provide instructor guides** in courses that contextualize topics and assessments and provide suggestions for student interaction.
- When designing an online course, **scaffold the learning** throughout the course and more specifically for a final or course project to help all students succeed in smaller incremental steps. For example, provide skill-building activities as formative practice prior to the assessment component.

Principle 2: Exploring, Affirming, and Embracing Diverse Voices and Students' Identities

Essential Question: In an attempt to serve all students equitably, how do the curriculum, course resources, student activities, and assessments affirm, celebrate, and validate historically marginalized individuals, groups, and students' diverse, multiple, and intersectional identities by supporting and normalizing these voices throughout the curriculum?

In designing effective and equitable online experiences for diverse learners, students' identities need to be represented and affirmed, which requires opportunities for both the instructor and learners to consider aspects of their own identities and how they intersect and affect the learning environment. While an individual may be perceived in certain contexts as a member of one group—a woman, for example—in reality, she has many possible identities, such as first-generation college student, a person of color, a nursing student, a mother, and more. Evans-Winters (2021) suggests that the ways these various identities overlap and intersect can influence the classroom learning environment and have an impact on the experience of individual students as well as groups within the cohort of students. Similarly, Grant & Zwier (2011) emphasize that embracing and exploring various aspects of learners' identities and how they intersect can help educators design effective interventions to support and promote advocacy for marginalized groups. To foster respect for one another's identities in the online classroom, discussion prompts and other reminders throughout the curriculum can encourage students to engage with someone who offers a different perspective, think about a viewpoint not previously considered, and imagine how someone else's life experiences might cause them to feel or think a certain way.

Online curriculum design that frames students' diverse experiences and perspectives as assets rather than deficits can promote engagement and persistence (Bendsen et al., 2018). Moreover, taking an intersectional perspective that recognizes, celebrates, and incorporates students' various identities in the learning experience can contribute to improved student outcomes (Grant & Zweir, 2011). Providing "respectful, empathetic, and inquisitive" opportunities for learning within an environment that is safe and supportive will also engage the learner to further understand intercultural competence outside of their own cultural understandings (Brooks & Grady, 2022).

Strategies that Support this Principle

- Provide learning resources (textbooks, articles, websites, media, etc.) that include authors/participants from a variety of cultural backgrounds.
- Provide learning resources (textbooks, articles, websites, media, etc.) that illustrate diverse perspectives and backgrounds.
- Provide case studies that highlight a variety of cultures and explore diverse ideas, opinions, perspectives, and experiences.
- Include a statement/attestation in every course that students are expected to demonstrate respect for others throughout the course.
- When designing a curriculum, work with subject matter experts from diverse cultural backgrounds to infuse multiple perspectives on topics and issues.
- Create role-playing discussions/assignments and encourage students to explore real-world issues/content from perspectives other than their own.
- Create learning experiences in which students can collaborate with their peers and incorporate their lived experiences that are aligned to the course content.

Principle 3: Valuing Each Student's Lived Experience

Essential Question: Do the course resources, student tasks, activities, and assessments create a space where knowledge is developed and co-constructed with students' lived experiences in a way that normalizes the need to share and critique?

Teaching from a social justice perspective promotes valuing all students' lived experiences. Nieto (2006) describes four components of social justice in education. First, it challenges, confronts, and disrupts misconceptions, untruths, and stereotypes that lead to structural inequality and discrimination based on race, social class, gender, and other social and human differences. Second, a social justice perspective means providing all students with the resources necessary to learn to their full potential. A third component of a social justice perspective is drawing on the talents and strengths that students bring to their education. And finally, "creating a learning environment that promotes critical thinking and supports agency for social change" (Nieto, 2006, pp. 6–7) is an essential component of social justice. These components of social justice in education are essential to creating a space where every student is afforded the opportunity to develop and co-construct knowledge that is connected in some way with their lived experiences. As a result, students can see how their life's journey connects to and applies to their education.

In addition to the social justice perspective, a necessary component of student success is a sense of belonging. A student's sense of belonging promotes better student experiences, satisfaction, and attainment as well as a lower rate of attrition (Peacock & Cowan, 2019). Ensuring that students feel as though they belong can result in positive outcomes for all stakeholders. However, the classroom has long been an environment in which instructors lecture and students listen—known as the transmittal model. In this model, the instructor, also known as the sage on the stage, is the one person in the room who is the expert who knows the content. The instructor imparts knowledge on the students, filling empty vessels once void of information (King, 1993). The transmittal model provides little to no opportunity for students to develop a sense of belonging or space for a student to connect the content with their lived experiences.

Acknowledging that every student has diverse personal, professional, academic, and cultural experiences, designing opportunities within the course for students to make connections and embrace their experiences in the classroom can improve a student's sense of belonging and engagement. Adult learning theory, or andragogy, states that the learner has a lifetime of rich experiences that are relevant to their learning (Merriam, 2001). Through the development of courses with intentional opportunities to share experiences and perspectives and to connect student experiences to the course content, "we can more fully realize a course design that engages difference as a valuable asset to learning. In this way, students are enacting valuable social justice work in small, yet meaningful, ways" (Richter, 2019). In turn, students may experience increased motivation and engagement as well as a greater sense of belonging when they are given opportunities to make personal connections to course content (Frymier & Shulman, 1995; The Glossary of Education Reform, 2013).

Student populations are more diverse, and their prior experiences are more varied. What instructional design strategies contribute to learning experiences that value students' lived experiences, celebrate students' differences, and align with the learning objectives and course outcomes?

Strategies that Support this Principle

- Include a statement/attestation in every course stating that students are expected to demonstrate respect for others throughout the course. A statement such as the one that follows could be included in the course syllabus or as an attestation that students complete at the beginning of each term:
    - **Note:** Remember to comply with the Code of Conduct when participating in classroom discussions and to always conduct yourself in a professional and respectful manner. As you engage with your colleagues, take the time to explore academic perspectives other than your own and reflect on your own perspectives as well.
- Use discussion for students to share their work and to give and receive constructive feedback.
- Example Discussion:
    - **Post** your poster presentation that includes a 2- to 3-minute discussion of the research highlights.
    - **Respond** to at least three of your peers with substantive feedback on their poster presentation. Include two or more of the following in your response:
    - Describe an insight you gained from their poster presentation and how you will incorporate that insight in future life, work, or academic experiences.
    - Describe at least one thing about their poster presentation that you thought they did well.
    - Describe at least one thing about their poster presentation you thought they could improve.
    - Provide at least one question you have about your colleague's research.
        - Provide opportunities for students to analyze concepts from a variety of perspectives. For example, students are asked to analyze business decisions based on both individualistic and collectivist approaches typically associated with Western and Eastern perspectives.

- Provide opportunities for students to take turns leading course discussions.
- Provide opportunities for students to develop meaningful and thoughtful discussion questions inspired by the course topics. The student-generated questions would require their peers to engage in deeper levels of critical thinking. For example, in a cross-cultural psychology course, ask students to post one meaningful, open-ended question that requires critical thinking about some aspect of individualism versus collectivism.
- When exploring new concepts, begin by having students connect these concepts with their own lived experiences. Teach from a place that decenters "expertise" from yourself to a place of shared understanding that takes your students' experiences into consideration.
- Allow students to locate and choose their own resources when exploring and unpacking a module or course concept. For example, on the topic of equity in higher education, ask students to find a recent example of a campus experiencing equity issues, explain the actions or policies stakeholders have implemented to address the issue(s), and evaluate the effectiveness of stakeholders' actions.
- Include resources from a variety of perspectives. Consider the perspectives and identities of your students and whether those are reflected in the learning resources provided. Where appropriate, invite your students to weigh in on the degree to which multiple perspectives are represented in the course resources and content.

Principle 4: Empowering Positive Social Change Agents

Essential Question: *How do the course's resources, student tasks, activities, and assessments promote, facilitate, and support collaborative alliances, action research, and projects that lead to student agency to effect positive social change?*

Online courses tend to be developed around overall course learning outcomes, with content and assignments carefully planned within the weeks or modules and timeline of the course. For instructors and curriculum designers, it can be challenging to release control of the planned content and pace of the curriculum. This is especially true in an online environment, where most communication tends to be asynchronous and where students generally appreciate the flexibility to plan ahead and complete what is required of them on their own time. However, allowing more flexibility in the curriculum to create true collaboration opportunities among students or between the instructor and students can provide a more engaging experience for both the learner and teacher alike. A flexible curriculum in which student input shapes the learning experience, can lead to the inclusion of circumstances, interests, and concerns of learners whose perspectives and experiences may be marginalized (Brooks & Grady, 2022).

Imagine an environmental science course in which students investigate climate or pollution issues in their local environment, and the class comes together to propose research-based solutions and actions that could contribute to addressing the local issue. This type of assignment, based on student choice and interest in an issue, not only contributes to academic engagement but can help students envision their potential professional identities (Bendsen et al., 2018; Boyd & Molloy, 2013). In addition, when working together to address an issue, students can form collaborative alliances, take action in their local community, bring attention to a societal problem, and ultimately contribute to positive social change. Creating an engaged, purpose-driven online community that values collaboration provides practice for students who will need these skills in their professional lives. Likewise, building community in the online classroom can reduce the sense of isolation associated with a fully remote learning environment.

While the typically asynchronous nature of online courses can often result in students feeling alone in their journey, the digital learning environment is well suited for expanding collaboration and communication beyond the "walls" of the learning management system. In addition to providing learning resources that connect students to a variety of perspectives, learning activities might require students to reach out to an institution or organization for information or connect with an individual in a different country to learn about a particular issue or interest. As Ritchie (2018) observes: "As students take control of their learning they seek information from sources and people, and the resulting web of connected practices are not limited to face-to-face encounters. Technology enables fast and easy connections across distances and cultures, and it is possible to engage with a wider, global learning community" (p. 201).

Strategies that Support this Principle

- Create discussions/assignments that provide students with the opportunity to apply discipline-specific knowledge and skills to real-world problems to enact positive social change. Include options for communication and collaboration with individuals or institutions outside of the classroom community.
- For example, a student identifies that their neighborhood lacks a proper drainage system when heavy rains occur. In collaboration with peers, they work with local water and city planners to explore potential solutions. Provide opportunities for students to reflect on their own learning and to extend their learning in ways that can contribute to positive social change. For example, in a teacher education program, ask teacher candidates to reflect on how their learning in a particular week, module, or unit will help them become a more effective teacher and, more broadly, how their effectiveness as an educator might contribute to the betterment of society.
- Ask students to demonstrate learning outcomes within the context of a topic or issue that is important to them.
- Expose students to learning resources that provide examples of social change agents addressing real-world problems.
- Include learning resources that identify real-world problems that need solutions.
- Provide synchronous opportunities for students to collaborate and discuss the topic or issue needing to be addressed for a particular assignment or discussion. Where appropriate, students may benefit from opportunities to role-play as different stakeholders involved in addressing the topic or issue.

Principle 5: Ensuring Multiple Means of Expression

Essential Question: *Are students offered multiple opportunities to demonstrate knowledge (via assessment strategies) in ways that are best aligned to their own unique abilities and strengths?*

Many educators are familiar with the concept of Universal Design for Learning (UDL), a curriculum design approach developed by CAST that focuses on removing or minimizing barriers to learning so all students have access to the curriculum. CAST (n.d.) describes UDL as "a framework to improve and optimize teaching and learning for all people based on scientific insights into how humans learn" and holds up UDL as "one of our core levers of change to help make learning inclusive and transformative for everyone" (para. 1-3).

According to the UDL framework, students should not only be provided with multiple types of representation of content, they should also be able to demonstrate their learning by showing what they know in ways that are more aligned to their strengths. Following UDL principles, the online environment should include a variety of ways to navigate the content and interact with others as well as offering a multiple formats and products students can create to demonstrate their achievement of learning outcomes (Houston, 2018). In addition, approaching online curriculum development through the lens of UDL can help address issues of inclusiveness and access (Cash et al., 2021; Dell et al., 2015) and promote a strengths-based approach for all students who may differ in their ableness, gender, race, ethnicity, or other aspect of their identity (Burgstahler & Cory, 2008). Similarly, students may have different preferences for how they learn and demonstrate their learning. So, providing alternative formats like videos, multimedia, and audio recordings rather than only text resources or paper assignments may engage more learners in more effective learning.

When courses are designed so that students have opportunities to choose assessment methods and strategies that are aligned to their own unique abilities, strengths, and preferences, and which demonstrate that they meet course and program learning outcomes, students have more agency and control of their learning (Houston, 2018; Boud & Molloy, 2013). Additionally, Houston (2018) suggests: "If integrated efficiently, the UDL framework has the potential to change the effectiveness of online learning and increase the success for all learners" (p. 97).

Strategies that Support this Principle

- Provide formative assessment opportunities such as a knowledge check or a self-check in which students can self-assess and determine where their strengths are and where they may need to focus more time.
- Provide multiple assessment format options that students can use to demonstrate their learning. For example, allow students to choose video, audio, work artifacts, and performance tasks as opposed to writing essays and papers.
- Ensure that all assessments are ADA compliant and/or offer alternate formats for students with diverse needs to be able to demonstrate their learning.
- Include the option for students to post video, audio, written, or graphical discussion posts.
- Provide a variety of opportunities for students to practice specific skills or knowledge needed prior to completing their graded assessment. For example, a law and public policy course requires very dense readings that are critical to student learning. To support and increase student success, create short interactive activities (e.g., drag and drop, fill in the blank, flashcards, etc.) that reinforce concepts and scaffold learning into smaller chunks in a more engaging manner than reading from a dense text.

Principle 6: Providing Meaningful Opportunities for Feedback for Growth

Essential Question: Are assessment and feedback provided in such a way that allows students to self-assess their own strengths, learning gaps, and direction to move forward?

The term *self-assessment* may inspire skepticism or feelings of unease in some higher education professionals for its reputation of inflated self-grading by students. However, self-assessment has been shown to be an important factor in enhancing student understanding of their own learning. Self-assessment as defined by Bourke (2018) is an activity in which students are required to examine, reflect, and build understanding about their own learning, yet it is not an isolated event. It is a part of the learning experience and "the social, cultural, and political contexts in which it occurs" (Bourke, 2018, p. 828). Self-assessment is a critical component to understanding one's own learning (Bourke, 2018) by developing a sense of agency about learning (Nieminen & Tuohilampi, 2020), self-regulation, and identity as a learner (Panadero & Alonso-Tapia, 2013).

An inclusive learning environment provides opportunities for students to participate in learning experiences by self-assessing their own strengths and learning gaps and identifying the direction for growth. For robust self-assessment, activities should specifically empower students to evaluate the knowledge they have gained and consider their relationship to that knowledge rather than simply asking for a general reflection on their learning (Bourke, 2018). This approach empowers students "as vehicles of their own learning and agents of their own change, requiring [them] not only to take an active role but to develop a new kind of a learner identity" (Nieminen et al., 2022, p. 97).

Strategies that Support this Principle

- Provide students with assessment rubrics to self-assess their work prior to submitting an assignment. Ask students to submit the completed rubric along with the assignment.
- Ask students to participate in developing evaluation criteria for an assignment. Then invite them to complete a self-evaluation against the criteria prior to submitting the assignment.
- Create a self-assessment pretest prior to initiating a learning experience, then compare it to the intended learning outcomes of the experience. Ask students to reflect on areas they may need to focus on during the learning experience and consciously attend to achieving that learning. After the learning experience, ask students to complete a posttest to assess their learning.
- Create interactive formative assessments that enable students to engage with the content prior to the summative assessment submission.
- Include reflection assignments that provide students with the opportunity to self-assess their strengths, learning gaps, and determine a direction to move forward.
- Create a brief survey at the end of an assignment. The survey may ask students to identify strategies or tools they used to prepare for or complete the assignment, concepts they found easy or difficult, and how they overcame challenges they experienced during the assignment.

Principle 7: Exploring Course Concepts Through the Lens of Historically Marginalized Individuals and Groups

Essential Question: How do the course's curriculum, instructional strategies, and central concepts incorporate historically marginalized individuals and groups?

As discussed in previous sections, students' sense of belonging can have a positive impact on retention and overall academic performance and achievement (Peacock & Cowan, 2019). Incorporating cultural diversity into the curriculum can nurture students' sense of belonging. According to Page (2021), supporting global engagement by broadening students' knowledge base and supporting students'

Designing an Inclusive Online Classroom

development in integrating multiple perspectives are additional benefits to offering a curriculum that is culturally diverse. When a broad range of views and perspectives are incorporated, students develop skills in discussing and analyzing diverse perspectives—their intercultural skills. In fact, when students of all ages are exposed to positive images of people from other cultures, negative associations tend to decline (Comprehensive Center Report, 2020). Clearly, exploring course concepts through the lens of historically marginalized individuals and groups can positively influence learners' perspectives and build appreciation and understanding of individuals different from themselves.

Similarly, instructors can benefit from widening their lens by exploring the realities of their students and incorporating them in the curriculum. *Reality pedagogy*, a term coined by Emdin (2014), is a method of teaching and learning that uses student realities as the starting point for instruction. Moll et al. (1992) explored the connection between curriculum and students' lives and found that students' homes are great sources of cultural and learning resources that can be incorporated into classroom instruction. Through reality pedagogy, the culture and lives of students become an integral part of the curriculum (Emdin, 2020), enabling students to personally connect with the learning process. Emdin (2020) defined a set of tools for instructors to use to initiate reality pedagogy:

1. **Co-generative dialogues:** Where teachers and students discuss the classroom, and both suggest ways to improve it.
2. **Coteaching:** Where students get opportunities to learn content and then teach the class.
3. **Cosmopolitanism:** Where students have a role in how the class operates and in what is taught.
4. **Context:** Where the neighborhood and community of the school is seen as part of the classroom.
5. **Content:** Where the teacher has to acknowledge the limitations of his/her content knowledge and work to build his/her content expertise with students (Emdin, 2014)

Incorporating historically marginalized individuals and groups through Emdin's tools for initiating reality pedagogy connects students to the content and makes what is being learned more relevant. This also aligns to andragogy and the tendency for adults to draw on their own life experience to assist in their learning (Knowles, 1980). The connection that students make between their lived experiences and the content is imperative to feeling a sense of belonging, satisfaction, and success.

Strategies that Support this Principle

- Provide learning resources (textbooks, articles, websites, media, etc.) that include authors, participants, and perspectives from historically marginalized groups.
- Provide case studies that include/address historically marginalized individuals or groups.
- Collaborate with subject matter experts from historically marginalized groups.
- Create role-playing discussions/assignments and have students look at real-world issues/content from the perspective of historically marginalized individuals or groups.
- Use artifacts or aspects of each student's culture as a stem for teaching the curriculum.
- Critically analyze the history and development of dominant perspectives (Page, 2021).
- Ask students to search or survey their family and/or community for artifacts or oral traditions that would support a given topic.
- Jigsaw activities: Provide opportunities for students to learn the content and then teach the content to their peers (The Bell Foundation, n.d.). With jigsaw activities, the class is divided into groups.

Within the groups, each student becomes an expert of a select part of a topic that they teach to the other members of the group.

Principle 8: Ensuring Designs are not Systemically Biased

Essential Question: *Is the course free of resources, student tasks, activities, and assessments that may be perceived as oppressive or reinforcing systemic biases and privilege? Is the course free of deficit-oriented, marginalizing, discriminatory, and racist ideologies?*

Examining curriculum design and content to avoid systemic bias requires a commitment by all stakeholders in the institution to explore underlying beliefs and assumptions, analyze the teaching and learning culture, and consider the root cause of barriers to student success (Bell, 2021). This commitment is required at all levels of the institution when students interact with faculty and staff, but the online classroom is a powerful example of where historically marginalized perspectives can be brought to the center and a diverse community of learners can expand their understanding of a variety of societal issues (Migueliz Valcarlos et al., 2020). As a first step, Migueliz Valcarlos et al. (2020) recommend "breaking with the hierarchy between educator and student" and using discussion boards "as spaces for knowledge creation in which students and educators co-constructed knowledge" (p. 354). For example, discussion prompts can be open ended, asking students to pose their own discussion questions about the course topics and inviting their peers to respond. Another approach might be having a student lead the discussion with the instructor acting as a participant along with the other students. Beisenherz et al. (2001) suggest that collaborative inquiry helps students achieve a deeper level of understanding and ability to monitor their learning. When students are asked to generate their own questions and engage others in discussion around a topic, they gain valuable practice in learning how to think about and gauge their understanding.

While a focus on the content and structure of the curriculum is essential, it is also important to consider intentional or unintentional faculty bias. Baker et al. (2018) report "a long-standing body of evidence indicates that students at all levels of education experience patterns of bias with respect to race, ethnicity, and gender in classrooms" (p. 5). Conaway & Bethune (2015) point out that most instructors do not see themselves as biased, but the effects of implicit unintentional bias are well documented and can harm students.

What can be done in the online classroom design to avoid implicit or unintentional bias on the part of the instructor? Tools in the online classroom can encourage equitable treatment of students. For example, Baker et al. (2018) suggest designing "online environments that guide instructors to engage with students in more equitable ways (e.g., dashboards that provide real-time feedback on the characteristics of their course engagement or short, embedded professional-development modules)" (pp. 25–26). Similarly, notes or announcements can remind instructors to provide timely feedback to all students and to review the quality of their feedback for "depth, validity, and warmth" (Conaway & Bethune, 2015, p. 175).

Strategies that Support this Principle

- Evaluate the curriculum (learning resources, discussions, assignments, introductions, lead-ins, rubrics, etc.) for anything that may be perceived as oppressive or reinforcing systemic biases and privilege or that may include deficit-oriented, marginalizing, discriminatory, and racist ideologies. Consider partnering with students and other stakeholders to get feedback on these potential issues in the curriculum.

Designing an Inclusive Online Classroom

- Include instructor notes or other tools that help instructors ensure that they are responding and providing feedback to students in an equitable way. This may include professional development modules for faculty.
- Design discussion boards that allow for open conversations and opportunities to include historically marginalized perspectives, individuals, and groups.
- Ask students to share a resource or an experience related to a course topic that provides a unique perspective that may not have been explored in the course resources.
- Expose students to learning resources that provide historical information about specific oppressed groups. For example, in a public policy course or civil rights unit, students might explore the significance of the 1969 Stonewall riots or the 1921 Tulsa race massacre to build empathy for and understanding of marginalized individuals and groups.

Principle 9: Empowering Appropriate Responses and Feedback to Perceived Inequities

Essential Question: Does the course have a space that allows students to provide feedback to instructors, and each other, when they feel not represented or valued?

Engaging in discourse related to inequities can be difficult and uncomfortable for all parties involved, whether those conversations are planned or unplanned. Educators have an important role in providing the space and the skills necessary for students to express their feelings and perceptions in an effective way.

Calls for "safe spaces" in educational settings have been echoing on campuses across the nation (Harless, 2018), but there may be disagreement about the necessity of providing those safe spaces. Harless (2018) believes higher education institutions have a moral imperative to respect students' dignity, an educational imperative to enhance deeper learning through safe exploration of ideas and perspectives, and a public imperative to fulfill the obligation of preparing students to be contributing members of society. Providing safe spaces for students to express their feelings and perspectives meets those imperatives.

Providing a safe space for discourse is an honorable aspiration, but how can educators create that environment for students to explore their perspectives and express their feelings in a way that respects all participants in the engagement? In some situations, instructors may respond to uncomfortable conversations by ignoring them, diverting attention, appeasing those involved, or simply ending the conversation. Sue (2016) advises against those avoidant behaviors and instead offers several strategies to instructors for creating an environment that invites open communication among students and faculty.

Strategies that Support this Principle

- Understand one's own racial and cultural identity. Carefully analyze one's values, beliefs, prejudices, and assumptions and publicly acknowledge or disclose personal biases and fears as a model of honest communication, vulnerability, and willingness to learn.
- Seek opportunities to interact with people who differ from you and engage in cultural discourse with others to increase your own comfort level with this type of discourse and learn how to instill it in your students.
- Acknowledge, understand, and openly discuss the emotions underlying uncomfortable conversations. Help students recognize hidden feelings in statements made by others.

- Embrace different communication styles and educate students on how to recognize them and respond to different styles.
- When engaged in discussion, control the *process* and not the content.
  - Actively prepare students by giving them strategies for engaging in difficult conversations with honor and respect.
  - Give students advanced warning through a video recording or written communication when a conversation may involve sensitive content and encourage them to use the strategies they have learned in order to respond in appreciative and respectful ways.
  - Show appreciation when students speak up and make themselves vulnerable in uncomfortable discussions to create a sense of trust and model the safety you are building.
  - Actively intervene if discussions come to an impasse or become destructive. Use the situation as a teachable moment and have others in the group actively observe the behaviors to refocus on the process of the conversation. For example, the instructor may ask: "What do you see happening in this dialogue?" "How might we change the approach to allow space for all voices to be heard?"

CONCLUSION

Designing inclusive learning experiences in any environment requires thoughtfulness and care, but curriculum design for the online classroom can present significant challenges due to the asynchronous nature of most instructor-to-student and student-to-student interactions. These types of interactions can interfere with students' "sense of belonging" and can cause "well-documented feelings of isolation, marginalization, alienation and loneliness" (Peacock, 2018, p. 1). This chapter provides a sampling of strategies to integrate the nine core principles of inclusive curriculum design identified. Online educators and curriculum designers will likely find that the principles overlap in some areas and build on one another. They provide a clear and research-based pathway to begin designing learning environments that incorporate students' strengths and assets, embrace diverse voices and identities, value lived experiences, empower positive social change agents, provide multiple avenues for expression, provide a variety of opportunities for feedback and growth, bring in perspectives of historically marginalized individuals and groups, and include opportunities for students to safely communicate when they feel undervalued or underrepresented. If higher education is to meet the challenge of examining and addressing the inequities that currently exist in its institutions, the online classroom environment is a promising area to make significant gains with the conscious effort and commitment of stakeholders.

REFERENCES

Baker, R., Dee, T., Evans, B., & John, J. (2018). *Bias in online classes: Evidence from a field experiment.* Stanford Center for Education Policy Analysis. https://cepa.stanford.edu/wp18-03

Bell, D. (2021). Becoming an anti-racist intuition: The challenges facing higher education. *International Journal of Multiple Research Approaches, 13*(1), 22–25. doi:10.29034/ijmra.v13n1commentary2

The Bell Foundation. (n.d.). *Great idea: Jigsaw activities*. https://www.bell-foundation.org.uk/eal-programme/guidance/effective-teaching-of-eal-learners/great-ideas/jigsaw-activities/#:~:text=What%20 are%20jigsaw%20activities%3F,then%20become%20the%20experts%20in

Beisenherz, P. C., Dantonio, M., & Richardson, L. (2001). The learning cycle and instructional conversations. *Science Scope*, *24*(4), 34–38.

Bendsen, A. H., Egendal, J., Jelsbak, V. A., Kristensen, M., Mikkelsen, T. R., & Pasgaard, N. J. (2018, November). Student engagement and perceptions of quality in flexible online study programs. *Proceedings of the European Conference on E-Learning*, 45–53. https://www.ucviden.dk/ws/portalfiles/portal/93048292/Presentation_ECEL_engagement_in_online_studies.pdf

Boud, D., & Molloy, E. (2013). Rethinking models of feedback for learning: The challenge of design. *Assessment & Evaluation in Higher Education*, *38*(6), 698–712. doi:10.1080/02602938.2012.691462

Bourke, R. (2018). Self-assessment to incite learning in higher education: Developing ontological awareness. *Assessment & Evaluation in Higher Education*, *43*(5), 827–839. doi:10.1080/02602938.2017.1411881

Burgstahler, S. E., & Cory, R. C. (2008). *Universal design in higher education: From principles to practice*. Harvard Education Press.

CAST. (n.d.). *About Universal Design for Learning*. https://www.cast.org/impact/universal-design-for-learning-udl

Cash, C. M., Cox, T. D., & Hahs-Vaughn, D. L. (2021). Distance educators' attitudes and actions towards inclusive teaching practices. *The Journal of Scholarship of Teaching and Learning*, *21*(2), 15–42. doi:10.14434/josotl.v21i2.27949

Comprehensive Center Network. (2020). *Tools and guidance for evaluating bias in instructional materials: A Region 8 Comprehensive Center report*. https://files.eric.ed.gov/fulltext/ED612040.pdf

Dell, C. A., Dell, T. F., & Blackwell, T. L. (2015). Applying universal design for learning in online courses: Pedagogical and practical considerations. *The Journal of Educators Online*, *13*(2), 166–192. doi:10.9743/JEO.2015.2.1

Desmond-Hellman, S., Garcia, M., & Voight, M. (2021). *Equitable value: Promoting economic mobility and social justice through postsecondary education*. Postsecondary Value Commission. https://postsecondaryvalue.org/wp-content/uploads/2021/07/PVC-Final-Report-FINAL-7.2.pdf

Emdin, C. (2014, April 2). 5 new approaches to teaching and learning: The next frontier. *HuffPost*. https://www.huffpost.com/entry/5-new-approaches-to-teaching-strategies_b_4697731?ir=India&adsSiteOverride=in

Emdin, C. (2020, July 24). Teaching isn't about managing behavior: It's about reaching students where they really are. *The Atlantic*. https://www.theatlantic.com/education/archive/2020/07/reality-pedagogy-teaching-form-protest/614554/

Evan-Winters, V. E. (2021). Race and gender intersectionality in education. In Oxford Research Encyclopedia. doi:10.1093/acrefore/9780190264093.013.1345

Frymier, A. B., & Shulman, G. M. (1995). "What's in it for me?": Increasing content relevance to enhance students' motivation. *Communication Education, 44*(1), 40–50. doi:10.1080/03634529509378996

Gering, C. S., Sheppard, D. K., Adams, B. L., Renes, S. L., & Morotti, A. A. (2018). Strengths-based analysis of student success in online courses. *Online Learning, 22*(3), 55–85. doi:10.24059/olj.v22i3.1464

Glossary of Education Reform. (2013, August 29). *Relevance.* https://www.edglossary.org/relevance/#:~:text=Advocates%20argue%20that%20personal%20relevance,even%20knowledge%20retention%20and%20recall

Grant, C. A., & Zwier, E. (2011). Intersectionality and student outcomes: Sharpening the struggle against racism, sexism, classism, ableism, heterosexism, nationalism, and linguistic, religious, and geographical discrimination in teaching and learning. *Multicultural Perspectives, 13*(4), 181–188. doi:10.1080/15210960.2011.616813

Harless, J. (2018). Safe space in the college classroom: Contact, dignity, and a kind of publicness. *Ethics and Education, 13*(3), 329–345. doi:10.1080/17449642.2018.1490116

Houston, L. (2018). Efficient strategies for integrating Universal Design for Learning in the online classroom. *Journal of Educators Online, 15*(3), 96–111. doi:10.9743/jeo.2018.15.3.4

King, A. (1993). From sage on the stage to guide on the side. *College Teaching, 41*(1), 30–35. doi:10.1080/87567555.1993.9926781

Knowles, M. S. (1980). *The modern practice of adult education: From pedagogy to andragogy.* Cambridge Adult Education.

Lee, A., Felten, P., Poch, R. K., Solheim, C., & O'Brien, M. K. (2017). *Teaching interculturally: A framework for integrating disciplinary knowledge and intercultural development.* Stylus Publishing.

Merriam, S. B. (2001). Andragogy and self-directed learning: Pillars of adult learning theory. *New Directions for Adult and Continuing Education, 2001*(89), 3–13. doi:10.1002/ace.3

Migueliz Valcarlos, M., Wolgemuth, J. R., Haraf, S., & Fisk, N. (2020). Anti-oppressive pedagogies in online learning: A critical review. *Distance Education, 41*(3), 345–360. doi:10.1080/01587919.2020.1763783

Moll, L. C., Amanti, C., Neff, D., & Gonzalez, N. (1992). Funds of knowledge for teaching: Using qualitative research to connect homes and classrooms. *Theory into Practice, 31*(2), 132–141. doi:10.1080/00405849209543534

Nieminen, J. H., & Tuohilampi, L. (2020). 'Finally studying for myself'–Examining student agency in summative and formative self-assessment models. *Assessment & Evaluation in Higher Education, 45*(7), 1031–1045. doi:10.1080/02602938.2020.1720595

Nieminen, J. H., Tai, J., Boud, D., & Henderson, M. (2022). Student agency in feedback: Beyond the individual. *Assessment & Evaluation in Higher Education, 47*(1), 95–108. doi:10.1080/02602938.2021.1887080

Nieto, S. (2006). *Teaching as political work: Learning from courageous and caring teachers.* https://files.eric.ed.gov/fulltext/ED497692.pdf

Panadero, E., & Alonso-Tapia, J. (2013). Self-assessment: Theoretical and practical considerations. When it happens, how it is acquired, and what to do to develop it in our students. *Electronic Journal of Research in Educational Psychology, 11*(2), 551–576. doi:10.14204/ejrep.30.12200

Ritchie, L. (2018). Opening the curriculum through open educational practices: International experience. *Open Praxis, 10*(2), 201–208. doi:10.5944/openpraxis.10.2.821

Page, C. (2021). Using content and learning resources that represent diverse perspectives, paradigms, or disciplinary approaches. In *Interculturalizing the curriculum*. Kwantlen Polytechnic University. https://kpu.pressbooks.pub/interculturalizingcurriculum/chapter/incorporate-content-and-learning-resources-that-represent-diverse-perspectives-paradigms-or-disciplinary-approaches/

Peacock, S. (2018). On discovering and profiting from the sense of belonging literature. *Journal Plus Education, 19*(1), 11–20.

Peacock, S., & Cowan, J. (2019). Promoting sense of belonging in online learning communities of inquiry in accredited courses. *Online Learning, 23*(2), 67–81. doi:10.24059/olj.v23i2.1488

Richter, J. (2019, December 3). *Decentering the classroom: Distributed expertise as social justice praxis in first year composition.* Digital Rhetoric Collaborative. https://www.digitalrhetoriccollaborative.org/2019/12/03/decentering-the-classroom-distributed-expertise-as-social-justice-praxis-in-first-year-composition/

Sue, D. W. (2016). *Race talk and the conspiracy of silence: Understanding and facilitating difficult dialogues on race.* John Wiley & Sons.

Thomas, L., Herbert, J., & Teras, M. (2014). A sense of belonging to enhance participation, success and retention in online programs. *The International Journal of the First Year in Higher Education, 5*(2), 69–80. doi:10.5204/intjfyhe.v5i2.233

Walden University. (n.d.). *The passion that drives us.* https://www.waldenu.edu/why-walden/social-change#mission

ADDITIONAL READING

Banks, J. A., & Banks, C. A. M. (Eds.). (2019). *Multicultural education: Issues and perspectives.* John Wiley & Sons.

Banning, M. (2019). Race, class, gender, and classroom discourse. In L. Parker, D. Deyhle, & S. Villenas (Eds.), *Race is … race isn't* (pp. 155–180). Routledge., doi:10.4324/9780429503504-8

Boothe, K. A., Lohmann, M. J., Donnell, K. A., & Hall, D. D. (2018). Applying the principles of universal design for learning (UDL) in the college classroom. *The Journal of Special Education Apprenticeship, 7*(3). https://files.eric.ed.gov/fulltext/EJ1201588.pdf

Cho, S., Crenshaw, K. W., & McCall, L. (2013). Toward a field of intersectionality studies: Theory, applications, and praxis. *Signs (Chicago, Ill.)*, *38*(4), 785–810. doi:10.1086/669608

Darling-Hammond, L. (2017). Teaching for social justice: Resources, relationships, and anti-racist practice. *Multicultural Perspectives*, *19*(3), 133–138. doi:10.1080/15210960.2017.1335039

Goldberg, A. E., & Allen, K. R. (2018). Teaching undergraduates about LGBTQ identities, families, and intersectionality. *Family Relations*, *67*(1), 176–191. doi:10.1111/fare.12224

Gutstein, E. (2007). "And that's just how it starts": Teaching mathematics and developing student agency. *Teachers College Record*, *109*(2), 420–448. doi:10.1177/016146810710900203

Ladson-Billings, G. (1995). But that's just good teaching! The case for culturally relevant pedagogy. *Theory into Practice*, *34*(3), 159–165. doi:10.1080/00405849509543675

Ladson-Billings, G. (2000). Culturally relevant pedagogy in African-centered schools: Possibilities for progressive educational reform. In D. S. Pollard & C. S. Ajirotutu (Eds.), *African-centered schooling in theory and practice* (pp. 187–198). Praeger.

Ladson-Billings, G. (2014). Culturally relevant pedagogy 2.0: A. K. A. the remix. *Harvard Educational Review*, *84*(1), 74–84. doi:10.17763/haer.84.1.p2rj131485484751

Ladson-Billings, G. (2021). Three decades of culturally relevant, responsive, & sustaining pedagogy: What lies ahead? *The Educational Forum*, *85*(4), 351–354. doi:10.1080/00131725.2021.1957632

Matias, C. E., & Mackey, J. (2016). Breakin' down whiteness in antiracist teaching: Introducing critical whiteness pedagogy. *The Urban Review*, *48*(1), 32–50. doi:10.100711256-015-0344-7

McLeod, J. (2011). Student voice and the politics of listening in higher education. *Critical Studies in Education*, *52*(2), 179–189. doi:10.1080/17508487.2011.572830

Smith, F. G. (2012). Analyzing a college course that adheres to the Universal Design for Learning (UDL) framework. *The Journal of Scholarship of Teaching and Learning*, *12*(3), 31–61. https://scholarworks.iu.edu/journals/index.php/josotl/article/view/2151

York, A., & Kirshner, B. (2015). How positioning shapes opportunities for student agency in schools. *Teachers College Record*, *117*(13), 103–118. doi:10.1177/016146811511701307

Yosso, T. J. (2005). Whose culture has capital? A critical race theory discussion of community cultural wealth. *Race, Ethnicity and Education*, *8*(1), 69–91. doi:10.1080/1361332052000341006

Zimmerman, T. D., & Nimon, K. (2017). The online student connectedness survey: Evidence of initial construct validity. *The International Review of Research in Open and Distributed Learning*, *18*(3), 25–46. doi:10.19173/irrodl.v18i3.2484

Section 3
Into Practice

Intentional design serves as the blueprint for creating inclusive environments in the online space. In this section, the authors explore how the theory and the conceptualization are put into practice.

Chapter 6
Advancing Equity, Diversity, and Inclusion Through the Transformation of Nursing Education

Todd A. Dickson
Walden University, USA

ABSTRACT

Diversity, equity, and inclusion are intimately connected to social determinants of health (SDOH). SDOH are crucial and can have a substantial impact on disparities in health outcomes. Nurses have a social mandate to address health disparities by recognizing social determinants of health and contributing to the development and implementation of initiatives to eliminate healthcare disparities for individuals, groups, and communities. This chapter defines the principles essential for addressing health equity and highlights the historical importance of nursing efforts in tackling health and healthcare disparities. Next, this chapter talks about the current state of various contextual elements that influence nursing education, with a focus on health equity and issues that will affect nursing education and the nursing workforce in the future.

INTRODUCTION

According to the American Nurses Association's (2015) Code of Ethics, respect for everyone's "innate dignity, worth, and unique attributes" is a foundational value that guides nurses' actions and attitudes. Nurses are tasked with addressing societal health requirements by assisting individuals, families, groups, and communities in achieving their optimal level of well-being (Perry et al., 2017). As such, nurses have a social mandate to address health equity, which is defined by Healthy People 2030 as "the attainment of the highest level of health for all people" (Office of Disease Prevention and Health Promotion, n.d.-a, para. 5). The concept of health equity indicates that everyone is valued equally, and societal efforts must

DOI: 10.4018/978-1-6684-5146-5.ch006

Advancing Equity, Diversity, and Inclusion Through the Transformation of Nursing Education

be focused on addressing inequalities and injustices and transforming healthcare to eliminate disparities. Respecting patients' preferences, values, and needs while engaging patients in active partnerships is central to patient-centered care (Kwame & Petrucka, 2021). The incorporation of diversity, equity, and inclusion (DEI) into nursing curricula is a prerequisite for professional development and practice across diverse settings and populations (Buchanan & O'Connor, 2020). This is intended to reflect the dynamic landscape of patient populations served by health systems and create a safe environment for teaching and learning while also improving the quality of nursing education (American Association of Colleges of Nursing, 2019). This chapter begins by defining the principles essential for addressing health equity and highlights the historical importance of nursing efforts in tackling health and healthcare inequities. Next, this chapter describes the current state of various contextual elements that influence nursing education, focusing on health equity and future issues for nursing education and the nursing workforce.

BACKGROUND

Diversity, Equity, Inclusion

The phrase diversity, equity, and inclusion (DEI) refers to a broad variety of individual, population, and social dimensions and is incorporated as one of the most visible principles in *The Essentials: Core Competencies for Professional Nursing Education* by the American Association of Colleges of Nursing (2021b). While all of them are concepts, identifying each conceptual feature leads to greater comprehension. Diversity describes individual differences (e.g., in life experiences, learning and working styles, personality types, etc.) and population characteristics (e.g., race, socioeconomic status, class, gender, sexual orientation, country of origin, ability, intellectual traditions, and perspectives as well as cultural, political, religious, and other affiliations) that significantly limit a major life activity, religious beliefs, and socioeconomic status (American Association of Colleges of Nursing, 2017). Equity is the ability to detect variations in the resources or knowledge required for individuals to participate fully in society, including access to higher education, with the intention of overcoming challenges to guarantee justice (Storch & Egbe, 2022). To have egalitarian systems, all individuals must be treated fairly and without artificial barriers, assumptions, or biases (Baron & Khullar, 2021). Inclusion refers to the environmental and institutional conditions that enable people from various backgrounds—including educators, students, staff, and administrators—to thrive. To be inclusive, environments must be intentional and embrace diversity, rather than simply tolerate it (American Association of Colleges of Nursing, 2021a; Bloomberg, 2021). In an inclusive setting, everyone strives to ensure that the perspectives and experiences of others are invited, embraced, acknowledged, and respected (American Association of Colleges of Nursing, 2021a). In DEI, structural racism and social justice are connected themes. The aims of diversity, equity, and inclusion (DEI) are not a destination but rather a journey, and they recognize growth in understanding as well as transition in nursing education. The comprehension of DEI-related topics is important for professional development and practice in a wide variety of contexts with different populations (American Association of Colleges of Nursing, 2021b).

Consequently, diversity, equity, and inclusion (DEI) are becoming more widely acknowledged as essential concepts in nursing education and practice (Stanford, 2020). Beyond acknowledging differences, DEI concepts address injustices, racism, marginalization, and structural factors that contribute to toxic environments (Greene-Moton & Minkler, 2020; Wright et al., 2021). To incorporate DEI into learning, nurses and other healthcare workers must first understand the policies and practices that affect the discrimination and marginalization of minority populations. Individual morals and ethics, including implicit and explicit biases and how they affect others, are explored in DEI concepts (Wright et al., 2021). The effects of biases on patient populations, institutions, and world perspectives are thoroughly examined.

Diversity, equity, and inclusion are independent, yet interconnected concepts. Incorporating these three concepts, equity is accomplished when unjust and preventable inequities between distinct groups of people are addressed by correcting the root causes and including the affected persons. According to the AACN's DEI position statement, it is necessary to ensure advancements in nursing education to address the pervasive health disparities in the United States. These improvements will ensure the preparation of nurses who can meet the needs of all people in a society that is becoming increasingly diverse (American Association of Colleges of Nursing, 2021a)

The introduction of DEI into nursing curricula is designed to reflect the changing landscape of patient populations served by health systems—and to establish a safe atmosphere for teaching and learning—while also increasing nursing education quality (American Association of Colleges of Nursing, 2019).

Health Equity

The notion of health equity suggests that every person should be provided with an equal opportunity to realize their full health potential and that none should be at a disadvantage in their efforts to improve their health. In addition, achieving health equity means that everyone—regardless of race, socioeconomic status, geography, or circumstance—has the same opportunity to live a healthy life (Centers for Disease Control and Prevention, 2022). For nursing students to graduate with a genuine understanding of the significance of health equity, it is the responsibility of nursing educators to ensure that students are well versed in how social justice, social determinants of health (SDOH), health disparities, and cultural competence all impact health equity (American Association of Colleges of Nursing, 2021b)

Social Justice

Social justice assumes that all people will get fair and equal treatment, wherein their rights are safeguarded, resources are distributed equitably, and choices are made without bias. In healthcare, this is frequently referred to as health equality, which is the reduction of health inequities and the pursuit of optimal health for all (American Association of Colleges of Nursing, 2021a). Racial minorities, women, LGBTQ+ individuals, and others with disadvantaged backgrounds have historically had limited access to healthcare or experienced trauma in healthcare institutions (Weinstein et al., 2017).

As a profession, nursing is founded on social justice engagement. Florence Nightingale pushed for India's famine alleviation and sought better circumstances for women. She contributed to the abolition of prostitution laws that were particularly severe on women and to expanding employment options for women (Prince Henry Hospital Nursing and Medical Museum, n.d.). She was among a long line of nurses who have worked to enhance access and establish health equity. Other examples include Lillian Wald, who coined the phrase "public health nurse" because she felt that public health nurses must address social and economic issues and care for sick individuals. In contrast to social commentators who believed that the poor were responsible for their poverty and sickness, Wald always stressed the human dignity of even the most destitute and impoverished families (Fee & Bu, 2010). Estelle Massey Riddle Osborne was an outstanding Black leader. She sought out and overcame racial prejudices at all levels in professional nursing, thereby empowering Blacks in nursing to rise above adversity and make significant contributions to all people's health and well-being. She also helped shape the history of professional nursing (Mosley, 2002). Historical African-American nurse Harriet Tubman was an abolitionist and women's rights activist who fought to bring about social justice and equal treatment of nurses, women, and slaves (Donnelly, 2016).

Health Disparities

Healthy People 2030 defines a health disparity as "a particular type of health difference that is closely linked with social, economic, and/or environmental disadvantage. Health disparities adversely affect groups of people who have systematically experienced greater obstacles to health based on their racial or ethnic group; religion; socioeconomic status; gender; age; mental health; cognitive, sensory, or physical disability; sexual orientation or gender identity; geographic location; or other characteristics historically linked to discrimination or exclusion" (U.S. Department of Health and Human Services, Office of Disease Prevention and Health Promotion, n.d., "Health Disparities Section",). Our country's commitment to equality is put to the test by these disparities.

While significant efforts have been made to reduce health disparities in the United States, gaps are still evident. Health disparities are frequently seen through the perspective of ethnicity and race, although they occur in other ways too. Disparities exist, for instance, concerning socioeconomic background, age, geographic area, language, gender, ability status, citizenship, gender expression, and sexual orientation. Disparities exist across the life span, from infancy through late adulthood (Artiga et al., 2020). There has never been a time in the United States without racial health disparities.

For the past 400 years, health disparities have contributed to broad gaps in health and life expectancy between African Americans and Whites (Hammonds & Reverby, 2019). In the years immediately after the Civil War, several factors contributed to the rise in the rates of illness and death among the newly emancipated Black citizens. These factors included the absence of plantation-based medical care, illness and disease epidemics brought on by starvation, disruption, a lack of employment, and the failure and unwillingness of a poorly developed and racist southern health system to fill the gap (Hammonds & Reverby, 2019). An understanding of past injustices on the part of nursing educators may inform current and future learning in clinical and classroom settings (Bleich et al., 2015).

Privilege, Bias, Structural Racism

The beginning, route, and destination of any journey are unique to each individual and impacted by privilege, bias, and structural racism.

Privilege

So many facets of a person's life may be connected with privilege, yet not everyone has access to or has the same level of advantage. This may include physical attributes, place of birth, and religious views (Sanchez, 2021). Someone who exerts a great effort to accomplish something may not understand that it was a privilege to do so, given that it would have been far more difficult or impossible for someone else. It is vital to recognize that privilege may exist in several areas and have invisible benefits that aid and facilitate the privileged individual. Shame may be associated with the existence or absence of a particular privilege and is personal and multifaceted. An honest evaluation of one's privileges is a critical first step in increasing awareness and taking action (Sanchez, 2021).

Bias

The Institute of Medicine (Altman et al., 2016) indicated that one of the leading causes of healthcare inequalities in the United States is the healthcare professionals' prejudice toward patients belonging to racial, ethnic, or cultural minorities (Williams & Wyatt, 2015). Bias occurs when a person or group fails to perceive the benefits of the privileges they possess and fails to consider the fact that others may not have access to the same possibilities (Sanchez, 2021). Implicit biases are unconscious or automatic attitudes toward people or stereotypes associated with them without conscious knowledge. Implicit biases among healthcare professionals are correlated with incomplete patient evaluation, inaccurate diagnosis and treatment recommendations, and less time spent on patient care, all of which contribute to poorer healthcare outcomes. Implicit bias can affect individual health and may facilitate maintaining or exacerbating health disparities (Committee on the Robert Wood Johnson Foundation Initiative on the Future of Nursing, at the Institute of Medicine., Robert Wood Johnson Foundation., & Institute of Medicine, 2011).

As the U.S. population continues to increase in diversity, nurses will need to be aware of their own implicit biases to interact with diverse patients with empathy and humility. Nurses have a responsibility to address the root causes of inequities and to advocate for policies that promote equity and the delivery of high-quality care to all. Nurse educators need to prepare nurses in addressing the social determinants of health, improving population health, and promoting health equity.

Structural Racism

Structural racism is a sophisticated structure that provides social benefits to some groups while conferring disadvantages on others, resulting in marginalization, poverty, and loss of opportunity for people of color. Structural racism comprises cultural ideas, historical legacies, institutions, and policies inside and across public and private entities, all of which intertwine to produce significant racial disparities in health outcomes. Structural racism refers to how our institutions (in healthcare, education, employment, housing, and public health) are designed to benefit the majority while disadvantaging minority communities. More precisely, it creates discrepancies in conditions between Whites and racial and ethnic minorities in the social determinants of health (SDOH), resulting in racial health disparities (Yearby, 2020).

Social Determinants of Health

Personal, social, economic, and environmental factors, all of which influence health, are referred to as health determinants in a broader sense (U.S. Department of Health and Human Services, Office of Disease Prevention and Health Promotion, n.d.). According to Healthy People 2030, "social determinants of health are the conditions in the environments where people are born, live, learn, work, play, worship, and age that affect a wide range of health, functioning, and quality-of-life outcomes and risks" (U.S. Department of Health and Human Services, Office of Disease Prevention and Health Promotion, n.d.). These SDOH contribute to wide health disparities and inequities. Nursing practices such as health assessment, health promotion, access to care, and patient teaching support improvements in health outcomes by addressing specific SDOH (Thornton & Persaud, 2018).

SDOH are closely related to diversity, equity, and inclusion. For example, poverty, unequal access to health care, lack of education, social stigma, and racism are all social determinants of health that cause or contribute to health inequities. Wakefield et al., 2021).

Cultural Humility

In the past few years, there has been a shift in nursing from cultural competency frameworks to cultural humility and cultural safety frameworks to create inclusive learning and practice settings (Foronda et al., in press). Healthcare providers' cultural humility can be associated with health equity, health disparities, and social justice. "Cultural humility" is defined as a process of introspection to realize personal and systemic bias and privilege that may lead to disparities in health (Ruud, 2018). Cultural competence suggests that the nurse or healthcare practitioner is the expert. In contrast, cultural humility means that the patient is the expert, fostering person-centered care and providing safe clinical environments (Ruud, 2018). When applied to educational contexts, cultural humility supports learner-centered instruction in safe learning environments. Cultural safety is a subjective sensation that can only be felt by the patient or student (Foronda et al., in press)

Cultural humility in nursing education means acknowledging, comprehending, and overcoming obstacles experienced by particular cultural groups to achieve positive educational and health outcomes (Foronda et al., in press). Students can benefit from theoretical and practicum coursework as well as experiential learning opportunities to increase their understanding of the relevance of cultural humility in their future patient interactions.

Social Determinants of Health and Disparities in Health Outcomes

The SDOH have a significant impact on population health, primary healthcare, and health policy. Under the Affordable Care Act, there was a major increase in health insurance coverage across demographic groups. Despite these advancements, people of color and low-income people are still at risk (Garfield et al., 2019).

In 2020, 31.6 million (9.7%) people of all ages lacked health insurance coverage in the United States (Cha & Cohen, 2022). Health insurance coverage is linked to improved healthcare and health outcomes and is a key measure of health care access (Cha & Cohen, 2022). Health insurance influences whether and when people receive essential healthcare services, where they receive them, and, therefore, how healthy they are. Uninsured individuals are considerably less likely than people with health insurance to receive preventative healthcare services and more likely to be hospitalized for disorders that could have been prevented (Garfield et al., 2019). Factors like this help to explain why certain people in the U.S. are healthier than others and why SDOH are connected with health disparities in particular communities (Centers for Disease Control and Prevention, 2022).

The research on health outcomes demonstrates that SDOH are crucial and can have a substantial impact on the health of a population. A review of the literature supported connections between the socioeconomic level, neighborhood, physical environment, and food environment on the one hand and health, social context, and diabetes-related outcomes on the other (Hill-Briggs et al., 2020). Inequalities in living and working situations as well as the environment in which people live have a significant impact on diabetes risk, diagnosis, and health outcomes (Hill-Briggs et al., 2020). Additionally, the amount of time an individual spends living in the resource-deprived contexts defined by poverty, lack of quality education, or healthcare access has a major impact on diabetes risk, diagnosis, and outcome inequalities.

In racial minority groups, illnesses such as hypertension, diabetes, renal disease, and cancer are widely prevalent. Latinos are also more prone to health disparities across several health conditions compared to non-Hispanic Whites (Families USA, 2018; see the infographic in Figure 1.1).

The COVID-19 pandemic has increased the incidence of disease and mortality among American Indians, Alaska natives, Blacks, and Hispanics. It has disproportionately impacted the financial stability, mental health, and well-being of racial minorities, low-income individuals, the LGBTQ+ community, and other marginalized groups (Artiga et al., 2020).

Maness et al. (2021) examined how systemic racism gives rise to differences in SDOH that affect differences in health outcomes, including COVID-19. Preliminary data showed higher COVID-19 mortality rates among African Americans than among Whites in the U.S. These deaths are perhaps linked to underlying conditions such as type 2 diabetes, hypertension, and asthma, of which African Americans have disproportionately higher rates than non-Hispanic Whites. According to the CDC (2022), older age and underlying medical conditions—such as chronic lung disease, asthma, heart conditions, immune-compromised states, severe obesity, diabetes, chronic kidney disease, and liver disease—are risk factors for serious illness when contracting COVID-19. These discrepancies are frequently the outcome of racial inequities among SDH in education, economic position, housing, neighborhood setting, and access to healthcare. When the risk of death from COVID-19 is higher in those with underlying health issues, it is obvious that African Americans will be more vulnerable than populations with lower rates of chronic disease.

NURSING PROFESSIONAL ORGANIZATIONS' RESPONSES

To address disparities in health, nurses must recognize the social determinants of health and contribute to the development and implementation of initiatives to eliminate healthcare disparities for individuals, groups, and communities.

Responding to this demand, nursing education organizations emphasize the need for diversity, equity, and inclusion in nursing and healthcare. For instance, the American Nurses Association constituted the National Commission to Address Racism in Nursing. The Commission's mission is to lead a national conversation by exploring the experiences of nurses of color to develop action-oriented strategies across the spectral range of curriculum, practice, political system, and research (American Nurses Association, 2021).

A 2020 report by the National Advisory Council on Nurse Education and Practice discussed the need for programs to support education and research in the SDOH within the nursing curricula to ensure that graduating nurses understand and incorporate the concepts of SDOH and that nursing faculty are prepared to teach them. Several national organizations have proposed the integration of nursing education with SDOH to prepare nurses to address the social determinants of health, improve population health, and advance health equity. The National Academies of Sciences, Engineering and Medicine (2021), in its report titled *The Future of Nursing, 2020–2030: Charting a Path to Achieve Health Equity* describe how the nursing profession will be required to adapt to societies' needs with a strong emphasis on the social determinants of health. In 2019, the National League for Nursing published its *Vision for Integration of the Social Determinants of Health Into Nursing Education Curricula,* which emphasizes the

Figure 1. Latino Health Inequities
Note. Reprinted with permission from Families USA. (2018).

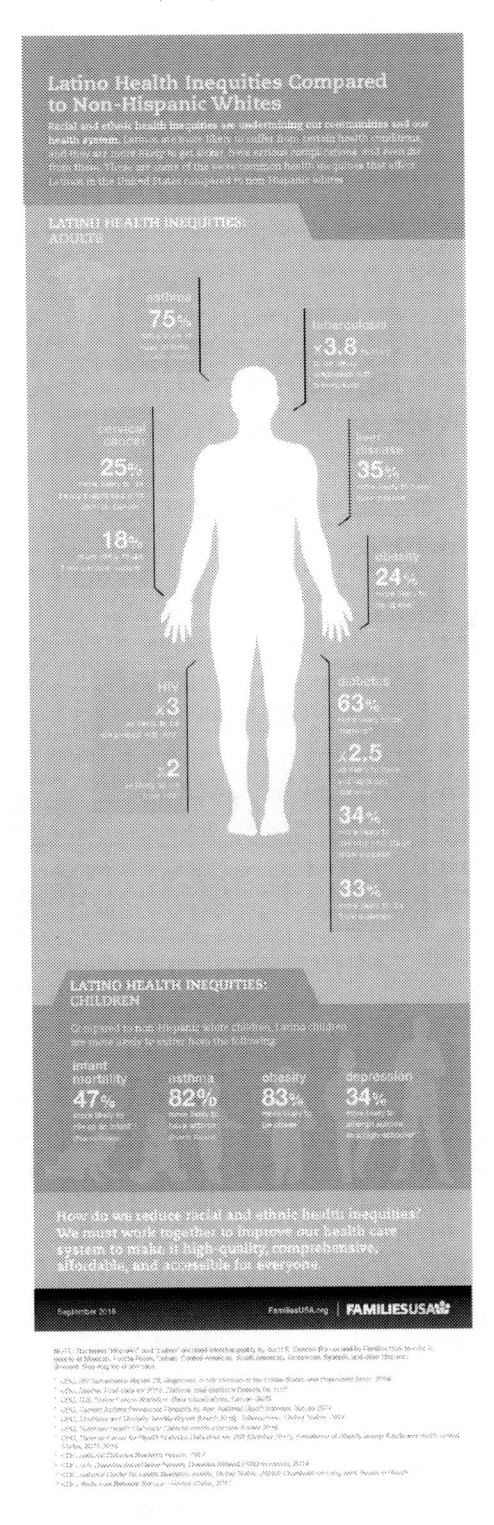

significance of the social determinates of health to the mission of professional nursing and offers recommendations on how nursing education should integrate SDOH. The American Association of Colleges of Nursing (2021b) published *The Essentials: Core Competencies for Professional Nursing Education*, which "provide a framework for preparing individuals as members of the discipline of nursing, reflecting expectations across the trajectory of nursing education and applied experience which are built on a strong foundation of a competency-based curriculum with diversity, equity, and inclusion as one of its most visible concepts" (p. 1).

Despite guidelines from several national organizations and numerous calls for including equity, population health, and SDOH in nursing education, these and related concepts are not currently well integrated into undergraduate and graduate nursing education Wakefield et al., 2021). Further, teaching the SDOH to students only as academic content, rather than through clinical experiences, does not equip them to conduct the necessary assessments and take actions to help society achieve health equity and eliminate disparities (National Advisory Council on Nurse Education and Practice, 2020).

Paths to Nursing Education

The Institute of Medicine in 2011 published *The Future of Nursing: Leading Change, Advancing Health*, which depicted professional nurses as well suited to meet many healthcare challenges. The success of healthcare professionals in delivering safe, effective, evidence-based, and patient-centered care depends on the future of nursing. The second key message in the report emphasized the need for nurses to achieve higher levels of education and training. The report also challenged the educational system to offer seamless academic progression.

Academic progression is not new to the nursing profession. In the 1920s, professional nursing associations recognized that nurses should seek higher education. Various options are now available for nurses to participate in lifelong learning and advance their education. Academic progression can lead to professional advancement, allowing nurses to improve practice outcomes using evidence-based practice (Altman et al., 2016).

Academic Degrees

The attainment of an academic degree demonstrates to society the mastery over a body of knowledge within a discipline. The bachelor's and the associate degrees are both undergraduate degrees. Though Master of Science programs indicate specialized graduate-level degrees, there are exceptions (e.g., a master's degree at the entry-level for a student with a bachelor's degree). A doctorate is an advanced postgraduate degree. Doctor of philosophy programs are research-oriented and produce graduate nurse scientists prepared to become researchers who can contribute to the body of nursing knowledge through direct research or theory creation. Doctor of nursing practice (DNP) programs are clinically oriented and equip nurses for advanced work in clinical practice rather than research or theory development. The DNP-prepared nurse possesses knowledge in the areas of scientific foundations of the practice, leadership, evidence-based practice translation, informatics, health and public policy, interprofessional skills, and population-focused healthcare. The focal point of a degree program is its role concentration.

Role Concentration

The advanced practice registered nurse is the most popular direct care role today. Currently, four roles can be distinguished by APRN direct care responsibilities: nurse practitioner (NP), clinical nurse specialist (CNS), certified nurse-midwife (CNM), and certified RN anesthetist (CRNA) (National Council of State Boards of Nursing, n.d.). Population-focused examples of NP role specialization include family (lifespan, traditionally primary care), pediatric (acute and primary care), neonatal, emergency, adult-gerontology (acute and primary care), women's health, and psychiatric mental health. Most state nursing boards require graduates who undertake these roles to pass national certification exams before they can be licensed to practice. Though national standards define the scope of practice, each state limits the extent to which the APRN functions. The second group of direct care nurses comprises the clinical nurse leader, the nurse educator, and the ambulatory care nurse. Like APRNs, these nurses are likely to interact with patients and their families.

Educational Delivery

Technology has influenced how learners attend school. Today, educational offerings are available in person, online, or as a combination. Nurses should be aware of their learning styles to determine which type of educational delivery setting is the best fit.

In-Person Environments

Universities that prescribe attendance at a predefined time and place create an in-person environment with a deliberate community of learners. In-person learners interact with their peers and faculty members in seminar discussions, classes, and group activities. Nurses with minimal computer skills may find the personal touch of in-person meetings more desirable.

Online

During the past decade, online programs have grown in popularity. Online learning is the newest frontier in education and offers flexibility to learners. There are advantages to online nursing programs over in-person education. For instance, online classes remove geographical restrictions and the need for students to arrive on campus at a prescribed time. They offer students the flexibility to learn at any time of the day. Highly organized and engaged learners perform well in online learning environments. The need for well-established, reputable, and accredited online programs for nurses to obtain a higher degree while working and balancing home life is a must in the academic realm to succeed in the future. Online nursing education opens the door to endless possibilities once seen as impossible for a working adult. Web-based learning experiences afford flexibility in providing content to students from various geographical regions and increase their reach to more students. Online instructional delivery systems may include self-directed (Leong et al., 2015) and independent study, web-based instruction, broadcast television/cable, interactive videoconferencing, and video streaming (Bradshaw & Hultquist, 2016). Educators must continue to evolve delivery mechanisms for online educational platforms to meet the changing dynamics in instructional design and technology as well as the need for workforce flexibility in training and learning.

Hybrid

A combination of the elements of in-person and online formats is known as a "hybrid approach." No single standard is available for hybrid education. The amount and frequency of face-to-face time can vary. The hybrid approach incorporates elements from both models (i.e., dedicated face-to-face time and the freedom to learn at a self-directed pace).

Many nurses view returning to school as nothing more than an opportunity to develop new knowledge. For some nurses, the choice to return to school and earn advanced degrees leads to greater mobility and practice options in the nursing profession, ultimately leading to better care and improved patient outcomes.

Educating Nurses to Address Health Equity and Social Determinants of Health

The nursing profession is tasked with addressing society's healthcare needs to assist individuals, families, and communities in attaining optimal health.

Nurses are well suited to address the SDOH with their patients, as more than 3.8 million registered nurses are practicing in the United States, making nursing the largest healthcare profession in the country (American Association of Colleges of Nursing, 2019b, 2021b; Wunnenberg, 2020). Nursing, which has more than three times the number of registered nurses as physicians in the United States, provides a wide range of healthcare services, including primary and preventive care provided by nurse practitioners who have received specialized training in areas like mental health, pediatrics, family health, women's health, and gerontological care (American Association of Colleges of Nursing, 2019b).

In addition, nurses are highly trusted healthcare professionals. They have topped the yearly list of occupations with the highest levels of honesty and ethics for the last 2 decades (Saad, 2022). Health promotion, access to care, and patient education are examples of nursing activities that help patients achieve better health outcomes.

Nurses alone are not sufficient to tackle SDOH, which require the collaboration of many health professionals, multiple sectors of society (e.g., education, justice, business, and employment), and local and federal governments (Andermann, & CLEAR Collaboration, 2016). Still, nurses are on the front line of clinical care and are uniquely positioned to serve as catalysts for change. To be truly effective, though, nurses need to be appropriately educated about SDOH and have adequate knowledge and tools to reduce the impact of SDOH on health outcomes (National Advisory Council on Nurse Education and Practice, 2020).

To assist nursing programs and faculty in educating students to address disparities in health in the U.S., nursing education organizations have provided guidelines, references, and resources. Educators will be challenged to evaluate their personal biases, the culture of their organizations, and the status of the curriculum they teach to improve health outcomes in the communities they serve (Sportsman, 2021).

Diversity in the Nursing Workforce

Demographic changes in the United States, nursing shortages, and ongoing health inequities require the education of nurses capable of addressing systematic racism and widespread injustices in healthcare. The current inequitable distribution of nurses in the United States, particularly in disadvantaged and marginalized urban and rural areas, impacts access to healthcare services across the spectrum, from preventive care to chronic disease management and therapeutic and responsive care. Diversity, equity, and inclusion promote nursing development by preparing graduates to increase access and care quality for underrepresented and medically underserved communities (American Association of Colleges of Nursing, 2019, 2021b).

According to the National Nursing Workforce Survey (2020), the RN workforce in 2020 is more demographically diverse and representative of the country's population than in any other year in which this study was previously conducted. Overall, the RN workforce is 81% White/Caucasian. In contrast, 72% of the U.S. population identifies as Caucasian (U.S. Census Bureau, n.d.) Although these data indicate that persons of color are not adequately represented in the RN workforce, as younger nurses have entered the workforce, they have introduced greater racial diversity by identifying as an under-represented minority. Nurses between 19 and 49 comprise 47% of all RNs but account for 49% of RNs who are Black/African American and more than 60% of RNs who are multiracial, Asian, Native Hawaiian, or other Pacific Islander (U.S. Census Bureau, n.d.).

The underrepresentation of racial and ethnic minority groups, as well as men, in the nursing profession, is a significant concern. To better meet the public's present and future health requirements and to provide more culturally relevant care, the nursing profession must become more diverse. To address this challenge, efforts to increase nurses' educational attainment must focus on diversifying the number of student nurses Wakefield et al., 2021).

Increasing the number minority nurses is crucial for addressing health disparities in minority communities because minority nurses familiar with the cultural and contextual conditions of diverse communities are much more likely to address the underlying causes of health disparities.

Minority nursing students have a better likelihood of retention, satisfaction, and enrollment in environments that support diversity and have diversified faculty composition. Institutions can demonstrate their commitment to diversity and inclusion by infusing health equity, health disparities, social justice, and cultural humility information into and across the curriculum. Diversity in the nursing field creates opportunities to provide excellent care, which improves patient satisfaction and psychological well-being. For example, a significant obstacle to Latino health is the lack of access to culturally competent healthcare. Substantial efforts are necessary to recruit additional Latinos in nursing. This would have a two-fold effect of strengthening the cultural competency of the service provided and providing more healthcare services to underserved communities (Hayes-Bautista et al., 2016).

Evidence That a More Diverse Workforce Will Result in a Better Outcomes

The U.S. Department of Health and Human Services Health Resources and Services Administration Bureau of Health Professions in 2006 published *The Rationale for Diversity in the Health Professions: A Review of the Evidence in 2006*. This seminal literature review identified two significant ways in which the diversity of healthcare providers will improve care for marginalized communities. Increased diversity in the nursing profession will benefit public health by increasing access to healthcare services for underserved populations and by enabling minority patients to receive care from nurses who share their race, ethnicity, or language. Patients' probability of getting appropriate care may be increased by race, ethnicity, and language concordance, which relates to improved patient-practitioner interactions and communications (U.S. Department of Health and Human Services Health Resources and Services Administration Bureau of Health Professions, 2006).

It is widely accepted that nursing education, health disparities, and the diversity of nurses have an intersecting linkage. A diversified nursing workforce can increase access to high-quality healthcare and health resources for all people and is a prerequisite for achieving health equity (Williams et al., 2014).

CONCLUSION

The future of health equity must include an adequate and purposeful implementation of nursing curricula and experiences that builds on past lessons and incorporates the current best practices to effectively train the next generation of the nursing workforce. To care for a complex, diverse population, a superficial understanding of health disparities, inequalities, and inequities is insufficient; changes must integrate cultural humility, structural causes of racism, inequities, and implicit biases that are deeply embedded in our society. Nurse educators are responsible for incorporating these concepts into the curriculum so that students are adequately prepared to address health equity, social justice, and SDOH as they navigate increasingly complex healthcare environments (Carter & Phillips, 2021).

REFERENCES

Altman, S. H., Stith Butler, A., & Shern, L. (Eds.). (2016). *Assessing progress on the institute of medicine report the future of nursing*. National Academies Press. doi:10.17226/21838

American Association of Colleges of Nursing. (2019). *AACN's vision for academic nursing. White paper.* https://www.aacnnursing.org/Portals/42/News/White-Papers/Vision-Academic-Nursing.pdf

American Association of Colleges of Nursing. (2021a). *Diversity, equity, and inclusion in academic nursing: AACN position statement.* https://www.aacnnursing.org/Portals/42/News/Position-Statements/Diversity-Inclusion.pdf

American Association of Colleges of Nursing. (2021b). *The essentials: Core competencies for professional nursing education. American Association of Colleges of Nursing.* https://www.aacnnursing.org/portals/42/downloads/essentials/essentials-draft-document.pdf

American Nurses Association (ANA). (2021, January 25). *Introducing the national commission to address racism in nursing.* https://www.nursingworld.org/news/news-releases/2021/leading-nursing-organizations-launch-the-national-commission-to-address-racism-in-nursing/

Andermann, A. (2016). Taking action on the social determinants of health in clinical practice: A framework for health professionals. *CMAJ, JAMC, 188*(17–18), E474–E483. doi:10.1503/cmaj.160177 PMID:27503870

Artiga, S., Orgera, K., & Pham, O. (2020, March 1). *Disparities in health and health care: Five key questions and answers.* Kaiser Family Foundation. https://files.kff.org/attachment/Issue-Brief-Disparities-in-Health-and-Health-Care-Five-Key-Questions-and-Answers

Baron, R. J., & Khullar, D. (2021). Building trust to promote a more equitable health care system. *Annals of Internal Medicine*, *174*(4), 548–549. doi:10.7326/M20-6984 PMID:33524292

Bleich, M. R., MacWilliams, B. R., & Schmidt, B. J. (2015). Advancing diversity through inclusive excellence in nursing education. *Journal of Professional Nursing*, *31*(2), 89–94. doi:10.1016/j.profnurs.2014.09.003 PMID:25839947

Bloomberg. (2021, October 27). *When addressing the abilities community, words matter and people come first*. https://www.bloomberg.com/company/stories/when-addressing-the-abilities-community-words-matter-and-people-come-first

Bradshaw, M. J., & Hultquist, B. L. (2016). *Innovative teaching strategies in nursing and related health professions*. Jones & Bartlett Learning.

Carter, B. M., & Phillips, B. C. (2021, February 01). Revolutionizing the nursing curriculum. *Creative Nursing*, *1*(1), 25–30. doi:10.1891/CRNR-D-20-00072 PMID:33574168

Centers for Disease Control [CDC]. (2022, May 2). *People with certain medical conditions*. https://www.cdc.gov/coronavirus/2019-ncov/need-extra-precautions/people-with-medical-conditions.html

Cha, A. E., & Cohen, R. A. (2022). Demographic variation in health insurance coverage: United states, 2020. *National Health Statistics Reports*, *169*, 1–15. doi:10.15620/cdc:113097 PMID:35166656

Committee on the Robert Wood Johnson Foundation Initiative on the Future of Nursing at the Institute of Medicine, Robert Wood Johnson Foundation, & Institute of Medicine (United States). (2011). *The future of nursing: Leading change, advancing health*. National Academies Press. https://www.ncbi.nlm.nih.gov/books/NBK209880/

Donnelly, G. (2016). In praise of Harriet Tubman; Nurse, spy, abolitionist. *Holistic Nursing Practice*, *30*(4), 191. doi:10.1097/HNP.0000000000000155 PMID:27309407

Families, U. S. A. (2018). *Latino health inequities compared to non-Hispanic whites*. https://www.familiesusa.org/resources/latino-health-inequities-compared-to-non-hispanic-whites/

Fee, E., & Bu, L. (2010). The origins of public health nursing: The henry street visiting nurse service. *American Journal of Public Health*, *100*(7), 1206–1207. doi:10.2105/AJPH.2009.186049 PMID:20466947

Foronda, C., Prather, S., Baptiste, D. L., & Luctkar-Flude, M. (2022, March 25). Cultural humility toolkit. *Nurse Educator*. Advance online publication. doi:10.1097/NNE.0000000000001182 PMID:35324491

Garfield, R., Orgera, K., & Damico, A. (2019, January 25). *The uninsured and the ACA: A primer – Key facts about health insurance and the uninsured amidst changes to the affordable care act - introduction*. Kaiser Family Foundation. https://www.kff.org/report-section/the-uninsured-and-the-aca-a-primer-key-facts-about-health-insurance-and-the-uninsured-amidst-changes-to-the-affordable-care-act-introduction/

Greene-Moton, E., & Minkler, M. (2020). Cultural competence or cultural humility? Moving beyond the debate. *Health Promotion Practice*, *21*(1), 142–145. doi:10.1177/1524839919884912 PMID:31718301

Hammonds, E. M., & Reverby, S. M. (2019). Toward a historically informed analysis of racial health disparities since 1619. *American Journal of Public Health, 109*(10), 1348–1349. doi:10.2105/AJPH.2019.305262 PMID:31483728

Hayes-Bautista, T. M., Schink, W., & Hayes-Bautista, D. E. (2016). Original research: Latino nurses in the united states an overview of three decades (1980–2010). *AJN. The American Journal of Nursing, 116*(2), 24–33. doi:10.1097/01.NAJ.0000480514.69683.ac PMID:26817552

Hill-Briggs, F., Adler, N. E., Berkowitz, S. A., Chin, M. H., Gary-Webb, T. L., Navas-Acien, A., Thornton, P. L., & Haire-Joshu, D. (2020). Social determinants of health and diabetes: A scientific review. *Diabetes Care, 44*(1), 258–279. doi:10.2337/dci20-0053 PMID:33139407

Leong, C., Louizos, C., Currie, C., Glassford, L., Davies, N. M., Brothwell, D., & Renaud, R. (2015). Student perspectives of an online module for teaching physical assessment skills for dentistry, dental hygiene, and pharmacy students. *Journal of Interprofessional Care, 29*(4), 383–385. doi:10.3109/13561820.2014.977380 PMID:25374378

Mosley, M. O. P. (2002). Great black nurses series: Estelle Massey Riddle Osborne. *The ABNF Journal, 13*(5), 114. PMID:12430505

National Academies of Sciences, Engineering, and Medicine. (2021). *The future of nursing 2020–2030: Charting a path to achieve health equity.* The National Academies Press. doi:10.17226/25982

Prince Henry Hospital Nursing and Medical Museum. (n.d.). *Florence Nightingale 1820-1910.* https://princehenryhospitalmuseum.org/florence-nightingale/

Ruud, M. (2018). Cultural humility in the care of individuals who are lesbian, gay, bisexual, transgender, or queer. *Nursing for Women's Health, 22*(3), 255–263. doi:10.1016/j.nwh.2018.03.009 PMID:29885714

Saad, L. (2022, January 12). *Gallup's annual ranking of professions for having high honesty and ethics.* https://news.gallup.com/poll/388649/military-brass-judges-among-professions-new-image-lows.aspx

Sanchez, M. (2021). Equity, diversity, and inclusion: Intersection with quality improvement. *Nursing Management, 52*(5), 14–21. doi:10.1097/01.NUMA.0000743408.29021.85 PMID:33908918

Sportsman, S. (2021, June 13). *Health disparities: What can nurse educators do?* Collaborative Momentum Consulting. https://collaborativemomentum.com/2021/06/13/health-disparities-what-can-nurse-educators-do/

Stanford, F. C. (2020). The importance of diversity and inclusion in the healthcare workforce. *Journal of the National Medical Association, 112*(3), 247–249. doi:10.1016/j.jnma.2020.03.014 PMID:32336480

Storch, E. A., & Egbe, D. (2022). 2022: Need for (much) greater equity and equality in behavioral health care. *Journal of Cognitive Psychotherapy, 36*(2), 99–101. doi:10.1891/JCP-2022-0001 PMID:35577520

Thornton, M., & Persaud, S. (2018). Preparing today's nurses: Social determinants of health and nursing education. *Online Journal of Issues in Nursing, 23*(3). Advance online publication. doi:10.3912/OJIN.Vol23No03Man05

United States Census Bureau. (n.d.). *Quickfacts: United states.* https://www.census.gov/quickfacts/fact/table/US/PST045221

United States Department of Health and Human Services Health Resources and Services Administration Bureau of Health Professions. (2006, October). *The rationale for diversity in the health professions: A review of the evidence.* https://docplayer.net/255577-The-rationale-for-diversity-in-the-health-professions-a-review-of-the-evidence.html

United States Department of Health and Human Services, Office of Disease Prevention and Health Promotion. (2021). *Healthy people 2030.* https://health.gov/healthypeople/objectives-and-data/social-determinants-health

Wakefield, M. K., Williams, D. R., Le Menestrel, S., & Lalitha Flaubert, J. (Eds.). (2021). *The future of nursing 2020-2030: Charting a path to achieve health equity.* The National Academies Press. doi:10.17226/25982

Weinstein, J. N., Geller, A., Negussie, Y., & Baciu, A. (Eds.). (2017). *Communities in action: Pathways to health equity.* The National Academies Press. doi:10.17226/24624

Williams, D. R., & Wyatt, R. (2015). Racial bias in health care and health: Challenges and opportunities. *Journal of the American Medical Association, 314*(6), 555–556. doi:10.1001/jama.2015.9260 PMID:26262792

Williams, S. D., Hansen, K., Smithey, M., Burnley, J., Koplitz, M., Koyama, K., Young, J., & Bakos, A. (2014). Using social determinants of health to link health workforce diversity, care quality and access, and health disparities to achieve health equity in nursing. *Public Health Reports, 129*(1, suppl2), 32–36. doi:10.1177/00333549141291S207 PMID:24385662

Wright, R., Baptiste, D. L., Booth, A., Addison, H., Abshire, M., Alvarez, D., Barrett, M., Hansen, B., Jenkins, E., Scarborough, S., Wright, E., Davidson, P. M., & Ramsey, G. C. (2021). Compelling voices of diversity, equity, and inclusion in prelicensure nursing students: Application of the cultural humility framework. *Nurse Educator, 46*(5), E90–e94. doi:10.1097/NNE.0000000000001094 PMID:34392249

Wunnenberg, M. (2020). Psychosocial bullying among nurse educators: Exploring coping strategies and intent to leave. *Journal of Nursing Scholarship, 52*(5), 574–582. doi:10.1111/jnu.12581 PMID:32735757

Yearby, R. (2020). Structural racism and health disparities: Reconfiguring the social determinants of health framework to include the root cause. *The Journal of Law, Medicine & Ethics, 48*(3), 518–526. doi:10.1177/1073110520958876 PMID:33021164

ADDITIONAL READING

National Advisory Council on Nursing. (2020). *Integration of social determinants of health in nursing education, practice, and research 16th report to the Secretary of Health and Human Services and the U.S. Congress.* https://www.hrsa.gov/sites/default/files/hrsa/advisory-committees/nursing/reports/nacnep-2019-sixteenthreport.pdf

Chapter 7
Strategies for Doctoral Student Readiness, Student-Centered Support, and Inclusion

Laura K. Lynn
Walden University, USA

Melanie Brown
Walden University, USA

Michelle Brown
Walden University, USA

Deborah Inman
Walden University, USA

ABSTRACT

Equity in education is instrumental to individual, local, national, and international progress. Walden University exemplifies this through a commitment to support doctoral students with various levels of prior experience. The university scales doctoral resources based on data and communication with stakeholders. Resulting from this effort, Walden has developed centralized academic support services. Students who use these services report better preparation to make progress in their doctoral programs; however, some students have struggled to find and access resources when they need them. In 2019, the concern was addressed through a collaborative planning summit and position paper to create a holistically supportive doctoral journey for all students. The resulting innovative approach is described, highlighting aspects used to foster inclusion through easy access and better preparation for our diverse student body. Recommendations for faculty and administrators looking to enhance their support strategy through increased inclusivity and improved student progress are shared.

DOI: 10.4018/978-1-6684-5146-5.ch007

INTRODUCTION

Universities and Academic Support

Equity and quality in education is a global priority (Organization for Economic Co-operation and Development, 2012). Equity in education refers to fairness, which represents *all* irrespective of any differences with the goal of access, participation, and progression in education (Parveen & Riffat-un-Nisa, 2019). In higher education, students often develop skills needed for academic success in areas such as writing, research, and study skills, both by learning from faculty in courses and by using instructional resources available outside the classroom (Balzer & London, 2019). Knowing how to provide access to these resources is critical to meet the needs of diversity, equity, and inclusion to ensure the success of all students. As noted by Kurfist (2022), "One of the primary goals of DEI in higher education is to create a learning environment where all students succeed and thrive…" (p.1)

In reviewing traditional and peer institutions, we have noticed that students access resources and guidance for academic support in a variety of departments known through faculty with specialized knowledge who are willing to offer guidance. For instance, departments that offer statistical support may do so through a centralized unit, such as a dedicated learning center, or within a mathematics department. Typically, students learn about instructional services through handbooks, webpages, or referrals from their faculty who noticed a deficit in students' work or if the students asked their faculty for help. Students' paths to accessing cocurricular support are often cumbersome and unclear. Several universities have Research Services departments or Writing Centers, but support provided and how to access it varies. This inconsistency can result in unintentionally providing less support for students who struggle to locate and use instructional resources outside the classroom or who find many resources but are overwhelmed and unsure how to select which materials best fit their learning needs at the time.

Inclusive Teaching and Learning

While there are many perspectives and definitions of inclusive teaching and learning (ITL), several universities are now taking a broader approach to ITL in contrast to the historical disabilities-oriented focus (Lawrie et al., 2017). This includes meeting students at varying levels of readiness and supporting instructors in collaboration with university colleagues across instructional departments to support these students. A shift in graduate education toward broad, inclusive support can be seen in the 2021 Council of Graduate Schools conference with a focus on students at the center. Sessions highlighted meeting students where they are and supporting diverse students. Lawrie et al.'s (2017) synthesis of recent literature argues that the trend of broad inclusivity encompasses a whole university approach that includes governance, instructors, developing learners, and curriculum and support services. Traditional institutions looking to expand and socialize resources among faculty and staff see the need for more agile and asynchronous support services to align better with the technical expectations and lifestyles of today's graduate students (James et al., 2021; Lim et al., 2019).

An important aspect of inclusivity is easy access. Students struggling to find resources and get assistance is an obstacle for resource utilization in universities (Tipton, 2001). Having a variety of resources for doctoral students is not enough, especially for working adult doctoral students. Accessible and transparent resources play a role in student persistence (Green, 2015). Ince et al. (2020) argued that just-in-time support for doctoral student researchers will help them better plan and produce research in a logical flow. For example, details on how to schedule tutoring appointments could be included in specific assignment instructions, not just the course syllabus, or the URL to an online tutoring schedule could be embedded in an online course. These strategies for broad inclusivity and accessibility align well with Walden University's commitment to student-centered learning.

Walden University was founded more than 50 years ago with the goal of offering greater access to graduate education, which historically had been restricted to members of a select group. The university's founders understood the potential of distance learning and set out to reshape access to high-quality education for working adult learners. The tagline, *An Education for Good*®, reflects the mission to provide a diverse community of adult learners with the knowledge, skills, and credentials to enact positive social change in their communities. As such, Walden is among the top accredited institutions for awarding doctoral degrees to both African American and Hispanic students (Walden University, n.d.-a).

Institutions of higher education should be thought leaders in advancing dedicated efforts that value diversity, equity, and inclusion (DEI), yet despite recent efforts, more can be done (Ely, 2021). Colleges and universities must demonstrate continual engagement with DEI initiatives. Clearly demonstrating that an institution values DEI sends a powerful message of commitment. Walden University began with a focus on inclusion, and today continues down the path of "intentional inclusivity." Diversity enriches us in powerful ways. Walden is committed to maintaining an inclusive organization that champions the uniqueness of each member of our community. Our students and faculty hail from a variety of ethnic, educational, and financial backgrounds. Walden's emphasis on intentional inclusivity creates an environment where all learners can thrive (Walden University, n.d.-b).

In this chapter, we will explore evolving efforts at Walden University, an online, broad-access admissions institution, to reimagine its cocurricular instructional support to help doctoral students develop skills for academic success, remain in their programs, and make timely progress to graduation.

The background section will show the history of Walden's data-informed approach to doctoral support services. The focus of the chapter will describe current and future initiatives in delivering cocurricular support to be inclusive of more students and to recognize their various learning needs at different points in their programs. Although this change is happening across the university, this chapter focuses on resources supporting doctoral students. As part of this discussion, information used to inform scaling to support a diverse and expanding population of doctoral students, including innovative and more effective modalities and access, will be discussed. The chapter will also include specific information on Walden's holistic doctoral journey and support by degree approach to integrate curricular and cocurricular support for all levels of readiness. We envision the takeaways in this chapter as of special potential value for new academic leaders, such as deans, program directors, and managers leading cocurricular instructional resources.

BACKGROUND

History of Centralized Doctoral Support

Student diversity, equity, and inclusion (DEI) at the university level, especially regarding doctoral students, have been of concern for many years. Walden University was established in 1970, originally dedicated to helping students at the all-but-dissertation (ABD) status to finish their degrees and then growing to support complete doctoral programs to provide more access to all students who were interested in pursuing a doctoral degree. From the 1970s to the 1990s, the university provided opportunities and supported students working through correspondence and in intensive residencies for which they researched, wrote, and received personalized support from faculty on their dissertations. To provide access and equity opportunities, Walden's initial approach to doctoral curriculum was a writing-based, independent model called Knowledge Area Modules (KAMs). In the 2000s, Walden integrated more standardized curriculum by offering research courses and mixed-model programs consisting of KAMs and courses, until all programs were fully course-based by 2017.

Cocurricular, instructional support grew in tandem with the university. To meet the needs of students who required more support to be successful and to meet individual needs (related to DEI concepts) to help with dissertation writing quality, the Form and Style review was established in 1996 as a required step in the doctoral capstone approval process. The university established the Walden University Writing Center in 2005 to address student writing needs in contexts beyond the dissertation as exhibited by its student body. Library services at Walden also evolved to be instructional and supportive, focused on developing students' information literacy skills. Librarians provide advising services appointments and resources to help students plan literature searches and ensure saturation in the breadth of their work.

As the doctoral programs grew with the emphasis on access, diversity, and inclusion, the university realized the need to provide a systematic approach as well as support for doctoral quality assurance. In 2007, the Center for Research Support was developed to provide research-oriented services for students and faculty, dissertation processing and approvals, grants and awards, and research ethics reviews of faculty and student research. That center, now the Office of Research and Doctoral Services, offers methodology advising services and consultation on research design selection and alignment, data collection and analysis, and review of abstract. The Academic Skills Center, founded in 2011, provides tutoring, peer mentoring, and administration of the university's doctoral writing assessment requirement. The CAEX program in the Academic Skills Center offers elective, skill-building support courses, seminars, and doctoral writing and revision workshops.

Although student satisfaction data shows that students who use support services find them effective for their progress, students also note interest in more timely and personally relevant resources. For instance, in a study on the learning preferences and support opportunities for Walden's African national students (Lynn & Adeoye, 2020), some students expressed great satisfaction with resources like the Walden Writing Center and library services, while others noted a desire for more personalized services and just-in-time resources where they could access a support person when they needed them. In reviewing our satisfaction data from multiple sources, certain outcomes were clear. First, students who used our support services found them very helpful and felt that support services helped them make progress and increased their likelihood of recommending Walden to future students. Second, students sometimes found it difficult to know where to find resources and were sometimes overwhelmed tracking them down. Some students were also unaware of resources that would be helpful for them.

To meet the needs of all students and ensure equity, adequacy, and inclusion for our diverse student body the need to develop more resources for student success became evident. During the nearly two decades these cocurricular departments have been in place, their staff and faculty have developed thousands of resources—videos, self-paced tutorials, webinars, downloadable PDFs, blog posts, podcasts, and website resources—to support doctoral students' skill development in research, writing, information literacy, statistics, study strategies, time management, and many other topics. Because these rich resources have been designed in different units over the years, they tend to overlap and can be redundant in ways that can confuse students trying to parse through all the materials available to them. This siloed structure has challenged us on how to match students with the instructional support they need at different points in their doctoral programs.

Over the years, cocurricular leaders have also sought ways to help more students use the instructional departments and resources available to them beyond the classroom. Of the more than 44,000 students who received Walden University's 2021 Student Satisfaction Survey, 9,889 (22%) responded (Walden University, Office of Institutional Effectiveness, 2022). Of that population, the following rated these cocurricular departments' services on effectiveness:

- Library: 5,455 students (55% of respondents; 12% of all students surveyed)
- Writing Center: 3,386 students (34% of respondents; 8% of all surveyed)
- Academic Skills Center: 1,519 students (15% of respondents; 3% of all surveyed)
- Center for Research Quality: 831 students (8% of respondents; 2% of all surveyed)

Making resources more accessible to doctoral students, who compose about 25% of the student body at Walden, would not necessarily result in more students completing the university's annual satisfaction survey. However, it could help us ensure that more doctoral students can engage with and learn from those resources, providing a more equitable foundation to help every student succeed in their doctoral program. The next section of this chapter addresses approaches that university administrators have taken to address the needs of our diverse student population, meeting equity and inclusion expectations, to help connect more doctoral students to the skill-building resources available to them to support their successful completion.

ADVANCING DOCTORAL SUPPORT FOR GREATER INCLUSION

At a large institution like Walden University, there are many milestones and stakeholder/support groups spanning the doctoral student journey, which stretches from identified prospect, to student, to candidate, to successful graduate and beyond. It is important to examine each phase for opportunities to improve the student experience and support success. Walden has long worked to understand how our diverse students move through the phases of doctoral education and often establishes teams that work to understand and create a framework for educational processes, including benchmarks and milestones to meet the needs of all students who come to Walden because of our mission for equity and access (Salter et al., 2013).

As Walden continues to expand access to education and provide opportunities for students to achieve their personal and professional goals, the conceptualization of the doctoral journey also expands (and evolves) along with the best approach to supporting students. The online setting provides many opportunities for technological innovation that supports individualized instruction at scale, and through continued efforts, the result is an integrated road map toward strategic innovation for doctoral success. This is extremely important to successfully address DEI concepts for all our students, keeping in mind the access many do or do not have to technology and realizing the potential for more student access through technology.

In 2019, Walden decided to more closely examine the doctoral experience to integrate skill building and meeting DEI student needs throughout the doctoral journey. A working group was established to analyze doctoral students' readiness to move through their doctoral journey timelines from prospect to graduate. The group carefully examined supports and services currently in place to support that journey

Strategies for Doctoral Student Readiness, Student-Centered Support, and Inclusion

and reported on recommendations for improvement (Salter et al., 2019). Framed by both the experiences of the team members and academic literature on doctoral student readiness—including diversity, equity and inclusion—the group presented the following "forms of readiness": academic, technology, reading, writing, research, capstone, and professional. Recommendations in the group's report included continuing efforts to streamline the organization and presentation of existing support for students, examining specific just-in-time, scaffolded by stage-in-the-program strategies, integrating (and coordinating) technological solutions for program and service delivery, and building opportunities for students to discuss their professional goals. The idea was to set expectations early, ready students' skills, proactively guide them, and support them through program completion (see Figure 1).

It is well known that doctoral students often experience challenges negotiating their doctoral journeys (Hutchings, 2017), and many of the team's recommendations supported a clearer, integrated experience with supports that meet students where they are. Also highlighted throughout the report was the need for early-program experiences in which students can practice and obtain feedback prior to capstone. The idea of developing a doctoral identity and/or identity as researchers early in the program is also supported in the literature (Caskey et al., 2020).

In the past 4 years, Walden has taken a strategic approach to organizing its doctoral support resources in ways to deliver them seamlessly to students. This section will provide an overview of some of the initiatives developed to help doctoral students better navigate and apply instructional support. These initiatives include the doctoral Walden Orientation and Welcome; the identification of doctoral competencies; the Doctoral Degree Coach™; and the doctoral companion courses, a series of five, one-credit courses offered at specific points during students' degree programs to help them develop skills needed at the capstone stage. These offerings include resources developed by Walden's various cocurricular support departments. Their innovation is in how they organize and present resources to students in a more curated, personalized way rather than simply having students visit disparate websites and select resources for themselves.

Figure 1. Visualizing doctoral student support across the journey
Note. Image credit: Jose Henriquez.

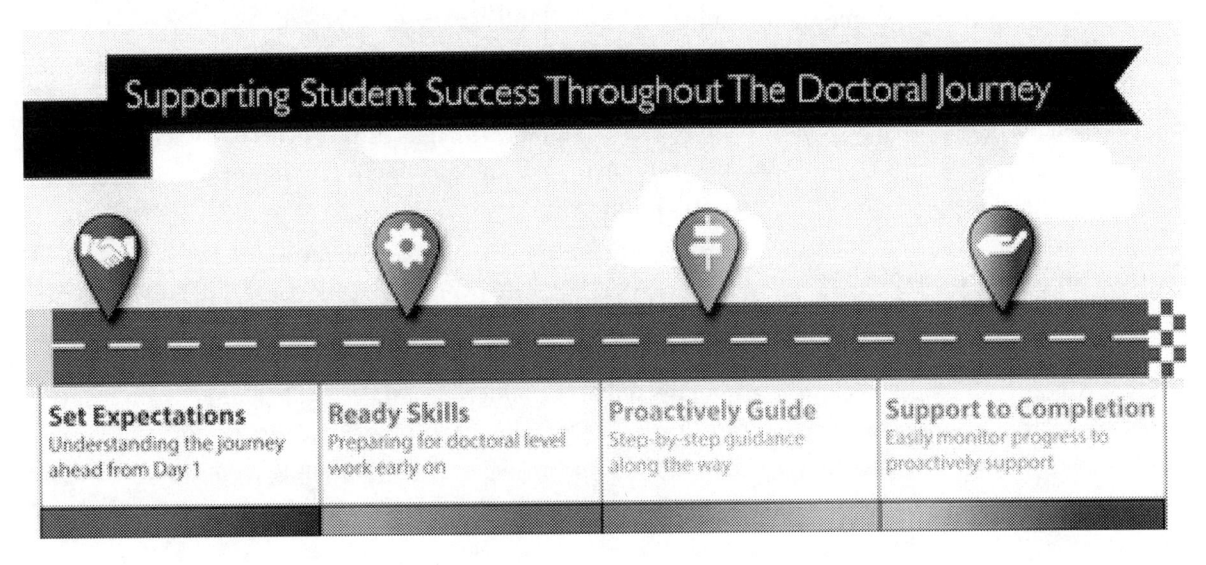

Doctoral Walden Orientation and Welcome

The Walden Orientation and Welcome (WOW) for doctoral students is designed to help students explore and become more familiar with Walden's online classroom and learn about support resources relevant to students in the first few months of their studies. Launched in summer 2021, the doctoral WOW replaced the previous orientation provided for graduate students in master's or doctoral programs at Walden. By streamlining WOW content to focus specifically on incoming doctoral students' needs (see Figure 2), this upgraded orientation provides those students with a curated, personally relevant first experience with the university.

Figure 2. A module from the doctoral the 'Walden Orientation and Welcome'
Note. Image credit: Walden University.

The doctoral WOW features a self-assessment in which students rate their confidence level with different topics pertinent to new doctoral students, including financial aid, time management, the university's doctoral writing assessment requirement, and using Walden's Doctoral Degree Coach™. When students rate their confidence level as *low* or *unsure* in a topic, they receive access to a self-paced resource about that topic to help them become more familiar with it. Students can also use the orientation course's practice environment to explore classroom navigation, Discussion boards, and assignment submissions.

In addition to becoming more comfortable with Walden's learning management system, new doctoral students can participate in a live Discussion board to interact with a doctoral peer mentor. Peer mentors are high-achieving Walden doctoral students who help new students build community, an approach to help incoming students feel less isolated in their online program.

Doctoral Competencies

Developed in 2019 as an outcome of a university-wide doctoral readiness summit, the Doctoral Competency Blueprint includes specific learning objectives common for all doctoral students within seven identified doctoral competency domains (see Figure 3). Domain-specific objectives are further categorized and scaffolded across the timeline of the doctoral journey—first term(s), middle terms, and capstone terms. The blueprint provides a foundation (or map) for supporting student success across the doctoral program timeline.

Strategies for Doctoral Student Readiness, Student-Centered Support, and Inclusion

Figure 3. Doctoral competencies resulting from the readiness summit
Note. Image credit: Jose Henriquez, Walden University.

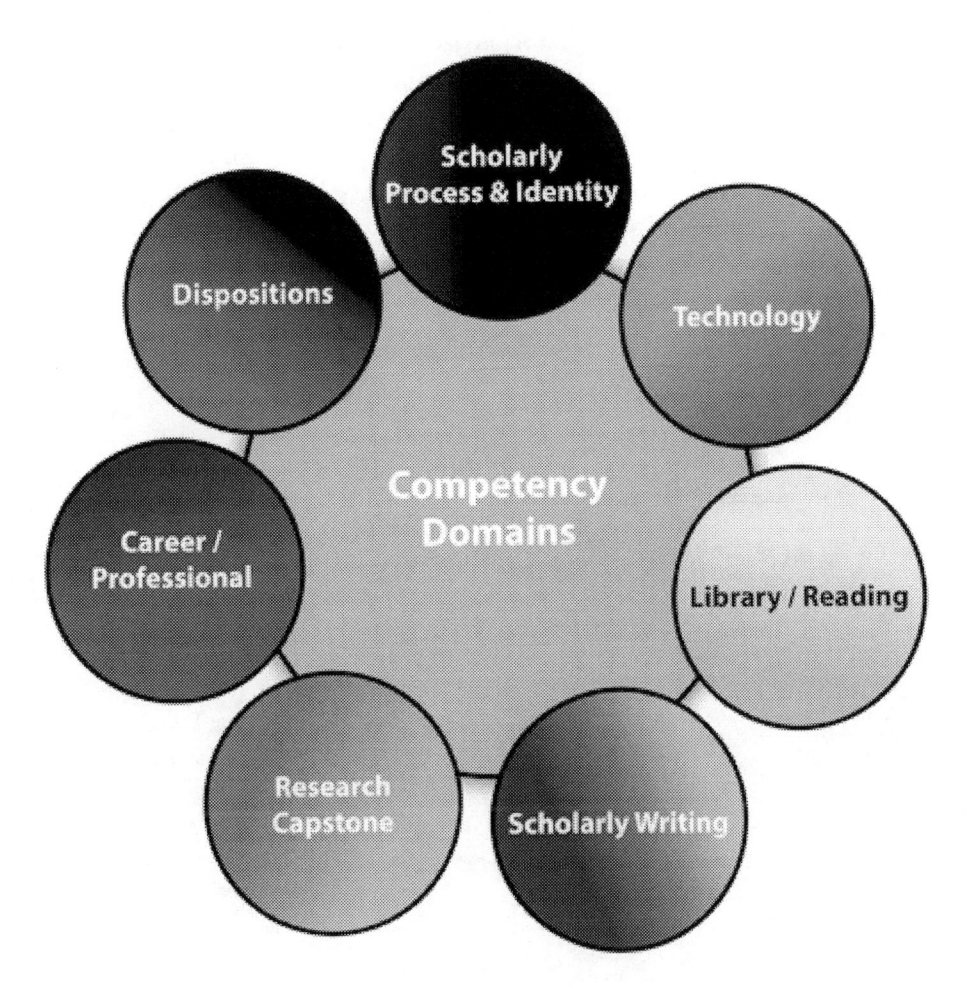

The Doctoral Competency Blueprint served as the foundation for future initiatives—both the doctoral capstone companion course concept as well as expanding the existing Doctoral Degree Coach™ to support doctoral students in their competency attainment from the beginning of their doctoral programs. Doctoral students work to establish their scholarly identities across the program timeline, with the end goal being successful completion of the doctoral capstone or project.

Doctoral Degree Coach™

Originally developed as the Doctoral Research Coach™ (DRC), the "coach" was a digital progress-tracking tool designed to support student progress and successful completion of the doctoral capstone. The DRC helps students stay on track by guiding them step-by-step through the doctoral capstone process with resources and help contacts for every step along the way. The tool is organized by stages of capstone development, milestones for capstone completion, and specific guidance for timing based on a goal completion date that students establish with their doctoral committee.

After its well-received pilot in 2018, access to the DRC was expanded in 2019 to all Walden doctoral students in the capstone or project study stages of their programs. From a faculty standpoint, the DRC tool is a valuable resource in helping to monitor progress and support mentoring throughout doctoral capstone or project stage. Used in tandem with the capstone course, the DRC can support goal setting each semester and elicit conversations on progress.

Recognizing an opportunity to support readiness throughout the journey, work began on an expansion of what was rebranded as the Doctoral Degree Coach™ (see Figure 4) to include doctoral skills and readiness content. Utilizing the doctoral competencies blueprint and working collaboratively with representatives from all support/stakeholder groups, scaffolded content was curated and provided for students to access and complete at their own pace, beginning in their first term as a doctoral student. The expanded Doctoral Degree Coach™ provides just-in-time, scaffolded by stage-in-the-program guidance and resources for students.

Figure 4. The dual-stage dashboard of the Doctoral Degree Coach™
Note. Image credit: Walden University.

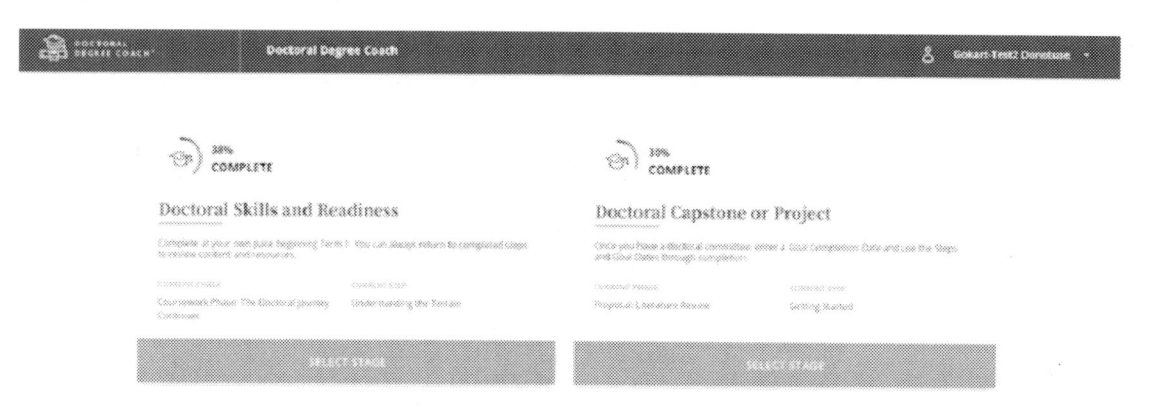

Using the guidance in the Doctoral Skills and Readiness portion of the Doctoral Degree Coach™, students in their first term can map out their course, plan for their future, and prepare their skills. Early on, students consider career goals and potential areas of research interest for their capstone or project. Later, students learn how to manage obstacles and strengthen their skills. To make the resource an integrated and comprehensive tool to support doctoral student progress and provide a unified experience, quick links to university resources and help contacts are provided and the content is conveniently positioned on the jumping-off point for all doctoral students—the student portal. This digital doorway is where new students also find their doctoral Walden Orientation and Welcome, which introduces them to the Doctoral Degree Coach™.

Doctoral Companion Courses

The doctoral companion courses were designed to complement the regular program of study, including program content courses, research courses, and residencies (where applicable) to prepare doctoral students for the dissertation/capstone phase. Students participate in scaffolded, comprehensive research projects anchored in real-world scenarios that model a research apprenticeship and provide opportunities for meaningful scholarly engagement.

Grounded in the seven doctoral competencies, the companion courses focus on developing skills and support the following series outcomes:

1. Evaluate the attitudes of oneself as a scholar-practitioner who conducts research within an academic community or professional practice.
2. Operate a variety of technologies to support the development of an independent doctoral capstone.
3. Critically evaluate the body of scholarly literature in a discipline with respect to the quality of research and consistency of conclusions.
4. Synthesize original research in an appropriate, discipline-relevant, scholarly voice following applicable standards and requirements for the program of study.
5. Design an independent capstone study that addresses a specified gap and results in positive social change.
6. Develop professional skills related to career development.
7. Approach scholarly work with dispositions that facilitate progress toward stated goals and collaboration.

The series begins with a *Welcome to the Capstone Journey* and then moves through *Building Knowledge and Skills* and ultimately concludes with the *Transition to Candidacy* course. Students participate in self-assessments that result in personalized resource recommendations. The "ebook" for each course is the Doctoral Degree Coach™ (see Figure 5).

This approach helps ensure consistency across the student experience. By providing this early-program, low-risk environment for students to practice academic and research skills, the companion courses help bridge the gap between coursework and independent research. Although developed as a standardized series, individual doctoral programs have the option to customize content and to include discipline-specific instructional resources in their departments' companion courses. Doctoral competency development is scaffolded to prepare students for the doctoral capstone phase.

Success by Degree and Students at the Center

"Success by Degree" is a strategic approach to reimagine how we provide support to students at the doctoral, master's, and bachelor's degree levels. Within each degree level, we imagine "Students at the Center," an instructional support model structured around a student's degree-program journey and its tasks. In this model, instructional support is scaffolded to build competencies relevant to the student's degree. By intentionally placing the student at the center in this approach to degree-specific skill-building instruction, support takes a more collaborative effort. With a renewed focus on a collaboration mindset, degree outcomes, and turning access into opportunity, the university is making additional strides in the continuous effort to examine opportunities for student success. While the other doctoral support initiatives described in this section have been rolled out, the Success by Degree approach and the Students at the Center model are currently in the planning and development phase.

Figure 5. Integration of the Doctoral Degree Coach™ in companion courses
Note. Image credit: Walden University.

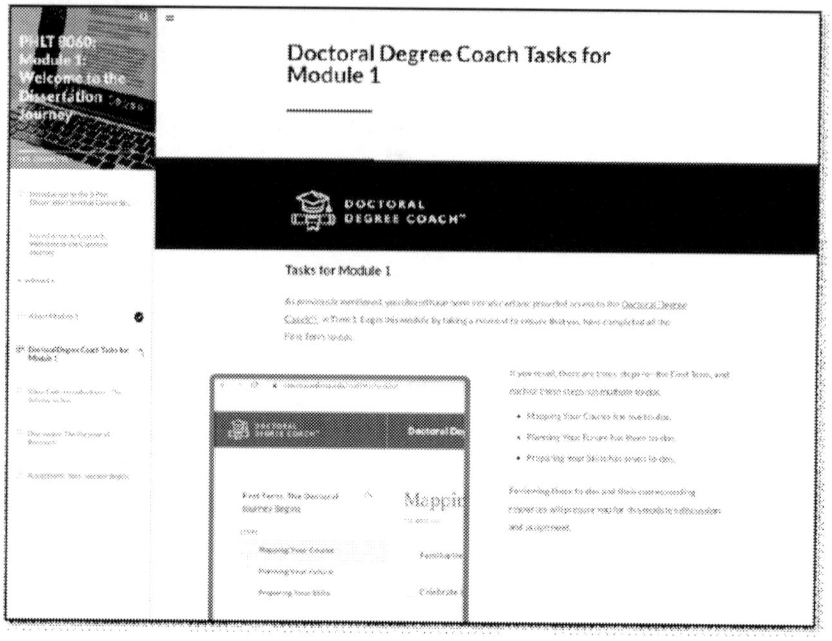

SOLUTIONS

Walden University began with a commitment to meeting the needs of doctoral learners who may experience barriers to completing their degrees in the traditional environment. As the university has grown and evolved it has maintained that legacy. Walden has more doctoral graduates than any other institution (National Center for Science and Engineering Statistics & National Science Foundation, 2021). Instead of limiting admission, Walden believes in meeting and guiding motivated students so they can reach their educational and career goals. In 2019, it became clear that "more and more" was not the solution, but rather where and how. Adapting in these ways requires cross-university commitment and collaboration. It also requires willingness for leadership to invest and encourage staff and department leaders to look at problems differently.

Data-based, continuous improvement has been essential for our path toward inclusive student support. Additionally, strong partnerships across academic programs with doctoral services have provided a robust flow of information regarding the impact of services and challenges faced. Regular meetings and review of policies, services, and impact have led to instructive adjustment. Tools like the doctoral coach have shown the effectiveness of early preparation and easy access to resources. Table 1 provides an annotated overview of Walden's social and instructional support initiatives scaffolded throughout students' doctoral programs.

Strategies for Doctoral Student Readiness, Student-Centered Support, and Inclusion

Setting Expectations
- Certified Doctoral Enrollment Specialists | All enrollment specialists working with potential doctoral students are trained and certified with key knowledge about the doctoral journey at Walden University.
- Walden Orientation & Welcome (WOW) | The Walden Orientation and Welcome helps to set the stage for what is to come. Students learn about Walden University—from our mission to our approach to doctoral education and more.

Preparing for the Journey
- Student Portal | The student portal is considered the main hub for students. From here, they access their academics, financial aid, student organizations, etc.
- Degree Coach—Skills & Readiness | The Skills and Readiness portion of the Doctoral Degree Coach™ includes important self-paced steps to ready our students early in their programs.
- Peer Mentors | New doctoral students can interact with a peer mentor in the doctoral WOW. Peer mentors are experienced Walden doctoral students who provide social support and tips for success.

Ensuring Readiness
- Companion Courses | The doctoral companion courses were developed to support readiness in all doctoral competencies and bridge the gap between coursework and capstone.
- Multi-Track Residency Experiences | The doctoral residency component of the doctoral journey includes multiple tracks to individualize the experiences and meet the needs of our students.
- Personalized Research Training | Our research training provides both the breadth and depth that students need to be successful.

Guiding Capstone Progress
- Degree Coach—Capstone or Project | The Capstone or Project portion of the Doctoral Degree Coach walks students through the capstone process from prospectus to proposal and through approval of the final study. Guidance, resources, and help contacts are only a click away.
- Progress-Oriented Capstone Course and Policies | The reimagined capstone experience provides term-by-term guidance along with the tools and resources to support timely completion.

Supporting Faculty
- Communication and Training | In collaboration with the Office of Teaching Learning Excellence, we support our faculty with the information and tools they need to promote student success.
- Support Resources | Faculty have access to the resources they will need for a strong teaching and mentoring culture.

Maintaining the Experience
- Student Experience | At the center of it all is a seamless doctoral student experience.
- Systems and IT | We ensure that our systems are integrated so that students can focus on their success.

CONCLUSION

Lessons learned from these doctoral improvements are now being reviewed at the undergraduate and master's levels. The undergraduate programs have developed an advisory committee, reviews data, and is working to provide real-time support based on what they have learned about their student body. They have also conducted a review of their services and practices in relation to National Institutes Guide for Historically Underserved Students. This work will help to increase support and provide degree-level practices targeted at student needs. Master's programs have not yet had a degree-level support strategy. However, with the Success by Degree/Students at the Center initiative, these programs will be applying the information gathering and governance practices of the doctoral programs to develop the right resources and modalities based on the common needs of our master's students while still providing specialized programmatic support.

Walden University is pleased to continue our tradition of data-based improvement and continues to look for ways to improve our practices to better meet the needs of our students. None of what has been accomplished thus far could have been accomplished without our shared mission and values and dynamic collaboration.

Some important lessons for administrators and program leaders from this work include the following:

1. **Collaborate and Listen**: Be sure to work closely with academic department staff, academic advising services, and university offices staff to understand data and have a sense of student experiences and needs. Also use meetings and governance groups to review data, strategies, and policy around student support to ensure that multiple stakeholders shape initiatives.
2. **Get the Data**: Make sure you have outcome data that can be linked to service utilization so you can track trends. Regularly collect satisfaction data and utilize data from multiple departments, including marketing, support services advisors, and other units so you can learn about both the academic experience and resource needs.
3. **Start Small and Scale Up**: With the resources you have, start with the most-needed services and use data and feedback to make a case for investments for more staff or expanded offerings.
4. **Emphasize Access**: Be innovative in thinking about how to get resources to students. You want to maximize students who can benefit, and to benefit they need to easily find these resources. Instead of searching, resources should come to students, through courses, portals, or tools they easily use every day in their program.

In the end, this effort is about equity, and we believe it is a worthy effort for all doctoral institutions. Equity should be addressed with inclusion as a priority. Walden has enjoyed meeting the challenge of support to ensure that more students have access to a doctoral degree to meet their goals. Our students come to us with a variety of experiences and levels of readiness, and we will continue to find ways to evolve to meet their needs. Walden's doctoral students, most of whom are working professionals, are faced with the challenges of balancing work, school, family, and other responsibilities. To have an integrated and personalized experience can make a difference in their ability to finish their doctoral programs and achieve their educational and personal goals, all of which supports Walden's mission of education for good.

REFERENCES

Adeoye, B., & Lynn, L. K. (2020, October 1). *Learning preferences and support opportunities for African national doctoral students* [Poster presentation]. Walden University Research Conference 2020. https://scholarworks.waldenu.edu/cgi/viewcontent.cgi?article=1046&context=researchconference

Balzer Carr, B., & London, R. (2019). The role of learning support services in university students' educational outcomes. *Journal of College Student Retention, 21*(1), 78–104. doi:10.1177/1521025117690159

Caskey, M. M., Stevens, D. D., & Yeo, M. (2020). Examining doctoral student development of a researcher identity: Using the Draw a Researcher Test. *Impacting Education, 5*(1). Advance online publication. doi:10.5195/ie.2020.92

Ely, E. (2021). Diversity, equity & inclusion statements on academic library websites. *Information Technology and Libraries, 40*(4), 1–22. doi:10.6017/ital.v40i4.13353

Hutchings, M. (2017). Improving doctoral support through group supervision: Analysing face-to-face and technology-mediated strategies for nurturing and sustaining scholarship. *Studies in Higher Education, 42*(3), 533–550. doi:10.1080/03075079.2015.1058352

Ince, S., Hoadley, C., & Kirschner, P. A. (2020). Research workflow skills for education doctoral students and postdocs: A qualitative study. *Journal of Academic Librarianship, 46*(5), 102172. doi:10.1016/j.acalib.2020.102172

James, E. A., Lanyon, S., Larson, S., & Oppong, J. (2021, December 1–4). *Building a new future for virtual academic support and professional development for graduate students: Investigating a consortium model* [Conference session]. Council of Graduate Schools 61st Annual Meeting. New Orleans, LA, United States. https://cgsnet.org/61st-annual-meeting/

Kurfist, A. (2022). *Student belonging: The next DEI frontier in higher education*. Hanover Research. https://www.hanoverresearch.com/insights-blog/student-belonging-the-next-dei-frontier-in-higher-education/

Lawrie, G., Marquis, E., Fuller, E., Newman, T., Qiu, M., Nomikoudis, M., Roelofs, F., & van Dam, L. (2017). Moving Towards Inclusive Learning and Teaching: A Synthesis of Recent Literature. *Teaching & Learning Inquiry: The ISSOTL Journal, 5*(1). Advance online publication. doi:10.20343/teachlearninqu.5.1.3

Lim, J., Covrig, D., Freed, S., De Oliveira, B., Ongo, M., & Newman, I. (2019). Strategies to assist distance doctoral students in completing their dissertations. *The International Review of Research in Open and Distributed Learning, 20*(5), 192–210. doi:10.19173/irrodl.v20i5.4532

National Center for Science and Engineering Statistics & National Science Foundation. (2021). *Doctorate recipients from U.S. universities: 2020*. https://ncses.nsf.gov/pubs/nsf22300/data-tables

Organization for Economic Co-operation and Development [OECD]. (2012). *Equity and quality in education: Supporting disadvantaged students and schools*. OECD Publishing. https://www.oecd.org/education/school/50293148.pdf

Parveen, I., & Riffat-un-Nisa, A. (2019). Equitable higher education: Students' perspective on access to resources, participation, and educational outcomes. *Bulletin of Education and Research, 41*(1), 185–201. https://files.eric.ed.gov/fulltext/EJ1217921.pdf

Salter, D., Ajsenberg, T., Ball, T., Bass, J., Brown, M., Picht, S., Pranke, D., Schneider, A., & Sullivan, K. (2019). *Readiness to succeed: Preparing the scholar-practitioner* [Unpublished internal report]. Walden University.

Salter, D., Larkin, G., Riedel, E., Schulz, W., Smeaton, G., & Westermann, J. (2013). *A framework for doctoral education: Milestones and benchmarks* [Unpublished internal report]. Walden University.

Tipton, C. J. (2001). Graduate students' perceptions of library support services for distance learners: A university system-wide study. *Journal of Library Administration, 32*(1–2), 393–408. doi:10.1300/J111v32n01_14

Walden University. (n.d.a). *Diversity & inclusion.* https://www.waldenu.edu/why-walden/diversity

Walden University. (n.d.b). *Why Walden.* https://www.waldenu.edu/why-walden

Walden University, Office of Institutional Effectiveness. (2022). *2021 student satisfaction survey outcomes* [Conference presentation]. National Faculty Meeting.

ADDITIONAL READING

Greene, M. (2015). Come hell or high water: Doctoral students' perceptions on support services and persistence. *International Journal of Doctoral Studies, 10,* 501–518. http://ijds.org/Volume10/IJDSv10p501-518Greene0597.pdf. doi:10.28945/2327

Johnson, L. M., Butler, J. T., & Johnston, L. R. (2012). Developing e-science and research services and support at the University of Minnesota health sciences libraries. *Journal of Library Administration, 52*(8), 754–769. doi:10.1080/01930826.2012.751291 PMID:23585706

Chapter 8
The Students We Have:
Compassionate Grading in Online Courses

D. Gabriela Johnson
Walden University, USA

Sara Makris
Walden University, USA

ABSTRACT

Students who choose to enter college in their twenties, thirties, and beyond face the challenges of balancing their academic experiences with busier lives, often with little social capital to guide them through the intricacies of college life. Students may feel overwhelmed, easily discouraged, or overlooked by people within their institution, including their professors. Instructors who, themselves, lack the experience of being first-generation college students may struggle to identify with the behaviors of the students they teach. They may see their roles as evaluators more than as partners or guides. The practice of compassionate grading and teaching can increase opportunities for trusting relationships to form among instructors and students, and for learning to occur.

INTRODUCTION

The authors assert the value of compassionate grading as a potential key to student retention in undergraduate programs. Because first-generation students —students who are the first members of their families to attend college—are more likely to drop out of undergraduate programs, compassionate grading may serve as a high-impact means for faculty engagement with students to support retention and address the problem of student attrition. Compassionate grading is defined and explained in the chapter, focusing on common misconceptions regarding the practice.

We underscore the value of feedback on academic work and, more importantly, how the feedback is delivered. Specifically, we consider the roles of tone, delivery, empathy, and subsequent action throughout the grading process. By linking scholarship on caring as a post-secondary level instructional tool

DOI: 10.4018/978-1-6684-5146-5.ch008

to definitions of empathy and compassion among college professors and undergraduate students, we illustrate the potential influence that compassionate grading can have on undergraduate success and retention in online programs.

BACKGROUND

In the United States, nearly 72% of students enrolled in 4-year private, for-profit universities are first generation students (RTI International, 2019). At one such institution—also the authors' home institution—78% of incoming undergraduate students have full- or part-time jobs, and almost half receive no financial support from their employers for educational expenses (Walden University, 2020). In addition to this, many in our predominantly female population are parents who, in addition to raising children, care for older family members.

First-generation adult undergraduates in online universities face well-documented challenges to persistence and retention through successful completion of bachelor's degrees (Seay, 2006). This population of students brings valuable life experiences and prior knowledge that their academic institutions may overlook. Many first-generation college students require support when connecting their existing strengths to academic study goals and their continued development as learners. As they manage competing personal and academic priorities at every turn, first-generation adult online learners may challenge many professors' instructional skillsets.

Undergraduate educators, who sometimes are admonished to "teach the students we *have*; not the students we *want*," may struggle to understand the meaning of this call to action. For lack of applicable references, many professors' teaching methods default to those they experienced as students. If they encounter limited success by default, professors may wonder how to better approach students whose behaviors are informed by different experiences, circumstances, and perspectives.

Among our institution's undergraduate population, 77% identify as female. The gender demographic is reflected in our faculty, which is 76% female. In terms of ethnicity and race, 35% of our students identify as Black or African American, and 43% identify as White. The faculty makeup differs here, with 19% identifying as Black or African American and 71% who are White (Walden, 2020). Intersectionality theory (Crenshaw, 1990) highlights the complexity of experience through the lens of identity. Though many faculty overlap with students in one aspect of their identities, they diverge in other essential ways. Faculty who may connect with students based on similar social classes of origin may diverge when it comes to experiences based in race and ethnicity. Faculty with similar ethnic backgrounds to their students may come from vastly different class and linguistic origins. Essential differences exist among faculty and their students in every case because of the inherent power differential they face. To address this imbalance, and to enable the primary goal of the pursuit of education—growth and development of learners—we offer some suggested methods for communication through feedback in the form of compassionate grading.

In this chapter, we detail scholarly observations on approaches to grading the work of first-generation undergraduate students. We build the case for operationalizing care in grading and giving feedback on assignments. The approach is based on compassion and empathy—concepts that are taking root in the literature on post-secondary teaching. Through descriptions of the philosophy and existing research on compassion in online and post-secondary settings, we lay the foundation for techniques used by faculty in our undergraduate program. We describe practices used within our general education program to enhance feelings of belonging among students and to remove obstacles that might otherwise hamper students' academic growth.

When the experiences and backgrounds of faculty and their students are significantly different, faculty can develop skills to help them address student needs in ways they may not automatically anticipate. With guidance and some reliable techniques, we believe that undergraduate faculty can teach across differences, build trust with their students, and support their successful acquisition of bachelor's degrees.

COMPASSIONATE TEACHING AND TEACHER EMPATHY

Teacher empathy is defined as "the degree to which instructors work to deeply understand students' personal and social situations, feel caring and concern in response to students' positive and negative emotions, and communicate their understanding and caring to students through their behavior" (Meyers et al., 2019, p. 161). It serves as the basis for compassionate teaching. As Sinclair et al. (2017) state, empathy denotes the ability to show understanding of another's feelings, acknowledge them, and respond appropriately. *Compassion* has been defined as "a deep awareness of the suffering of another coupled with the wish to relieve it" (Nunberg & Newman, 2011). According to Berkley's Greater Good Science Center (n.d.), ". . . while empathy refers more generally to our ability to take the perspective of and feel another person's emotions, compassion is when those feelings and thoughts include the desire to help" (para. 2).

Sinclair et al. (2017) distinguish compassion as separate from empathy as follows: Unlike empathy, which describes an emotional state, compassion involves activity that aims to alleviate suffering in others. Meyers et al. (2019) explain that instructors who are high in teacher empathy "identify and remove obstacles to learning" (p. 162). Thus, compassionate teaching encourages an empathetic instructor to understand students' situations and alleviate students' concerns and stress by removing obstacles to learning. White and Ruth-Sahd (2020) define *compassionate teaching* as teaching that "involves faculty awareness of student suffering, followed by a sympathetic concern, and then a wish to see relief" (p. 7). The authors link compassionate teaching in this case to student loss and grief. In addition, a compassionate disposition can also embody acknowledgment of the stressors of students' daily lives, such as the impacts of working full time, serving as a caregiver, and managing financial burdens.

According to Johnson, Killion, and Oomen (2005), connection and communication with faculty are primary contributors to student satisfaction. Of additional importance, instructors' social presence, defined by Garrison et al. (2000) as "the ability of participants in a community of inquiry to project themselves socially and emotionally, as 'real' people (i.e., their full personality), through the medium of communication being used" (p. 94).

Instructors play a key role in defining student experiences in academic institutions. Thus, students' likelihood of remaining enrolled and persisting at their academic institutions may hinge, in large part, on the quality of their relationships with their instructors. Considering the anxiety adult students experience and the influence of teacher interaction on student satisfaction, faculty who work with undergraduate online students may see benefits to engagement in compassionate teaching, an approach that begins with empathy.

Avoiding Grade Inflation

Though compelling, the idea of compassionate grading risks misinterpretation. Instructors may perceive that one way to alleviate a student's stress and remove obstacles to learning is to lower the academic standards of a course to help the student earn better grades and feel more successful. Such practices constitute artificial grade inflation—an increase to grade point average (GPA) without increasing achievement (Potter & Nyman, 2001). When grades are inflated, students receive higher marks without showing higher levels of mastery (Finefter-Rosenbluh & Levinson, 2015).

While grade inflation has negative connotations in academic circles, instructors may have reasons they consider helpful to give a student more points than the student earned in an assignment. Finefter-Rosenbluh and Levinson (2015) explain that instructors may think that giving higher grades constitutes an expression of care toward their students, suggesting that instructors may inflate grades "due to concern for their students' psychology, motivation and life prospects" (p. 11), to alleviate students' outside pressure to achieve high grades, and to keep from harming students psychologically or professionally.

Teachers often feel that assigning students lower grades will negatively affect students' self-image, causing them to feel incapable and give up learning (Cushman, 2003). The lowering of academic standards, however, signifies sympathy rather than empathy (Meyers et al., 2019). Sympathy is an emotional, pity-based response to a distressing situation, which lacks the relational understanding of empathy (Sinclair et al., 2017). A sympathetic response focuses only on a student's immediate needs without considering their future need: preparation for future academic courses and life outside of the university, where they will be held to higher standards.

While the intention behind it may seem compassionate, doling out points irrespective of the quality of students' work may result in adverse consequences to learning and academic self-concept. Grade inflation does not engender a realistic awareness among students of their actual degree of academic performance (Chowdhury, 2018). It instead causes students to misunderstand their capabilities, leading to a false sense of preparation, knowledge, and skills. This is particularly detrimental when students take a prerequisite course, only to move to a higher-level course possessing a mistaken sense of mastery of the content. Grade inflation "can deteriorate the work ethic of students" (Chowdhury, 2018, p. 88). In other words, if students see that high grades are awarded easily, they may rightly feel that they do not have to work as hard in a class, and they may carry that attitude with them to subsequent courses. Per Gershenson (2020): "studies have found that college students study for less time—by as much as 50 percent—when they expect the average class grade to be an A rather than a C" (p. 15).

It is worth mentioning that other motivations prompt faculty to inflate grades. Some want to avoid the extra work of having to justify and explain their low grades to students (Cushman, 2003). In some cases, instructor concern about the influence of student evaluations on their own professional prospects has been cited as a cause for the inflation of grades. Per Culver (2010), "many faculty believe that they are, at least until they are tenured, held hostage by students because they believe that lower student grades will result in lower course evaluations, a key element in their faculty evaluation process related to tenure and promotion" (p. 331). However, data are inconclusive when it comes to demonstrating that higher grades lead to better faculty evaluations. Studies like Culver's (2010) concluded that the quality of engagement of the student, as well as larger workloads and higher levels of difficulty of courses, are associated with *higher* ratings of faculty in evaluations. Smith, Cook, and Buskist (2011), however, found that teachers who tend to be more lenient in grading subjectively may receive better student evaluations of their performance.

The Students We Have

Mastery Learning

The noted detrimental effects of grade inflation make it a problem worth analyzing when considering compassionate teaching practices without dismissing the faculty's real concern for the relationship between student evaluations and their prospects. Chowdhury (2018) summarizes the problem in this way: ". . . if grades are a form of academic currency, then grade inflation results in the devaluation of that currency. Grade inflation erodes confidence in the whole system of academic evaluation, devaluing all grades and even the degrees to which they lead" (p. 86).

If awarding high grades unearned through high-quality student work (the proverbial "A for effort") is not a compassionate teaching practice, how might faculty approach grading and point assignments in compassionate ways that remove obstacles to learning? One compassionate practice is to focus on mastery learning and to develop grading practices and classroom policies that foster it. Simply put, mastery learning is achieved when competency criteria for the assignment are met.

In the most traditional form of mastery learning [. . .], students are provided with attempts (as many as are necessary, theoretically) to demonstrate mastery of each learning competency and are then presented with feedback. If mastery is not demonstrated, the feedback guides learning progress and provides specific corrective activities to target the conceptual gaps the student needs to bridge. (Bekki et al., 2012, p. 1)

Mastery learning contrasts with another approach: performance learning.

Teachers who hold a performance orientation will focus on competence-based judgments of student learning, mainly presented as grades, and tend to select easy tasks for students that allow them to obtain a good grade. On the other hand, a learning-oriented teacher focuses on creating greater opportunities for students to learn and improve their understanding. [. . .] In contrast with performance goals that place emphasis on grades, learning-orientated teachers consider grades as less important and rather require students to be persistent and to persevere to achieve their learning success. (Arsyad Arrafii, 2020, p. 481)

Mastery learning is the brainchild of Benjamin Bloom. His work famously challenged the once-standard belief that, in the "normal" curve of a grading system, only a small percentage of students should be able to learn what is being taught. In 1968, Bloom proposed that the achievement distribution should look very different from the normal grading curve. Following much subsequent scholarship and practice prompted by Bloom's theory, Guskey (2010) proposed that when instructors set favorable learning conditions and sufficient time, students can consistently reach a high level of achievement. Then, a mastery learning philosophy encouraged accuracy and rigor in faculty assessment of student work while also allowing students to develop their understanding of concepts through practice. While specific competencies vary according to discipline, pedagogical approaches informed by a mastery learning philosophy can be generalized.

Per Bekki, Dalrymple, and Butler (2012), students attained "higher levels of achievement and had more confidence in the material" (p. 1) when participating in courses delivered with a mastery approach. Bloom's work focused largely on individual student characteristics and how curricula and assessments could accommodate those to enable student success. Recommended strategies included allowing students to learn at their own pace, assigning each student a personal tutor, and supplementing instruction with alternative teaching methods.

STRATEGIES FOR IMPLEMENTING COMPASSIONATE GRADING

An authentic, mastery-based approach to a course requires a complete rethinking of curriculum and assessment. In many online courses, instructors do not have the autonomy to change assignments or develop alternative assessments to fully accommodate students' learning styles and abilities. However, there is a strategy developed by Bloom that might foster mastery learning if incorporated into the grading practices of today's online courses: the inclusion of "correctives" within faculty feedback.

Bloom, Hastings, and Madaus (1971) included correctives in their formative assessments. The term *correctives* denotes "explicit, targeted suggestions of what students must do to correct their learning difficulties and master the desired learning outcomes" (Guskey, 2010, p. 53). Instructors supplement the standard feedback they provide students on assignments by adding correctives. Guskey (2005) describes standard feedback as diagnostic and prescriptive, stating that it reinforces "precisely what students were expected to learn, identifies what was learned well, and describes what needs to be learned better" (p. 6). Per Guskey (2005), feedback paired with correctives provides more significant improvement in learning.

Active Listening

When instructors cannot award points for late work because a final deadline has passed, for example, Meyers et al. (2019) advise that they practice actively listening to their students' frustration or disappointment. *[E]nsuring a student feels understood is an important way to communicate empathy to an individual student, particularly when prioritizing student learning makes it impossible to make an exception to a course policy* (p. 161).

When instructors have a mastery-based perspective, they understand the roles that effective feedback and compassionate teaching practices and policies play. An instructor who applies compassionate teaching principles can be especially precise regarding scores on assignments; this practice is, in fact, necessary to call students' attention to deficiencies in their work that need to be addressed. Instructors can explain to their students exactly how they earn their scores and what to do if they are unhappy with their grades while maintaining high-quality standards of the work they expect from students.

Effective Feedback

Feedback from faculty has been found to influence how students feel about themselves, whether positive or negative, and how they learn (Nicol & Macfarlane-Dick, 2006). Additionally, faculty feedback has a positive impact on learning gains. However, all forms of feedback are not necessarily helpful, so instructors who understand the qualities of effective feedback may have an advantage when it comes to enhancing their students' learning.

Effective feedback is constructive and emotionally sensitive, and it is delivered in a manner designed to avoid causing students shame, dejection, or disappointment (Eraut, 2006). Effective feedback is also helpful, clear, and understandable (Elson et al., 2006). It is described additionally as "prompt, meaningful and give[s] students an opportunity to rethink and rework the errors of their efforts" (Helterbran, 2005, p. 262). Effective feedback "contains a clearly stated goal, evidence about where the student is at the time of the . . . assessment, and a method for the student to reach that goal" (DeWeese, 2011, p. 3). Per Sadler (1989), the necessary conditions for students to benefit from feedback in academic tasks include:

The Students We Have

1. That students understand what good performance is (what goal or standard is being achieved),
2. How their current performance relates to good performance, and
3. How to close the gap between their current performance and good performance ().

Effective feedback allows students to improve their work, thus earning higher grades; it also allows students to understand what qualities may be lacking from their work. Nicole and Macfarlane-Dick (2006) propose, too, that effective feedback "delivers high-quality information to students about their learning; encourages teacher and peer dialogue around learning and encourages positive motivational beliefs and self-esteem" (p. 205).

Feedback should not merely state the strengths and weaknesses of the assignment but should also offer corrective advice in a non-authoritative tone (Lunsford, 1997). Feedback should be constructed as a dialogue between instructor and student rather than solely as a transmission of information (Nicole and Macfarlane-Dick, 2006): "Feedback as dialogue means that the student not only receives initial feedback information but also has the opportunity to engage the teacher in discussion about that feedback" (p. 210). With effective feedback, students gain the knowledge to discuss their grades with their instructor, and they also develop a feeling of empowerment to improve their performance. By providing exemplars of good performance, instructors guide students to understand the marking criteria more thoroughly, especially when instructors accompany the exemplars with meaningful formative feedback (Orsmond et al., 2002). As Nicol and Macfarlane-Dick (2006) explain: "Exemplars are effective because they make explicit what is required, and they define a valid standard against which students can compare their work" (p. 206).

In connection with compassionate teaching practices and a mastery learning approach, a key accompaniment to effective feedback is that faculty offer students opportunities to address the errors of their efforts by, for example, resubmitting assignments in which they received unsatisfactory grades. The effectiveness of feedback can only be measured by permitting students to close the feedback loop—in other words, by responding to the feedback they receive. Per Nicol and Macfarlane-Dick (2006): "In higher education, most students have little opportunity to directly use the feedback they receive to close the performance gap, especially in the case of planned assignments. Invariably they move on to the next assessment task soon after feedback is received" (p. 213).

Effective Feedback in Action

The following example of feedback encompasses strategies described in the paragraphs above. Taken from one of the authors' classes, an assignment prompt read,

Write a professional biography to introduce yourself in a medium such as LinkedIn or other professional websites.

In response to this prompt, one student submitted a personal biography in which he described his childhood and a favorite trip he had taken with his wife. The student's submission did not meet the criteria of assignment, earning a minimal—failing—score. The instructor's response included the following elements of effective feedback:

- **Describing what the student did well:** *Mel [a pseudonym], your paper was interesting to read and, as far as a biography goes, it helped me to know you better and I enjoyed reading about your trip to Germany. How interesting!*
- **Explaining what the student needs to do differently:** *This paper, however, was meant to highlight your professional life, rather than your personal life, which is why you received such a poor grade.*
- **Validating both student's emotions and the importance of mastering this concept:** *But fear not! I would like for you to resubmit your paper because I want you to have a product that you would be able to include in your LinkedIn profile right away. So, let's talk about how to improve on this product.*
- **Reteaching the original concept:** *When you write a professional biography the first thing you need to consider is your audience. Your audience here is potential employers because this is a sort of personal statement to "sell" yourself. Like a personal biography, it will include information about you, but the focus is on what you have done, your education, and your skills and accomplishments. It can also capture and represent your passions, causes, and activities. So, your childhood, for example, should not be a part of it.*
- **Providing "correctives" to help the student understand how to correct their assignment:** *As you rewrite, I want you to think about questions like these:*
  - What is your professional experience?
  - What skills do you possess that would make you an asset to an organization?
  - What experiences have you had that have changed you as a professional or given you an edge over other candidates?
  - What are your best personality traits that would make you a great employee?
  - What is your education?
- **Setting a goal and outlining a clear path toward it:** *Can you resubmit this in 2 days? Is that a reachable goal? If not, let's have a conversation about your schedule and come up with a plan.*

Instructional language may not sufficiently prepare all students for proficient completion of an assignment. Students may misinterpret an instructor's expectations for a multitude of reasons. When this occurs, targeted, honest, and encouraging feedback allows the student to understand how to better achieve the task's learning objective—in this case, to write a professional biography rather than a personal one. Upon receiving such feedback, Mel resubmitted the assignment and wrote a professional biography that met all requirements and expectations, resulting in a much-improved final score. Well-meaning faculty sometimes offer feedback that is not explicit enough for students to grasp. Statements such as "your discussion needs more detail" or "your paragraph does not make sense" do not provide sufficient guidance to inform thorough revision. Operating under the assumption that students' original submissions constitute their best efforts, instructors must then assume that the initial prompt provided inadequate information to support successful completion of the assignment.

While the authors do not advocate that all student work be eligible for resubmission, we stress that allowing students to reattempt an assignment fulfills the idea that learning is mastery and that compassionate teaching can be practiced in online classrooms. A resubmission policy of only those assignments that earn a D or below could limit the number of assignments a faculty member needs to regrade. In the pursuit of true mastery learning, faculty might also consider the resubmission of higher-scoring assignments at their students' request on a case-by-case basis. In essence, compassionate teaching practice

The Students We Have

may support the notion that no assignment is fully summative; instead, all assignments have formative elements within a reasonable time expectation.

Compassionate teaching consists of awarding students the grades they earn, accompanied by plenty of effective feedback and opportunities to revise and resubmit work. Another compassionate teaching practice is greater lenience in late policies. Submitting work on time is a necessary skill that students need to develop. As Meyers et al. (2019) recommend, however, instructors could

> *. . . use their understanding of students when formulating late policies. Submitting work on time is an important skill for students to master before graduation, but students need help to develop that skill. Instructors higher in teacher empathy would provide greater flexibility to students taking introductory level courses than to students taking upper-level courses. In this way, instructors can scaffold students' learning of the skill [. . .] Building flexibility into due dates and explaining the rationale behind policies communicate to students that the instructor is aware of the challenges students face (p. 165).*

As Meyers et al. (2019) explain, "instructors high in teacher empathy can use tokens to communicate they understand the lives of college students, but still set limits on how many second chances students can have" (p. 161). With the understanding that certain compassionate practices can create more work for instructors—allowance of resubmissions and institution of flexible late policies, for example—Meyers et al. (2019) propose a system of tokens. In this system, students receive a certain number of tokens at the beginning of a course that they can exchange for resubmissions or late submissions of assignments without penalty. The instructor decides the number of tokens, which is stated clearly at the beginning of the class. It is a practical way to set boundaries around faculty's time while creating a compassionate atmosphere for the students.

Additionally, instructor feedback should focus on mastery of the learning as outlined in the learning outcomes. College English and composition courses tend to include learning outcomes that promote Standard Academic English (SAE) and academic writing mechanics. Faculty in courses outside of those disciplines should not penalize students for using what MacSwan (2020) labels their "home language" instead of "school language." Yet, in contrast to the 1974 Students' Right to Their Own Language (SRTOL) resolution adopted by the Conference on College Composition and Communication (CCCC), linguistically marginalized students continue to suffer unfair grading practices in academic settings because of their perceived lack of SAE skills (Weaver, 2019).

When faculty focus on message over mechanics, students who speak nonstandard English at home or for whom English is not their first language—who are less proficient in SAE—feel more comfortable communicating in an online classroom and providing their honest understanding of the learning material. MacSwan (2020) warns against the assumption that only academic language effectively discusses issues within the classroom. This perspective of language in the classroom fits within the mastery learning paradigm because it encourages moving "language education beyond an atheoretical product-process orientation and toward one that is socially situated, and which seeks to include rather than exclude diverse language backgrounds in classroom settings" (p. 34). In other words, students will express themselves more freely if they can do so with ease and without fear of penalty, even if that means using their *home language*.

As Eilers (2019) explains, language is "an integral part of identity" (p. 14). Penalizing students for failing to write in SAE may fail to acknowledge—thus dismissing—their identities. Instructors must consider that dialects of English such as AAVE, Appalachian English, and Chicano English have consistent and complex grammar rules of their own and that Standard English is, in fact, just another dialect of the English language—the dialect of academia, as it were. Faculty can reframe students' use of their home dialects' grammar as "wrong," and instead, take a neutral perspective on this choice. A compassionate and inclusive teaching strategy may accommodate grammar and spelling deviations from SAE, so long as they do not obscure meaning. In courses that do not teach academic writing—including the mechanics of SAE—students' use of their home dialects should not constitute a source of unnecessary penalties in grading.

Rubrics can serve to emphasize language as a means of communication of a message, regardless of its SAE accuracy. Instructors can develop rubric criteria for writing and formatting in ways that support this ideology. In keeping with the meaning-first approach, "Format and Writing" sections should not count for more than 8% to 15% of the final point total on a written assignment. Table 1 offers examples of the writing row for a 1000-level course rubric.

Notice that spelling and grammar deviations from SAE are only penalized to the extent that they obscure meaning and detract from clear communication. Instructors who teach marginalized populations cannot afford to assume that nonstandard English is "less communicative, less effective, less professional" than SAE (Inoue, 2021, p.18). The focus on meaning before mechanics creates space for students to comfortably explore concepts and develop ease in the discipline. Like other elements of effective feedback, rubrics can serve as tools for compassionate grading.

Table 1. Writing row of a 1000-level course rubric

Developing	Meets Expectations	Exceeds Expectations
There are multiple spelling, grammar, and/or punctuation deviations from Standard Academic English that affect clear communication with others within the context.	Posts contain few spelling, grammar, and/or punctuation deviations from Standard Academic English. OR these deviations do not affect clear communication within the context.	Any spelling, grammar, and/or punctuation deviations from Standard Academic English are minor and do not affect clear communication within the context.

CONCLUSION

First-generation adult undergraduate students in the United States are choosing to enter online degree programs because of their flexibility. Such programs are available to students regardless of geographic location. Their open-access admissions and asynchronous learning experiences offer opportunities for students to schedule classwork around competing personal and professional priorities. Despite increased accessibility of higher education, it is unclear whether faculty are better prepared to support academic achievement among first-generation students—students who are the first members of their families to attend college. Participation in an undergraduate program in adulthood, particularly as a first-generation college student, requires courage.

First-generation adult undergraduates may doubt their readiness for the demands of academic work. They may feel that their rich life experiences are undervalued by faculty who focus exclusively on completing assignments within specified parameters. Faculty may believe that strict grading policies are the best means to demonstrate rigor and inspire a serious commitment to schoolwork among students. Such beliefs might be based on experiences instructors had as students, experiences on which they rely for the schema that informs their teaching practices.

The ease and comfort of such instructors within the academic world may obscure a clear sense of how their first-generation students could be feeling. Left alone, this situation may enable misunderstanding and alienation among instructors and their first-generation adult online students. The combination of self-doubt on the part of students and rigidity among faculty may, unfortunately, set the scene for students' premature departure from college. This chapter has examined the potential of compassionate grading to bolster academic growth in first-generation adults attending open-access online undergraduate programs.

As an expression of active caring, compassionate grading—including the use of tools like active listening, effective feedback, and equitable rubric design—can help build first-generation students' confidence in their academic strengths. Compassionate grading may also enable the creation of a safe, nurturing space for academic development and creativity. If adopted broadly across entire academic programs, compassionate grading may even support student retention through successful completion of bachelor's degrees.

REFERENCES

Arsyad Arrafii, M. (2020). Grades and grade inflation: Exploring teachers' grading practices in Indonesian EFL secondary school classrooms. *Pedagogy, Culture & Society, 28*(3), 477–499. doi:10.1080/14681366.2019.1663246

Bekki, J. M., Dalrymple, O., & Butler, C. S. (2012, October 3–6). *A mastery-based learning approach for undergraduate engineering programs* [Conference publication]. 2012 Frontiers in Education Conference Proceedings, Seattle, WA, United States. 10.1109/FIE.2012.6462253

Bloom, B. S. (1968). Learning for mastery. Instruction and curriculum. Regional Education Laboratory for the Carolinas and Virginia, topical papers and reprints, number 1. *Evaluation Comment, 1*(2). https://programs.honolulu.hawaii.edu/intranet/sites/programs.honolulu.hawaii.edu.intranet/files/upstf-student-success-bloom-1968.pdf

Bloom, B. S., Hastings, J. T., & Madaus, G. (1971). *Handbook on formative and summative evaluation of student learning.* McGraw-Hill.

Chowdhury, F. (2018). Grade inflation: Causes, consequences and cure. *Journal of Education and Learning, 7*(6), 86–92. doi:10.5539/jel.v7n6p86

Crenshaw, K. (1989). Demarginalizing the intersection of race and sex: A Black feminist critique of antidiscrimination doctrine, feminist theory and antiracist politics. *University of Chicago Legal Forum, 1989*(1), 8. https://chicagounbound.uchicago.edu/uclf/vol1989/iss1/8

Culver, S. (2010). Course grades, quality of student engagement, and students' evaluation of instructor. *International Journal on Teaching and Learning in Higher Education, 22*(3), 331–336. https://files.eric.ed.gov/fulltext/EJ938568.pdf

Cushman, T. (2003). Who best to tame grade inflation? *Academic Questions, 16*(4), 48–56. doi:10.100712129-003-1063-1

DeWeese, S. V., & Randolph, J. J. (2011, February 14). *Effective use of correctives in masterly learning* [Paper presentation]. Association of Teacher Educators National Conference, Orlando, FL, United States. https://files.eric.ed.gov/fulltext/ED523991.pdf

Eilers, A. M. (2019). *Incorporating African American vernacular English in education: Fostering linguistic diversity within Mississippi K-12 classrooms* [Honors thesis, University of Mississippi]. eGrove. https://egrove.olemiss.edu/hon_thesis/1025/

Elson, R. J., Gupta, S., & Krispin, J. (2018). Students' perceptions of instructor interaction, feedback, and course effectiveness in a large class environment. *Journal of Instructional Pedagogies, 20.* https://files.eric.ed.gov/fulltext/EJ1178738.pdf

Eraut, M. (2006). Feedback. *Learning in Health and Social Care, 5*(3), 111–118. doi:10.1111/j.1473-6861.2006.00129.x

Finefter-Rosenbluh, I., & Levinson, M. (2015). What is wrong with grade inflation (if anything)? *Philosophical Inquiry in Education, 23*(1), 3–21. doi:10.7202/1070362ar

Garrison, D. R., Anderson, T., & Archer, W. (1999). Critical inquiry in a text-based environment: Computer conferencing in higher education. *The Internet and Higher Education, 2*(2–3), 87–105. doi:10.1016/S1096-7516(00)00016-6

Gershenson, S. (2020). *Great expectations: The impact of rigorous grading practices on student achievement.* Thomas B. Fordham Institute. https://fordhaminstitute.org/national/research/great-expectations-impact-rigorous-grading-practices-student-achievement

Greater Good Science Center. (n.d.). What is compassion? *Greater Good Magazine.* https://greatergood.berkeley.edu/topic/compassion/definition#what-is-compassion

Guskey, T. R. (2005, April 11–15). *Formative classroom assessment and Benjamin S. Bloom: Theory, research, and implications* [Paper presentation]. Annual Meeting of the American Educational Research Association, Montreal, Canada. https://files.eric.ed.gov/fulltext/ED490412.pdf

Guskey, T. R. (2010). Lessons of mastery learning. *Educational Leadership, 68*(2), 52–57. https://www.researchgate.net/publication/236273526_Lessons_of_Mastery_Learning

Helterbran, V. R. (2005). Lifelong or school-long learning: A daily choice. *The Clearing House: A Journal of Educational Strategies, Issues and Ideas, 78*(6), 261–263. doi:10.3200/TCHS.78.6.261-264

Inoue, A. B. (2021). *Above the well: An antiracist literacy argument from a boy of color.* The WAC Clearinghouse & Utah State University Press. doi:10.37514/PER-B.2021.1244

International, R. T. I. (2019). *First-generation college students: Demographic characteristics and postsecondary enrollment.* NASPA. https://firstgen.naspa.org/files/dmfile/FactSheet-01.pdf

Lunsford, R. F. (1997). When less is more: Principles for responding in the disciplines. *New Directions for Teaching and Learning, 1997*(69), 91–104. doi:10.1002/tl.6908

MacSwan, J. (2020). Academic English as standard language ideology: A renewed research agenda for asset-based language education. *Language Teaching Research, 24*(1), 28–36. doi:10.1177/1362168818777540

Meyers, S., Rowell, K., Wells, M., & Smith, B. C. (2019). Teacher empathy: A model of empathy for teaching for student success. *College Teaching*, *67*(3), 160–168. doi:10.1080/87567555.2019.1579699

Nicol, D., & Macfarlane-Dick, D. (2006). Formative assessment and self-regulated learning: A model and seven principles of good feedback practice. *Studies in Higher Education*, *31*(2), 199–218. doi:10.1080/03075070600572090

Nunberg, G., & Newman, E. (2011). *The American heritage dictionary of the English language* (5th ed.). Houghton Mifflin Harcourt. https://ahdictionary.com/word/search.html?q=compassion

Orsmond, P., Merry, S., & Reiling, K. (2002). The use of exemplars and formative feedback when using student derived marking criteria in peer and self-assessment. *Assessment & Evaluation in Higher Education*, *27*(4), 309–323. doi:10.1080/0260293022000001337

Sadler, D. R. (1989). Formative assessment and the design of instructional systems. *Instructional Science*, *18*(2), 119–144. doi:10.1007/BF00117714

Seay, S. (2006). Strategies for success: Improving the academic performance of low-income adult and first-generation students in online General Education Courses. *The Journal of Continuing Higher Education*, *54*(3), 22–35. doi:10.1080/07377366.2006.10401222

Sinclair, S., Beamer, K., Hack, T. F., McClement, S., Bouchal, S. R., Chochinov, H. M., & Hagen, N. A. (2017). Sympathy, empathy, and compassion: A grounded theory study of palliative care patients' understandings, experiences, and preferences. *Palliative Medicine*, *31*(5), 437–447. doi:10.1177/0269216316663499 PMID:27535319

Smith, D. L., Cook, P., & Buskist, W. (2011). An experimental analysis of the relation between assigned grades and instructor evaluations. *Teaching of Psychology*, *38*(4), 225–228. doi:10.1177/0098628311421317

Walden University. (2020). *Executive summary (DATA)*. https://www.waldenu.edu/about/data/summary

Weaver, M. M. (2019). "I still think there's a need for proper, academic, Standard English": Examining a teacher's negotiation of multiple language ideologies. *Linguistics and Education*, *49*, 41–51. doi:10.1016/j.linged.2018.12.005

White, K. A., & Ruth-Sahd, L. A. (2020). Compassionate teaching strategies amid the COVID-19 pandemic. *Nurse Educator*, *45*(6), 294–295. doi:10.1097/NNE.0000000000000901 PMID:32658092

ADDITIONAL READING

Johnston, J., Killion, J., & Oomen, J. (2005). Student satisfaction in the virtual classroom. *The Internet Journal of Allied Health Sciences and Practice*, *3*(2), 1–7.

Chapter 9
The SPII–Hub and Other Initiatives to Advance Online Engagement

Rebecca L. Jobe
Walden University, USA

Katherine Strang
Adtalem Global Education, USA

ABSTRACT

This chapter reviews some of the essential ingredients in creating a post-secondary online learning environment that is diverse, inclusive, and promotes connection and engagement across the program lifecycle. Various initiatives to build student engagement and connection are discussed. The authors also argue that while most of the attention on engagement in the educational setting focuses on student engagement, equal consideration must be given to faculty and staff engagement to create the optimal environment.

A diverse mix of voices leads to better discussions, decisions, and outcomes for everyone. —Sundar Pichai, CEO of Alphabet Inc.

INTRODUCTION

The decision to obtain a higher education degree requires many sacrifices. In the long-term view, a student's decision to pursue a degree is often made to increase one's financial position, career opportunities, and personal and family well-being; however, in the short-term, students often must sacrifice in these same areas. This multiyear commitment is, therefore, weighed heavily, and institutions must not only prepare students with support resources to be successful, they must also provide an inclusive and welcoming learning environment that lays the foundation for success and promotes the skills and abilities needed to work in a diverse workforce.

DOI: 10.4018/978-1-6684-5146-5.ch009

The SPII-Hub and Other Initiatives to Advance Online Engagement

Engagement in the online environment is critical to success, and feelings of isolation are often manifested in disconnection in the classroom and other university spaces. Engagement is a component of inclusiveness; if students are not able or willing to interact through the curriculum, clubs, committees, or policy making within the university, key perspectives and voices are missing. Likewise, if faculty and staff lack opportunity to engage within the organization, diverse viewpoints risk being left out. Miller (2021) asserts that:

Inclusion elicits the best effort and broadest perspectives—intellectual, cultural, experiential—of all involved, and elevates the performance of an organization by bringing the diversity inherent in its members to bear.

As such, neither an organization nor the members within it can reach their fullest potential unless they are inclusive, and inclusivity is not enough; they must also be engaging. This chapter reviews some of the essential ingredients in creating a post-secondary online learning environment that is diverse, inclusive, and promotes connection and engagement across the program lifecycle.

BACKGROUND

Whether in a traditional campus-based program or an online platform, students' perceptions of a university and their place in it begin forming long before they step into their first class. Every touch point and experience leading up to that start lays the foundation for a student's identity with the institution, commitment to achieving their goals, and future success in the program. Thus, universities must prioritize the onboarding process by creating opportunities for students to learn about the institution, understand its mission, see how they fit within it and how their goals can be realized, and connect with others (peers, faculty, and staff) sharing in their journey.

Walden's First-Year Student Progress (FYSP) strategic plan (see Figure 1; Jobe et al., 2016) casts a brighter light upon the onboarding experience of new students preparing to start their programs. Through this plan and the methodology developed to identify gaps in the student experience and address those gaps in an empirical way, multiple initiatives were launched (many of which were aimed at the onboarding stage, prior to the first course). These initiatives focused specifically on increasing connectedness, preparedness, and setting expectations.

Students should be provided with an orientation experience prior to starting their coursework not only to help them understand what is expected and where they can find support if they need it, but to instill a sense of confidence that they have made the right choice and can be successful in the online environment and their field of study (Jobe et al., 2018). Ferrer et al. (2022) found that student attitude to online learning was an important factor in motivation and engagement and that "both individual- and institutional-level contributions are required to cultivate positive experiences for students within online learning environments and usage of online learning tools in order to improve their attitude to online learning" (p. 335). Furthermore, studies suggest that students who complete a timely, supportive, and informative online orientation are better prepared to meet expectations and more likely to persist in their coursework and remain in their program of study (Mensch, 2017; Robichaud, 2016; Stoebe, 2020).

Figure 1. First-Year Student Progress (FYSP) methodology
Note. Image Credit: Jose Henriquez, Walden University.

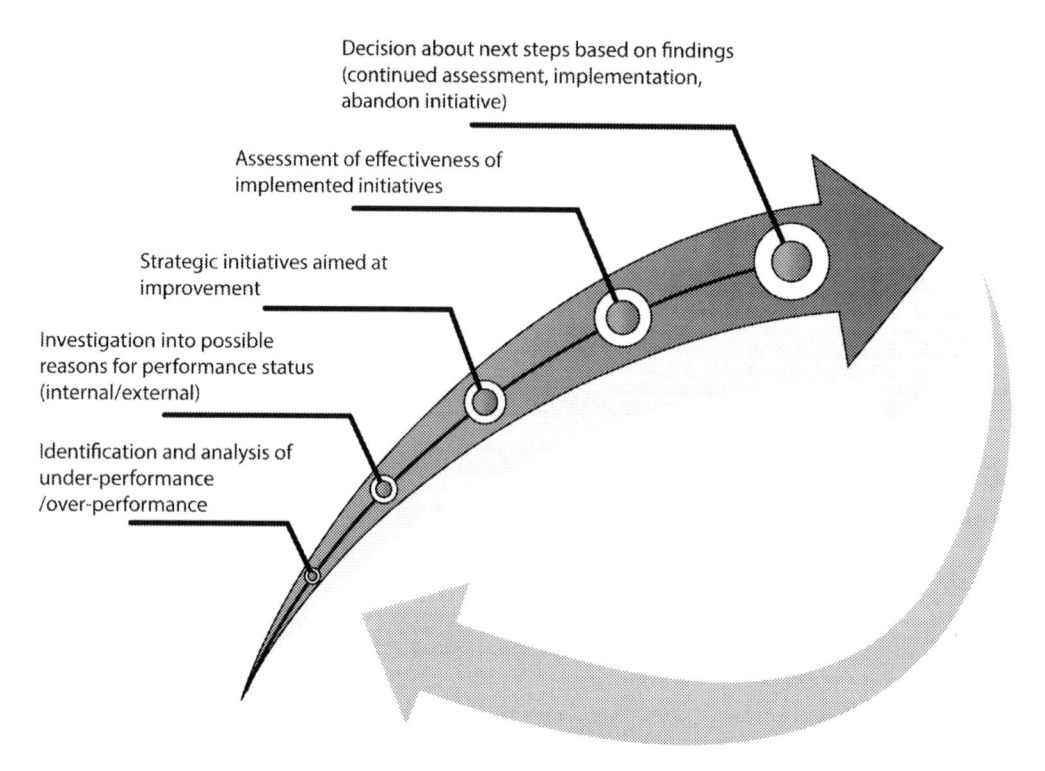

Decision about next steps based on findings (continued assessment, implementation, abandon initiative)

Assessment of effectiveness of implemented initiatives

Strategic initiatives aimed at improvement

Investigation into possible reasons for performance status (internal/external)

Identification and analysis of under-performance /over-performance

Walden's student readiness orientation was recently updated to focus not only on readiness, but on creating a welcoming and supportive environment. The Walden Orientation and Welcome (WOW) includes videos from university leadership and alumni, who welcome students into the Walden community and convey the message that students have the support they need to be successful (see Figure 2). Degree- and program-specific versions of the WOW are customized for students. For example, a doctoral student will learn about residency experiences and a candidate in a licensure program can learn about their specific licensing requirements.

A Pulse Check quiz in the WOW asks students about their level of comfort and confidence related to the online learning environment, university support resources (library, Writing Center, financial aid, etc.), specific details about their degree program, and other relevant information. If students indicate discomfort or lack of confidence in a particular area, the quiz feedback links them to an interactive multimedia resource where they can learn more in an engaging way. Data from the Pulse Checks (see Figure 3) can also indicate to university leadership where students need more support and guidance.

Other initiatives within the Walden FYSP strategic plan have included the development of a peer mentoring model. New students are paired with advanced students who can provide tips for success, direct experience about the program, and answers to questions they may have as they learn to navigate the institution. The peer mentoring model was shown to improve retention, and new students were highly satisfied with the resource. Because students often feel anxiety about the next course in their program, especially during their first year, Course Preview videos were created to make students aware of the supports available to them and some of the tools that would help them be successful. According

The SPII-Hub and Other Initiatives to Advance Online Engagement

to Jobe et al., 2018, "overall retention and enrollment into the targeted, desired courses were better in the course preview group" (p. 118). Due to the success of the Course Previews, the idea was extended to other areas of programs where Course Jumpstarts were provided as synchronous virtual events that were recorded for those who opted to watch them "on demand." These events featured course faculty, who offer a look ahead and highlight interesting topics and learning opportunities. Quantitative findings showed that students who attended the jumpstart either live or on demand felt much more prepared for their upcoming course than those who did not attend.

Figure 2. Walden Orientation and Welcome (WOW) home page
Note. Image credit: Walden University.

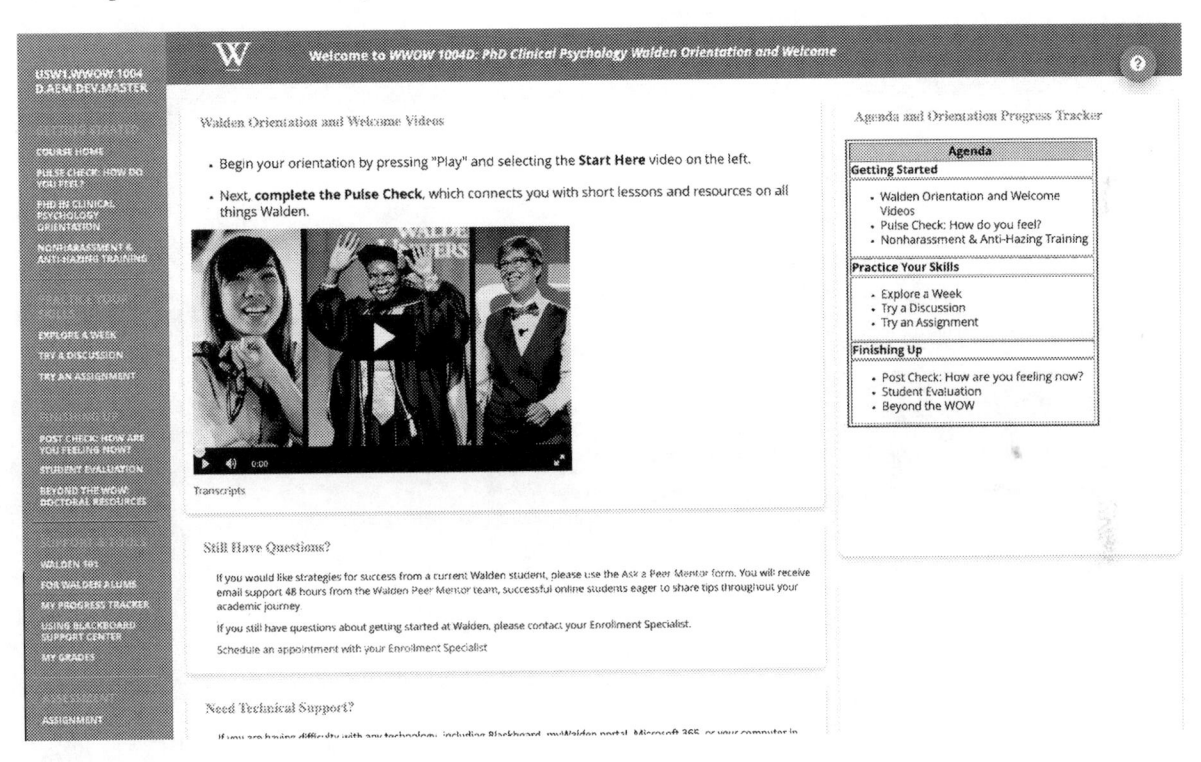

Students were asked to share their perceptions of the jumpstart (see Figure 4). Qualitative responses also supported the notion that jumpstarts better prepared students by setting expectations and building confidence for the course ahead. Below is a sample of those responses.

- "The best aspect is outlining the task by the week with requirements and expectations. I am less nervous about starting, as I have not been in an English classroom setting in 20+ years."
- "In my opinion, the jumpstart was thorough and provided a sense of relief to know how the class will be formatted and what to expect as a student. This is a positive approach to prepare students for the class."
- "This is my 5th course at [institution] and I am really nervous. The professor made me feel like I can do well in this course. I work really hard and try my best to do my work with a spirit of excel-

lence. This jumpstart took the edge off and I will do my very best to follow all that was advised. Thank You!!"
- "The best aspect of the course jumpstart was the examples given of what we will cover, the way the week to week will run, and the questions and answers at the end."
- "I feel better prepared and like to know my expectations before starting."

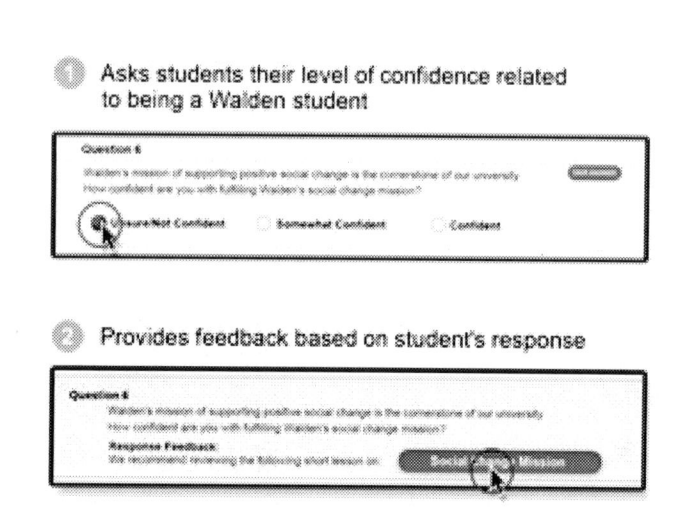

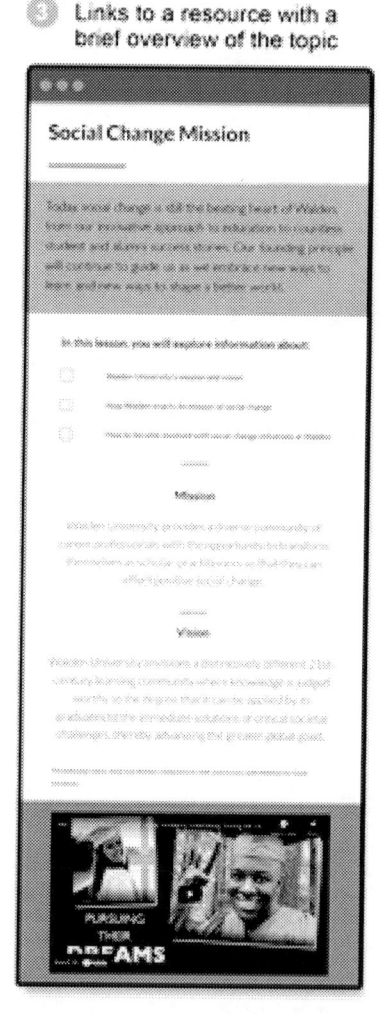

Figure 3. Sample Walden pulse check question with feedback
Note. Image credit: Jose Henriquez, Walden University.

Figure 4. Course jumpstart survey responses
Note. Image credit: Jose Henriquez, Walden University.

	Live	On Demand	Non-Attendee	Total
N	41	55	94	190
Mean	4.46a	4.13b	3.78c	4.03
Std.	0.67	0.90	1.13	1.02

a and c and b and c significantly different at p<.05; a and b were not significantly different

ENGAGING STUDNETS IN THE CLASSROOM

Just as inclusive and engaging practices should be used to help students persist from course to course, those same approaches should remain a priority within the online classroom. Recognizing and addressing the unique challenges of the online learning environment is an important first step. *Unlike* in campus-based programs, the online student does not *walk* into the first day of class, make eye contact with his/her peers, choose a seat that is comfortable for engaging and learning, or see and hear the professor. One could argue that the online classroom is a completely distinct environment and experience, one that is more different than it is similar to a campus classroom and, thus, requires particular characteristics to ensure effective engagement. According to Ferrer et al. (2022), "Many institutions have failed to understand the unique requirements of online education delivery in contrast to the traditional on-campus model as they have transitioned from one to the other, and have equated the two in terms of how it is delivered and the time and staff required to do so effectively" (p. 333).

With all the opportunities to connect with and engage students during their programs, certainly the most critical space is inside the classroom. Creating dynamic, interactive courses that challenge students, promote critical thinking, and advance their knowledge can take many forms, depending on the individual students and the learning context. When students feel connected to a community of learners (peer-to-peer and student-to-instructor) and can align their learning to real-world problems and situations they tend to be more satisfied with their experience and successful in their learning (Kara, 2019; Ornelles, 2019). This connection to one another and the content occurs when there is a focus on "establishing a learning climate that values trust, support, collaboration, and respect, as well as aligning course content with learners' needs" (Ornelles, 2019, p. 549). Discussion board prompts can be designed to encourage students to share their unique perspectives related to course content, which provides a forum for all students to be exposed to and consider diverse perspectives. It is also an opportunity to reinforce appropriate ways to interact with one another in an online environment by providing guidelines for engagement and even requiring students to indicate their agreement to abide by the criteria prior to opening the discussion forum.

Synchronous Discussions

The asynchronous nature of online education allows students the flexibility to complete their assignments when and where it is convenient for them. For that reason, the discussion board is not always an entirely dynamic interchange of ideas because people post at different times and responses may lag between postings. The use of synchronous discussions can provide a welcome change. Based on some positive "live" virtual meetings in a principal licensure program, the program director and faculty decided to try offering several synchronous discussions throughout a course that students had the option of attending live or viewing the recordings and responding afterward. All students who responded to the survey were either "extremely satisfied" or "satisfied" with the synchronous discussion and all would like to participate in synchronous discussions in each course (see Figure 5 below).

Figure 5. Satisfaction survey responses for synchronous discussion experience
Note. Image credit: Ness, 2020.

Q3 Please rate your satisfaction with the synchronous discussion call:

#	Answer	%	Count
1	Extremely Satisfied	68.8%	11
2	Satisfied	31.2%	5
3	Neutral	0.00%	0
4	Dissatisfied	0.00%	0
5	Extremely Dissatisfied	0.00%	0
	Total	100%	16

Q4 Would you like to participate in synchronous discussions in each course?

#	Answer	%
1	Yes	100%
2	No	0.0%
	Total	100%

Students were asked, "What went well or what did you like about the synchronous discussion call(s)?" Some of their responses included the following:

- "It was good to connect with everyone and to see them. Helped to form a sense of community."
- "I enjoyed sharing my thoughts with others and them sharing with me."
- "I really enjoy being able to hear and see the enthusiasm."
- "Connections and collaboration"

- "It was great to connect with classmates who are going through the program and really develop an understanding of their path, knowledge, and experiences. I felt that I got FAR more out of the synchronous discussions than I do discussion posts."
- "I enjoyed the opportunity to hear and see the level of excitement and passion for education in the faces of my peers. It was also a pleasure to engage in scholarly conversation with peers and to witness how closely professional goals and personal ethics intertwined."
- "I like the interaction. It added relationships and personality to those you are in the class with. You get to understand each person and who they are."
- "I thoroughly enjoy the personalization that synchronous discussions bring to the class. I am the type of learner that prefers to be hands on and face to face. When I have a question or a comment, I like to address it in real time, to real faces."

In addition to connecting with the instructor and colleagues in various types of discussions and forums, offering multiple ways for students to engage with content and to demonstrate learning is an inclusive approach that honors each individual student's strengths. For example, students may be provided the option to demonstrate their learning by creating a video or audio segment rather than being required to submit a written response for every assignment. *(Please see Chapter 5 for a more detailed discussion of strategies for designing an inclusive online classroom.)*

Engaging Students Outside the Classroom

While higher education students' primary focus should be the program of study, the college experience encompasses a lot more than just attending classes. Creating space for students to enhance critical-thinking skills and social dynamics is important to the overall development needed to advance in the workplace. Of course, campus-based institutions have numerous ways to engage and connect students outside the classroom, from football games and trivia nights to Greek life and social clubs. Even the layout of a campus can promote relationships and social connection as shown in Figure 6. Creating engaging spaces outside the classroom are vital to student life, not only for a positive college experience but also to increase student success (Fish et al., 2016).

This highlights a key challenge for online institutions who do not have the benefit of a physical location with these additional social spaces. With no Saturday football game and no campus quad wherein to gather, online universities must find other creative ways to bring their students together and build connection within their community. For example, Walden University has created Facebook groups and online clubs (e.g., academic, cultural, hobby and interest-area clubs) to strengthen students' identity with the institution and their peer group. Diversity, equity, and inclusion–specific student organizations that the university has established—such as the Multicultural and International Student Club, Student Veterans Association, and Walden Women in Technology to name a few—further aid connectedness, retention, and a positive student experience. While creating opportunities to connect may be a greater challenge for online institutions, there is an added benefit. Given the digital nature of the "campus environment," data about where students are engaging (or not) is more readily available and can be used to help university leadership and faculty be more deliberatively inclusive and welcoming. Pacansky-Brock et al. (2020) use the term "humanizing strategies" to characterize how the online environment can take advantage of "welcoming visuals and warm asynchronous communications to establish positive first impressions, trust between the instructor and students, and a culture of care in the online environment" (p. 2).

Figure 6. Students connect and engage in a traditional campus environment
Note. Image credit: Svyatoslav Lypynskyy/Adobe Stock.

Keeping Online Students Engaged "Outside the Walls" of the University

Online institutions face additional challenges in keeping students connected as compared to their campus-based counterparts. As such, engagement is a key ingredient not only within the "walls" of the institution, but also in the interactions outside the institution that may ultimately impact persistence and academic success. The world has become very distracting, with people being pulled in many directions. Institutions are, therefore, further challenged by the competing priorities and cognitive overload that encompasses their students and threatens successful completion of their degree programs. Use of social media has become a primary activity of daily life. In 2016, Pew Research Center statistics showed that more than 90% of adults aged 18–49 used one or more social media sites within the last year. Facebook, Twitter, Instagram, Pinterest, Snapchat, and other social media platforms have become not only commonplace in our society but are now a major avenue for socializing, information gathering, political discourse, and other forms of social interaction. Additionally, research has shown that social media can have contrasting effects on student success; it can be utilized in ways to enhance the academic experience, or it can be disruptive to learning (Zachos et al., 2018).

Given the high usage of social media, Walden University recognized the fact that students are spending a great deal of time on social media sites (and, therefore, outside of Walden). Thus, the question becomes: How does the institution continue to connect with students while they are using these platforms and how do you keep students focused on their educational goals? One strategy that Walden employed involved teaming up with a company, Motimatic™, to *nudge* thoughts and behaviors that helped keep students on track. For example, a student may peruse Facebook for an hour. But in the margins of the

The SPII-Hub and Other Initiatives to Advance Online Engagement

site, they see inspirational messages about the power of education or practical tips about contacting the Writing Center for help with organizing a paper. These targeted messages replaced advertisements that are typically seen when browsing the site. Therefore, even though the student is not within the campus community at that time, they are still receiving important messages about their academic pursuits and reminders about their educational goals. This strategy resulted in an increase in early-term retention, and that finding was even larger for students who were identified as "at risk" based on current grade in their course.

The Student Progress Insights and Innovation (SPII) Hub

As evidenced in the previous sections, Walden University has a long history of research and thought leadership in student progress and retention. For more than a decade, Walden has prioritized identifying barriers to student success and developing initiatives to address those challenges (Jobe et al., 2016). Similarly, Walden strives to find innovative solutions to improve student learning and continuously offer an engaging and inspiring student experience. While most of the attention on engagement in the educational setting focuses on *student engagement*, equal consideration must be given to *faculty and staff engagement* to create the optimal environment. The idea of building an internal space to communicate best practices and cutting-edge research to promote positive student outcomes was the culmination of Walden's participation in the Higher Learning Commission's Persistence and Completion Academy. A parallel effort to build a platform in which faculty and staff could collaborate and innovate resulted in a combined effort to develop the Student Progress Insights and Innovation (SPII) Hub.

The SPII Hub was created to capture the initiatives, research, and learnings across the university related to student engagement and persistence. It includes three main sections: Find Research, Contribute Research, and Collaborate & Innovate (see Figure 7 below). Find Research is a knowledge base for presentations, articles, white papers, and other resources related to student progress and includes internal and external resources designed for easy access with multiple parameters for filtering a search. This area provides a historical record of internal findings and insights gained from pilots and initiatives as well as external research that supports the approaches, strategies, or principles presented. Contribute Research is a place for Walden colleagues to contribute white papers, presentations, initiatives, published research, and other items using a submission form. Once the resource is submitted, the content is vetted and curated before becoming part of the collection. Finally, Collaborate & Innovate is an evolving community forum to innovate, ideate, and collaborate around student progress efforts. The interactive platform was designed to "democratize" innovation where anyone can share an idea, "like" a post, start a discussion, or conduct a poll.

As part of Walden's social change mission and recent focus on inclusive teaching and learning, the Collaborate & Innovate area became a critical tool for bringing faculty and staff together around common challenges in the online classroom related to creating a sense of belonging and an inclusive teaching and learning environment (see Figures 8 and 9).

Challenge questions that faculty and staff were invited to address included the following:

- What does "inclusive" teaching and learning mean for you at Walden?
- What do you do to promote inclusion in your classes?
- Tell your story when you felt included.
- How to handle "hot" conversations while making all participants feel heard?

- How would you coach this colleague? (case study)
- "What form transforms?" Share your story about a transformation you've seen in your class.

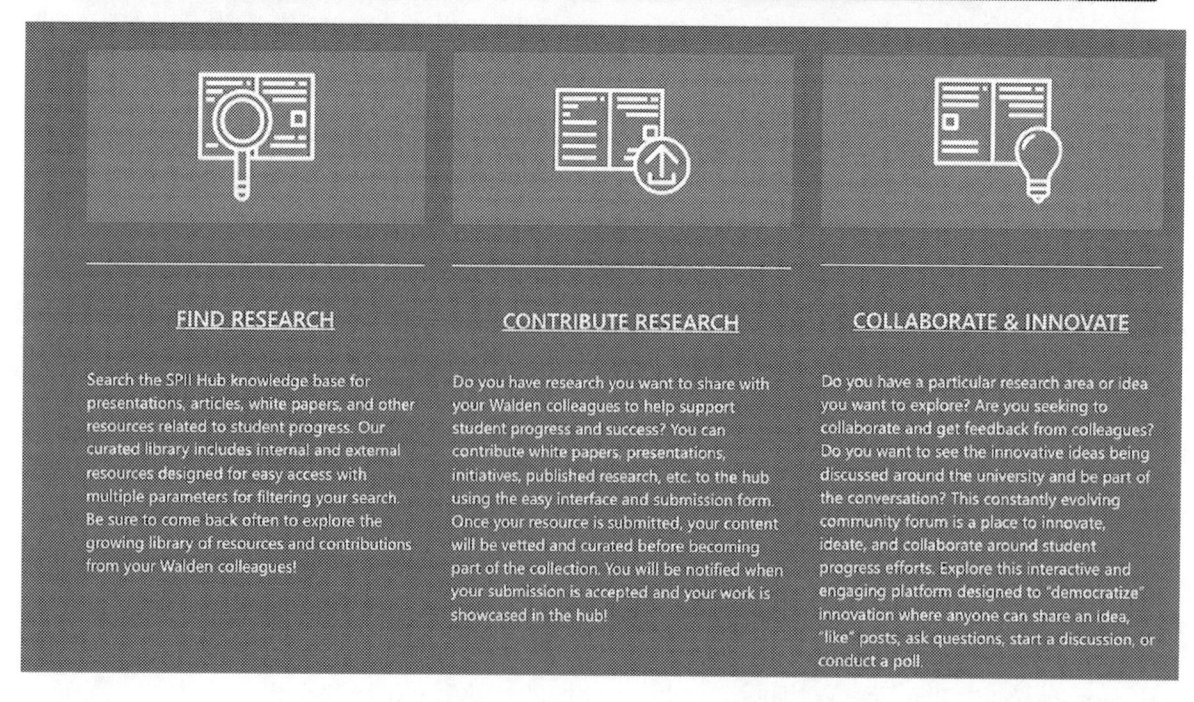

Figure 7. SPII Hub home page showing platform architecture
Note. Image credit: Walden University.

Figure 8. 'Collaborate & Innovate' discussion prompt
Note. Image credit: Walden University.

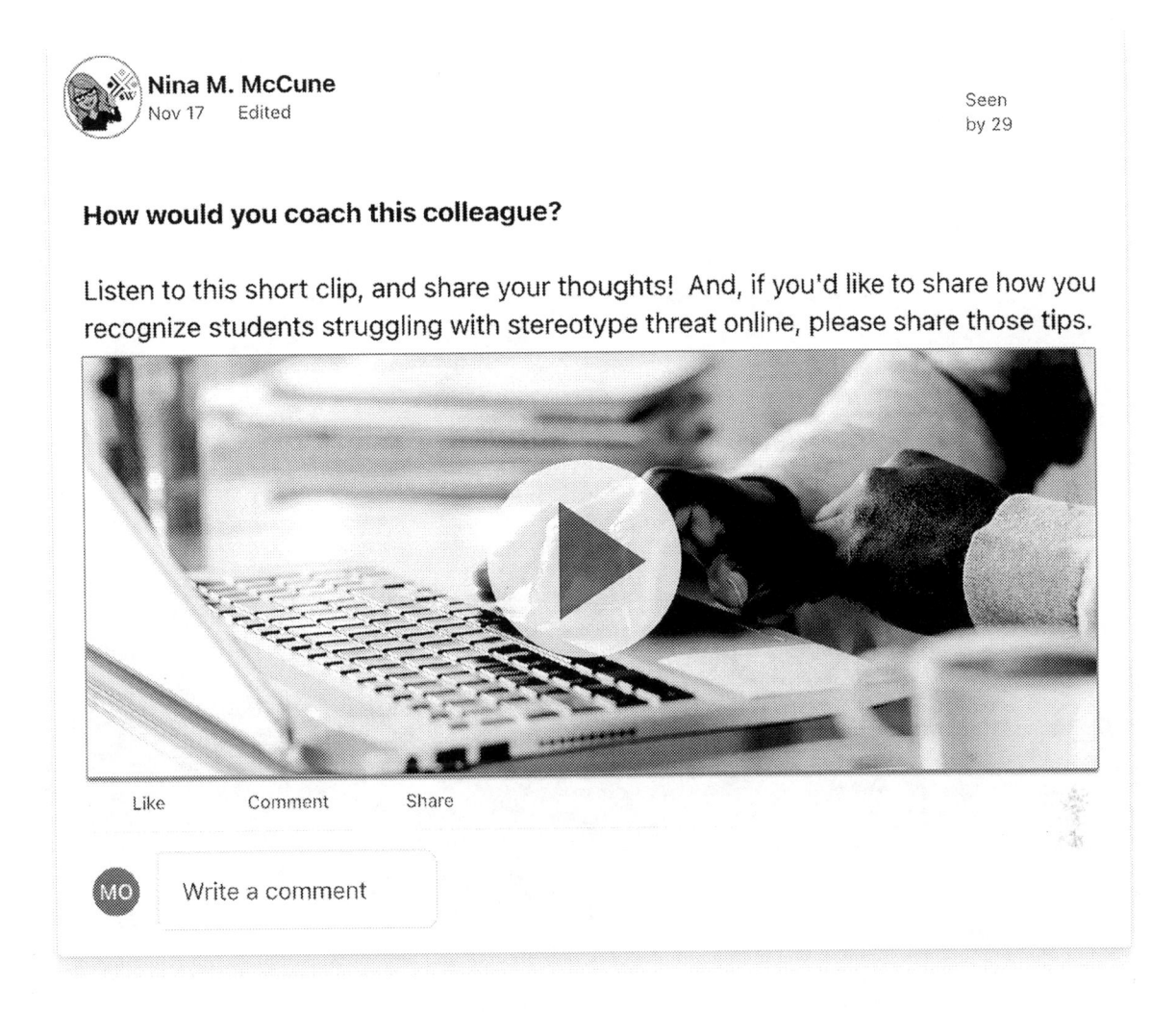

CONCLUSION

Holistic Engagement

Above all, meeting students "where they are" and providing the support they need to engage with the curriculum and the university to achieve their goals should be a top priority. As technology advances and more tools become available to know students better and anticipate their needs, educators will be more prepared to address expected and unexpected challenges in a student's learning journey. In addition, creating a space like the SPII Hub can provide an environment in which faculty and staff across the university share effective practices to promote student engagement and success, add to the collective thought leadership around important issues like inclusive teaching and learning, and innovate to address issues and challenges in a community forum.

Figure 9. Excerpt of SPII Hub collaborative discussion among Walden faculty
Note. Image credit: Walden University.

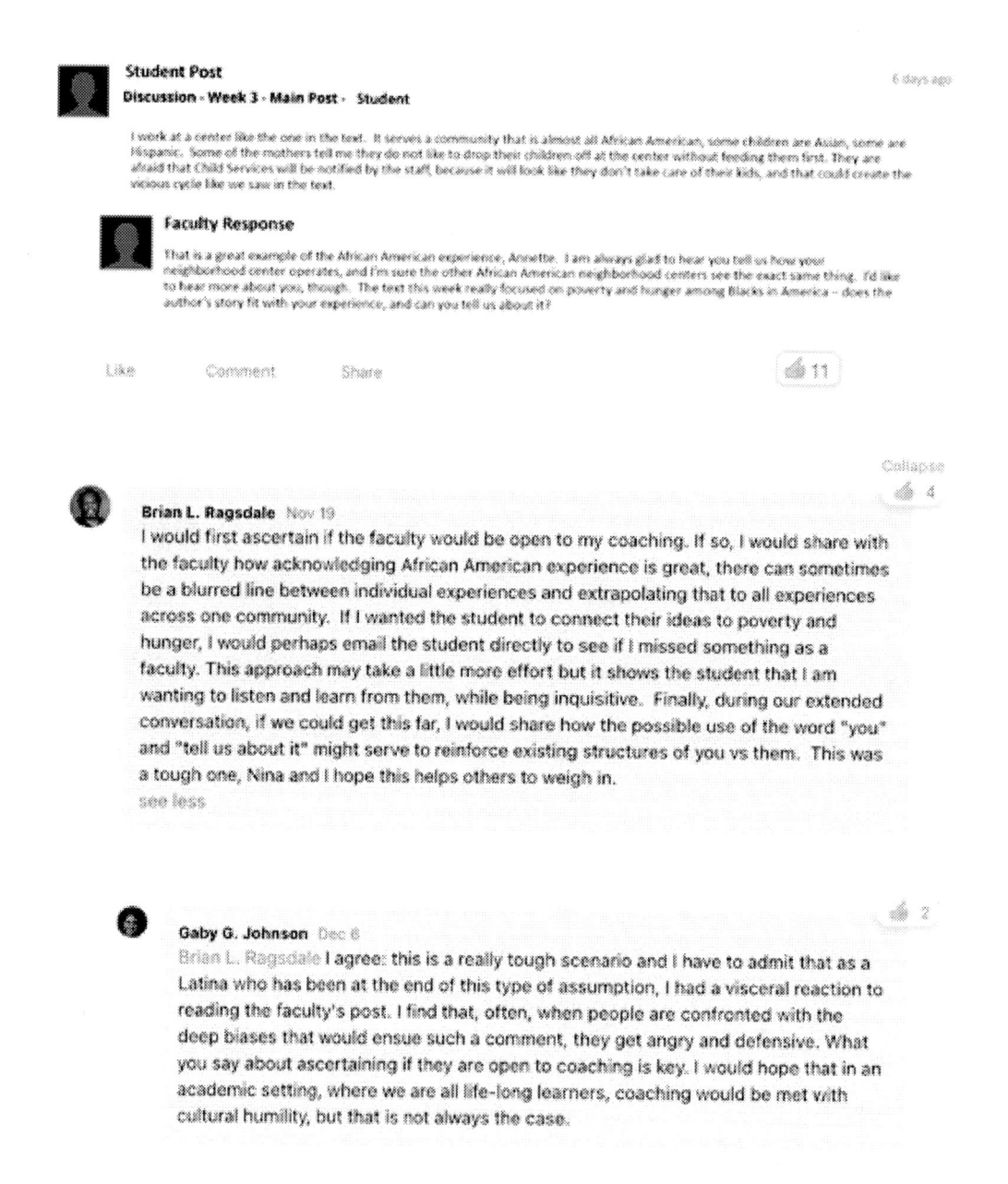

As discussed in this chapter, inclusivity must be a core thread within the tapestry of university policy, processes, and experience. From the first contact a prospective student has with the institution through graduation (and beyond), and among the faculty and staff as they work together to deliver an exceptional educational experience, engagement is key to fostering a fully inclusive environment.

REFERENCES

Ferrer, J., Ringer, A., Saville, K., Parris, M. A., & Kashi, K. (2022). Student' motivation and engagement in higher education: The importance of attitude to online learning. *Higher Education*, *83*(2), 317–338. doi:10.100710734-020-00657-5

Fish, M. C., Gefen, D. R., Kaczetow, W., Winograd, G., & Futtersak-Goldberg, R. (2016). Development and validation of the college campus environment scale (CCES): Promoting positive college experiences. *Innovative Higher Education*, *41*(2), 153–165. doi:10.100710755-015-9337-4

Jobe, B. (2016). The first year: A cultural shift towards improving student progress. *Higher Learning Research Communications*, *6*(1), 10–20. doi:10.18870/hlrc.v6i1.305

Jobe, R. L., Lenio, J., & Saunders, J. (2018). The first year: Bridging content and experience for online adult learners. *The Journal of Continuing Higher Education*, *66*(2), 115–121. doi:10.1080/07377363.2018.1469074

Kara, M., Erdoğdu, F., Kokoc, M., & Cagiltay, K. (2019). Challenges faced by adult learners in online distance education: A literature review. *Open Praxis*, *11*(1), 5–22. doi:10.5944/openpraxis.11.1.929

Mensch, S. (2017). Improving distance education through student online orientation classes. *Global Education Journal*, *2017*(1), 1–6. http://www.aabri.com/OC09manuscripts/OC09092.pdf

Ness, S. (2020, October). *Synchronous discussions in a principal licensure program* [Unpublished raw data]. Walden University, The Richard W. Riley College of Education and Leadership.

Ornelles, C., Ray, A. B., & Wells, J. C. (2019). Designing online courses in teacher education to enhance adult learner engagement. *International Journal on Teaching and Learning in Higher Education*, *31*(3), 547–557.

Pacansky-Brock, M., Smedshammer, M., & Vincent-Layton, K. (2020). Humanizing online teaching to equitize higher education. *Current Issues in Education (Tempe, Ariz.)*, *21*(2), 1–21.

Pew Research Center. (2017) *Demographics of social media usage and adoption in the United States*. https://fs.wp.odu.edu/dchapman/2017/02/14/demographics-of-social-media-users-and-adoption-in-the-united-states-pew-research-center/

Robichaud, W. (2016). Orientation programs to increase retention in online community college courses. *Distance Learning*, *13*(2), 57–64.

Stoebe, A. (2020). The effect of new student orientations on the retention of online students. *Online Journal of Distance Learning Administration*, *23*(2), 1–9.

Zachos, G., Paraskevopoulou-Kollia, E.-A., & Anagnostopoulos, I. (2018). Social media use in higher education: A review. *Education Sciences*, *8*(4), 194. doi:10.3390/educsci8040194

Section 4
Measuring Inclusive Teaching and Learning

How can a university measure the efficacy of its diversity, equity, and inclusion initiatives?

Chapter 10
A Framework to Measure Inclusion

Rebecca L. Jobe
Walden University, USA

Nina M. McCune
https://orcid.org/0000-0001-5339-9383
Walden University, USA

Laura K. Lynn
Walden University, USA

ABSTRACT

Inclusive learning environments create a well-rounded education that initiates and amplifies the diverse experiences of all students. In higher education, this requires that all learning spaces, from the point of onboarding and classrooms through social clubs and completion, are designed in ways that promote the active participation of learners, and that students feel a sense of purpose, belonging, and safety to engage fully in the academic process. Institutions working to integrate and assess inclusive teaching and learning need to carefully consider their institutional mission and understand the history and potential challenges of developing systemic, structural inclusion within their organization. Successfully measuring inclusion requires clear operational definitions and comprehensive evaluation that includes both quantitative and qualitative assessment. This chapter reviews the importance of creating an inclusive environment in higher education, the barriers that arise, and the need for reliable and valid means of measuring its effectiveness.

INTRODUCTION

Diversity is a fact, but inclusion is a choice we make every day. —Nellie Borrero, senior global inclusion and diversity managing director with Accenture

DOI: 10.4018/978-1-6684-5146-5.ch010

Higher education is a driving sector for cultural and economic advancement. College and universities are in a unique position to help shape an emerging educated population for a changing, diverse workforce. Kruse et al. (2018) noted:

Given the growing diversity of US colleges and universities and the desire of many higher education institutions to promote inclusivity, there is a great need to create a systematic, dynamic, organized, and multifaceted approach to cultural competency work in higher education. (p. 737)

Because this need and desire exist, it is crucial that organizations establish clear definitions and metrics for measuring inclusion that fit within their cultural framework. This chapter will explore that aspect of the equation, starting with the importance of inclusive learning environments and the challenges that arise, including engagement and dynamics within the organization. Ensuring the online learning environment is inclusive—or any learning environment is inclusive—requires a cross-institutional approach to implement and assess.

BACKGROUND

Positive Outcomes of Inclusive Environments

The need to create an inclusive environment in an organization is both a moral and a practical one. Inclusive learning environments create a well-rounded education that initiates and amplifies the diverse experiences of all students. In higher education, this requires that all learning spaces, from the point of onboarding and classrooms through social clubs and completion, are designed in ways that promote the active participation of learners and that students feel a sense of purpose, belonging, and safety to engage fully in the academic process. Years of research decisively show how exclusion through biases or perpetuating stereotype threat negatively impact academic performance (American Psychological Association, 2006) and psychological and physical health (Blascovich et al., 2001; Cohen et al., 2006; Cohen et al., 2009; Eisenberger et al., 2003). Years of research have also uncovered plentiful evidence that efforts to increase marginalized students' sense of belonging and achievement lead to increases in both long-lasting academic success and life-long learning among students (Boswell, 2004; Engstrom & Tinto, 2008; Goldrick-Rab, 2010; Graziano et al., 2016). When a university admits students, it tacitly agrees to create opportunities to share ideas, critically think, collaborate openly with others, and benefit from the richness that comes from learning in a diverse community. Put simply, it is a moral obligation for an institution to deliver an exceptional experience to its students that promotes the most academic and professional growth.

In recent years, this institutional obligation has deepened to what Witham et al. (2015) call an *equity imperative*, to "provide the most empowering forms of learning to all who enroll in college, not just to the most fortunate among our students" (p. vii). With increasing focus on both facts that postsecondary opportunities are relegated to students enrolling from the highest-earning families (Cahalan et al., 2021, p. 39) and outcomes show students with the least amount of income complete the fewest academic credentials (Cahalan et al., 2021, p. 181), institutions must consider how to live up to the promise of higher education. Since Harry S. Truman ordered the first federal study on the social and economic impacts of segregation in 1947, and since the 1966 Coleman Report's finding of profound achievement gaps between

A Framework to Measure Inclusion

White and Black students, educators in 2022 continue to grapple with ensuring equitable opportunity for all students, regardless of background or socioeconomic status. Witham et al. (2015) continue that:

while the individual benefits higher education affords provide clear justification for making equity in access and success a moral imperative of a democratic society, the larger social benefits that derive from having a highly educated workforce make the equity imperative not only a moral one but an economic and political one as well…the population of young people on whom the nation's future depends will increasingly be comprised of children from groups who have been historically excluded from, tracked out of, and served most poorly by existing higher education structures. (pp. 6–7)

In addition to the social benefits of a highly educated workforce, postsecondary institutions benefit from creating sustainable inclusive environments in an immediate, tangible way. From an institutional perspective, Bourke and Dillon (2018) shared findings that organizations with inclusive cultures are two times as likely to exceed financial targets and six times more likely to be innovative and agile as compared to non-inclusive businesses. For the longevity and stability of institutional value, it is essential to model inclusivity across all units and operations. As Fuentes and colleagues (2020) aptly observe, "the primary aim of inclusion is to leverage the cultural capital that all students bring into the classroom" (p. 71). That is to say, the varied beliefs, values, and backgrounds of learners brought together with "a sense of solidarity" (Mezirow, 1996, p. 170) results in transformative education. Not only is social and economic capital improved for students, but an increase in cultural capital results in many gains, including successful graduates that are prepared to *thrive* and *lead* in a diverse workforce.

The Problem of Measuring Confidently

Since 2015, initiatives like the Equity Scorecard™ from the Center for Urban Education at the Rossier School of Education at the University of Southern California, and in collaboration with the Association of American Colleges and Universities (AAC&U), provide templates to measure current and future states of equity in higher education institutions. Workshops and working groups have introduced a number of schools across the United States to the fact that racially disaggregating student data reveals racialized disparities in retention and completion, how to conduct policy reviews to remove (often unwitting) barriers for student success, and how to design targets to meet equity goals (AAC&U, 2015). The measures include a mathematical formula (Bensimon et al., 2016) similar to calculating achievement gaps across racial, gender, or other disaggregation of student identities. This assessment results in a specific number of students who must achieve a certain level of proficiency to earn a passing grade (for example, 20 more Hispanic students must earn a C or better in a certain class) to achieve *equity*. While this formula is compelling because it identifies a clear body of students to engage, motivate, and support, the math leaves us puzzled as to how to create a sustainable environment where those target students respond in a way that we hope and at a time that enrolled student demographics are constantly shifting.

In 2020, the world experienced events at a scale not seen in years. The COVID-19 pandemic lockdowns forced people into quarantine and social isolation, as threats of an evolving virus loomed large, echoing practices long forgotten, like that announced in a 1918 Louisiana newspaper that "all of the public schools…both day and night, will be closed on Wednesday, and continued closed [*sic*], until further notice, on account of the prevalence of influenza and its continued spread" (New Orleans States, p. 1). Limited contact with others outside a so-called pandemic bubble became the *new* normal. Within months of quarantines and lockdowns, the United States and the world—despite the widely reported rapid spread of the virus—saw unprecedented social and civil unrest in response to the death of an unarmed Black man, George Floyd, in Minneapolis while in police custody. Societal fear was high for both safety and security of our neighborhoods *and* a new virus that scientists raced to understand. Supply chains once ensuring the steady delivery of everything, from food to car parts to toilet paper, stalled as precipitously as an increasing number of producers of those goods (and those who deliver them) were unable to work.

The full impact of this pandemic likely will not be known for decades; we do know, however, that one immediate consequence reverberates throughout all higher education. As students were forced to engage in learning experiences online, the rapid transition to internet-based education exposed the fragility of educators learning new technology. Often, face-to-face courses did not work well in the rapid transition to online teaching, where creating inclusive learning environments was often an afterthought (Cash et al., 2021). Potentially, one outcome of this pandemic performance is realized in higher education: new and continuing enrollments have plummeted in the past 2 years (United States Department of Education, & National Student Clearinghouse Research Center, 2021a; 2021b). Among the groups least likely to persist include students of color and students over the age of 25 (Torres, 2021). These groups typically identified in the calculus as those required to persist and complete in order to reach equity. While previous formulas designed to achieve equity have intended to close equity or achievement gaps, those formulas can in no way adapt and respond to the institutional reality that they are losing the very students needed to close those gaps. Institutions need other ways to measure the efficacy of their efforts in creating inclusive environments. But how is *inclusivity* measured?

Unlike the data produced in the Center for Urban Education's "equity gap calculation" (n.d.), which helps identify targets for improving racialized student achievement and outcomes, measuring inclusion is a trickier calculus. Feeling included is just that—the subjective, fuzzy metric of *a feeling*. Feelings can change based on the time of day, amount of time since one has last eaten, the weather, or any number of fluctuations of fancy. Yet, in diversity (measured through student headcount data) and equity (possibly measured by the Center for Urban Education's equity gap calculator), inclusion remains an elusive but important factor to understand and measure. Akin to the Equity Scorecard™, Bensimon designed an earlier Diversity Scorecard (2004); and Williams et al. (2005) introduced an Inclusive Excellence Scorecard, both of which relied on the targeted calculus of achieving equity. Given the changing nature of student demographics, and external and uncontrollable conditions that influence those demographics, such models may fall short of achieving their goal.

Additionally, institutions can disaggregate student data based on self-identified attributes like race and ethnicity for those students who so identified on an application for federal financial aid or at the time of matriculation, all of which relies on racial and ethnic categories defined by the United States' Office of Management and Budget, the entity that standardizes the language used to collect and present federal data on race and ethnicity. The categories have been in place since 1997, identifying that the terms "Black or African American," for example, are a single category (United States Office of Management and Budget, 1997, p. 58, 787). The Department of Education issued its guidance to use both terms (United States Department of Education, 2008) in an attempt to recognize that many who identify as Black have a non-African ethnic origin or lineage, including individuals with a lineage tracing back to Afro-Caribbean nations like Haiti or Jamaica. Since the 1791 Haitian Revolution, for example, Louisiana, and New Orleans specifically, has had a large non-African Black population. This example of a non-African Black population exists not only in Louisiana, but across the United States. Or the definition for *Hispanic* engages a broad swath of geographic affiliation and an anthropological pan-ethnicity

A Framework to Measure Inclusion

without attribution to race (United States Office of Management and Budget, 1997, p. 58, 786). The definition of Hispanic belies the complexity and variation of linguistic or regional affiliations, without establishing clear understanding of who has this identity (Hugo Lopez et al., 2021). In these examples, and without considering how an individual having *both* an African American parent and a Hispanic parent might self-identify, the difficulty of relying on racial categories to pronounce accurate tallies of racially disaggregated student data becomes clear: The data do not necessarily represent the full complexity of race and ethnicity. The authors find it important to reconsider measuring inclusion outside of the equity calculators given these compounding issues and the limitations of existing formulas.

Diversity and inclusion are clearly intertwined, but it is essential that we also detangle them for the purposes of research and advancing our knowledge and application in higher education. Institutions provide the best learning environment when they are both diverse and inclusive, but without deliberate efforts to ensure this, some may find that they are diverse but not inclusive while others may be inclusive but not diverse. Unfortunately, diversity without inclusion may do more harm than good. Students from marginalized groups may feel out of place, unable to connect, or even threatened by a heterogeneous-seeming majority demographic. They may avoid speaking up in class or lose interest in pursuing their goals. On the other hand, inclusion without diversity may create a homogenous environment where the richness of cultural differences is lost and groupthink is promoted.

Diversity is commonly defined as quantifiable information related to identity, such as demographics or characteristics associated with a person, group, or organization. In higher education, diversity in student population is often represented by the mix of race, ethnicity, gender, marital status, geographic location, age, religious affiliation, and other like variables. While these measures still have some inherent subjectivity in terms of how people identify or choose to self-identify on federal financial aid applications or respond (or not) to requests for such information, they still provide a basis for how a population is characterized and, thus, the depth of cultural and social richness brought to the learning environment. Winter (2014) asserts that diversity is much easier to achieve than inclusion; diversity can be interpreted as a noun (aligning people into representative categories) that can be mandated, whereas inclusion is a verb that gets at the heart of the cultural style and feel of an organization. The challenge then becomes operationally defining what we mean by "inclusivity" and developing metrics that accurately reflect that definition. The authors add to these standard definitions that diversity contributes to a process of better learning, only realized through active, intentional inclusive teaching and learning.

Walden University's Office of Inclusive Teaching and Learning has identified a broad shape of such inclusive environments: *Inclusive teaching* is an intentional practice and conscious awareness of the diverse social, cultural, and community identities and lived experiences of all learners. Inclusive teaching includes a variety of strategies to fully activate student strengths and occurs in environments that draw relevant, meaningful connections to their lives and the professional dispositions they develop. The goal is to ensure learners know Walden values the inherent worth, humanity, and dignity of every learner engaged in the learning process. By sharing knowledge and expertise through mutual inquiry, *inclusive learning* empowers and connects each learner with multiple perspectives and ways of thinking to the practices that can benefit a variety of cultures and contexts. In this space, students build upon existing knowledge and advance lifelong skills to create positive social change in local, national, and global communities. Being included means one feels accepted and valued. Creating an inclusive learning space is the *act* of developing a supportive environment that fosters those feelings. In other words, inclusion is the way one utilizes and benefits from the diverse population at an institution.

It follows that assessing inclusivity must involve measuring one's perception of the environment and assessing the learning environment in both a quantitative and qualitative way. A multifaceted approach can address both the data of diversity in student headcount, for example, as well as the feeling of inclusion, compounded not only by the issues raised above, but also by the varying impact of context and perception. A faculty member may set up what they deem as a very inclusive classroom that is based on a set of best practices for engaging a diverse group, but if students do not *feel* like they belong or that they are free to safely share their viewpoints, then the degree of inclusivity is low. Only through a multifaceted, layered analysis can the feeling of inclusivity be measured with confidence.

Barriers to Inclusivity

The benefits of creating inclusive learning environments are clear and empirically supported. However, various types of organizations are faced with factors that interfere with inclusivity and institutions of higher education are not immune. These factors range from highly manageable to less controllable and present threats to an institution's ability to realize its full potential.

Perhaps one of the most crucial barriers to inclusivity is lack of engagement (for a more in-depth review, see Chapter 9, "The SPII-Hub and Other Initiatives to Advance Online Engagement"). In a university setting, this is two-fold. First, students must have opportunities to bring their rich experiences and backgrounds to the educational environment and feel safe in doing so. They must see opportunities to advance their own goals in a cooperative, supportive atmosphere. They must be able to view academic questions and social problems through their lenses and bring to light new ways of advancing knowledge areas. Similarly, faculty and staff must have opportunities to bring their rich experiences and backgrounds to the educational environment and feel safe doing so. They must seek ways to include *all* students and foster an environment that helps each advance their goals, and they must help students navigate their programs of study, articulating expectations and opportunities for support for engaged learning (Athanases et al., 2016). It is not enough for institutions to attract and enroll a diverse student and faculty body. For a course experience to be truly rich, that diversity of cultures and perspectives must come to light in the discussions and interactions of the classroom. This is not simply icing on the proverbial cake; rather, it *is* the cake. It is, in fact, a central part of what makes higher education . . . indeed . . . *higher*.

Much attention has focused on organizational culture and structure as a barrier to inclusivity over the past decades; for the scope of this chapter, we will recap only the high-level issues in play. Importantly, Berger and Milem (2000) championed understanding organizational behavior as a multidimensional entity in order to develop and operationalize diversity goals. This approach to organizational change often requires multidimensional leadership (Eddy, 2010) that encourages change across several units throughout an institution. A school's culture and practices, without question, can support or interfere with any number of goals intended to change the organization for the better. Entrenched practices and roles have an incredible impact on improving diverse, inclusive environments, especially if those practices and roles have little incentive to make change. It is critical that institutions articulate the vision, mission, and intention of these initiatives and create strong, sustainable strategic plans (see Chapter 14, "Sustainable Strategic Planning for Inclusive Online Teaching and Learning") to meet the complex demands of integrating student and financial services, academics, library and learning resources, and technology support (among others) for inclusivity to become a reality.

OPERATIONALIZING INCLUSION

Practical (Quantitative) Implementations

Three critical steps to the measurement of inclusion are establishing clear definitions, determining the right metrics, and developing valid and reliable ways of measuring them. While arguments can be made based on research questions for how one chooses to operationalize inclusion, a common definition would benefit the ability to compare results and generalize as we delve deeper into this important construct in higher education. This is the primary argument for the need for a systematic framework to assess the extent to which a learning environment is inclusive and, more specifically, areas where inclusivity may be low and able to be improved.

To create a systematic framework to assess inclusivity, we must first know what "inclusive" looks like and be able to articulate that in a quantifiable, measurable way. Gaudiano (2019) astutely explains that "inclusion is invisible to those who enjoy it, because inclusion reflects the absence of negative incidents that make one feel excluded." As educators and students, we know the feeling of connectedness to our peers, our faculty, the curriculum, and the university. Likewise, we can readily spot a situation that feels "exclusive" and does not foster a healthy exchange of ideas. But beyond the feeling of being included (or the absence of feeling excluded), do we really know what factors create an optimal, inclusive experience?

To solve this problem, the simplest, first step to measure inclusivity is surveying the immediate stakeholders. The following questions are intended to frame issues that each institution may value or consider most important, and may be structured to capture responses on a Likert scale or as a yes/no binary:

- How are students experiencing the online environment?
- Do they see themselves in the curriculum?
- Do they feel valued, seen, and heard in the learning spaces?
- Are they asked to incorporate their lived experiences into their work?
- Are resources provided that represent a range of human experience and perspective, not just the canonical necessities of a discipline?
- If students experience hostility, microaggression, or stereotype threat, what opportunities are there to engage and respond? Do they engage in those opportunities and feel issues are resolved?
- What kinds of interaction and feedback do the instructors provide, and within what timeframe?
- Do instructors feel supported and valued in their work?

In this line of questions, a practical observation emerges: All stakeholders must feel supported and valued throughout the learning process and each institution will create those spaces befitting to organizational structure and mission. Everyone engaged in the learning process must sense the value in the exercise of education. However, those spaces must be created with the assumption they must continue to evolve and adapt in order to respond to and provide for the ever-changing needs and intersectional identities of the stakeholders. Creating meaningful engagement in online spaces is never a one-and-done scenario. Points of engagement require continual efficacy assessment and revision.

That is to say, a process of measuring inclusivity must involve assessing student and faculty perceptions of the learning environments, both in terms of content and materials and accessibility in the online space. And this process must be iterative. Such information can be aggregated from student satisfaction surveys, end-of-course surveys, or faculty engagement surveys. Depending on the method of survey administration, data could be gathered with identification numbers, allowing for the data to be disaggregated racially, by gender, by degree level, or by faculty discipline; then this data could be anonymized for further analysis. Often, dissatisfaction arises in any situation because we, as humans, are inclined to operate (often unwittingly) with bias and are prone to poorly manage conflict arising from that bias.

If stakeholders experience some sort of issues needing resolution during the educational process, and assuming guidelines or policy exist to mediate issues that create a less-than-inclusive environment, surveying those who engage in that such mediation would be helpful. This is akin to a customer effort score (Dixon et al., 2010) that measures how much effort was needed to resolve an issue and if that issue was resolved satisfactorily. Especially in an online environment, understanding if faculty and students feel seen and heard is critical to continually supporting inclusive environments.

Toward a More Holistic Assessment of Inclusivity

As higher education institutions continue to prioritize both diversity and inclusion, there is a need for researchers to develop assessment strategies that triangulate multiple sources that can easily translate in action. There are some new and innovative assessments that integrate organizational reflection and engage multiple stakeholders. New measures, such as the Inclusive Management in Tertiary Institutions Scale, or IMTIS (Solis-Grat et al., 2022), provide promise with supporting institutional objectives to better understand how inclusion is perceived from all perspectives of the educational system—students, faculty, staff, and administrators. Such measures help show the complexity of the relationship between diversity and inclusion as well as the multifaceted nature of inclusive environments.

Additionally, the *Diversity and Inclusion Self-Assessment* adapted by the National Association of Colleges and Employers (NACE) (n.d.) provides a guided process for self-review and identifying opportunities for improvement. This tool requires multiple roles within and across the institution to consider, providing an opportunity for group discussion and reflection. No one tool adequately measures inclusivity, but the NACE assessment is one example of an approach to investigating current environments. Similarly, Walden University has partnered with the National Institutes of Historically-Underserved Students (NIHUS) to review and apply the NIHUS self-assessment tool to evaluate our inclusivity efforts to support all undergraduate students within the institution. As described in Chapter 11 ("Assessing Institutional Readiness: A Collaboration"), assessment is conducted by multiple leadership stakeholders resulting in a robust strategy to gather student and faculty partnership information and leverage that information for meaningful improvement.

Measuring Inclusion Inclusively: Qualitative Assessment and Stakeholder Engagement

To approach assessment holistically, more traditional measures and self-assessments need to be considered along with qualitative approaches. This can ensure that the "why" "how" and "what next" are answered in partnership with those living through the teaching and learning experiences. To connect research and evaluation with organizational change and improvements, Walden has prioritized using participatory approaches to stakeholder-engaged research.

In 2021, Walden University introduced new grading turnaround policies for many of its courses. To understand the lived faculty experience with grading timeline policies, a participatory action research (PAR) study was undertaken for one high-impact course. The PAR methodology was identified as an approach that would include and empower full- and part-time faculty—as members of the team most directly impacted by the policy—in understanding and improving the situation through reflection and action (MacDonald, 2012). Through PAR, faculty and academic leaders sought to answer this question: *What can we learn and understand about faculty behaviors, challenges, and support needs for improving grading and feedback turnaround without compromising quality and learning outcomes?*

Participation in the study was voluntary and would involve recursive practices aimed at exploration, knowledge construction, and action (McIntyre, 2008), including, attendance at three different focus group sessions throughout a term, optional one-to-one meetings with the lead researcher, and completion of weekly reflection and goal surveys. Of the 23 faculty scheduled to teach the course, 95.6% were part-time faculty and 69.5% of the total faculty chose to participate in the study. The high participation is an indication of the desire to be included in developing the key, strategic takeaways culled from the process and the decision that would be implemented going forward.

Generally, the findings of the study indicated the behaviors, challenges, and support needs among faculty participants were varied and unique to each individual's circumstances. However, while the focus of the study was on grading turnaround behaviors, challenges, and support needs, faculty expressed that being included in the PAR lent to their feeling less isolated, finding common ground, supporting and encouraging one another, and moving together toward a shared goal.

CONCLUSION

Systematic inclusion efforts could also forestall or prevent the widening of *equity gaps*, a more profound problem than just a target population needing inclusion. Whereas traditional educational nomenclature has been explored and defined—like an *achievement gap* (Coleman et al., 1966) and the *opportunity gap* (Diamond, 2006; Pendakur, 2016)—the term *equity gap* has not been fully defined in its most damning dimension. An equity gap not only encompasses the racial imbalance in student achievement outcomes, it also represents ongoing harm to the student, incurred while attempting to achieve academic outcomes, and persisting after the student leaves the institution without completion. For example, students who incur student loan debt without completing a degree or certificate program experience financial harm that could haunt them well beyond their academic experience (Samans et al., 2017; University of Southern California Equity Research Institute and PolicyLink, 2020). Access to higher-paying jobs, adequate and stable housing, and good healthcare often rely on academic success culminating in a credential. Without such credentials, economic and social mobility remain elusive. Postsecondary institutions can help close these gaps, though systemic, inclusive initiatives must be aimed at supporting student achievement and ensuring their efficacy through careful assessment, reflection, and refitting. In sum, not only do structural, but inclusive interventions also bolster institutional performance metrics, those practices enhance human capital and communities and, thereby, forestall future equity gaps.

Institutions working to integrate and assess inclusive teaching and learning need to carefully consider their institutional mission and understand the history and potential challenges of developing systemic, structural inclusion within their organization. The authors of this chapter advocate thoughtful self-reflection regarding opportunities and barriers within a given organization. With that in mind, a measurement approach needs to be planned carefully and in a holistic manner. Structured assessments should be applied through collaborative conversation with multiple stakeholders and lead to further strategy or adjustments. That is to say, to successfully measure inclusion requires not only the assessment of an environment, but a review and adjustment of the systems around those environments. Measuring inclusion requires multiple points of reconsideration and readjustment, as our collective contexts shift within and outside of higher education settings. There is room for institutions to add to the literature and create new considerations and self-assessments from their experiences. It is a frustrating conclusion that there is no one-size-fits-all approach, or one clear scorecard model, and that each unique institution must rely on many factors to calculate the success of inclusivity. It is our sincere hope to spark broader, and even more nuanced conversation around such assessments. The authors also advocate for the power of qualitative and stakeholder-informed approaches. Incorporating participatory action research into such approaches can lead to meaningful, organizational learning and change with the added benefits of creating a greater sense of inclusion from stakeholders in the process along with the benefits that manifest in inclusive environments.

REFERENCES

American Psychological Association. (2006, July 15). *Stereotype threat widens achievement gap: Reminders of stereotyped inferiority hurt test scores.* https://www.apa.org/research/action/stereotype

Association of American Colleges and Universities. (2015). *Step up and lead for equity: What higher education can do to reverse our deepening divides.* https://www.aacu.org/publication/step-up-and-lead-for-equity-what-higher-education-can-do-to-reverse-our-deepening-divides

Athanases, S. Z., Achinstein, B., Curry, M. W., & Ogawa, R. T. (2016). The promise and limitations of a college-going culture: Toward cultures of engaged learning for low-SES Latina/o youth. *Teachers College Record, 118*(7), 1–60. https://doi.org/10.1177/016146811611800708

Bensimon, E. M. (2004). The diversity scorecard: A learning approach to institutional change. *Change: The Magazine of Higher Learning 36*(1), 45–52. doi:10.1080/00091380409605083

Bensimon, E. M., Dowd, A. C., & Witham, K. (2016). Five principles for enacting equity by design. *Diversity & Democracy, 19*(1). http://ftla.laccdssi.org/files/2017/01/Five-Principles-for-Enacting-Equity-by-Design-1-4.pdf

Berger, J. B., & Milem, J. F. (2000). Organizational behavior in higher education and student outcomes. In J. C. Smart (Ed.), *Higher education: Handbook of theory and research* (Vol. 15, pp. 238–338). Agathon.

Blascovich, S. J., Spencer, D. Q., & Steele, C. (2001). African Americans and high blood pressure: The role of stereotype threat. *Psychological Science, 12*(3), 225–229. https://doi.org/10.1111/1467-9280.00340

Boswell, K. (2004). Bridges or barriers? *Change: The Magazine of Higher Learning, 36*(6), 22–29. doi:10.1080/00091380409604240

Bourke, J., & Dillon, B. (2018). The diversity and inclusion revolution: Eight powerful truths. *Deloitte Review, 22,* 82–95. https://www2.deloitte.com/content/dam/insights/us/articles/4209_Diversity-and-inclusion-revolution/DI_Diversity-and-inclusion-revolution.pdf

Cahalan, M. W., Addison, M., Brunt, N., Patel, P. R., & Perna, L. W. (2021). *Indicators of higher education equity in the United States: 2021 historical trend report*. The Pell Institute for the Study of Opportunity in Higher Education. http://pellinstitute.org/downloads/publications-Indicators_of_Higher_Education_Equity_in_the_US_2021_Historical_Trend_Report.pdf

Cash, C. M., Cox, T. D., & Hahs-Vaughn, D. L. (2021). Distance educators attitudes and actions towards inclusive teaching practices. *The Journal of Scholarship of Teaching and Learning, 21*(2), 15–42. https://doi.org/10.14434/josotl.v21i2.27949

Center for Urban Education. (n.d.). *Closing racial equity gaps*. https://bit.ly/3qZbzIC

Cohen, G. L., Garcia, J., Apfel, N., & Master, A. (2006). Reducing the racial achievement gap: A social-psychological intervention. *Science, 313*(5791), 1307–1310. https://doi.org/10.1126/science.1128317

Cohen, G. L., Garcia, J., Purdie-Vaughns, V., Apfel, N., & Brzustoski, P. (2009). Recursive processes in self-affirmation: Intervening to close the minority achievement gap. *Science, 324*(5925), 400–403. https://doi.org/10.1126/science.1170769

Coleman, J. S., Campbell, E. Q., Hobson, C. J., McPartland, J., Mood, A. M., Weinfeld, F. D., & York, R. L. (1966). *Equality of educational opportunity* [Summary report]. United States Department of Health, Education, and Welfare, Office of Education & National Center for Educational Statistics. https://bit.ly/36owcWO

Diamond, J. B. (2006). Still separate and unequal: Examining race, opportunity, and school achievement in "integrated" suburbs. *The Journal of Negro Education, 75*(3), 495–505. https://www.jstor.org/stable/40026817

Dixon, M., Freeman, K., & Toman, N. (2010, July–August). Stop trying to delight your customers. *Harvard Business Review, 88*(7–8), 116–122. https://hbr.org/2010/07/stop-trying-to-delight-your-customers

Dowd, A. C. (2007). Community colleges as gateways and gatekeepers: Moving beyond the access "saga" toward outcome equity. *Harvard Educational Review, 77*(4), 1–13. https://doi.org/10.17763/haer.77.4.1233g31741157227

Eddy, P. L. (2010). *Community college leadership: A multidimensional model for leading change*. Stylus Publishing.

Eisenberger, N. I., Lieberman, M. D., & Williams, K. D. (2003). Does rejection hurt? An fMRI study of social exclusion. *Science, 302*(5643), 290–292. https://doi.org/10.1126/science.1089134

Engstrom, C., & Tinto, V. (2008). Access without support is not opportunity. *Change: The Magazine of Higher Learning, 40*(1), 46–50. doi:10.3200/CHNG.40.1.46-50

Fuentes, M. A., Zelaya, D. G., & Madsen, J. W. (2021). Rethinking the course syllabus: Considerations for promoting equity, diversity, and inclusion. *Teaching of Psychology, 48*(1), 69–79. https://doi.org/10.1177%2F0098628320959979

Gaudiano, P. (2019, April 23). Inclusion is invisible: How to measure it. *Forbes*. https://www.forbes.com/sites/paologaudiano/2019/04/23/inclusion-is-invisible-how-to-measure-it/?sh=269ccef2a3d2

Goldrick-Rab, S. (2010). Challenges and opportunities for improving community college student success. *Review of Educational Research, 80*(3), 437–469. https://doi.org/10.3102/0034654310370163

Graziano, J., Schlesinger, M. R., Kahn, G., & Singer, R. (2016). A workbook for designing, building, and sustaining learning communities. *Learning Communities Research and Practice, 4*(1), Article 6. https://files.eric.ed.gov/fulltext/EJ1112853.pdf

Hugo Lopez, M., Krogstad, J. M., & Passel, J. S. (2021, September 23). *Who is Hispanic?* Pew Research Center. https://www.pewresearch.org/fact-tank/2021/09/23/who-is-hispanic/

Kruse, S. D., Rakha, S., & Calderone, S. (2018). Developing cultural competency in higher education: An agenda for practice. *Teaching in Higher Education, 23*(6), 733–750. https://doi.org/10.1080/13562517.2017.1414790

MacDonald, C. (2012). Understanding participatory action research: A qualitative research methodology option. *Canadian Journal of Action Research, 12*(2), 34–50. https://doi.org/10.33524/cjar.v13i2.37

McIntyre, A. (2008). *Participatory action research*. Sage Publications.

Mezirow, J. (1996). Contemporary paradigms of learning. *Adult Education Quarterly, 46*(3), 158–172. https://doi.org/10.1177%2F074171369604600303

National Association of Colleges and Employers. (n.d.). *Diversity and inclusion self-assessment*. https://www.csuci.edu/careerdevelopment/employers/documents/diversity-inclusion-self-assessment.pdf

New Orleans States. (1918, October 8). *City schools closed to halt flu spread*. https://bit.ly/3oEoKxi

Pendakur, V. (2016). Two distinct paths and a missed opportunity. In V. Pendakur (Ed.), *Closing the opportunity gap. Identity-conscious strategies for retention and student success* (pp. 1–9). Stylus Publishing.

Samans, R., Blanke, J., Drzeniek Hannoun, M., & Corrigan, G. (2017). *Insight report: The inclusive growth and development report*. World Economic Forum. https://www3.weforum.org/docs/WEF_Forum_IncGrwth_2017.pdf

Solis-Grant, M. J., Espinoza-Parçet, C., Sepúlveda-Carrasco, C., Pérez-Villalobos, C., Rodríguez-Núñez, I., Pincheira-Martínez, C., Gómez-Varela, J. P., & Aránguiz-Ibarra, D. (2022). Inclusion at universities: Psychometric properties of an inclusive management scale as perceived by students. *PLoS One, 17*(1), e0262011. https://doi.org/10.1371/journal.pone.0262011

Torres, R. (2021, January 26). 2021: A new year and a new beginning for our education system, learners, and the workforce. *National Student Clearinghouse Research Center*. https://bit.ly/3FtTYkc

United States Department of Education. (2008, August). *New race and ethnicity guidance for the collection of federal education data*. http://bit.ly/2NKfKJX

United States Department of Education, & National Student Clearinghouse Research Center. (2021a, July 8). *College persistence rate drops an unprecedented 2 percentage points*. https://bit.ly/3v10uKn

United States Department of Education, & National Student Clearinghouse Research Center. (2021b, July 8). *Persistence and retention. Fall 2019 beginning cohort*. https://bit.ly/3DkmjaI

United States Office of Management and Budget. (1997, October 30). *Revisions to the standards for the classification of federal data on race and ethnicity.* http://bit.ly/3rbDQvT

University of Southern California Equity Research Institute and PolicyLink. (2020a). *The national equity atlas.* https://nationalequityatlas.org/

Williams, D. A., Berger, J. B., & McClendon, S. B. (2005). *Toward a model of inclusive excellence and change in postsecondary institutions.* American Association of Colleges and Universities. https://drdamonawilliams.com/daw-item/towards-a-model-of-inclusive-excellence-and-change-in-post-secondary-institutions/

Witham, K. A., Malcolm-Piqueux, L., Dowd, A. C., & Bensimon, E. M. (2015). *America's unmet promise. The imperative for equity in higher education.* Association of American Colleges and Universities.

ADDITIONAL READING

Alexandra, V., Ehrhart, K. H., & Randel, A. E. (2021). Cultural intelligence, perceived inclusion, and cultural diversity in workgroups. *Personality and Individual Differences, 168*(110285), 110285. Advance online publication. doi:10.1016/j.paid.2020.110285

President's Committee on Civil Rights. (1947). *To secure these rights: The report of president's committee on civil rights.* United States Government Printing Office. https://teachingamericanhistory.org/document/to-secure-these-rights-the-report-of-the-presidents-committee-on-civil-rights/

The Chronicle of Higher Education. (2022). *The demographic cliff: Surviving enrollment challenges* [Special issue]. https://connect.chronicle.com/rs/931-EKA-218/images/DemographicCliff_Syntellis_KeyTakeaways_v1.pdf

Winters, M. F. (2014). From diversity to inclusion: An inclusion equation. In B. M. Ferdman & B. R. Deane (Eds.), *Diversity at work: The practice of inclusion* (pp. 205–228). John Wiley & Sons.

Chapter 11
Assessing Institutional Readiness:
A Collaboration

Kristin Bundesen
Walden University, USA

Christopher Gilmer
West Virginia University Potomac State College, USA

Latara O. Lampkin
Florida State University, USA

Laura K. Lynn
Walden University, USA

ABSTRACT

This chapter examines, introduces, and documents the exploration and initial review of an institutional self-assessment toolkit designed to query and instigate discussion of how institutions perceive equity as they serve "historically-underserved" undergraduate students. A pilot of the toolkit, developed by the National Institutes for Historically Underserved Students (NIHUS), was evaluated by a working group of the Undergraduate Advisory Council within Walden University. The working group generated feedback to the NIHUS on the toolkit and considered potential wider adoption across undergraduate education within the university. This exploration and collaboration continues.

INTRODUCTION

In order to serve its undergraduate students equitably, Walden University's leadership sought to adopt an equity assessment tool to inform and enhance current policies and practices toward providing an equitable and inclusive student experience. While exploring options, a collaboration formed between Walden

University and the National Institutes for Historically Underserved Students (NIHUS), and Walden's School for Interdisciplinary Undergraduate Studies agreed to review and revise a tool kit for assessing diversity, equity, and inclusion (DEI). A key component of this collaboration would be the ability to assess university awareness of DEI across all student demographic categories and organizational findings of the toolkit. Walden University's commitment to social change requires that it continuously examine the many layers of the student experience in order to fulfill that mission. Walden undergraduate students are all adult learners, and the experience is primarily online. Identifying and engaging university stakeholders is a key first step in addressing DEI in the student experience.

At the start of the collaboration, described below, the tool kit was in a pilot phase. NIHUS was in the process of working with partner institutions to test its approach in the field. Those partners are traditional brick and mortar universities, including several historically black colleges and universities (HBCUs). This collaboration focused on testing the pilot version of the toolkit for use in an online environment. The hope was that Walden's feedback to NIHUS would be adapted to online learning environments, and that Walden University could assess the tool kit's appropriateness for supporting the larger university goals of consistently improving DEI processes and policies.

The balance of this chapter will introduce the two collaborating groups, include the reasoning behind the NIHUS development of the tool kit, a description of how the tool kit was assessed by the university, and commentary on the findings. The outcome is that of continued collaboration, and continued benefit from improving and expanding the tool kit, both as an instrument the NIHUS can offer to multiple universities within the United States, and by wider deployment within Walden University. As with the collaboration described here, this paper is also collaborative. There are four authors: Dr. Bundesen represents the perspective of the Walden undergraduate community and Dr. Lynn brings in the perspective of student academic and research support; Dr. Gilmer is the NIHUS founder and president, and Dr. Lampkin grounded tool kit in extant literature. The bibliographic material for this chapter informed the development of the tool kit, and is the work of Dr. Lampkin. As the collaboration described here was experiential, external citations are not required to substantiate the process described.

BACKGROUND

Walden University is a member of Adtalem Global Education (NYSE: ATGE) and was founded in 1970 to support adult learners in achieving their academic goals. Walden University now offers more than 100 online degree and certificate programs and is accredited by the Higher Learning Commission. Approximately 55,000 students from across the U.S. and approximately 115 countries are enrolled and pursuing a certificate, bachelor's, master's, or doctoral degree online at Walden. The average age of a Walden student is 40, and approximately 75% identify as female. According to fall 2020 data (Walden University, n.d.), students enrolled in full-time graduate programs are predominantly Black or African American female (32.2%), followed by White female (30.3%) and Black or African American male (7.61%).

The Walden Undergraduate Student Profile

Students enrolled in full-time undergraduate programs are most commonly White female (48.2%), followed by Black or African American female (16.3%) and Hispanic or Latino female (7.38%). Undergraduate degrees offered include Bachelor of Science in nursing, psychology, business administration and management, public administration and social services, education, communications, interdisciplinary studies, and health services. Undergraduate programs are delivered almost entirely online.

The university pursues a broad undergraduate admissions standard that allows students with non-standard academic backgrounds to access higher education. However, adult students and online education are increasing across the academic spectrum due to the changing economic landscape with the COVID-19 pandemic serving as an accelerator for socially distanced education that online environments support. Walden students are required to have completed high school or to have successfully passed a General Education Development test (GED). This broad access supports the university's commitment to education as social change. Students who want to pursue a degree, should be able to do so even if they have been unsuccessful in the past or have not believed (or were told that they were not up to) the challenge of higher education. Although the profile of the larger university is distinctly different than other NIHUS partners, the undergraduate population overwhelmingly falls within the NIHUS profile of the historically underserved.

School of Interdisciplinary Undergraduate Studies

The School of Interdisciplinary Undergraduate Studies (SIUS) houses the B.S. in Communications, the B.S. in Interdisciplinary Studies, and the general education courses for all undergraduate degree programs within Walden. Excluding the undergraduate nursing programs, approximately 90% of new students take their first term course under the auspices of SIUS before moving on to other general education courses and their core program studies. In 2021, SIUS launched *The Academy* for students with no previous higher education credits, many of whom are first-generation college students. *The Academy* is a fixed program of study comprising general education courses roughly equivalent to the first year of study at a traditional community college. *Academy* students are cohorted in class sections with dedicated faculty and advisors. At the end of the program, students move into their degree concentrations.

Within SIUS, we respect our students by accepting and teaching the students we have, not the students we imagine. Consequently, the concept of student readiness is sidelined. There is no such thing as an underprepared student, as this presupposes an equity in K–12 education, reflected in the GED exam, that does not exist. Therefore, there is no universal standard of preparedness for higher education, which should be a life-long experience regardless. This philosophical approach underpins how SIUS supports the broad admissions standard. If a student has committed to the process of further education, they are ready.

The Global COVID-19 Pandemic Heightens DEI Awareness

It may be of interest to readers that the collaboration between NIHUS and Walden took place during the global pandemic of 2019–2021. While many higher education and K–12 institutions were making urgent and sometimes awkward transitions to online instruction, Walden's long-standing status as an online institution meant that the academic experience was primarily one of continuity for faculty and academic leaders. There was a modest increase in enrollment as students who found themselves unemployed or underemployed searched for institutions like Walden to support newly conceived or previously shelved educational goals. At the same time, continuing students' lives were dramatically impacted. Those that were able to—or required to—work from home also became home teachers who supported children engaged in the new experience of online schooling and cared for elders or worried about them in care facilities compounded by limited access to medical and mental health care for themselves and their

Assessing Institutional Readiness

families. Sites for information gathering and data collection, such as libraries or residencies, were no longer open or available, which impacted assignments for some programs and degree levels.

The university had a rapid response approach and determined that in all cases flexibility was needed and policies were adjusted. Program leaders communicated this widely and announcements were provided in classrooms. At the same time, academic support service offerings increased and additional outreach was provided to ensure that students' questions were answered and exceptions and flexibility was given.

The urgent attention needed during the pandemic generated heightened awareness of issues of equity. Adjusting one policy to support students during this time opened opportunities to review other areas where equity was assumed or had been overlooked. This push to provide the best possible experience for our students during the health crisis energized leaders within the university to advance exploration of DEI across all services. Hence, the timing for the NIHUS/Walden collaboration was unfortunate but fortuitous.

Demand for access to devices within families and households was at a premium. As the typical Walden undergraduate student is also a parent, these parent/students were sharing their computers and other productivity devices with their children to support online schooling. Prior to the pandemic, one or two devices may have served a household. During the pandemic there was demand for a device for each child as well as the parent/student and possible partner working from home. A family of two adults and three children was hoping for five devices and enough bandwidth to support concurrent video calls and content. Compounding this was a simultaneous shortage of tablet- and Chromebook-style devices.

With restricted mobility, students were unable to use a "third space," such as a coffee shop to do schoolwork. Privacy and quiet within households were also at a premium. This was captured in a photograph in *The New York Times* of a woman sitting on the floor of a closet with a phone to her ear changing a child's clothes while a partner was using a laptop at a desk to work remotely. The gender disparity was distressing.

Then there was the illness. Any family member diagnosed with COVID became a full-time responsibility for the household. Isolation protocols were almost impossible to maintain in close quarters, and inevitably more family members would contract the illness. The long recovery period, including exhaustion and impaired mental focus, negatively impacted successfully completing schoolwork. At Walden University, the undergraduate terms are only 6 weeks. Normally, students take a single class at a time, but some circumstances may lead to students taking two classes concurrently. The effect of the illness and general pandemic restrictions and protocols forced the university to reevaluate late policies and application of incompletes for those students unable to maintain the fast pace of schoolwork through no fault of their own. Walden had to address the socioeconomic disparities revealed and exacerbated by the global pandemic.

The National Institutes for Historically Underserved Students

The National Institutes for Historically Underserved Students (NIHUS) is committed to seeing each student as an individual, not a statistic. Every student who commits to further education should be supported in achieving their goals. Some professions require bachelor's or advanced degrees. It is just as noble and appropriate for others to complete short-term workforce credentialing programs or associate degrees and then move directly into the workforce. What matters is every student's right to choose and to be supported.

Research, technical assistance centers, and programs widely and successfully exist to serve distinct populations of historically underserved students. NIHUS was established in 2016 to fill an unmet need for an academic center of national scope that focuses on researching the common barriers experienced by historically underserved students, the many intersections of historically underserved identities within individuals and among groups and developing and sharing solutions to common barriers across institutions.

West Virginia University at Parkersburg (WVUP), collaborating with its foundation and numerous national partners, became the lead agent of NIHUS in July 2018 when it welcomed the founder of NIHUS as the university's president. An ad-hoc group of historically underserved students and their champions from 26 states and the District of Columbia have hosted several national think tanks broadly exploring issues of diversity, equity, and inclusion (DEI), drafting and ratifying *A Declaration on the Rights of Historically Underserved Students*, which is shared freely with colleges and universities nationwide. Collaborators include historically black colleges and universities (HBCUs), Hispanic-serving institutions (HSIs), adult-serving universities, tribal colleges, Appalachian colleges, private liberal arts colleges, and other higher educational, pre-K–12 educational, healthcare, civil rights, artistic, and philanthropic partners with a commitment to the diversity of historically underserved students. Delegates to NIHUS events have included the president of the National Association for the Advancement of Colored People (NAACP), a senior representative of the Obama Administration, an American Book Award–winning poet, a Tony-winning actor, university and college presidents and faculty members, high-level representatives of numerous national educational organizations, and, most importantly, a broad and deep representation of historically underserved students.

The Institutes are built on three interconnected pillars: aspire, learn, lead. The underlying assumption of the Institutes is that all students and families served are fully committed to the education of self and society. Underserved students are recruited to seek higher education, supported as they complete their education, and prepared to lead in their communities after graduation. In addition, the Institutes encourages and supports the development of innovative strategies for college success by other institutions of higher education and shares its own resources broadly. It is recognized nationally as a repository of knowledge and as a training and technical resource to other universities, colleges, schools, and businesses.

The mission of NIHUS is to research and identify common barriers to educational equity and success for all historically underserved students; to develop and disseminate research-based solutions to these barriers; and to recruit, retain, and graduate more of those students who are currently being overlooked or failed by American higher education. Sample populations served include, but are not limited to:

- First-generation college students
- Racial and ethnic "minority" groups such as Hispanic/LatinX/Latine Americans, African Americans, and American Indians/Native Americans
- Historically disenfranchised sex and gender minorities—women and transgendered
- Young men of color and young women of color
- Disabled/differently-abled
- LGBTQ+
- Socioeconomically challenged
- Veterans
- Adults reentering or entering college
- Academically underprepared
- International students and immigrants

Assessing Institutional Readiness

- Undocumented students

NIHUS works to identify through research and practice other groups of historically underserved students and bring them into its research and service programs. Ultimately, the Institutes will provide a comprehensive web of support for all historically underserved students.

The Institutes

There are four interrelated institutes operating under one umbrella:

1. *The Institute for Social Justice in Higher Education:* Focuses on civil rights issues advocating for historically underserved and disenfranchised student populations.
2. *The Institute for Curricular Reform in Higher Education:* Curricular and other materials based on research and best practices that can be shared with colleges and universities as texts by publishers have become prohibitively expensive for most vulnerable students. This Institute also focuses on development of culturally relevant pedagogies.
3. *The Institute for Research and Best Practices in Higher Education:* Uses research-based models to test the theories and develop tools that emerge from the other Institutes and validate the efficacy of the work. It is the dissemination arm to share cross-institute resources with the broader education community.
4. *The Institute for Pre–K Through Adult Education Partnerships in Higher Education:"* Builds primary/secondary/higher education partnerships and a continuum of best practices. This Institute focuses on familial education and develops its resources with familial education as its central tenet.

Development of the Assessment Tool Kit

Supported by the research capacity of the U.S. Department of Education–funded Regional Educational Lab Southeast at Florida State University, *The Institute for Research and Best Practices in Higher Education* developed NIHUS's first product—a tool kit crafted by delegates that can be used by colleges and universities nationwide to assess their own readiness to serve historically underserved students. The uniqueness of the research-based tool kit lies in its "by us, for us" development process. Underserved students and their advocates, researchers in collaboration with practitioners representing highly diverse cultural perspectives, have developed the product to ensure its cultural relevance, appropriateness, and likelihood to be implemented. The primary desired outcome is for the tool kit to be used by colleges and universities to promote honest, thoughtful, and often difficult dialogue among all internal stakeholder groups to accurately assess the institution's readiness to serve underserved students. The belief is that progress cannot be made until an institution engages in deep and reflective self-assessment and owns any challenges or limitations it might find. At a later time, and to the degree that institutions using the tool are comfortable sharing their findings, NIHUS hopes to conduct a research study correlating and analyzing findings across institutions. The collaboration with Walden is part of this process.

Three instruments have been developed so far: an in-depth institutional tool, a more cursory institutional tool, and a tool to assess readiness to serve one specific student population—veterans. The veterans' tool was deliberately chosen for development as the first population-specific instrument because veterans exist across virtually every other category of underserved students and this was thought to be the most inclusive and far-reaching population-specific instrument. Walden University's initial evaluation of the tool kit did not include the veteran's tool although it is acknowledged that this tool could generate the most wide-reaching assessment of an institution's effectiveness in terms of equity given the demographic's presence across multiple areas of the student experience. The plan is to develop population-specific instruments for the other population groups identified by NIHUS, including race, gender, first-generation, sexual orientation, etc.

Based on the 2016 *Becoming a Student-Ready College* by McNair et al., the tool explores four primary categories:

1. Demonstrating belief in students
2. Leadership values and organizational culture
3. Promoting inclusive excellence to support student success
4. Building student readiness through promoting effective partnerships

The tool kit focusses on laws, policies, procedures, and practices, including the differences in these constructs and how they overlap. An assessment scoring guide leads individuals through a series of guiding questions to a consensus rating process in which domains are rated as having no evidence, some evidence, or exemplar evidence for success. Stakeholders are asked to identify common priorities, to assess what resources are currently attributed to accomplish those priorities, and what additional resources will be necessary to accomplish them. A series of "Look Fors" based on the hundreds of years of combined experience possessed by the NIHUS development team sets the institutional findings within a broader context.

PILOTING THE ASSESSMENT TOOLKIT

The NIHUS Perspective

Several HBCUs, a tribal college, an Appalachian college, a community college, and an HSI have partnered to conduct student focus groups to vet the tool for piloting, and several of these institutions, primarily small institutions with a focus on teaching and service, are preparing for larger-scale pilots. NIHUS is pleased to have collaborated with Walden University, as Walden holds internal stakeholder discussions on the tool kit working toward a broader adoption. NIHUS is especially interested in partnering with Walden University because Walden is a different kind of institution than most of the founding NIHUS partners. Walden is large and online, enrolls a broadly diverse student body, and offers significant graduate programs, whereas most of NIHUS's founding partners are primarily undergraduate institutions. Walden possesses significant research history and capacity; was founded on the principles of social justice and equity, which are at the core of NIHUS; and is both national and international in scope. The NIHUS and Walden's School of Interdisciplinary Undergraduate Studies (SIUS) share the ethos that no student should be reduced to a statistic and that every student who commits to higher education should become a graduate. This alignment of values tethered the collaboration.

Comparing the Walden pilot experience with the pilot experience of the more traditional NIHUS partner institutions will deepen and broaden feedback as NIHUS builds out the remaining components of the tool kit and makes revisions that are always part of the pilot phase of any project (note: "pilot"

Assessing Institutional Readiness

refers to the assessment of the early version of the NIHUS tool kit by Walden). Walden also provides a development laboratory for the tool kit since Walden's profile is different than that of other partners and there is a likely need for Walden to tailor the tool kit to meet the needs of its stakeholders. The goal, then, will be to maintain the integrity of the tool kit and its purpose while allowing for an implementation process that is more than just replication across similar institutions. It also includes room for appropriate tailoring of the instruments in the future as NIHUS and its expanding network of partners take the tool kit from the pilot phase to the mass dissemination phase, which will hopefully result in hundreds of colleges and universities nationwide using the "by us, for us" approach to identify, address, and provide the equal and equitable educational experiences that historically underserved students deserve.

The Walden Perspective

The School of Interdisciplinary Undergraduate Studies (SIUS) was already in the process of a comprehensive assessment of how to serve students through diversity, equity, and inclusion. This involved revisioning the online classroom design, increasing the use of open-source materials, faculty development on compassion and empathy in the classroom—areas of research interest for two of our faculty—and building closer relationships across stakeholders within the university. Interest in the NIHUS assessment tool, underpinned by faculty research interests, offers a potential method for expanding that work in a structured manner. As such, piloting the tool was of interest to SIUS.

As part of Walden's implementation of shared governance, the Walden University Undergraduate Education Advisory Council serves in an advisory capacity to the chief academic officer and senior academic leadership, providing feedback and recommendations in areas that support the expression of the Walden University mission and vision across undergraduate programs. The council is co-chaired by the dean of SIUS and the academic program director for the bachelor's in business administration. This council includes undergraduate academic program directors for each undergraduate discipline and general education as well as representatives from Product Strategy Innovation and Design, the Office of Faculty Development, the Academic Skills Center, the Office of Student Affairs, and the Office of Institutional Effectiveness. The advisory council meets regularly to discuss issues common to the undergraduate experience regardless of discipline. As such, working groups are formed to investigate or develop approaches to strengthen the undergraduate student experience in areas such as writing across the curriculum, undergraduate policies, and DEI. Similar councils with different charters and missions exist throughout the university.

In 2021, the Undergraduate Education Advisory Council formed a working group to evaluate an early iteration, a pilot, of the NIHUS self-assessment tool kit, described below, and explore its appropriateness to Walden's unique environment and student population. The working group was composed of six members: the co-chair of the advisory council and dean of SUIS; the academic program director developing *The Academy*; the SIUS associate director of curriculum and assessment; and two full-time faculty members, one of whom is also a current Ph.D. student. The dean of research quality served as evaluator and assessment consultant. The goal was to provide NIHUS with feedback on its pilot version of the tool kit and to consider ways to adapt it to the Walden undergraduate environment. The working group approached this task deliberatively and worked directly with the assessment creators to gain deeper understanding of the tool kit and how to best approach the review. With the use of the supportive guide provided within the tool kit, participants considered what might fit for assessing DEI within the Walden undergraduate experience.

The Working Group's Approach to Assessing the Tool Kit

The working group met regularly throughout 2021, a pandemic year also marked by civil unrest, evaluating the tool kit one section at a time. Each part was evaluated for relevance to the online environment, adult learners, and ease of engagement for potential participants. Comments, drafts, information, and resources were shared on a Microsoft Teams site. Each of the sections of the NIHUS institutional self-assessment tool kit were discussed by the entire group in video meetings, group chat, and email. Members worked together on one section and then independently on subsequent sections, bringing their reflections back to the larger working group. The responses were then summarized and shared back to the NIHUS advisory board and tool kit development team.

Through conversation and individual engagement, participants determined evidence, areas of strengths, and places where the program and the wider university have opportunities. Additional reflection led to discussions on how this tool kit could lead to further inquiry and inform DEI improvements within undergraduate programs.

Each member of the working group participated as a subject engaged in the assessment process from individual perspectives. This work was completed one section at a time followed by group meetings to provide feedback on the tool itself and the relevance and usefulness of the tool for broader deployment.

The group's findings were summarized and presented to the board of the NIHUS at the end of 2021 for its review. Summative findings were also shared with the full Walden Undergraduate Advisory Council (see below).

THE SELF-ASSESSMENT TOOL KIT

The NIHUS Think Tanks served as idea incubators for the assessment tool kit, which led to further grounding in extensive research of the literature. (A partial listing of this literature is available in the bibliography below.)

The assessment is broken into four domains (McNair et al., 2016):

1. Demonstrating belief in students
2. Leadership values and organizational culture
3. Making excellence inclusive to support student success
4. Building student readiness through effective partnerships

For each domain, fixed variables or behaviors were explored:

1. **Laws** – Federal laws are the same for all U.S. institutions, but state and local laws may vary considerably and be applicable to some programs of study. Laws represent a fundamental measure of compliance guiding the development of policies and procedures.
2. **Policies** – Policies govern individual institutions' procedures and practices. These are usually set by senior leadership and given authority by the endorsement of the provost, chief academic officer and/or president of the institution.

3. **Procedures** – Procedures are the implementation patterns of laws and policies. They can vary widely within an institution and may have limited relevance to a subset of programs or even a single program.
4. **Practices** – Practices are the results of implementation or lack thereof of laws, policies, and procedures. Practices are found in the day-to-day occurrences within each institution.

For each domain and variable or behavior, participants were prompted to include examples as evidence. "Delving Deeper" questions were provided to guide discussions.

The Walden Working Group's Response to the First Domain

The Walden working group's reaction to and assessment of the first domain is described here. Focus was placed on the largest component of the Walden undergraduate experience: general education within SIUS. The tool kit language is presented first and then the Walden response is provided for each variable and/or behavior. Additional domains are summarized below but not described in detail. Here, we present our guidance for *Domain 1: Demonstrating Belief in Students*:

Variables/Behavior Prompts:

- **Laws** – What laws are in place to demonstrate belief in students?
- **Policies** – What policies are in place to demonstrate a belief in students?
- **Procedures** – What procedures are in place to demonstrate beliefs in students?
- **Practices** – What practices are in place to demonstrate beliefs in students?

Delving Deeper Guiding Questions:

- How does the institution value and affirm the cultural capital of underserved students?
- What biases or stereotypes may be standing in the way?
- What do our students' own stories tell us about the work the institution needs to do?
- How does the institution ensure that the underserved students receive the appropriate amount of challenge and support to ensure their success without marginalizing these students?
- What can the institution learn from our success and failures and from other institutions working to increase underserved student success?

Variable 1: Laws

The legal variable exposed limited perspectives within the faculty and differences between faculty and leadership understanding that may lead to confusion, especially in the implementation of policies as practices. Faculty and the doctoral student on the working group were aware of policies, but not necessarily the legal ramifications or restrictions that inform those policies. Without that broader understanding, the implementation of policies can vary widely and create inequitable student experiences. Responses about laws that demonstrate making excellence inclusive were more nuanced the higher up the participant's job title. The higher the title, the more aware participants were of laws affecting and underlying policies such as the Second Morrill Act of 1890, Title VI of the Civil Rights Act of 1964, or the Higher Education Act of 1965. Conversely, the participants who were also active teaching faculty were well versed in the practices and nuances of The Family Educational Rights and Privacy Act (1974) familiarly known as FERPA, as opposed to academic leaders, who may not have been in the classroom for years or subject to repeated faculty development training on this act. When the NIHUS tool is more widely piloted by diverse institutions, we suspect this pattern will be repeated.

All working group participants, regardless of responsibility level, were aware of the Americans With Disabilities Act (1990) requirements, as there had been a recent set of communications and policy development within SIUS regarding ADA compliance, including color choices for faculty-to-student communications, testing of GIFs to keep image speed and repetition within defined guidelines, and the requirement of captioning for moving image content and screencasts. Whether the practices continue to reflect the policy will be a matter of ongoing communication and faculty development activities. ADA awareness was considered positive evidence for an inclusive student experience. But there may be more work to do on understanding additional laws that inform policies.

Variable 2: Policies

As discussed above, due to the pandemic and the rapid response by Walden's upper leadership to amend policies affecting student success, the participants of the working group were acutely aware of shifting policies and procedures for both the submission of late work and extending grace periods for incompletes during 2021. At the same time, socializing these changing policies was challenging. Some faculty who were only minimally affected by the pandemic were initially resistant to adopting these new policies. During the course of the year concurrent with the assessment of the pilot tool kit, even the most traditionally minded faculty saw the need for employing these flexible approaches. The very few who didn't, resigned. This was deemed disappointing but appropriate, leaving a more cohesive faculty that shared the new approaches to student equity. Alertness to understanding each student's situation and challenges, combined with leadership's active support, substantially changed the faculty as instructors. Consequently, the evidence supporting this variable/behavior was newly energized but appropriate for the time. Without the pandemic, compelling positive evidence of DEI-informed policies may have been weaker.

Variable 3: Procedures

As the new policies gained traction, procedures developed to support them. A by-product of having to create new processes was increased communication across institutional stakeholders. Academic advisors, senior faculty, and leadership reached out across teams in search of solutions for individual students and circumstances. Academic advisors were overwhelmed with student requests and needed more frequent and urgent input from faculty and leadership. In turn, faculty were fielding more appeals from students in difficult situations.

Variable 4: Practices

The communication channel between full-time academic faculty and leaders and adjunct faculty, called "contributing faculty" within Walden, opened up and increased in volume starting in 2020 and continuing through this writing. Contributing faculty reached out to leadership more frequently to verify and test what leeway was allowable. As the pandemic shifts, this communication channel has maintained its strength. There was also increased communication between faculty and their students as each situation

Assessing Institutional Readiness

was disclosed, discussed, and addressed. Faculty started using voice and text with their students more frequently to circumvent pressures on computers and tablets as well as internet bandwidth.

The intensity of developing procedures under pandemic pressure naturally led to codifying successful responses to student needs. As one faculty member created a practice for late submission of student work, it was shared to other faculty, either directly from colleague to colleague or from faculty to leadership and back out to faculty.

Given the demands of the pandemic, the participants focused primarily on these issues when piloting the self-assessment tool. Since the pilot ended, additional practices are being socialized, including the maxim to "believe the student." Faculty no longer ask students for proof of illness or death in the family as a prerequisite to establishing recovery plans. We recognize that no matter what words students use to ask for extensions, they are in distress. The best way to support a student in stressful situations is to create and offer a way to recover. Should the working group revisit this domain in what is optimistically called the post-pandemic environment, additional procedures and policies similar to "believe the student" would figure more prominently. SIUS was already on the path to these practices, but the pandemic lent urgency to their implementation.

This positive evidence was reassuring to the working group. As with most self-reflection, it can be difficult to identify where blind spots exist. A pandemic should not be the reason DEI is pursued. The rapid and prolonged confluence, though, made it hard to tease apart evidence that was less flattering. In this respect, it was useful to have a stakeholder and researcher, Dr. Lynn, who works outside the undergraduate programs, facilitate discussions and bring an objective perspective to the table.

Domain 1: "Delving Deeper" Questions

As previously mentioned, the participants found the "Delving Deeper" questions key to reflecting on SIUS's institutional readiness to support the underserved student. Following are summaries of the working group's discussion based on the tool kit's "Delving Deeper" questions for the first domain/assessment area, *Demonstrating Belief in Students*. These summaries have been shaped by Walden's director and dean of the Center for Research Quality, who also facilitated the discussions.

How does the Institution Value and Affirm the Cultural Capital of Underserved Students?

Affirming the cultural capital of students is a key component of valuing equity, diversity, and inclusion. Walden University is committed to these values and is making efforts to move in the right direction toward supporting them by creating working groups attached to governance councils that will discuss strategies to foster more equity, diversity, and inclusion. The working group collaborating with NIHUS is one example of this. These working groups, however, are not student focused specifically, nor do they always acknowledge the cultural capital these students bring to the institution. Hopefully, these working groups will empower faculty and staff to learn how to connect with students. Knowing how to listen to students better will allow faculty to understand students' perspectives, to demonstrate affirmation of students' identities and values, and to recognize students' cultural capital.

What Biases or Stereotypes May be Standing in the Way?

Some of the biases and stereotypes that stand in the way of affirming a students' cultural capital may be a result of the fact that most of our faculty, administrators, and staff are White and middle to upper class. This perspective may influence how faculty perceive aspects of underserved students' academic behavior and responses. For example, late work submissions may be perceived as laziness and a result of the student lacking time management skills rather than as a result of students having multiple jobs to make ends meet or a lack of access to internet and equipment. Plagiarism may be perceived as deliberate cheating rather than a cultural difference in understanding of "cheating" or an act of nerves and desperation by a student who is struggling to keep their head above water. Faculty may assume students understand their directions, comments, and feedback based on a Eurocentric understanding of culture and language use and jargon, expect students to write in standard English, and misinterpret cultural customs around power dynamics, asking for help, and solving personal obstacles. Because biases and stereotypes are not limited to ethnicity or nationality and culture is a wider concept than ethnic background or race, biases can also exist around students' disability, gender identity, and other cultural differences.

What do our Students' Own Stories Tell Us About the Work the Institution Needs to do?

Our students want accommodations for religious holidays and longer breaks between terms to guard against exhaustion. Many students seem confused about the services available to them, such as accommodations for disabilities, mental health disorders, and other personal issues. Our data shows that certain groups of students must go above and beyond what others do to complete assignments, attend residencies, and pay tuition. We need to listen to these students and find out how to lessen this burden for them. Students do not always understand instructors' tone, particularly when the instructor uses formal language in written communication and comes across as uncaring. Students talk about a fear of retaliation if they complain and feel alienated by instructors who seem to arbitrarily enforce policy even in the face of extenuating circumstances outside of the classroom.

How does the Institution Ensure that the Underserved Students Receive the Appropriate Amount of Challenge and Support to Ensure Their Success Without Marginalizing these Students?

Walden students are not considered traditional. Most of them are adults who work full time, care for children or aging parents, are not White and middle class, and require financial aid to afford their education. It is important to note this because it will define what we mean by "challenge" and "support" as we answer this question. We need to define those terms in ways that reflect our specific population. We need to focus on the feedback we receive from students. If they ask for extra help and support, faculty should listen carefully and not rush to judgment or respond as if we know better from our position.

Walden's strategies not to marginalize students include not permitting faculty to ask students about their disabilities or disclose any personal information about a student to other students. We have a robust procedure for students to obtain accommodations if they need them, and our faculty is trained to support this process. We have a broad-access, open-enrollment policy and a well-developed process of recruiting and enrolling students with plenty of support from advisors. We are careful as an institution to be sensitive to environmental concerns, such as creating flexible policies for students around COVID or natural disaster that may be affecting our students in large numbers. We offer an ombuds process and a grievance process, and we uphold student-centered laws like the Americans With Disabilities Act, Age Discrimination Act of 1975, FERPA, Title VI of the Civil Rights Act of 1964, and Title IX of the Education Amendment.

Lastly in this context, we also are careful to update our courses to align with the latest theories in pedagogy for educational technology and compassionate, empathetic teaching. We have some room for growth, however. There is a sense that faculty will do most of the heavy lifting in challenging students while not marginalizing them, but we need the help of university services focused on students and more training for faculty in this area.

Additional Areas of Reflection

Above are summaries of the working group's reflection to the first section of the NIHUS tool kit pilot, both as subjects and as assessors of the tool kit itself. This paper does not allow for a full report of the pilot assessment experience through all four of the tool kit's domains and variables. However, some additional questions posed by the tool kit with the working group's responses may be of interest to the reader and are included here.

What are the Essential Understandings and Preconditions That Enable Campus Leaders to Support Student Success by Leveraging the Ecosystem That Surrounds Their Campuses?

Students are individuals. Continual faculty development and communications is needed, to keep part-time contributing faculty (adjuncts) connected to shifting approaches and priorities in dealing with vulnerable students. At Walden, it is understood that student support, especially student support services and the like, are crucial for our students, many of whom have concerns about such areas as financial aid, work, veteran services, disability services, recognition of family responsibilities (children, aging parents, etc.).

In SIUS, the Undergraduate Faculty Training (UGFT) course, designed for newly hired undergraduate faculty, is one part of the university's commitment to continuous improvement. Through continual revision, the latest policies and practices are included in the training so new faculty are up to speed on the current approaches to DEI. The institution is aware and committed to ongoing faculty training in rationale, cultural context, and the nature of holistic strategy and extends this to deans and academic leaders. Moreover, SIUS's increased focus on fostering and maintaining updated undergraduate general education learning outcomes is important because undergraduate general education students need not only time but also strategies for maximizing that time in order to achieve established learning outcomes.

Who are Today's College Students, and What Institutional and Interpersonal Dynamics can Influence Their Success on College Campuses?

The COVID pandemic has had an impact, but there has not been a major shift in the overall undergraduate student body. Perhaps a small percentage of students are now saying that they are also hoping to earn master's degrees at Walden. Faculty serve as cheerleaders for these goals, especially given the fact that many of our students are the first in their families to pursue college degrees (that aspect is not new to the institution, but it is increasing).

Faster response to student frustration is needed. Students can be frustrated at inconvenient times for leaders and faculty. One faculty member reported receiving four emails from a student between midnight and 6 a.m., each expressing more frustration than the one before and demanding that work that had been submitted at midnight be graded immediately. The faculty member had been asleep and gently pointed that out to the student. Improved communication around financial aid, timing, disbursement amounts, limits, and the details of the process are needed. Even a temporary delay of 3 or 4 days can cause undue stress, especially when students are relying on disbursements to pay for groceries as well as tuition.

The Walden student body, and especially the undergraduate general education student, is diverse in every way: nontraditional students who generally are older than age 24; have children and/or aging parents; and are low income, first generation, and working. Institutions of higher education need to be flexible because adult students have busy lives with multiple responsibilities. In addition, international students may have contexts and responsibilities that are not as familiar to U.S.-based instructors. There may also be a disconnect between students' and faculty timing for school and/or work—their noon may be a faculty member's midnight.

CONCLUSION

How Can Campus Leaders Create Partnerships that Work?

At Walden, potential partnerships are handled outside the academic realm. This is likely not unique to Walden, and other institutions may not be leveraging faculty community ties to build institutional relationships.

Another area of opportunity would be participatory action research, which can lead to both continuous improvement and meaningful engagement with stakeholders. In addition, there need to be systems in place for listening to students and faculty and understanding their lives. Bringing employers into the conversation opens the discussion further to consideration of tuition reduction or reimbursement plans and flexible work schedules. This would be especially relevant for programs that support needed workforce skills that employers have identified.

How Can Leaders Make the Most of Creative Tensions in the Community?

Leaders can provide opportunities for the exchange of ideas by meeting to discuss what initiatives may arise or even capitalizing on underutilized, already existing ideas. Leaders also can create opportunities for safe discussions and community listening by gathering information and ensuring that diverse perspectives are shared. Leaders also can refocus the institution's attention on breaking down barriers to student success and provide productive outlets for frustration with administrative processes by streamlining these processes and breaking down silos. Faculty/staff cross-functional working groups and structured catch-up plans for students who have fallen behind are a great way to start.

Conclusion

The consensus is that the NIHUS has developed a strong mechanism for sparking and facilitating discussions of diversity, equity, and inclusion that challenges received wisdom and assumptions about what diversity, equity, and inclusion mean as well as the varied levels and touchpoints that put students at the center of program-wide initiatives, operational processes, and practices.

Participants agreed that this was a unique assessment tool that was useful for academic administrators and program leaders to engage in a reflection process and identify some broad gaps where more resources are needed or students could be better served or in more effective ways. The need for the student voice in an asynchronous online university is clear but difficult to organize. Students who are doing schoolwork during their lunch break on a work computer or who are coming off a 12-hour shift and still needing to make dinner and put the kids to bed are the voices most needed but hardest to ask for.

Reflecting on these areas brought light to current strategies in SIUS, where the university has alignment for strategically supporting historically underserved students. This reflection also indicated what is systemic and organized within the program and university versus what is instructor or department dependent.

We recognize that reviewing this tool and providing feedback to NIHUS is a valuable contribution to their work and understanding of how an organization like Walden University could apply this tool. Additionally, this is an important step in understanding how the school serves diverse students and what can be improved. This work helped define a clear path for using this guide with an expanded group of undergraduate stakeholders. Other degree levels, including our doctoral programs, could also benefit greatly from this effort. Below is a summary of the concrete plans and directions stemming from this experience

For SIUS, the tool will be adapted for institutional self-reflection based on the recommendations and experience from this pilot. Beyond administrative reflection, additional essential stakeholders will engage in a similar process using an adaptation of this guide. The consensus of the working group would be to apply tools and methods of participatory action research, or PAR, (McIntyre, 2007) as follows:

1. Develop a series of questions, or slightly amend the NIHUS tool kit questions, that stakeholder groups can use to review consideration of policies, practices, and resources.
2. Hold discussion sessions to review documentation and synthesize findings. It is important that stakeholder representatives are co-evaluators/researchers in coming to common understanding and that this is a true experience of engagement with everyone having a voice.
3. Stakeholder teams would include diverse representation within separate stakeholder groups, including full-time and part-time faculty, undergraduate students, academic advisors, and other support service teams.

Within the PAR approach, it will be important not only to understand perspectives on student experiences and university recommendations but also specifically learn what faculty and administrators need to do to better serve and support historically underserved students.

PAR is very appropriate for Walden's purpose in engaging stakeholders as equal partners with a clear voice in the decisions resulting from the assessment. Additionally, it supports learning and change that is iterative, ensuring that inclusivity work is not a point-in-time activity. Instead, it is then embedded within the organizational culture through a continuous improvement process with updates, report outs, and strategy refinement (McIntyre, 2007). Aspects of the PAR concept are also highly aligned with processes embedded in the NIHUS tool kit for self-reflection and assessment.

This work is an example of Walden University's commitment to being inclusive in our process of assessing and truly understanding ways our degree levels and programs can continue to improve in efforts to be a broadly inclusive institution. Beyond SIUS, the process reflection and further strategy sparked by this tool is needed across the university. After further integration and application with SIUS, a working group will be developed for doctoral programs that uses an updated guide and a participatory action research study will be applied. The collaboration and support between the National Institutes for Historically-Underserved Students and Walden's School of Interdisciplinary Undergraduate Studies has been valuable for both organizations. The hope is that the collaboration will continue to the benefit of students beyond these two institutions.

REFERENCES

McIntyre, A. (2007). *Participatory action research*. SAGE Publications.

McNair, T. B., Albertine, S., Cooper, M. A., McDonald, M., & Major, T. Jr. (2016). *Becoming a student-ready college: A new culture of leadership for student success*. Jossey-Bass.

Walden University. (n.d.). *Diverse and inclusive*. https://www.waldenfacts.com/#section3

ADDITIONAL READING

Anderson, M. B. L. (2018). *A seat at the table: African American youth's perceptions of K-12 education*. UNCF. https://cdn.uncf.org/wp-content/uploads/reports/Advocacy_ASATTBro_4-18F_Digital.pdf?_ga=2.110064460.877671887.1655900854-1650829736.1655900854

Association of American Colleges and Universities. (2015). *Committing to equity and inclusive excellence: A campus guide for self-study and planning*. https://files.eric.ed.gov/fulltext/ED556762.pdf

Baber, L. D., Castro, E. L., & Bragg, D. D. (2010). *Measuring success: David Conley's college readiness framework and the Illinois college and career readiness act*. Office of Community College Research and Leadership at the University of Illinois at Urbana-Champaign. https://files.eric.ed.gov/fulltext/ED513397.pdf

Baber, L. D., & Common, B. (2010). "Keep seeing the options.... don't give up": How males of color in a college and career readiness intervention portray their high school-to-college transition experiences. Office of Community College Research and Leadership at the University of Illinois at Urbana-Champaign. https://occrl.illinois.edu/docs/librariesprovider2/ccr/options.pdf

Barnett, E. A., & Bragg, D. D. (2006). Academic pathways and increased opportunities for underserved students: Crosscutting themes and lessons learned. *New Directions for Community Colleges*, 2006(135), 101–107. doi:10.1002/cc.252

Bragg, D. D., Kim, E., & Barnett, E. A. (2006). Creating access and success: Academic pathways reaching underserved students. *New Directions for Community Colleges*, *2006*(135), 5–19. doi:10.1002/cc.243

Bryk, A. S., Gomez, L., & Grunow, A. (2011). *Getting ideas into action: Building networked improvement communities in education.* Carnegie Foundation for the Advancement of Teaching. https://www.carnegiefoundation.org/resources/publications/getting-ideas-action-building-networked-improvement-communities-education/

Carnegie Foundation. (2017). *How a networked improvement community improved success rates for struggling college math students.* Carnegie Foundation for the Advancement of Teaching. https://www.carnegiefoundation.org/wp-content/uploads/2017/01/pathways_vignette_01-13-17.pdf

Castleman, B. L., Arnold, K., & Lynk Wartman, K. (2012). Stemming the tide of summer melt: An experimental study on the effects of post-high school summer intervention on low-income students' college enrollment. *Journal of Research on Educational Effectiveness*, *5*(1), 1–17. https://eric.ed.gov/?id=EJ952097. doi:10.1080/19345747.2011.618214

Castro, E. L. (2013). Racialized readiness for college and career: Toward an equity-grounded social science of intervention programming. *Community College Review*, *41*(4), 292–310. doi:10.1177/0091552113504291

Clouse, W. A. (2012). The effects of non-compulsory freshman seminar and core curriculum completion ratios on post-secondary persistence and baccalaureate degree attainment (Publication No. 3523633) [Doctoral dissertation, University of Colorado at Colorado Springs]. ProQuest Dissertations and Theses database.

Conley, D. T., Drummond, K. V., de Gonzalez, A., Rooseboom, J., & Stout, O. (2011). *Reaching the goal: The applicability and importance of the common core state standards to college and career readiness.* https://achievethecore.org/content/upload/2011_ReachingtheGoal-FullReport.pdf

Cunningham, A., Park, E., & Engle, J. (2014). *Minority-serving institutions: Doing more with less.* Institute for Higher Education Policy.

Del Siegle, E., Gubbins, J., O'Rourke, P., Langley, S. D., Mun, R. U., Luria, S. R., Little, C. A., McCoach, B., Knupp, T., Callahan, C. M., & Plucker, J. A. (2016). Barriers to underserved students' participation in gifted programs and possible solutions. *Journal for the Education of the Gifted*, *39*(2), 103–131. doi:10.1177/0162353216640930

Domina, T. (2009). What works in college outreach: Assessing targeted and schoolwide interventions for disadvantaged students. *Educational Evaluation and Policy Analysis*, *31*(2), 127–152. doi:10.3102/0162373709333887

Ferretti, R. P., & Eisenman, L. T. (2010). Commentary: Delivering educational services that meet the needs of all students. *Exceptional Children*, *76*(3), 378–383. doi:10.1177/001440291007600308

Folk, A. L. (2018). Drawing on students' funds of knowledge: Using identity and lived experience to join the conversation in research assignments. *Journal of Information Literacy*, *12*(2), 44–59. doi:10.11645/12.2.2468

Green, D. (2006). Historically underserved students: What we know, what we still need to know. *New Directions for Community Colleges, 2006*(135), 21–28. doi:10.1002/cc.244

Gupta, A., Garg, D., & Kumar, P. (2018). Analysis of students' ratings of teaching quality to understand the role of gender and socio-economic diversity in higher education. *IEEE Transactions on Education, 61*(4), 319–327. doi:10.1109/TE.2018.2814599

Jamelske, E. (2009). Measuring the impact of a university first-year experience program on student GPA and retention. *Higher Education, 57*(3), 373–391. https://eric.ed.gov/?id=EJ825726. doi:10.100710734-008-9161-1

Johnson, G. (2021, October 28–29). *Compassionate teaching strategies in digital classrooms for adult online students* [Conference presentation]. 28th National HBCU faculty development network conference. Virtual.

Kezar, A. J., & Lester, J. (2009). *Organizing higher education for collaboration: A guide for campus leaders*. Jossey-Bass.

Kinzie, J., Gonyea, R., Shoup, R., & Kuh, G. D. (2008). Promoting persistence and success of underrepresented students: Lessons for teaching and learning. *New Directions for Teaching and Learning, 2008*(115), 21–38. doi:10.1002/tl.323

Murphy, T. E., Gaughan, M., Hume, R., & Moore, S. G. Jr. (2010). College graduation rates for minority students in a selective technical university: Will participation on summer bridge contribute to success? *Educational Evaluation and Policy Analysis, 32*(1), 70–83. doi:10.3102/0162373709360064 PMID:23136456

Office of Teaching and Learning Excellence. (2021, September 7). *"Catch-up plans" as a demonstration of empathy in the student-instructor relationship* [Video]. YouTube. https://www.youtube.com/watch?v=bSVnTsurJsM

Prystowsky, R. J., Herrera, J., Crowley, C., Lowery-Hart, R., & Fannon, S. (2017). Grabbing third rails: Courageous responses to persistent equity gaps. *Liberal Education, 103*(2), 44.

Rendón, L. I. (2006). *Reconceptualizing success for underserved students in higher education*. National Postsecondary Education Cooperative. https:// nces.ed.gov/NPEC/pdf/resp_Rendon.pdf

Roderick, M., Nagaoka, J., & Coca, V. (2009). College readiness for all: The challenge for urban high schools. *The Future of Children, 19*(1), 185–210. doi:10.1353/foc.0.0024 PMID:21141710

Schroeder, C. M. (2011). *Coming in from the margins: Faculty development's emerging organizational development role in institutional change*. Stylus Publishing.

Visher, M. G., Weiss, M. J., Weissman, E., Rudd, T., & Wathington, H. D. (2012). The effects of learning communities for students in developmental education: A synthesis of findings from six community colleges. National Center for Postsecondary Research. https://www.mdrc.org/sites/default/files/LC%20A%20Synthesis%20of%20Findings%20FR.pdf

Weiss, M. J., Visher, M. G., & Wathington, H. (2010). *Learning communities for students in developmental reading: An impact study at Hillsborough Community College.* National Center for Postsecondary Research. https://www.mdrc.org/sites/default/files/full_424.pdf

Wilkerson, S. L. (2008). An empirical analysis of factors that influence the first year to second year retention of students at one large, Hispanic Serving institution (HSI) (Publication No. 3333787) [Doctoral dissertation, Texas A&M University]. ProQuest Dissertations and Theses database.

Chapter 12
Developing a Rubric for a Person-Centered Approach to Teaching in Inclusive Online Learning Spaces

William C. Schulz III
https://orcid.org/0000-0001-8560-5540
Walden University, USA

Juli K. Konopa
https://orcid.org/0000-0003-3753-579X
Walden University, USA

ABSTRACT

In this chapter, the authors discuss the benefits of developing and deploying a care-oriented, person-centered rubric for supporting effective online learning relationships. The process by which the rubric was developed at the university and a detailed faculty-focused rubric are presented as part of a larger inclusive teaching and learning standards framework, and the implications of utilizing both the rubric and ITL frame for future faculty recruiting, development, and assessment are discussed.

INTRODUCTION

One of the challenges in implementing a person-centered, inclusive teaching and learning environment, either for in-person or online learning, is identifying the specific actions and behaviors of faculty and students that contribute to the creation of healthy learning relationships and finding a proximate way to measure these behaviors in an online setting.

Inclusive teaching at Walden is an intentional practice and requires conscious awareness of the diverse social, cultural, and community identities and lived experiences of all learners. Inclusive teaching includes a variety of strategies to fully activate student strengths, and it occurs in environments that

DOI: 10.4018/978-1-6684-5146-5.ch012

Developing a Rubric for a Person-Centered Approach to Teaching in Inclusive Online Learning Spaces

draw relevant, meaningful connections to their lives and the professional dispositions they develop. The goal is to ensure that learners know Walden values the inherent worth, humanity, and dignity of every learner engaged in the learning process.

In this chapter, we will discuss both the need for and the collaborative process by which Walden University has developed a learning-relationship & faculty-oriented rubric that aligns with and supports Walden's larger inclusive teaching and learning strategy. This rubric builds on Walden's faculty quality appreciation indicators, Walden's hallmarks of quality framework, and its historic commitments to best practices in online learning.

The general outline and the detailed elements of the integrated, inclusive teaching and learning faculty quality rubric will be presented. It is important to note that the logic and elements of the rubric flow from the learning model that was presented in Chapter 1 ("Developing a Learning Model for Caring, Inclusion and Social Change in an Online Environment"), where we discuss more broadly how an inclusive teaching and learning perspective can help faculty and staff be more responsive in supporting all its learners, particularly those from traditionally marginalized populations who are less likely to understand the hidden curriculum of higher education (Austin et al., 2021; Delvin & McKay, 2018).

The behavioral elements described in the rubric algin with both Walden's inclusive teaching and learning model and also frameworks and practices that seek, like the American Association of Colleges and Universities, "inclusive excellence [that] emphasizes student intellectual and social development and the need to create a welcoming community that values cultural differences" (Chun & Evans, 2010, p. 2).

The rubric elements inform our expectations of faculty, but this chapter does not go into detail about how to specifically develop culturally competent teaching and learning practices, which is a subject worthy of a book-length treatment itself (Darby & Lang, 2019). Rather, we conclude the chapter with a general discussion of the implications for future faculty recruiting and development.

BACKGROUND

In Chapter 1 ("Developing a Learning Model for Caring, Inclusion and Social Change in an Online Environment"), the diagram below was presented to illustrate how Walden's learning model supports its inclusive teaching and learning (ITL) strategy:

As you review the diagram, note how four of the five threads are highly process- and relationship-focused and address the *how* of Walden's learning model. As such, each element is highly dependent on and assumes that the human beings at the heart of these relationships have the capabilities to be inclusive, respectful, curious, reflective, and caring of others.

The model requires, in particular, that faculty come to the learning relationship prepared to not only be experts in content, but also empathetic, person-centered servant leaders who can help welcome (Ahn & Davis, 2020) and guide students in their learning within an online, multi-contextual, multicultural, and inclusive teaching and learning environment. Faculty too, must also be capable of and comfortable with supporting learning relationships within the context of an online community of appreciative mutual inquiry (Garrison et al., 2000; Swan, 2004), as discussed in Chapter 2 ("Digital Appreciative Inquiry for Inclusion").

This is a lot to ask of faculty, who are among the most important frontline professionals that represent their university in countless moments of truth (Carlzon, 1989) when they engage with their learners/students each day.

Figure 1. How Walden's Learning Model Supports its ITL Strategy
Note. Image credit: Nina M. McCune, Walden University.

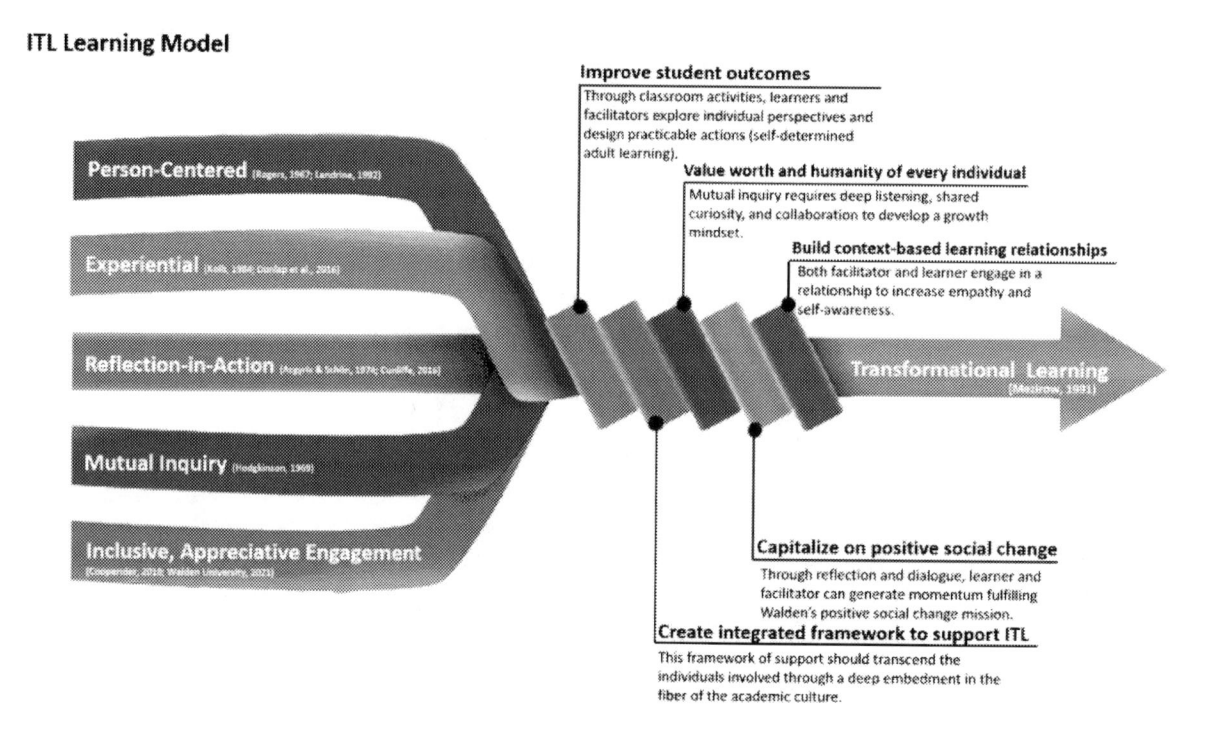

ITL Learning Model

Moments of Truth in Higher Education

Jan Carlzon, in his 1989 book, *Moments of Truth: New Strategies for Today's Customer-Driven Economy*, addressed the challenges of moving a traditional, heavily regulated Scandinavian airline into one that could be responsive, in real-time, to the needs of the people it served. As Tom Peters notes in the forward to the book (Carlzon, 1989, p. vii):

Everyone wants to be treated like an individual... After all, the first (and every) 15-second encounter between a passenger and the frontline people, from ticket agent to flight attendant, sets the tone of the entire company in the mind of the customer. This is what Carlzon calls "the moment of truth."

Thirty-three years later, whether you are a faculty member, work in the bursar's office, are a program manager, or serve as dean of an academic department, it is impossible not to acknowledge that a certain *customerization* has come to all higher education and that the observations of Jan Carlzon and Tom Peters are relevant to us today. Those that pay for our educational services come to each of our universities with a strong customer mindset and with the expectations that their individual needs can and will—even must—be met by those in higher education.

You may not like the idea of *student as customer*, but the truth is that our potential students (customers), and then our enrolled students, DO think of themselves first as customers. (Personally, we like to think of them as *clients* and *shared learners* and *not* customers or students.) So, what does Carlzon, the airlines, and customers like this have to do with education?

Developing a Rubric for a Person-Centered Approach to Teaching in Inclusive Online Learning Spaces

A university, in key aspects, is very much like an airline: They both offer relative commodities (a byproduct of regulation and accreditation) that are perishable in time (seats or seat-time offered in a term), that require an array of large-scale information technology and sophisticated software programs. These programs need to be able to talk to one other to allow for seamless scheduling, staffing, billing, etc. And, in both cases, the software programs must help frontline professionals provide very high-touch, fast-moving, individualized personal service.

Likewise, the most important resources in both an airline and a university are the people who engage with those customers/students/clients/passengers and who serve them at the frontline. Especially when things go wrong, the ability of those people on the frontline of the university to meet a moment of truth can make the difference between keeping a customer/learner/client or losing them to a competitor. Worse still is if that person abandoned their educational plans altogether, which would be both a personal and a societal loss.

To push the comparison even further, once a flight/course is launched—and we have diverse groups of people who don't know one another confined within a space, must follow explicit rules and instructions, and have a wide range of expectations for how they should be taken care of during the journey—an immense amount of pressure is put on the flight crew/faculty/advisors to get it right, now and always.

Layer this real-time pressure with the cultural notion that *the customer is always right*, and it is no surprise that tensions rise when even small things go wrong during a flight/course. These tensions can elevate to outright conflict (exacerbated, of course, by those differences in expectations within the flight/section—consider flying in the COVID era).

So, what is the solution to these challenges? How can we support the frontline staff, especially the faculty in the case of higher education, so that they can, in turn, best support those who are paying for their services but might not always appreciate those services?

How can we help our faculty be more person centered in real-time, especially in an online context?[1]

In the next sections, we'll briefly explore some of the structural challenges to being person centered within an online context and review how Walden supports its faculty generally. Then we'll present our person-centered, inclusive teaching and learning rubric, which is deeply informed by our learning model. We will then discuss how this rubric informs our faculty development and performance management processes—all aimed at enabling our faculty to meet difficult moments of truth.

Structural Challenges to Meeting the Moments of Truth in Online Higher Education

Before we explore the ways a person-centered, inclusive teaching and learning rubric can help us support faculty (and thus learners), it's important to note that if you teach in a purely online context, as Walden faculty do, there are structural challenges that make being person centered even more difficult than it is within a direct face-to-face learning context.

In online learning, especially in those contexts where such learning is provided in a dominant, or fully asynchronous fashion, the largest and most obvious challenge to building strong and consistent person-centered relationships is that technology mediates them and presses us into what seems like one- or two-dimensional worlds of gray scale, rather than a full-color, three-dimensional world. The convenience of asynchronous online engagement comes at the price of losing many, if not all, non-verbal communication queues and meaning that is often conveyed through verbal pitch and tone and the trust and mutual vulnerability that happens when someone is sharing the same physical space with you.

That is, it is much easier to potentially understand a whole person that is proximate with you than one that has been flattened into a mostly two-dimensional world dominated by the written word. While being face to face can come with its challenges of implicit bias triggers, overall, it is likely easier to build a person-to-person connection—and more trust—when you share physical spaces.

Likewise, and this holds for both online and on-ground teaching and learning, another structural challenge is the speed and scale at which most courses/learning experiences are offered. Programs are built so that learners can potentially progress through them quickly (via 6- or 8-week, full-credit courses, for example), and in combination with relatively large section sizes for many core or required courses, the combination of a short flight with many passengers can make it difficult to be personal.

So, what behaviors and behavioral strategies might mitigate some of these challenges so that faculty have more of an ability to offer a trustworthy, caring, person-centered, diverse, and inclusive learning and working environment? How can we support faculty so they can better serve each learner and create a learning climate in which others can achieve their goals, find success, and make inspiring contributions to our global society?

The first step is to recognize that faculty, including today's online faculty, must go beyond being competent content managers and purveyors of knowledge. They must also be masters of relationship building and must exhibit the traits of transformational leaders who "engage with others in such a way that leaders and followers raise one another up to higher levels of motivation and morality" (Bogler et al., 2013, p. 379).

The second step is to recognize that it is the university's responsibility to explicitly identify, recruit for, develop, and reward faculty when they put caring, inclusive, person-centered behaviors into action. In the remainder of this chapter, we will briefly review how Walden supports its faculty generally, then we will focus on how we developed a learning-relationship & faculty-oriented rubric that aligns with and supports Walden's larger inclusive teaching and learning strategy. This rubric builds on Walden's faculty quality appreciation indicators, Walden's hallmarks of quality framework, and our historic commitments to best practices in online learning.

Finally, we will share the specific elements of the integrated, inclusive teaching and learning faculty quality rubric, and the implications for future faculty recruiting and development will be discussed.

Preparing Our Frontline Faculty for Moments of Truth

Over the years, Walden University has made several important investments in supporting the teaching excellence of its faculty. Walden's Office of Teaching and Learning Excellence (OTLE) maintains a staff of experts that supports high-quality online teaching and learning by engaging the faculty and academic leadership and providing a number of services, including offering a robust onboard training and development program, many self-paced professional development modules, and live webinars and coaching, among others.

The OTLE, and academic leadership, is supported by the Faculty Administration Advisory Council (FAAC), which informs, develops, and recommends policy, practice, and procedure under the oversight of the Office of the Provost. Members engage in discussion about topics including, faculty development, satisfaction, and teaching/learning success; teaching culture and adherence to teaching models and practices espoused by Walden and its faculty; faculty performance and quality standards and their measurement; and improvement of the student experience through instruction, mentoring, and other faculty roles. The council has three working groups: Faculty Onboarding, Training, and Development; Instructional Quality and Student Learning; and Faculty Experience.

As Walden has developed its inclusive teaching and learning strategy and accompanying learning model, it has relied on the work and input of the FAAC as well as the input of the staff of the Office of Teaching and Learning Excellence to improve elements and tools designed to support the ITL strategy. One of the most important contributions from the OTLE/FAAC team was the development of Walden's faculty quality appreciation standards, which are a foundational element of our ITL practices.

Development of Walden's Faculty Quality Appreciation Framework

As part of their ongoing mission to support faculty quality and to provide leadership and a voice on faculty quality issues and standards, staff members from the Office of Teaching and Learning Excellence were joined in 2018 by faculty and staff representatives and academic leadership in a 3-day summit centered on faculty key performance metrics and faculty quality standards.

The team's analysis process was guided using an Appreciative Inquiry approach, as described by Morgan, et al., (2022, forthcoming):

An Appreciative Inquiry Summit (AIS) was used as the method to build on existing strengths and uphold a culture rooted in social change, branching into positive leadership (Cameron, 2008). Use of Appreciative Inquiry (AI) allowed for the exploration of dialogic assessment of quality in teaching and learning during that time (Powley et al., 2004). The process was grounded in the key AI Principles encouraging asset-focused, inclusive co-construction of an ideal result...

The AIS began with a provost welcome and review of the call-to-action. The facilitator discussed the AI approach and tenets for engagement. The summit team was told this would be a summit powered by positive leadership and positive education. The summit team would be considering the whole system of whole individuals. Team members would self-manage, share stories, encourage the ideas of others, listen, and engage in mutual inquiry. Team members would honor diversity, embrace various forms of expression or creativity, and embrace the unknown. They would find common ground and opportunities where their strengths and imaginations come together.

The AIS resulted in the formation of three working groups focused on faculty quality standards and competencies, faculty performance data, and faculty peer observation. What started as a summit of 20 individuals morphed into 120 working groups, subgroups, and university experts contributing to a deep and systemic, 18-month review of Walden's quality teaching standards and expectations to ensure outcomes and action plans were values based, faculty driven, and student centered.

During that period, the Faculty Quality Standards working group conducted a review of literature pertaining to standards for faculty quality and performance and wrote annotated bibliographies for more than 40 articles. Through the review, the group discovered the quality standards identified in the literature were already infused within the culture of Walden and existing policies as well as practices exhibited by many faculty members, but the standards were not clearly outlined in university documentation relating to expectations for faculty performance.

In order to provide faculty with additional guidance, the group developed a faculty quality goal statement and a framework for key faculty roles that was composed of quality standards, quality indicators, and evidence of quality performance. Table 1 presents the quality appreciation framework.

Table 1. Walden University faculty quality framework

Walden University Faculty Quality Framework	
Walden University aims to recruit, hire, retain high quality faculty and help all faculty improve their performance by bringing the faculty voice to the university at a level that informs decision making as well as standards and policy revision, development, and implementation. Faculty members should use this model as a guide for performance achievement as well as growth and development. It can also be used as a guide for professional accountability, to develop annual work plans, and to summarize performance for performance assessment/review processes.	
Quality Standards:	Represent quality guidelines in the areas of instructional engagement, scholarship, and service that will serve as a guide for Walden University faculty performance, growth and development, annual work plans, and annual performance assessment/review.
Quality Indicators:	Represent behaviors that demonstrate understanding and or mastery of a standard/competency area. Faculty do not have to demonstrate all behaviors listed as quality indicators. Rather, these are examples of the types of activities in which faculty who demonstrate competency in this category might exhibit.
Evidence of Quality Performance:	Represent documentation/evidence items that may be used to support faculty performance, growth, and development.

The overarching goal was that faculty members use this model as a guide for performance achievement, growth, and development as well as for professional accountability. It was also intended that the model could help faculty develop annual work plans and summarize their performance for performance assessment/review processes.

The quality standards were categorized into performance areas of instructional engagement, scholarship, and service. Next, the group reviewed the university's existing key performance indicators (KPIs) by faculty role and aligned them to statements summarizing quality indicators as revealed in the literature. The quality indicators represent behaviors that demonstrate understanding and or mastery of a standard/competency area and serve as examples of the types of activities in which faculty who demonstrate competency in each category might exhibit.

However, the group realized it wasn't sufficient to outline the framework, the standards, and the key performance indicators. It is just as important, group members reasoned, for faculty and university supervisors to be able to recognize quality performance when they see it or exhibit it. The result was the addition of direct measures of quality performance expressed as evidence items within the standards and performance indicators alignment matrix.

The group presented the proposed framework, standards, and performance indicators to stakeholders at various levels across the university to gather feedback and validate the model for the five primary faculty roles. Throughout these discussions, the overarching goals were to ensure the competencies thoroughly and accurately addressed all categories of instruction, key performance indicators reflected quality, student views about faculty quality were addressed, and there was a consistent faculty voice throughout the framework.

Developing a Rubric for a Person-Centered Approach to Teaching in Inclusive Online Learning Spaces

In January 2020, the recommendations and specific faculty appreciation quality indicators (see the tables later in this chapter that includes these FQIs) were formally considered and approved by Walden's university-level academic governance committee, which set the stage for incorporating them into the larger, inclusive teaching and learning framework that is discussed below.

TOWARD A PERSON-CENTERED, FACULTY-FOCUSED RUBRIC TO SUPPORT MORE EFFECTIVE ONLINE LEARNING

In Chapter 1 ("Developing a Learning Model for Caring, Inclusion and Social Change in an Online Environment"), we presented Walden's inclusive teaching and learning model in some detail and reviewed the model briefly in the introduction to this chapter. One of the five core threads of that model is that Walden is committed to ensuring that our faculty and staff take a person-centered approach to teaching, learning, and all the supporting functions that support learners.

Recall that the core elements of a person-centered approach to supporting learning relationships are:

- There must be *congruence* between the learner and facilitator.
  - Presence
  - Realness (authenticity)
  - Genuineness (general courtesy)
- There must be a *level of regard* between the learner and facilitator.
  - Active listening
  - Positive recognition
  - Timeliness in feedback and engagement
  - Contextual and culturally competent feedback
- There must be *empathy in the relationship* between the learner and the facilitator.
  - Reflective callouts
  - Overall caring approach

Why Taking a Person-Centered Approach is so Important

Carl Rogers argues that through our curriculum and teaching we must reach the whole person and seek to understand and engage with the whole person and their learning context (Landrine, 1992). Hence, this is a person-centered approach, not merely a student-centered approach in which faculty and support staff, working together, help to unlock the client's or the learner's untapped potential. It is everyone's job in the university, through the lenses of this person-centered approach, to provide on-the-spot customization when we can so that learners understand we see them as individuals and that we're working to help them learn best. The goal of expecting and supporting faculty and staff to work within this person-centered frame is to help create a community of care that leads our learners to be trusting of us and more willing to engage in the often-painful process of genuine and transformational learning. Figure 2 illustrates how a person-centered approach might help us reach those goals.

In each and every learning relationship there are both transactional and transformational elements of teaching that support learning. However, if we think of the relationship between teacher and learner as being that of two magnets, how they orient toward one another makes all the difference as to whether the relationship will attract deeper, more transformational learning, which is a core goal of universities whose mission is tied to helping students become leaders for social change.

The Shallows of a Transactional Approach to Teaching & Learning

If an instructor, or the environment in which an instructor must work, puts a premium and focus on the more *transactional elements of teaching*, or what might be thought of as a work-centered approach to teaching, then they spend the bulk of their time focused on the work of the student, and they take a more instrumental approach to the learning relationship. They might be more content- and product-oriented than process-oriented, and their responses to student inquiries may lack contextual depth. Finally, they may provide limited access via prescribed office hours. Given some of the structural challenges we described earlier, particularly the scale and speed issues, a transactional approach to teaching that focuses primarily on evaluating and responding to technical needs is rational but ultimately may be self-defeating in that learners may actually require more of a work-focused instructor's time because learners are not connecting to the tasks and get frustrated with a perceived lack of support.

From the learner's perspective, a transaction-work-oriented learning environment provides shallow soil for transformation. While there are, in fact, many students who are perfectly satisfied with transactional, shallow learning, when a university ties its mission to educating learners so that they can then affect social change, an approach such as the default is not acceptable.

For in such transactional environments, it is unlikely that learners will be able to overcome the fears that are an inherent part of learning. Many students, particularly first-generation and traditionally marginalized learners, come to the university and need help in learning to become a university learner (Christie et al., 2008; Collier & Morgan, 2008), and those needs cannot be met with a transactional approach to teaching.

If learners come to the learning relationship with fear, anxiety, and low trust, then they often exhibit fight or flight reactions to transactional, evaluative feedback that they perceive as judging them as people. Their trust further erodes, and they exhibit more external locus-of-control behaviors that can lead to confrontations with faculty and a polarizing, repelling magnet learning relationship.

Interestingly, even when faculty are committed to a more person-centered approach, the nature of most academics' analytic and evaluative training can work against them! One of the authors of this chapter was recently working with a doctoral student and was reviewing an early draft of their dissertation proposal. The author found themselves deeply involved in providing feedback on the logic and the structure of the work and then sent the suggestions and edits to the chair.

Upon a second look at the feedback, they thought, 'Oh dear, that was really technical feedback that could be received as overly critical.' They had done nothing within the feedback to acknowledge that this draft was much improved over the very first draft and that it was becoming easier to see where the emerging/new scholar was making original connections. Falling back into old patterns of being highly analytical and transactional—without taking the time to recognize the improving development of the learner—is easy to do, which is why being person centered first is key.

Figure 2. Incorporating a person-centered approach to teaching—a magnet for improving learning
Note. Image credit: Jose Henriquez, Walden University.

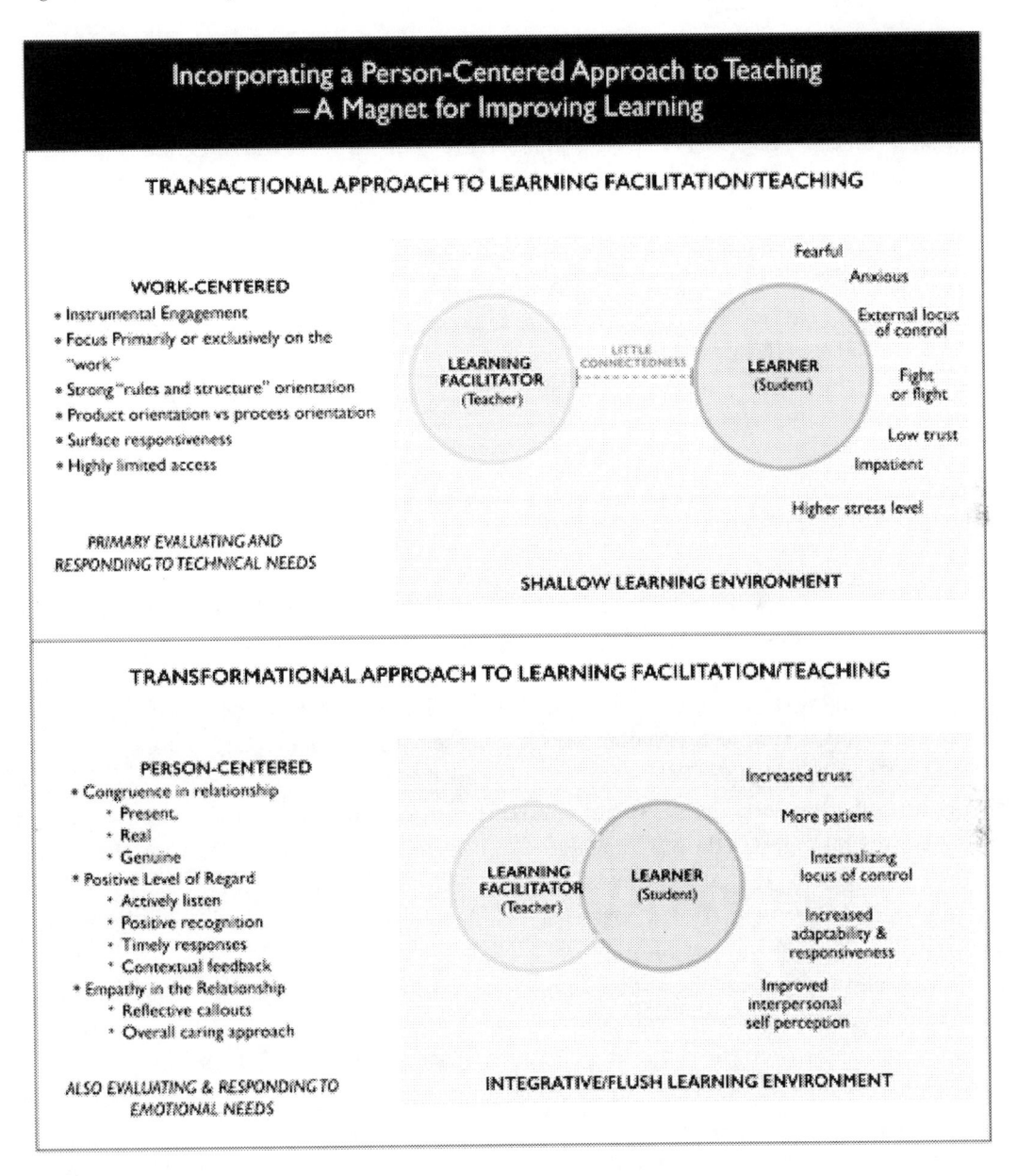

Starting Within a Person-Centered Transformational Approach for More Fertile Learning

While much of the day-to-day work faculty do to support their learners leans toward being transactional, the underlying context for that work—the learning relationship itself—can make a very big difference in how effective the transactional work winds up being from the perspective of the learner. If a faculty member must provide critical, difficult feedback to a learner, it is far more likely to be received, and perhaps even acted upon, if the learner trusts the motives of the faculty member and believes that the faculty cares for them as an individual.

For if a faculty member comes to each of their learners within the spirit of being person centered, of being present, real, and genuine, with a willingness to actively listen and recognize the positives in their learner, as someone who values that learner's unique experiences in the world and demonstrates an overall caring attitude with empathic sensitivity—it is much more likely to lead to an integrated and more fertile learning environment. With the belief that their faculty care, students will develop an increased trust and willingness to share their experiences and listen to others and will be more patient with themselves and less likely to give up when learning is painful. All these potentially beneficial individual outcomes also support more inclusive and engaging learning for all.

Upon reading this, you might observe that *this is just good teaching*, and not much more needs to be said about it. But it is clear that, as online programs continue to grow and the learning population continues to become more diverse, having a more formal framework to exercise person-centered learning could be helpful.

THE PERSON-CENTERED RUBRIC

We have argued, to this point, that taking a person-centered, humanizing (Pacansky-Brock, et. al., 2020) approach to inclusive online teaching and learning can help move the dial toward more transformational learning and increased persistence and completion by learners. Research supports this conclusion and suggests that recognizing learners as unique individuals with distinct experiences—being person centered—is both possible and valued in online learning (Leners & Sitzman, 2006; Mann, 2014; Vanslambrouck et al., 2016; Williams, 2017).

This research also suggests that there are specific behaviors and actions that course designers and faculty can take to create the conditions for a humanized online learning experience, and these behaviors align very cleanly with the Rogersian-based constructs outlined earlier in this chapter. Table 2 presents these person-centered, faculty-oriented constructs and then offers a preliminary way to operationalize them for inclusive teaching and learning.

Table 2 illustrates the major elements of the Rogers model and shows for each the operational construct and some examples of demonstrated behaviors for that construct. Some primary sources are also provided.

The major construct of congruence is broken into three subcomponents, which include general courtesy, presence, and realness. The easiest of these measures to practice and observe is general courtesy, but in the online environment it is all too easy to dispense with the small steps of saying 'hello' or 'thank you' in an email response chain. In situations where there may be potential disagreement or conflict, it is even more important to have established a basic relationship based in courtesy so that things do not escalate quickly because of small misunderstandings.

Likewise, in almost all the research on faculty engagement in the online classroom, having faculty establish a sense of presence in both the social and informal learning spaces is important (Robinson et al., 2020). Being available for substantive engagement in various learning spaces within the online classroom and demonstrating an active presence is a prerequisite for person-centered learning. Interestingly, there is research that shows that the quality of faculty engagements within the classroom are far more important than the quantity (Schindler & Burkholder, 2014), and the Rogersian construct of level of regard, which we will discuss shortly, helps inform the behaviors that support quality engagement.

Table 2. An operational construct rendering of a person-centered approach to inclusive teaching and learning

Rogers Relationship Inventory Construct	Operational Construct	Demonstrated Behaviors	Resources
Congruence: Genuineness	*General Courtesy*	Personal greeting, please, thank you, you are welcome, no ALL CAPS	Brockmeir-Sommers & Martin (2020); Leners & Stizman (2006)
Congruence: Presence	*Presence*	Substantive engagement within section	Robinson, et al (2020)
Congruence: Authenticity	*Realness*	Sharing genuine life/professional experiences	Brockmeir-Sommers & Martin (2020)
Level of Regard	*Active listening*	Call-back student work, incorporation of ideas in responses	Swan, et al (2020)
Level of Regard	*Positive recognition*	Showing genuine appreciation, acknowledge ideas, contributions	Swan, et al (2020)
Level of Regard	*Timeliness*	Timely response to Q/A or DQ questions	Robinson, et al. (2020); Swan, et al (2020)
Level of Regard	*Contextual/culturally competent feedback*	Sensitivity to uniqueness, cultivating acceptance of differences in others	Brockmeir-Sommers & Martin (2020)
Empathy	*Reflective callouts*	Demonstrating concern for student's well-being	Leners & Stizman 20060
Empathy	*Caring approach*	Personal interest in goals/aspirations, encouraging the best in others	Robinson, et al. (2020); Leners & Sitzman (2006)

Another important factor in establishing congruence is for one to be able to present an authentic online persona in which others perceive you to be real and genuine. One of the easiest ways to do this is to integrate professional and personal stories into the online classroom, when appropriate. If there are informal spaces, such as a Class Café within the online course, it is important that faculty members engage in such spaces and respond to their learners' stories as well (through active listening, see below).

As noted above, being present is not enough, as quality of engagement is more important than quantity (and there can be too much of certain kinds of faculty presence). The three elements of the level of regard construct begin to address what quality engagement looks like within a person-centered learning relationship.

Four elements inform level of regard: timeliness of engagement, active listening, positive recognition, and contextually and culturally competent feedback. There is substantial research within the field of online, care-oriented teaching—primarily originating from the nursing education field—that shows that learners perceive timeliness of feedback as among the strongest indicators that faculty care about them (Leners & Sitzman, 2006). This is associated with presence, of course, and is a way for faculty to demonstrate both a level of regard and congruence in a person-centered relationship.

Assuming that one is present, being able to listen deeply and actively to learners is also a prerequisite to building a strong learning relationship. Again, this applies to both the formal learning spaces—such as Discussion areas or within feedback on papers and other assignments—as well as in the less formal Class Café. Calling back specifics of the learner's assignment or writing and incorporating those ideas into responses is one way to model active listening in the online environment.

Providing positive recognition for the work of learners is also a way to demonstrate level of regard and to bring quality to a learning relationship. Positive recognition is an active strategy in response to active listening. Even though learners will not always make the strongest contributions, showing genuine appreciation and acknowledgment for ideas and contributions is an important element in building trust.

Within an inclusive teaching and learning environment, the fourth element of level of regard becomes very important and is, perhaps, one of the most difficult elements to put into practice. Being able to provide contextual and culturally competent feedback and engagement is one of the cornerstones of being inclusive and helping to build a sense of belonging among the learning community. If a faculty member establishes genuine and authentic presence and listens actively to learners, it is likely that they will pick up interesting and relevant cues about their learners and what is important to them. Likewise, in many online course designs, learners are invited to share information about themselves, and their peers can learn why they are taking a particular course and what it means to them.

It is important that faculty develop strategies for incorporating this kind of information into the feedback they provide within the online classroom context. Being sensitive to uniqueness, cultivating acceptance and differences in others, and recognizing that many of our learners come from traditionally marginalized communities, are steps in showing level of regard and being inclusive.

Finally, it is important overall that faculty members demonstrate concern for their learners' well-being and take a genuine approach to demonstrating interest in their learners' goals and aspirations and encouraging the best in others. These behaviors align with a general sense of being empathetic.

An Exploratory Line-Item Rubric to Support Person-Centered Learning: Thoughts

Given this preliminary exploration of Rogers's relationship inventory concepts, with broad operational constructs outlined, the next step was to develop a more prescriptive rubric that could be used for assessing person-centered engagement in historical online sections (retrospectively). In the following section, we present some of the details of this preliminary rubric, which is but one part of a larger, inclusive teaching and learning rubric (course development aspects are presented in Chapter 5, "Designing an Inclusive Online Classroom") that will be shared in the final section of this chapter. It is important to note that, at the time of this book's publication, Walden was early in its implementation of the use of this rubric in practice, so this chapter and section do not include in-action examples.

During the development of this more prescriptive, person-centered rubric, some faculty who we shared the rubric with during open-access webinars expressed concerns that such a rubric would routinize or oversimplify complex behaviors in ways that would negatively impact some faculty who had teaching and communication styles that were not compatible with this approach but that were still valuable in teaching complex concepts and supporting learners at the doctoral dissertation stage.

After careful consideration, it was our team's (inclusive teaching and learning advisory council) thoughts that the kinds of person-centered behaviors we are addressing are core to effective inclusive teaching and that we would develop both robust orientation and professional development modules to support faculty in their efforts to continuously improve in building effective learning relationship as teachers.

Few of the desired behaviors outlined in the person-centered approach to inclusive teaching and learning are technically difficult, nor do they take excessive amounts of time above other more transactional engagements—they are more aligned with *how* to engage rather than *how much*. In those areas, particularly around learning to provide contextual and culturally competent feedback and where more professional development may be needed, the university is committing significant resources via its overall inclusive teaching and learning strategy (see Chapter 14, "Sustainable Strategic Planning for Inclusive Online Teaching and Learning").

An Exploratory Line-Item Rubric to Support Person-Centered Learning: First Draft

In this section, a more detailed, line-item rubric is presented in three tables (Table 3, Table 4, and Table 5). This is an early draft of the rubric, and it is the one being used to do the retrospective analysis on past course engagements:

The Person-Centered Rubric Embedded as an Element of a Larger ITL Frame

One of the goals of using a more detailed, person-centered behavioral rubric is to have a starting place from which to identify and assess behaviors (and skills) that relate directly to person-to-person engagments but that are also core elements to a more broad, inclusive teaching and learning framework. In Chapter 5 ("Designing an Inclusive Online Classroom"), a nine-standard, inclusive teaching and learning frame (ITL Frame) is presented, and the implications of that frame are discussed relative to course design. In this section of the current chapter, we'll use the same ITL Frame to put elements of the person-centered teaching and learning rubric into a larger context.

Table 6 presents the nine standards of Walden's ITL Frame along with their essential questions as well as elements from the person-centered rubric described above. Also, Walden's faculty appreciation quality framework (discussed earlier in this chapter) are aligned with the standards. This table provides the larger, more holistic set of elements that support Walden's inclusive teaching and learning model and related expectations for faculty engagement.

It is important to note that these standards, the essential questions, the faculty quality appreciation indicators and the caring, person-centered engagement elements have all been developed collaboratively over the past 10 years (with an ITL emphasis within the past year) among Walden's academic leadership, our faculty and inclusive teaching and learning advisory councils, our institutional effectiveness office, and our formal governance committees.

Interestingly, when the ITL Frame standards were developed and we bounced our current faculty engagement standards and practices against it nearly 90% of the specific behaviors and appreciation elements aligned directly with the ITL standards. Those that did not focused primarily on the standards relating to systemic bias and exploring course content through the lens of historically marginalized groups (see Chapter 5, "Designing an Inclusive Online Classroom").

Having said that, there has been great reward in bringing the entire ITL Frame to life and to see where it reveals shortcomings in Walden's curricular development and in its recruiting and professional development of faculty, to which we now turn.

Developing a Rubric for a Person-Centered Approach to Teaching in Inclusive Online Learning Spaces

Table 3. *Person-centered engagement rubric: congruence details*

Person-Centered Teaching Evaluation Rubric

Rogers Relationship Inventory Construct	Operational Construct	Demonstrated Behaviors	0 - Not Acceptable	1 - Needs Improvement	2 - Acceptable	3 - Strong
Congruence-Genuineness	General Courtesy	Personal greeting, please, thank you, you are welcome, no ALL CAPS	Prima fascia rudeness at any time	Inconsistent in application; transactional/canned responses with little context	Generally consistent in application; contextual responses	End-to-end, consistent in all engagements, warm, enthusiastic, requests begin with 'please,' end with 'thank you,' use student's preferred first name and/or pronouns, inclusive/inviting
Congruence-Presence	Presence	Substantive engagement within section	Questions ignored or nonresponsive replies; not regularly engaged in classroom (via announcements, discussions, etc.) in alignment with program policies	Inconsistent classroom engagement either in frequency or quality	Consistently addresses student questions in a timely fashion and participates in classroom in meaningful ways in multiple places with regularity and aligned with program policies; some use of announcements, though not regularly	Consistent use of timely, relevant, and succinct announcements; context-specific responses to questions in Q/A and DQ areas that promote student learning and critical thinking; video incorporated; follow-up questions asked, enables deeper synthesis of important learning outcomes; is present outside of classroom when students need
Congruence-Authenticity	Realness	Sharing genuine life/professional experiences	No engagement outside of direct/technical content or APA/writing focus	Provides a biography that outlines professional and academic experience; inconsistent in commentary or sharing of professional experiences; mechanical in interactions in the classroom	Posts a biography and greeting that establishes relevant professional and academic experience; sets appropriate expectations for respectful interactions in the classroom, offers professional expertise and experience as part of discussions or feedback, demonstrates appropriate flexibility and understanding of student situations and needs	Clear and context-appropriate integration of experiential or professional stories; interacts with students on a human-to-human level by demonstrating flexibility or understanding, consideration of students' perspectives, demonstrating courage in challenging commonly held perspectives, respectful and inclusive of different experiences in ways that help students develop broader and richer understanding of the concepts and how those apply to real situations; effectively uses media or video to introduce themselves and motivate students

Developing a Rubric for a Person-Centered Approach to Teaching in Inclusive Online Learning Spaces

Table 4. *Person-centered engagement rubric: level of regard details*

Person-Centered Teaching Evaluation Rubric

Rogers Relationship Inventory Construct	Operational Construct	Demonstrated Behaviors	0 - Not Acceptable	1 - Needs Improvement	2 - Acceptable	3 - Strong
Level of Regard	Active Listening	*Call-back student work, incorporation of ideas in responses and feedback*	No context-specific responses	Inconsistent in quality of responses; responses often are short (refer to the rubric) or terse and do not fully support the learner's question	Responses are context specific, with some indications/examples of call-back.	Responses paraphrase student's words/ideas, advance engagement with follow-up question; synthesizes important points and seeks further student engagement in the conversation
Level of Regard	Positive Recognition	*Showing genuine appreciation, acknowledge ideas, contributions*	No recognition of student work, contributions	Sometimes acknowledges student work and contributions to the learning environment	Consistently acknowledges the ideas students share and contributions they make to discussions. Provides positive and authentic feedback to students that highlights at least one area in which they did well	Responses geared to make student feel appreciated; acknowledge student ideas/creativity/learning/contributions
Level of Regard	Timeliness	*Timely response to Q/A or DQ questions*	Questions ignored or nonresponsive replies	Responses are late relative to KPI expectation	Responses meet KPI expectation	Responses almost or always exceed KPI expectation
Level of Regard	Contextual/Culturally Competent Feedback	*Sensitivity to uniqueness, cultivating acceptance of differences in others*	No context- or no specific context to how work could be improved, why it should be	Instructor does not regularly provide specific feedback to each student.	Feedback is specific to each student and as appropriate, demonstrates sensitivity to the uniqueness of every student (i.e., it is possible to tell that the instructor read the student's work).	Context for improvement is clear, how to fix is included, why important is included, sandwich method, de-escalation language, inclusive tone. Feedback, if acted upon, will further the student's ability to improve, think critically, and at a level appropriate to the degree level

Table 5. Person-centered engagement rubric: empathy details

Rogers Relationship Inventory Construct	Operational Construct	Demonstrated Behaviors	Person-Centered Teaching Evaluation Rubric — Criteria & Scale			
			0 - Not Acceptable	1 - Needs Improvement	2 - Acceptable	3 - Strong
Empathy	Reflective Callouts	Demonstrating concern for student's well-being	No acknowledgements of student's feelings (when expressed)	Responses are blunt, do not move engagement forward	Smile (emoticon or other indicator), soothing language	Reflective callout of student's feelings; be forgiving of posts that might be rude; patient responses with no escalation; responses indicate compassion and understanding
Empathy	Caring Approach	Professional and personal interest in goals/aspirations; encouraging the best in others	No contextually specific response to student posts about goals/aspirations			Reflective callouts that support student goals/aspirations with concrete responses

Table 6. Faculty engagement elements of an ITL standards framework

Spring 2022

Standard	Title	Essential Question	Faculty/Student Interaction			
			Statement Form: Faculty Focus (Current Faculty Quality Appreciation Indicators)	Statement Form: Faculty Focus (Person-Centered Care Rubric Element)	Primary Place of Action	Primary Learning Model Thread
			STUDENT-FOCUSED: PROCESS ORIENTED			
1	Building on Students' Individual Strengths and Assets	How do the course resources, student tasks, activities, assessments, and instructional strategies build on students' individual strengths and assets while also supporting their needs?	Supports student success through frequent, regular, and proactive communication with students and other quality teaching/mentoring strategies based on individual student needs Personalizes grades on assignments and Discussion posts to reflect the quality of student work Provides responses and feedback to students throughout the learning process that are constructive, detailed, and timely	Level of Regard: Positive Recognition: Show genuine appreciation, acknowledge ideas, contributions	Need new space beyond the Class Café where faculty can obtain knowledge of students' strengths	Person-centered, positive regard, congruence
Standard	Title	Essential Question	Statement Form: Faculty Focus (Current Faculty Quality Appreciation Indicators)	Statement Form: Faculty Focus (Person-Centered Care Rubric Element)	Primary Place of Action	Primary Learning Model Thread

continues on following page

Developing a Rubric for a Person-Centered Approach to Teaching in Inclusive Online Learning Spaces

Table 6. Continued

Spring 2022			Faculty/Student Interaction			
Standard	Title	Essential Question	Statement Form: Faculty Focus (Current Faculty Quality Appreciation Indicators)	Statement Form: Faculty Focus (Person-Centered Care Rubric Element)	Primary Place of Action	Primary Learning Model Thread
STUDENT-FOCUSED: PROCESS ORIENTED						
2	Exploring, Affirming, and Embracing Diverse Voices and Student Identities	In an attempt to serve ALL students equitably, how do the curriculum, instructional strategies, course resources, student activities, and assessments affirm, celebrate, and validate historically marginalized individuals, groups, and students' diverse, multiple, and intersectional identities by supporting and normalizing these voices throughout the curriculum?	Demonstrates caring and empathy for students Provides course content and feedback that encourages students to view and consider diverse perspectives Demonstrates effective communication techniques that considers cultural differences Supports development of learning community, creates an atmosphere of mutual respect, shared learning, and is proactive in initiating interactions with students	Caring Approach: Professional & personal interest in goals/aspirations; encouraging the best in others	Discussions/Assignments	Inclusive, appreciative engagement; mutual inquiry
3	Valuing Each Student's Lived Experience	Do the course resources, student tasks, activities, assessments, and instructional strategies create a space where knowledge is developed and co-constructed with students' lived experiences in a way that normalizes the need to share, critique, review, and renew?	Encourages the sharing of diverse student experiences and facilitates opportunities for students to learn from one another so all students benefit	Level of Regard: Positive recognition: Show genuine appreciation, acknowledge ideas, contribution Level of Regard: Culturally competent feedback—sensitivity to uniqueness, cultivating acceptance of diffferences in others	Discussions/Assignments	Mutual inquiry; experiential; inclusive and appreciative engagement
Standard	Title	Essential Question	Statement Form: Faculty Focus (Current Faculty Quality Appreciation Indicators)	Statement Form: Faculty Focus (Person-Centered Care Rubric Element)	Primary Place of Action	Primary Learning Model Thread
4	Empowering Positive Social Change Agents	How do the course resources, student tasks, activities, assessments, and instructional strategies promote, facilitate, and support collaborative alliances, action research, and projects that lead to student agency to effect positive social change?	Engages in instruction that prepares students as agents of social change Supports students in adapting to university, degree-level, and disciplinary expectations	Level of Regard: Active Listening: Call-back student work, incorporation of ideas in feedback Congruence-Authenticity: Realness— sharing genuine life/professional experiences	Discussions/Assignments	Experiential, reflection-in-action (reflexive practitioner)
5	Ensuring Multiple Means of Expression	Are students offered multiple opportunities to demonstrate knowledge (via assessment strategies) in ways that are best aligned to their own unique abilities and strengths?	Uses a variety of technology tools to enhance instructional engagement and learning processes	Presence: Substantive engagement	Assignment choice sets	Inclusive, appreciative engagement; mutual inquiry

continues on following page

Developing a Rubric for a Person-Centered Approach to Teaching in Inclusive Online Learning Spaces

Table 6. Continued

Spring 2022				Faculty/Student Interaction		
Standard	Title	Essential Question	Statement Form: Faculty Focus (Current Faculty Quality Appreciation Indicators)	Statement Form: Faculty Focus (Person-Centered Care Rubric Element)	Primary Place of Action	Primary Learning Model Thread
STUDENT-FOCUSED: PROCESS ORIENTED						
Standard	Title	Essential Question	Statement Form: Faculty Quality (Current Faculty Quality Appreciation Indicators)	Statement Form: Faculty Focus (Person-Centered Care Rubric Element)	Primary Place of Action	Primary Learning Model Thread
6	Providing Meaningful Feedback for Growth	Are assessment and feedback provided in such a way that allows students to self-assess their own strengths, learning gaps, and direction to move forward?	Demonstrates awareness of the dispersed nature of the university and maintains flexibility with regard to availability. Demonstrates proactive techniques in outreach to and follow-up with students to address student performance issues. Provides feedback specific to student work designed to improve the student's performance in the mastery of the course content as well as in other academic areas, such as the development of critical thinking and writing skills, and problem solving. Meets deadlines for classroom engagement, including grading, responding to students, and interacting with students in the classroom	Level of Regard: Timeliness: Timely response to Q/A or DQ questions. Level of Regard: Active Listening: Call-back student work, incorporation of ideas in feedback	All course elements	Reflection-in-Action
CONTENT ORIENTED						
7	Exploring Course Concepts Through the Lens of Historically Marginalized Individuals and Groups	How do the course's curriculum, instructional strategies, and central concepts incorporate the following? (List of marginalized groups)	Encourages the sharing of diverse student experiences and facilitates opportunities for students to learn from one another so all students benefit		Discussion/ Assignments	Experiential, mutual inquiry
Standard	Title	Essential Question	Statement Form: Faculty Focus (Current Faculty Quality Appreciation Indicators)	Statement Form: Faculty Focus (Person-Centered Care Rubric Element)	Primary Place of Action	Primary Learning Model Thread

continues on following page

Developing a Rubric for a Person-Centered Approach to Teaching in Inclusive Online Learning Spaces

Table 6. Continued

Spring 2022			Faculty/Student Interaction		
Standard	Title	Essential Question	Statement Form: Faculty Focus (Current Faculty Quality Appreciation Indicators)	Statement Form: Faculty Focus (Person-Centered Care Rubric Element)	Primary Place of Action	Primary Learning Model Thread
STUDENT-FOCUSED: PROCESS ORIENTED					
SYSTEMIC IMPROVEMENT ORIENTED					
8	**Ensuring Designs Are Not Systemically Biased**	Is the course free of resources, student tasks, activities, assessments, and instructional strategies that may be perceived as oppressive or reinforcing systemic biases and privilege, deficit-oriented, marginalizing, discriminatory, and/or racist ideologies?		Congruence: Genuineness—General courtesy Empathy: Caring Approach—Professional and personal interest in goals/aspirations; encouraging the best in others	All course elements	Mutual inquiry
9	**Empowering Appropriate Responses and Feedback to Perceived Inequities**	Does the course have a space that allows students to raise concerns, critique and engage in healthy-diverse dialog where differences can be explored, and provide feedback to instructors and each other when they feel maltreated and not represented or heard?	Provides open-minded, balanced feedback that is both summative and formative and is receptive to student responses. Uses a variety of instructional techniques, tools, technologies, and communication strategies that support diverse students and promote student engagement and learning. Exercises good judgment and accepts responsibility to promote integrity, transparency, and ethical conduct in all service activities. Uses a professional tone when communicating with students. Uses Walden email accounts and Walden media for all communication with Walden students	Level of Regard: Active listening	'Let's Talk' public space; additional private anon space (POPIn?)	Reflection-in-Action

205

CONCLUSION

As we seek to roll out our inclusive teaching and learning strategy and the frameworks and tools related to it, such as the teaching and learning rubrics shared in this chapter, there are a few implications, challenges, and opportunities that arise.

The first is that we need to develop similar frameworks, expectations, and systems across all staff at the university. The challenge of meeting a moment of truth exists for everyone, always, and these rubrics have been developed primarily with the direct learning relationship at its focus. Having said that, however, the basic person-centered elements of congruence, level of regard, and empathy apply to all relationships in general. Additionally, specific operational constructs for those elements could be developed for those serving learners in a staff capacity.

Another important implication is that our academic leaders and faculty representatives need to work closely with our university's human resource leaders to develop a robust, fair, and valid performance management application of these concepts into our faculty professional development and evaluation systems and that those systems should be oriented within a positive psychology/person-centered approach.

The way the university supports and engages with its faculty and staff models what we should expect of those faculty and staff when supporting learners. For our inclusive teaching and learning model to take root and thrive, the organizational culture that supports our faculty and staff must be consistent with the ideas and principles outlined in this chapter. Such alignment should ensure that our recruiting systems through to our performance management systems clearly reward the behaviors outlined in this chapter.

Finally, the university must invest resources that can help bridge gaps in both our understanding of and practice in person-centered engagement and leadership. We need to develop and offer robust professional development for emotional intelligence skills, which have been discussed in Chapter 3 ("Using an Emotional Intelligence Learning System for Person-Centered Curriculum Development and Teaching"), and we must take an appreciative inquiry approach in helping our people develop those skills.

By doing so, it will help each of us meet the challenges of our educational moments of truth! Will each of us be ready?

REFERENCES

Ahn, M. Y., & Davis, H. H. (2020). Four domains of students' sense of belonging to university. *Studies in Higher Education*, *45*(3), 622–634. doi:10.1080/03075079.2018.1564902

Bogler, R., Caspi, A., & Roccas, S. (2013). Transformational and passive leadership: An initial investigation of university instructors as leaders in a virtual learning environment. *Educational Management Administration & Leadership*, *41*(3), 372–392. doi:10.1177/1741143212474805

Brockmier-Sommers, D. K., & Martin, J. L. (2020, June 16). *Using empathy, genuineness and unconditional positive regard to build safety for discussing difficult topics in the online classroom* [Online conference session]. OLC Innovate. https://onlinelearningconsortium.org/olc-innovate-2020-session-page/?session=8507&kwds=

Cameron, K. (2008). *Positive leadership: Strategies for extraordinary performance*. Berrett-Koehler Publishers.

Carlzon, J. (1989). *Moments of truth*. Ballinger Publishing.

Chun, E., & Evans, A. (2010, February 8). Linking diversity and accountability through accreditation standards. *Hispanic Outlook*. http://ednachun.com/wp/articles/

Darby, F., & Lang, J. M. (2019). *Small teaching online: Applying learning science in online classes*. John Wiley & Sons.

Garrison, D. R., Anderson, T., & Archer, W. (2000). Critical inquiry in a text-based environment: Computer conferencing in higher education model. *The Internet and Higher Education*, 2(2–3), 87–105. doi:10.1016/S1096-7516(00)00016-6

Leners, D. W., & Sitzman, K. (2006). Graduate student perceptions: Feeling the passion of caring online. *Nursing Education Perspectives*, 27(6), 315–319. PMID:17256656

Mann, J. C. (2014). A pilot study of RN-BSN completion students' preferred instructor online classroom caring behaviors. *The ABNF Journal*, 25(2), 33–39. PMID:24855803

Morgan, A. M., Jobe, R. L., Konopa, J. K., & Downs, L. D. (2022). Quality assurance, meet quality appreciation: Using appreciative inquiry to define faculty quality standards. *Higher Learning Research Communications*, 12(1), 98–111. https://scholarworks.waldenu.edu/cgi/viewcontent.cgi?article=1301&context=hlrc

Pacansky-Brock, M., Smedshammer, M., & Vincent-Layton, K. (2020). Humanizing online teaching to equitize higher education. *Current Issues in Education (Tempe, Ariz.)*, 21(2). https://cie.asu.edu/ojs/index.php/cieatasu/article/view/1905

Powley, E. H., Fry, R. E., Barrett, F. J., & Bright, D. S. (2004). Dialogic democracy meets command and control: Transformation through the appreciative inquiry summit. *The Academy of Management Executive*, 18(3), 67–80. doi:10.5465/ame.2004.14776170

Robinson, H., Al-Freih, M., & Kilgore, W. (2020). Designing with care: Towards a care-centered model for online learning design. *The International Journal of Information of Learning Technology*, 37(3), 99–108. doi:10.1108/IJILT-10-2019-0098

Rogers, C. (1969). Freedom to learn: A view of what education might become. Charles E. Merrill Publishing.

Schindler, L. A., & Burkholder, G. J. (2014). Instructional design and facilitation approaches that promote critical thinking in asynchronous online discussions: A review of the literature. *Higher Learning Research Communications*, 4(4), 11–29. doi:10.18870/hlrc.v4i4.222

Swan, K. (2004). *Relationships between interactions and learning in online environments*. The Sloan Consortium. https://www.immagic.com/eLibrary/ARCHIVES/GENERAL/SLOANCUS/S041202C.pdf

Swan, K., Chen, C.-C. B., & Bockmier-Sommers, D. K. (2020). Relationships between Carl Rogers' person-centered education and the community of inquiry framework: A preliminary exploration. *Online Learning*, 24(3). Advance online publication. doi:10.24059/olj.v24i3.2279

Vanslambrouck, S., Chang, Z., Tondeur, J., Phillipsen, B., & Lombaerts, K. (2016, October). Adult learners' motivation to participate and perception of online and blended environments. *Proceedings of the 15th European Conference on E-Learning*, 750–757. https://www.researchgate.net/publication/309490567_Adult_learners'_motivation_to_participate_and_perception_of_online_and_blended_environments

Williams, L. S. (2017). The managed heart: Adult learners and emotional presence online. *The Journal of Continuing Higher Education, 65*(2), 124–131. doi:10.1080/07377363.2017.1320204

ADDITIONAL READING

Austen, L., Pickering, N., & Judge, M. (2021). Student reflections on the pedagogy of transitions into higher education, through digital storytelling. *Journal of Further and Higher Education, 45*(3), 337–348. doi:10.1080/0309877X.2020.1762171

Devlin, M., & McKay, J. (2018). Teaching inclusively online in a massified university system. *Widening Participation and Lifelong Learning: the Journal of the Institute for Access Studies and the European Access Network, 20*(1), 146–166. doi:10.5456/WPLL.20.1.146

Dillon, R. S., & Stines, P. W. (1996). A phenomenological study of faculty-student caring interactions. *The Journal of Nursing Education, 35*(3), 113–118. doi:10.3928/0148-4834-19960301-06 PMID:8676206

Dunlap, J. C., Verma, G., & Johnson, H. L. (2016). Presence+Experience: A framework for the purposeful design of presence in online courses. *TechTrends, 60*(2), 145–151. doi:10.100711528-016-0029-4

Hodgkinson, H. L. (1969). Walden U.: A working paper. *Soundings: An Interdisciplinary Journal, 52*, 172–185. https://scholarworks.waldenu.edu/cgi/viewcontent.cgi?article=1000&context=university_history

Simonson, C. L. S. (1996). Teaching caring to nursing students. *The Journal of Nursing Education, 35*(3), 100–104. doi:10.3928/0148-4834-19960301-04 PMID:8676204

ENDNOTE

[1] Note: the concept person-centered is introduced in chapter 1, and we'll use those same ideas in this chapter but with the caveat that person-centered is also the way we'll finesse the customer/client learner/student issue as well. We serve people, whole persons, so we'll talk about being person-centered from here on.

Section 5
Systems of Practice

What systems must be considered to operationalize and institutionalize inclusive practices?

Chapter 13
Framing Higher Education Through the Social Determinants of Health

Aimee Ferraro
Walden University, USA

ABSTRACT

The mission and organizational structure of a university can employ a variety of frameworks to address diversity, equity, and inclusion. In this chapter, the guiding principles of one online university, and how reframing its approach to higher education through the Social Determinants of Health, allowed the institution to respond to the call for action around educational justice, health equity, and healthier communities. Examples of how to encourage interdisciplinary collaboration and integrate social determinants of health into curricula are provided.

INTRODUCTION

The COVID-19 pandemic has renewed awareness in the persistent and growing inequities in health, education, employment, and living conditions. Compounded by war, political conflict, social unrest, and climate change, the problems faced by societies today are complex, systemic, and interdependent. Compagnucci and Spigarelli (2020) argue that universities are poised to respond and adapt by adding a "third mission" aimed at transferring knowledge and technologies to industry and to society at large (p. 1). Boyer (1990) asserts that universities in the United States have "their own distinctive mission" (p. xiii), which is essentially a "moral mission" (p. 7) that should be directly related to "the realities of contemporary life" (p. 13). They go on to say, "[a]t no time in our history has the need been greater for connecting the work for the academy to the social and environmental challenges beyond the campus" (Boyer, 1990, p. xii). Boyer wrote over 30 years ago, and the observation contains lasting merit.

DOI: 10.4018/978-1-6684-5146-5.ch013

Universities have taken many approaches to adopting a third mission that addresses diversity, equity, and inclusion. Chamberlain University developed (and trademarked) the Social Determinants of Learning™ (SDOL™) as "an actionable model to address learning disparities and expand learning opportunities to support nursing student diversity, equity, and inclusion" (Sanderson et al, 2021, p. 7). The SDOL™ provide a framework to describe the "socially imposed forces which are causative factors that influence learning and life" (Sanderson et al., 2021, p.7). This framework includes physical health, psychosocial health, economic stability, physical environment/community, social environment/community, and self-motivation. Similarly, accredited medical schools are required to train students to recognize the Social Determinants of Health (SDOH) so they are better able to address the root causes of health inequities (Sharma et al., 2018). The manner in which each university meets this requirement differs greatly, with some institutions offering as little as single didactic lessons and service-learning opportunities (Witten & Maskarinec, 2015), while others provide mentorship, collaborative longitudinal service with community partners, career seminars, and research (Bakshi et al., 2015; Furin, et al., 2006; O'Brien, et al., 2014). This chapter describes the approach of one online university to meaningfully address diversity, equity, and inclusion through a mission and institutional structure framed by the Social Determinants of Health.

Guiding Principles of Walden University

The founders of Walden University sought to build a learning community in which knowledge could be applied to solve key societal challenges (Hodgkinson, 1969). Their vision was to empower students to make a difference in their communities, their professions, and on a global scale through positive social change. This mission powered the university through its first 50 years and lays the foundation for the next phase of its interdisciplinary approach to higher education.

Figure 1 illustrates how Walden University has conceptualized its own distinctive mission, vision, and purpose. Based on the mission for social change and the value of educational justice, Walden University has framed its schools and programs around the SDOH. The overall purpose is to improve educational equity and create healthier communities.

BACKGROUND

Social Change

Walden University was founded in 1970 by two teachers, Bernie and Rita Turner, who wanted a way for adults in the workforce to pursue a doctoral degree (Walden University, 2017). In collaboration with Harold Hodgkinson, the three set out to develop a university rooted in mutual inquiry and social change. The first mission stated: "Walden University provides a diverse community of career professionals with the opportunity to transform themselves as scholar/practitioners so that they may transform society" (Hodgkinson, 1969, p. 1). Over time, the mission was slightly altered to end with ". . . so that they can effect positive social change" (Walden University, 2022).

For more than 50 years, Walden University has been committed to fostering social change through the education of a diverse community of career professionals who share a passion to improve the world. The university defines social change as:

Figure 1. Guiding principles of Walden University
Note. The central part of this image is a modification of a graphic in the public domain (United States Department of Health and Human Services. Office of Disease Prevention and Health Promotion, n.d.). This image illustrates how the social determinants of health (SDOH) are at the heart of educational justice and healthy communities initiatives at Walden. Image credit: Jose Henriquez, Walden University.

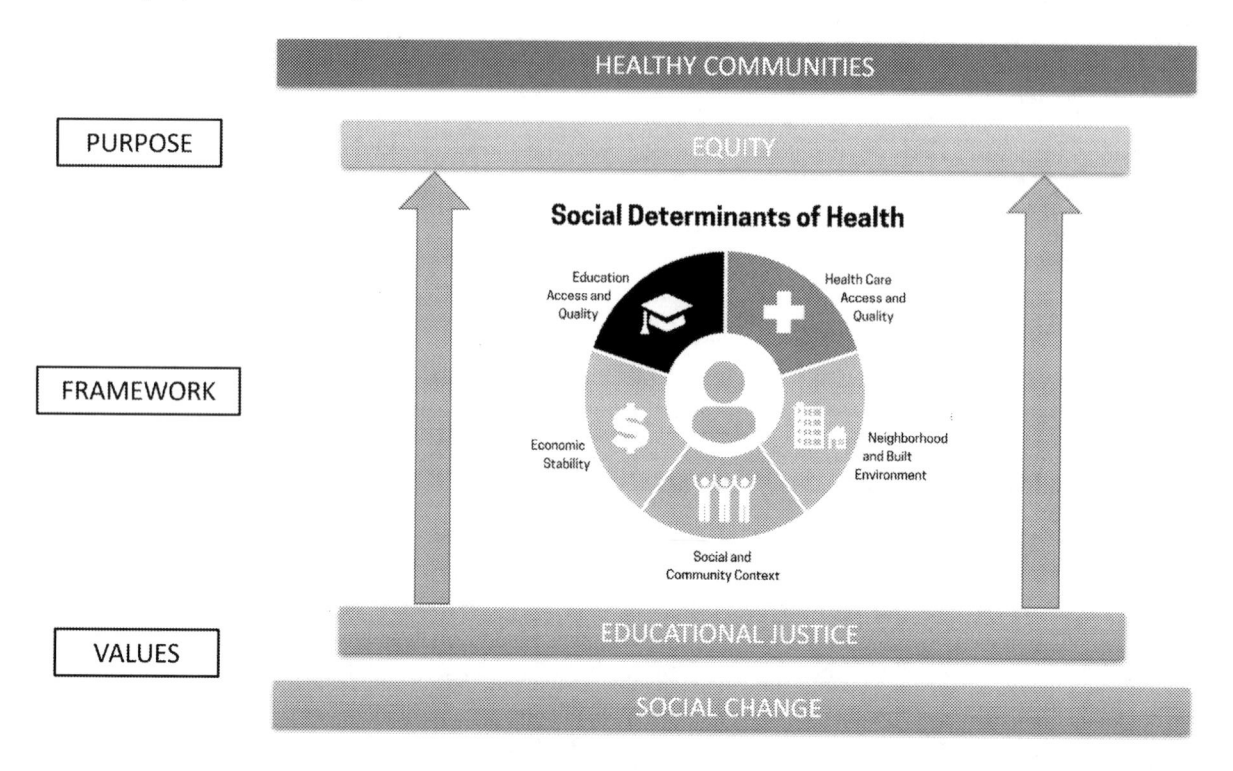

A deliberate process of creating and applying ideas, strategies, and actions to promote the worth, dignity, and development of individuals, communities, organizations, institutions, cultures, and societies. Positive social change results in the improvement of human and social conditions. (Hodgkinson, 1969, p. 2)

    This definition closely aligns with the core vision of the SDOH, placing diversity, equity, inclusion, and health for all at the forefront. Even so, the concept of social change has proven to be almost indefinable. Based on a comprehensive literature review on social change and interviews with faculty, students, and alumni, a university task force discovered that there was no consensus about what positive social change meant in an educational setting (Yob et al., 2016). For some, social change might be actualized through political activism, like writing letters to the editor or protesting; for others it comes through raising awareness or funding for a particular cause (Yob & Ferraro, 2012). It was concluded that students and faculty need training and tools to turn scholarly knowledge and personal passion into scholarship, advocacy, civic engagement, political action, and other forms of social change. A follow-up faculty task force was tasked with creating *The Curriculum Guide for Social Change*, which provided a matrix for mapping social change in courses (Yob et al., 2016). This matrix focused on curricula, rather than university-wide culture, and provided unique qualities that allowed assessment of social change features on a course-by-course and program-by-program basis.

Walden established the Center for Social Change in 2017 with the purpose of being "a connective hub that promotes, facilitates, and supports collaborative alliances, action research, and projects that lead to purposeful action for sustainable positive social change" (Walden University, 2021). The center was charged with managing the Fellowship in Research and Applications in Social Change, Global Days of Service, Scholars for Change video contest, Talks for Good, community partner training, faculty research and dissemination grants, and the *Journal of Social Change* (Walden University, 2017). The Center for Social Change champions the guiding principles of the university by empowering changemakers, building community, elevating social change, and addressing diversity, equity, and inclusion in all its offerings.

Educational Justice

Another one of Walden University's core values is to "support diversity and multiculturalism within [students'] profession, communities, and society" (Walden University, n.d., para. 7). This commitment to educational justice is demonstrated in Walden's broad access admissions policies and practices that attract a wide variety of students, including those who are historically underserved and often marginalized in traditional higher education spaces. While the health and healthcare-focused portions of the university curriculum explicitly address health equity, Walden actively addresses intentional curricular design across programs to enable a more just/inclusive/equitable educational experience. Curricula are designed according to the Walden University Hallmarks and quality indicators, which require that learning is collaborative, inspiring, diversity oriented, and conducive to positive social change. Walden's Inclusive Teaching and Learning Strategic Plan sets out a clear objective to, "[e]nsure our community knows that we value the inherent worth, the humanity, and the dignity of every individual engaged in the learning process" (Lindell et al., 2021, p. 5). The values of diversity, inclusion, and justice are embedded across curriculum and governance structures of the university and are covered in more depth in other chapters of this book.

SOCIAL DETERMINANTS OF HEALTH

The Social Determinants of Health (SDOH), as a concept, has been widely used in the field of public health. More recently, the concept has been applied to nursing and medicine to understand the health impact of social, economic, and environmental factors. It is a concept that was interdisciplinary from its inception. Students at Walden University learn about the historical roots of the SDOH to ensure that they fully understand the breadth of its utility in addressing social, cultural, educational, economic, environmental, and health inequities. Students are also exposed to key figures and seminal research on the SDOH so they can contribute to research and practice in their field of study.

The fundamental concept of SDOH dates back thousands of years to when the first philosophers and physicians attempted to explain the root causes of illness and disease. Societies have changed their approach to health and wellness based on belief systems, scientific advancements, and changing prevalence of diseases over time. Some of the first ideas related to the SDOH came during the medieval period in Europe (approximately 500–1500 AD). Changing patterns of agricultural production produced greater population density, and urbanization expanded due to increased trade with societies of the Middle East (Rotberg & Rabb, 1985). However, these social, economic, and demographic factors combined to create new opportunities for the spread of infections such as plague, leprosy, tuberculosis, and influenza

(Porter, 2001). Some of the greatest suffering in the Middle Ages was caused by bubonic plague, also known at the Black Death, which continued to haunt western Europe until the 18th century (Park, 1993). During this time, governments in Italy, England, and France began to implement quarantines and isolation of the sick, recognizing that social disorder, overcrowding, and person-to-person contact may be the culprit of Black Death (Porter, 2001). However, the prevailing belief at the time was that contagious diseases were transmitted through "miasma," or bad air arising from decayed organic matter (Sterner, 2007). Some of the first public health policies were aimed at halting miasmatic infection through street cleaning and sewage systems to get rid of foul-smelling air (Cipolla, 1992). Even though miasma theory was eventually disproved, it helped establish the connection between poor sanitation and disease, which is one of the SDOH we still combat today.

The miasma theory persisted until the cholera epidemic of London in the mid-1800s, when John Snow posited the cause of disease was from an unknown "germ" that was spreading through contaminated water (Snow, 1856). This alternative germ theory was later confirmed by German bacteriologist Robert Koch when he identified the *Vibrio cholerae* that causes tuberculosis (Rockett, 1999, p. 7). It had immediate implications for medicine and public health, resulting in advances in vaccinations and antibiotics that brought about dramatic declines in infectious diseases during the next 100 years (Egger, 2012). Germ theory also extended its relevance to public health through the concept of the epidemiologic triad, which asserts that all three corners of the public health triangle—host, agent, and environment—must be addressed to control a disease outbreak (Rockett, 1999, p. 10). John Snow's removal of the Broad Street pump during the cholera outbreak in London demonstrated the impact of addressing two corners of the triangle: agent (germ) and environment (pump).

Disease patterns changed dramatically during the late Industrial Era (20th century). In 1900, the three leading causes of death were pneumonia, tuberculosis, and diarrhea and enteritis—all communicable diseases (Centers for Disease Control, 1999). By 2000, the three leading causes of death were heart disease, cancer, and stroke—all chronic diseases (World Health Organization, 2020). This epidemiologic transition progressed from "the age of pestilence and famine, through the age of receding pandemics, and culminated in the age of degenerative and man-made diseases" (Rockett, 1999, p. 9). Rockett (1999) further asserts that the United States and many other industrialized countries are in a fourth "hybristic" stage, in which "personal behavior and lifestyle influence the patterns and levels of disease and injury" (p. 9). "Social pathologies," such as homicide, cirrhosis of the liver, suicide, and HIV/AIDS are now among the leading killers in the United States. Along with these changing disease patterns came new theories to explain them, including the web of causation, ecosocial theory, and the SDOH (Krieger, 1994, Krieger, 2001b).

One of the first empirical studies examining SDOH was conducted by Louise Rene Villerme between 1823 and 1834 in the city of Mulhouse, France. Villerme (1840) found that more affluent and educated people had a life expectancy more than 10 years greater than factory workers. In 1848, Rudolf Virchow investigated a typhus epidemic in Upper Silesia and criticized the social conditions that fostered the disease (Schultz, 2008). In one of the first examples of "social medicine," Virchow outlined a revolutionary program of social reconstruction, including full employment, higher wages, establishment of agricultural cooperatives, and universal education (Taylor & Rieger, 1985). Virchow's attempts to reform healthcare link directly to current developments in the political economy of health and social justice.

Later in the 19th century, Emile Durkheim examined how suicide rates differed by social factors such as marital status, religion, and military status. Durkheim (1897) concluded that suicide can have origins in social causes rather than individual temperament. Researchers continued to demonstrate the association between social factors and death throughout the early 20th century (Chapin, 1924; Coombs, 1941). The understanding that health is influenced by more than just biological causes is also illustrated in the fact that "social" was included in the definition of health when the World Health Organization (WHO) was founded in 1948 (World Health Organization, n.d., para. 1).

The roots of the term "Social Determinants of Health" can be traced back to 1960, when a medical sociologist named Leonard Syme formed the Human Ecology Study Section, later named the Epidemiology Study Section, at the National Institutes of Health (Syme, 2005). His work focused on sociocultural factors and coronary heart disease (Syme et al., 1964). Other notable researchers were John Cassel and Herman Tyroler, who studied the health consequences of urbanization and industrialization (Cassel & Tyroler, 1961; Tyroler & Cassel, 1964). During the next several decades, Syme mentored dozens of researchers and spawned a new subfield of epidemiology called social epidemiology, which focuses on social phenomena such as socioeconomic stratification, social networks and support, discrimination, work demands, and neighborhood segregation on health outcomes like functional status, disability, and well-being (Berkman & Kawachi, 2000).

It is important to recognize the most prominent social epidemiologists, as many of them were instrumental in the development of the SDOH framework later on. In the 1970s, Lisa Berkman worked with Leonard Syme on a longitudinal study of Alameda County residents that showed an association between lack of social ties and increased mortality (Berkman & Syme, 1979). Syme (2005) is quoted as saying "Berkman's study . . . really began to establish the field of social determinants" (p. 7). Berkman later published the first textbook on social epidemiology with Ichiro Kawachi (Berkman & Kawachi, 2000). Nancy Krieger is one of the most prolific social epidemiologists, with many of her studies focusing on social class and racial discrimination (Krieger, 1990; Krieger, 2000; Krieger & Sidney, 1996). She wrote several textbooks that are seminal to the field, including the *Glossary for Social Epidemiology* (Krieger, 2001a). Another student of Leonard Syme is Michael Marmot. The two worked together on epidemiological studies of coronary heart disease and stroke among Japanese men living in Japan, Hawaii, and California during the 1970s (Marmot et al., 1975). By the 1990s, Marmot shifted to research on health inequalities among British civil servants through the Whitehall II study (Marmot et al., 1991). In 1998, Marmot and Richard Wilkinson were commissioned by the WHO to summarize the scientific evidence on SDOH. The book, called *The Solid Facts: Social Determinants of Health* (Wilkinson & Marmot, 1998), marked the beginning of translating research into policy and action to address SDOH such as stress, unemployment, social support, addiction, food, and transport.

Several years later, the WHO launched the Commission on Social Determinants of Health (CSDH) to "contribute to a long-term process of incorporating the SDOH into planning, policy, and technical work" around the world (Marmot, 2005, p. 1099). Based on several years of global, cross-organizational collaboration (WHO, 2008), the final report addressed "all the factors and conditions in which people are born, grow, work, live and age in relation to the wider set of forces and systems that shape their daily lives" (Marmot, 2004, p.1099). More specifically, social determinants related to daily living conditions included educational equity, the living environment, fair employment and decent work, social protection across the life-course, and universal healthcare. Social determinants related to power and money, and resources included health equity in government policies and systems, fair financing, market responsibility, gender equity, political empowerment (inclusion and voice), and good global governance (WHO, 2008).

Soon after, the CSDH developed the Social Determinants of Health Conceptual Framework (WHO, 2010) to better understand the complexity of factors that define health. The CSDH stated:

Having health framed as a social phenomenon emphasizes health as a topic of social justice more broadly. Consequently, health equity (described by the absence of unfair and avoidable or remediable differences in health among social groups) becomes a guiding criterion or principle. (WHO, 2010, p. 4)

The CSDH conceptual framework (see Figure 2) defined structural and intermediary determinants that impact on equity in health and well-being (WHO, 2010). Structural determinants include socioeconomic and political context, policies, culture and societal values, socioeconomic position, and other demographic factors. Intermediary determinants include material circumstances, behaviors, biological and psychosocial factors, and the health system. The WHO report ends with several examples of interventions to address social stratification, vulnerability, and unequal consequences (WHO, 2010, p. 62). The SDOH conceptual framework operationalizes the factors that influence health equity and provides an action plan for positive social change.

The U.S. Department of Health and Human Services (DHHS) incorporated SDOH into its Healthy People 2020 initiative with a new goal to "create social and physical environments that promote good health for all" (Koh et al., 2011). The hope was that the social determinants approach could enhance collective efforts to improve population health. Ten years later, the Healthy People 2030 initiative went one step further and established five domains to organize SDOH around economic stability, education access and quality, healthcare access and quality, neighborhood and built environment, and social and community context (U.S. Department of Health and Human Services & Office of Disease Prevention and Health Promotion, 2020). The five domains of the SDOH (illustrated in Figure 1) highlight the importance of addressing "upstream" factors to reduce health disparities.

Figure 2. Social determinants of health conceptual framework
Note. Reprinted from World Health Organization (2010) with permission.

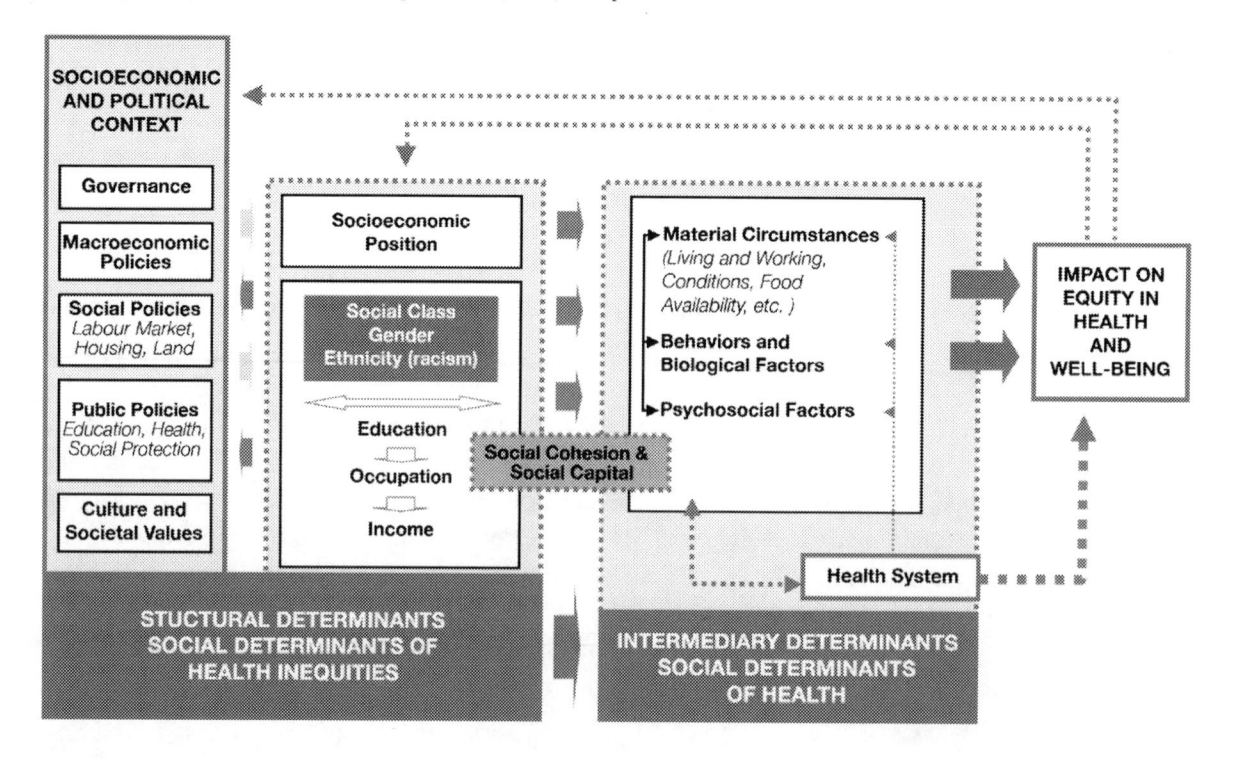

Economic Stability

Issues related to economic stability include the ability to access resources to fulfill basic needs, food insecurity, stable and safe housing, and adequate income (U.S. Department of Health and Human Services & Office of Disease Prevention and Health Promotion, 2020).

Education Access and Quality

Issues related to education access and quality include length and quality of education, availability of early learning opportunities, literacy, and workforce development opportunities such as interprofessional prevention education in health professions training programs (U.S. Department of Health and Human Services & Office of Disease Prevention and Health Promotion, 2020).

Healthcare Access and Quality

Issues related to healthcare access and quality include financing of and access to healthcare delivery systems, access to primary care and prevention services, and access to affordable health insurance (U.S. Department of Health and Human Services & Office of Disease Prevention and Health Promotion, 2020).

Neighborhood and Built Environment

Issues related to neighborhood and built environment include access to green spaces, provision of safe transportation, improvement in quality of housing, and elimination of air pollution and toxic pollutants (U.S. Department of Health and Human Services & Office of Disease Prevention and Health Promotion, 2020).

Social and Community Context

Issues related to social and community context include structural and systemic racism, incarceration, discrimination, exposure to trauma and violence, social cohesion, and civic engagement (U.S. Department of Health and Human Services & Office of Disease Prevention and Health Promotion, 2020).

Interdisciplinary Approach to Higher Education

To date, the fields of public health, nursing, and medicine have arguably made the most concerted efforts to utilize the SDOH to improve health equity. However, most of the issues addressed in the SDOH framework are related to other disciplines, such as education, counseling, social work, policy, urban planning, and business, among others. Therefore, interdisciplinary training, research, and practice is imperative to addressing all aspects of the SDOH. Walden University has recognized the need to rethink the structure of its schools and programs to better address the complex, systemic issues that impact diversity, equity, inclusion, and the health of communities.

Walden University was originally structured according to traditional academic disciplines, including schools of business, counseling, education, health sciences, nursing, public policy, psychology, social work, and undergraduate studies. Under Walden's new structure, historically differentiated programs are now housed together to encourage interdisciplinary collaboration around the SDOH. For example, to tackle issues related to healthcare access and quality, programs in nursing, social work, counseling, and clinical psychology have been placed together. To address issues related to education access and quality, education programs are now paired with health education and promotion, a program that was traditionally placed with public health and health services. Programs in human services and criminal justice have been partnered to focus on issues related to social and community context. In another major shift, programs in public health have been placed with public policy to harness the strengths of both disciplines to address all five domains of the SDOH at the population level.

Walden University has also utilized multiple online teaching approaches—content building, knowledge acquisition, and collaborative (Badia et al., 2017)—to integrate the SDOH into its curricula. For example, the nursing program developed an animated video about the history of SDOH and the public health program developed an interactive module covering important terms and concepts related to the framework. Both resources were made available to the entire Walden community to allow content building, knowledge acquisition, and collaboration, especially for students, faculty, and staff who are not familiar with the SDOH.

In nursing and medical education, the focus of SDOH is typically on gaining perspective about the social factors that impact health (Sharma et al., 2018). In an online university, the focus can broaden into teaching students about how to frame their research around SDOH or apply factors in the framework to policy and practice. For example, in one public health course at Walden University, students participate in a discussion about an observable example of SDOH in their daily life and they develop a research question that could potentially examine it. Another assignment has students identify three upstream factors related to a health topic of their choice, explain how they might measure these upstream factors, and specify which component of the SDOH framework each upstream factor addresses. These assignments aim to prepare students to conduct their own research on SDOH, which is a powerful way that online universities can contribute to improving the complex issues facing society.

CONCLUSION

Responding to the Call

There are several reasons why a university should consider framing curricula and organizational structure around the SDOH. The first is to respond to the call for educational justice (Lazăr, 2020; Levin, 2009; Warren, 2014) and the United Nations Education Steering Committee's goals for inclusive and equitable quality education and lifelong learning for all (UNESCO, 2015). UNESCO's new vision for education is captured by sustainable development goal (SDG) 4 to "ensure inclusive and equitable quality education and promote lifelong learning opportunities for all" (UNESCO, 2015, p. iii). It was inspired by a "humanistic vision of education and development based on human rights and dignity; social justice; inclusion; protection; culturally, linguistic and ethnic diversity; and shared responsibility and accountability" (UNESCO, 2015, p. iii). Educational justice, diversity, and inclusion intersect with the objectives of the SDOH.

Secondly, framing higher education around the SDOH also responds to a call for action issued by the World Health Organization (WHO) in 2008 and the National Academy of Sciences, Engineering, and Medicine (NASEM) in 2016. In *A Framework for Educating Health Professionals to Address the Social Determinants of Health*, NASEM (2016) stated the following:

Making the Social Determinants of Health a core component of all health professionals' lifelong learning pathways will engender in them the competence, skill, and passion to take action, independent of their role and position in the health system, on these crucial contributors to individual and community health, and enhance their ability to identify, engage, and partner with others to take this action. The Social Determinants of Health can and should be integral to all health professional education and training. (p. 3)

NASEM (2016) recommended that educational organizations "should foster an enabling environment that supports and values the integration of the framework's principles into their mission, culture, and work" (p. 91). By framing the mission and organization of an institution around the SDOH, universities can provide students a transformative learning experience so they can contribute to positive social change, improve equity, and create healthier communities around the world.

The National League for Nursing (NLN) issued a similar call to action in its *Vision for Integration of the Social Determinants of Health into Nursing Education Curricula* living document (NLN, 2019). NLN argues that "failing to intentionally integrate the SDOH throughout a program of learning and limiting exposure to newly developed tools and guidelines for assessment have unintended consequences" (p. 4), including unequal quality of care for vulnerable populations and disproportionate distribution of disease (Francis et al., 2018). Thus, universities must use evidence-based approaches to teaching and learning strategies related to SDOH, thread SDOH education throughout the program of learning in varied educational settings (e.g., classroom, practice settings, and simulation-learning environments), and create partnerships with community agencies to intentionally expose students to real-world experiences related to SDOH (NLN, 2019, p. 6). In other words, it is not sufficient to just teach one course on SDOH. Universities must establish supportive infrastructure, comprehensive curricula, longitudinal training, and evidence-based research on the SDOH to make a significant impact on health outcomes, health equity, and social justice.

The final rationale for framing higher education around a framework like the SDOH relates to the need for interdisciplinary collaboration and action to realize the mission of a university. Bollela and colleagues (2015) demonstrated that effective application of interdisciplinary and interprofessional education has potential downstream benefits in improving health outcomes, reducing health inequalities, and promoting health equity. Major international organizations have also recognized the importance of a cross-sectoral approach to achieve global and national improvements in health, education, and sustainable development. The 2030 Agenda for Sustainable Development (United Nations, 2015) provided the impetus and architecture for the United Nations Educational, Scientific and Cultural Organization (UNESCO) and the World Health Organization (WHO) to work in closer collaboration. The alignment of higher education with SDOH through an interdisciplinary perspective provides an opportunity to address the need for educational justice, health equity, and healthier communities.

REFERENCES

Badia, A., Garcia, C., & Meneses, J. (2017). Approaches to teaching online: Exploring factors influencing teachers in a fully online university. *British Journal of Educational Technology*, *48*(6), 1193–1207. doi:10.1111/bjet.12475

Bakshi, S., James, A., Hennelly, M. O., Karani, R., Palermo, A.-G., Jakubowski, A., Ciccariello, C., & Atkinson, H. (2015). The human rights and social justice scholars program: A collaborative model for preclinical training in social medicine. *Annals of Global Health*, *81*(2), 290–297. doi:10.1016/j.aogh.2015.04.001 PMID:26088098

Berkman, L. F., Kawachi, I., & Glymour, M. M. (Eds.). (2000). *Social epidemiology*. Oxford University Press.

Berkman, L. F., & Syme, S. L. (1979). Social networks, host resistance, and mortality: A nine-year follow-up study of Alameda County residents. *American Journal of Epidemiology*, *109*(2), 186–204. doi:10.1093/oxfordjournals.aje.a112674 PMID:425958

Bollela, V. R., Germani, A. C. C. G., de Holanda Campos, H., & Amaral, E. (Eds.). (2015). *Community-based education for the health professions: Learning from the Brazilian experience*. https://www.academia.edu/22090649/COMMUNITY_BASED_EDUCATION_FOR_THE_HEALTH_PROFESSIONS_Learning_from_the_Brazilian_Experience

Boyer, E. L. (1990). *Scholarship reconsidered: Priorities of the professorate*. Carnegie Foundation for the Advancement of Teaching.

Cassel, J., & Tyroler, H. A. (1961). Epidemiological studies of culture change. I. Health status and recency of industrialization. *Archives of Environmental Health*, *3*(1), 25–33. doi:10.1080/00039896.1961.10662969 PMID:13691334

Centers for Disease Control and Prevention. (1999). Achievements in public health, 1900–1999: Control of infectious diseases. *MMWR*, *48*(29), 621–629. https://www.cdc.gov/mmwr/preview/mmwrhtml/mm4829a1.htm#:~:text=In%201900%2C%20the%20three%20leading,than%205%20years%20(1) PMID:10458535

Chapin, C. V. (1924). Deaths among taxpayers and nontaxpayers income tax, Providence, 1865. *American Journal of Public Health*, *4*(8), 647–651. doi:10.2105/AJPH.14.8.647-a PMID:18011285

Cipolla, C. M. (1992). *Miasmas and disease: Public health and environment in the pre-industrial age*. Yale University Press. doi:10.12987/9780300156928

Compagnucci, L., & Spigarelli, F. (2020). The third mission of the university: A systematic literature review on potentials and constraints. *Technological Forecasting and Social Change*, *161*(120284), 120284. Advance online publication. doi:10.1016/j.techfore.2020.120284

Coombs, L. C. (1941). Economic differentials in causes of death. *Medical Care*, *1*(3), 246–255.

Egger, G. (2012). In search of a germ theory equivalent for chronic disease. *Preventing Chronic Disease*, *9*(E95). Advance online publication. doi:10.5888/pcd9.110301 PMID:22575080

Furin, J., Farmer, P., Wolf, M., Levy, B., Judd, A., Paternek, M., Hurtado, R., & Katz, J. (2006). A novel training model to address health problems in poor and underserved populations. *Journal of Health Care for the Poor and Underserved, 17*(1), 17–24. doi:10.1353/hpu.2006.0023 PMID:16520503

Hodgkinson, H. L. (1969). Walden u. *Soundings: An Interdisciplinary Journal, 52,* 172–185. https://scholarworks.waldenu.edu/cgi/viewcontent.cgi?article=1000&context=university_history

Koh, H. K., Piotrowski, J. J., Kumanyika, S., & Fielding, J. S. (2011). Healthy people: A 2020 vision for the social determinants approach. *Health Education & Behavior, 38*(6), 551–557. doi:10.1177/1090198111428646 PMID:22102542

Krieger, N. (1990). Racial and gender discrimination: Risk factors for high blood pressure? *Social Science & Medicine, 30*(12), 1273–1281. doi:10.1016/0277-9536(90)90307-E PMID:2367873

Krieger, N. (1994). Epidemiology and the web of causation: Has anyone seen the spider? *Social Science & Medicine, 39*(7), 887–903. doi:10.1016/0277-9536(94)90202-X PMID:7992123

Krieger, N. (2000). Discrimination and health. In L. F. Berkman & I. Kawachi (Eds.), *Social epidemiology* (pp. 36–75). Oxford University Press.

Krieger, N. (2001a). A glossary for social epidemiology. *Journal of Epidemiology and Community Health, 55*(10), 693–700. doi:10.1136/jech.55.10.693 PMID:11553651

Krieger, N. (2001b). Theories for social epidemiology in the 21st century: An ecosocial perspective. *International Journal of Epidemiology, 30*(4), 668–677. doi:10.1093/ije/30.4.668 PMID:11511581

Krieger, N., & Sidney, S. (1996). Racial discrimination and blood pressure: The CARDIA Study of young black and white adults. *American Journal of Public Health, 86*(10), 1370–1378. doi:10.2105/AJPH.86.10.1370 PMID:8876504

Lazăr, M. L. (2020). Ensuring access to education through inclusion and equity. *Romanian Journal of School Psychology, 13*(26), 32–38.

Levin, H. M. (2009). The economic payoff to investing in educational justice. *Educational Researcher, 38*(1), 5–20. doi:10.3102/0013189X08331192

Lindell, A., Morgan, A., Sugarman, B. H., Tervala, D. J., Westermann, J., Strang, K. P., Costner, K. L., Ingram, M. N., Powell, M., McCune, N. M., Jobe, R. L., Dixon-Saxon, S., Subocz, S., & Schulz, W. (2021, December 2). *Beyond the social determinants of learning™: A Walden University position paper.* https://scholarworks.waldenu.edu/white_papers/3

Marmot, M. (2004). *The status syndrome: How your social standing affects your health and life expectancy.* Bloomsbury. doi:10.1111/j.1740-9713.2004.00058.x

Marmot, M. (2005). Social determinants of health inequalities. *Lancet, 365*(9464), 1099–1104. doi:10.1016/S0140-6736(05)71146-6 PMID:15781105

Marmot, M. G., Smith, G. D., Stansfeld, S., Patel, C., North, F., Head, J., White, I., Brunner, E., & Feeney, A. (1991). Health inequalities among British civil servants: The Whitehall II study. *Lancet, 337*(8754), 1387–1393. doi:10.1016/0140-6736(91)93068-K PMID:1674771

Marmot, M. G., Syme, S. L., Kagan, A., Kato, H., Cohen, J. B., & Belsky, J. (1975). Epidemiologic studies of coronary heart disease and stroke in Japanese men living in Japan, Hawaii and California: Prevalence of coronary and hypertensive heart disease and associated risk factors. *American Journal of Epidemiology*, *102*(6), 514–525. doi:10.1093/oxfordjournals.aje.a112189 PMID:1202953

National League for Nursing. (2019). NLN releases a vision for integration of social determinants of health into nursing education curricula. *Nursing Education Perspectives*, *40*(6), 390. doi:10.1097/01.NEP.0000000000000597 PMID:31644458

O'Brien, M. J., Garland, J. M., Murphy, K. M., Shuman, S. J., Whitaker, R. C., & Larson, S. C. (2014). Training medical students in the social determinants of health: The health scholars program at Puentes de Salud. *Advances in Medical Education and Practice*, *5*, 307–314. doi:10.2147/AMEP.S67480 PMID:25278787

Park, C. (1993). The Black Death. In K. F. Kiple (Ed.), *The Cambridge World History of Human Disease* (pp. 612–615). Cambridge University Press. doi:10.1017/CHOL9780521332866.078

Porter, D. (2001). *Health civilization and the state: A history of public health from ancient to modern times*. Routledge.

Rockett, I. R. H. (1999). Population and health: An introduction to epidemiology. *Population Bulletin*, *54*(4), 1–44. https://www.prb.org/wp-content/uploads/1999/12/Population-Bulletin-54.4PopHealthEpidemiology.pdf PMID:12295687

Rotberg, R. J., & Rabb, T. K. (Eds.). (1985). *Hunger and history: The impact of changing food production and consumption patterns on society*. Cambridge University Press.

Sanderson, C. D., Hollinger-Smith, L. M., & Cox, K. (2021). Developing a social determinants of learning™ framework: A case study. *Nursing Education Perspectives*, *42*(4), 205–211. doi:10.1097/01.NEP.0000000000000810 PMID:33935243

Schultz, M. (2008). Rudolf Virchow. *Emerging Infectious Diseases*, *14*(9), 1480–1481. doi:10.3201/eid1409.086672

Sharma, M., Pinto, A. D., & Kumagai, A. K. (2018). Teaching the social determinants of health: A path to equity or a road to nowhere? *Academic Medicine*, *93*(1), 25–30. doi:10.1097/ACM.0000000000001689 PMID:28445214

Sterner, C. S. (2007). A brief history of miasmic theory. *Bulletin of the History of Medicine*, *22*, 747.

Syme, S. L. (2005). Historical perspective: The social determinants of disease – some roots of the movement. *Epidemiologic Perspectives & Innovations*, *2*(2), 1–7. doi:10.1186/1742-5573-2-2

Syme, S. L., Hyman, M. M., & Enterline, P. E. (1964). Some social and cultural factors associated with incidence of coronary heart disease. *Journal of Chronic Diseases*, *17*(3), 277–289. doi:10.1016/0021-9681(64)90155-9 PMID:5878595

Taylor, R., & Rieger, A. (1985). Medicine as social science: Rudolf Virchow on the typhus epidemic in Upper Silesia. *International Journal of Health Services*, *15*(4), 547–559. doi:10.2190/XX9V-ACD4-KUXD-C0E5 PMID:3908347

Tyroler, H. A., & Cassel, J. (1964). Health consequences of culture change: The effect of urbanization on coronary heart mortality in rural residents. *Journal of Chronic Diseases, 17*, 167–177. doi:10.1016/0021-9681(64)90053-0 PMID:14123834

UNESCO. (2015). *Education 2030: Incheon declaration and framework for action for the implementation of sustainable development goal 4.* http://uis.unesco.org/sites/default/files/documents/education-2030-incheon-framework-for-action-implementation-of-sdg4-2016-en_2.pdf

United States Department of Health and Human Services, Office of Disease Prevention and Health Promotion. (n.d.). *Healthy People 2030. Social determinants of health.* https://health.gov/healthypeople/priority-areas/social-determinants-health

United States Department of Health and Human Services & Office of Disease Prevention and Health Promotion. (2020). *Healthy People 2030.* https://health.gov/healthypeople/objectives-and-data/social-determinants-health

Villerme, L. (1840). *Tableau d'etat physique et moral des ouvriers* (Vol. 2). Renouard.

Walden University. (2017). *Walden 2020: A vision for social change.* https://www.waldenu.edu/-/media/Walden/files/about-walden/walden-university-2017-social-change-report-final-v-2.pdf?la=en

Walden University. (n.d.). *Social change: The passion that drives us.* https://www.waldenu.edu/why-walden/social-change

Walden University Center for Social Change. (n.d.). *About us.* https://academicguides.waldenu.edu/social-change/about-us

Warren, M. R. (2014). Transforming public education: The need for an educational justice movement. *New England Journal of Public Policy, 26*(1), 1–16. https://scholarworks.umb.edu/nejpp/vol26/iss1/11

Wilkinson, R. G., & Marmot, M. (Eds.). (2003). *Social determinants of health: The solid facts.* World Health Organization. https://apps.who.int/iris/bitstream/handle/10665/326568/9789289013710-eng.pdf?sequence=1&isAllowed=y

Witten, N. A. K., & Maskarinec, G. G. (2015). Privilege as a social determinant of health in medical education: A single class session can change privilege perspective. *Hawai'i Journal of Medicine & Public Health: a Journal of Asia Pacific Medicine & Public Health, 74*(9), 297–301. https://www.ncbi.nlm.nih.gov/pmc/articles/PMC4578164/#:~:text=By%20incorporating%20a%20single%20class,a%20social%20determinant%20of%20health PMID:26468425

World Health Organization. (2010). *A conceptual framework for action on the social determinants of health.* https://apps.who.int/iris/bitstream/handle/10665/44489/?sequence=1

World Health Organization. (2020). *The top 10 causes of death.* https://www.who.int/news-room/fact-sheets/detail/the-top-10-causes-of-death

World Health Organization. (n.d.). *Frequently asked questions.* https://www.who.int/about/frequently-asked-questions

World Health Organization Commission on Social Determinants of Health. (2008). *Closing the gap in a generation: Health equity through action on the social determinants of health.* https://www.who.int/teams/social-determinants-of-health/equity-and-health/commission-on-social-determinants-of-health

Yob, I. M., Danver, S. L., Kristensen, S., Schulz, W., Simmons, K., Brashen, H. M., Krysiak, R. S., Kiltz, L., Gatlin, L., Wesson, S., & Penland, D. R. (2016). Curriculum alignment with a mission of social change in higher education. *Innovative Higher Education, 41*(3), 203–219. doi:10.100710755-015-9344-5

Yob, I. M., & Ferraro, A. (2013). Political engagement in higher education curricula. *Journal of Social Change, 5*(1), 1–10. doi:10.5590/JOSC.2013.05.1.01

ADDITIONAL READING

Adtalem. (n.d.). *About us.* https://www.adtalem.com/about-us

Lawrence, M. G., Williams, S., Nanz, P., & Renn, O. (2022). Characteristics, potentials, and challenges of transdisciplinary research. *One Earth, 5*(1), 44–61. doi:10.1016/j.oneear.2021.12.010

Chapter 14
Sustainable Strategic Planning for Inclusive Online Teaching and Learning

Sue Subocz
Walden University, USA

Heidi Chumley
Ross University School of Medicine, Barbados

Sri Banerjee
https://orcid.org/0000-0002-6872-4983
Walden University, USA

Myrna Cano-Wolfbrandt
https://orcid.org/0000-0002-3170-1972
Arizona State University, USA

ABSTRACT

It may indeed be time to stop strategic planning, at least as it has most typically been considered and conducted, in favor of approaches that focus on articulating visions for a future built on the individual and collective experiences of learners and future learners of an institution. Instead, it may be time to create operational plans designed to sustain a culture of community commitment and ensure an inclusive teaching and learning environment. Such an inclusive teaching and learning environment is founded on (1) an understanding of learners as whole people with pasts that must be honored throughout the learning process, (2) a set of complex social circumstances that must be considered in the design and delivery of learning experiences, and (3) a future that is unpredictable and ever-changing.

INTRODUCTION

As institutions of higher education look to ensure inclusive and equitable quality education programs, they create strategic plans to guide future efforts. These initiative-level strategic plans are often in the context of a larger university strategic plan. As larger university strategic plans may be written from a university growth lens, it is important to recognize where inclusive teaching and learning supports university growth. Inclusive teaching and learning, which strives to support individual students, has the added advantages of broadening the attractiveness of a university to prospective students, improving student retention, and may serve to attract donor interest. Leaders who are building strategic plans to promote inclusive teaching and learning can tie their key approaches to larger movements around new student growth, student retention, diversity, and equity initiatives.

Strategic plans in general vary in their ability to guide universities towards their vision in support of their mission. Popular narratives hold that up to 90% of strategic plans fail in implementation. While this may be an exaggeration that does not account for more recent advances in the field of strategic planning (Cândido & Santos, 2015), such critical views outlining difficulties with strategic planning in higher education are not new. Strategic planning at institutions of higher education is so notoriously subject to failure that a recent article in *Inside Higher Ed* (Eckel & Trower, 2019) suggests institutions stop strategic planning altogether, in favor of focusing more fully on the strategy itself. Others (Gordon & Fischer, 2015) infer that management motivations for strategic planning are grounded more in external influence and/or to simply comply with accreditation checklists, resulting in very few strategic achievements.

Strategic planning for inclusive teaching and learning shares these challenges and must consider the additional complexities that arise when truly striving for inclusivity. Building on the literature around strategic planning, we propose three reasons why inclusive teaching and learning strategic planning initiatives fail (see Figure 1).

1. Strategic plans were built from a narrow world view with a lack of surfacing of underlying assumptions and perspectives.
2. Strategic plans fail to address the variety of lived experiences current and prospective students face outside of the ever-changing classroom environment.
3. Strategic plans were created for linear instead of complex systems, assuming that the same macro or micro events will affect people and programs similarly.

Together, these shortcomings lead to strategic plans that are incapable of surviving even small perturbances to the educational system.

To address these challenges, particularly in institutions serving working professional and/or non-traditional age learners, institutional leaders have the opportunity to create achievable and sustainable strategic plans by adjusting their vantage point and focusing more time and energy on understanding the full student (and prospective student) experience. Too often institutional leaders overly consider the employee and organizational stakeholders, systems, and processes in the planning process. These plans may include tidy phrases such as "putting students at the center" or "being student-centric" to address the learner as the stakeholder, using only broad survey data or the voices of a handful of students involved in the planning process superficially. When taking such approaches, the starting point is institution-centric, with students playing only a small role in influencing a substantial institutional infrastructure that already exists – largely to support its own great weight.

Figure 1. An illustration of the three reasons why inclusive teaching and learning strategic planning initiatives fail
Note. Image credit: Sri Banerjee, Walden University.

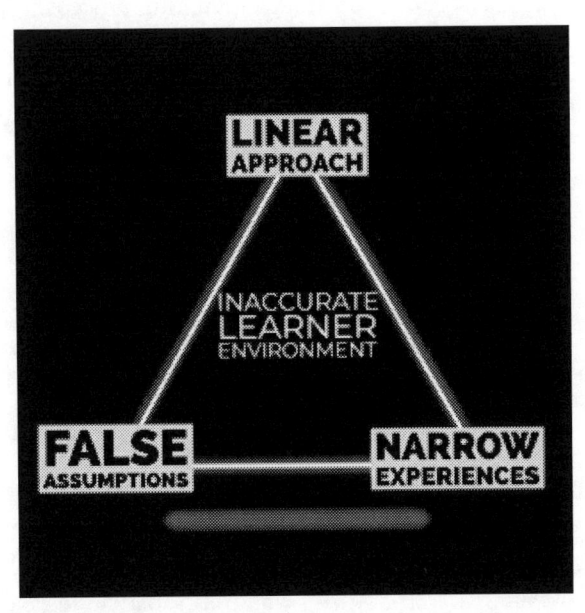

What if the planning process started with the learners as full persons, and began to seek to have the university understand the larger context from which learning can arise truly and deeply? What if strategic thinking started with the commitment to serve *whole* learners. Not just names and faces who sit in classrooms, but people. People with past experiences that create a worldview unique to each of them. Not just educational pasts, but the entire set of experiences and lived contexts that brought them to your institution. People with whole lives that influence each individual's opportunity at success in their present learning environment. Not just the learning environment they find on campus or online, but the learning environment allowed by their whole lived experience in the present. People with dreams that extend beyond a classroom. Dreams to better their own lives, the lives of their families, and the lives in their communities. What if inclusive teaching and learning strategies recognized the development of both the referential self, and the indexical self, as Hope Landrine (1992) suggests (see Chapter 1, "Developing a Learning Model for Caring, Inclusion and Social Change in an Online Environment")?

Re-framing in this way takes courage. While many institutions began because they saw a need to improve the lives in their communities, the massive growth in higher education has led so many institutions far afield from these original intentions. Not through maliciousness or callousness, but simply as a manifestation of the challenges of growth. As challenges arose, they designed institutional solutions to meet the challenges. Most often, these solutions resulted in "more" within the institution. More tutoring. More advising. More intrusive advising. More guided pathways and more information on the website. More remedial courses. More, more, more.

The result of these efforts have often led to unfocused, untestable solutions that allow us to check boxes on our plans without gaining the impact we desire. And the very students we have been seeking to help are the ones who have little opportunity to engage in "more" anything when these solutions are tested through the lens of students' whole lives. This effect is magnified when considering the whole lives of working adult professionals; so, for institutions serving returning adult students these solutions, while well intentioned, are particularly wasteful.

We propose that through a person-centered strategic planning process focused on knowing students – whole students – institutions can address the challenges of strategic planning in ways that will create sustainable systems focused on *building better rather than building more*. This approach addresses the three challenges above while giving primary consideration to building better systems that consider where learners have come from through their lived experiences, what they are experiencing concurrent with the institutional experience, and the dreams they hold for their future selves.

ADDRESSING CHALLENGE 1

Moving from a Narrower to a Broader World View by Taking a Holistic View of the Learners' Past Experiences

Strategic plans are often built from a narrow world view in which many important underlying assumptions go unnoticed. Perhaps one of the most important assumptions a university makes is that it knows who it serves and who its students are.

But is this so? In an increasingly diverse world, where it is critical to be culturally competent to be authentically inclusive, does your university take the time, and invest in the resources necessary to truly understand the lived experiences of each person thinking about attending, or enrolled in the university?

Individuals have unique sets of experiences that combine to shape their thinking. This might make it seem overwhelming to even attempt to address the prior lived experiences of students when making strategic plans. There are several ways in which institutions can begin, however.

First, there are experiences that transcend unique individuals and are shared by cohorts. Shared experiences can come from a similar geographic location, identification with a specific race/ethnicity or gender, comparable socioeconomic positions, a shared generation, or experiencing a similar highly impactful event. Thus, a first step in taking a person-centered approach to strategy, paradoxically, is to understand potential shared group effects more deeply as embedded context.

A second step would be to seek to identify and to understand differences between the university's leadership team's and its students' breadth of world view. It is critical to map actual and desired life experiences of current and prospective students against those of the leadership team most involved in the strategic planning process, including those who will be responsible for executing on the plan. Experiences selected for the mapping exercise should differ by university based on local context and mission. Some examples of current students' experiences may include self or parent immigrant to the U.S., belonging to a racial minority, living at or below poverty level, prior attendance at multiple colleges, parenting a young child, non-binary gender, home insecurity, and so on. Creating a simple grid can provide important insights. As shown in Table 1 below, the decision-makers lack two life experiences common to their students.

Many leadership teams will not have members with all, or even many of the noted life experiences that students experience every day. There are insights to be realized by simply identifying the experiences common in students that are rare to be experienced by leadership. This realization brings unconsciousness to consciousness, an early step in understanding similarities and differences. If experiences are discovered that are important for leadership to understand, there are several ways to broaden one's perspective.

Sustainable Strategic Planning for Inclusive Online Teaching and Learning

Table 1. Decision-makers need to consider, but do not share, some of the life experiences of their students

	Current students	**Leadership / decision-makers**
Self / parent immigrant to US	+++	-
Belonging to a racial minority	++++	+
Living at or below poverty level	+++	-
Parenting a young child and taking care of elders	+	++
LGBTQ	++	+

Note. This table offers the kinds of mapping to differentiate between the actual and desired life experiences of current and prospective students against the lived experiences of a leadership team. The plus and minus signs could indicate the prevalence of an attribute within a campus community, with more "+" plus signs indicating a proportionally higher instance of a certain attribute; a "-" minus sign likewise indicates a proportionally lower instance of a certain attribute.

1. **Gain exposure:** The University of Kansas, which serves students from many rural counties, takes faculty on a Wheat State Tour, to provide insight into students' experiences prior to college. In an online learning environment, this might mean regional events, leveraging the experiences of local adjunct faculty, alumni, and students to understand the communities in which they live and work.
2. **Engage with experts:** Ross University School of Medicine engaged with Historically Black Colleges and Universities to improve recruiting and support of Black students. This dialogue resulted in changing the scholarship structure and creating better networking opportunities.
3. **Meet your students and alumni:** don't just to ask for donations or leverage them for marketing! Student advisory boards, student government associations, and alumni associations present great opportunities to meet the people behind the learning.

One can "meet" students and understand their interests by seeing what they create organically also. Student clubs and organizations can seem like a nice-to-have opportunity, particularly in online or adult learning environments. However, when allowed to flourish, such clubs and organizations create opportunities for students to engage with others with shared experiences.

- **Action Step:** Take time to understand your students' whole lives by visiting their communities, engaging with experts, and/or leveraging student and alumni organizations to listen.

These organizations not only create a way to acknowledge their pasts, but also provide great insights into the kinds of experiences that need to be considered in the planning process. At Walden University, for example, students have formed clubs for veterans, LGBTQ+ students, and multicultural and international students. When leaders listen closely to those students rather than tallying a list of co-curriculars, we can gain valuable insights.

Moving from a narrower to a broader worldview can be accomplished by articulating common life experiences in your student body, uncovering the differences in their experiences compared to those of the leadership team, and taking steps to better understand common student experiences. This understanding lays important groundwork for development of a strategic plan to promote inclusive teaching and learning. In our experience, the breadth of worldview, when divergent from that of the students, is almost invariably too narrow; however, the possibility exists that it can be too wide. There is a difference between educational programming that strives to broaden students' world views and life experiences and that which does so with a strong regard for understanding students' current world views and prior life experiences. For strategic planning, the latter is the preferred approach.

ADDRESSING CHALLENGE 2

Addressing the Variety of Experiences Students Face Outside of the Ever-Changing Classroom Environment by Taking an Inclusive Approach Informed by Factors Identified as the Social Determinants of Learning

Understanding the past experiences of learners and the communities in which they live and work is one important part of coming to know your learners as you begin your strategic planning process. Creating a connection between those past experiences and learners' communities provides an opportunity to more fully examine the holistic environment in which they are currently operating – and trying to learn.

Such ideas for considering the whole student experience are not new. A newly advanced framework may offer the necessary framework to allow for broader implementation of what may have seemed nebulous in the past. This new framework, Social Determinants of Learning™ (SDOL™) creates a clear path for understanding current or desired student population for immediate impact and an ongoing framework to continuously understand the students' current world view and prior life experiences (Sanderson et al., 2021). Or, an alternate framework animates an active approach to considering a student's lived experience through developing a university wide community of care is explored in the epilogue to this book (see Chapter 16).

Moving beyond the information and into action, a thorough understanding of what it means to create an inclusive teaching and learning environment helps bridge the divide from understanding learners to creating curricula, learning experiences, and outcomes that allow the best opportunity for the most learners to succeed.

To create the whole student experience, it sometimes is important to understand potential health risks that may be affecting specific segments of the student population. Students who have been negatively impacted from having no access to in-person learning due to the COVID pandemic of 2020 are disproportionately low-income and students of color (Levinson et al. 2021; Mahmood, 2021). According to Healthy People 2030 (n.d.) the Social Determinants of Health (SDOH) were designed to identify and "create social and physical environments that promote good health for all" (para. 3). This model clusters the significant social structures impacting lived experiences (see Figure 2) and allows observers to identify both areas of strength and deficit to intervene where appropriate.

The SDOH greatly affect health inequities experienced primarily by marginalized communities, and education, and educational justice, is the direct link between the SDOH and the SDOL™ that impacts the well-being and the quality of life throughout one's lifespan. The domains of the SDOL™ framework focus on physical health, psychosocial health, physical environment, social environment, economic stability, and self-motivation (Sanderson et al., 2021). The lack of in-person learning exacerbates the hardships experienced by students. Those hardships may include such things as family stress, separation from peers, anxiety, inaccessibility of digital tools, etc. Educational opportunities have the potential to transform lives for the better, by enabling socioeconomic mobility, reducing inequality, improving equity,

Sustainable Strategic Planning for Inclusive Online Teaching and Learning

and increasing one's ability to make well-informed decisions to positively impact their societal needs and improve overall health equity (Bleser, 2022; McGill, 2016).

Figure 2. The social determinants of health
Note. This image is in the public domain (United States Department of Health and Human Services. Office of Disease Prevention and Health Promotion, n.d.).

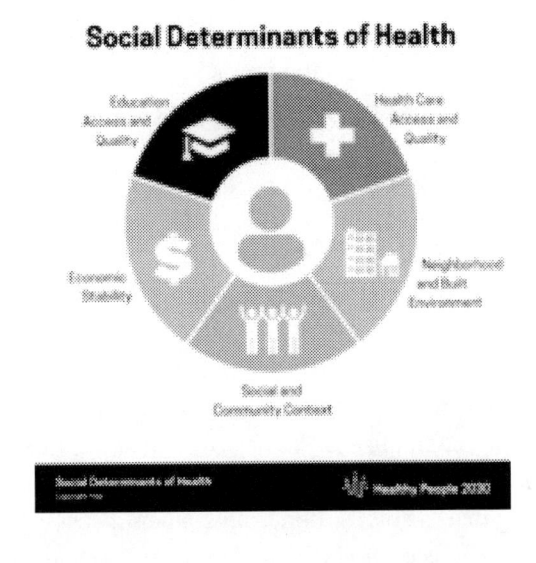

Action Steps:

- Add to typical demographic data, information about each of the SDOLs, may need to add metrics
- Identify the most important SDOLs for your current and desired student population
- Map most important SDOLs to your current educational approach (when classes are taught, what is needed to access, approach to building self-motivation and resilience, etc.

Putting the Information into Practice Through a Focus on Inclusive Teaching and Learning

One does not need to delve too deeply into these sorts of analyses to make some good assumptions in how to leverage social determinants of learning in the design and delivery of curriculum. One such assumption is that institutions must be purposeful in ensuring an inclusive teaching and learning environment to account for differences relative to the social determinants of learning. What is inclusive teaching and learning (ITL) and why does it matter?

ITL is a fundamental characteristic in ensuring equitable access to learning, health equity, and social justice. It promotes the success of all students, including students from marginalized groups who are often overlooked. Establishing sustainable approaches to ensure equitable access to learning increases students' sense of belonging, helps them recognize their strengths, provides them with the tools to overcome the challenges and barriers they face and increases completion and graduation rates. For ITL to be successful, it requires inclusive planning, designing, delivery methods, and evaluation of learning outcomes.

The pandemic of the early 2020s highlighted the differential educational experiences of learners and taught us that schools, colleges, and universities must develop guiding principles and sustainable development goals to ensure equitable access, student success, and high-quality learning. To do so, there must be an understanding of what that encompasses. How do we make certain that all students and teachers are experiencing an inclusive teaching and learning environment and how do we make that experience sustainable? Failing to address the all-encompassing needs that have come to light from the pandemic is sure to exacerbate the social and academic disparities already experienced by marginalized communities. Historically, there exists an achievement gap between students from marginalized populations and students who do not belong to those populations. Addressing these disparities through inclusive practices can form the solid base necessary for sustainable strategic plans.

Marginalized populations include multiple ethnic groups, those with learning, mental, linguistic, or physical conditions, veteran status, LGBTQ+ identities, felons and current parolees, and varying socioeconomic status. Another assumption that can be made is that marginalized populations, who are seeing both relative and absolute population growth, are unfortunately more likely to be excluded from economic, societal, and educational opportunities than other populations despite being "just as capable and full of potential" (Wilkinson, 2020). The opportunity has presented itself to develop purposeful, inclusive teaching practices to respond and address the diverse needs of learners without excluding the needs of those who are most marginalized. This involves making modifications to the curriculum, approaches, and delivery of learning content to acknowledge these differences and ensure design and delivery is proactive in ensuring that the backgrounds and experiences of each learner are not just a valued part of the process. In fact, there needs to be an understanding that the educational process *depends* on those differences and backgrounds.

There are several instructional strategies that can be implemented to ensure a person-centered approach to support the learning of all students. What is important to note, when implementing new or revised strategies, is that we ensure the content is accessible to all learners, is understandable, and that additional resources are available if needed. Even the most effective teaching strategies, despite their good intentions, have the potential to exclude learners. In the online environment, educators must consider their students' access or familiarity with digital tools. According to Goudeau et al. (2021), more than 40% of working-class families in the United States either did not have a laptop or desktop computer or access to broadband internet. For those families who do have access to digital tools, many of the lessons require downloading, printing, and or scanning. This significantly excludes those students who may not have access to these types of digital tools or may be sharing one home computer with multiple family members, who, during the pandemic, were also working or learning from home. This example reiterates the duality that while developing online content may increase an audience for online learning for some, it simultaneously eliminates access to educational content for others.

The Academic Development and Diversity Team (2021) at Sheffield Hallam University in Sheffield, England have developed five principles listed below for an inclusive learning experience. By considering the various challenges or barriers faced by diverse populations of students, these principles offer tools to minimize their impact and facilitate higher online learner engagement. The principles encourage higher education institutions to be:

1. Flexible and open to change

Sustainable Strategic Planning for Inclusive Online Teaching and Learning

2. Equitable, consistent, and accessible
3. Working in collaboration with students and stakeholders
4. Personalizing interactions and recognizing that successful teaching and learning is measured by personal difference
5. Embracing diversity

These principles can be applied to teaching practices, curriculum design, delivery methods, and evaluation processes and are supported by the teaching and learning tips included in other chapters of this book (Chapters 4, 5, and 6 are especially helpful in illuminating these topics). While these may seem most pertinent to instructional design, these foundational concepts can also provide a common language that can be used throughout the institution.

For purposes of strategic planning, the most important takeaway is that inclusive teaching and learning considers all aspects of the student experience, such as student background, culture, prior knowledge, motivations, and abilities. The use of real-world examples in the classroom environment and throughout the student service experience promotes engagement, makes connections between courses and content, and helps students reevaluate prior viewpoints (as discussed in the learning model presented in Chapter 1 in this book). The use of personal stories, values, and beliefs as they pertain to the content also aids in having students, staff and faculty learn about and from one another. Personal sharing includes recognizing one's failures as well as their successes. Failure is only failure if one does not learn from it. Guided reflection on failure can be a tool for learning or professional development.

Faculty support should also be considered when devising and evaluating strategic plans. Supporting and empowering students in their success is crucial and faculty who feel supported and cared for will have a higher probability of ensuring that success. Engaging with faculty – deeply engaging through dialogue and meeting them where they are – offers an opportunity to share strategies on what is working and what is not, to give and receive feedback, but most importantly to verify that faculty from diverse groups are succeeding and thriving. Administrators model responsible strategic human resource planning when they are conducting reviews of this nature rather than simply counting numbers in demographic categories.

Further, there are lessons from inclusive teaching and learning practices that can be applied in strategic planning. Most notably, it is important to recognize that strategic plans, just like learning experiences, are developed based on unconscious biases. This leads to another assumption that can be made in the strategic planning process -- every individual has unconscious/implicit bias. Biases are natural, based on one's lived experiences and context, cultural contours and norms, prevalence of media, and community standards.

According to the Association of Executive Search and Leadership Consultants (2020), some of the most common types of biases that can affect the student and/or educator experience are listed below:

- **Confirmation bias** – Favors or prefers to trust in the ideas or beliefs that confirm existing beliefs and what we may think we know about a certain topic. Using positive or negative preconceived notions about a population of students can impact their learning and faculty development.
- **Self-serving bias** – Attributes one's successes and positive outcomes to one's own doing, and failures and negative outcomes to other individuals or factors.
- **In-group bias** – Unfairly favors, supports, or protects students or peers because they identify with one's own group (ingroup). For example: gender, ethnicity, occupation, economic and social

position, race, etc., as opposed to those who are outside of one's own group (outgroup). It is also possible to hold a bias against individuals who are in one's own group.
- **Out-group bias** – Assigning negative categorizations, feelings, or ideas about students or peers because they are not part of one's own group.

(See Chapter 15 for more on cognitive biases that impact inclusive teaching and learning.) Educational leaders must recognize that unconscious bias or unconscious decision making, can have an impact on the strategic planning process as well as the learning environment. Recognizing bias and how it affects the student experience is vital to strategic planning, student success and accessibility. Promoting an inclusive, positive learning environment impacts how an educator views and communicates with their students and peers and helps in recognizing students' biases and opening opportunities for safe and healthy dialogue.

When educators demonstrate cultural awareness by recognizing and reflecting on personal biases, they can, in turn, evaluate interpersonal communication that will reflect cultural knowledge and promote equity and civility in the classroom and can acknowledge that all students and peers involved in conversations bring with them a multitude of ideas, attitudes, feelings, and opinions. Effective dialogue allows all involved to express their ideas or opinions without fear of judgment and exposes all to relevant information. Teachers have a responsibility to present person-centered strategies for speaking across differences in the inclusive learning environment. In this regard, teachers should?

- Model mutual respect for the feelings, wishes, rights, traditions, or the background of others. During discussion or classroom collaboration, teachers must demonstrate honoring and regarding another person's basic humanity. Feelings of disrespect often take place when there is a focus on how others are different from ourselves. Those feelings can be counteracted by looking for ways we may be similar or focusing on how those differences can create understanding without excusing another's behavior, we can try to sympathize, even empathize, with them.
- Practice active listening, which consists of listing without interrupting, making eye contact, and using body language.
- Listen without judgment and confirm understanding by repeating what was heard to ensure one understands what was meant.
- Empathize: place yourself in someone else's shoes.
- Show students how to compare opposing views rather than disagreeing.

Without this kind of dialogue, strategic plans are doomed to stagnate, if not fail completely.

Finally, it is also reasonable to assume that students with significant challenges relative to the social determinants of learning will come with a fixed-mindset or deficit mentality. Without care and attention, this type of deficit thinking can impact the attitudes of faculty and staff. Students who hold a fixed mindset believe their talents or qualities are permanent and change is not possible. Promoting a growth mindset is an important component of a sustainable strategic planning effort in that every member of the learning community must believe that students can succeed in accomplishing their goals, regardless of the background of social determinants of learning. Teachers can foster this through feedback, mentorship, and learning opportunities. This gives students the tools to recognize their challenges or barriers and how to overcome them (Amayo, 2020). Promoting a growth mindset helps students believe they can develop their skills or qualities over time despite their biases or experiences, and it allows faculty and staff the same opportunity.

ADDRESSING CHALLENGE 3

Future-Proof Your Strategic Plan by Using Systems Approaches that Moderate Complexity and Frameworks that Acknowledge Events Do Not Affect People and Programs Similarly

The actions taken to understand your learners is key to creating and sustaining an inclusive environment. It should also be evident that there will be a broad range of reactions to the same event. Many of the same practices can support ongoing engagement with learner communities to ensure that disparate impacts are being continuously evaluated.

Sustainability Dimensions

When working on a plan for inclusive education, sustainable education practices should be central to the effort. Though the meaning of sustainability can vary – and sustainability is such a broad topic – there are several facets of the concept that should be incorporated into your inclusive educational strategy.

The first is that such strategies should reflect all three elements of the United Nations' tripartite, interconnected, sustainability framework, known as ESG (Environmental, Social, and Governance), in which strategic planners must think beyond the environmental realm when considering sustainable practices.

Even within the extensive list of sustainable development goals, the ESG framework is the guiding paradigm of these goals (United Nations, 2019). These approaches move away from comforting averages and toward the consideration of how actions in each of these dimensions impact individuals across myriad intersecting and diverging dimensions.

In the world of higher education, this translates to an emphasis on integrating sustainable methods of meeting learners' needs so as to improve the whole-student-as-individual participant experience. According to the U.N. Cooperation Framework, integration requires a systems-based understanding and collective action and awareness of longer "time horizons" (U.N., 2019). Additionally, it is important to note that sustainable development does not imply solely focusing on economic growth of nations or universities, as this would promote existing inequities further. There is a notion that there are trade-offs that must be considered between unbridled economic growth and social justice.

The Association for the Advancement of Sustainability in Higher Education has created a transparent, self-reporting framework which can be assessed using the Sustainability Tracking, Assessment, and Rating System (STARS). This system has been designed to inspire higher education to lead the sustainability transformation. According to working groups at Columbia University, sustainability is a culture which must be fostered, and sustainability should be the starting point for initiatives and planning, looking at least 10 years into the future (Sustainable Columbia, 2022). They have also attempted to align their brand with environmental sustainability by creating a separate "Sustainable Columbia." The creation of this name demonstrates this institutional commitment.

Still, most current thinking about sustainability is mired in discussions primarily aimed at environmental goals. Many of these environmental sustainability challenges are areas in which distance education can provide positive contributions, given the existential threats that climate change pose to humanity. For instance, energy needed to heat and cool buildings is significantly reduced, as are carbon emissions from transportation, paving the way for an environmentally sustainable future.

How then, does a leader consider sustainability as a way of being that encompasses not only the environmental aspects of sustainable systems but also the people aspects? From an environmental perspective, sustainability considerations are contextualized within the confines of scarcity. This additional consideration can lead to a more realistic understanding of sustainability as one of the reasons that there are barriers to maximize the utility of resources. In the discipline of economics, the consideration of scarce resources is fundamental. Tipping points vary in that the scarcity of natural resources is considered as a primary upper limit based on which sustainability averts reaching these points. This leads to an important conclusion: Where the two seemingly disparate conversations converge is in the interest of addressing any sources that have caused uneven distribution of wealth and power, thereby creating an environment in which the impact of events becomes vastly different based on this distribution.

These principles of sustainability then can be applied to curricular considerations and inclusive education. It is important to address any sources that have caused uneven distribution of wealth and power, but it also is critical to create a plan that is inclusive in nature that is sustainable.

So how does an institutional leader go about such a lofty, yet somewhat mercurial goal? The solution may sound like one that many have tried in the past, with varying degrees of success – and yet the SWOT (strengths, weaknesses, opportunities, and threats) analysis, when approached with some discipline, can be quite effective. Such discipline can be achieved through appreciative-inquiry based models, which are referenced in Chapter 2 (Digital Appreciative Inquiry for Inclusion), such as a scenario-based planning model. This disciplined, scenario-based planning model will offer leaders the opportunity to create sustainable plans by modeling and understanding the systemic effects of an increasingly diverse and polarized world:

Utilize Effective Scenario Planning

In order to develop scenario-based lists of strengths, weaknesses, opportunities and threats to the learners and future learners of the institution. And, to prepare for the future, it is especially important to understand and make sense of the future. Ramirez and Wilkinson (2016) provided the idea of "future-less" future, where we mitigate potential failures in planning by framing and reframing potential future scenarios. To understand imagined possibilities requires important considerations. Thinking about contrasting approaches to imagined futures, there are multiple perspectives which are important to consider when thinking about the principle of sustainability. The main issue with using forecasting is that the future is often considered a continuation of the past, which many current world events show clearly is not necessarily true.

The principles of effectuation and types of uncertainty are extremely important in characterizing a sustainability plan. More specifically, causation focuses on one variable and its effect. However, when thinking of effectuation, it is important to explore multiple risk factors and causal interrelationships at the same time (Alsaadi, 2021). When the distribution of a system is unknown or there is no distribution that can sufficiently describe the future then this is known as Knightian Uncertainty as is outlined in the table below. Researchers have found that certain models can also explain resource shocks during particular time periods (Shillebeeckx et al., 2019), which is an important consideration in the field of education. Another approach is to use different problem-solving methods of effectuation which can then be used to ideate what-if scenarios and other decision-making (see Table 2).

Table 2. Description of various types of uncertainty

	Risk/Statistical Uncertainty	Knightian Uncertainty
Nature of Future	Distribution (known versus unknown)	Future has no distribution
Probability	Known	Unclassifiable instances
Method to deal with Uncertainty	Analysis and Estimation	Effectuation

In such an environment, leaders would do well to acknowledge that the future cannot be predicted and that even if it could, that future would be different for each individual experiencing it. Just as past micro and macro events are felt differently by different people, so will future events. This is especially important when thinking about sustainability. In this unpredictable environment scenario planning provides the flexibility of thinking of alternatives to identify strengths, to take full advantage of opportunities and to address weaknesses and threats.

Use key experiences common to your students and important social determinants of learning in your context to identify key issues to address with scenario planning. For example, a key issue may be decreasing student debt, increasing access to education, etc.

- Consider major external factors that could impact higher education, such as:
  - a redistribution of wealth and/or power
  - a disproportionately available technological advantage
  - a significant change in life expectancy or quality of life
  - a significant social or political event
- Create two or three reasonable scenarios. How the scenarios come to pass is less important than the outcome that creates an impact. For example, use an outcome such as less income for discretionary spending as the scenario, instead of what might lead to less discretionary spending.
- Understand your institutions' current strengths and weaknesses and how they will play out in each scenario.
- Develop an approach that will best address the key issues in the most likely scenarios.

Leverage Risk Modeling to Aid in Developing Priorities to Address Threats

When creating an inclusive sustainability plan, if probability distributions of the future can be assigned, then inferences about potential outcomes can be made. Usually, in the discipline of epidemiology, the future is viewed as "risk" and central to this is the idea of causation (Wilkinson & Ramirez, 2019). However, thinking of risks as possibilities, then similar calculations can be made of the future. When the nature of the risk is known, then the future is assigned concrete risks. This way, there are known distributions that can be characterized and calculated (Johnson & Hörisch, 2021). When using a statistical approach, the ability to make specific inferences about the future and calculate is crucial in that it provides better opportunities for specific sustainability plans. However, the issue is that future depiction is not always quantifiable. This has classically been true for decision-making paradigms that gained traction due to the confluence of the core competency movement and process management.

Part of this is understanding how to collectivize risk. We define *collectivization of risk* as the mitigation of individual risk through cooperation and the establishment of collective responsibility for educational provision. Risk is collectivized by creating structures that absorb the risk of exclusion from education and the social exclusion that can result. Successful collectivization of educational risk requires a shared assessment of mutual vulnerability to external shocks.

This all may sound somehow magical to many higher education leaders. And surely, the outcomes of this sort of future-proofing projections of the future and addressing risk through collectivizing is not a skillset ordinarily found at institutions.

- **Action Step:** Engage with futurist and risk planning experts to prioritize based on risk. Make specific note that this is not about predicting the future of higher education. It is about predicting the future worldview our learners will have experienced as they enter and about the holistic environment in which they will be engaging as they strive to learn.

Embed Priorities into Operating Models, Particularly with Respect to Technologies

Strategic plans that sit to the side of operations are almost guaranteed to fail. An operating model is especially important to articulate in relation to a university due to the presence of various business models within which operations function in education. The operating model not only is an abstraction and visual of how the business runs but also how this delivers value to beneficiaries and stakeholders - it is the embodiment of the strategic plan on a daily basis! The operating model provides an abstraction on how the educational institution is functioning which then can guide the development of sustainability plan for inclusive teaching and learning. When combining principles of education in various operating models, it is important to incorporate concepts from various disciplines as well.

Another concept that is critical to defining and implementing an effective operating model is to have a shared, and clear value proposition. The strength of models with clearly articulated and understood value propositions is that they provide clarity on what should be the central focus in operations: supporting all elements of the university in taking care of students, all students. The interaction with stakeholders with and for students is what drives the goals of the emerging venture or innovation. Very few approaches are value or student-centered. By identifying the benefits of the plan as it is tailored to specific student demographics sustainability can be better ensured. Specifically, when considering value propositions, it is important to know how value propositions or innovations can be made sustainable and incorporated into the larger plan. If the strategic plan is built as proposed previously, through the student lens, but the operating models continue to be viewed through an institutional lens, then the strategic goals will never be realized.

In the 21st century, it would be impossible to embed sustainability into the operating model without considering of the role of technology, especially in distance education. Due to this, it is important to understand and discuss the role of technology in a sustainability plan. It is imperative to offer specific guidance on how technology can be harnessed and leveraged in order to meet the demands of online distance education (Uygur et al., 2020). For instance, students who may have learning disabilities, technology can especially meet the needs of these students. Therefore, from the perspective of technology, the communication of information is conducted using technology as well. The infrastructures must not only be able to tolerate increasing demands but also have mechanisms to handle potential interruptions in service or threats to cybersecurity.

It is important to provide specific considerations to technology in sustainability in the digital context. A major component of sustainability in technology is how societies adopt novel technologies (Liu et al., 2020). The Technology Acceptance Model (TAM) is an important stepwise framework that specifically outlines the ways in which to achieve sustainability (Marangunić & Granić, 2015). This is important in technology because there is a flux of communication and information technology that will continue to better guide the inclusive use of technology.

As artificial intelligence technology gains momentum in education, facial recognition, and various other types of technologies have become commonplace in the student experience (Chen et al., 2020). However, with the ubiquitous nature of artificial intelligence, conscious efforts of sustainable implementation of inclusive practices with careful considerations and management of biases will be even more important.

Various types of artificial intelligence are beginning to further revolutionize learning. Currently in education, there are three types of applications of artificial intelligence a) personal tutors, b) intelligent support for collaborative learning, and c) intelligent virtual reality. For instance, the word suggestions provided for emails and documents will need to be offered in diverse datasets so that thought can be aided in a tailored manner. Another example of application of artificial intelligence are the usage of chatbots. Recent research indicates chatbots – when used meaningfully – can bring just in time support and improve retention (Weissman, 2022). Higher education is on the cusp of harnessing the power of big data and embracing the revolution that artificial intelligence is bringing. According to Klutka et al. (2018), personalized learning tailored to individuals' needs is increasing not only retention and improving outcomes but decreasing time to completion and increasing access.

Consider Change Adaptability in the Context of Disparate Outcomes

Consider this global view of sustainability, which has evolved over time based on the nature of change adaptability viewed through the lens of disparate outcomes. At the turn of the 21st century, globally there was a need to extensively evaluate the education system. One major development that took place a bit earlier was that in December of 1992, the UN General Assembly established the United Nations Commission on Sustainable Development (CSD) which had utilized a participatory approach and was beginning to outline the importance of a sustainability lens. In less than a decade, as a result of the most extensive evaluation conducted of the education system, the Dakar Framework for Action was created. The Dakar Framework for Action (UNESCO, 2000) was the initial attempt to create a collective commitment for achieving actionable goals and objectives with lasting sustainable results. This extensive framework included considerations of inclusivity as part of the initial framework from Dakar and subsequently the millennium development goals but did not create enough investment in higher education. Therefore, there was a need to better understand how the dynamics of higher education were changing.

While the establishment of the sustainable development goals better inform education, people are experiencing more educational inequities after their implementation (Giangrande et al., 2019). Very few individuals in low-and-middle income countries have attained higher education due to lack of government investment and minimal public/private partnerships. Within the United States, there are persistent gaps based on gender, race, and socioeconomic status in higher education achievement leading to struggling communities. The same outcomes can be expected at the institutional level without a disciplined approach to analyzing the rate of change and the impact of change across different groups of learners.

Globally, through the years 2000 to 2020, higher education enrollment has more than doubled from 100 million to 220 million (The World Bank, 2021), and the economic returns for pursuing higher education have proven to have the greatest impact out of all types of education, providing a 17% increase in earnings after graduation. More recently, the crisis stemming from the pandemic had affected enrollment as well, making pandemic considerations important when creating a sustainability framework. Distance education received much attention when social distancing measures were leading students to look for options, yet there were great disparities in how effective these options proved to be based on the experience the institution had with distance education. Those institutions who had been involved creating online distance education for years were able to provide a foundation for other schools to follow.

Another important trend is the idea that investment in higher education is greatest in high income countries such as the United States. As a result, as a global leader in education, we can demonstrate how in our strategic design for inclusivity, we can focus on potential international students – but only if done in the contexts and with the discipline of continuous application of the students' individual and collective experiences.

Embed the Student-Focused Lens in all Aspects of the Learning Process

Including the curriculum, the delivery of curriculum and services, and the learning experience, embedding is crucial. Of particular importance to sustainability is the notion we will call here "flexibilization," or the active process of ensuring openness to flexibility and adaptability in all aspects of the learning environment.

Case Study: Case Scenario-Embedded Flexibilization for Sustainability

As the learner journeys through the curriculum by taking courses over a period of time, they enter a different part of the journey, where they take the experiences and course learning and translate this to addressing novel issues and concepts. While the classic structure of the classroom may be suited for traditional instruction, the research phase requires creativity in curricular development such as to allow flexibility in thought but then also provide some guidelines to promote innovative thinking within some parameters. The nature of flexibility allowed can be for unforeseen circumstances or flexibility in learning format to accommodate various learning styles which can be considered built into the curriculum or embedded. While the nature of flexibility is usually well understood, there is little agreement in the process to build flexibility or embed flexibilization. Due to the exploratory nature of research within the parameters of university guidelines, there is a need for negotiation.

Consider some perspectives drawn from the experiences of a faculty member mentoring learners for many long-term research commitments (master's or doctoral theses), a situation in which it is important to identify deadlines that are especially important for students' personal goals and also to continually reassess targets as they go through this crucial journey. However, the alignment of expected timelines from the learner with what is possible realistically is often challenging. Relative cultural perceptions of time are different based on occupation or cultural background. Initially, if this is the first time conducting research, students may have the unrealistic sense that a doctoral dissertation (for instance) can be completed in a little over a year and is similar to a lengthy class assignment.

Background

The dissertation process is a segment of the student journey which requires creative planning and structuring as a system must be in place which fosters creativity as much as provide the parameters needed for the student to follow a set of standards. While it is difficult to standardize such a creative process, due to the variability of the types and topics of dissertations selected an attempt is made to create systems. In this case study, we will explore how the system that is created to help the student is disturbed due to a process-level unforeseen circumstance. Next, we will show how some embedded flexibilization can aid in helping the student succeed within the dissertation journey.

When conducting research, students often find that the timelines between different obligations are difficult to manage especially due to the uncertain nature of the dissertation process. With structured and embedded flexibilization, this can be addressed in a specific manner.

One student who was both a military veteran and attended medical school, was writing about the topic of mental health issues such as suicide and substance use. He had a very strong clinical background as he had been trained in a Caribbean school. However, he needed assistance in developing the methodological approach of the study. He lost his father during the dissertation journey which took a toll on him. Initially we had submitted to the IRB a longitudinal study about suicidal ideation and depression assessed using Beck's Depression Inventory. However, subsequently we had to modify the topic because the initial dataset had been removed from National Survey on Drug Use on Health.

Scenario planning using the five steps outlined within this chapter can aid in better mentoring the student who is writing a dissertation. At this juncture, for a faculty member, it is important to start thinking in terms of scenario planning, by assessing both the strengths and weaknesses of the learner to plan on the direction of the study. One of the strengths of my student is the ability to comprehend the quantitative skills, so this means the student would be able to understand methodological changes more easily than his peers. However, due to delays and discouraging life events one weakness was that time was against the student. Some opportunities are the ability to harness additional knowledge that student gained from medical school to reformulate the design and think creatively on how to improve the study. This can then lead to the creation of a SWOT analysis from the perspective of the university (see Table 3).

Table 3. Strengths-weaknesses-opportunities-threats (SWOT) analysis from learner perspective

Strengths	Weaknesses
Quantitative knowledge	Time

In thinking of futures and possibilities, it is important to think of a research design that addresses similar questions but will not require collecting new data. Applying scenario planning, the ideal future was to successfully complete the study by assessing the effect of policy during the same time period and then finding if there was an impact in mental health outcomes. While this was an opportunity to rethink the details of the study, it is important to provide the learner with an opportunity to think about potential methodological innovations. This process of re-thinking is important because it gives the learner the opportunity to think about new possibilities. One possibility was to conduct a new study in a different dataset or collect original study. All of these options were explored and discussed as feasible. However, when we were providing priorities, one primary consideration was time to completion since we identified this as a potential weakness in step 1.

As described above, in most considerations, time should be specifically evaluated as part of risk. Each scenario carries risk in terms of loss of interest, methodological complications, and feasibility if proposing a new primary study at this stage in the dissertation phase as seen in step 2. The future with the least risk is to conduct a slightly different secondary data analysis which addresses a similar research question.

Embedding critical considerations into the operating model is important. Including vast varieties of readily accessible datasets can be an area that, if embedded within the operating model, can allow students many options to readily access a variety of secondary data analysis. Hubs of research and even data lakes can provide students options which would then save time when unforeseen delay occur.

Overall, as provided in Steps 4 and 5 (above) it is not only important to keep in mind the importance of change adaptability, but also it is important to embed this adaptability and flexibilization into the classroom. Therefore, having a repository of resources where many quick clips can provide guidance in specific methodological areas, this can aid student progress. This type of resource repository is currently being used through a coaching program but also can be improved with specialized resources.

After applying scenario planning, it is important to take these steps and proceed with some additional considerations. For instance, ethics is an important area that requires attention whenever conducting research. If there is special need to change the procedure at a time when this should be finalized, then there should be special and unexpected process-level considerations for next best steps:

1. Due to the thesis being now in data collection phase, the IRB must be notified of procedural changes
2. Where these changes must occur within the dissertation should be provided clearly.
3. If time will be a factor, then have an alternative plan on what other aspect to work on so that time is not wasted. Additionally, adjust goals.

The system provides clear guidelines in the context of the expected progression of the dissertation. However, when unexpected procedural or life events take place, then it is difficult to embed these aspects of uncertainty within the classroom. As suggested in step 5 of scenario planning, tailored and embedded flexibilization in this context may mean providing a place where there could be a way to have a plan in place when difficulties in data collection or access arise. While within the case study it is not evident how frustrating the process can be. When the student creates and builds a whole study for years around one dataset, if this dataset is no longer accessible without advanced notice, this can create incredible disruption for student completion. The student must be advised to revisit the literature, so that other procedures could be explored, including other datasets. Other datasets may prove costly, insofar as many datasets are available with fees. Additional fees ensure additional time – if a student opts to engage a new (fee-based) dataset, the chair may need to find additional special expertise regarding costs and procedures.

In going through the National Survey on Drug Use and Health (NSDUH), the same student had to procedurally use sample weights due to representativeness of the sample. This technique only works with this dataset. If a list of these techniques is embedded within the classroom, for those individuals who are interested in complex samples or advanced statistical techniques can have access to robust techniques and multiple freely and paid available data software package options.

The advantage with data analytics is that there are many opportunities for embedded flexibilization. When preparing for medical board exams, when the learner gets a question incorrect, they then view the video on the topic to learn more about it in familiar training exercises. Similarly, if programs were to join efforts, since the methods chapter is very similar for one NSDUH thesis to another, this can then be provided as an additional template. Having consulting groups that specialize in datasets and broad topics also have the additional advantage of covering multiple topic areas cross-disciplinarily.

Embedded flexibilization may look like integrating an additional artificial intelligence technique to rank the predictors within a model. If they are interested in integrating artificial intelligence into their modeling, learners can have a place their to give them a quick place to run an Artificial Intelligence (AI) model for any dissertation using regression, the most widely used technique in use for theses.

When uncertainties arise, and a particular student no longer has access to a dataset, it is important to counsel the student as well. The next best step is to communicate with the student the expectations from the context of process. However, there is a lot of reassurance involved within the initial talk. To assure sustainability, the committee chair had to ensure that the mentor believes in the learner's abilities to create a more fulfilling learning experience. Due to the subjective and individual nature of evaluations from committee members during the revision phases, this requires varying degrees of change adaptability according to the individual styles on the part of the learner and the mentor. Understanding that having a broad global perspective is excellent for leading others whether a mentor or an instructor; however, the level to which to apply a broad perspective is limited (Banerjee & Ragon, 2020). According to researchers at Walden University, the level of influence of change adaptability varies so it is especially important to meet the needs of students, where it is most needed (Lindell et al., 2021). To ensure sustainability, it is especially important to ask about expectations but also communicate the realistic timelines depending on the topic, familiarity with the topic and research, and also any personal milestones.

CONCLUSION

It may indeed be time to stop strategic planning – at least as it has most typically been considered and conducted – in favor of approaches that focus on articulating visions for a future built on the individual and collective experiences of learners and future learners of an institution, and then developing operational plans to sustain a culture of community commitment to ensure an inclusive teaching and learning environment. Such an inclusive teaching and learning environment is founded on principles of empathy and understanding of learners as whole people with pasts that must be honored throughout the learning process, a set of social circumstances that must be considered the design and delivery of learning experiences and a future that is unpredictable and ever-changing.

While nothing can ensure the success of strategic planning efforts, surely the continuous improvement of processes and dispositions in the formulation of strategy and the plans to support them must continue. We have provided some action-oriented considerations for all parts of the institution to consider, particularly with regards to the notion that such a culture must emphasize the concept we describe here as "flexibilization," the active process of ensuring openness to flexibility and adaptability in all aspects of the learning environment. When combined with the myriad approaches to inclusive design across all units of an institution, this approach to learning environment delivery can ensure the operationalization of the design throughout the learning experience itself.

REFERENCES

Academic Development and Diversity Team. (2022, May 10). *Inclusive pedagogy and practice.* Sheffield Hallam University. https://blogs.shu.ac.uk/add/inclusive-pedagogy-and-practice/#II

Amayo, J., Heron, S., Spell, N., & Gooding, H. (2021). Twelve tips for inclusive teaching. *MedEdPublish, 10*(81). Advance online publication. doi:10.15694/mep.2021.000081.1

The Association for the Advancement of Sustainability in Higher Education. (n.d.). https:www.aashe.org/

Association of Executive Search and Leadership Consultants. (n.d.). *Checking your blind spot: Ways to find and fix unconscious bias. Executive Talent.* https://www.aesc./insights/magazine/article/checking-your-blind-spots

Banerjee, S., & Ragon, B. (2020, October 1–2). *Assessing the effect of global mindset on the development of leadership competency* [Paper presentation]. Walden University Research Conference 2020. https://scholarworks.waldenu.edu/researchconference/2020/papers/10/

Bleser, W. K. (2021). *Pandemic-driven health policies to address social needs and health equity.* Robert Wood Johnson Foundation. https://www.rwjf.org/en/library/research/2022/03/pandemic-driven-health-policies-to-address-social-needs-and-health-equity.html

Cândido, C. J. F., & Santos, S. P. (2015). Strategy implementation: What is the failure rate? *Journal of Management & Organization, 21*(2), 237–262. doi:10.1017/jmo.2014.77

Chen, L., Chen, P., & Lin, Z. (2020). Artificial intelligence in education: A review. *IEEE Access: Practical Innovations, Open Solutions, 8,* 75264–75278. doi:10.1109/ACCESS.2020.2988510

Eckel, P., & Trower, C. (2019, February 14). Stop planning! *Insider Higher Ed.* https://www.insidehighered.com/views/2019/02/14/colleges-need-rethink-strategic-planning-opinion

Gordon, G., & Fischer, M. (2015). Strategic planning in public higher education: Management tool or publicity platform? *Educational Planning, 22*(3), 5–17.

Goudeau, S., Sanrey, C., Stanczak, A., Manstread, A., & Darnon, C. (2021). Why lockdown and distance learning during the COVID-19 pandemic are likely to increase the social class achievement gap. *Nature Human Behaviour, 5*(10), 1273–1281. doi:10.103841562-021-01212-7 PMID:34580440

Granić, A., & Marangunić, N. (2019). Technology acceptance model in educational context: A systematic literature review. *British Journal of Educational Technology, 50*(5), 2572–2593. doi:10.1111/bjet.12864

Landrine, H. (1992). Clinical implications of cultural differences: The referential versus the indexical self. *Clinical Psychology Review, 12*(4), 401–415. doi:10.1016/0272-7358(92)90124-Q

Levinson, M., Geller, A. C., & Allen, J. G. (2021). Health equity, schooling hesitancy, and the social determinants of learning. *The Lancet Regional Health-Americas, 2*(100032), 1–6. doi:10.1016/j.lana.2021.100032

Lindell, A., Morgan, A., Sugarman, B. H., Tervala, D. J., Westermann, J., Strang, K. P., Costner, K. L., Ingram, M. N., Powell, M., McCune, N. M., Jobe, R. L., Dixon-Saxon, S., Subocz, S., & Schulz, W. (2021, December 2). *Beyond the social determinants of learning™: A Walden University position paper.* https://scholarworks.waldenu.edu/white_papers/3

Liu, Q., Geertshuis, S., & Grainger, R. (2020). Understanding academics' adoption of learning technologies: A systematic review. *Computers & Education, 151*(103857), 103857. Advance online publication. doi:10.1016/j.compedu.2020.103857

Mahmood, S. (2021). Instructional strategies for online teaching in COVID-19 pandemic. *Human Behavior and Emerging Technologies, 3*(1), 199–203. doi:10.1002/hbe2.218

Marangunić, N., & Granić, A. (2015). Technology acceptance model: A literature review from 1986 to 2013. *Universal Access in the Information Society, 14*(1), 81–95. doi:10.100710209-014-0348-1

McGill, N. (2016). Social determinants of health: Education attainment linked to health throughout life span. *American Journal of Public Health, 106*(10), 1719. https://dialnet.unirioja.es/servlet/articulo?codigo=6821697

Sanderson, C. D., Hollinger-Smith, L. M., & Cox, K. (2021). Developing a social determinants of learning™ framework: A case study. *Nursing Education Perspectives, 42*(4), 205–211. doi:10.1097/01.NEP.0000000000000810 PMID:33935243

Sustainable Columbia. (n.d.). *Sustainable Columbia: Plan 2030.* https://sustainable.columbia.edu/content/plan-2030

UNESCO. (2000). *The Dakar framework for action.* https://sustainabledevelopment.un.org/content/documents/1681Dakar%20Framework%20for%20Action.pdf

United Nations. (2019). *United nations sustainable development cooperation framework guidance.* https://unsdg.un.org/resources/united-nations-sustainable-development-cooperation-framework-guidance

United States Department of Education, National Center for Education Statistics. (n.d.). *Achievement gaps.* https://nces.ed.gov/nationsreportcard/studies/gaps

United States Department of Health and Human Services. Office of Disease Prevention and Health Promotion. (n.d.). *Healthy People 2030. Social determinants of health.* https://health.gov/healthypeople/priority-areas/social-determinants-health

Uygur, M., Ayçiçek, B., Doğrul, H., & Yanpar Yelken, T. (2020). Investigating stakeholders' views on technology integration: The role of educational leadership for sustainable inclusive education. *Sustainability, 12*(24), 10354. doi:10.3390u122410354

Weissman, S. (2022, March 18). Chat bots bypass 'communication clutter' to help students. *Insider Higher Ed.* https://www.insidehighered.com/news/2022/03/18/new-study-explores-how-use-chat-bots-retain-students

The World Bank. (2021, October 22). *Higher education.* https://www.worldbank.org/en/topic/tertiaryeducation#1

ADDITIONAL READING

Annan-Diab, F., & Molinari, C. (2017). Interdisciplinarity: Practical approach to advancing education for sustainability and for the sustainable development goals. *International Journal of Management Education*, *15*(2), 73–83. doi:10.1016/j.ijme.2017.03.006

Banerjee, S., Burkholder, G., Sana, B., & Szirony, G. M. (2020). Social Isolation as a predictor for mortality: Implications for COVID-19 prognosis. MedRxiv. doi:10.1101/2020.04.15.20066548

Birnbaum, H. J., Stephens, N. M., Townsend, S. S. M., & Hamedani, M. G. (2021). A diversity ideology intervention: Multiculturalism reduces the racial achievement gap. *Social Psychological & Personality Science*, *12*(5), 751–759. doi:10.1177/1948550620938227

Dalton, E. M., Lyner-Cleophas, M., Ferguson, B. T., & McKenzie, J. (2019). Inclusion, universal design and universal design for learning in higher education: South Africa and the United States. *African Journal of Disability*, *8*(1), 1–7. doi:10.4102/ajod.v8i0.519 PMID:31392169

Dwyer, C. (2018, September 7). 12 common biases that affect how we make everyday decisions. *Psychology Today*. https://www.psychologytoday.com/us/blog/thoughts-thinking/201809/12-common-biases-affect-how-we-make-everyday-decisions

Egron-Polak, E. (2018). Sustainable development goals: A new framework for the future of international higher education? *World Education News & Reviews*, 37–41. https://wenr.wes.org/2018/02/sustainable-development-goals-a-new-framework-for-the-future-of-international-higher-education

Eiriz, V., Gonçalves, M., & Areias, J. S. (2017). Inter-organizational learning within an institutional knowledge network: A case study in the textile and clothing industry. *European Journal of Innovation Management*, *20*(2), 230–249. doi:10.1108/EJIM-11-2015-0117

Henry, H. F., & Suk, W. A. (2017). Sustainable exposure prevention through innovative detection and remediation technologies from the NIEHS superfund research program. *Reviews on Environmental Health*, *32*(1–2), 35–44. doi:10.1515/reveh-2016-0037 PMID:28212109

Hogan, K. A., & Sathy, V. (2020, April 7) 8 ways to be more inclusive in your Zoom teaching. *The Chronicle of Higher Education*. https://www.chronicle.com/article/8-ways-to-be-more-inclusive-in-your-zoom-teaching/

Mascini, P., & van der Veen, R. (2021). The privatization of work-related risk control. *Zeitschrift für Sozialreform*, *66*(3), 195–206. doi:10.1515/zsr-2020-0009

Owens, T. L. (2017). Higher education in the sustainable development goals framework. *European Journal of Education*, *52*(4), 414–420. doi:10.1111/ejed.12237

Passey, D. (2017). Developing inclusive practices with technologies for online teaching and learning: A theoretical perspective. *Bordón. Revista De Pedagogía*, 25–40. doi:10.13042/.2017.53523

Rahimi, B., Nadri, H., Afshar, H. L., & Timpka, T. (2018). A systematic review of the technology acceptance model in health informatics. *Applied Clinical Informatics*, *9*(3), 604–634. doi:10.1055-0038-1668091 PMID:30112741

Ramaswamy, M., Marciniuk, D. D., Csonka, V., Colò, L., & Saso, L. (2021). Reimagining internationalization in higher education through the United Nations sustainable development goals for the betterment of society. *Journal of Studies in International Education*, 25(4), 388–406. doi:10.1177/10283153211031046

Salloum, S. A., Alhamad, A. Q. M., Al-Emran, M., Monem, A. A., & Shaalan, K. (2019). Exploring students' acceptance of e-learning through the development of a comprehensive technology acceptance model. *IEEE Access: Practical Innovations, Open Solutions*, 7, 128445–128462. doi:10.1109/ACCESS.2019.2939467

Sandars, J., Correia, R., Dankbaar, M., de Jong, P., Goh, P. S., Hege, I., Masters, K., Oh, S.-Y., Patel, R., Premkumar, K., Webb, A., & Pusic, M. (2020). Twelve tips for rapidly migrating to online learning during the COVID-19 pandemic. *MedEdPublish*, 9(1). Advance online publication. doi:10.15694/.2020.000082.1

Schillebeeckx, S. J., Merrill, R. K., & George, G. (2019, July). Can competitive advantage be sustainable under Knightian uncertainty? A resource-capital perspective. *Academy of Management Annual Meeting Proceedings*, 2019(1), 13516. 10.5465/AMBPP.2019.13516abstract

Schmid, M. E., Gillian-Daniel, D. L., Kraemer, S., & Kueppers, M. (2016). Promoting student academic achievement through faculty development about inclusive teaching. *Change: The Magazine of Higher Learning*, 48(5), 16–25. doi:10.1080/00091383.2016.1227672

Schwartz, R., Vassilev, A., Greene, K., Perine, L., Burt, A., & Hall, P. (2022). *Towards a standard for identifying and managing bias in artificial intelligence*. National Institute of Standards and Technology. https://nvlpubs.nist.gov/nistpubs/SpecialPublications/NIST.SP.1270.pdf

United Nations Statistics Division. (n.d.). *Ensure inclusive and equitable quality education and promote lifelong learning opportunities for all*. https://unstats.un.org/sdgs/report/2021/goal-04/

United States Department of Health and Human Services. Office of Disease Prevention and Health Promotion. (2022, February 6). *Social determinants of health*. https://www.healthypeople.gov/2020/topics-objectives/topic/social-determinants-of-health

United States Environmental Protection Agency. (n.d.). *Sustainability*. https://www.epa.gov/sustainability

Chapter 15
Equity in the Online Space?
A Multi-Systems Perspective

Nina M. McCune
https://orcid.org/0000-0001-5339-9383
Walden University, USA

ABSTRACT

As postsecondary institutions develop equity-minded approaches to improve minoritized and marginalized student retention and completion, most literature, case study, and discourse focuses on traditional, on ground, and/or residential schools and courses. More intentional and urgent focus must happen in the online space both in terms of institutional planning, practice, and strategy and in terms of individual/ professional development. All individuals navigate systems using sets of ingrained, implicit, or cognitive biases. In postsecondary education, these biases impact student success. For any postsecondary institution with online course or program delivery, individual and organizational development opportunities must target these biases and create space for double-loop learning in order to achieve an equity-minded approach to organizational change.

INTRODUCTION

Since the first televised committee hearings in 1948, and especially the 1954 Army-McCarthy hearings, House members have sometimes engaged in political theatrics, airing political grievances, or advancing specific platforms or agendas (Troy, 2015). The historic 2022 hearings in the United States Senate Committee on the Judiciary for Ketanji Brown Jackson, the first African American woman nominated for an associate justice appointment to the Supreme Court were no different and showcased profound cognitive biases that inform interpersonal interactions as they pertain to education. Senator Ted Cruz, a Cuban American man, asked Brown Jackson about their affiliation with a private school in Washington, D.C. Reinforcing recent negative and politicized characterizations of critical race theory within legal scholarship (Bell, 1976; 1980; Delgado & Stefancic, 1998), Cruz stated "no one should be discriminated against because of race" (United States Senate Committee on the Judiciary, 2022, 06:08:43) and held up

DOI: 10.4018/978-1-6684-5146-5.ch015

Equity in the Online Space?

a book the school may have in its collection, *Antiracist Baby* by author Ibram Kendi (2020). As aides swapped out different poster-size facsimiles of pages from the book, Cruz continued:

The book says babies are taught [emphasis in original] to be racist or antiracist, there is no neutrality. Another portion of the book, they recommend that babies confess [emphasis in original] when being racist...do you agree with this book that it's being taught to kids that babies are racist? (United States Senate Committee on the Judiciary, 2022, 06:09:47)

While the question strays from the scope of legal and judicial training and practices, or as Brown Jackson stated, "these ideas do not come up in my work as a judge" (United States Senate Committee on the Judiciary, 2022, 06:13:08), Cruz's remarks are noteworthy. Not only do the remarks crystallize a political and rhetorical undercurrent aimed at all levels of education, they also highlight an inherent reaction to disavow or eschew any form of unflattering or problematic biases that shape our perceptions, interpretations, preferences, and proclivities in all sorts of interpersonal interactions. While many may agree that individuals should not be discriminated against because of race (or other attributes), some may agree with Cruz that discussing uncomfortable topics like one's own racism, sexism, homophobia, or religious bigotry is something entirely disagreeable and unwanted. Individuals often accuse others of operating with biases while claiming themselves to be bias-free (Wang & Jeon, 2020), especially since "there is a contrasting tendency for people in privileged groups to deny the existence of bias" for others (West & Eaton, 2019, p. 111). Not acknowledging or grappling with one's own biases, rather than understanding how deeply ingrained biases inform our behavior, is a much easier and more comfortable route to navigating social life and establishing a (hopefully favorable) public persona. While the above exchange could suggest some sort of *correct* or *incorrect* educational experience, and while unsuccessfully identifying what that experience should entail, Cruz's comments emphasize the profound need for explicitly and specifically sharing our intended understandings of certain key words and ideas, while concomitantly explaining how a shared concept is intended to shape an educational experience. Most importantly, the exchange highlights how cognitive biases can place issues within and around education at the center of an ideological maelstrom.

"There's no such thing as neutral education. Education either functions as an instrument to bring about conformity or freedom" (Freire, 1970/2018, p. 219). Writing within their lived context of legislated barriers for class-exclusive education in 1960s Brazil (Mendonca, 2020), Freire posited that those "leaders who do not act dialogically, but insist on imposing their decisions, do not organize the people – they manipulate them. They do not liberate, nor are they liberated: they oppress" (1970/2018, p. 178). Whereas I am not contending an exchange from an isolated Senate subcommittee hearing necessarily demonstrates a larger, coordinated effort to impose reactionary and misinformed decisions on which books and what kind of curriculum are available for American students, I am concerned that American postsecondary educational institutions specifically must engage a level of clarity and intentionality in our online learning spaces if one of the goals is to create equitable access to and outcomes for all students.

At a time when state legislators are, in fact, intruding in postsecondary curriculum (Moody, 2022) in a way that identifies certain ideas as "divisive" and threatening funding if such ideas or frameworks are included in coursework (AAC&U, 2022; Intellectual Freedom, 2022; Intellectual Diversity, 2022), it is imperative to understand what drives the actions and need to regulate ideas and analytic lenses. These legislative actions run counter to national efforts of the last decade in postsecondary education of improving equity outcomes for students of color across the United States to increase access to high-quality education, to innovate how minoritized students see themselves in the curriculum and the professions to which they aspire, and to ensure the promise of increased social and economic mobility for all students. Together with Jobe and Lynn (see Chapter 10: "A Framework to Measure Inclusion"), I highlight this *equity imperative* within higher education whereby "the larger social benefits that derive from having a highly educated workforce make the equity imperative not only a moral one but an economic and political one as well" (Witham et al., 2015, p. 6) rather than perpetuate a system with racially disadvantageous and disproportionate outcomes for students of color (Cahalan et al., 2021) that reinforces similar class and race-based educational models akin to those of Cold War Brazil or Jim Crow America. For all the swirling questions around the education and equity, I narrow the focus of this chapter, and call for clarity of two key concepts: what *equity* entails for online education within and among the systems of postsecondary institutions and what individual *biases* persist in those distance education spaces that can confound inclusion and equity efforts.

To be sure, such a call—and the attendant literature exploring what equity entails—is not new. The context of online education and a continually unfulfilled promise of equity in higher education, however, offers modifications to those existing narratives. Searches for literature addressing all components of online learning, equity, and postsecondary education return few results in comparison to other bodies of research on equity and postsecondary education. Most of what is returned for online learning, equity, and postsecondary education has been written since March of 2020, when the COVID-19 pandemic forced almost all forms of communication and learning to be conducted online. In other words, the field of exploring the dynamics between designing and attaining equity outcomes in the postsecondary online space are relatively new. As such, it may be worthwhile to review earlier discussions on equity or, more appropriately, discussions *around* equity in the postsecondary space in general.

Of note, the first dedicated publication on educational equity did not define the term. In 1963, the peer-reviewed journal *Equity & Excellence in Education* launched with a mission of exploring "what equity and justice may look like or do for historically marginalized populations" (Taylor & Francis Online, n.d.). Without explicating what equity in education is, the first issue contained articles on desegregation legislation (Editor, 1963a) and busing (Editor, 1963b) as well as other pieces that focused on racial and socioeconomic barriers to education and advancement (Baron, 1963; Countryman, 1963; Deutsch, 1963; Douglas, 1963). Rather than define *equity*, the authors articulate an *absence of equity* within the democratic process of education and point to the continued disenfranchisement of minoritized students and stakeholders, especially in urban schools. Douglas (1963) poignantly outlines specific interactions that are not only not conducive to learning but also points to factors beyond the control of school administrators, teachers, parents, and students. The sheer number of students in a majority-Black school means many cannot enjoy the limited amount of free milk or food. Inadequate restroom facilities relative to the vast size of the school population mean many students are unable to concentrate on schoolwork or show what Douglas (1963) finds many interpret as "just plain orneriness" (p. 20) toward learning. In other words, the inaugural edition highlighted the outcome of racialized segregation and resource rationing on education of minoritized student populations across the United States and pointed to how stereotyping perceived-as-ornery or otherwise disengaged students of a particular race can work toward continued marginalization.

BACKGROUND

Educational Equity: What Is the Goal?

Despite the plethora of literature and conference presentations on equity in postsecondary education in the past decade, it is quite possible there is no one complete definition of equity. It very well may be that each institution must engage in internally focused inquiry to define *equity* as an outcome of the education process as it pertains to that specific institution. Each institution has unique student demographic matriculants and enrollments, discrete student demographics specific to each program, and differing student demographic patterns of retention and completion within those programs and within the institution. Each institution has its unique set of policies and procedures that may create barriers (unwittingly) to enrollment, retention, and/or completion, including internal policies and requirements of accrediting bodies.[1] Each institution has varying readiness and ability to diversify its faculty and administrative personnel, often tied to budget or even tenure lines. Given these three dominating factors, institutions must carefully and strategically plan (see Chapter 14: "Sustainable Strategic Planning for Inclusive Online Teaching and Learning") to ensure equitable outcomes. But what is *equity* in postsecondary education beyond a statistical definition tied to racially disaggregated demographics in graduation rates or program performance? More specifically, what is equity in the *online setting*? While equity is linked to constructs of *justice* and *fairness* (Dowd & Bensimon, 2015), Le Grand (1991) warns that *equity* is a broad, not easily defined term. Sometimes, "the search for acceptable definitions of equity is in fact a futile one" (p. 7). Perhaps that sense of futility comes from the fact that equity is what Jencks (1988) calls "elastic" (p. 533), insofar as it spans several ideological and philosophical positions, resulting in both complementary and competing frameworks. For the purposes of exploring how institutions can define and, therefore, create a platform to achieve equity, three propositions of equity allow for a deeper understanding of educational equity outcomes in postsecondary online learning.

Resource Distribution

Most scholarship interprets equity, justice, and fairness (Adams, 1963; Le Grand, 1991; Nozick, 1974) synonymously. One form of equity proposes the idea as divisions of a mythical pie, where equity as a practice of distributing resources is equity itself. In this proposition, equity, justice, and fairness are normative matters that are measured by the distribution and allocation of available resources. The pastry metaphor follows that a person or entity receives a share of a resource based on what they deserve. Often the share of resources received is based on merit, for example, efficiently distributing resources based on the amount of effort expended (Milne, 1986). Or resources are distributed based on the value of the work and contribution to a social product (Riley, 1989). Or resources may be distributed as a form of compensation that reflect the value of both the amount of effort expended and the contribution to a social product (Dick, 1975). In this proposition, individuals are motivated by a perception of "relative justice" (Adams, 1963, p. 422) to receive larger shares of the resource. Considering equity through a lens of distributing a (limited number of) resources is well articulated in Rawls (1971), where those with equal needs require the distribution of equal resources, such as equal educational resources. Likewise, those with greater needs should receive greater resources, for example, "social and economic inequalities are to be arranged…to the greatest benefit of the least advantaged" (Rawls, 1971, p. 302). Understanding equity in terms of resource distribution aligns neatly with any manner of arguments for funding public school districts, with metrics ranging from pairing more funding with schools with higher test scores or more graduates. Yet, allowing equity to be defined by resources, and thus by cost or expenditure, falls quite short of the promise of higher education to improve all graduates' social and economic mobility.

Democratic Participation

Rather than merit-based transactions, another proposition of equity considers equity as a process, where authentic public participation of all citizens will achieve equitable outcomes (Gould, 1996; Howe, 1994; Verba, 2006). A fundamental aspect of this process is removing barriers to educational access, necessitating that "individuals are afforded equal opportunities to obtain an education" (Howe, 1994, p. 27). Throughout American history, educational goals have been informed by a three-way tension between democratic equality (building a responsible citizenry), social efficiency (training workers), and social mobility (allowing individuals to compete for improvements) (Larabee, 1997). Additionally, as schools adopted neoliberal efficiency models akin to those of private business and enterprise (Hayes, 2016; Levin et al., 2018), the goal of democratic equality was replaced by the need to train *more* workers and to create *more* social mobility (Callahan, 1964; Doherty, 2007; Larabee, 1997). These policies have had the impact of reducing equal access to education, given the fact they focused on career development and not the well-rounded training that responsible citizens require. If a certain sector of employees is not desirable, for example, entire swaths of individuals would be excluded from workforce-focused training.

The history of so-called equal education in the United States is forever tainted by the structural practices born out of *Plessy v. Ferguson* (1896), the legacies of Jim Crow, and the two separate 1954 and 1955 *Brown v. Board of Ed* rulings. Equal education in the American context has endured a patchwork of contentious narratives about resources, funding, and student achievement. It is far too easy to assume that by the year 2022 educational systems have worked out the kinks of racialized and racializing practices. As recently as 2019, one-third of all K–12 public school districts in the state of Louisiana, for example, were under active federal desegregation orders, with many highly segregated districts producing unequal outcomes for White and Black students (Butkus, 2019; Groeger et al., 2018). While such efforts to enforce integration and cure segregation in the K–12 space exist throughout the state, its capital city of Baton Rouge witnessed an unsuccessful secession attempt of an entire White neighborhood, specifically to preserve White schools (Runnel, 2016). Not only are notions of equal educational access wholly unrealized, the impacts such contests create on the promise of equality, let alone equity, build futures of immeasurable damage to the integrity of all things *equal*.

Not only must we question *who* continues to enjoy equality in education, post-*Brown* notions of *what* students learn flounder under the fallacy of equality. Curricula and educational practices and policies are themselves the product of dominant, hegemonic norms, including groupings of race (White), gender (male), class (middle-class), ability (able-bodied individuals), sexual orientation (heterosexual), and creed (Christian). These norms create educational goods "worth wanting" (Howe, 1994, p. 30), despite the fact these educational goods have been formulated without the full participation of nondominant groups. Almost 70 years after the *Brown* decisions, schools serving large populations of minoritized students are often underfunded, under-resourced, and understaffed, making delivering education and achieving its promises a struggle for all stakeholders. According to Sen (1999), we (humans) respond to differentiation and diversity in opposition to the demands of sameness. That is to say, the metric of interpersonal comparison, even when trying to achieve equal distributions, needs to take human diversity as a central concern. Capabilities, which represent the freedoms to achieve combinations of socially valued perfor-

Equity in the Online Space?

mance and production (Sen, 1999), are the tools one needs to succeed socially and economically. Thus, linking equity to fairness and participation in democracy fall short and leave us without clarity of what dimensions educational equity may have.

Structural Transformation

It is only within recent history that institutions and practitioners have considered structurally transforming educational institutions to achieve educational equity. The otherwise noble framework of democratic equality and social mobility as postsecondary educational outcomes—perhaps inadvertently—produces a hegemonic, "majoritarian" narrative that mythologizes the fallacy that "educational structures provide equal opportunity and social mobility...and attribute[s] unequal participation and achievement in education to the cultural pathologies and deficits of minoritized groups" (Dowd & Bensimon, 2015, p. 15). Or those believing and reproducing this fallacious hegemony may claim that unequal achievement is due to other deficits, such as inadequate college preparation, student motivation, self-efficacy, goal-directness, and so on (Bensimon, 2005; 2007). Providing an intellectual architecture for the standard of equity as structural transformation, Bensimon and colleagues develop not only persuasive scholarship arguing why equity and equity outcomes are vital to education, they also develop clear pathways for institutional engagement and transformational equity work. Shifting from those deficit-minded attributions (e.g., students enter colleges unprepared), this scholarship encourages addressing such cultural or personal inadequacies at a macro, or institutional, level. "While individual change agents can exert a powerful influence on the lives of individual students, unless inequity in educational outcomes is framed from the perspective of institution-wide communal responsibility, it is impossible to discuss how it can be prevented" (Bensimon, 2006, p. 21). In an institutional review and dialog, patterns may emerge, showing barriers to access of equal educational opportunities. More importantly, however, data show "forms of stratification in the kinds of opportunities students have *within* college" (Witham et al., 2015, p. 9; italics in original) persist.

This approach assumes institutions have a degree of readiness and are comfortable with critically assessing and discussing racially disaggregated data and assess and shed deficit mindsets whereby "deficit-minded individuals construe unequal outcomes as originating from students' characteristics, [and] equity minded individuals will reflect on institution-based dysfunctions and consider their own roles and responsibilities...in the production of equitable educational outcomes" (Bensimon, 2006, p. 4). This kind of discourse further assumes administrators and postsecondary practitioners are ready and able to hold discussions of racialized education, and divest of "repressive tolerance" (Brookfield, 2003, pp. 501–502) that reinforces, perhaps unwittingly, a White, Eurocentric perspective on everything from course content to post-graduation expectations. On a macro level, then, the discomfort of acknowledging institutional practices that disadvantage entire student populations of a school may arouse a similar reaction to Cruz's during Brown Jackson's nomination hearings. While I agree with Bensimon and colleagues that institutions must develop equity-minded systems, I wonder how those systems may be operationalized in the online space.

EDUCATIONAL EQUITY IN THE ONLINE SPACE

In order to achieve equity in postsecondary education, institutions and structures must transform. This work will be done one institution at a time, with each institution having different missions and visions, student and faculty populations, and aptitudes and readiness for the work. Just as there are myriad consultants and offices that focus on diversity and inclusion, there are no clear lists of how equity can be achieved. The work requires deep thought and attention to how institutions create barriers for students or how institutions could begin (even simple, no-cost) initiatives to support and reach out to students that have not seen themselves in curriculum, have had trouble making on-time payments, or have so many competing demands on their schedule that school tends to be seen as a luxury. But higher education is not a luxury for the few, it is a necessary means to economic advancement. The U.S. Bureau of Labor Statistics repeatedly reports that earning a bachelor's degree correlates to higher—at least a 67% increase—income (2020) when compared to those with no college degree. Earning a graduate degree escalates that figure, especially within specific fields (Carnevale et al., 2019). This kind of economic mobility is one of the promises of higher education, one that has been unattainable for the countless thousands of students who have withdrawn from institutions and foreclosed on higher education due to inflexible policies and practices, or because professions tend to perpetuate hegemonic identities (especially in those programs with high costs) and exclude minoritized populations, or because marginalized students see little value competing against rigid, majoritarian interpretations of sometimes unnecessarily hagiographic disciplinary texts.

Considering the United States has approximately 4,000 postsecondary institutions (National Center for Education Statistics, 2021), an institution-by-institution transformation is unwieldy and wildly varying in approach and potential impact. Yet, it is precisely this kind of wide-scale transformation that is necessary for minoritized and marginalized students to achieve the many dimensions within the promise of higher education. Educational equity demands attention to and contextualization of stakeholder pluralities, differences, and needs stemming from multiple group identities (race, gender and gender identity, creed). Educational equity within the proposition of structural transformation demands remedies within systems of education, especially within the online delivery of learning. While this seems an impossible task, the National Association of System Heads (NASH) adopted an equity framework in 2020 that encourages public colleges and universities to "confront longstanding systemic inequity and visibly stand for the values of inclusive excellence. In addition to identifying and removing barriers to equity, systems and their constituent campuses should be anti-racist" (n.d.-a, para. 1). The framework provides guiding questions and essential practices for public postsecondary systems to enact systemic transformation, including public commitment, dedicated leadership, equitable policies and curriculum, and intentional and inclusive community engagement.

The NASH equity framework does not explicitly consider online learning, however. In a separate set of strategic initiatives, the organization states an intention to further study eLearning and alternate modes of learning delivery (National Association of System Heads, n.d.-b, para. 12). The disconnect between on-ground work toward structural transformation and creating equity outcome in online models remains unexplored. Whereas organizations like Quality Matters and the Online Learning Consortium have created sets of best practices and course design scorecards, serving more than 1,500 institutions combined (Online Learning Consortium, n.d., para. 1; Quality Matters, n.d., para. 2), very little literature has focused on how online faculty and schools with online courses can read and respond to the cues of students experiencing stereotype threat or imposter syndrome, how to build community in online spaces

Equity in the Online Space?

to promote retention, or how to reduce negative self-efficacy of students already thinking a college or graduate degree might be out of reach. Campus after campus has invested in wrap-around services to ensure students feel cared for and supported, but those services rarely transfer to a digital experience—before, during, or after the COVID-19 pandemic.

What systems, then, can disrupt the policies and practices that could lead to early withdrawals, failing grades, or even just a lack of engagement from minoritized and marginalized students? Dowd (2007) describes institutional opportunities to explore structural innovation and change to improve student outcomes and success, identify practices to promote equity across different sectors of an institution, and examine campus culture. As succinct as my paraphrasing of Dowd's work is, these three elements are crucial in the online as well as on-ground educational setting. To that end, several chapters of this book investigate designing online classrooms (see Chapters 4, 5, and 6), and include calls to create spaces where minoritized and marginalized students can envision themselves as leaders and innovators, solving the multifaceted problems of today and tomorrow. Curriculum design, while critical to engage students and faculty alike to develop and practice the competencies, standards, and ethics required in any profession, is but one path toward achieving equity outcomes.

Structural transformation in the online space requires a deep understanding of how online practices and policies impact students. For example, students who register late in a semester tend to experience higher rates of failure and withdrawal much more frequently in online courses (Pathak, 2019), or uncompromising assignment due dates ensure students with heavy family and work responsibilities will not succeed (Schacter et al., 2021). Both policy examples can not only thwart academic progress but also cost students thousands of dollars for a negative reward. From a systems perspective, the most important question to consider is whether a policy privileges the institution (or an institutional actor) or the student. Policies could include broader laptop loaner programs or practices of joining with internet service providers to ensure all potential matriculants have the ability to join classes online. This is the least of the systems needed to ensure equitable online education (Laufer et al., 2021). Such framing can guide policy revisions and practices to develop and promote student success at a macro level. *Individual* practice, however, falls in the realm of school culture and the willingness to engage in equity work on a micro level.

Given that most interactions between the student and institutional actors online are conducted asynchronously through web or email communication, each institutional representative remains simultaneously dissociative and anonymous (Suler, 2015) yet can be perceived by the student to be *the* most critical to academic success. If a student receives responses from institutional actors, like faculty or department chairs, that communication may signal an "only" reaction, whereby the student sees the individual responding to requests for information or assistance as the only institutional actor responding as such. Should the student perceive responses as helpful or competent to navigate a situation, that student may continue to request information from the institutional actor that goes beyond their role (for example, asking faculty about financial aid matters or issues related to personal mental health). At that point, this form of social presence (Kreijns et al., 2020) may become distorted and, depending on the response of the institutional actor, either remain helpful to the student or become contentious as requests for information or assistance are unfulfilled (Yu et al., 2020). In other words, while the call for institutions to examine these systems (Bensimon, 2006; Witham et al., 2015) is paramount, the need for individual double-loop learning (examined in greater detail in the following section) is an efficient approach to instituting changes, and must be explicitly addressed in and tailored to the online space.

Practical Implications: The Individual Is Key

Developing equity-minded systems requires a certain amount of double-loop learning (Argyris & Schön, 1978) to change "the attitudes, values, beliefs, and practices of individuals to bring about enduring results" (Bensimon, 2005, p. 104). Double-loop learning requires not only learning about a certain concept or practice, applying the learning, and then reflecting on the outcome; it also requires changing mental models to achieve a desired result (Argyris, 1991). Often, organizational actors need a nudge to understand that the outcome of a certain practice may not meet the needs of the situation. Improving equity outcomes requires that intuitional actors change from deficit-thinking (the student is lacking in some way for not being able to understand how to sign up for classes, for example) to what Bensimon calls equity-mindedness. This involves understanding how exclusionary and racialized practices have impacted students of color and taking "personal and institutional responsibility for the success of their students" (University of Southern California, n.d.). Such a transformation is simultaneously private and public, beginning with an individual considering how cognitive biases inform personal decisions and interactions in their public, institutional role.

Tagg (2007) finds higher education practitioners are resistant to changing procedures within schools because they do not perceive their individual efforts running counter to the school mission or that their individual actions necessarily promote student success. Individuals perceive fulfilling a mandate or job prescripts based on unquestioning habits of the way work has always been performed. Whereas individuals may begin to identify inefficiencies or unintended consequences of their actions, few actively seek to correct such issues (Tagg, 2010). For example, academic officers may not realize how policies for applying for graduation, transferring credit hours, or even requesting financial aid may privilege one set of students over another or privilege administrative convenience over what actually benefits students. Those staff members must re-examine and investigate what is not working for different student populations—specifically based on disaggregated data and student reaction and commentary—to restructure inequitable policies. This work is necessary to have personnel "assume responsibility for the elimination of unequal results" (Bensimon, 2005, p. 105) and develop an "access perspective" that enables institutional actors "to be more fully informed about the extent to which underrepresented students have access to…compete for academic advancement" (Bensimon et al., 2006, p. 147) and create equity outcomes within the school.

The institutional opportunity, then, is to learn to solve for equity outcomes in higher education iteratively. The multiple systems within an institution must align with an equity-driven mission. If institutions are to succeed in achieving equity outcomes, every office and officer must align with that mission. For example, bursars can reconsider the wording of late-payment notices to be more inclusive and fairer or offer micro-loans to students facing unplanned expenses such as car repairs or emergency room visits that compromise a student's ability to remain enrolled. Everyone within a bursar's office, however, plays a role in advancing the equity-driven mission.

Persistent Biases in Online Spaces

Without effective programs for double-loop learning and development, there is little incentive for individuals to change behaviors that have led to poor institutional outcomes. Practitioners across the school may be content to continue working—and navigating conflict that results from that work—without change (Tagg, 2010). As it turns out, we are all human. Humans are prone to conflict. And sometimes, humans handle conflict poorly—perhaps unintentionally, perhaps without good reason. And sometimes, as exemplified in the exchange initiated by Cruz during Brown Jackson's nomination hearings, humans are resistant to exploring how their own individual preferences or biases lay at the very foundation of conflict management (Gullo & Beachum, 2020). The Stanford Center for Educational Policy Analysis (CEPA) led a ground-breaking analysis showing faculty biases unequivocally include racial and gender preference in the online space insofar as instructors are 94% more likely to respond to forum posts by White male students (Baker et al., 2018). Studies like this must continue to be conducted to reproduce these findings, and studies pertaining to additional biases must begin for institutions to design and implement effective equity-minded, double-loop learning opportunities.

Manoogian and Benson (2016) designed a cognitive bias codex, sorting more than 180 cognitive biases into four categories. These categories are ordered according to the lenses employed to navigate situations that require us to either remember information, sift through too much information or construe meaning from too little information, or make rapid decisions based on the information we have processed. These categories are further delineated into subgroupings and dimensions comprising the mental activities employed in each main group. Many of these biases may be more pertinent to face-to-face educational settings; however, several deserve our attention in the online space. For example, an instructor facing a heavy set of grading may essentialize student responses based on readability of font—something that may be auto-generated based on the latest upgrade to an operating system. Or instructors may stereotype students in discussion forums along racial or gender identities, perhaps unwittingly narrowing the focus of a discussion on identity traits. Although instructors may object, claiming they do not know the gender or racial identity of their students, a study from CEPA examined 124 discussion forums and found instructors are 94% more likely to answer comments posted by White male students than any other students, and comments posted by White females are more likely to receive a response from White female peers (2018). Such a finding has vast implications for creating equity in the online space, most importantly that racial and gender biases are inherent bias blind spots for online instructors in that "even knowing that one is *generally* susceptible to a bias is consistent with one's believing, on the specific occasion one considers the matter, that one is not displaying a bias" (Kenyon & Beaulac, 2014, p. 346; italics in original). Understanding racial and gender bias and how these biases operate in the online space are a critical first step for both instructors and all higher education practitioners as a part of organizational learning when committing to equity-minded systems that support online learning.

Consider the category of how higher education practitioners must remember information, and the filters or biases that inform what information gets remembered, and in what way or in what context the information is remembered. For example, an advisor who has worked with hundreds of students may operate with certain stereotypical biases (students who are unable to readily declare a major will not be able to graduate in 4 years) or implicit stereotypes and prejudices (students from a certain income bracket tend not to succeed, perhaps spending too much time with them is not a wise move in my 8-hour day). Or instructors may employ leveling and sharpening when navigating a conflict with a student by thinking through similar past scenarios. By remembering or excluding small details of what happened in a prior situation, an instructor may generalize an approach for the current situation that undercuts an appropriate solution. Especially for practitioners who may have served an institution for a lengthy period, remembering and recalling are innate to performing job functions (Tagg, 2010).

At times when practitioners need to respond quickly to situations—due to rapidly approaching deadlines, the need to solve a conflict immediately, or even the perception of needing to complete grading a virtual stack of papers quickly—biases can inform how decisions are made. An instructor racing through what may seem like poorly constructed essays may be practicing illusory superiority or the Lake Wobegon effect, whereby the instructor is confident the assignment instructions were clear, and it is, in fact, the students who just need to work harder to earn the degree of sophistication and knowledge competency the instructor has. Or employing the macabre constant bias (Antibi, 2003), the instructor has already determined there is a fixed number of poor, average, and excellent assignment submissions and will mark papers according to that scheme without individualized (slower) consideration of each student's work. Or, in an instance in which a staff member engages with a failing student who requires several emails to clarify a question, staff may practice escalation of commitment or sunk-cost fallacy, as they may assume spending more time trying to remedy the issue is futile because the student just is not receiving the information. This fallacy is detrimental more often to students of color (Cook, 2017), and requires specific training to recognize and mitigate.

Any researcher may succumb to a confirmation bias, practiced when too much competing information interferes with what is already understood or desirable about a certain outcome. Likewise, selective perception can inadvertently prompt instructors to reach out to a favorite student (Van Auken, 2013), or a student affairs officer may be more likely to respond more quickly to a student they believe is agreeable and friendly. Perhaps the most insidious issues with cognitive biases in education come when decisions are made with scant information. The assumptions any individual makes about others create tenuous and often incorrect bases to articulate any kind of action, and if those actions occur when making decisions about a student's continued enrollment or success in an academic course or program, they can be devastating. Authority and publication biases (McClain et al., 2021) can cause a grade to plummet and, when operating concomitantly with racial or gender biases, also can be operating at cross purposes with equity-minded strategies.

These are but a few examples of areas where organizational learning and development can coalesce. Whereas institutions may create equity strategies and identify equity goals, it is the individuals in academic support units, student services, or the academic disciplines that are responsible in educational settings to actively employ those strategies and goals. In the online space especially, where students may struggle with motivation to continue that often goes undetected, it is critical individuals are afforded space to critically reflect and understand how these kinds of biases impact even the smallest or briefest of interactions. To that end, colleges and universities must also be mindful of engaging with any kind of artificial intelligence to supplant or enhance digital human interaction. During the pandemic, concerns around academic integrity prompted many institutions to use digital test-proctoring services. One consideration around any form of digital service, whether chatbots (Weisman, 2022) or proctoring, is the degree to which trained human beings are engaged in the process (Asep & Bandung, 2019). For example, proctoring services relying on algorithms measuring eye movements through video may contain biases and incorrectly attribute instances of academic dishonesty at a higher rate to students of color (Cabreros, 2022; Clark, 2021; Carozza & Gennaro, 2021). While it may seem Sisyphean for institutions to organize training and development opportunities that consider both individual biases and biases expressed through artificial intelligence (an extension of individual biases), the more biases impacting online education are addressed and researched, the more the damaging impacts of those biases can be mitigated and reduced.

CONCLUSION

Before the COVID-19 pandemic, more often than not, literature relating to online teaching and learning focused on best practices. Organizations like Quality Matters and the Online Learning Consortium created scorecards to measure the navigability of online courses and the clarity used to deliver content and align learning outcomes. Scores of institutions adopted those best practices, often requiring faculty interested in teaching online to complete training and design courses incorporating the practices and technologies that could boost student engagement. It is almost inconceivable in the post-pandemic era to imagine a time when faculty considered online teaching optional and could elect to teach online. For those faculty resistant to online teaching, there were concerns of the quality of education or the engagement and honesty of students (Glass, 2017; Krug et al., 2016; Mitchell & Geva-May, 2009) submitting work from afar. Some faculty believed teaching online to be less rigorous (Smidt et al., 2014), or even downright lazy (Porter, 2004). Since the pandemic, however, it is hard to imagine how any postsecondary institution can remain competitive and attractive without robust online offerings. What was once considered a disruptive innovation (Windes & Lesht, 2014) is now a mainstay due to the rapid transition to online teaching and learning at the beginning of the COIVD pandemic. Faculty and staff must receive ample opportunity for robust development and reflection to establish equity-minded practices that ensure all students achieve the promises of higher education. All systems—faculty, individual offices, leadership, etc.—must perceive its policies through lenses of equity and students' lived experience to identify and dismantle barriers to success.

Yet, online teaching and learning spaces have not been clearly identified as areas of focus in national equity imperative discourses. These online spaces require modifications to services and instruction and, as such, require deeper consideration of how individual institutional participants are readied to operate in a way that supports equity initiatives. Articulating institutional goals around equity may produce some good dialogue, but good dialogue alone does not provide enough motivation to change behaviors and practices.

Good dialogue is not a matter of smoothness of operation or elimination of error...its goodness is inherent in the ways in which error is continually interpreted and corrected, incompatibility and incongruity are continually engaged, and conflict is continually confronted and resolved. (Argyris & Schön, 1978, p. 146)

To be sure, the call for systemic change in postsecondary education comes from observed data of racially discrepant education outcomes, and often the underlying cause brings discomfort to the individual and embarrassment to the institution. To counter the popular adage, it may *not* be the one squeaky wheel that gets the proverbial grease – that one squeaky wheel may be "viewed as a systemic issue rather than simply an isolated indicator" (Zabawski, 2019, para. 7) of one part needing repair. Yet, not all individuals wish to engage in the uncomfortable discussions around systemic racism and the biases blindly operating within structural practices. These bias blind spots, however, drive the need to explore more deeply how individual practitioners impact educational institutions, and it is precisely these explorations that offer the opportunity for authentic double-loop learning. Education is never a neutral act, as Freire pointed out. Not only did Freire believe that education was a political act intended to transform all involved in the learning process, but that "the educator also has the duty of not being neutral" (Horton et al., 1990, p. 180). We live in a time of incredible political derision and division, one that places educational equity in great danger. We will be wholly unable to achieve equity outcomes if we do not address the unique issues that impact our online educational experiences, and we must be unencumbered to design institutional experiences that support equity goals.

REFERENCES

Adams, J. S. (1963). Toward an understanding of inequity. *Journal of Abnormal and Social Psychology*, *67*(5), 422–436. doi:10.1037/h0040968 PMID:14081885

American Association of Colleges and Universities. (2022, June 8). *Statement by AAC&U and PEN America regarding recent legislative restrictions on teaching and learning.* https://www.aacu.org/newsroom/statement-regarding-recent-legislative-restrictions-on-teaching-and-learning

Antibi, M. A. (2003). *La constante macabre, ou, comment a-t-on découragé des générations d'élèves.* Math'Adore.

Argyris, C. (1991, May). Teaching smart people how to learn. *Harvard Business Review*, *69*(3), 99–109. https://hbr.org/1991/05/teaching-smart-people-how-to-learn

Argyris, C., & Schön, D. (1978). *Organizational learning: A theory of action perspective.* Addison-Wesley Publishing Co.

Asep, H. S. G., & Bandung, Y. (2019, July 9–10). A design of continuous user verification for online exam proctoring on m-learning. *2019 International Conference on Electrical Engineering and Informatics*, Bandung, Indonesia. 10.1109/ICEEI47359.2019.8988786

Baker, R., Dee, T. S., Evans, B., & John, J. (2018). *Bias in online classes: Evidence from a field experiment* (CEPA Working Paper No. 18–03). Stanford Center for Education and Policy Analysis. https://cepa.stanford.edu/sites/default/files/wp18-03-201803.pdf

Baron, H. (1963). History of Chicago school segregation to 1953. *Equity & Excellence in Education*, *1*(1), 17–20. doi:10.1080/0020486630010106

Bell, D. A. Jr. (1976). Serving two masters: Integration ideas and client interests in school desegregation litigation. *The Yale Law Journal*, *85*(4), 470–516. doi:10.2307/795339

Bell, D. A. JrBoard of Education and the Interest-Convergence Dilemma. (1980). Brown v. board of education and the interest-convergence dilemma. *Harvard Law Review*, *93*(3), 518–533. doi:10.2307/1340546

Bensimon, E. M. (2005). Closing the achievement gap in higher education: An organizational learning perspective. *New Directions for Higher Education*, *131*(131), 99–111. doi:10.1002/he.190

Bensimon, E. M. (2006). Learning equity-mindedness: Equality in educational outcomes. *Academic Workplace*, *17*(1), 2–6, 18–21. https://cpb-us-e1.wpmucdn.com/sites.usc.edu/dist/6/735/files/2016/01/Bensimon_Learning-Equity-Mindedness-Equality-in-Educational-Outcomes.pdf

Bensimon, E. M. (2007). The underestimated significance of practitioner knowledge in the scholarship of student success. *The Review of Higher Education*, *30*(4), 441–469. doi:10.1353/rhe.2007.0032

Bensimon, E. M., Hao, L., & Tomas Bustillos, L. (2006). Measuring the state of equity in public higher education. In P. Gándara, G. Orfield, & C. L. Horn (Eds.), *Expanding opportunity in higher education: Leveraging promise* (pp. 143–164). State University of New York Press.

Brookfield, S. D. (2003). Racializing the discourse of adult education. *Harvard Educational Review, 73*(4), 497–523. doi:10.17763/haer.73.4.a54508r0464863u2

Butkus, N. (2019, May 17). *Separate and unequal: School segregation in Louisiana 65 years after Brown v. board.* Louisiana Budget Project. https://bit.ly/2L1xAXV

Cabreros, I. (2022, March 27). Why an algorithm can never truly be 'fair.' *Los Angeles Times*. https://www.latimes.com/opinion/story/2022-03-27/algorithms-unfair-racial-bias-math

Cahalan, M. W., Addison, M., Brunt, N., Patel, P. R., & Perna, L. W. (2021). *Indicators of higher education equity in the United States: 2021 historical trend report.* The Pell Institute for the Study of Opportunity in Higher Education, Council for Opportunity in Education & Alliance for Higher Education and Democracy of the University of Pennsylvania. http://pellinstitute.org/downloads/publications-Indicators_of_Higher_Education_Equity_in_the_US_2021_Historical_Trend_Report.pdf

Callahan, R. E. (1964). *Education and the cult of efficiency: A study of the social forces that have shaped the administration of the public schools.* University of Chicago Press. doi:10.7208/chicago/9780226216904.001.0001

Carnevale, A. P., Cheah, B., & Van Der Werf, M. (2019). *A first try at ROI: Ranking 4,500 colleges.* Georgetown University, Center for Education and the Workforce. https://1gyhoq479ufd3yna29x7ubjn-wpengine.netdna-ssl.com/wp-content/uploads/College_ROI.pdf

Carozza, L., & Gennaro, S. (2021). Post-pandemic pedagogy. Compassionate and caring course curriculum in the digital university. In J. M. Valenzano III, (Ed.), *Post-pandemic pedagogy: A paradigm shift* (pp. 57–72). Lexington Books.

Clark, M. (2021, April 8). Students of color are getting flagged to their teachers because testing software can't see them. *The Verge*. https://www.theverge.com/2021/4/8/22374386/proctorio-racial-bias-issues-opencv-facial-detection-schools-tests-remote-learning

Conwill, W. L. (2009). Factors affecting the presence of African American males in counseling and psychology training program faculties. In H. T. Frierson, J. H. Whyche, & W. Pearson, Jr. (Eds.) Black American males in higher education: Research, programs, and academe (Vol. 6, pp. 287–316). Emerald Group Publishing. doi:10.1108/S1479-3644(2009)0000007017

Cook, C. (2017). 20th Pauline Cerasoli lecture: The sunk cost fallacy. *Journal of Physical Therapy Education, 31*(3), 10–14. doi:10.1097/00001416-201731030-00005

Council for Accreditation of Counseling and Related Educational Programs. (2016). *2016 CACREP standards.* https://www.cacrep.org/for-programs/2016-cacrep-standards/

Countryman, P. (1963). The Philadelphia experiment. *Equity & Excellence in Education, 1*(1), 14–16. doi:10.1080/0020486630010104

Delgado, R., & Stefancic, J. (1998). Critical race theory: Past, present, and future. *Current Legal Problems, 1*(51), 467–491. doi:10.1093/clp/51.1.467

Deutsch, M. (1963). The disadvantaged child and the learning process. *Equity & Excellence in Education, 1*(1), 11–12. doi:10.1080/0020486630010102

Dick, J. C. (1975). How to justify a distribution of earnings. *Philosophy & Public Affairs, 4*(3), 248–272. https://www.jstor.org/stable/2265085

Doherty, R. A. (2007). Education, neoliberalism and the consumer citizen: After the golden age of egalitarian reform. *Critical Studies in Education, 48*(2), 269–288. doi:10.1080/17508480701494275

Douglas, P. H. (1963). Teaching in a ghetto school. *Equity & Excellence in Education, 1*(1), 20–21. doi:10.1080/0020486630010107

Dowd, A. C. (2007). Community colleges as gateways and gatekeepers: Moving beyond the access 'saga' toward outcome equity. *Harvard Educational Review, 77*(4), 1–13. doi:10.17763/haer.77.4.1233g31741157227

Dowd, A. C., & Bensimon, E. M. (2015). *Engaging the "race question": Accountability and equity in U.S. higher education.* Teachers College Press.

Freedom, I. Fla. Stat. 2022-72 § 4 (2022). https://legiscan.com/FL/bill/H0007/2022

Freire, P. (2018). Pedagogy of the oppressed (M. Bergman Ramos, Trans.; 50th anniversary ed.). Bloomsbury Academic. (Original work published 1970)

Glass, C. (2017). Self-expression, social roles, and faculty members' attitudes towards online teaching. *Innovative Higher Education, 42*(3), 239–252. doi:10.100710755-016-9379-2

Gould, C. (1996). Diversity and democracy: Representing differences. In S. Benhabib (Ed.), *Democracy and difference: Contesting the boundaries of the political* (pp. 171–186). Princeton University Press. doi:10.1515/9780691234168-010

Groeger, L. V., Waldman, A., & Eads, D. (2018, October 16). *Miseducation. Is there racial inequality at your school?* ProPublica. https://bit.ly/3r3T3Pp

Gullo, G., & Beachum, F. (2020). Framing implicit bias impact reduction in social justice leadership. *Journal of Educational Leadership and Policy Studies, 3*(3). https://files.eric.ed.gov/fulltext/EJ1251975.pdf

Hayes, K. N. (2016). Neoliberalism in historical light: How business models displaced science education goals in two eras. *Educational Leadership and Administration: Teaching and Program Development, 27*, 1–19. https://files.eric.ed.gov/fulltext/EJ1094418.pdf

Horton, M., Bell, B., Gaventa, J., & Peters, J. M. (1990). *We make the road by walking: Conversations on education and social change.* Tempe University Press.

Howe, K. R. (1994). Standards, assessment, and equality of educational opportunity. *Educational Researcher, 23*(8), 27–33. doi:10.2307/1176860

Intellectual Diversity, S. D. Codified Laws § 13-53-53 (2022). https://sdlegislature.gov/Statutes/Codified_Laws/2042844

Jencks, C. (1988). Whom must we treat equally for educational opportunity to be equal? *Ethics*, *98*(3), 518–533. doi:10.1086/292969

Kendi, I. X. (2020). *Antiracist baby* (A. Lukashevsky, Illus.). Kokila.

Kenyon, T., & Beaulac, G. (2014). Critical thinking education and debiasing. *Informal Logic*, *34*(4), 341–363. doi:10.22329/il.v34i4.4203

Kreijns, K., Xu, K., & Weidlich, J. (2022). Social presence: Conceptualization and measurement. *Educational Psychology Review*, *34*(1), 139–170. doi:10.100710648-021-09623-8 PMID:34177204

Krug, K. S., Dickson, K. W., Lessiter, J. A., & Vassar, J. S. (2016). Faculty attitudes for changing a university's core and structure. *International Journal of Higher Education*, *5*(2), 63–73. doi:10.5430/ijhe.v5n2p63

Larabee, D. F. (1997). Public goods, private goods: The American struggle over educational goals. *American Educational Research Journal*, *34*(1), 39–81. doi:10.3102/00028312034001039

Laufer, M., Leiser, A., Deacon, B., de Brichambaut, P. P., Fecher, B., Kobsda, C., & Hesse, F. (2021). Digital higher education: A divider or bridge builder? Leadership perspectives on edtech in a COVID-19 reality. *International Journal of Educational Technology in Higher Education*, *18*(1), 1–17. doi:10.118641239-021-00287-6 PMID:34778538

Le Grand, J. (1991). *Equity and choice: An essay in economics and applied philosophy*. Routledge. doi:10.4324/9780203400098

Levin, J. S., Martin, M. C., López Damián, A. I., & Hoggatt, M. J. (2018). Preservation of community college logic: Organizational responses to state policies and funding practices in three states. *Community College Review*, *46*(2), 197–220. doi:10.1177/0091552118758893

Manoogian, J., III, & Benson, B. (2016, September 5). *The cognitive bias codex. 180+ biases*. https://upload.wikimedia.org/wikipedia/commons/6/65/Cognitive_bias_codex_en.svg

Matters, Q. (n.d.). *Helping you deliver on your online promise*. https://www.qualitymatters.org/

McClain, M. B., Callan, G. L., Harris, B., Floyd, R. G., Haverkamp, C. R., Golson, M. E., Longhurst, D. N., & Benallie, K. J. (2021). Methods for addressing publication bias in school psychology journals: A descriptive review of meta-analyses from 1980 to 2019. *Journal of School Psychology*, *84*, 74–94. doi:10.1016/j.jsp.2020.11.002 PMID:33581772

Mendonca, A. L. (2020). Understanding the perpetuation of inequalities in Brazilian K–12 public and private schools from a historical perspective. *Educational Considerations*, *42*(2), 1–13. doi:10.4148/0146-9282.2189

Milne, H. (1986). Desert, effort and equality. *Journal of Applied Philosophy*, *3*(2), 235–243. doi:10.1111/j.1468-5930.1986.tb00423.x

Mitchell, B., & Geva-May, I. (2009). Attitudes affecting online learning implementation in higher education institutions. *Journal of Distance Education, 23*(1), 71–88. https://files.eric.ed.gov/fulltext/EJ836033.pdf

Moody, J. (2022, June 6). A grab for power. *Inside Higher Ed.* https://www.insidehighered.com/news/2022/06/06/draft-legislation-shows-desantis-plan-control-higher-ed

National Association of System Heads. (n.d.-a) *NASH equity action agenda.* https://nashonline.org/

National Association of System Heads. (n.d.-b) *Strategic initiatives.* https://nashonline.org/strategic-initiatives/

Nozick, R. (1974). *Anarchy, state, and utopia.* Basic Books.

Online Learning Consortium. (n.d.). *OLC institutional membership.* https://onlinelearningconsortium.org/join/institutional/

Pathak, B. K. (2019). Study of e-learning outcomes: The role of late-registration and self-selection. *E-Journal of Business Education & Scholarship of Teaching, 13*(1), 13–19. https://files.eric.ed.gov/fulltext/EJ1239138.pdf

Plessy v. Ferguson, 163 U.S. 537 (1896). https://supreme.justia.com/cases/federal/us/163/537/

Porter, L. R. (2004). *Developing an online curriculum: Technologies and techniques.* Information Science Publishing. doi:10.4018/978-1-59140-136-0

Rawls, J. (1971). *A theory of justice.* Harvard University Press. doi:10.4159/9780674042605

Report on five cities. (1963). *Equity & Excellence in Education, 1*(1), 3–10. doi:10.1080/0020486630010101

Riley, J. (1989). Justice under capitalism. In J. W. Chapman (Ed.), *Markets and justice* (pp. 122–162). New York University Press.

Schacter, H. L., Brown, S. G., Daugherty, A. M., Brummelte, S., & Grekin, E. (2021, December 1). Creating a compassionate classroom. *Inside Higher Ed.* https://www.insidehighered.com/advice/2021/12/01/compassionate-teaching-yields-most-benefits-opinion

Sen, A. (1999). *Development as freedom.* Oxford University Press.

Smidt, E., McDyre, B., Bunk, J., Li, R., & Gatenby, T. (2014). Faculty attitudes about distance education. *IAFOR Journal of Education, 2*(2), 181–209. https://files.eric.ed.gov/fulltext/EJ1080364.pdf

Suler, J. R. (2015). *Psychology of the digital age: Humans become electric.* Cambridge University Press. doi:10.1017/CBO9781316424070

Tagg, J. (2007). Double-loop learning in higher education. *Change: The Magazine of Higher Learning, 39*(4), 36–41. doi:10.3200/CHNG.39.4.36-41

Tagg, J. (2010). The learning-paradigm campus: From single- to double-loop learning. *New Directions for Teaching and Learning, 123*(123), 51–61. doi:10.1002/tl.409

Taylor & Francis Online. (n.d.). *Equity & Excellence in Education: Aims and scope.* https://bit.ly/3r6GPWk

Troy, T. (2015, Fall). Reclaiming the congressional hearing. *National Affairs, 25*, 62–77. https://tevitroy.org/17877/reclaiming-the-congressional-hearing

Two cities evaluate busing. (1963). *Equity & Excellence in Education, 1*(1), 13. doi:10.1080/0020486630010103

United States Bureau of Labor Statistics. (2021, April 21). *Education pays. Earnings and unemployment rates by educational attainment, 2020.* https://www.bls.gov/emp/chart-unemployment-earnings-education.htm

United States Department of Education, National Center for Education Statistics. (2021). *Digest of Education Statistics 2020* [Table 310.20]. U.S. Department of Education. https://www.nces.ed.gov/programs/digest/d20/tables/dt20_301.20.asp?current=yes

United States Senate Committee on the Judiciary. (2022, March 22). *The nomination of Ketanji Brown Jackson to be an associate justice of the supreme court of the United States (day 2)* [Video]. https://www.judiciary.senate.gov/meetings/03/14/2022/the-nomination-of-ketanji-brown-jackson-top-be-an-associate-justice-of-the-supreme-court-of-the-united-states-day-2

University of Southern California Center for Urban Education. (n.d.). *Equity mindedness.* https://cue.usc.edu/equity/equity-mindedness/

Van Auken, S. (2013). Using an exemplar to teach attitudinal formation, attitudinal change and consumer defense mechanisms: The motel selection problem. *Journal of Advertising Education, 17*(2), 39–42. doi:10.1177/109804821301700206

Verba, S. (2006). Fairness, equality, and democracy: three big words. *Social Research: An International Quarterly of Social Sciences 73*(2), 499–540. https://dash.harvard.edu/bitstream/handle/1/2640592/verba_2006.pdf

Virginia Department of Planning and Budget. (2016, March 27). *Economic impact analysis. 18 VAC 115-20 regulations governing the practice of professional counseling department of health professions.* https://townhall.virginia.gov/L/GetFile.cfm?File=25%5C4259%5C7390%5CEIA_DHP_7390_vE.pdf

Wang, Q., & Jeon, H. J. (2020). Bias in bias recognition: People view others but not themselves as biased by preexisting beliefs and social stigmas. *PLoS One, 15*(10), e0240232. Advance online publication. doi:10.1371/journal.pone.0240232 PMID:33035252

Weisman, S. (2022, March 18). Chat bots bypass 'communication clutter' to help students. *Inside Higher Ed.* https://www.insidehighered.com/news/2022/03/18/new-study-explores-how-use-chat-bots-retain-students

West, K., & Eaton, A. A. (2019). Prejudiced and unaware of it: Evidence for the Dunning-Kruger model in the domains of racism and sexism. *Personality and Individual Differences, 146*, 111–119. doi:10.1016/j.paid.2019.03.047

Windes, D. L., & Lesht, F. L. (2014). The effects of online teaching experience and institution type on faculty perceptions of teaching online. *Online Journal of Distance Learning Administration, 17*(1).

Witham, K. A., Malcolm-Piqueux, L., Dowd, A. C., & Bensimon, E. M. (2015). *America's unmet promise. The imperative for equity in higher education.* Association of American Colleges & Universities.

Yu, J., Huang, C., Han, Z., He, T., & Li, M. (2020). Investigating the influence of interaction on learning persistence in online settings: Moderation or mediation of academic emotions? *International Journal of Environmental Research and Public Health*, *17*(7), 2320. doi:10.3390/ijerph17072320 PMID:32235547

Zabawski, E. (2019). The squeaky wheel. Various interpretations of a proverb [Editorial]. *Tribology & Lubrication Technology*, *75*(7), 8. https://digitaleditions.walsworth.com/publication/?m=5716&i=595223&view=articleBrowser&article_id=3404572&ver=html5

ENDNOTE

[1] For example, the Council for Accreditation of Counseling and Related Educational Programs (CACREP) requires specific faculty-to-student ratios, ensuring a low number of students (CACREP, 2016, Section 3) are observed by a low number of specific kinds of credentialed and currently licensed faculty (CACREP, 2016, Section 1). Such a requirement ensures program cost will remain elevated and thereby exclude historically minoritized populations (Conwill, 2009; Virginia Department of Planning and Budget, 2016).

Section 6
Closing Thoughts

Intentional inclusive environments impact more than the institution and more than the student. Entire communities can experience positive social change.

Chapter 16
The Social Determinants of Changemakers:
A Commitment to Inclusive Teaching and Learning and a Positive Social Change Mission

Nina M. McCune
https://orcid.org/0000-0001-5339-9383
Walden University, USA

William C. Schulz III
https://orcid.org/0000-0001-8560-5540
Walden University, USA

ABSTRACT

The closing chapter of this edited edition puts forward a theory of the social determinants of changemakers – those learners supported by an inclusive educational institution, empowered to create positive social change in the world. Building on previous social change and social determinants scholarship, and through intentional and inclusive institutional organization, planning, and support, this framework is not only possible for postsecondary education institutions to drive positive social change – it is the call to action of our time.

INTRODUCTION

In this edited collection, Walden University has shared its story and process of creating a caring and inclusive teaching and learning environment in an online postsecondary institution. Rather than understanding equity through policy reviews and racially disaggregated data that may have only a short-term impact on educational justice (see Chapter 15: "Equity in the Online Space? A Multi-Systems Perspective"), the authors have explored how this unique online institution, with a mission of positive social change,

DOI: 10.4018/978-1-6684-5146-5.ch016

The Social Determinants of Changemakers

has built, and continues to build, a space for multiple-stakeholder reflection and engagement using a methodology of person-centered, appreciative inquiry, toward the goal of creating long-term caring and inclusive teaching and learning environments that ultimately lead to our learners actively participating in creating a healthier world (see Chapters 1 and 2: "Developing a Learning Model for Caring, Inclusion & Social Change in an Online Environment" and "Digital Appreciative Inquiry for Inclusion").

The authors understand that creating equity and educational justice is an inclusive process unique to each institution, specific to its learners and its mission, and urgent for the communities they serve (see Chapters 14 and 11: "Sustainable Strategic Planning for Inclusive Online Teaching and Learning" and "Assessing Institutional Readiness: A Collaboration"). Inclusive teaching and learning at Walden University is an intentional practice that requires that the entire institution and its members develop a conscious awareness of the diverse social, cultural, and community identities and lived experiences of all learners.

Inclusive teaching includes a variety of strategies to fully activate learner strengths, and it occurs in environments that draw relevant, meaningful connections to their lives and the professional dispositions they develop (see Chapters 4, 5, and 12: "Success and Failures in the Development of an Inclusive Online Learning Environment," "Designing an Inclusive Online Classroom," and "Developing a Rubric for a Person-Centered Approach to Teaching in Inclusive Online Learning Spaces"). The goal is to ensure learners (1) know that Walden values the inherent worth, humanity, and dignity of every learner engaged in the learning process; (2) will be prepared and empowered to share knowledge and expertise through mutual inquiry that connects each of them with multiple perspectives and ways of thinking; and (3) that their experiences at Walden enhance their ability to take actions that can benefit a variety of communities, cultures, and contexts.

In this space, learners build upon existing knowledge and advance lifelong skills to create positive social change in local, national, and global communities (see Chapters 6 and 7: "Advancing Equity, Diversity, and Inclusion through the Transformation of Nursing Education" and "Strategies for Doctoral Student Readiness, Student-Centered Support, and Inclusion). Walden, thus, connects our efforts at building and supporting an inclusive teaching and learning environment with our institutional mission and dedication to drive positive social change more broadly through striving for educational justice (see Chapters 8 and 9: "The Students We Have: Compassionate Grading in Online Courses" and "The SPII Hub and Promoting Online Engagement") and supporting the benefits that society gains through such justice.

BACKGROUND

Reshaping our Frames of Engagement in the World

As members of the Walden community continue to work collaboratively to bring our vision of inclusive teaching and learning to life, substantial opportunities and challenges remain before all postsecondary practitioners, including how to strengthen our curriculum to be more inclusive and to empower social change agents—and to do so at scale and in a timely, flexible manner. But the road map outlined in this volume and the process commitments that Walden has made will see those challenges met, and they have provided a new frame from which this institution can continue to learn and grow that is focused on educational justice and social change more broadly. This is a frame that can be adopted by other postsecondary institutions as well.

In Chapter 13, "Framing Higher Education Through the Social Determinants of Health," Dr. Aimee Ferraro shared that Walden has taken major steps to reorganize academic college and departmental structures so that the university could be more effective in providing learners with opportunities to connect learning systemically and across disciplines, address complex social challenges, and exercise specific skills related to the advancement of positive social change. By observing those events and phenomena whose outcomes are socially determined, specific interventions can be operationalized to reduce, or at least mitigate, events with negative outcomes for communities. For example, within the past decade, scientists and public health practitioners have observed the strongest predictor of one's overall health and life expectancy correlates to zip codes (Agarwal et al., 2015; Bhatt, 2018; Graham, 2016; Holmes et al., 2018; Liu et al., 2022; Orminski, 2021; Roeder, 2014). The collective discourse around these kinds of findings have enabled researchers to develop and share publicly the tools to inform and situate fact-based and context-specific programming, policies, or interventions to address inequities. One example of this is the University of Wisconsin School of Medicine and Public Health's *Neighborhood Atlas* (n.d.), which shares measures of neighborhood disadvantage. Using such information allows for more targeted and potentially more efficacious cures to improve outcomes for specific populations, and it allows postsecondary institutions to engage those resources in programs to solve complex problems.

Similar tools exist, such as the *Opportunity Atlas* (Opportunity Insights, n.d.), which measures social mobility, and the University of Southern California's *National Equity Atlas* (2022), which relays racially disaggregated economic data for specific cities and regions across the United States. Such data can be used in education—both K–12 and postsecondary sectors—to better understand not only the context and communities our learners come from but to better support those learners as they complete educational programs. These two tools are equally useful for learners, faculty, and administrators engaging in research around issues of diversity, equity, and inclusion.

The current SDOH framework originated through observations about community health during the industrial revolution (Virchow, 1848). This modern version (World Health Organization, 2010) encompasses multiple indicators that impact individual and community health, including lack of education, stigma, structural and systemic racism, and social and cultural norms (Centers for Disease Control and Prevention, 2019, para. 4–5). The SDOH framework highlights inequities that are unjust, unnecessary, and avoidable because they are caused by socially determined policies and practices that result in different outcomes for different groups (Braveman & Gruskin, 2003). Such inequities are produced and reproduced within certain systems and continue to benefit privileged groups and disadvantage vulnerable and marginalized groups (Prättälä & Puska, 2012). Different outcomes among groups with different levels of advantage or disadvantage tend to be significant, frequent, and predictable; differing outcomes are not incidental or unforeseeable. Such structural inequities are important to contrast with those inequities that occur outside of what is otherwise socially determined.

Some examples are differing outcomes of uncontrollable factors like climate, availability of resources based on geography and topography, biological factors (e.g., physiological or chemical conditions), outcomes based on decisions under an individual's direct control/choice, and those random outcomes that defy correlation and causation. The social determinants, in other words, are those socially constructed elements that we can observe and mitigate, albeit with interventions often requiring changes to systems and structures (social, cultural, political, economic) to address "multidimensional [inequities]…most often caused by multiple factors that intersect and interact in complex ways varying across contexts and time" (Robertson, 2016, p. 347). This distinction between inequitable and inevitable socially determined outcomes has prompted the development of other social determinants frameworks, including a social determinants of equity framework (SDoE). The SDoE considers and measures factors such as socioeconomic status, education, neighborhood and physical environment, employment, and social support networks. The SDoE also takes into account access to healthcare (Artiga & Hinton, 2018; Braveman, 2006; Robertson, 2016), often leading to politically interpreted and value-based findings, especially since, as Gudeva Nikovska and Tozija (2014) point out, inequities and inequitable outcomes occur and persist in both wealthy and poor countries worldwide.

Other branching frameworks have been identified (see Figure 1), including the aforementioned social determinants of equity (SDoE). Most recently, frameworks have extended beyond health and healthcare and include two that are important for the intended outcomes of inclusive teaching and learning in postsecondary spaces. First, a social determinants of learning framework (SDOL™) identifies causative social and structural factors that impact learning in postsecondary institutions and encourage further research on interventions to eliminate root-cause factors of racialized educational outcome and achievement discrepancies (Sanderson et al., 2021). Second, a social determinants of education framework (SDoED) considers targeted academic integration, persistence, and discipline-specific values that different learner populations need to reach their full potential (Fortes et al., 2022). The SDoED situated within nursing education incorporates recent discourse on identifying specific kinds of learner support—including emotional intelligence, lifestyle, and social support—for different learner populations with differing academic, social, or financial needs (Browman et al., 2017; Fortes et al., 2022) to close achievement gaps between those different learner populations.

Figure 1. A genesis of social determinants frameworks
Note. This figure illustrates a recent proliferation of types and kinds of social determinants frameworks. It is by no means exhaustive. The social determinants of changemakers (SDoΔ) stems from previous scholarship, as indicated in the figure. Image credit: Nina M. McCune, Walden University.

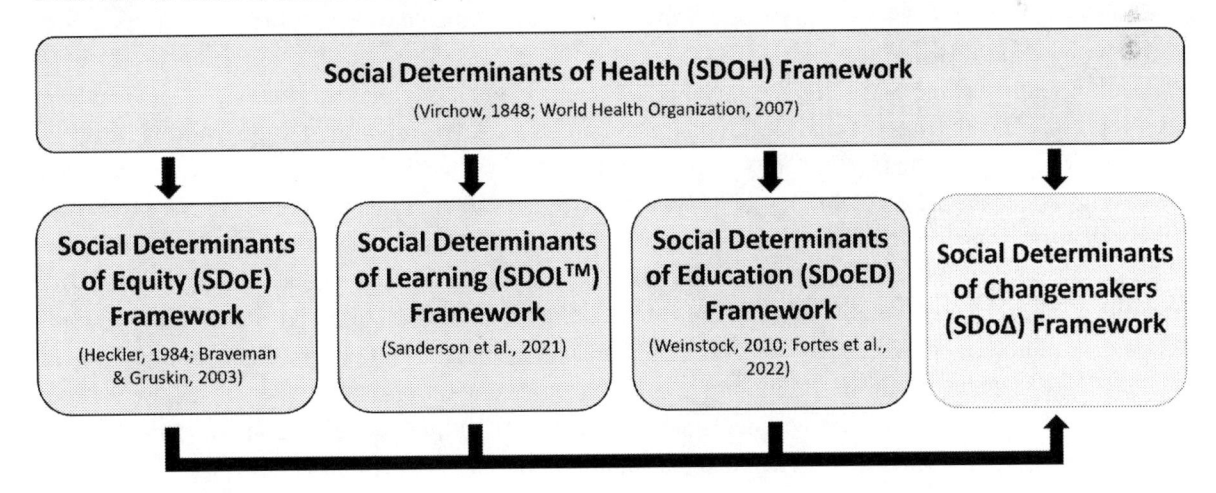

THE SOCIAL DETERMINANTS OF CHANGEMAKERS

A Framework for Positive Social Change

In response to proliferating social determinants frameworks, Lindell et al. (2021) recommend future frameworks must be broad and elaborated in order "to address justice and equity, globally, across the educational lifespan to reflect an emphasis… [on] …health and healthcare equity… [and on] creating educational equity and justice" (p. 6). To be sure, this is the call of our time: to transform higher education and to explore all options to increase and ensure equitable outcomes for all learners in postsecondary education. We must do this in a way that is diligent, fact based, and attentive to the needs of different types of learners. In light of this call, it seems fitting to close this edited collection with a socially determined framework that can realize outcomes of equitable and just education, and ultimately, the outcome of positive social change. By understanding each individual holistically—that each individual expresses their intellectual, emotional, and physical well-being in a number of ways—postsecondary institutions can harness collective creative energies and resources and effect change to improve sociable, just, and fair conditions for learners and the communities that learners go on to serve.

In the pursuit of those aims, individuals will engage in any number of processes to create the economic, social, and political conditions in which they can exercise freedoms to be and do (Sen, 1999; 2004; Nussbaum 2000), and to live dignified and autonomous lives, reasonably secure from identifiable and socially determined hazards that threaten, victimize, and oppress them. The fact that individuals are willing to use their own time and effort to create and realize prosperous, fair, and just communities reveals the value they would place on such public conditions. As the individual pursues shared values of a good and just society, they are enabled to participate more robustly in the economic, social, and political life of that society. And more often than not, it is up to individuals to inspire others in order to mobilize such change. Postsecondary institutions are perfectly situated to support this kind of personal growth and community development.

Positive social change is "a deliberate process of creating and applying ideas, strategies, and actions to promote the worth, dignity, and development of individuals, communities, organizations, institutions, cultures, and societies" (Walden University, n.d., para. 2). This definition undergirds an approach to creating inclusive and equitable learning spaces, insofar as those spaces emerge from a *deliberate process* that *promotes the inherent worth, dignity*, and humanity of all engaged in the learning process. "A social determinants effort addresses social change through the development of greater equity… [by creating] a fairer, more equitable community that deals with discrimination and other equity issues" (Brennan Ramirez et al., n.d., para. 17–20). Changemakers operate within numerous communities at once, the least of which are those communities seeking change and the communities targeted for change. Changemakers are also supported within communities of care within educational institutions that can offer the intellectual, academic, financial, social, and emotional support that learners at all stages of development require. Figure 2 illustrates how a SDoΔ framework operates and is akin to participator action research, a form of research often suited to education environments.

The Social Determinants of Changemakers

Figure 2. The Social Determinants of Changemakers (SDoΔ) framework
Note. In this framework, the central figure is an individual embodying social change. The individual is borne of a series of socially determined elements – including mental and physical health, economic stability, social supports, socio-cultural context, and a built environment. The individual brings a certain degree of social mobility as they matriculate at an educational environment that promotes the inherent worth, dignity, and humanity of all engaged in the learning process. This individual's lived experience is honored and incorporated into the learning process, especially insofar as the individual learns how to change those systems and structures currently preventing their growth or career advancement, akin to what Mezirow (1978) calls a disorienting dilemma. Here, a community of care mobilizes academic support and addresses learner needs to develop a scholar practitioner who can create positive social change. This framework of transformational learning advances the individual's social mobility, stemming from those innovations of positive social change carried out in the individual's local context or community. This model is cyclical, insofar as those who experience equitable education, and realize the positive impact they can have because of this experience, become lifelong learners (Casey & Patrick, 2020; Lopes & Carreira, 2020; McDuff et al., 2020; Wienclaw, 2021), creating continual improvement and positive social change. Image credit: Nina M. McCune, Walden University.

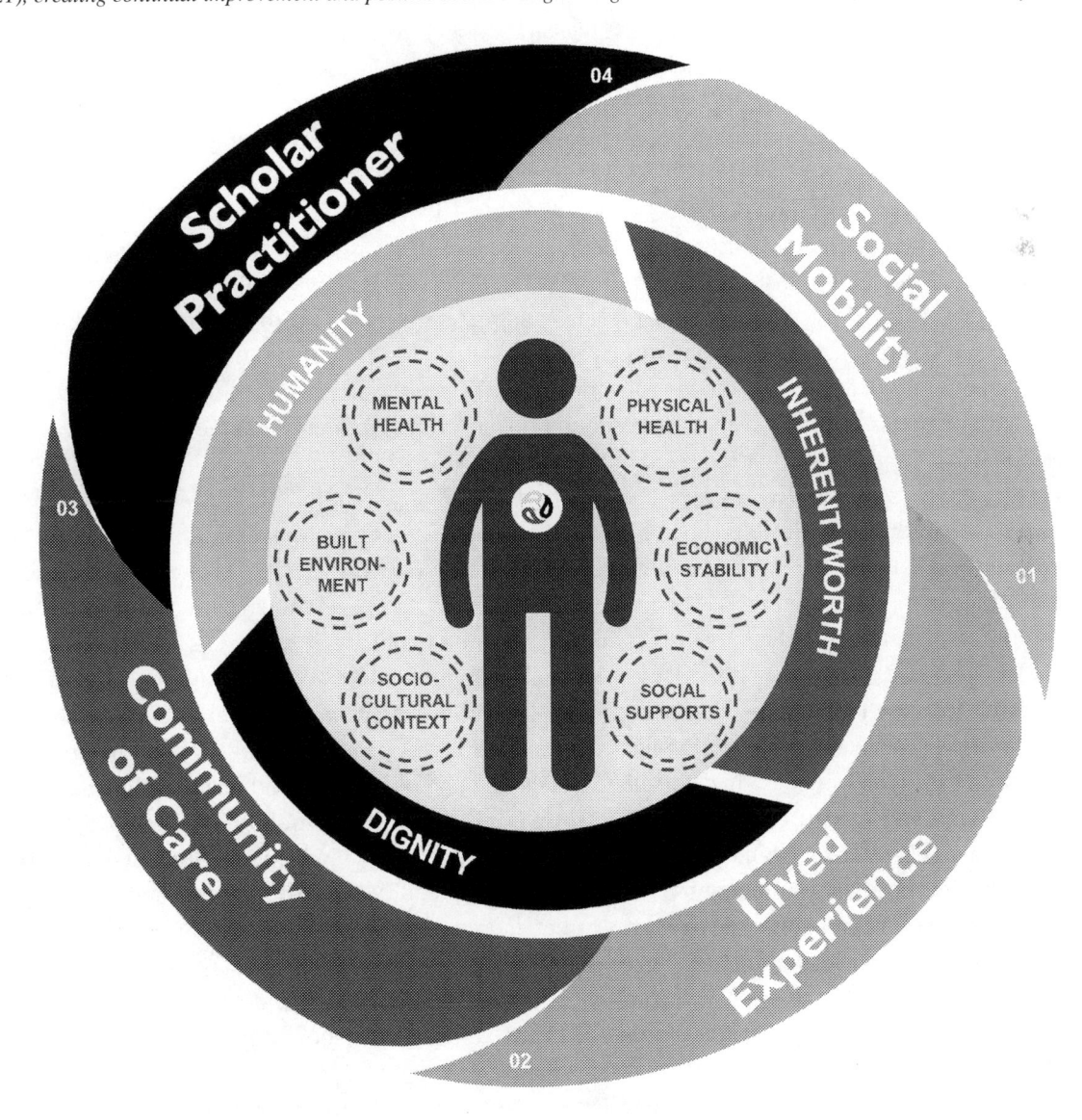

Theory Into Practice: What a Social Determinants of Changemakers Framework Considers

The SDoΔ framework engages an understanding of **social mobility** from an individual's inherent social capital and capabilities (Nussbaum, 2000), insofar as an individual's social capital is a means toward advancing towards full functioning (Sen, 1999; 2004) and social mobility (Coleman, 1988). Social mobility is expressed as individuals engage in actions that have (what is perceived as) the best outcomes. Individuals invest in relationships assuming they will benefit from such investments – individuals calculate and determine which actions they will take with respect to the quantity and quality of the social relationships in which they are involved. While there are "innumerable cultural influences which thwart and misdirect the rational activity…the mind has a functional drive for use just as surely as do muscles and the rest of the body and it will be used on whatever content is available" (Steward, 1951, p. 36). Postsecondary institutions have the opportunity to operationalize innately rational actors as long as curricular and co-cocurricular programming explicates why learning is important (e.g., creating positive social change) and, in doing so, impacts social mobility.

"This form of social capital depends on two elements: trustworthiness of the social environment… and the actual extent of obligations held" (Coleman, 1988, p. 102). In the postsecondary context, learners entering an institution need to be supported through the academic, social, and financial supports (Fortes et al., 2022) in a way that both (a) creates and recreates trust, and (b) explicates the reciprocal obligations of parties engaged in the learning process. Establishing and maintaining trust is critical to a thriving community of practice (Woods-Jaeger et al., 2022), especially in educational settings that may overwhelm learners and researchers with confounding and compounding academic demands. Trust can be established through honoring the **lived experiences** of learners as part of institutional practice and, as a result, learners are able to better see themselves in professions (Bjørnskov & Méon, 2013; White et al., 2022) where they can create positive social change and further develop autonomy and agency. The latter is embedded within course design and course delivery (see Chapter 5, "Designing an Inclusive Online Classroom," and Chapter 4, "Success and Failures in the Development of an Inclusive Online Learning Environment"), and the former is found throughout the lifecycle of the learner experience (for example, Chapter 7, "Strategies for Doctoral Student Readiness, Student-Centered Support, and Inclusion," or Chapter 1, "Developing a Learning Model for Caring, Inclusion & Social Change in an Online Environment"). Especially in a learning environment that prizes positive social change, changemakers are exposed to an array of socially determined issues that can be impacted by learner engagement and action. As learners advance through the SDoΔ framework, their social mobility increases as they engage. Coleman (1988) understands social capital as a collective asset and a public good, where actions of individuals benefit the whole and that "the public goods quality of most social capital means…it is an important resource for individuals and may affect greatly their ability to act and their perceived quality of life. They have the capability of bringing into being" (p. 118). Practices that ensure that learners are seen and heard holistically—where the inherent worth, humanity, and dignity of each learner is preserved—create an environment that fosters further development of social capital and, thus, increases social mobility.

This theoretical background is animated through an institution's **community of care**, in which all available resources are deployed to support and nurture learner development and growth. In advancing DEI in the online space, specific technological tools can be used efficaciously, like chatbots for tutoring (Walden University, 2021) or engaging platforms for learner discourse (see Chapter 9, "The SPII Hub and Other Initiatives to Advance Online Engagement"). In a community of care, members are aware that individuals come from a lived context described by individual experience, their physical and mental health, and their socio-cultural contexts and social supports of family and friends as well the implications of their physical or built environment (refer to the zip code discussion above) and their economic stability. These conditions must be part and parcel of institutional indices that may be appropriately named as *thrive indexes*: How can institutions use the data they have to promote learner success and learner well-being? Mühlpachr (2008) underscores this idea: "we need to analyze the changes of educational climate in the social environment…as the consequence of worldwide changes and process characteristic for post-modern society… [like the] ever growing demands on the individual" (p. 67). Such a holistic approach must be an integral part of postsecondary institutional collections of data and deployed in such a way as to establish norms of care for the changemakers and the communities that schools serve. In this model, equity mindsets are operationalized and encourage learners and scholar practitioners to "positively affect the fundamental aim of expanding choice and enhancing one's quality of life" (Gil et al., n.d., p. 3) because the focus is on engaging communities to enact positive social change.

At the time of its conceptualization, Walden incorporates a **scholar-practitioner** model that melds scholarly research with learner expertise as skilled practitioners in their fields insofar as most learners know "more about some things than faculty do… [both faculty and learners are] free to learn from each other" (Hodgkinson, 1969, p. 175). This approach to learning reflects "ways of thinking and understanding the world which are contextual and participatory, and which reflect the socialness of the human condition" (Miller, 1997, p. 58) and are critical for changemakers to thrive. Learners receive guidance and support while they investigate those innovations and interventions that can have positive impact (Yob, 2018). Although Coleman (1988) held a rather pessimistic view that the changemaker sees little benefit of the change, decades earlier, Stewart (1951) pointed to the most important outcome of social change—that of the culmination of progress and advancement that impacts the targeted community, the institution supporting change, and the changemaker:

[existing deficits are] exceedingly durable and change slowly. The rapidity and nature of change depends on quite a number of determinants—physical environment, rational determinant and various cultural factors. Whether the change is periodic and violent, gradual, in successful or unsuccessful directions depends upon the enlightenment of the group and its leadership. (p. 38)

In an environment valuing the inherent worth, dignity, and humanity of all engaged in the learning process—including the communities in which changemakers operate—social change can be realized through steadfast application of agreed-upon practices with fact patterns of producing equity outcome. Or, as Nussbaum (2006) clarifies, those who cultivate the capacity for change, develop "an ability to see themselves as not simply citizens of some local region or group, but also, and above all, as human beings bound to all other human beings by ties of recognition and concern" (p. 389). By developing such bonds of recognition and concern, the changemaker not only achieves a goal of positive social change, but continues to advance individual social mobility, and continues to advance solutions for collective social change.

CONCLUSION

Implications for the Social Determinants of Changemakers

While Walden may not be alone in the field of developing changemakers (Brennan Ramierez et al., n.d.; James, 2020; Mogford et al., 2011), the school carries with it a 50-year mission of positive social change. The SDOH framework, and its offshoots (SDoE, SDOL™, SDoED) build active models of interrogating inequities. It is unconscionable to reproduce inequity in higher education; it is unreasonable to continue with systems and structures while purporting growth; it is incongruous with any standard of practice to reproduce or cause harm for educational participants. Thus, through intentional and inclusive institutional organization, planning, and support, it is possible for postsecondary education to drive positive social change. Walden prepares changemakers to create—and to continue to create—positive social change. To that end,

the University actively addresses intentional curricular design across the portfolio to enable a more just/ inclusive/equitable educational experience...learning is collaborative, inspiring, diversity-oriented, and conducive to positive social change...[programs] infuse positive social change activities throughout the curriculum. Social change components are integrated with the development of courses; alignment with the social change mission is tracked in all programs. (Lindell et al., 2021, p. 5)

As citizens, we all take part in socially constructing and socially determining how change is made, and social change is an outcome of all the determinants frameworks considered in this epilogue. Importantly, higher education must fulfill its promise of social mobility and work toward creating a society that not only values our ability to meet basic needs, earn a living, take care of health, and learn throughout our lives. We also must value the way we treat and are treated by others as well as the justice and fairness of the institutions we rely on to protect us from victimization and discrimination. This edition highlights the approach to how we educate and support learners to be changemakers to impact communities so that our learners don't just learn, they make a difference.

REFERENCES

Agarwal, S., Menon, V., & Jaber, W. A. (2015). Residential zip code influences outcomes following hospitalization for acute pulmonary embolism in the United States. *Vascular Medicine, 20*(5), 439–446. doi:10.1177/1358863X15592486 PMID:26163399

Artiga, S., & Hinton, E. (2018, May 10). *Beyond health care: The role of social determinants in promoting health and health equity.* Kaiser Family Foundation. https://www.kff.org/racial-equity-and-health-policy/issue-brief/beyond-health-care-the-role-of-social-determinants-in-promoting-health-and-health-equity/

Bhatt, J. (2018, May 16). *Your zip code, your health.* American Hospital Association. https://www.aha.org/news/insights-and-analysis/2018-05-16-your-zip-code-your-health

Bjørnskov, C., & Méon, P.-G. (2013). Is trust the missing root of institutions, education, and development? *Public Choice, 157*(3–4), 641–669. doi:10.100711127-013-0069-7

Braveman, P. (2006). Health disparities and health equity: Concepts and measurement. *Annual Review of Public Health, 27*(1), 167–194. doi:10.1146/annurev.publhealth.27.021405.102103 PMID:16533114

Braveman, P., & Gruskin, S. (2003). Defining equity in health. *Journal of Epidemiology and Community Health, 57*(4), 254–258. doi:10.1136/jech.57.4.254 PMID:12646539

Brennan Ramirez, L. K., Baker, E. A., & Metzler, M. (n.d.). *Addressing social determinants of health in your community*. Community Tool Box. https://ctb.ku.edu/en/table-of-contents/overview/models-for-community-health-and-development/social-determinants-of-health/main

Browman, A. S., Destin, M., Carswell, K. L., & Svoboda, R. C. (2017). Perceptions of socioeconomic mobility influence academic persistence among low socioeconomic status students. *Journal of Experimental Social Psychology, 72*, 45–52. doi:10.1016/j.jesp.2017.03.006

Casey, K., & Patrick, S. (2020). *A promise for equitable futures: Enabling systems change to scale educational and economic mobility pathways*. Aurora Institute. https://files.eric.ed.gov/fulltext/ED611660.pdf

Centers for Disease Control and Prevention. (2019, December 19). *NCHHSTP social determinants of health*. https://cdc.gov/nchhstp/socialdeterminants/faq.html#what-are-social-determinants

Coleman, J. S. (1988). Social capital in the creation of human capital. *American Journal of Sociology, 94*, S95–S120. https://www.jstor.org/stable/2780243. doi:10.1086/228943

Fortes, K., Latham, C. L., Vaughn, S., & Preston, K. (2022). The influence of social determinants of education on nursing student persistence and professional values. *Journal of Professional Nursing, 39*, 41–53. doi:10.1016/j.profnurs.2021.11.011 PMID:35272832

Gil, H., Mannen, D., Cama, R., & Mainero, C. (n.d.). *The community living model*. https://www.countyhealthrankings.org/sites/default/files/media/document/documents/webinars/The%20Community%20Living%20Model%20White%20Paper%20-%20Gil%2C%20Mannen%2C%20Cama%2C%20and%20Mainero%20-%202-7-17.pdf

Graham, G. N. (2016). Why your ZIP code matters more than your genetic code: Promoting healthy outcomes from mother to child. *Breastfeeding Medicine, 11*(8), 396–397. doi:10.1089/bfm.2016.0113 PMID:27513279

Gudeva Nikovska, D., & Tozija, F. (2014). Social determinants of equity in access to healthcare for tuberculosis patients in republic of Macedonia – Results from a case-control study. *International Journal of Health Policy and Management, 3*(4), 199–205. doi:10.15171/ijhpm.2014.89 PMID:25279382

Hodgkinson, H. L. (1969). Walden U: A working paper. *Soundings: An Interdisciplinary Journal, 52*(2), 172–185. https://scholarworks.waldenu.edu/cgi/viewcontent.cgi?article=1000&context=university_history

Holmes, J. R., Tootoo, J. L., Chosy, E. J., Bowie, A. Y., & Starr, R. R. (2018). Examining variation in life expectancy estimates by ZIP code tabulation area (ZCTA) in Hawaii's four main counties, 2008–2012. *Preventing Chronic Disease, 15*(E114), 1–3. doi:10.5888/pcd15.180035 PMID:30240571

James, T. A. (2020, November 10). *Physicians as advocates for social change*. Harvard Medical School. https://postgraduateeducation.hms.harvard.edu/trends-medicine/physicians-advocates-social-change

Lindell, A., Morgan, A., Sugarman, B. H., Tervala, D. J., Westermann, J., Strang, K. P., Costner, K. L., Ingram, M. N., Powell, M., McCune, N. M., Jobe, R. L., Dixon-Saxon, S., Subocz, S., & Schulz, W. (2021, December 2). *Beyond the social determinants of learning™: A Walden University position paper.* https://scholarworks.waldenu.edu/white_papers/3

Liu, E. F., Rubinsky, A. D., Pacca, L., Mujahid, M., Fontil, V., DeRouen, M. C., Fields, J., Bibbins-Domingo, K., & Lyles, C. R. (2022, February). Examining neighborhood socioeconomic status as a mediator of racial/ethnic disparities in hypertension control across two San Francisco health systems. *Circulation: Cardiovascular Quality and Outcomes, 15*(2), e008256. doi:10.1161/CIRCOUTCOMES.121.008256 PMID:35098728

Lopes, A. S. P. P., & Carreira, P. M. R. (2020). Adult workers in higher education: Enhancing social mobility. *Education + Training, 62*(9), 1101–1117. doi:10.1108/ET-03-2018-0056

McDuff, N., Hughes, A., Tatam, J., Morrow, E., & Ross, F. (2020). Improving equality of opportunity in higher education through the adoption of an Inclusive Curriculum Framework. *Widening Participation and Lifelong Learning: the Journal of the Institute for Access Studies and the European Access Network, 22*(2), 83–121. doi:10.5456/WPLL.22.2.83

Mezirow, J. (1978). *Education for perspective transformation: Women's reentry programs in community colleges.* Center for Adult Education, Teachers College, Columbia University.

Miller, S. (1997). Futures work: Recognising [sic] the social determinants of change. *Social Alternatives, 16*(1), 57–58.

Mogford, E., Gould, L., & DeVoght, A. (2011). Teaching critical health literacy in the US as a means to action on the social determinants of health. *Health Promotion International, 26*(1), 4–13. doi:10.1093/heapro/daq049 PMID:20729240

Morgan, A. M., Jobe, R. L., Konopa, J. K., & Downs, L. D. (2022). Quality assurance, meet quality appreciation: Using appreciative inquiry to define faculty quality standards. *Higher Learning Research Communications, 12*(1), 98–111. doi:10.5590/HLRC.2022.12.1.1301

Mühlpachr, P. (2008). Social determinants of education in the postmodern society. *Santalka: Filologija, Edukologija, 16*(4), 61–67. https://repozytorium.amu.edu.pl/bitstream/10593/14522/1/KSE_2_4_2013_Pavel_Muhlpachr.pdf

Nussbaum, M. (2000). Women's capabilities and social justice. *Journal of Human Development, 1*(2), 219–247. doi:10.1080/713678045

Nussbaum, M. (2006). Education and democratic citizenship: Capabilities and quality education. *Journal of Human Development, 7*(3), 385–395. doi:10.1080/14649880600815974

Opportunity Insights. (n.d.). *The opportunity atlas.* https://www.opportunityatlas.org/

Orminski, E. (2021, June 30). *Your zip code is more important than your genetic code.* National Community Reinvestment Coalition. https://ncrc.org/your-zip-code-is-more-important-than-your-genetic-code/

Prättälä, R. S., & Puska, P. (2012). Social determinants of health behaviours [sic] and social change. *European Journal of Public Health, 22*(2), 166. doi:10.1093/eurpub/ckr211 PMID:22241756

Robertson, K. N. (2016). Considering the social determinants of equity in international development evaluation guidance documents. *The Canadian Journal of Program Evaluation, 30*(3), 344–373. doi:10.3138/cjpe.30.3.07

Roeder, A. (2014, August 4). *Zip code better predictor of health than genetic code*. Harvard T. H. Chan School of Public Health. https://www.hsph.harvard.edu/news/features/zip-code-better-predictor-of-health-than-genetic-code/

Sanderson, C. D., Hollinger-Smith, L. M., & Cox, K. (2021). Developing a social determinants of learning™ framework: A case study. *Nursing Education Perspectives, 42*(4), 205–211. doi:10.1097/01.NEP.0000000000000810 PMID:33935243

Sen, A. (1999). *Development as freedom*. Oxford University Press.

Sen, A. (2004). *Rationality and freedom*. The Belknap Press of Harvard University Press. doi:10.2307/j.ctv1dv0td8

Stewart, B. (1951). Some determinants of social change. *The Journal of Social Psychology, 33*(1), 33–49. doi:10.1080/00224545.1951.9921799

University of Southern California Equity Research Institute and PolicyLink. (2022). *The national equity atlas*. https://nationalequityatlas.org/

University of Wisconsin School of Medicine and Public Health. (n.d.). *About the neighborhood atlas®*. https://www.neighborhoodatlas.medicine.wisc.edu/

Virchow, R. (1985). *Collected essays on public health and epidemiology* (Vol. 1). Science History Publications. (Original work published 1848)

Walden University. (2017). *Walden 2020. A vision for social change report*. https://www.waldenu.edu/-/media/walden/files/about-walden/walden-university-2017-social-change-report-final-v-2.pdf?rev=5ded98a6d84e4a0096d02c9ec0f458af&hash=3CBA4D20AF7FA7F23BC21D69B2A9EB37

Walden University. (2021). *Walden University's AI-powered Tutor: Julian™*. https://www.waldenu.edu/news-and-events/events/walden-universitys-ai-powered-tutor-julian

Walden University. (n.d.). *Walden and social change*. https://academicguides.waldenu.edu/social-change/mission

White, M. L., Henderson, D. F., Smith, S. G., & Bell, M. P. (2022). A new look at an old problem: A positive psychology lens on discrimination – identity builders and work-related outcomes. *Human Resource Management Review, 32*(3), 1–15. doi:10.1016/j.hrmr.2021.100858

Wienclaw, R. A. (2021). *Adult education as social capital*. Salem Press Encyclopedia.

Woods-Jaeger, B., Kleven, L., Sexton, C., O'Malley, D., Cho, B., Bronston, S., McGowan, K., & Starr, D. (2022, May 23). Two generations thrive: Bidirectional collaboration among researchers, practitioners, and parents to promote culturally responsive trauma research, practice, and policy. *Psychological Trauma: Theory, Research, Practice, and Policy*. Advance online publication. doi:10.1037/tra0001209 PMID:35604710

World Health Organization, Commission on Social Determinants of Health. (2010). *A conceptual framework for action on the social determinants of health.* https://apps.who.int/iris/bitstream/handle/10665/44489/9789241500852_eng.pdf

Yob, I. M. (2018). Conceptual framework for a curriculum in social change. *Journal of Social Change, 10*(1), 71–80. doi:10.5590/JOSC.2018.10.1.06

ADDITIONAL READING

Heckler, M. (1984, January). *Report of the secretary's task force on black & minority health* (Vol. 1). https://minorityhealth.hhs.gov/assets/pdf/checked/1/ANDERSON.pdf

Weinstock, D. M. (2010). Can thinking about justice in health help us in thinking about justice in education? *Theory and Research in Education, 8*(1), 79–91. doi:10.1177/1477878509356344

Compilation of References

Academic Development and Diversity Team. (2022, May 10). *Inclusive pedagogy and practice.* Sheffield Hallam University. https://blogs.shu.ac.uk/add/inclusive-pedagogy-and-practice/#II

Adams, J. S. (1963). Toward an understanding of inequity. *Journal of Abnormal and Social Psychology, 67*(5), 422–436. doi:10.1037/h0040968 PMID:14081885

Adeoye, B., & Lynn, L. K. (2020, October 1). *Learning preferences and support opportunities for African national doctoral students* [Poster presentation]. Walden University Research Conference 2020. https://scholarworks.waldenu.edu/cgi/viewcontent.cgi?article=1046&context=researchconference

Agarwal, S., Menon, V., & Jaber, W. A. (2015). Residential zip code influences outcomes following hospitalization for acute pulmonary embolism in the United States. *Vascular Medicine, 20*(5), 439–446. doi:10.1177/1358863X15592486 PMID:26163399

Ahn, M. Y., & Davis, H. H. (2020). Four domains of students' sense of belonging to university. *Studies in Higher Education, 45*(3), 622–634. doi:10.1080/03075079.2018.1564902

AlFuqaha, I. N. (2013). Pedagogy redefined: Frameworks of learning approaches prevalent in the current digital information age. *Journal of Educational Technology, 10*(1), 36–45. https://eric.ed.gov/?id=EJ1101795

Altman, S. H., Stith Butler, A., & Shern, L. (Eds.). (2016). *Assessing progress on the institute of medicine report the future of nursing.* National Academies Press. doi:10.17226/21838

Amayo, J., Heron, S., Spell, N., & Gooding, H. (2021). Twelve tips for inclusive teaching. *MedEdPublish, 10*(81). Advance online publication. doi:10.15694/mep.2021.000081.1

American Association of Colleges and Universities. (2022, June 8). *Statement by AAC&U and PEN America regarding recent legislative restrictions on teaching and learning.* https://www.aacu.org/newsroom/statement-regarding-recent-legislative-restrictions-on-teaching-and-learning

American Association of Colleges of Nursing. (2019). *AACN's vision for academic nursing. White paper.* https://www.aacnnursing.org/Portals/42/News/White-Papers/Vision-Academic-Nursing.pdf

American Association of Colleges of Nursing. (2021a). *Diversity, equity, and inclusion in academic nursing: AACN position statement.* https://www.aacnnursing.org/Portals/42/News/Position-Statements/Diversity-Inclusion.pdf

American Association of Colleges of Nursing. (2021b). *The essentials: Core competencies for professional nursing education.* American Association of Colleges of Nursing. https://www.aacnnursing.org/portals/42/downloads/essentials/essentials-draft-document.pdf

American Nurses Association (ANA). (2021, January 25). *Introducing the national commission to address racism in nursing*. https://www.nursingworld.org/news/news-releases/2021/leading-nursing-organizations-launch-the-national-commission-to-address-racism-in-nursing/

Andermann, A. (2016). Taking action on the social determinants of health in clinical practice: A framework for health professionals. *CMAJ, JAMC, 188*(17–18), E474–E483. doi:10.1503/cmaj.160177 PMID:27503870

Antibi, M. A. (2003). *La constante macabre, ou, comment a-t-on découragé des générations d'élèves*. Math'Adore.

Argyris, C. (1991, May). Teaching smart people how to learn. *Harvard Business Review, 69*(3), 99–109. https://hbr.org/1991/05/teaching-smart-people-how-to-learn

Argyris, C., & Schön, D. (1974). *Theory in practice: Increasing professional effectiveness*. Jossey Bass.

Argyris, C., & Schön, D. (1978). *Organizational learning: A theory of action perspective*. Addison-Wesley Publishing Co.

Arroyo, A. T., & Gasman, M. (2014). An HBCU-based educational approach for Black college student success: Toward a framework with implications for all institutions. *American Journal of Education, 121*(1), 57–85. doi:10.1086/678112

Arsyad Arrafii, M. (2020). Grades and grade inflation: Exploring teachers' grading practices in Indonesian EFL secondary school classrooms. *Pedagogy, Culture & Society, 28*(3), 477–499. doi:10.1080/14681366.2019.1663246

Artiga, S., & Hinton, E. (2018, May 10). *Beyond health care: The role of social determinants in promoting health and health equity*. Kaiser Family Foundation. https://www.kff.org/racial-equity-and-health-policy/issue-brief/beyond-health-care-the-role-of-social-determinants-in-promoting-health-and-health-equity/

Artiga, S., Orgera, K., & Pham, O. (2020, March 1). *Disparities in health and health care: Five key questions and answers*. Kaiser Family Foundation. https://files.kff.org/attachment/Issue-Brief-Disparities-in-Health-and-Health-Care-Five-Key-Questions-and-Answers

Asep, H. S. G., & Bandung, Y. (2019, July 9–10). A design of continuous user verification for online exam proctoring on m-learning. *2019 International Conference on Electrical Engineering and Informatics*, Bandung, Indonesia. 10.1109/ICEEI47359.2019.8988786

Association of Executive Search and Leadership Consultants. (n.d.). *Checking your blind spot: Ways to find and fix unconscious bias. Executive Talent*. https://www.aesc./insights/magazine/article/checking-your-blind-spots

Badia, A., Garcia, C., & Meneses, J. (2017). Approaches to teaching online: Exploring factors influencing teachers in a fully online university. *British Journal of Educational Technology, 48*(6), 1193–1207. doi:10.1111/bjet.12475

Baker, R., Dee, T. S., Evans, B., & John, J. (2018). *Bias in online classes: Evidence from a field experiment* (CEPA Working Paper No. 18–03). Stanford Center for Education and Policy Analysis. https://cepa.stanford.edu/sites/default/files/wp18-03-201803.pdf

Baker, R., Dee, T., Evans, B., & John, J. (2018). *Bias in online classes: Evidence from a field experiment*. Stanford Center for Education Policy Analysis. https://cepa.stanford.edu/wp18-03

Bakshi, S., James, A., Hennelly, M. O., Karani, R., Palermo, A.-G., Jakubowski, A., Ciccariello, C., & Atkinson, H. (2015). The human rights and social justice scholars program: A collaborative model for preclinical training in social medicine. *Annals of Global Health, 81*(2), 290–297. doi:10.1016/j.aogh.2015.04.001 PMID:26088098

Balzer Carr, B., & London, R. (2019). The role of learning support services in university students' educational outcomes. *Journal of College Student Retention, 21*(1), 78–104. doi:10.1177/1521025117690159

Compilation of References

Banerjee, S., & Ragon, B. (2020, October 1–2). *Assessing the effect of global mindset on the development of leadership competency* [Paper presentation]. Walden University Research Conference 2020. https://scholarworks.waldenu.edu/researchconference/2020/papers/10/

Baron, H. (1963). History of Chicago school segregation to 1953. *Equity & Excellence in Education*, *1*(1), 17–20. doi:10.1080/0020486630010106

Baron, R. J., & Khullar, D. (2021). Building trust to promote a more equitable health care system. *Annals of Internal Medicine*, *174*(4), 548–549. doi:10.7326/M20-6984 PMID:33524292

Beisenherz, P. C., Dantonio, M., & Richardson, L. (2001). The learning cycle and instructional conversations. *Science Scope*, *24*(4), 34–38.

Bekki, J. M., Dalrymple, O., & Butler, C. S. (2012, October 3–6). *A mastery-based learning approach for undergraduate engineering programs* [Conference publication]. 2012 Frontiers in Education Conference Proceedings, Seattle, WA, United States. 10.1109/FIE.2012.6462253

Bell, D. (2021). Becoming an anti-racist intuition: The challenges facing higher education. *International Journal of Multiple Research Approaches*, *13*(1), 22–25. doi:10.29034/ijmra.v13n1commentary2

Bell, D. A. Jr. (1976). Serving two masters: Integration ideas and client interests in school desegregation litigation. *The Yale Law Journal*, *85*(4), 470–516. doi:10.2307/795339

Bell, D. A. JrBoard of Education and the Interest-Convergence Dilemma. (1980). Brown v. board of education and the interest-convergence dilemma. *Harvard Law Review*, *93*(3), 518–533. doi:10.2307/1340546

Bendsen, A. H., Egendal, J., Jelsbak, V. A., Kristensen, M., Mikkelsen, T. R., & Pasgaard, N. J. (2018, November). Student engagement and perceptions of quality in flexible online study programs. *Proceedings of the European Conference on E-Learning*, 45–53. https://www.ucviden.dk/ws/portalfiles/portal/93048292/Presentation_ECEL_engagement_in_online_studies.pdf

Bensimon, E. M. (2006). Learning equity-mindedness: Equality in educational outcomes. *Academic Workplace*, *17*(1), 2–6, 18–21. https://cpb-us-e1.wpmucdn.com/sites.usc.edu/dist/6/735/files/2016/01/Bensimon_Learning-Equity-Mindedness-Equality-in-Educational-Outcomes.pdf

Bensimon, E. M. (2005). Closing the achievement gap in higher education: An organizational learning perspective. *New Directions for Higher Education*, *131*(131), 99–111. doi:10.1002/he.190

Bensimon, E. M. (2007). The underestimated significance of practitioner knowledge in the scholarship of student success. *The Review of Higher Education*, *30*(4), 441–469. doi:10.1353/rhe.2007.0032

Bensimon, E. M., Hao, L., & Tomas Bustillos, L. (2006). Measuring the state of equity in public higher education. In P. Gándara, G. Orfield, & C. L. Horn (Eds.), *Expanding opportunity in higher education: Leveraging promise* (pp. 143–164). State University of New York Press.

Berger, W. (2014). *A more beautiful question: The power of inquiry to spark breakthrough ideas*. Bloomsbury.

Berkman, L. F., Kawachi, I., & Glymour, M. M. (Eds.). (2000). *Social epidemiology*. Oxford University Press.

Berkman, L. F., & Syme, S. L. (1979). Social networks, host resistance, and mortality: A nine-year follow-up study of Alameda County residents. *American Journal of Epidemiology*, *109*(2), 186–204. doi:10.1093/oxfordjournals.aje.a112674 PMID:425958

Bhatt, J. (2018, May 16). *Your zip code, your health.* American Hospital Association. https://www.aha.org/news/insights-and-analysis/2018-05-16-your-zip-code-your-health

Bjørnskov, C., & Méon, P.-G. (2013). Is trust the missing root of institutions, education, and development? *Public Choice, 157*(3–4), 641–669. doi:10.100711127-013-0069-7

Bleich, M. R., MacWilliams, B. R., & Schmidt, B. J. (2015). Advancing diversity through inclusive excellence in nursing education. *Journal of Professional Nursing, 31*(2), 89–94. doi:10.1016/j.profnurs.2014.09.003 PMID:25839947

Bleser, W. K. (2021). *Pandemic-driven health policies to address social needs and health equity.* Robert Wood Johnson Foundation. https://www.rwjf.org/en/library/research/2022/03/pandemic-driven-health-policies-to-address-social-needs-and-health-equity.html

Bloom, B. S. (1968). Learning for mastery. Instruction and curriculum. Regional Education Laboratory for the Carolinas and Virginia, topical papers and reprints, number 1. *Evaluation Comment, 1*(2). https://programs.honolulu.hawaii.edu/intranet/sites/programs.honolulu.hawaii.edu.intranet/files/upstf-student-success-bloom-1968.pdf

Bloom, B. S., Hastings, J. T., & Madaus, G. (1971). *Handbook on formative and summative evaluation of student learning.* McGraw-Hill.

Bloomberg. (2021, October 27). *When addressing the abilities community, words matter and people come first.* https://www.bloomberg.com/company/stories/when-addressing-the-abilities-community-words-matter-and-people-come-first

Bogler, R., Caspi, A., & Roccas, S. (2013). Transformational and passive leadership: An initial investigation of university instructors as leaders in a virtual learning environment. *Educational Management Administration & Leadership, 41*(3), 372–392. doi:10.1177/1741143212474805

Bollela, V. R., Germani, A. C. C. G., de Holanda Campos, H., & Amaral, E. (Eds.). (2015). *Community-based education for the health professions: Learning from the Brazilian experience.* https://www.academia.edu/22090649/COMMUNITY_BASED_EDUCATION_FOR_THE_HEALTH_PROFESSIONS_Learning_from_the_Brazilian_Experience

Boud, D., & Molloy, E. (2013). Rethinking models of feedback for learning: The challenge of design. *Assessment & Evaluation in Higher Education, 38*(6), 698–712. doi:10.1080/02602938.2012.691462

Bourke, R. (2018). Self-assessment to incite learning in higher education: Developing ontological awareness. *Assessment & Evaluation in Higher Education, 43*(5), 827–839. doi:10.1080/02602938.2017.1411881

Boyer, E. L. (1990). *Scholarship reconsidered: Priorities of the professorate.* Carnegie Foundation for the Advancement of Teaching.

Bradshaw, M. J., & Hultquist, B. L. (2016). *Innovative teaching strategies in nursing and related health professions.* Jones & Bartlett Learning.

Braveman, P. (2006). Health disparities and health equity: Concepts and measurement. *Annual Review of Public Health, 27*(1), 167–194. doi:10.1146/annurev.publhealth.27.021405.102103 PMID:16533114

Braveman, P., & Gruskin, S. (2003). Defining equity in health. *Journal of Epidemiology and Community Health, 57*(4), 254–258. doi:10.1136/jech.57.4.254 PMID:12646539

Brennan Ramirez, L. K., Baker, E. A., & Metzler, M. (n.d.). *Addressing social determinants of health in your community.* Community Tool Box. https://ctb.ku.edu/en/table-of-contents/overview/models-for-community-health-and-development/social-determinants-of-health/main

Compilation of References

Brockmier-Sommers, D. K., & Martin, J. L. (2020, June 16). *Using empathy, genuineness and unconditional positive regard to build safety for discussing difficult topics in the online classroom* [Online conference session]. OLC Innovate. https://onlinelearningconsortium.org/olc-innovate-2020-session-page/?session=8507&kwds=

Brookfield, S. D. (2003). Racializing the discourse of adult education. *Harvard Educational Review*, *73*(4), 497–523. doi:10.17763/haer.73.4.a54508r0464863u2

Browman, A. S., Destin, M., Carswell, K. L., & Svoboda, R. C. (2017). Perceptions of socioeconomic mobility influence academic persistence among low socioeconomic status students. *Journal of Experimental Social Psychology*, *72*, 45–52. doi:10.1016/j.jesp.2017.03.006

Burgstahler, S. E., & Cory, R. C. (2008). *Universal design in higher education: From principles to practice*. Harvard Education Press.

Butkus, N. (2019, May 17). *Separate and unequal: School segregation in Louisiana 65 years after Brown v. board*. Louisiana Budget Project. https://bit.ly/2L1xAXV

Cabreros, I. (2022, March 27). Why an algorithm can never truly be 'fair.' *Los Angeles Times*. https://www.latimes.com/opinion/story/2022-03-27/algorithms-unfair-racial-bias-math

Cahalan, M. W., Addison, M., Brunt, N., Patel, P. R., & Perna, L. W. (2021). *Indicators of higher education equity in the United States: 2021 historical trend report*. The Pell Institute for the Study of Opportunity in Higher Education, Council for Opportunity in Education & Alliance for Higher Education and Democracy of the University of Pennsylvania. http://pellinstitute.org/downloads/publications-Indicators_of_Higher_Education_Equity_in_the_US_2021_Historical_Trend_Report.pdf

Callahan, R. E. (1964). *Education and the cult of efficiency: A study of the social forces that have shaped the administration of the public schools*. University of Chicago Press. doi:10.7208/chicago/9780226216904.001.0001

Cameron, K. (2008). *Positive leadership: Strategies for extraordinary performance*. Berrett-Koehler Publishers.

Cândido, C. J. F., & Santos, S. P. (2015). Strategy implementation: What is the failure rate? *Journal of Management & Organization*, *21*(2), 237–262. doi:10.1017/jmo.2014.77

Canning, N. (2010). Playing with heutagogy: Exploring strategies to empower mature learners in higher education. *Journal of Further and Higher Education*, *34*(1), 59–71. doi:10.1080/03098770903477102

Carlzon, J. (1989). *Moments of truth*. Ballinger Publishing.

Carnevale, A. P., Cheah, B., & Van Der Werf, M. (2019). *A first try at ROI: Ranking 4,500 colleges*. Georgetown University, Center for Education and the Workforce. https://1gyhoq479ufd3yna29x7ubjn-wpengine.netdna-ssl.com/wp-content/uploads/College_ROI.pdf

Carozza, L., & Gennaro, S. (2021). Post-pandemic pedagogy. Compassionate and caring course curriculum in the digital university. In J. M. Valenzano III, (Ed.), *Post-pandemic pedagogy: A paradigm shift* (pp. 57–72). Lexington Books.

Carter, B. M., & Phillips, B. C. (2021, February 01). Revolutionizing the nursing curriculum. *Creative Nursing*, *1*(1), 25–30. doi:10.1891/CRNR-D-20-00072 PMID:33574168

Casey, K., & Patrick, S. (2020). *A promise for equitable futures: Enabling systems change to scale educational and economic mobility pathways*. Aurora Institute. https://files.eric.ed.gov/fulltext/ED611660.pdf

Cash, C. M., Cox, T. D., & Hahs-Vaughn, D. L. (2021). Distance educators' attitudes and actions towards inclusive teaching practices. *The Journal of Scholarship of Teaching and Learning*, *21*(2), 15–42. doi:10.14434/josotl.v21i2.27949

Caskey, M. M., Stevens, D. D., & Yeo, M. (2020). Examining doctoral student development of a researcher identity: Using the Draw a Researcher Test. *Impacting Education*, *5*(1). Advance online publication. doi:10.5195/ie.2020.92

Cassel, J., & Tyroler, H. A. (1961). Epidemiological studies of culture change. I. Health status and recency of industrialization. *Archives of Environmental Health*, *3*(1), 25–33. doi:10.1080/00039896.1961.10662969 PMID:13691334

CAST. (n.d.). *About Universal Design for Learning*. https://www.cast.org/impact/universal-design-for-learning-udl

Centers for Disease Control [CDC]. (2022, May 2). *People with certain medical conditions*. https://www.cdc.gov/coronavirus/2019-ncov/need-extra-precautions/people-with-medical-conditions.html

Centers for Disease Control and Prevention. (1999). Achievements in public health, 1900–1999: Control of infectious diseases. *MMWR*, *48*(29), 621–629. https://www.cdc.gov/mmwr/preview/mmwrhtml/mm4829a1.htm#:~:text=In%201900%2C%20the%20three%20leading,than%205%20years%20(1) PMID:10458535

Centers for Disease Control and Prevention. (2019, December 19). *NCHHSTP social determinants of health*. https://cdc.gov/nchhstp/socialdeterminants/faq.html#what-are-social-determinants

Cha, A. E., & Cohen, R. A. (2022). Demographic variation in health insurance coverage: United states, 2020. *National Health Statistics Reports*, *169*, 1–15. doi:10.15620/cdc:113097 PMID:35166656

Chapin, C. V. (1924). Deaths among taxpayers and nontaxpayers income tax, Providence, 1865. *American Journal of Public Health*, *4*(8), 647–651. doi:10.2105/AJPH.14.8.647-a PMID:18011285

Cheddadi, S., & Bouache, M. (2021, August 17–21). *Improving equity and access to higher education using artificial intelligence* [Conference presentation]. 16th International Conference on Computer Science & Education, Lancaster, UK. 10.1109/ICCSE51940.2021.9569548

Chen, L., Chen, P., & Lin, Z. (2020). Artificial intelligence in education: A review. *IEEE Access: Practical Innovations, Open Solutions*, *8*, 75264–75278. doi:10.1109/ACCESS.2020.2988510

Chetty, R., Hendren, N., & Katz, L. F. (2016). The effects of exposure to better neighborhoods on children: New evidence from the moving to opportunity experiment. *The American Economic Review*, *106*(4), 855–902. doi:10.1257/aer.20150572 PMID:29546974

Chowdhury, F. (2018). Grade inflation: Causes, consequences and cure. *Journal of Education and Learning*, *7*(6), 86–92. doi:10.5539/jel.v7n6p86

Christie, H., Tett, L., Cree, V. E., Hounsell, J., & McCune, V. (2008). 'A real rollercoaster of confidence and emotions': Learning to be a university student. *Studies in Higher Education*, *33*(5), 567–581. doi:10.1080/03075070802373040

Chun, E., & Evans, A. (2010, February 8). Linking diversity and accountability through accreditation standards. *Hispanic Outlook*. http://ednachun.com/wp/articles/

Cipolla, C. M. (1992). *Miasmas and disease: Public health and environment in the pre-industrial age*. Yale University Press. doi:10.12987/9780300156928

Clark, M. (2021, April 8). Students of color are getting flagged to their teachers because testing software can't see them. *The Verge*. https://www.theverge.com/2021/4/8/22374386/proctorio-racial-bias-issues-opencv-facial-detection-schools-tests-remote-learning

Cohrs, J. C., Christie, D. J., White, M. P., & Das, C. (2013). Contributions of positive psychology to peace: Toward global well-being and resilience. *The American Psychologist*, *68*(7), 590–600. doi:10.1037/a0032089 PMID:24128320

Coleman, J. S. (1988). Social capital in the creation of human capital. *American Journal of Sociology*, *94*, S95–S120. https://www.jstor.org/stable/2780243. doi:10.1086/228943

Collier, P. J., & Morgan, D. L. (2008). Is that paper due today?: Differences in first-generation and traditional college students' understandings of faculty expectations. *Higher Education*, *55*(4), 425–446. doi:10.100710734-007-9065-5

Committee on the Robert Wood Johnson Foundation Initiative on the Future of Nursing at the Institute of Medicine, Robert Wood Johnson Foundation, & Institute of Medicine (United States). (2011). *The future of nursing: Leading change, advancing health*. National Academies Press. https://www.ncbi.nlm.nih.gov/books/NBK209880/

Compagnucci, L., & Spigarelli, F. (2020). The third mission of the university: A systematic literature review on potentials and constraints. *Technological Forecasting and Social Change*, *161*(120284), 120284. Advance online publication. doi:10.1016/j.techfore.2020.120284

Comprehensive Center Network. (2020). *Tools and guidance for evaluating bias in instructional materials: A Region 8 Comprehensive Center report*. https://files.eric.ed.gov/fulltext/ED612040.pdf

Conwill, W. L. (2009). Factors affecting the presence of African American males in counseling and psychology training program faculties. In H. T. Frierson, J. H. Whyche, & W. Pearson, Jr. (Eds.) Black American males in higher education: Research, programs, and academe (Vol. 6, pp. 287–316). Emerald Group Publishing. doi:10.1108/S1479-3644(2009)0000007017

Cook, C. (2017). 20th Pauline Cerasoli lecture: The sunk cost fallacy. *Journal of Physical Therapy Education*, *31*(3), 10–14. doi:10.1097/00001416-201731030-00005

Coombs, L. C. (1941). Economic differentials in causes of death. *Medical Care*, *1*(3), 246–255.

Cooperrider, D. L. (2018). A time for action: Appreciative inquiry, positive peace and the making of a Nobel nomination. *AI Practitioner*, *20*(1), 7–18. doi:10.12781/978-1-907549-34-2-2

Cooperrider, D. L., & Srivastva, S. (1987). Appreciative inquiry in organizational life. *Research in Organizational Change and Development*, *1*, 129–169.

Cooperrider, D. L., & Whitney, D. (2005). *Appreciative inquiry: A positive revolution in change*. Berrett-Koehler Publishers.

Cooperrider, D. L., Whitney, D. D., & Stavros, J. (2008). *The appreciative inquiry handbook: For leaders of change*. Berrett-Koehler Publishers.

Council for Accreditation of Counseling and Related Educational Programs. (2016). *2016 CACREP standards*. https://www.cacrep.org/for-programs/2016-cacrep-standards/

Countryman, P. (1963). The Philadelphia experiment. *Equity & Excellence in Education*, *1*(1), 14–16. doi:10.1080/0020486630010104

Crenshaw, K. (1989). Demarginalizing the intersection of race and sex: A Black feminist critique of antidiscrimination doctrine, feminist theory and antiracist politics. *University of Chicago Legal Forum*, *1989*(1), 8. https://chicagounbound.uchicago.edu/uclf/vol1989/iss1/8

Crooks, N., Smith, A., & Lofton, S. (2021). Building bridges and capacity for Black, Indigenous, and scholars of color in the era of COVID-19 and Black Lives Matter. *Nursing Outlook*, *69*(5), 892–902. doi:10.1016/j.outlook.2021.03.022 PMID:34092370

Crowley, D. M., Scott, J. T., Long, E. C., Green, L., Giray, C., Gay, B., Israel, A., Storace, R., McCauley, M., & Donovan, M. (2021). Cultivating researcher-policymaker partnerships: A randomized controlled trial of a model for training public psychologists. *The American Psychologist, 76*(8), 1307–1322. doi:10.1037/amp0000880 PMID:35113595

Csikszentmihalyi, M. (1990). *Flow: The psychology of optimal experience.* Harper and Row.

Culver, S. (2010). Course grades, quality of student engagement, and students' evaluation of instructor. *International Journal on Teaching and Learning in Higher Education, 22*(3), 331–336. https://files.eric.ed.gov/fulltext/EJ938568.pdf

Cunliffe, A. L. (2016). On becoming a critically reflexive practitioner redux: What does it mean to "be" reflexive? *Journal of Management Education, 40*(6), 740–746. doi:10.1177/1052562916668919

Cushman, T. (2003). Who best to tame grade inflation? *Academic Questions, 16*(4), 48–56. doi:10.100712129-003-1063-1

Darby, F., & Lang, J. M. (2019). *Small teaching online: Applying learning science in online classes.* John Wiley & Sons.

Delgado, R., & Stefancic, J. (1998). Critical race theory: Past, present, and future. *Current Legal Problems, 1*(51), 467–491. doi:10.1093/clp/51.1.467

Dell, C. A., Dell, T. F., & Blackwell, T. L. (2015). Applying universal design for learning in online courses: Pedagogical and practical considerations. *The Journal of Educators Online, 13*(2), 166–192. doi:10.9743/JEO.2015.2.1

Desmond-Hellman, S., Garcia, M., & Voight, M. (2021). *Equitable value: Promoting economic mobility and social justice through postsecondary education.* Postsecondary Value Commission. https://postsecondaryvalue.org/wp-content/uploads/2021/07/PVC-Final-Report-FINAL-7.2.pdf

Deutsch, M. (1963). The disadvantaged child and the learning process. *Equity & Excellence in Education, 1*(1), 11–12. doi:10.1080/0020486630010102

Devlin, M., & McKay, J. (2018). Teaching inclusively online in a massified university system. *Widening Participation and Lifelong Learning: the Journal of the Institute for Access Studies and the European Access Network, 20*(1), 146–166. doi:10.5456/WPLL.20.1.146

DeWeese, S. V., & Randolph, J. J. (2011, February 14). *Effective use of correctives in masterly learning* [Paper presentation]. Association of Teacher Educators National Conference, Orlando, FL, United States. https://files.eric.ed.gov/fulltext/ED523991.pdf

DiAngelo, R. (2018). *White fragility: Why it's so hard for white people to talk about racism.* Beacon Press.

Dick, J. C. (1975). How to justify a distribution of earnings. *Philosophy & Public Affairs, 4*(3), 248–272. https://www.jstor.org/stable/2265085

Doherty, R. A. (2007). Education, neoliberalism and the consumer citizen: After the golden age of egalitarian reform. *Critical Studies in Education, 48*(2), 269–288. doi:10.1080/17508480701494275

Donnelly, G. (2016). In praise of Harriet Tubman; Nurse, spy, abolitionist. *Holistic Nursing Practice, 30*(4), 191. doi:10.1097/HNP.0000000000000155 PMID:27309407

Douglas, P. H. (1963). Teaching in a ghetto school. *Equity & Excellence in Education, 1*(1), 20–21. doi:10.1080/0020486630010107

Dowd, A. C. (2007). Community colleges as gateways and gatekeepers: Moving beyond the access 'saga' toward outcome equity. *Harvard Educational Review, 77*(4), 1–13. doi:10.17763/haer.77.4.1233g31741157227

Dowd, A. C., & Bensimon, E. M. (2015). *Engaging the "race question": Accountability and equity in U.S. higher education*. Teachers College Press.

Drake, R., & Ogelsby, A. (2020). Humanity is not a thing: Disrupting white supremacy in k-12 social emotional learning. *Journal of Critical Thought and Praxis*, *10*(1), 1–22. doi:10.31274/jctp.11549

Dunlap, J. C., Verma, G., & Johnson, H. L. (2016). Presence+Experience: A framework for the purposeful design of presence in online courses. *TechTrends*, *60*(2), 145–151. doi:10.100711528-016-0029-4

Eckel, P., & Trower, C. (2019, February 14). Stop planning! *Insider Higher Ed*. https://www.insidehighered.com/views/2019/02/14/colleges-need-rethink-strategic-planning-opinion

Egger, G. (2012). In search of a germ theory equivalent for chronic disease. *Preventing Chronic Disease*, *9*(E95). Advance online publication. doi:10.5888/pcd9.110301 PMID:22575080

Eilers, A. M. (2019). *Incorporating African American vernacular English in education: Fostering linguistic diversity within Mississippi K-12 classrooms* [Honors thesis, University of Mississippi]. eGrove. https://egrove.olemiss.edu/hon_thesis/1025/

Elson, R. J., Gupta, S., & Krispin, J. (2018). Students' perceptions of instructor interaction, feedback, and course effectiveness in a large class environment. *Journal of Instructional Pedagogies*, *20*. https://files.eric.ed.gov/fulltext/EJ1178738.pdf

Ely, E. (2021). Diversity, equity & inclusion statements on academic library websites. *Information Technology and Libraries*, *40*(4), 1–22. doi:10.6017/ital.v40i4.13353

Emdin, C. (2014, April 2). 5 new approaches to teaching and learning: The next frontier. *HuffPost*. https://www.huffpost.com/entry/5-new-approaches-to-teaching-strategies_b_4697731?ir=India&adsSiteOverride=in

Emdin, C. (2020, July 24). Teaching isn't about managing behavior: It's about reaching students where they really are. *The Atlantic*. https://www.theatlantic.com/education/archive/2020/07/reality-pedagogy-teaching-form-protest/614554/

Epstein, S. (1998). *Constructive thinking: The key to emotional intelligence*. Praeger Publishers.

Epstein, S. (2012). Emotional intelligence from the perspective of cognitive-experiential self-theory. *The International Journal of Transformative Emotional Intelligence*, *1*, 108–120. http://eitri.org/2015/11/14/emotional-intelligence-from-the-perspective-of-cognitive-experiential-self-theory/

Eraut, M. (2006). Feedback. *Learning in Health and Social Care*, *5*(3), 111–118. doi:10.1111/j.1473-6861.2006.00129.x

Evans-Amalu, K., & Claravall, E. B. (2021). Inclusive online teaching and digital learning: Lessons learned in the time of pandemic and beyond. *Journal of Curriculum Studies Research.*, *3*(1), i–iii. doi:10.46303/jcsr.2021.4

Evan-Winters, V. E. (2021). Race and gender intersectionality in education. In Oxford Research Encyclopedia. doi:10.1093/acrefore/9780190264093.013.1345

Families, U. S. A. (2018). *Latino health inequities compared to non-Hispanic whites*. https://www.familiesusa.org/resources/latino-health-inequities-compared-to-non-hispanic-whites/

Fee, E., & Bu, L. (2010). The origins of public health nursing: The henry street visiting nurse service. *American Journal of Public Health*, *100*(7), 1206–1207. doi:10.2105/AJPH.2009.186049 PMID:20466947

Ferrer, J., Ringer, A., Saville, K., Parris, M. A., & Kashi, K. (2022). Student' motivation and engagement in higher education: The importance of attitude to online learning. *Higher Education*, *83*(2), 317–338. doi:10.100710734-020-00657-5

Finefter-Rosenbluh, I., & Levinson, M. (2015). What is wrong with grade inflation (if anything)? *Philosophical Inquiry in Education, 23*(1), 3–21. doi:10.7202/1070362ar

Fish, M. C., Gefen, D. R., Kaczetow, W., Winograd, G., & Futtersak-Goldberg, R. (2016). Development and validation of the college campus environment scale (CCES): Promoting positive college experiences. *Innovative Higher Education, 41*(2), 153–165. doi:10.100710755-015-9337-4

Fornaciari, C. J., & Lund Dean, K. (2014). The 21st-century syllabus: From pedagogy to andragogy. *Journal of Management Education, 38*(5), 701–723. doi:10.1177/1052562913504763

Foronda, C., Prather, S., Baptiste, D. L., & Luctkar-Flude, M. (2022, March 25). Cultural humility toolkit. *Nurse Educator*. Advance online publication. doi:10.1097/NNE.0000000000001182 PMID:35324491

Fortes, K., Latham, C. L., Vaughn, S., & Preston, K. (2022). The influence of social determinants of education on nursing student persistence and professional values. *Journal of Professional Nursing, 39*, 41–53. doi:10.1016/j.profnurs.2021.11.011 PMID:35272832

Freedom, I. Fla. Stat. 2022-72 § 4 (2022). https://legiscan.com/FL/bill/H0007/2022

Freire, P. (2018). *Pedagogy of the oppressed* (M. Bergman Ramos, Trans.; 50th anniversary ed.). Bloomsbury Academic. (Original work published 1970)

Frymier, A. B., & Shulman, G. M. (1995). "What's in it for me?": Increasing content relevance to enhance students' motivation. *Communication Education, 44*(1), 40–50. doi:10.1080/03634529509378996

Fuentes, M. A., Zelaya, D. G., & Madsen, J. W. (2021). Rethinking the course syllabus: Considerations for promoting equity, diversity, and inclusion. *Teaching of Psychology, 48*(1), 69–79. doi:10.1177/0098628320959979

Furin, J., Farmer, P., Wolf, M., Levy, B., Judd, A., Paternek, M., Hurtado, R., & Katz, J. (2006). A novel training model to address health problems in poor and underserved populations. *Journal of Health Care for the Poor and Underserved, 17*(1), 17–24. doi:10.1353/hpu.2006.0023 PMID:16520503

Galán, C. A., Tung, I., Call, C., Boness, C. L., Bowdring, M., Mcphee, J., & Savell, S. M. (2021, July 20). *Anti-racist approaches to ensure the retention and success of BIPOC graduate students in psychology* [Conference session]. American Psychological Association Conference. 10.1037/e505642022-001

Gardner, J. (1961). *Excellence: Can we be equal and excellent too?* Harper & Brothers.

Gardner, J. (1963). *Self-renewal: The individual and the innovative society*. W. W. Norton.

Garfield, R., Orgera, K., & Damico, A. (2019, January 25). *The uninsured and the ACA: A primer – Key facts about health insurance and the uninsured amidst changes to the affordable care act - introduction*. Kaiser Family Foundation. https://www.kff.org/report-section/the-uninsured-and-the-aca-a-primer-key-facts-about-health-insurance-and-the-uninsured-amidst-changes-to-the-affordable-care-act-introduction/

Garrison, D. R., Anderson, T., & Archer, W. (1999). Critical inquiry in a text-based environment: Computer conferencing in higher education. *The Internet and Higher Education, 2*(2–3), 87–105. doi:10.1016/S1096-7516(00)00016-6

Gering, C. S., Sheppard, D. K., Adams, B. L., Renes, S. L., & Morotti, A. A. (2018). Strengths-based analysis of student success in online courses. *Online Learning, 22*(3), 55–85. doi:10.24059/olj.v22i3.1464

Gershenson, S. (2020). *Great expectations: The impact of rigorous grading practices on student achievement*. Thomas B. Fordham Institute. https://fordhaminstitute.org/national/research/great-expectations-impact-rigorous-grading-practices-student-achievement

Gil, H., Mannen, D., Cama, R., & Mainero, C. (n.d.). *The community living model.* https://www.countyhealthrankings.org/sites/default/files/media/document/documents/webinars/The%20Community%20Living%20Model%20White%20Paper%20-%20Gil%2C%20Mannen%2C%20Cama%2C%20and%20Mainero%20-%202-7-17.pdf

Glass, C. (2017). Self-expression, social roles, and faculty members' attitudes towards online teaching. *Innovative Higher Education, 42*(3), 239–252. doi:10.100710755-016-9379-2

Glossary of Education Reform. (2013, August 29). *Relevance.* https://www.edglossary.org/relevance/#:~:text=Advocates%20argue%20that%20personal%20relevance,even%20knowledge%20retention%20and%20recall

Goleman, D. (1995). *Emotional intelligence: Why it can matter more than IQ* (10th Anniversary). Bantom Books.

Gordon, G., & Fischer, M. (2015). Strategic planning in public higher education: Management tool or publicity platform? *Educational Planning, 22*(3), 5–17.

Goudeau, S., Sanrey, C., Stanczak, A., Manstread, A., & Darnon, C. (2021). Why lockdown and distance learning during the COVID-19 pandemic are likely to increase the social class achievement gap. *Nature Human Behaviour, 5*(10), 1273–1281. doi:10.103841562-021-01212-7 PMID:34580440

Gould, C. (1996). Diversity and democracy: Representing differences. In S. Benhabib (Ed.), *Democracy and difference: Contesting the boundaries of the political* (pp. 171–186). Princeton University Press. doi:10.1515/9780691234168-010

Graham, G. N. (2016). Why your ZIP code matters more than your genetic code: Promoting healthy outcomes from mother to child. *Breastfeeding Medicine, 11*(8), 396–397. doi:10.1089/bfm.2016.0113 PMID:27513279

Granić, A., & Marangunić, N. (2019). Technology acceptance model in educational context: A systematic literature review. *British Journal of Educational Technology, 50*(5), 2572–2593. doi:10.1111/bjet.12864

Grant, C. A., & Zwier, E. (2011). Intersectionality and student outcomes: Sharpening the struggle against racism, sexism, classism, ableism, heterosexism, nationalism, and linguistic, religious, and geographical discrimination in teaching and learning. *Multicultural Perspectives, 13*(4), 181–188. doi:10.1080/15210960.2011.616813

Greater Good Science Center. (n.d.). What is compassion? *Greater Good Magazine.* https://greatergood.berkeley.edu/topic/compassion/definition#what-is-compassion

Greene-Moton, E., & Minkler, M. (2020). Cultural competence or cultural humility? Moving beyond the debate. *Health Promotion Practice, 21*(1), 142–145. doi:10.1177/1524839919884912 PMID:31718301

Groeger, L. V., Waldman, A., & Eads, D. (2018, October 16). *Miseducation. Is there racial inequality at your school?* ProPublica. https://bit.ly/3r3T3Pp

Gudeva Nikovska, D., & Tozija, F. (2014). Social determinants of equity in access to healthcare for tuberculosis patients in republic of Macedonia – Results from a case-control study. *International Journal of Health Policy and Management, 3*(4), 199–205. doi:10.15171/ijhpm.2014.89 PMID:25279382

Gullo, G., & Beachum, F. (2020). Framing implicit bias impact reduction in social justice leadership. *Journal of Educational Leadership and Policy Studies, 3*(3). https://files.eric.ed.gov/fulltext/EJ1251975.pdf

Guskey, T. R. (2005, April 11–15). *Formative classroom assessment and Benjamin S. Bloom: Theory, research, and implications* [Paper presentation]. Annual Meeting of the American Educational Research Association, Montreal, Canada. https://files.eric.ed.gov/fulltext/ED490412.pdf

Guskey, T. R. (2010). Lessons of mastery learning. *Educational Leadership, 68*(2), 52–57. https://www.researchgate.net/publication/236273526_Lessons_of_Mastery_Learning

Hammonds, E. M., & Reverby, S. M. (2019). Toward a historically informed analysis of racial health disparities since 1619. *American Journal of Public Health, 109*(10), 1348–1349. doi:10.2105/AJPH.2019.305262 PMID:31483728

Hanstedt, P. (2018). *Creating wicked students: Designing courses for a complex world*. Stylus Publishing.

Harless, J. (2018). Safe space in the college classroom: Contact, dignity, and a kind of publicness. *Ethics and Education, 13*(3), 329–345. doi:10.1080/17449642.2018.1490116

Hayes, K. N. (2016). Neoliberalism in historical light: How business models displaced science education goals in two eras. *Educational Leadership and Administration: Teaching and Program Development, 27*, 1–19. https://files.eric.ed.gov/fulltext/EJ1094418.pdf

Hayes-Bautista, T. M., Schink, W., & Hayes-Bautista, D. E. (2016). Original research: Latino nurses in the united states an overview of three decades (1980–2010). *AJN. The American Journal of Nursing, 116*(2), 24–33. doi:10.1097/01.NAJ.0000480514.69683.ac PMID:26817552

Helterbran, V. R. (2005). Lifelong or school-long learning: A daily choice. *The Clearing House: A Journal of Educational Strategies, Issues and Ideas, 78*(6), 261–263. doi:10.3200/TCHS.78.6.261-264

Herie, M. A. (2013). Andragogy 2.0? Teaching and learning in the global classroom: Heutagogy and paragogy. *Global Citizen Digest, 2*(2), 8–14. https://www.centennialcollege.ca/pdf/global_citizen_digest/volume-2-issue-2.pdf

Hill-Briggs, F., Adler, N. E., Berkowitz, S. A., Chin, M. H., Gary-Webb, T. L., Navas-Acien, A., Thornton, P. L., & Haire-Joshu, D. (2020). Social determinants of health and diabetes: A scientific review. *Diabetes Care, 44*(1), 258–279. doi:10.2337/dci20-0053 PMID:33139407

Hodgkinson, H. L. (1969). Walden u. *Soundings: An Interdisciplinary Journal, 52*, 172–185. https://scholarworks.waldenu.edu/cgi/viewcontent.cgi?article=1000&context=university_history

Hodgkinson, H. L. (1969). Walden U.: A working paper. *Soundings: An Interdisciplinary Journal, 52*, 172–185. https://scholarworks.waldenu.edu/cgi/viewcontent.cgi?article=1000&context=university_history

Hodgkinson, H. L. (1969). Walden U.: A working paper. *University History, 1*. https://scholarworks.waldenu.edu/university_history/1

Hodgkinson, H. L. (1969). Walden U: A working paper. *Soundings: An Interdisciplinary Journal, 52*(2), 172–185. https://scholarworks.waldenu.edu/cgi/viewcontent.cgi?article=1000&context=university_history

Holmes, J. R., Tootoo, J. L., Chosy, E. J., Bowie, A. Y., & Starr, R. R. (2018). Examining variation in life expectancy estimates by ZIP code tabulation area (ZCTA) in Hawaii's four main counties, 2008–2012. *Preventing Chronic Disease, 15*(E114), 1–3. doi:10.5888/pcd15.180035 PMID:30240571

Horton, M., Bell, B., Gaventa, J., & Peters, J. M. (1990). *We make the road by walking: Conversations on education and social change*. Tempe University Press.

Houston, L. (2018). Efficient strategies for integrating Universal Design for Learning in the online classroom. *Journal of Educators Online, 15*(3), 96–111. doi:10.9743/jeo.2018.15.3.4

Howe, K. R. (1994). Standards, assessment, and equality of educational opportunity. *Educational Researcher, 23*(8), 27–33. doi:10.2307/1176860

Hutchings, M. (2017). Improving doctoral support through group supervision: Analysing face-to-face and technology-mediated strategies for nurturing and sustaining scholarship. *Studies in Higher Education, 42*(3), 533–550. doi:10.1080/03075079.2015.1058352

Ince, S., Hoadley, C., & Kirschner, P. A. (2020). Research workflow skills for education doctoral students and postdocs: A qualitative study. *Journal of Academic Librarianship*, *46*(5), 102172. doi:10.1016/j.acalib.2020.102172

Inoue, A. B. (2021). *Above the well: An antiracist literacy argument from a boy of color*. The WAC Clearinghouse & Utah State University Press. doi:10.37514/PER-B.2021.1244

Intellectual Diversity, S. D. Codified Laws § 13-53-53 (2022). https://sdlegislature.gov/Statutes/Codified_Laws/2042844

International Association of Universities. (n.d.). *Equitable access, success and quality in higher education: A policy statement by the International Association of Universities*. https://www.iau-aiu.net/IMG/pdf/iau_policy_statement_on_equitable_access_final_version_august_2008_eng_0.pdf

International, R. T. I. (2019). *First-generation college students: Demographic characteristics and postsecondary enrollment*. NASPA. https://firstgen.naspa.org/files/dmfile/FactSheet-01.pdf

James, E. A., Lanyon, S., Larson, S., & Oppong, J. (2021, December 1–4). *Building a new future for virtual academic support and professional development for graduate students: Investigating a consortium model* [Conference session]. Council of Graduate Schools 61st Annual Meeting. New Orleans, LA, United States. https://cgsnet.org/61st-annual-meeting/

James, T. A. (2020, November 10). *Physicians as advocates for social change*. Harvard Medical School. https://postgraduateeducation.hms.harvard.edu/trends-medicine/physicians-advocates-social-change

Jencks, C. (1988). Whom must we treat equally for educational opportunity to be equal? *Ethics*, *98*(3), 518–533. doi:10.1086/292969

Jobe, B. (2016). The first year: A cultural shift towards improving student progress. *Higher Learning Research Communications*, *6*(1), 10–20. doi:10.18870/hlrc.v6i1.305

Jobe, R. L., Lenio, J., & Saunders, J. (2018). The first year: Bridging content and experience for online adult learners. *The Journal of Continuing Higher Education*, *66*(2), 115–121. doi:10.1080/07377363.2018.1469074

Johnson, B. A. (2014). Transformation of online teaching practices through implementation of appreciative inquiry. *Online Learning*, *18*(3).

Johnson, D. J., Chuang, S. S., & Glozman, J. (2022). Identity formation and re-formation: Resistance, growth, and emerging pathways for immigrant youth and their families. In D. J. Johnson, S. S. Chuang, & J. Glozman (Eds.), *Re/formation and identity: The intersectionality of development, culture, and immigration* (pp. 1–15). Springer International Publishing. doi:10.1007/978-3-030-86426-2_1

Kara, M., Erdoğdu, F., Kokoc, M., & Cagiltay, K. (2019). Challenges faced by adult learners in online distance education: A literature review. *Open Praxis*, *11*(1), 5–22. doi:10.5944/openpraxis.11.1.929

Kendi, I. X. (2020). *Antiracist baby* (A. Lukashevsky, Illus.). Kokila.

Kenyon, T., & Beaulac, G. (2014). Critical thinking education and debiasing. *Informal Logic*, *34*(4), 341–363. doi:10.22329/il.v34i4.4203

King, A. (1993). From sage on the stage to guide on the side. *College Teaching*, *41*(1), 30–35. doi:10.1080/87567555.1993.9926781

Knowles, M. S. (1980). *The modern practice of adult education: From pedagogy to andragogy*. Association Press.

Koh, H. K., Piotrowski, J. J., Kumanyika, S., & Fielding, J. S. (2011). Healthy people: A 2020 vision for the social determinants approach. *Health Education & Behavior*, *38*(6), 551–557. doi:10.1177/1090198111428646 PMID:22102542

Kolb, D. A. (1984). *Experiential learning: Experience as the source of learning and development.* Prentice-Hall.

Kreijns, K., Xu, K., & Weidlich, J. (2022). Social presence: Conceptualization and measurement. *Educational Psychology Review*, *34*(1), 139–170. doi:10.100710648-021-09623-8 PMID:34177204

Krieger, N. (1990). Racial and gender discrimination: Risk factors for high blood pressure? *Social Science & Medicine*, *30*(12), 1273–1281. doi:10.1016/0277-9536(90)90307-E PMID:2367873

Krieger, N. (1994). Epidemiology and the web of causation: Has anyone seen the spider? *Social Science & Medicine*, *39*(7), 887–903. doi:10.1016/0277-9536(94)90202-X PMID:7992123

Krieger, N. (2000). Discrimination and health. In L. F. Berkman & I. Kawachi (Eds.), *Social epidemiology* (pp. 36–75). Oxford University Press.

Krieger, N. (2001a). A glossary for social epidemiology. *Journal of Epidemiology and Community Health*, *55*(10), 693–700. doi:10.1136/jech.55.10.693 PMID:11553651

Krieger, N. (2001b). Theories for social epidemiology in the 21st century: An ecosocial perspective. *International Journal of Epidemiology*, *30*(4), 668–677. doi:10.1093/ije/30.4.668 PMID:11511581

Krieger, N., & Sidney, S. (1996). Racial discrimination and blood pressure: The CARDIA Study of young black and white adults. *American Journal of Public Health*, *86*(10), 1370–1378. doi:10.2105/AJPH.86.10.1370 PMID:8876504

Krug, K. S., Dickson, K. W., Lessiter, J. A., & Vassar, J. S. (2016). Faculty attitudes for changing a university's core and structure. *International Journal of Higher Education*, *5*(2), 63–73. doi:10.5430/ijhe.v5n2p63

Kurfist, A. (2022). *Student belonging: The next DEI frontier in higher education.* Hanover Research. https://www.hanoverresearch.com/insights-blog/student-belonging-the-next-dei-frontier-in-higher-education/

Landrine, H. (1992). Clinical implications of cultural differences: The referential versus the indexical self. *Clinical Psychology Review*, *12*(4), 401–415. doi:10.1016/0272-7358(92)90124-Q

Larabee, D. F. (1997). Public goods, private goods: The American struggle over educational goals. *American Educational Research Journal*, *34*(1), 39–81. doi:10.3102/00028312034001039

Laufer, M., Leiser, A., Deacon, B., de Brichambaut, P. P., Fecher, B., Kobsda, C., & Hesse, F. (2021). Digital higher education: A divider or bridge builder? Leadership perspectives on edtech in a COVID-19 reality. *International Journal of Educational Technology in Higher Education*, *18*(1), 1–17. doi:10.118641239-021-00287-6 PMID:34778538

Lawrie, G., Marquis, E., Fuller, E., Newman, T., Qiu, M., Nomikoudis, M., Roelofs, F., & van Dam, L. (2017). Moving Towards Inclusive Learning and Teaching: A Synthesis of Recent Literature. *Teaching & Learning Inquiry: The ISSOTL Journal*, *5*(1). Advance online publication. doi:10.20343/teachlearninqu.5.1.3

Lazăr, M. L. (2020). Ensuring access to education through inclusion and equity. *Romanian Journal of School Psychology*, *13*(26), 32–38.

Le Grand, J. (1991). *Equity and choice: An essay in economics and applied philosophy.* Routledge. doi:10.4324/9780203400098

Lee, A., Felten, P., Poch, R. K., Solheim, C., & O'Brien, M. K. (2017). *Teaching interculturally: A framework for integrating disciplinary knowledge and intercultural development.* Stylus Publishing.

Leners, D. W., & Sitzman, K. (2006). Graduate student perceptions: Feeling the passion of caring online. *Nursing Education Perspectives*, *27*(6), 315–319. PMID:17256656

Leong, C., Louizos, C., Currie, C., Glassford, L., Davies, N. M., Brothwell, D., & Renaud, R. (2015). Student perspectives of an online module for teaching physical assessment skills for dentistry, dental hygiene, and pharmacy students. *Journal of Interprofessional Care*, 29(4), 383–385. doi:10.3109/13561820.2014.977380 PMID:25374378

Levin, H. M. (2009). The economic payoff to investing in educational justice. *Educational Researcher*, 38(1), 5–20. doi:10.3102/0013189X08331192

Levin, J. S., Martin, M. C., López Damián, A. I., & Hoggatt, M. J. (2018). Preservation of community college logic: Organizational responses to state policies and funding practices in three states. *Community College Review*, 46(2), 197–220. doi:10.1177/0091552118758893

Levinson, M., Geller, A. C., & Allen, J. G. (2021). Health equity, schooling hesitancy, and the social determinants of learning. *The Lancet Regional Health-Americas*, 2(100032), 1–6. doi:10.1016/j.lana.2021.100032

Lim, J., Covrig, D., Freed, S., De Oliveira, B., Ongo, M., & Newman, I. (2019). Strategies to assist distance doctoral students in completing their dissertations. *The International Review of Research in Open and Distributed Learning*, 20(5), 192–210. doi:10.19173/irrodl.v20i5.4532

Lindell, A., Morgan, A., Sugarman, B. H., Tervala, D. J., Westermann, J., Strang, K. P., Costner, K. L., Ingram, M. N., Powell, M., McCune, N. M., Jobe, R. L., Dixon-Saxon, S., Subocz, S., & Schulz, W. (2021, December 2). *Beyond the social determinants of learning™: A Walden University position paper*. https://scholarworks.waldenu.edu/white_papers/3

Liu, E. F., Rubinsky, A. D., Pacca, L., Mujahid, M., Fontil, V., DeRouen, M. C., Fields, J., Bibbins-Domingo, K., & Lyles, C. R. (2022, February). Examining neighborhood socioeconomic status as a mediator of racial/ethnic disparities in hypertension control across two San Francisco health systems. *Circulation: Cardiovascular Quality and Outcomes*, 15(2), e008256. doi:10.1161/CIRCOUTCOMES.121.008256 PMID:35098728

Liu, Q., Geertshuis, S., & Grainger, R. (2020). Understanding academics' adoption of learning technologies: A systematic review. *Computers & Education*, 151(103857), 103857. Advance online publication. doi:10.1016/j.compedu.2020.103857

Lopes, A. S. P. P., & Carreira, P. M. R. (2020). Adult workers in higher education: Enhancing social mobility. *Education + Training*, 62(9), 1101–1117. doi:10.1108/ET-03-2018-0056

Low, G. R., & Hammett, R. D. (2021). *Transformative emotional intelligence for a positive career and life*. Emotional Intelligence Learning Systems. https://pubhtml5.com/tene/fdpa

Lunsford, R. F. (1997). When less is more: Principles for responding in the disciplines. *New Directions for Teaching and Learning*, 1997(69), 91–104. doi:10.1002/tl.6908

MacSwan, J. (2020). Academic English as standard language ideology: A renewed research agenda for asset-based language education. *Language Teaching Research*, 24(1), 28–36. doi:10.1177/1362168818777540

Mahmood, S. (2021). Instructional strategies for online teaching in COVID-19 pandemic. *Human Behavior and Emerging Technologies*, 3(1), 199–203. doi:10.1002/hbe2.218

Mann, J. C. (2014). A pilot study of RN-BSN completion students' preferred instructor online classroom caring behaviors. *The ABNF Journal*, 25(2), 33–39. PMID:24855803

Manoogian, J., III, & Benson, B. (2016, September 5). *The cognitive bias codex. 180+ biases*. https://upload.wikimedia.org/wikipedia/commons/6/65/Cognitive_bias_codex_en.svg

Marangunić, N., & Granić, A. (2015). Technology acceptance model: A literature review from 1986 to 2013. *Universal Access in the Information Society*, 14(1), 81–95. doi:10.100710209-014-0348-1

Marmot, M. (2004). *The status syndrome: How your social standing affects your health and life expectancy.* Bloomsbury. doi:10.1111/j.1740-9713.2004.00058.x

Marmot, M. (2005). Social determinants of health inequalities. *Lancet, 365*(9464), 1099–1104. doi:10.1016/S0140-6736(05)71146-6 PMID:15781105

Marmot, M. G., Smith, G. D., Stansfeld, S., Patel, C., North, F., Head, J., White, I., Brunner, E., & Feeney, A. (1991). Health inequalities among British civil servants: The Whitehall II study. *Lancet, 337*(8754), 1387–1393. doi:10.1016/0140-6736(91)93068-K PMID:1674771

Marmot, M. G., Syme, S. L., Kagan, A., Kato, H., Cohen, J. B., & Belsky, J. (1975). Epidemiologic studies of coronary heart disease and stroke in Japanese men living in Japan, Hawaii and California: Prevalence of coronary and hypertensive heart disease and associated risk factors. *American Journal of Epidemiology, 102*(6), 514–525. doi:10.1093/oxfordjournals.aje.a112189 PMID:1202953

Matters, Q. (n.d.). *Helping you deliver on your online promise.* https://www.qualitymatters.org/

McClain, M. B., Callan, G. L., Harris, B., Floyd, R. G., Haverkamp, C. R., Golson, M. E., Longhurst, D. N., & Benallie, K. J. (2021). Methods for addressing publication bias in school psychology journals: A descriptive review of meta-analyses from 1980 to 2019. *Journal of School Psychology, 84*, 74–94. doi:10.1016/j.jsp.2020.11.002 PMID:33581772

McDuff, N., Hughes, A., Tatam, J., Morrow, E., & Ross, F. (2020). Improving equality of opportunity in higher education through the adoption of an Inclusive Curriculum Framework. *Widening Participation and Lifelong Learning: the Journal of the Institute for Access Studies and the European Access Network, 22*(2), 83–121. doi:10.5456/WPLL.22.2.83

McGill, N. (2016). Social determinants of health: Education attainment linked to health throughout life span. *American Journal of Public Health, 106*(10), 1719. https://dialnet.unirioja.es/servlet/articulo?codigo=6821697

McIntyre, A. (2007). *Participatory action research.* SAGE Publications.

McNair, T. B., Albertine, S., Cooper, M. A., McDonald, M., & Major, T. Jr. (2016). *Becoming a student-ready college: A new culture of leadership for student success.* Jossey-Bass.

Mendonca, A. L. (2020). Understanding the perpetuation of inequalities in Brazilian K–12 public and private schools from a historical perspective. *Educational Considerations, 42*(2), 1–13. doi:10.4148/0146-9282.2189

Mensch, S. (2017). Improving distance education through student online orientation classes. *Global Education Journal, 2017*(1), 1–6. http://www.aabri.com/OC09manuscripts/OC09092.pdf

Merriam, S. B. (2001). Andragogy and self-directed learning: Pillars of adult learning theory. *New Directions for Adult and Continuing Education, 2001*(89), 3–13. doi:10.1002/ace.3

Meyers, S., Rowell, K., Wells, M., & Smith, B. C. (2019). Teacher empathy: A model of empathy for teaching for student success. *College Teaching, 67*(3), 160–168. doi:10.1080/87567555.2019.1579699

Mezirow, J. (1978). *Education for perspective transformation: Women's reentry programs in community colleges.* Center for Adult Education, Teachers College, Columbia University.

Mezirow, J. (1991). *Transformative dimensions of adult learning.* Jossey-Bass.

Migueliz Valcarlos, M., Wolgemuth, J. R., Haraf, S., & Fisk, N. (2020). Anti-oppressive pedagogies in online learning: A critical review. *Distance Education, 41*(3), 345–360. doi:10.1080/01587919.2020.1763783

Miller, S. (1997). Futures work: Recognising [sic] the social determinants of change. *Social Alternatives, 16*(1), 57–58.

Compilation of References

Milne, H. (1986). Desert, effort and equality. *Journal of Applied Philosophy, 3*(2), 235–243. doi:10.1111/j.1468-5930.1986.tb00423.x

Mitchell, B., & Geva-May, I. (2009). Attitudes affecting online learning implementation in higher education institutions. *Journal of Distance Education, 23*(1), 71–88. https://files.eric.ed.gov/fulltext/EJ836033.pdf

Mogford, E., Gould, L., & DeVoght, A. (2011). Teaching critical health literacy in the US as a means to action on the social determinants of health. *Health Promotion International, 26*(1), 4–13. doi:10.1093/heapro/daq049 PMID:20729240

Moll, L. C., Amanti, C., Neff, D., & Gonzalez, N. (1992). Funds of knowledge for teaching: Using qualitative research to connect homes and classrooms. *Theory into Practice, 31*(2), 132–141. doi:10.1080/00405849209543534

Moody, J. (2022, June 6). A grab for power. *Inside Higher Ed.* https://www.insidehighered.com/news/2022/06/06/draft-legislation-shows-desantis-plan-control-higher-ed

Moores, T. T., Change, J. C.-J., & Smith, D. K. (2004). Learning style and performance: A field study of Is students in an analysis and design course. *Journal of Computer Information Systems, 45*(1), 77–85. doi:10.1080/08874417.2004.11645819

Morgan, A. M., Jobe, R. L., Konopa, J. K., & Downs, L. D. (2022). Quality assurance, meet quality appreciation: Using appreciative inquiry to define faculty quality standards. *Higher Learning Research Communications, 12*(1), 98–111. https://scholarworks.waldenu.edu/cgi/viewcontent.cgi?article=1301&context=hlrc

Morgan, A. M., Jobe, R. L., Konopa, J. K., & Downs, L. D. (2022). Quality assurance, meet quality appreciation: Using appreciative inquiry to define faculty quality standards. *Higher Learning Research Communications, 12*(1), 98–111. doi:10.5590/HLRC.2022.12.1.1301

Mosley, M. O. P. (2002). Great black nurses series: Estelle Massey Riddle Osborne. *The ABNF Journal, 13*(5), 114. PMID:12430505

Mühlpachr, P. (2008). Social determinants of education in the postmodern society. *Santalka: Filologija, Edukologija, 16*(4), 61–67. https://repozytorium.amu.edu.pl/bitstream/10593/14522/1/KSE_2_4_2013_Pavel_Muhlpachr.pdf

National Academies of Sciences, Engineering, and Medicine. (2021). *The future of nursing 2020–2030: Charting a path to achieve health equity.* The National Academies Press. doi:10.17226/25982

National Association of System Heads. (n.d.-a) *NASH equity action agenda.* https://nashonline.org/

National Association of System Heads. (n.d.-b) *Strategic initiatives.* https://nashonline.org/strategic-initiatives/

National Center for Science and Engineering Statistics & National Science Foundation. (2021). *Doctorate recipients from U.S. universities: 2020.* https://ncses.nsf.gov/pubs/nsf22300/data-tables

National League for Nursing. (2019). NLN releases a vision for integration of social determinants of health into nursing education curricula. *Nursing Education Perspectives, 40*(6), 390. doi:10.1097/01.NEP.0000000000000597 PMID:31644458

Ndumu, A., & Walker, S. (2021). Adapting an HBCU-inspired framework for Black student success in U.S. LIS education. *Education for Information, 37*(9/10), 1–11. doi:10.3233/EFI-211511

Nelson, D. B., & Low, G. R. (2011). *The skills for career and life effectiveness assessment.* https://doscale.com/

Nelson, D. B., & Low, G. R. (2014). *Lifestyle type indicator.* https://eilearningsys.com/?page_id=142

Nelson, D. B., Low, G. R., & Hammett, R. D. (2007). *Personal excellence map.* Emotional Intelligence Learning Systems. https://eilearningsys.com/?page_id=218

Nelson, D. B., & Low, G. R. (2004). *Emotional intelligence: Achieving academic and career excellence.* Pearson Higher Education.

Nelson, D. B., & Nelson, K. W. (1984). *Relationship skills map: Positive assessment of relationship and intimacy skills.* Emotional Intelligence Learning Systems.

Ness, S. (2020, October). *Synchronous discussions in a principal licensure program* [Unpublished raw data]. Walden University, The Richard W. Riley College of Education and Leadership.

Nicol, D., & Macfarlane-Dick, D. (2006). Formative assessment and self-regulated learning: A model and seven principles of good feedback practice. *Studies in Higher Education, 31*(2), 199–218. doi:10.1080/03075070600572090

Nieminen, J. H., Tai, J., Boud, D., & Henderson, M. (2022). Student agency in feedback: Beyond the individual. *Assessment & Evaluation in Higher Education, 47*(1), 95–108. doi:10.1080/02602938.2021.1887080

Nieminen, J. H., & Tuohilampi, L. (2020). 'Finally studying for myself'–Examining student agency in summative and formative self-assessment models. *Assessment & Evaluation in Higher Education, 45*(7), 1031–1045. doi:10.1080/02602938.2020.1720595

Nieto, S. (2006). *Teaching as political work: Learning from courageous and caring teachers.* https://files.eric.ed.gov/fulltext/ED497692.pdf

Nozick, R. (1974). *Anarchy, state, and utopia.* Basic Books.

Nunberg, G., & Newman, E. (2011). *The American heritage dictionary of the English language* (5th ed.). Houghton Mifflin Harcourt. https://ahdictionary.com/word/search.html?q=compassion

Nussbaum, M. (2000). Women's capabilities and social justice. *Journal of Human Development, 1*(2), 219–247. doi:10.1080/713678045

Nussbaum, M. (2006). Education and democratic citizenship: Capabilities and quality education. *Journal of Human Development, 7*(3), 385–395. doi:10.1080/14649880600815974

O'Brien, M. J., Garland, J. M., Murphy, K. M., Shuman, S. J., Whitaker, R. C., & Larson, S. C. (2014). Training medical students in the social determinants of health: The health scholars program at Puentes de Salud. *Advances in Medical Education and Practice, 5*, 307–314. doi:10.2147/AMEP.S67480 PMID:25278787

Online Learning Consortium. (n.d.). *OLC institutional membership.* https://onlinelearningconsortium.org/join/institutional/

Opportunity Insights. (n.d.). *The opportunity atlas.* https://www.opportunityatlas.org/

Orem, S. (n.d.). *The five principles of appreciative coaching.* http://www.saraorem.com/5-principles/

Organization for Economic Co-operation and Development [OECD]. (2012). *Equity and quality in education: Supporting disadvantaged students and schools.* OECD Publishing. https://www.oecd.org/education/school/50293148.pdf

Orminski, E. (2021, June 30). *Your zip code is more important than your genetic code.* National Community Reinvestment Coalition. https://ncrc.org/your-zip-code-is-more-important-than-your-genetic-code/

Ornelles, C., Ray, A. B., & Wells, J. C. (2019). Designing online courses in teacher education to enhance adult learner engagement. *International Journal on Teaching and Learning in Higher Education, 31*(3), 547–557.

Orsmond, P., Merry, S., & Reiling, K. (2002). The use of exemplars and formative feedback when using student derived marking criteria in peer and self-assessment. *Assessment & Evaluation in Higher Education, 27*(4), 309–323. doi:10.1080/0260293022000001337

Compilation of References

Owen, H. (2017). 'The best PLD I've ever had': Reconceptualising professional learning and development. *Professional Development in Education*, *43*(1), 57–71. doi:10.1080/19415257.2015.1085890

Pacansky-Brock, M., Smedshammer, M., & Vincent-Layton, K. (2020). Humanizing online teaching to equitize higher education. *Current Issues in Education (Tempe, Ariz.)*, *21*(2), 1–21.

Page, C. (2021). Using content and learning resources that represent diverse perspectives, paradigms, or disciplinary approaches. In *Interculturalizing the curriculum*. Kwantlen Polytechnic University. https://kpu.pressbooks.pub/interculturalizingcurriculum/chapter/incorporate-content-and-learning-resources-that-represent-diverse-perspectives-paradigms-or-disciplinary-approaches/

Panadero, E., & Alonso-Tapia, J. (2013). Self-assessment: Theoretical and practical considerations. When it happens, how it is acquired, and what to do to develop it in our students. *Electronic Journal of Research in Educational Psychology*, *11*(2), 551–576. doi:10.14204/ejrep.30.12200

Park, C. (1993). The Black Death. In K. F. Kiple (Ed.), *The Cambridge World History of Human Disease* (pp. 612–615). Cambridge University Press. doi:10.1017/CHOL9780521332866.078

Parveen, I., & Riffat-un-Nisa, A. (2019). Equitable higher education: Students' perspective on access to resources, participation, and educational outcomes. *Bulletin of Education and Research*, *41*(1), 185–201. https://files.eric.ed.gov/fulltext/EJ1217921.pdf

Pathak, B. K. (2019). Study of e-learning outcomes: The role of late-registration and self-selection. *E-Journal of Business Education & Scholarship of Teaching*, *13*(1), 13–19. https://files.eric.ed.gov/fulltext/EJ1239138.pdf

Peacock, S. (2018). On discovering and profiting from the sense of belonging literature. *Journal Plus Education*, *19*(1), 11–20.

Peacock, S., & Cowan, J. (2019). Promoting sense of belonging in online learning communities of inquiry in accredited courses. *Online Learning*, *23*(2), 67–81. doi:10.24059/olj.v23i2.1488

Pew Research Center. (2017) *Demographics of social media usage and adoption in the United States*. https://fs.wp.odu.edu/dchapman/2017/02/14/demographics-of-social-media-users-and-adoption-in-the-united-states-pew-research-center/

Plessy v. Ferguson, 163 U.S. 537 (1896). https://supreme.justia.com/cases/federal/us/163/537/

Porter, D. (2001). *Health civilization and the state: A history of public health from ancient to modern times*. Routledge.

Porter, L. R. (2004). *Developing an online curriculum: Technologies and techniques*. Information Science Publishing. doi:10.4018/978-1-59140-136-0

Powley, E. H., Fry, R. E., Barrett, F. J., & Bright, D. S. (2004). Dialogic democracy meets command and control: Transformation through the appreciative inquiry summit. *The Academy of Management Executive*, *18*(3), 67–80. doi:10.5465/ame.2004.14776170

Prättälä, R. S., & Puska, P. (2012). Social determinants of health behaviours [sic] and social change. *European Journal of Public Health*, *22*(2), 166. doi:10.1093/eurpub/ckr211 PMID:22241756

Prince Henry Hospital Nursing and Medical Museum. (n.d.). *Florence Nightingale 1820-1910*. https://princehenryhospitalmuseum.org/florence-nightingale/

Ragoonaden, K., & Mueller, L. (2017). Culturally responsive pedagogy: Indigenizing curriculum. *Canadian Journal of Higher Education*, *47*(2), 22–46. doi:10.47678/cjhe.v47i2.187963

Rawls, J. (1971). *A theory of justice*. Harvard University Press. doi:10.4159/9780674042605

Report on five cities. (1963). *Equity & Excellence in Education, 1*(1), 3–10. doi:10.1080/0020486630010101

Richter, J. (2019, December 3). *Decentering the classroom: Distributed expertise as social justice praxis in first year composition*. Digital Rhetoric Collaborative. https://www.digitalrhetoriccollaborative.org/2019/12/03/decentering-the-classroom-distributed-expertise-as-social-justice-praxis-in-first-year-composition/

Riley, J. (1989). Justice under capitalism. In J. W. Chapman (Ed.), *Markets and justice* (pp. 122–162). New York University Press.

Ritchie, L. (2018). Opening the curriculum through open educational practices: International experience. *Open Praxis, 10*(2), 201–208. doi:10.5944/openpraxis.10.2.821

Rittel, H. W. J., & Webber, M. M. (1973). Dilemmas in a general theory of planning. *Policy Sciences, 4*(2), 155–169. doi:10.1007/BF01405730

Robertson, K. N. (2016). Considering the social determinants of equity in international development evaluation guidance documents. *The Canadian Journal of Program Evaluation, 30*(3), 344–373. doi:10.3138/cjpe.30.3.07

Robichaud, W. (2016). Orientation programs to increase retention in online community college courses. *Distance Learning, 13*(2), 57–64.

Robinson, H., Al-Freih, M., & Kilgore, W. (2020). Designing with care: Towards a care-centered model for online learning design. *The International Journal of Information of Learning Technology, 37*(3), 99–108. doi:10.1108/IJILT-10-2019-0098

Rockett, I. R. H. (1999). Population and health: An introduction to epidemiology. *Population Bulletin, 54*(4), 1–44. https://www.prb.org/wp-content/uploads/1999/12/Population-Bulletin-54.4PopHealthEpidemiology.pdf PMID:12295687

Roeder, A. (2014, August 4). *Zip code better predictor of health than genetic code*. Harvard T. H. Chan School of Public Health. https://www.hsph.harvard.edu/news/features/zip-code-better-predictor-of-health-than-genetic-code/

Rogers, C. (1969). Freedom to learn: A view of what education might become. Charles E. Merrill Publishing.

Rotberg, R. J., & Rabb, T. K. (Eds.). (1985). *Hunger and history: The impact of changing food production and consumption patterns on society*. Cambridge University Press.

Ruud, M. (2018). Cultural humility in the care of individuals who are lesbian, gay, bisexual, transgender, or queer. *Nursing for Women's Health, 22*(3), 255–263. doi:10.1016/j.nwh.2018.03.009 PMID:29885714

Ryff, C. D., & Keyes, C. L. (1995). The structure of psychological well-being revisited. *Journal of Personality and Social Psychology, 69*(4), 719–727. doi:10.1037/0022-3514.69.4.719 PMID:7473027

Saad, L. (2022, January 12). *Gallup's annual ranking of professions for having high honesty and ethics*. https://news.gallup.com/poll/388649/military-brass-judges-among-professions-new-image-lows.aspx

Sadler, D. R. (1989). Formative assessment and the design of instructional systems. *Instructional Science, 18*(2), 119–144. doi:10.1007/BF00117714

Salter, D., Ajsenberg, T., Ball, T., Bass, J., Brown, M., Picht, S., Pranke, D., Schneider, A., & Sullivan, K. (2019). *Readiness to succeed: Preparing the scholar-practitioner* [Unpublished internal report]. Walden University.

Salter, D., Larkin, G., Riedel, E., Schulz, W., Smeaton, G., & Westermann, J. (2013). *A framework for doctoral education: Milestones and benchmarks* [Unpublished internal report]. Walden University.

Compilation of References

Sanbonmatsu, L., Ludwig, J., Katz, L. F., Gennetian, L. A., Duncan, G. J., Kessler, R. C., Adam, E., McDade, T. W., & Tessler Lindau, S. (2011, November). *Moving to opportunity for fair housing demonstration program. Final impacts evaluation.* United States Department of Housing and Urban Development, Office of Policy Development and Research. http://www.huduser.org/publications/pdf/MTOFHD_fullreport_v2.pdf

Sanchez, M. (2021). Equity, diversity, and inclusion: Intersection with quality improvement. *Nursing Management, 52*(5), 14–21. doi:10.1097/01.NUMA.0000743408.29021.85 PMID:33908918

Sanderson, C. D., Hollinger-Smith, L. M., & Cox, K. (2021). Developing a social determinants of learning™ framework: A case study. *Nursing Education Perspectives, 42*(4), 205–211. doi:10.1097/01.NEP.0000000000000810 PMID:33935243

Schacter, H. L., Brown, S. G., Daugherty, A. M., Brummelte, S., & Grekin, E. (2021, December 1). Creating a compassionate classroom. *Inside Higher Ed.* https://www.insidehighered.com/advice/2021/12/01/compassionate-teaching-yields-most-benefits-opinion

Schindler, L. A., & Burkholder, G. J. (2014). Instructional design and facilitation approaches that promote critical thinking in asynchronous online discussions: A review of the literature. *Higher Learning Research Communications, 4*(4), 11–29. doi:10.18870/hlrc.v4i4.222

Schön, D. A. (1984). *The reflective practitioner: How professionals think in action* (1st ed.). Basic Books.

Schultz, M. (2008). Rudolf Virchow. *Emerging Infectious Diseases, 14*(9), 1480–1481. doi:10.3201/eid1409.086672

Seay, S. (2006). Strategies for success: Improving the academic performance of low-income adult and first-generation students in online General Education Courses. *The Journal of Continuing Higher Education, 54*(3), 22–35. doi:10.1080/07377366.2006.10401222

Seligman, M. (2018). PERMA and the building blocks of well-being. *The Journal of Positive Psychology, 13*(4), 333–335. doi:10.1080/17439760.2018.1437466

Sen, A. (1999). *Development as freedom.* Oxford University Press.

Sen, A. (2004). *Rationality and freedom.* The Belknap Press of Harvard University Press. doi:10.2307/j.ctv1dv0td8

Shaeffer, K. (2021, December 10). *America's public school teachers are far less racially and ethnically diverse than their students.* Pew Research Center. https://www.pewresearch.org/fact-tank/2021/12/10/americas-public-school-teachers-are-far-less-racially-and-ethnically-diverse-than-their-students/

Sharma, M., Pinto, A. D., & Kumagai, A. K. (2018). Teaching the social determinants of health: A path to equity or a road to nowhere? *Academic Medicine, 93*(1), 25–30. doi:10.1097/ACM.0000000000001689 PMID:28445214

Sinclair, S., Beamer, K., Hack, T. F., McClement, S., Bouchal, S. R., Chochinov, H. M., & Hagen, N. A. (2017). Sympathy, empathy, and compassion: A grounded theory study of palliative care patients' understandings, experiences, and preferences. *Palliative Medicine, 31*(5), 437–447. doi:10.1177/0269216316663499 PMID:27535319

Smidt, E., McDyre, B., Bunk, J., Li, R., & Gatenby, T. (2014). Faculty attitudes about distance education. *IAFOR Journal of Education, 2*(2), 181–209. https://files.eric.ed.gov/fulltext/EJ1080364.pdf

Smith, D. L., Cook, P., & Buskist, W. (2011). An experimental analysis of the relation between assigned grades and instructor evaluations. *Teaching of Psychology, 38*(4), 225–228. doi:10.1177/0098628311421317

Sportsman, S. (2021, June 13). *Health disparities: What can nurse educators do?* Collaborative Momentum Consulting. https://collaborativemomentum.com/2021/06/13/health-disparities-what-can-nurse-educators-do/

Stanford, F. C. (2020). The importance of diversity and inclusion in the healthcare workforce. *Journal of the National Medical Association, 112*(3), 247–249. doi:10.1016/j.jnma.2020.03.014 PMID:32336480

Sterner, C. S. (2007). A brief history of miasmic theory. *Bulletin of the History of Medicine, 22,* 747. Syme, S. L. (2005). Historical perspective: The social determinants of disease – some roots of the movement. *Epidemiologic Perspectives & Innovations, 2*(2), 1–7. doi:10.1186/1742-5573-2-2

Stewart, B. (1951). Some determinants of social change. *The Journal of Social Psychology, 33*(1), 33–49. doi:10.1080/00224545.1951.9921799

Stoebe, A. (2020). The effect of new student orientations on the retention of online students. *Online Journal of Distance Learning Administration, 23*(2), 1–9.

Storch, E. A., & Egbe, D. (2022). 2022: Need for (much) greater equity and equality in behavioral health care. *Journal of Cognitive Psychotherapy, 36*(2), 99–101. doi:10.1891/JCP-2022-0001 PMID:35577520

Sue, D. W. (2016). *Race talk and the conspiracy of silence: Understanding and facilitating difficult dialogues on race.* John Wiley & Sons.

Suler, J. R. (2015). *Psychology of the digital age: Humans become electric.* Cambridge University Press. doi:10.1017/CBO9781316424070

Sustainable Columbia. (n.d.). *Sustainable Columbia: Plan 2030.* https://sustainable.columbia.edu/content/plan-2030

Swan, K. (2004). *Relationships between interactions and learning in online environments.* The Sloan Consortium. https://www.immagic.com/eLibrary/ARCHIVES/GENERAL/SLOANCUS/S041202C.pdf

Swan, K., Chen, C.-C. B., & Bockmier-Sommers, D. K. (2020). Relationships between Carl Rogers' person-centered education and the community of inquiry framework: A preliminary exploration. *Online Learning, 24*(3). Advance online publication. doi:10.24059/olj.v24i3.2279

Syme, S. L., Hyman, M. M., & Enterline, P. E. (1964). Some social and cultural factors associated with incidence of coronary heart disease. *Journal of Chronic Diseases, 17*(3), 277–289. doi:10.1016/0021-9681(64)90155-9 PMID:5878595

Tagg, J. (2007). Double-loop learning in higher education. *Change: The Magazine of Higher Learning, 39*(4), 36–41. doi:10.3200/CHNG.39.4.36-41

Tagg, J. (2010). The learning-paradigm campus: From single- to double-loop learning. *New Directions for Teaching and Learning, 123*(123), 51–61. doi:10.1002/tl.409

Taylor & Francis Online. (n.d.). *Equity & Excellence in Education: Aims and scope.* https://bit.ly/3r6GPWk

Taylor, R., & Rieger, A. (1985). Medicine as social science: Rudolf Virchow on the typhus epidemic in Upper Silesia. *International Journal of Health Services, 15*(4), 547–559. doi:10.2190/XX9V-ACD4-KUXD-C0E5 PMID:3908347

The Association for the Advancement of Sustainability in Higher Education. (n.d.). https:www.aashe.org/

The Bell Foundation. (n.d.). *Great idea: Jigsaw activities.* https://www.bell-foundation.org.uk/eal-programme/guidance/effective-teaching-of-eal-learners/great-ideas/jigsaw-activities/#:~:text=What%20are%20jigsaw%20activities%3F,then%20become%20the%20experts%20in

The World Bank. (2021, October 22). *Higher education.* https://www.worldbank.org/en/topic/tertiaryeducation#1

Thomas, L., Herbert, J., & Teras, M. (2014). A sense of belonging to enhance participation, success and retention in online programs. *The International Journal of the First Year in Higher Education, 5*(2), 69–80. doi:10.5204/intjfyhe.v5i2.233

Compilation of References

Thornton, M., & Persaud, S. (2018). Preparing today's nurses: Social determinants of health and nursing education. *Online Journal of Issues in Nursing, 23*(3). Advance online publication. doi:10.3912/OJIN.Vol23No03Man05

Tipton, C. J. (2001). Graduate students' perceptions of library support services for distance learners: A university system-wide study. *Journal of Library Administration, 32*(1–2), 393–408. doi:10.1300/J111v32n01_14

Troy, T. (2015, Fall). Reclaiming the congressional hearing. *National Affairs, 25*, 62–77. https://tevitroy.org/17877/reclaiming-the-congressional-hearing

Two cities evaluate busing. (1963). *Equity & Excellence in Education, 1*(1), 13. doi:10.1080/0020486630010103

Tyroler, H. A., & Cassel, J. (1964). Health consequences of culture change: The effect of urbanization on coronary heart mortality in rural residents. *Journal of Chronic Diseases, 17*, 167–177. doi:10.1016/0021-9681(64)90053-0 PMID:14123834

UNESCO. (2000). *The Dakar framework for action.* https://sustainabledevelopment.un.org/content/documents/1681Dakar%20Framework%20for%20Action.pdf

UNESCO. (2015). *Education 2030: Incheon declaration and framework for action for the implementation of sustainable development goal 4.* http://uis.unesco.org/sites/default/files/documents/education-2030-incheon-framework-for-action-implementation-of-sdg4-2016-en_2.pdf

United Nations. (2019). *United nations sustainable development cooperation framework guidance.* https://unsdg.un.org/resources/united-nations-sustainable-development-cooperation-framework-guidance

United States Bureau of Labor Statistics. (2021, April 21). *Education pays. Earnings and unemployment rates by educational attainment, 2020.* https://www.bls.gov/emp/chart-unemployment-earnings-education.htm

United States Census Bureau. (n.d.). *Quickfacts: United states.* https://www.census.gov/quickfacts/fact/table/US/PST045221

United States Department of Education, National Center for Education Statistics. (2021). *Digest of Education Statistics 2020* [Table 310.20]. U.S. Department of Education. https://www.nces.ed.gov/programs/digest/d20/tables/dt20_301.20.asp?current=yes

United States Department of Education, National Center for Education Statistics. (n.d.). *Achievement gaps.* https://nces.ed.gov/nationsreportcard/studies/gaps

United States Department of Health and Human Services & Office of Disease Prevention and Health Promotion. (2020). *Healthy People 2030.* https://health.gov/healthypeople/objectives-and-data/social-determinants-health

United States Department of Health and Human Services Health Resources and Services Administration Bureau of Health Professions. (2006, October). *The rationale for diversity in the health professions: A review of the evidence.* https://docplayer.net/255577-The-rationale-for-diversity-in-the-health-professions-a-review-of-the-evidence.html

United States Department of Health and Human Services, Office of Disease Prevention and Health Promotion. (2021). *Healthy people 2030.* https://health.gov/healthypeople/objectives-and-data/social-determinants-health

United States Department of Health and Human Services, Office of Disease Prevention and Health Promotion. (n.d.). *Healthy People 2030. Social determinants of health.* https://health.gov/healthypeople/priority-areas/social-determinants-health

United States Department of Health and Human Services. Office of Disease Prevention and Health Promotion. (n.d.). *Healthy People 2030. Social determinants of health.* https://health.gov/healthypeople/priority-areas/social-determinants-health

United States Government Accountability Office. (2022, June 16). *K-12 education: Student population has significantly diversified, but many schools remain divided along racial, ethnic, and economic lines* (GAO-22-104737). https://www.gao.gov/products/gao-22-104737

United States Senate Committee on the Judiciary. (2022, March 22). *The nomination of Ketanji Brown Jackson to be an associate justice of the supreme court of the United States (day 2)* [Video]. https://www.judiciary.senate.gov/meetings/03/14/2022/the-nomination-of-ketanji-brown-jackson-top-be-an-associate-justice-of-the-supreme-court-of-the-united-states-day-2

University of Southern California Center for Urban Education. (n.d.). *Equity mindedness.* https://cue.usc.edu/equity/equity-mindedness/

University of Southern California Equity Research Institute and PolicyLink. (2022). *The national equity atlas.* https://nationalequityatlas.org/

University of Wisconsin School of Medicine and Public Health. (n.d.). *About the neighborhood atlas®.* https://www.neighborhoodatlas.medicine.wisc.edu/

Uygur, M., Ayçiçek, B., Doğrul, H., & Yanpar Yelken, T. (2020). Investigating stakeholders' views on technology integration: The role of educational leadership for sustainable inclusive education. *Sustainability, 12*(24), 10354. doi:10.3390u122410354

Van Auken, S. (2013). Using an exemplar to teach attitudinal formation, attitudinal change and consumer defense mechanisms: The motel selection problem. *Journal of Advertising Education, 17*(2), 39–42. doi:10.1177/109804821301700206

Vanslambrouck, S., Chang, Z., Tondeur, J., Phillipsen, B., & Lombaerts, K. (2016, October). Adult learners' motivation to participate and perception of online and blended environments. *Proceedings of the 15th European Conference on E-Learning,* 750–757. https://www.researchgate.net/publication/309490567_Adult_learners'_motivation_to_participate_and_perception_of_online_and_blended_environments

Vega, D., & Moore, J. L. III. (2018). Access to gifted education among African-American and Latino males. *Journal for Multicultural Education, 12*(3), 237–248. doi:10.1108/JME-01-2017-0006

Verba, S. (2006). Fairness, equality, and democracy: three big words. *Social Research: An International Quarterly of Social Sciences 73*(2), 499–540. https://dash.harvard.edu/bitstream/handle/1/2640592/verba_2006.pdf

Villerme, L. (1840). *Tableau d'etat physique et moral des ouvriers* (Vol. 2). Renouard.

Virchow, R. (1985). *Collected essays on public health and epidemiology* (Vol. 1). Science History Publications. (Original work published 1848)

Virginia Department of Planning and Budget. (2016, March 27). *Economic impact analysis. 18 VAC 115-20 regulations governing the practice of professional counseling department of health professions.* https://townhall.virginia.gov/L/GetFile.cfm?File=25%5C4259%5C7390%5CEIA_DHP_7390_vE.pdf

Walden University Center for Social Change. (n.d.). *About us.* https://academicguides.waldenu.edu/social-change/about-us

Walden University, Office of Institutional Effectiveness. (2022). *2021 student satisfaction survey outcomes* [Conference presentation]. National Faculty Meeting.

Walden University. (2017). *Walden 2020. A vision for social change report.* https://www.waldenu.edu/-/media/walden/files/about-walden/walden-university-2017-social-change-report-final-v-2.pdf?rev=5ded98a6d84e4a0096d02c9ec0f458af&hash=3CBA4D20AF7FA7F23BC21D69B2A9EB37

Walden University. (2017). *Walden 2020: A vision for social change.* https://www.waldenu.edu/-/media/Walden/files/about-walden/walden-university-2017-social-change-report-final-v-2.pdf?la=en

Walden University. (2020). *Executive summary (DATA).* https://www.waldenu.edu/about/data/summary

Walden University. (2021). *Walden University's AI-powered Tutor: Julian™*. https://www.waldenu.edu/news-and-events/events/walden-universitys-ai-powered-tutor-julian

Walden University. (2022). *Walden university catalog*. https://catalog.waldenu.edu/content.php?catoid=193&navoid=74971

Walden University. (n.d.). *Diverse and inclusive*. https://www.waldenfacts.com/#section3

Walden University. (n.d.). *Social change: The passion that drives us*. https://www.waldenu.edu/why-walden/social-change

Walden University. (n.d.). *The passion that drives us*. https://www.waldenu.edu/why-walden/social-change#mission

Walden University. (n.d.). *Vision, mission, and goals*. https://catalog.waldenu.edu/content.php?catoid=147&navoid=47257

Walden University. (n.d.). *Walden and social change*. https://academicguides.waldenu.edu/social-change/mission

Walden University. (n.d.a). *Diversity & inclusion*. https://www.waldenu.edu/why-walden/diversity

Walden University. (n.d.b). *Why Walden*. https://www.waldenu.edu/why-walden

Wang, Q., & Jeon, H. J. (2020). Bias in bias recognition: People view others but not themselves as biased by preexisting beliefs and social stigmas. *PLoS One*, *15*(10), e0240232. Advance online publication. doi:10.1371/journal.pone.0240232 PMID:33035252

Warren, M. R. (2014). Transforming public education: The need for an educational justice movement. *New England Journal of Public Policy*, *26*(1), 1–16. https://scholarworks.umb.edu/nejpp/vol26/iss1/11

Weaver, M. M. (2019). "I still think there's a need for proper, academic, Standard English": Examining a teacher's negotiation of multiple language ideologies. *Linguistics and Education*, *49*, 41–51. doi:10.1016/j.linged.2018.12.005

Weinstein, J. N., Geller, A., Negussie, Y., & Baciu, A. (Eds.). (2017). *Communities in action: Pathways to health equity*. The National Academies Press. doi:10.17226/24624

Weisman, S. (2022, March 18). Chat bots bypass 'communication clutter' to help students. *Inside Higher Ed*. https://www.insidehighered.com/news/2022/03/18/new-study-explores-how-use-chat-bots-retain-students

Weissman, S. (2022, March 18). Chat bots bypass 'communication clutter' to help students. *Insider Higher Ed*. https://www.insidehighered.com/news/2022/03/18/new-study-explores-how-use-chat-bots-retain-students

West, K., & Eaton, A. A. (2019). Prejudiced and unaware of it: Evidence for the Dunning-Kruger model in the domains of racism and sexism. *Personality and Individual Differences*, *146*, 111–119. doi:10.1016/j.paid.2019.03.047

White, K. A., & Ruth-Sahd, L. A. (2020). Compassionate teaching strategies amid the COVID-19 pandemic. *Nurse Educator*, *45*(6), 294–295. doi:10.1097/NNE.0000000000000901 PMID:32658092

White, M. L., Henderson, D. F., Smith, S. G., & Bell, M. P. (2022). A new look at an old problem: A positive psychology lens on discrimination – identity builders and work-related outcomes. *Human Resource Management Review*, *32*(3), 1–15. doi:10.1016/j.hrmr.2021.100858

Wienclaw, R. A. (2021). *Adult education as social capital*. Salem Press Encyclopedia.

Wilkinson, R. G., & Marmot, M. (Eds.). (2003). *Social determinants of health: The solid facts*. World Health Organization. https://apps.who.int/iris/bitstream/handle/10665/326568/9789289013710-eng.pdf?sequence=1&isAllowed=y

Williams, D. R., & Wyatt, R. (2015). Racial bias in health care and health: Challenges and opportunities. *Journal of the American Medical Association*, *314*(6), 555–556. doi:10.1001/jama.2015.9260 PMID:26262792

Williams, L. S. (2017). The managed heart: Adult learners and emotional presence online. *The Journal of Continuing Higher Education, 65*(2), 124–131. doi:10.1080/07377363.2017.1320204

Williams, S. D., Hansen, K., Smithey, M., Burnley, J., Koplitz, M., Koyama, K., Young, J., & Bakos, A. (2014). Using social determinants of health to link health workforce diversity, care quality and access, and health disparities to achieve health equity in nursing. *Public Health Reports, 129*(1, suppl2), 32–36. doi:10.1177/00333549141291S207 PMID:24385662

Windes, D. L., & Lesht, F. L. (2014). The effects of online teaching experience and institution type on faculty perceptions of teaching online. *Online Journal of Distance Learning Administration, 17*(1).

Witham, K. A., Malcolm-Piqueux, L., Dowd, A. C., & Bensimon, E. M. (2015). *America's unmet promise. The imperative for equity in higher education*. Association of American Colleges & Universities.

Witten, N. A. K., & Maskarinec, G. G. (2015). Privilege as a social determinant of health in medical education: A single class session can change privilege perspective. *Hawai'i Journal of Medicine & Public Health: a Journal of Asia Pacific Medicine & Public Health, 74*(9), 297–301. https://www.ncbi.nlm.nih.gov/pmc/articles/PMC4578164/#:~:text=By%20 incorporating%20a%20single%20class,a%20social%20determinant%20of%20health PMID:26468425

Woods-Jaeger, B., Kleven, L., Sexton, C., O'Malley, D., Cho, B., Bronston, S., McGowan, K., & Starr, D. (2022, May 23). Two generations thrive: Bidirectional collaboration among researchers, practitioners, and parents to promote culturally responsive trauma research, practice, and policy. *Psychological Trauma: Theory, Research, Practice, and Policy*. Advance online publication. doi:10.1037/tra0001209 PMID:35604710

World Health Organization Commission on Social Determinants of Health. (2008). *Closing the gap in a generation: Health equity through action on the social determinants of health*. https://www.who.int/teams/social-determinants-of-health/equity-and-health/commission-on-social-determinants-of-health

World Health Organization, Commission on Social Determinants of Health. (2010). *A conceptual framework for action on the social determinants of health*. https://apps.who.int/iris/bitstream/handle/10665/44489/9789241500852_eng.pdf

World Health Organization. (2010). *A conceptual framework for action on the social determinants of health*. https://apps.who.int/iris/bitstream/handle/10665/44489/?sequence=1

World Health Organization. (2020). *The top 10 causes of death*. https://www.who.int/news-room/fact-sheets/detail/the-top-10-causes-of-death

World Health Organization. (n.d.). *Frequently asked questions*. https://www.who.int/about/frequently-asked-questions

Wright, R., Baptiste, D. L., Booth, A., Addison, H., Abshire, M., Alvarez, D., Barrett, M., Hansen, B., Jenkins, E., Scarborough, S., Wright, E., Davidson, P. M., & Ramsey, G. C. (2021). Compelling voices of diversity, equity, and inclusion in prelicensure nursing students: Application of the cultural humility framework. *Nurse Educator, 46*(5), E90–e94. doi:10.1097/NNE.0000000000001094 PMID:34392249

Wunnenberg, M. (2020). Psychosocial bullying among nurse educators: Exploring coping strategies and intent to leave. *Journal of Nursing Scholarship, 52*(5), 574–582. doi:10.1111/jnu.12581 PMID:32735757

Yearby, R. (2020). Structural racism and health disparities: Reconfiguring the social determinants of health framework to include the root cause. *The Journal of Law, Medicine & Ethics, 48*(3), 518–526. doi:10.1177/1073110520958876 PMID:33021164

Yob, I. M. (2018). Conceptual framework for a curriculum in social change. *Journal of Social Change, 10*(1), 71–80. doi:10.5590/JOSC.2018.10.1.06

Compilation of References

Yob, I. M., Danver, S. L., Kristensen, S., Schulz, W., Simmons, K., Brashen, H. M., Krysiak, R. S., Kiltz, L., Gatlin, L., Wesson, S., & Penland, D. R. (2016). Curriculum alignment with a mission of social change in higher education. *Innovative Higher Education*, *41*(3), 203–219. doi:10.100710755-015-9344-5

Yob, I. M., & Ferraro, A. (2013). Political engagement in higher education curricula. *Journal of Social Change*, *5*(1), 1–10. doi:10.5590/JOSC.2013.05.1.01

Yu, J., Huang, C., Han, Z., He, T., & Li, M. (2020). Investigating the influence of interaction on learning persistence in online settings: Moderation or mediation of academic emotions? *International Journal of Environmental Research and Public Health*, *17*(7), 2320. doi:10.3390/ijerph17072320 PMID:32235547

Zabawski, E. (2019). The squeaky wheel. Various interpretations of a proverb [Editorial]. *Tribology & Lubrication Technology*, *75*(7), 8. https://digitaleditions.walsworth.com/publication/?m=5716&i=595223&view=articleBrowser&article_id=3404572&ver=html5

Zachos, G., Paraskevopoulou-Kollia, E.-A., & Anagnostopoulos, I. (2018). Social media use in higher education: A review. *Education Sciences*, *8*(4), 194. doi:10.3390/educsci8040194

About the Contributors

Nina M. McCune has served as faculty and in leadership positions, with an increasing focus on interventions that strengthen equity outcomes. In 2020, she was awarded a NISOD Award for Teaching Excellence, and the Sean and Jennifer Eplett Reilly Chancellor's Endowed Professorship at Baton Rouge Community College, due in part to an Equity Institute she launched to improve persistence and completion within general education course outcomes. In 2021, she joined Walden University as the Associate Dean for Inclusive Teaching and Learning environments, where she collaborates and directs systemic transformations that elevate the inherent worth, dignity, and humanity for all involved in the learning process. Dr. McCune holds an EdD in Adult Learning and Development with a specialization in Community College Leadership from Northwestern State University in Louisiana, a MA in the Social Sciences with a concentration on History, and a BA in Germanic Languages and Literature from the University of Chicago.

* * *

Sri Banerjee has nearly 20 years of experience in the areas of Public Health and Global Health. He has worked at the Centers for Disease Control in the area of infectious diseases and has worked on public health projects worldwide. Additionally, he has conducted award-winning research in the areas of HIV and chronic diseases and has experience writing grant proposals. He has conducted geospatial analysis to determine the presence of food deserts. His experience as a public health consultant and serving on the board of directors of public health organizations help in providing a practical front line perspective to the learning of public health. Also, he has experience in advising students about public health projects. He has also coauthored and published more than 50 research articles in prestigious journals such as the Lancet, and the Journal of American Medical Association with emphasis on global health, social epidemiology, cancer, and injury prevention. More recently, his research has received widespread attention from prominent media outlets such as Yahoo News, Healthline, HealthDigest, and MSN Health News. He uses his medical clinical expertise and his research acumen to guide his students.

Melanie Brown, Ph.D., is the Director of Doctoral Academic Support in the Office of Academic Support and Instructional Services at Walden University. Over her 15 years in higher education, she has taught writing and literature as a faculty member and led co-curricular instruction in learning centers. Her research interests include learning strategies, student retention, and workplace culture and communication.

About the Contributors

Michelle Brown, Ed.D., serves as the Director of Doctoral Committee Support and Student Progress within Walden's Office of Research and Doctoral Services. In this role, she supports university-wide strategies and initiatives related to the doctoral student journey—from doctoral skills and readiness to research support through capstone completion. In her more than 20 years in higher education, Michelle has served as a program director, research coordinator, and associate professor for doctoral programs in educational leadership. Current research interests include online instruction and tools to support student research.

Kristin Bundesen earned her doctorate at the University of Nottingham, UK. Her first degree was in Drama & Dance from Bard College. She maintains an active research agenda both presenting and publishing for the academic and lay audience. She serves as Associate Dean for the School of Interdisciplinary Undergraduate Studies at Walden University and has been honored with the Center for Faculty Excellence Award. She served as scholar of record for the First Folio! The Book That Gave Us Shakespeare for the state of New Mexico, supported by the National Endowment for the Humanities and The Folger Shakespeare Library, and was a founding board member of the International Shakespeare Center, Santa Fe, New Mexico. She was the founding Executive Director of the Southwest Mississippi Center for Culture & Learning at Alcorn State University, the oldest land-grant HBCU in the nation.

Myrna Cano-Wolfbrandt began her career in education as an elementary teacher and special education provider. She moved on to instructional design and faculty professional development in higher education. Faculty, student, and colleague success is a primary reason she continues to have an interest in the field of instructional design, intergroup dialogue training, and leadership development. She designs courses, webinars, and presentations in diversity, inclusion, equity (DEI), communication practices, change management processes, faculty development, microaggressions, and curriculum assessment tools to promote an inclusive learning environment. Her experience includes leading an engaged, high-performing team using critical thinking skills and intergroup dialogue processes to foster a positive and high-quality working and learning environment. She earned a Bachelor of Science in Psychology from the University of Texas-El Paso, a Masters in Curriculum and Instruction from Arizona State University, and a Doctorate in Educational Leadership and Administration from Northern Arizona University with a specialty in intergroup dialogue and diversity/inclusion initiatives. She currently teaches Masters of Education courses and mentors doctoral students throughout their dissertation process. She and her husband live in Tucson, AZ, are avid hikers, and would like to eventually hike the entire Arizona Trail.

Heidi Chumley, MD, MBA, is a family physician by training with 20 years of leadership experience in medical education in non-profit and for-profit institutions. She completed medical school, residency, and an academic leadership fellowship at University of Texas Health Science Center, San Antonio. After serving 5 years on the UTHSC-SA faculty, she was recruited to the University of Kansas School of Medicine where she became Senior Associate Dean, Medical Education and Associate Vice Chancellor for Interprofessional Education. She was then selected to be the Executive Dean at American University of the Caribbean School of Medicine where she served almost 9 years before moving into the Dean role at Ross University School of Medicine. Her career has been focused on medical education, specifically increasing opportunity for students from disadvantaged backgrounds to become physicians.

Todd A. Dickson, DNP, APRN, PMHNP-BC, FNP-BC is a core faculty member at Walden University in the Master of Science in Nursing psychiatric mental health nurse practitioner program. He currently serves on the board of the Minnesota Chapter of the American Psychiatric Nurses Association and co-chairs the Walden University College of Nursing Inclusive Teaching and Learning Committee as well as the College of Nursing Advanced Practice Nursing Program Diversity and Inclusion Committee. He is board certified as both a Psychiatric Mental Health Nurse Practitioner (PMHNP) and Family Nurse Practitioner (FNP) with over 30 years of experience practicing nursing. He maintains an active private practice specializing in the treatment of adults with psychiatric and co-occurring substance use disorders. His research and clinical practice interest areas include addictions, eliminating health disparities among historically marginalized communities, and LGBTQ+ mental health.

Aimee Ferraro has over 20 years of experience conducting inter-disciplinary and mixed-methods research in a variety of public health settings. She holds a dual B.A. in Biology and Psychology from Johns Hopkins University, an M.P.H. from George Washington University, and a Ph.D. in Health and Behavioral Sciences from the University of Colorado at Denver. Dr. Ferraro joined Walden University's faculty in 2008, became Senior Core Faculty in 2018, and was awarded the Faculty Excellence Award for the School of Health Sciences in 2019. Dr. Ferraro teaches courses in Epidemiology, SPSS, Biostatistics and Applied Research in addition to mentoring doctoral study research in the DrPH and PhD in Public Health programs. Professionally, she has worked as an ethnographer and applied epidemiologist on studies related to drug use, HIV, STDs, Hepatitis C, Zika and COVID-19. After completing a CDC/CSTE Applied Epidemiology Fellowship with the Pennsylvania Department of Health, Dr. Ferraro has been conducting research on infectious and vector-borne diseases internationally. In 2017, she was awarded the Research and Applications in Social Change Grant and named a Fellow of Walden's Center for Social Change for her study about the socio-ecological factors impacting Zika virus transmission in shantytowns of Lima, Peru. In 2020, Dr. Ferraro received a Faculty Research Initiative Grant to support a study on the life of Peruvians during the COVID-19 pandemic. Dr. Ferraro's work has been published in Morbidity and Mortality Weekly Report, Pediatrics, International Health, and Vaccines.

Chris Gilmer is currently interim President of West Virginia University Potomac State College and Founder of the National Institutes for Historically-Underserved Students. Previously, he was President of West Virginia University at Parkersburg, Vice President for Academic Affairs at Adams State University, the oldest federally designated Hispanic-Serving Institution in Colorado, and several leadership positions within the HBCU network. He has consulted with the U.S. Department of Education's regional education labs and comprehensive technical assistance networks. As a first-generation student, he earned his Ph.D. in English at The University of Southern Mississippi.

Richard Hammett is a founding faculty member of the Emotional Intelligence Training & Research Institute and editor of EITRI's journal, the International Journal of Transformative Emotional Intelligence. He teaches graduate research and supervises doctoral research for Walden University's Richard W. Riley College of Education and Leadership.

About the Contributors

Deborah Inman has been with Walden University since 2013 and serves as the Director of Research Quality Management within the Office of Research and Doctoral Services. She oversees doctoral student quality assurance, research support services for doctoral students, and doctoral faculty training. She collaborates university-wide with doctoral program leadership to build consensus for substantive student progress, identify and address quality research concerns, and develop strategies for improvement for all research policy related issues. She has education research, policy and evaluation experience in local, state, national and international arenas. Current research interest includes evolving needs in higher education and faculty mentoring for student success.

Rebecca L. Jobe, Ph.D., is Dean, Student Progress and Completion at Walden University. She has worked in higher education as a researcher, faculty member, and administrator for over 20 years and has many professional publications and presentations in areas of psychology (physiology, emotion, motivation, personality, and social influence), research design, and most recently in the areas of student progress and retention in online higher education. She earned her Ph.D. from the University of Tennessee in psychology (emphasis in social and health psychology research), Masters from Western Illinois University (experimental psychology), and Bachelor's degrees from the University of Missouri (B. S in Psychology, B.A. in English, and B.S.Ed in Secondary Education).

Gabriela D. Johnson is a native of Quito, Ecuador, and has lived in the USA for almost 30 years. She is faculty at Walden University in the School of Interdisciplinary Undergraduate Studies. Ms. Johnson earned her B.A. in Communication Education from MidAmerica Nazarene University and her M.A. in Communication Studies from the University of Kansas. She is currently a Ph.D. Candidate in Education with a specialization in Educational Technology and Design at Walden University. D. Gabriela's career in Education spans more than twenty years and includes high school and college teaching and leadership. She has won multiple teaching awards, including Walden's Center for Faculty Excellence Award for teaching and service to the university. Her research interests focus on topics concerning diversity, equity, and inclusion in online Education. She volunteers as a curator of diverse and inclusive curricula for homeschooling families.

Laura Karl, Ed.D., is a pedagogical and andragogical professional with over 30 years in the educational field. Her educational experience spans over elementary/middle school classrooms as a 1-8 classroom teacher and technology instructional specialist as well as a university student teaching supervisor and a university professor. She has presented at a variety of workshops and seminars focusing on the professional development of teachers. Dr. Karl earned her Ed.D from Walden University and a Master of Education in Instructional Technology from the University of Texas at El Paso. Currently, Dr. Karl is a Director of Learning Solutions for Walden University/Adtalem Global Education, Inc. where she oversees the design, development, and implementation of academic programs through close collaboration with institutions and academic leadership of partner institutions. As Dr. Karl leads and supervises product design and development teams, she also leads the collaborative effort with institutional leaders where she consults on online strategy, program positioning, and the integration of learning models into the curriculum experience. Dr. Karl maintains a level of expertise in instructional design, curriculum design, online learning, adult learning theory, and andragogy/pedagogy to support program and course development.

Juli K. Konopa, Ph.D., has been with Walden University since 2010. In her role as Director of Academic Operations in the Office of Academic Affairs, she collaborates on university-wide change management initiatives and supports the implementation of technology solutions that innovate and improve student, faculty, and staff experiences. Additionally, she oversees the planning and delivery of academic events and communications and designs and implements operational process improvements across academic units. She earned a B.S. in General Business Administration, an M.S. in Training and Development, and an Ed.S. in Industrial and Vocational Education from the University of Wisconsin-Stout and holds a Ph.D. in Education from the University of Minnesota. With over 25 years of experience in post-secondary education, she has served in various roles including program director for undergraduate, graduate, and doctoral programs, faculty for business, marketing, and post-secondary teacher education, curriculum developer, post-secondary and secondary student teaching supervisor, research advisor for graduate and doctoral students, change lead/champion, and assessment coordinator. Dr. Konopa has delivered numerous presentations and workshops focused on online teaching, learning, and teacher preparation, faculty development, student engagement, problem-based learning, communities of practice, and career clusters and pathways in local, state, national, and international arenas.

Latara O. Lampkin is a Senior Research Associate at Florida State University (FSU). As a policy and research scholar, her research spans both PreK-12 and higher education and is largely conducted through collaborative partnerships with practitioners and policy-makers. For the past decade, Dr. Lampkin has been engaged in large-scale, federally funded technical assistance and research projects conducted in partnership with local and state educational agencies and higher education institutions that focus on local implementation of policy and reform efforts, particularly aimed to increase the educational outcomes for underserved student populations. These projects have produced rigorous, policy and practice-relevant resources to inform initiatives and innovations to inform pre-service and in-service training for educators and researchers and to increase student outcomes across the PreK-20 continuum, including at Historically Black Colleges and Universities. Dr. Lampkin also develops and brokers partnerships with other Minority Serving Institutions, non-profit, and community-based organizations to leverage research-practice-community partnerships to enhance the access, use, and dissemination of tailored, evidence-based resources and strategies to improve student outcomes for diverse student populations.

Gary R. Low is Professor Emeritus of Education, Texas A&M University-Kingsville, founding faculty of the Emotional Intelligence Training and Research Institute (EITRI), patron and life member of the Forum for EI Learning (FEIL) in India, consulting psychologist, researcher, and author. He is co-creator and developer of the research derived, person-centered, relationship focused, skills-based learning system and theory of transformative emotional intelligence (TEI).

Laura K. Lynn, Ph.D., has been with Walden University since 2003 and has overseen the research functions for the university since 2010. In her role as Dean, she has led several initiatives to enhance strategy for doctoral education and initiated many essential services. She has extensive experience in applied research and program evaluation and has consulted with many non-profits and community programs. Additional areas of research and scholarship include graduate student research self-efficacy, resource and support needs for international students, and inclusive assessment strategies.

About the Contributors

Sara Makris is the dean of the School of Interdisciplinary Undergraduate Studies and the interim dean of The Richard W. Riley College of Education and Human Sciences at Walden University. She received her Ph.D. in Curriculum and Instruction from the University of Maryland, College Park, and her M.A. in Leadership in Teaching from the University of Notre Dame of Maryland. She has taught and served as department chair in public secondary schools in Baltimore, Maryland, and she has taught undergraduate and graduate courses in topics ranging from research to teaching for social justice. Her scholarship focuses on teacher identity and education, and inclusive teaching practice.

Tina Marshall-Bradley is an Academic Coordinator in the Master of Science in Education (MSED) program in the Riley College of Education and Leadership at Walden University where she works with the core courses. Dr. Marshall-Bradley's professional experiences have been rich and varied to include being the founding dean of a school of education; working at the state level on regulatory issues; holding faculty positions at state and private colleges as well as at a military college; working at the Giza plateau in Cairo, Egypt, and working at NASA's Langley Research Center. She has worked in the area of educator preparation for the past twenty-five years. Her current research focuses on quality services for students underserved by the education system, comparative education and equity in education. She completed a funded interdisciplinary research project on skills of the future and is currently working on teacher efficacy on applying issues of social justice.

Ann M. Morgan is a board-certified leadership and life coach in the Twin Cities of Minnesota who uses Appreciative Inquiry as a coach and consultant for businesses, non-profit and religious organizations, and individuals. An educator and administrator in higher education for over 20 years, Ann continues to teach as a professor of human behavior, emotional intelligence, and lifespan development.

Kathleen Morrison's passion for education and the power it brings to people to improve communities has spanned all age levels and delivery methods. She has had the privilege of exploring learning with young people in the K-12 classroom, publishing curriculum materials in print and digitally, and designing curriculum in the online higher education space.

Kathe Pelletier has spent the last 20 years in higher education innovation of some form or another. Kathe's entry point into higher ed was in an adult-serving institution that was fully online, and most of her work since then has been oriented around combining evidence-based practice with innovative delivery models. She has held roles in many different areas including advising, curriculum and instructional design, competency based education, and academic support. Dr. Pelletier's dissertation, "Improving Cross-Institutional Collaboration in the Curriculum and Course Development Process Using Appreciative Inquiry," solidified her love for AI as a method for positive change. She is currently the director of the teaching and learning program at EDUCAUSE, a non-profit membership organization that serves higher ed IT professionals.

William C. Schulz, III is currently an Associate Dean of Academic Research, Progress and Completion and was the Founding Director of Walden University's Center for Social Change. He was previously an Associate Dean of Walden's School of Management and was founding Director of the Tagliatela School of Business and Leadership at Albertus Magnus College. Dr. Schulz is an award-winning scholar in the fields of Strategic Management and Entrepreneurship, whose book, Creating Value Through Skill-Based Strategic Thinking and Entrepreneurial Leadership (Schulz & Hofer, Pergamon, 1999) has received critical acclaim. He earned a Ph.D. in Strategic Management from the University of Georgia, and a Master of Arts in Political Science & Public Policy from Indiana University. Will has been at Walden university for 15 years, and shares its passion to help motivated scholar-practitioners across all disciplines develop the skills needed to be effective agents for social change and good in the world.

Katherine Strang is an education professional who has enjoyed over 30 years of curriculum and product design and development for K-12 and higher education. She is passionate about finding innovative ways to improve online teaching and learning and create a welcoming and engaging learning environment.

Susan Subocz is the Associate President and Provost of Walden University, responsible for leading academic programs online for diverse adult learners. With more than 20 years of experience in higher education, she has led efforts to transform academic governance to an engaged stakeholder model, creating new opportunities for collaborative and innovative approaches to student retention and progress, particularly in areas of university-wide approaches to doctoral research and early term retention for undergraduate students. She has published numerous papers on teaching, education innovation, and academic quality. She is also a frequent speaker on digital experiences in higher education, academic quality, and leveraging innovation in technology to improve student experience and success. A first-generation college graduate, Dr. Subocz earned both her PhD in Education, Instructional Design for Online Learning, and her Master of Science in Education from Capella University. She earned a Master of Science in Civil Engineering from the University of Maryland. Dr. Subocz is also a graduate of the U.S. Coast Guard Academy, where she earned her Bachelor of Science degree in Civil Engineering before going on to serve 26 years in the Coast Guard and Coast Guard Reserve.

Kristi Trapp earned a Ph.D. in Learning, Design, and Technology from the University of Georgia. She has developed computer-based training for the U.S. Air Force and curriculum for several institutions including Walden University, the University of Miami, and Torrens University.

Index

A

ADA compliance 176
adult undergraduates 126, 134
andragogy 3-5, 7, 12, 14, 19, 21-22, 73, 76, 80, 85, 90
appreciative engagement 13, 54

B

barriers 13, 24, 34, 66, 68-70, 73, 76, 82, 86, 95, 120, 147, 153, 155, 158, 161-162, 170, 180, 183, 232, 234, 236, 249-254, 259
bias 30-31, 33, 36, 39, 64, 68, 72, 75, 86, 88-89, 94, 96-99, 109, 160, 190, 199, 233-234, 244, 247-249, 257-260, 262-263, 265
Black Indigenous People of Color (BIPOC) 63

C

care 15, 24, 26, 28, 32, 35, 39, 42, 56-57, 59, 88, 95-99, 102-109, 125-126, 128, 136-137, 145, 168, 178, 189, 193, 196-197, 207, 217, 219-221, 230, 234, 238, 272-276
caring 1, 11-12, 17, 26, 41, 46, 48, 91, 125, 127, 135, 187, 190, 193, 196, 199, 207-208, 227, 261, 268-269, 274
change 1-5, 11-15, 20-22, 24, 26-28, 30-31, 34-35, 37-38, 40-41, 43-48, 51, 53-55, 58, 60, 63, 65-72, 74-76, 79, 81-84, 88, 102, 104, 107, 112, 119, 130, 144, 147, 156-158, 160, 162-163, 165, 167-168, 181, 184, 187, 191, 193-194, 210-213, 216, 219-220, 223-224, 227, 232, 234-235, 237, 239, 242-243, 247-248, 253, 255-256, 259, 262, 264-265, 268-270, 272-280
Co-Curricular Support 110
cognitive bias 248, 257, 263
congruence 12, 47, 57, 186, 193, 196-197, 200, 206
courtesy 12, 193, 196
Cultural competence 96, 99, 107

cultural humility 99, 105-109
culture 2, 28, 37-38, 73, 85-86, 92, 104, 121, 135, 145, 153, 158, 162, 172, 174, 178, 181-182, 190-191, 206, 212, 216, 219-220, 223, 225, 233, 235, 243, 255
curriculum design 75-76, 78, 82, 86, 88, 233, 255

D

design strategies 75-76, 80
development 1-3, 7, 10, 12-15, 17, 21-24, 26, 29, 37, 40-41, 43-46, 48, 55, 60, 63-66, 69-70, 73, 80, 83, 85, 87, 90, 94-95, 100, 102, 105, 111, 113, 117, 119, 123, 126, 135, 140, 145, 151, 164, 167-168, 170-174, 176, 179, 184, 186-187, 189-192, 194, 198-199, 206, 212, 215, 217-219, 223, 227, 229, 232-233, 235, 238-240, 244-248, 252, 256, 258-259, 262, 264, 269-270, 272, 274, 276, 278-279
diversity 3, 10, 24, 29, 32-33, 35-36, 38, 57, 64-70, 73, 75-76, 84, 94-96, 98-100, 102, 104-109, 111-113, 115, 123-124, 136, 139, 145, 153-154, 156-158, 160, 162-165, 167, 170, 173, 177, 181, 184, 191, 207, 210-213, 217-218, 226, 232-233, 244, 246, 249, 252, 254, 262-263, 269-270
doctoral readiness 110, 116
doctoral support 112, 114-115, 119, 123

E

education 5, 8, 10-13, 16, 21-26, 28-29, 34-36, 38, 41, 44, 46, 48, 60-61, 63-67, 71-76, 79-82, 84, 86-92, 94-96, 98-100, 102-104, 106-112, 114, 121-124, 126, 131-138, 143-145, 147, 151, 153-160, 162-173, 175, 178-180, 182-184, 187-189, 191, 197, 206-208, 210-211, 213-214, 216-224, 226-227, 230, 232, 235-240, 244-265, 268-273, 276-280
educational justice 2, 63, 210-213, 218-219, 221, 223, 230, 268-269
emotional intelligence 12, 17, 40-45, 48, 51, 55-56,

59-61, 206, 271
emotional intelligence system 40, 42
emotional skills 40, 46-48, 51, 53, 61
empathy 3-4, 12, 15, 33, 41, 47, 56-59, 87, 98, 125-128, 130, 133, 137, 173, 184, 193, 202, 206, 243
engagement 12-15, 17-19, 24-26, 29-30, 32, 34-35, 43, 50, 54, 60, 64-66, 78, 80-81, 84, 86-87, 89, 96, 112, 119, 125, 127-128, 135, 138-139, 143, 146-147, 149-151, 153-154, 158-160, 174, 180-181, 189, 191-193, 196-202, 206, 212, 217, 224, 232-233, 235, 253-255, 259, 269, 274-275
equity 2, 24, 29, 31, 63-64, 66-67, 69-70, 72-73, 75-76, 81, 94-96, 98-100, 102, 104-106, 108-115, 122-123, 145, 153-157, 161-163, 165-170, 172-173, 176-177, 181-182, 184, 210-213, 215-217, 219, 221-222, 224-226, 230-231, 234, 244, 248-265, 268-272, 275-277, 279
equity outcomes 248-251, 253, 255-256, 259
equity-minded 248, 253, 256-259
experiential 1, 6-7, 15-18, 22-23, 41, 46, 57, 99, 139, 167

F

faculty engagement 125, 159, 196, 199, 202
first-generation 21, 78, 125-126, 134-137, 168, 170, 172, 194
flexibilization 240-243
future 24, 27-28, 33, 38, 52-53, 59, 64, 66, 68, 80, 94-95, 97-100, 102-103, 105-109, 112-113, 117-118, 123, 128, 139, 155, 161, 173, 184, 186-187, 190, 225-226, 228, 235-238, 241-243, 246, 262, 272

H

health disparities 94, 96-100, 105-106, 108-109, 216, 277
health equity 94-96, 98-100, 102, 104-106, 108-109, 210, 213, 215-217, 219, 224, 231, 244, 276-277
health outcomes 94, 98-100, 104, 215, 219, 241
healthy communities 210, 212
heutagogy 4-7, 12, 15, 19, 21, 23
higher education 11, 21-26, 29, 34-36, 38, 41, 60, 63, 71-74, 76, 81, 84, 87-92, 95, 102, 111-112, 123-124, 131, 134-138, 145, 151, 153-160, 162-165, 168, 170-172, 175, 180, 183-184, 187-189, 206-208, 210-211, 213, 217-219, 224, 226-227, 232, 235, 237-240, 244-247, 250, 252, 254, 256-257, 259-265, 270, 272, 276, 278
Holistic Engagement 149

I

inclusion 1-3, 10, 13, 24-26, 28-31, 33-38, 41-44, 58, 63-64, 66-69, 73, 75-76, 81, 94-96, 99-100, 102, 105-106, 108-115, 122-124, 130, 138-139, 145, 147, 153-165, 167, 170, 173, 177, 181, 187, 193, 210-213, 215, 217-218, 221, 227, 236, 246, 250, 254, 269-270, 274
Inclusive Assessment 166
Inclusive Support Services 110
inclusive teaching 1-8, 10-11, 13, 15-16, 18, 20, 37, 40-42, 59-60, 70, 89, 111, 134, 147, 149, 153, 157, 161, 163, 186-187, 189-191, 193, 196-199, 206, 213, 225-227, 229-234, 238, 243-244, 247, 268-269, 271
inclusive teaching and learning 1-8, 10-11, 13, 15-16, 18, 20, 37, 40-42, 59-60, 70, 111, 147, 149, 153, 157, 161, 186-187, 189-191, 193, 196-199, 206, 213, 225-227, 229-234, 238, 243, 268-269, 271
inclusive teaching and learning model 1, 3-8, 11, 15-16, 20, 40, 59-60, 187, 193, 199, 206
inclusiveness 83, 139
inclusivity 26-27, 34, 63-64, 70, 75, 110-112, 139, 150, 153-160, 162, 181, 226, 239-240
innovation 26-28, 35, 57, 114-115, 147, 173, 238, 246, 255, 259
Institutional Leadership 225

L

Level-of-Regard 186

M

measurement 13, 153, 159, 161, 190, 263, 277
Meier 125
mentoring 23, 48, 50, 54, 113, 118, 121, 138, 140, 190, 240-241
Moments of Truth 42, 186-190, 206-207
mutual inquiry 1, 4, 8, 10-15, 18, 157, 187, 191, 211, 269

N

National Institutes for Historically Underserved Students 166-167, 169

O

onboarding 138-139, 153-154, 191

Index

online classroom 14, 18, 42, 70, 75-76, 78, 82, 86, 88, 90, 116, 133, 143, 145, 147, 173, 196-199, 206-207, 269, 274

online learning 2, 5, 8-10, 13, 22-23, 36, 42, 50, 58, 63, 74, 76, 83, 90-91, 103, 138-140, 143, 151, 154, 167, 186-187, 189-190, 193, 196, 207, 229, 232, 247-251, 254, 257, 259, 264, 269, 274

open-access 125, 134-135, 198

operationalize 158-159, 196, 274

organizational development 24, 26, 184, 248

organizational learning 162, 248, 257-258, 260

orientation 25, 29, 54-55, 95, 97, 115-116, 118, 121, 129, 133, 138-141, 151, 172, 198, 252

P

participatory action research 160, 162, 164, 180-182

PERL 40, 44-46, 48, 50, 54

person-centered 1-2, 11-13, 17, 23, 38, 40-44, 46-48, 50, 54, 56, 59-60, 99, 186-187, 189-190, 193-202, 206-208, 228, 232, 234, 269

person-centered learning 2, 12-13, 40, 46, 50, 186, 196-199

Planning Frameworks 225

postsecondary education 75, 89, 184, 248-251, 254, 259, 268, 272, 276

postsecondary institutions 155, 161, 165, 248, 250, 254, 268-272, 274

presence 8, 10, 12, 16-17, 21, 41, 48, 127, 172, 193, 196-198, 208, 238, 255, 261, 263

privilege 86, 94, 97-99, 223, 256

Program Development 63, 262

R

Reflection-in-Action 1, 18, 20

research 2-3, 5, 8, 10, 14, 21-23, 27, 29, 37-38, 40-41, 43-46, 48, 54, 63, 65-66, 72-73, 76, 80-81, 88-92, 99-100, 102, 108-109, 111, 113-115, 117-119, 121, 123-124, 126, 136, 146-147, 151, 154, 156-157, 159-162, 164-165, 167, 170-174, 177, 180-185, 196-197, 207, 211, 213, 215, 217-219, 224, 239-244, 246, 250, 261, 263, 265-266, 270-272, 275, 278-280

retention 23, 25-26, 28, 73, 84, 90-91, 105, 123, 125-126, 135, 140-141, 145, 147, 151, 155, 164, 184-185, 226, 239, 248, 251, 255

Rogers 4, 11-12, 22-23, 27, 38, 40, 44, 46-48, 59, 186, 193, 196, 198, 207

S

social change 1-5, 11, 15, 20, 41, 65-72, 74-76, 79, 81-82, 88, 112, 119, 147, 157, 167-168, 187, 191, 193-194, 210-213, 216, 219-220, 223-224, 227, 262, 268-270, 272-280

social determinants 11, 15, 22, 42, 61, 94, 96, 98-100, 104, 106, 108-109, 210-213, 215-216, 219, 221-224, 230-231, 234, 237, 244-245, 247, 268, 270-274, 276-280

Social Determinants of Health 11, 15, 94, 96, 98-100, 104, 106, 108-109, 210-213, 215-216, 219, 221-224, 230-231, 245, 247, 270, 277-278, 280

social justice 71, 79-80, 89, 91-92, 94-97, 99, 105-106, 171-172, 214, 216, 218-220, 231, 235, 262, 268, 278

social media 31, 33, 146, 151

strategic planning 11, 158, 199, 225-228, 230, 233-234, 243-244, 251, 269

strengths-based 13, 15, 26, 38, 75-76, 83, 90

Structural racism 94-95, 97-98, 109

student engagement 89, 135, 138, 147, 149, 259

student progress 110, 117-118, 138-140, 147, 151, 242

student success 63, 70, 72-73, 79, 83, 86, 90, 113, 116, 119, 121, 129, 137-138, 145-147, 155, 164, 172, 174-176, 179-180, 182, 232, 234, 248, 255-256, 260

Student-Centered Support 110, 269, 274

sustainability 24, 28, 34, 225, 235-240, 243-247

System Accountability 63

systemic bias 75, 86, 99, 199

T

Teacher Feedback 125

teaching practices 22, 89, 125, 129-131, 135, 163, 232-233

technology 5, 20, 24-25, 28-30, 32, 34-35, 38, 41, 67, 74, 82, 103, 114-115, 123, 145, 149, 156, 158, 179, 189, 207, 220, 238-239, 244-247, 263, 266

training 3, 29, 33, 36, 44, 46, 69, 72, 102-104, 121, 170, 176, 179, 190-191, 194, 212-213, 217, 219-222, 242, 249, 252, 258-259, 261, 278

transformational learning 3, 5, 7, 13, 15, 41, 44, 60, 193-194, 196, 273

Transformative EI 46, 49, 60

U

universal design for learning 30, 32, 38, 82, 89-92, 246

317

W

Walden University 1-2, 4-6, 9, 19, 23-24, 40, 42-43, 47, 49, 52, 60, 63-67, 69-74, 76, 91, 94, 110, 112-114, 116-118, 120-126, 137-138, 140-143, 145-151, 153, 157, 160, 166-167, 169, 172-173, 177, 181-182, 186-188, 190, 192, 195, 210-213, 217-218, 221, 223, 225, 227, 229, 243-245, 248, 268-269, 271-274, 278-279

workplace 24-26, 28-29, 34-35, 37-38, 145, 260

Recommended Reference Books

IGI Global's reference books are available in three unique pricing formats:
Print Only, E-Book Only, or Print + E-Book.

Shipping fees may apply.

www.igi-global.com

Participatory Pedagogy: Emerging Research and Opportunities

ISBN: 9781522589648
EISBN: 9781522589655
© 2021; 156 pp.
List Price: US$ **155**

Transformative Pedagogical Perspectives on Home Language Use in Classrooms

ISBN: 9781799840756
EISBN: 9781799840763
© 2021; 282 pp.
List Price: US$ **185**

Advancing Online Course Design and Pedagogy for the 21st Century Learning Environment

ISBN: 9781799855989
EISBN: 9781799856009
© 2021; 382 pp.
List Price: US$ **195**

Deep Fakes, Fake News, and Misinformation in Online Teaching and Learning Technologies

ISBN: 9781799864745
EISBN: 9781799864752
© 2021; 271 pp.
List Price: US$ **195**

Enhancing Higher Education Accessibility Through Open Education and Prior Learning

ISBN: 9781799875710
EISBN: 9781799875734
© 2021; 252 pp.
List Price: US$ **195**

Connecting Disciplinary Literacy and Digital Storytelling in K-12 Education

ISBN: 9781799857709
EISBN: 9781799857716
© 2021; 378 pp.
List Price: US$ **195**

Do you want to stay current on the latest research trends, product announcements, news, and special offers?
Join IGI Global's mailing list to receive customized recommendations, exclusive discounts, and more.
Sign up at: **www.igi-global.com/newsletters**.

Publisher of Timely, Peer-Reviewed Inclusive Research Since 1988

IGI Global
PUBLISHER of TIMELY KNOWLEDGE

www.igi-global.com   Sign up at www.igi-global.com/newsletters   facebook.com/igiglobal   twitter.com/igiglobal   linkedin.com/igiglobal

Ensure Quality Research is Introduced to the Academic Community

Become an Evaluator for IGI Global Authored Book Projects

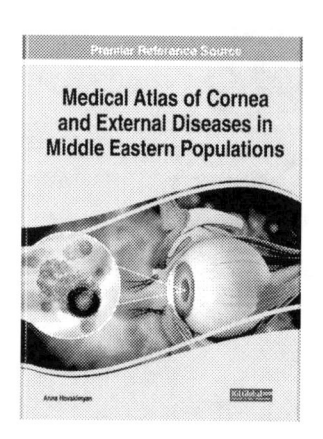

The overall success of an authored book project is dependent on quality and timely manuscript evaluations.

Applications and Inquiries may be sent to:
development@igi-global.com

Applicants must have a doctorate (or equivalent degree) as well as publishing, research, and reviewing experience. Authored Book Evaluators are appointed for one-year terms and are expected to complete at least three evaluations per term. Upon successful completion of this term, evaluators can be considered for an additional term.

If you have a colleague that may be interested in this opportunity, we encourage you to share this information with them.

Increase Your Manuscript's Chance of Acceptance
IGI Global Author Services

Copy Editing & Proofreading

Professional, native English language copy editors improve your manuscript's grammar, spelling, punctuation, terminology, semantics, consistency, flow, formatting, and more.

Scientific & Scholarly Editing

A Ph.D. level review for qualities such as originality and significance, interest to researchers, level of methodology and analysis, coverage of literature, organization, quality of writing, and strengths and weaknesses.

Figure, Table, Chart & Equation Conversions

Work with IGI Global's graphic designers before submission to enhance and design all figures and charts to IGI Global's specific standards for clarity.

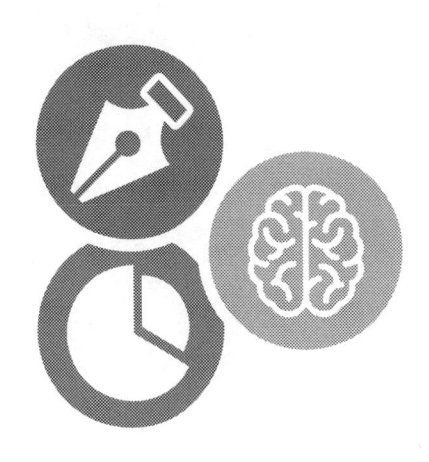

- Professional Service
- Quality Guarantee & Certificate
- Timeliness
- Affordable Pricing

What Makes IGI Global Author Services Stand Apart?

Services/Offerings	IGI Global Author Services	Editage	Enago
Turnaround Time of Projects	3-5 Business Days	6-7 Busines Days	6-7 Busines Days
Pricing	Fraction of our Competitors' Cost	Up to 2x Higher	Up to 3x Higher

Learn More or Get Started Here:

For Questions, Contact IGI Global's Customer Service Team at cust@igi-global.com or 717-533-8845

IGI Global
PUBLISHER of TIMELY KNOWLEDGE
www.igi-global.com

6,600+ E-BOOKS.
ADVANCED RESEARCH.
INCLUSIVE & ACCESSIBLE.

IGI Global e-Book Collection

- **Flexible Purchasing Options** (Perpetual, Subscription, EBA, etc.)
- Multi-Year Agreements with **No Price Increases** Guaranteed
- **No Additional Charge** for Multi-User Licensing
- No Maintenance, Hosting, or Archiving Fees
- Transformative **Open Access Options** Available

Request More Information, or Recommend the IGI Global e-Book Collection to Your Institution's Librarian

Among Titles Included in the IGI Global e-Book Collection

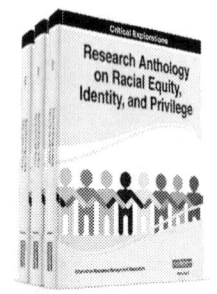

Research Anthology on Racial Equity, Identity, and Privilege (3 Vols.)
EISBN: 9781668445082
Price: US$ 895

Handbook of Research on Remote Work and Worker Well-Being in the Post-COVID-19 Era
EISBN: 9781799867562
Price: US$ 265

Research Anthology on Big Data Analytics, Architectures, and Applications (4 Vols.)
EISBN: 9781668436639
Price: US$ 1,950

Handbook of Research on Challenging Deficit Thinking for Exceptional Education Improvement
EISBN: 9781799888628
Price: US$ 265

Acquire & Open

When your library acquires an IGI Global e-Book and/or e-Journal Collection, your faculty's published work will be considered for immediate conversion to Open Access *(CC BY License)*, at no additional cost to the library or its faculty *(cost only applies to the e-Collection content being acquired)*, through our popular **Transformative Open Access (Read & Publish) Initiative**.

For More Information or to Request a Free Trial, Contact IGI Global's e-Collections Team: eresources@igi-global.com | 1-866-342-6657 ext. 100 | 717-533-8845 ext. 100

Have Your Work Published and Freely Accessible
Open Access Publishing

With the industry shifting from the more traditional publication models to an open access (OA) publication model, publishers are finding that OA publishing has many benefits that are awarded to authors and editors of published work.

- **Freely Share Your Research**
- **Higher Discoverability & Citation Impact**
- **Rigorous & Expedited Publishing Process**
- **Increased Advancement & Collaboration**

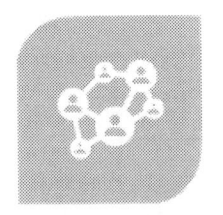

Acquire & Open

When your library acquires an IGI Global e-Book and/or e-Journal Collection, your faculty's published work will be considered for immediate conversion to Open Access *(CC BY License)*, at no additional cost to the library or its faculty *(cost only applies to the e-Collection content being acquired)*, through our popular **Transformative Open Access (Read & Publish) Initiative**.

- Provide Up To **100%** OA APC or CPC Funding
- Funding to Convert or Start a Journal to **Platinum OA**
- Support for Funding an **OA Reference Book**

IGI Global publications are found in a number of prestigious indices, including Web of Science™, Scopus®, Compendex, and PsycINFO®. The selection criteria is very strict and to ensure that journals and books are accepted into the major indexes, IGI Global closely monitors publications against the criteria that the indexes provide to publishers.

WEB OF SCIENCE™   **Compendex**   **Scopus®**
PsycINFO®   **IET Inspec**

Learn More Here:

For Questions, Contact IGI Global's Open Access Team at openaccessadmin@igi-global.com

IGI Global
PUBLISHER of TIMELY KNOWLEDGE
www.igi-global.com